Islamic Scholarship in Africa

Series information:
RELIGION IN TRANSFORMING AFRICA
ISSN 2398-8673

Series description
The series is open to submissions that examine local or regional realities on the complexities of religion and spirituality in Africa. Religion in Transforming Africa will showcase cutting-edge research into continent-wide issues on Christianity, Islam and other religions of Africa; Traditional beliefs and witchcraft; Religion, culture & society; History of religion, politics and power; Global networks and new missions; Religion in conflict and peace-building processes; Religion and development; Religious rituals and texts and their role in shaping religious ideologies and theologies. Innovative, and challenging current perspectives, the series provides an indispensable resource on this key area of African Studies for academics, students, international policy-makers and development practitioners.

Please contact the Series Editors with an outline or download the proposal form at www.jamescurrey.com.

Dr Barbara Bompani, Reader in Africa and International Development, University of Edinburgh: b.bompani@ed.ac.uk
Dr Joseph Hellweg, Associate Professor of Religion, Department of Religion, Florida State University: jhellweg@fsu.edu
Professor Ousmane Kane, Prince Alwaleed Bin Talal Professor of Contemporary Islamic Religion & Society, Harvard Divinity School: okane@hds.harvard.edu
Dr Emma Wild-Wood, Senior Lecturer, African Christianity and African Indigenous Religions, University of Edinburgh: emma.wildwood@ed.ac.uk

Previously published titles in the series are listed at the back of this volume.

Islamic Scholarship in Africa

New Directions and Global Contexts

Edited by
Ousmane Oumar Kane

JC JAMES CURREY

James Currey
is an imprint of
Boydell & Brewer Ltd
PO Box 9, Woodbridge
Suffolk IP12 3DF (GB)
www.jamescurrey.com
and of
Boydell & Brewer Inc.
668 Mt Hope Avenue
Rochester, NY 14620–2731 (US)
www.boydellandbrewer.com

First published in hardback 2021
Paperback edition 2023

First published in paperback in Africa in 2021 by
Cerdis
Nord Foire Cité
Marine Villa 91
Dakar
Senegal
www.cerdis.org

British Library Cataloguing in Publication Data
A catalogue record for this book is available from the British Library

ISBN 978-1-84701-231-9 (James Currey hardback)
ISBN 978-0-9986263-4-5 (Cerdis paperback edition)
ISBN 978-1-84701-230-2(James Currey paperback)

This publication is printed on acid-free paper

To Sister Khadija and Nanouna

Contents

Part IV: *'Ajamī*, Knowledge Transmission, and Spirituality

Illustrations

Notes on Contributors

Chanfi Ahmed trained in Islamic Studies and in History. He is a Lecturer on the History of the Indian Ocean and on the History of Islam in Africa and Asia at the Institute for Asian and African Studies at Humboldt University of Berlin-Germany. He received his PhD in History at the EHESS (École des Hautes Études en Sciences Sociales) in Paris. His research areas are history and anthropology of Islam in Africa and the history of the Muslim world in general. He has written on a variety of topics related to Islam in Africa, including Sufi revival, Muslim preachers, Islamic education, Islamic faith-based NGOs and Salafism. His books include *AfroMecca in History. African Societies, Anti-Black Racism, and Teaching in al-Haram Mosque in Mecca* (Newcastle: Cambridge Scholar, 2019), *Preaching Islamic Revival in East Africa* (Newcastle: Cambridge Scholar, 2018), and *West African 'Ulamā' and Salafism in Mecca and Medina: Jawab al-Ifriqi – The Response of the African* (Leiden: Brill, 2015).

Caitlyn Bolton is a PhD candidate in Cultural Anthropology at the Graduate Center of the City University of New York. Her research focuses on international Islamic development organizations working in education in Zanzibar and the role of religion and religious knowledge in their approaches to progress and social change. She has a BA in Anthropology and Africana Studies from Bard College and a MA in Near Eastern Studies from New York University, and has worked at Harvard Kennedy School's Middle East Initiative and the Cordoba Initiative on issues related to Islamic law and the modern state.

Laura L. Cochrane is Professor of Anthropology at Central Michigan University. She teaches topics within African studies, cultural and linguistic anthropology, the anthropology of religion, and ethnographic methods. Her longitudinal ethnographic research in Senegal (since 2003) concerns local development, religious discourse, and artisanal production, all in the contexts of economic challenges and environmental shifts. She is the author of *Weaving through Islam in Senegal* (Carolina Academic Press, 2012), *Everyday Faith in Sufi Senegal* (London and New York: Routledge, 2017) and *Adventure as Education: John W. Bennett and*

Anthropology in the Early Twentieth Century (Carolina Academic Press, 2019). She has also published articles in the journals *Anthropology* and *African Studies*.

Jeremy Dell has been a Lecturer in African History at the University of Edinburgh since January 2020, following his completion of a Modern Intellectual History (MIH) post-doctoral fellowship at Dartmouth College. He received his PhD in History at the University of Pennsylvania in 2018, with a dissertation titled 'Saving Tradition: Genres of Islamic Knowledge in Senegal and the Western Sahel'. He has had articles published in *Islamic Africa* and *Journal of African History* and is currently converting his thesis into a book.

Antonio de Diego González is Assistant Professor of Philosophy at Universidad Pablo de Olavide. He received an MA in Contemporary History (2015) and a PhD (2016) on the History and Doctrines of the Tijaniyya Tariqa in Contemporary West Africa at the Universidad de Sevilla. His research focuses on intellectual history and epistemological problems in Islamic contemporary societies. He is author of *Ley y Gnosis. Historia intelectual de la tariqa Tijaniyya* (Granada: Editorial Universidad de Granada, 2020) and *Populismo Islámico* (Córdoba: Almuzara, 2020).

Farah El-Sharif is a PhD student at Harvard University's Near Eastern Languages and Civilizations Department. Her research focuses on the modern (nineteenth and twentieth century) intellectual, mystical and legal history of West Africa and the Levant. Farah completed her undergraduate degree in Culture and Politics at Georgetown University's School of Foreign Service in 2009 and received her MA from the Graduate Theological Union in Berkeley, California in 2013. She received the 'Rising Scholar' award from the International Institute for Islamic Thought in Herndon, VA, the Kenneth W. Russell Fellowship from the American Center for Oriental Research in Amman, Jordan and the Alwaleed bin Talal Fellowship at Harvard University. She has also served on the editorial board of *The Muslim 500: The World's Most Influential Muslims*, a publication produced by the Royal Islamic Institute of Islamic Thought in Amman, Jordan.

Britta Frede has been a Postdoctoral Research Fellow at the research programme 'Africa Multiple – Cluster of Excellence' at Bayreuth University (Germany) since 2019. She previously held posts at Leibniz Zentrum Moderner Orient (ZMO, Berlin), Free University (BGSMCS, Berlin) and Humboldt University (IAAW, Berlin). She has also been a member of the editorial board of *Islamic Africa* since 2015.

Dahlia E.M. Gubara is an Assistant Professor in the Civilization Studies Program at the American University of Beirut. Her work is principally concerned with the production and transmission of knowledge in, and about, the Islamic tradition, and is regionally focused on the Middle East and Africa. She studied Law at the School of Oriental and African Studies, University of London, concentrating on Islamic jurisprudence, and later History at Columbia University, New York, where her doctoral work explored the Cairene mosque-seminary of al-Azhar and the orders of knowledge in the long eighteenth century. She has published articles in the *Journal of Arabic Literature* and in *Comparative Studies of South Asia, Africa and the Middle East*.

Abdulkadir Hashim is a Senior Lecturer in Sharia and Islamic Studies in the Department of Philosophy and Religious Studies at the University of Nairobi and an Advocate of the High Court of Kenya. He is Head of Department of Sharia, Faculty of Law, Zanzibar University. He has published articles in several refereed journals and contributed book chapters on Muslim personal law and Muslim intellectual contributions along the East African coast.

Hannah Hoechner is a Lecturer in Education and International Development at the School of International Development, University of East Anglia. Her research seeks to shed light on the diversity and dynamism of Islamic schooling practices in contexts of ongoing social change. As part of her work in Nigeria, with nine Qur'anic students she produced the participatory docu-drama *Duniya Juyi Juyi / How life goes*, which won the AFRICAST 2012 Special Award 'Participatory Video for Development'. Hannah's current work includes Muslim immigrant communities in the West and their relationships with their homelands. She is the author of *Qur'anic Schools in Northern Nigeria: Everyday Experiences of Youth, Faith, and Poverty* (Cambridge University Press, 2018).

Ousmane Oumar Kane is the first Prince Alwaleed Bin Talal Professor of Contemporary Islamic Religion and Society at Harvard Divinity School and Professor of African and African American Studies. He has been an Associate Professor of International and Public Affairs at Columbia University's School of International and Public Affairs since 2002. Kane studies the history of Islamic religious institutions and organizations since the eighteenth century, and he is engaged in documenting the intellectual history of Islam in Africa. He is the author of *Muslim Modernity in Postcolonial Nigeria* (Brill, 2003), *The Homeland Is the Arena: Religion, Transnationalism and the Integration of Senegalese Immigrants in America* (Oxford University Press, 2011), and *Beyond Timbuktu: An Intellectual History of Muslim West Africa* (Harvard University Press, 2016).

Lidwien Kapteijns is Kendall/Hodder Professor of History at Wellesley College, where she has taught African and Middle Eastern history for more than thirty years. Educated in The Netherlands, she also studied Somali Language and Literature under B.W. Andrzejewski at the School of Oriental and African Studies in London. Before turning to Somali studies in c. 1986, she lived and worked in the Sudan and published about late precolonial Sudanese history, including a source publication titled *After the Millennium: Diplomatic Correspondence from Wadai and Dar Fur on the Eve of Colonial Conquest, 1885–1916* (with Jay Spaulding) (East Lansing, Michigan: African Studies Center, 1988). Her books also include *Clan Cleansing in Somalia: The Ruinous Legacy of 1991* (Philadelphia: University of Pennsylvania Press, 2013).

Yunus Kumek is Religious Studies Coordinator and Lecturer at the Philosophy and Humanities Department at SUNY Buffalo State, where he also completed his PhD. He completed a postdoctoral fellowship at Harvard Divinity School. Kumek's research interests include theological and anthropological studies of Islamic peoples and cultures, mysticism, Sufism, the anthropology of education and medicine, science and religion, critical analysis of sacred texts as well as the cultural studies approach of religious literacy. His books include *International Teachers in American Schools* (Washington, DC: Rethink Institute, 2011) and *Compendium: Spiritual Care Through Muslim Ethnographic Studies* (Amherst, NY: Sage Chronicle, 2019).

Khadim Ndiaye studied at the universities of Dakar, Geneva and Quebec in Montreal (UQAM) and is currently conducting research in history at the University of Sherbrooke in Canada. He is the author of several articles and a book in French about the Senegalese historian Cheikh Anta Diop.

Oludamini Ogunnaike is an Assistant Professor of Religious Studies at the University of Virginia. He teaches courses on Islam, Islamic Philosophy, Spirituality and Art, as well as African and African Diasporic Religions. He holds a PhD in African Studies and the Study of Religion from Harvard University, and spent a year as a postdoctoral fellow at Stanford University's Abbasi Program in Islamic Studies. Dr Ogunnaike's research examines the philosophical dimensions of postcolonial, colonial and precolonial Islamic and indigenous religious traditions of West and North Africa, especially Sufism and Ifa, and he maintains a digital archive of West African Sufi poetry. He is the author of *Deep Knowledge: Ways of Knowing in Sufism and Ifa, Two West African Intellectual Traditions* (Philadelphia: Penn State University Press, 2020).

Ebrima Sall is Executive Director of Trust Africa and the immediate past Executive Secretary of the Council for the Development of Social Science Research in Africa (CODESRIA). He holds a PhD in Sociology from the University of Paris 1 Panthéon-Sorbonne, and has held senior positions in other institutions, including those of Senior Researcher at the Nordic Africa Institute in Uppsala, Sweden, and Director of the Centre for the Promotion of Village Savings and Credit Associations in The Gambia. He was promoted to Maître de Conférences (Associate Professor) in sociology-demography by the French National Universities Council in 1992.

Alessandra Vianello is an independent scholar and researcher. She lived and worked in Somalia from 1970 to 1990 and has specialized in the history and culture of Brava, on the Benadir coast of Somalia, especially Brava's Bantu language Chimiini or Chimbalazi. She edited the two-volume *Servants of the Sharia: The Civil Register of the Qadis' Court of Brava, 1893–1900* (with Mohamed Kassim, Brill, 2006) and (with Lidwien Kapteijns and Mohamed M. Kassim) '*Stringing Coral beads*': *A Source Publication of Chimiini Texts and English Translations* (Leiden: Brill, 2018).

Ismail Warscheid is a tenured researcher at the National Center for Scientific Research (Centre National de la Recherche Scientifique, CNRS) in Paris. He received his training in History and Arabic Studies at the University of Geneva and the Ecole des Hautes Etudes en Sciences Sociales in Paris, from which he obtained his PhD in 2014. Combining methodologies from history, social and legal anthropology as well as philology, his research deals primarily with the cultural and social history of North and West Africa, with a strong emphasis on the study of Islamic legal texts. He is currently developing a research project that engages in a comparative analysis of Islamic law's role in the construction of social order within pre-modern Saharan and Sahelian societies. Among his recent publications are *Droit musulman et société: la justice islamique dans les oasis du Grand Touat (Algérie) aux XVIIe–XIXe siècles* (Brill, 2017) and 'The Persisting Spectre of Cultural Decline: Historiographical Approaches to Muslim Scholarship in the Early Modern Maghreb' (*Journal of the Economic and Social History of the Orient*, 2017).

Zachary Wright is Associate Professor of History and Religious Studies at Northwestern University in Qatar. He received his PhD in History from Northwestern University, his MA in Arabic Studies, Middle East History, from the American University in Cairo, and his BA in History from Stanford University. His book publications include *Realizing Islam: The Tijaniyya in North Africa and the Eighteenth-Century Muslim World* (University of North Carolina Press,

2020), *Jihad of the Pen: the Sufi Literature of West Africa* (with R. Ware and A. Syed, American University in Cairo Press, 2018), and *Living Knowledge in West African Islam: the Sufi Community of Ibrahim Niasse* (Brill, 2015). He has also translated a number of West African Arabic texts into English, such as Shaykh Ibrahim Niasse's primary work on Sufism, *The Removal of Confusion Concerning the Saintly Seal* (Fons Vitae, 2010, reprint 2019).

Note on Transliteration and Calendar

We have sought to make the transliteration as consistent as possible without modifying bibliographic titles or changing known usages. Arabic long vowels and emphatic letters have been transliterated according to standard norms of transliteration, with the exception of well-known Arabic words in the English language which we maintained in their best-known form. We have opted for Sufi (instead of Ṣūfī), Islam (instead of Islām), Ramadan (instead of Ramaḍān) except when mentioned otherwise in bibliographic titles.

For the Muslim Holy Book and derived adjective, we have transliterated 'Qur'ān' and 'Qur'ānic' except when mentioned otherwise in bibliographic titles. We have also maintained names of famous people in their best-known form, thus Ibrahim Niasse (instead of Ibrāhīm Niyās), Gamal Abdel Naser (instead of Jamāl 'Abd al-Nāsir) except when mentioned otherwise in bibliographic titles.

Names of places have also been kept in their known orthography, thus Madinat Nasr (not Madīnat al-Naṣr) and Hadiqatul Dawliya (not Ḥadīqat al-dawliyya).

In most cases, we have pluralized with an 's' Arabic words known in English. Thus we opted for '*qāḍīs*', '*ḥadīths*', '*du'ās*' instead of the Arabic plural form '*quḍāt*', '*aḥādīth*', '*ad'iya'*. Some chapters have used the Gregorian calendar only and others have used both dates of the Gregorian calendar and their equivalent in the Islamic calendar, which starts with the year of emigration (*Hijra* in Arabic) of Prophet Muḥammad from Mecca to Medina in 622. For example: 1741–42 (1154 A.H.). Finally, the 'ayn has been transcribed ['] and the marker of feminity [h] final has been omitted. For example we have opted for *qaṣīda* and not *qaṣīdah.*

Abbreviations

ACI	African Citation Index
ACT	American College Testing
AKDN	Aga Khan Development Network
AKF	Aga Khan Foundation
b.	bin, i.e. son of
bt.	bint, i.e. daughter of
c.	circa
CE	Current Era
CODESRIA	Council for the Development of Social Science Research in Africa
d.	died
FLN	Front de Libération Nationale
GHA	*General History of Africa*
HDS	Harvard Divinity School
ICT	information and communications technology
IDEAs	International Development Economics Associates
IQRABA	IQRA Bilingual Academy
ISERI	Islamic University in Nouakchott
lit.	literally
n.p.	no publisher
NYFACS	New York French American Charter School
SABS	Senegalese American Bilingual School
SAT	Scholastic Aptitude Test
Sh.	Shaykh
trans.	translator
vss.	verses
WACA	West African College of the Atlantic

Acknowledgements

In 2012, I was appointed to the Alwaleed Bin Talal chair of Contemporary Islamic Religion and Society, whose mission is to contribute to the development of the field of Islam in sub-Saharan Africa and especially its intellectual history. Pursuing such an objective required mobilizing a community of scholars and students around extra-curricular activities such as conferences, symposia, lecture series, etc. This in turn requires financial and logistical resources.

I was fortunate that Harvard University provided such resources, and many colleagues near and far agreed to join us in an ongoing intellectual conversation around an annual conference series and an annual lecture series on Islam in Africa, both of which I initiated, and which have been meeting regularly in the last several years. This volume is the product of the first two conferences: 'Texts, Knowledge and Practice: The Meaning of Scholarship in Muslim Africa', convened in February 2017, and 'New Directions in the Study of Islamic Scholarship in Africa', in October 2017. A follow-up volume on Africa, Globalization and the Muslim World, based on the third annual conference, 'West Africa and the Maghreb' (September 2018), and the fourth, 'Africa, Globalization, and the Muslim World' (September 2019, the last co-organized with Zekeria Ould Ahmed Salam at Northwestern University), is forthcoming as a special issue of the journal *Religions*. In addition to the annual conference, the Islam in Africa lecture series provides a platform for the discussion of cutting-edge research in the field of Islam in Africa and brings authors of newly published books and advanced PhD students to campus to discuss their work.

For tirelessly and generously pumping money to make these activities happen, I gratefully acknowledge the financial support of many schools, departments, institutes and centres at Harvard, including Harvard Divinity School, the Hutchins Center, the Alwaleed Bin Talal Program of Islamic Studies, the Department of African and African American Studies, the Center for African Studies, the Provostial Fund for the Arts and the Humanities, the Weatherhead Center for International Affairs at Harvard University and the Radcliffe Institute.

Heartfelt thanks are offered to David Hempton, the Dean of the Divinity School, and Janet Gyatso, the Academic Dean, for their constant support. The Office of Academic Affairs of Harvard Divinity School has also provided unflinching logistical support, from booking flights and hotel rooms, and dinner tables in restaurants, to producing posters, arranging for venues, and video-recording the events for wide dissemination. I especially would like to acknowledge the support of Matthew Turner, Marlon Cumming, Jennifer Conforti, Bob Deveau, Karin Grundler Whitacker, Herchel Blemur and Kristin Gunst.

A number of colleagues at Harvard University have been very supportive of our activities, including Charles Hallisey, Leila Ahmed, Henry Louis Gates Jr, Emmanuel Akyempong, Jacob Olupona, Kimberly Patton, Stephanie Paulsell and Frank Clooney.

Several of our graduate students, some of whom have now become colleagues, have been part of this conversation. I would like to thank Ayodeji Ogunnaike, Oludamini Ogunnaike, Kimberly Wortmann, Farah El-Sharif, Armaan Siddiqi, Matthew Steele, Norbert Litoing, Abtsam Saleh and Adnan Wood-Smith. Mamadou Diouf, Souleymane Bachir Diagne, Mahmood Mamdani, Zachary Wright of Northwestern University in Qatar and Zekeria Ould Ahmed Salem, who co-organized the fourth Islam in Africa conference, have been wonderful conversation partners and friends for well over a decade.

I am very grateful to Jaqueline Mitchell, Commissioning Editor at James Currey, for her keen interest in this project and guidance during the preparation of the manuscript, as well as to my co-editors of the Religion in Transforming Africa series for their feedback on the project. I thank all the reviewers of the volume for their useful suggestions.

Finally, I thank my family, and especially Sister Khadija, for her tireless effort in hosting conference and lecture series participants.

To her, and our assistant Nanouna, this collective volume is dedicated.

INTRODUCTION

Where Have We Been and Where Are We Going in the Study of Islamic Scholarship in Africa?

Ousmane Oumar Kane

> When I performed my first pilgrimage to Mecca in 1937, sixteen Muslim scholars from different parts of the World and I were invited for dinner by King Sa'ūd b. 'Abd al-'Azīz of Saudi Arabia. During our conversation, one Egyptian scholar apparently impressed by my erudition, asked me where I lived in Egypt. I replied that I have never been to Egypt. Surprised, he then asked me where I did study, and I replied with my father in Senegal. He then asked when my father did graduate from Egypt? I replied he never studied in Egypt. He studied only with his own father. Sadly, the Egyptian scholar believed that it is only in Al-Azhar that one can acquire solid Islamic knowledge.
>
> Shaykh Ibrahim Niasse

To introduce this collection of essays, a personal note is much in order! In July 2012, I was appointed to the Alwaleed Professorship of Contemporary Islamic Religion and Society at Harvard Divinity School (HDS) to develop the field of Islam in sub-Saharan Africa, and especially its intellectual history. One of the first courses I taught was entitled 'Readings in the Islamic Archive of Africa'. Its purpose was to explore the intellectual production of Arabophone intellectuals, especially those from West Africa. I contacted the librarian of HDS to order the relevant course material. He informed me that he specialized in Christianity and did not have the expertise to deal with Arabic books, and referred me to the Middle Eastern librarian at the Widener Library of Harvard University. The latter could not order Arabic books from sub-Saharan Africa because he specialized in the Middle East and North Africa, but referred me in turn to his colleague the librarian of sub-Saharan Africa, who could not order Arabic books either. Since Arabic was supposedly not a language of sub-Saharan Africa, it did not fall within her field.[1] This difficulty of acquiring books had of course confronted graduate students working on Islam in Africa before my arrival at Harvard. To solve the problem without stepping on anybody's toes, the Dean of HDS offered some of his discretionary funds to acquire the books that I needed. A kind gesture – but it did not address the root of the problem.

This anecdote speaks volumes about the ways in which the academic division of labour in the study of Africa in Western universities makes the study of the Islamic scholarship of sub-Saharan Africa difficult. This problem is not specific to Harvard. It is the same everywhere, and is further illustrated by the programming of centres of African Studies and centres of Middle Eastern Studies. The former focus on sub-Saharan Africa and typically exclude North Africa, and the latter centre their programming on North Africa and some parts of Western Asia. In fact, the roots of this particularly regional division lie in the racial bias of Enlightenment European thinkers such as Hegel,[2] who felt the need to separate a 'black' and uncivilized Africa from one that contributed to and shared some of Europe's Mediterranean heritage. Thus, the interconnections between these two regions are largely ignored. Such a division and its underlying assumptions overlook the fact that for centuries the Islamic faith and the Arabic language cemented relations between large populations in the Maghreb, the Sahara, and West Africa. Furthermore, to this day many African Muslims imagine and understand their communities in ways that directly contradict this largely Western division of sub-Saharan Africa and North Africa.

It is now well known that, with the spread of Arabic literacy, African scholars developed a rich tradition of debate over orthodoxy and meaning in Islam. The colonization of the African continent at the turn of the twentieth century and the establishment of European colonial rule and Western types of schools did not eradicate the Islamic scholarly tradition in Africa. It rested on the faulty assumption that the Sahara was a physical barrier to intellectual exhange between a literate North Africa and an oral sub-Saharan Africa. The growth of literacy in Arabic in sub-Saharan Africa was not at all disconnected from centres of Islamic learning elsewhere in the Muslim world. As will be obvious to the readers of this volume, West African scholars participated in the development of virtually every field of Islamic sciences. Some of the essays featured in this volume constitute major

[1] The situation has now thankfully changed at Harvard and we are grateful to the librarian of sub-Saharan Africa for her diligence in ordering books that we need.

[2] In an infamous series of lectures he delivered on the philosophy of world history in 1822–23, Hegel claimed that Africa south of the Sahara was 'outside history'. See Georg Wilhelm Friedrich Hegel, *The Philosophy of History* (New York: Willey Book Co., 1900) 99.

contributions to astronomy (chapter 2),[3] political theory (chapter 5),[4] philosophy (chapter 6),[5] and jurisprudence (chapter 7),[6] to cite just a few. In addition, a glance at the curriculum and the writings of scholars of sub-Saharan Africa, including those who never travelled beyond their homeland, shows that many of them were extremely learned, but also engaged with the works of authors from all over the Muslim world, proving that they had long been integrated in a global network of intellectual exchange.

For most of the twentieth century, this literary tradition had remained unknown to the Western world and scholarship outside a small circle of specialists. At the turn of the twenty-first century, however, many commendable efforts have been made to document this literary tradition. Dozens of doctoral dissertations have been produced on Islamic scholarship in Africa. They have documented the rise of clerical lineages in sub-Saharan Africa, the role of these lineages in societal reform and state building from the sixteenth to the nineteenth centuries, and their intellectual production. In addition, dozens of catalogues of sub-Saharan African Islamic manuscripts have been produced, and thousands of Arabic manuscripts digitalized, some of them even translated into European languages.[7]

Despite this huge scholarly endeavour, Islamic scholarship in black Africa had remained invisible in the larger field of Islamic studies and African studies, but also in major debates of the social sciences. Between 2004 and 2016, the publication of three volumes of essays gave significant visibility to the study of Islamic

[3] Dahlia Gubara, 'Muhammad al-Kashnāwī and the Everyday Life of the Occult', presents the Durr al-manẓum by Muḥammad al-Kashnāwī from Nigeria, which 'displays extensive knowledge of scientific and cosmological theories that had prevailed over the centuries in all of the Islamic, Christian and Jewish traditions, as well as their precursors in classical Antiquity'.

[4] Ismail Warscheid, '"Those Who Represent the Sovereign in his Absence": Muslim Scholarship and the Question of Legal Authority in the Pre-Modern Sahara (Southern Algeria, Mauritania, Mali), 1750–1850', featuring the *Kitāb al-Bādiya* by Muḥammad al-Māmi (d. 1865–66), which is a major contribution of a Saharan scholar to political theory and to the development of Islamic legal thought.

[5] Oludamini Ogunnaike, 'Philosophical Sufism in the Sokoto Caliphate: The Case of Shaykh Dan Tafa', examines the work of Shaykh Dan Tafa (d. 1864) to show that the study of philosophy is part and parcel of the intellectual history of West Africa.

[6] Farah el-Sharif, '"If all the Legal Schools were to Disappear": ʿUmar Tāl's Approach to Jurisprudence in *Kitāb al-Rimāḥ*', which is one of the most important – yet understudied – works of the nineteenth century in the Muslim world.

[7] See Ousmane Kane, *Beyond Timbuktu. An Intellectual History of Muslim West Africa* (Cambridge: Harvard University Press, 2016) chapter 1. Charles Stewart and Bruce Hall have put online a database of more than 20,000 manuscripts, giving a good idea of the breadth of Islamic scholarship in the Sahel. See https://waamd.lib.berkeley.edu/home https://waamd.lib.berkeley.edu/home. Accessed 1 March 2020.

erudition in Africa. The first, edited by Scott Reese,[8] is entitled *The Transmission of Learning in Muslim Africa* and the second, by Shamil Jeppie and Souleymane Bachir Diagne, *The Meanings of Timbuktu.*[9] The latter came out of an international conference convened at the University of Cape Town in South Africa, in which the most prominent scholars who shaped the field of Islamic scholarship in Africa in the last fifty years participated, including John Hunwick, Sean O'Fahey, Charles Stewart, Abdel Wedoud Ould Cheikh, Yahya Ould el-Bara, Timothy Cleveland, Shamil Jeppie, Murray Last, and others. Many 'traditional' scholars of Timbuktu like Hamu al-Arawānī, 'Abd al-Qādir Haidara, also attended the conference and authored chapters in the resulting collective volume. Themes they explored included the Timbuktu libraries, African Arabic literature as a source of history, and the biographies of prominent scholars of Timbuktu. The third, edited by Robert Launay,[10] is entitled *Islamic Education in Africa: Writing Boards and Blackboards.* Since the publication of these books, the field has grown considerably and attracted younger, talented scholars whose work is transforming not just the larger field of Islamic studies and African studies, but is also beginning to inform debates in many disciplines in the social sciences. Dozens of articles and monographs have been produced, documenting various aspects of this intellectual tradition, but there has been no recent state-of-the art volume.

To take stock of these developments, I convened an international conference entitled 'Texts, Knowledge, and Practice: The Meaning of Scholarship in Muslim Africa' at HDS in February 2017, which brought together twenty-five scholars from twenty-one universities in Europe, the Middle East, Africa, and the United States.[11] Drawn from a variety of disciplines including history, Islamic studies, anthropology, philosophy, religious studies, and political science, these conference participants explored the literary cultures expressed in the Arabic language or in African languages written with the Arabic script. Like the pioneers in the field, participants refuted the notion that Muslim societies in black Africa were essentially oral prior to the European colonial conquest of the turn of the twentieth century. Their analysis of the movement of texts and ideas across and between West and North Africa through the Sahara and between East Africa

[8] Scott Reese (ed.), *The Transmission of Learning in Muslim Africa* (Leiden: Brill, 2004).

[9] Shamil Jeppie and Souleymane Bachir Diagne (eds.), *The Meanings of Timbuktu* (Cape Town: Human Sciences Research Council, 2008).

[10] Robert Launay (ed.), *Islamic Education in Africa: Writing Boards and Blackboards* (Bloomington: Indiana University Press, 2016).

[11] I acknowledge the assistance of Matthew Steele, a PhD candidate at the Department of Near Eastern Languages and Civilizations, Harvard University for the planning of this conference.

and the Arabian Peninsula across the Rea Sea and the Indian Ocean further confirmed that Muslim scholars south of the Sahara have never been isolated. On the contrary, they have long interacted and been integrated with other parts of the Muslim world.

In October 2017, I hosted a follow-up workshop at the Radcliffe Institute at Harvard University. Entitled 'New directions in the study of Islamic scholarship in Africa', it brought together half of the scholars who attended the February 2017 international conference and a few more to continue the conversation started in the previous February. This volume results from the conference and follow-up workshop. Panelists assessed the achievements in the study of Islamic scholarship in Africa, addressed the limitations in the emerging scholarship, and charted new directions for the field. Among the issues that they interrogated, the following were paramount: are sub-Saharan Africans mainly consumers of knowledge produced elsewhere or have they contributed as equal partners to knowledge production? Is the textuality versus orality paradigm relevant in African Islamic scholarship? Is *'Ajamī* essentially about the transmission of basic religious knowledge? What is the relevance of this Islamic scholarship for larger debates in the social sciences about epistemology, postcolonial, and decolonial studies? Last but not least, are scholars working in the field of Islamic scholarhip in Africa on the cutting edge of the debates about the epistemology of knowledge production?

Sub-Saharan Scholars and the Production and Global Transmission of Islamic Knowledge

The emerging literature addresses the intellectual linkages between Arabs and Africans by looking at the movement of sub-Saharan Africans to major centres of learning in North Africa and the Arabian Peninsula to study and perform the pilgrimage. Yet, there was also movement in the opposite direction when Berbers and Arabs came to study among black African shaykhs. Furthermore, many prominent sub-Saharan African scholars taught in Fez, Egypt, and the Holy Lands. The workshop challenged the implicit assumption that sub-Saharan Africans tend to be junior partners in these intellectual relations.

The vignette in the introduction (Figure 0.1) features the Senegalese Shaykh Ibrahim Niasse (1900–75), a towering figure of twentieth-century African Islam, whose following runs in the millions in the African continent and beyond.[12] He

[12] A dozen monographs have been devoted to the impact of his teaching and his disciples in Africa in English or French. Notable among them are Cheikh Niang, 'Le transnational pour argument. Socio-anthropologie historique du mouvement confrérique tidjane de Cheikh Ibrahim Niasse (Sénégal, Niger, Nigeria)', PhD diss. in Anthropology, Université de Toulouse, 2014; Oludamini Ogunnaike, *Deep Knowledge: Ways*

Fig. 0.1 Shaykh Ibrahim Niasse (Credit: Djim Diop)

occupied prominent positions in pan-Islamic organizations such as the World Muslim League, the World Muslim Congress based in Karachi, Pakistan, and the Research Academy of the Al-Azhar University, and made major interventions in all important matters affecting the affairs of the global Muslim community. Shaykh Ibrahim taught in the Wolof language to his Senegalese disciples and in Arabic to Arabic-speaking Mauritanian students and non-Senegalese African disciples.[13] Yet, the Egyptian scholar he met in Mecca could not possibly

of Knowing in Sufism and Ifa, Two West African Intellectual Traditions (Penn State University Press, forthcoming); Adam Barnes, 'A comparative spirituality of liberation: The Anti-Poverty Struggles of the Poverty Initiative and the Tijaniyya of Kiota', PhD diss., Union Theological Seminary New York, 2014; Zachary Wright, *Living Knowledge in West African Islam: The Sufi Community of Ibrahim Niasse* (Leiden: E.J. Brill, 2014); Rudiger Seeseman, *The Divine Flood: Ibrahim Niasse and the Roots of a Twentieth-century Sufi Revival* (Oxford: Oxford University Press, 2011); Antonio de Diego González, *Ley y Gnosis. Historia Intelectual de la ṭarīqa Tijāniyya* (Granada: Editorial Universidad de Granada, 2020); Yasir Anjola Quadri, 'The Tijaniyyah in Nigeria. A Case Study', PhD diss., Arabic and Islamic Studies, University of Ibadan, 1981; Britta Frede, *Die Erneuerung der Tiğānīya in Mauretanien. Popularisierung religiöser Ideen in der Kolonialzeit.* ZMO Studien; 31. (Berlin: Schwarz-Verlag, 2014); Abdul Ganiy Muhammad Raji Abiodin, 'Shaykh Ibrahim Niass: His Revival of the Tijaniyya Sufi order and response to colonialism', PhD diss., International Islamic University Malaysia, 2016. For Arabic sources, see following footnote.

[13] One of his Arabic-speaking disciples has collected and edited his entire work, consisting of a multi-volume exegesis of the Qur'ān in Arabic; an encyclopedia of his prominent disciples in Africa, and the collection of all his poetry and poems written in praise of him in Arabic. On his exegesis of the Qur'ān, see Ibrahim Niasse, *Fī Riyāḍ al-Tafsīr li'l-Qur'ān al-Karīm* (M. Ibn al-Shaykh ʿAbdullāh, compiled and edited, 2014). Muḥammad ibn al-Shaykh ʿAbdullāh, *Mādhā ʿan al-Shaykh Ibrāhīm* (Lemden Mauritania, Muḥammad ibn al-Shaykh ʿAbdullāh, 2014). On his disciples, see Muḥammad ibn al-Shaykh ʿAbdullāh, *Rijāl wa Adwār fī Ẓill Ṣāḥib al-Fayḍah al-Tijānīyah: Al-Milaff al-Gharb Ifrīqī.* (Lemden Mauritania: Muḥammad ibn

have imagined that he (or for that matter his father) could receive advanced learning outside Al-Azhar, let alone in West Africa.

Yet, that Shaykh Ibrahim acquired his knowledge with his father in Senegal, and his father with his grandfather, stands to reason. Before the erection of colonial borders in West Africa, there existed wide translocal scholarly networks in the Sahelian region, within which texts and scholars circulated unrestrained, and any text could be taught in any region. The analysis of the core curriculum of Islamic studies in the Sahel[14] reveals that the same works were taught in North Africa, Egypt, and West Africa. Shaykh Abdallah Niasse (1845–1922), the father and teacher of Shaykh Ibrahim, also acquired all his knowledge in Senegal. Yet, he did receive honorary knowledge certification in Egypt during his pilgrimage to Mecca in 1891. As was the custom with scholars visiting Egypt, Shaykh Abdallah, according to his Mauritanian biographer Muḥammad b. ʿAbdallāh b. Muḥammad b. al-Ṣaghīr al-ʿAlawī,[15] met with Al-Azhar *ʻUlamā'*. After extensive conversation with him, they awarded him honorary certificates (*ijāza al-tabarruk*)[16] acknowledging his competence in Islamic sciences. Furthermore, the fact that

---

al-Shaykh ʿAbdullāh, 2014); Muḥammad ibn al-Shaykh ʿAbdullāh, *Rijāl wa Adwār fī Ẓill Ṣāḥib al-Fayḍah al-Tijānīyah: Al-Milaff al-Mūrītānī.* (Lemden Mauritania: Muḥammad ibn al-Shaykh ʿAbdullāh, 2014); Muḥammad ibn al-Shaykh ʿAbdullāh, *Rijāl wa adwār fī ẓill Ṣāḥib al-Fayḍa al-Tijānīya: Al-Milaff al-Singhālī.* (Lemden Mauritania: Muḥammad ibn al-Shaykh ʿAbdullāh, 2014). On his poetry, Muḥammad ibn al-Shaykh ʿAbdullāh, *Āfāq al-Shiʿr fī al-Shaykh Ibrāhīm Niyās* (Lemden Mauritania: Muḥammad ibn al-Shaykh ʿAbdullāh, 2018. (Vols. 1–6).

14 See for example Deddoud Ould Abdallah, *Dawr al-Shanāqiṭa fi-nashr al-thaqāfa al-'arabiyya al-islāmiyya bi-Gharb Ifrīqiyya ḥattā nihāyat al-ḳarn al-thāmina ʻashar li ʻl-mīlād, Annales de la Fac. des Lettres et des Sciences Humaines de l'Univ. de Nouakchott,* 1989, 13–33; A.D.H. Bivar; Mervyn Hiskett, 'The Arabic Literature of Nigeria to 1804: a provisional account', *Bulletin of the School of Oriental and African Studies,* xxv, 1962, 104–48; Mervyn Hiskett, 'Materials related to the state of learning among the Fulani before their jihad', *Bulletin of the School of Oriental and African Studies*, 19, 3, 1957, 550–78; Bruce Hall; Charles Stewart, 'The Historic "Core Curriculum" and The Book Market in Islamic West Africa,' in Graziano Krätli; Ghislaine Lydon (dirs.), *The Trans-Saharan Book Trade* (Leiden and Boston: Brill, 2011) 109–74; Thierno Ka, *Ecole de Pir-Saniokhor et culture arabo-islamique au Sénégal du XVIIe au XXe siècle* (Dakar: GIA, nd).

15 Muḥammad b. ʿAbdallāh b. Muḥammad b. al-Ṣaghīr al-ʿAlawī, *Muṭrib al-sāmiʿīn al-nāẓirīn fī manāqib al-Shaykh al-Ḥājj ʿAbdallāh b. al-Sayyid Muḥammad* (Kaolack, Senegal: Maktabat al-Nahḍa, 2004).

16 In Islamic learning there exist two types of certificates. The first is a licence to teach a book given by a master to a student who studied a book with him, and the second *ijāza al-tabarruk* or honorary certification is given to peers in recognition of their erudition.

the author of the unique and extensive biography of Shaykh Ibrahim's father was a prominent Arab scholar testifies to the close interactions and intellectual friendship between scholars of different parts of West Africa. The city of Kaolack, where Shaykh Ibrahim Niasse grew up, was an economic and intellectual hub at the turn of the twentieth century. It attracted scholars from West and North Africa, some of whom were the guests of his father. All this proves that the Niasse family had been at the cutting edge of Islamic scholarship for generations and were a living contradiction of the balkanization of sub-Saharan Africa in the academy as well as in the perspective of many Arabs like the Egyptian scholar from the beginning of this introduction.

It is true that Al-Azhar has been a major centre of Islamic learning for over a thousand years and attracted students from all over the world, including black Africans. The first residence (*riwāq*)[17] for West African students and pilgrims was established in Al-Azhar in the mid-thirteenth century for Borno students and pilgrims (Riwāq al-Burnīya). In the eighteenth century, three of the twenty-five residences of Al-Azhar hosted students from West-Central Africa. The above-mentioned Riwāq al-Burnīya for students of the Borno Region of Central Africa,[18] the Riwāq al-Dakārinah for students from Takrūr, Sinnār, and Darfūr, and other places in the Sudan and Central Africa,[19] and the Riwāq Dakārnah Sāliḥ for students from the Lake Chad Region of Africa[20] are a testament to the long-standing presence of sub-Saharan Africans in the most prestigious institutions of higher Islamic education. But Muslims from black Africa have also been prominent teachers at Al-Azhar, and for that matter, other major centres of Islamic learning all over the world. Two centuries before Shaykh Ibrahim Niasse, Muhammad Al-Kashnāwī (d. 1741), whose biography Dahlia Gubara covers in this volume, received his entire education in present day northern Nigeria[21] before travelling to the Holy Lands and settling in Al-Azhar, where he stayed till the end of his life. Yet, he taught many people in Egypt. His name was immortalized by a necrology featured in one of the most renowned historical works of Ottoman Egypt:

[17] As noted by Dahlia Gubara, 'Al-Azhar and the Orders of Knowledge', 33: *riwāq* pl. *arwiqa* in Arabic 'are the basic administrative units – denoting residential and study quarters of students – around which al-Azhar remains organized, and are mostly classified according to the students'. See also Bayard Dodge, 'Principal Units of the Riwāq system', in Dodge, *Al-Azhar. A Millennium of Muslim Learning* (Washington, DC: The Muslim Institute, 1961), Appendix IV, 201–07.

[18] Dodge, *Al-Azhar*, 203.

[19] Dodge, *Al-Azhar*, 202.

[20] Dodge, *Al-Azhar*, 205.

[21] See Dahlia Gubara, chapter 2 of this volume; and Gubara, 'Al-Azhar and the Orders of Knowledge', 257–58.

the *'Ajā'ib al-Āthār fi al-tarājim wal akhbār* ('The Marvellous Compositions of Biographies and Events') by 'Abd al-Raḥmān al-Jabartī (1753–1825).[22]

There are tales of other influential West African teachers in North Africa. Ahmad Baba al-Timbukti (d. 1627) was one of them.[23] Deported to Morocco following the Saadian invasion of Songhay, he resided there between May 1594 and February 1608. During his stay, he taught in the most reputed schools in Marrakesh. His students included luminaries such as Aḥmad b. Muḥammad al-Maqqarī al-Tilimsāni (d. 1041/1632), the author of *Nafḥ al-tīb min ghusn al-Andalūs al-raṭīb wa-dhikr wazīrihā Lisān al-Dīn ibn al-Khaṭīb* ('The Breath of Perfume from the Branch of Flourishing Al-Andalūs and Memories of its Vizier Lisān al-Dīn ibn al-Khaṭīb'), the most imporant reference work on the intellectual history of Muslim Spain; Ibn Abi Nu'aym al-Ghassani, qadi of Fez (d. 1032/1623); and Ibn al-Qāḍī, qadi of Meknes (d. 1025/1616).[24] A leading authority in Mālikī jurisprudence, Ahmad Baba authored a much-cited bibliographic dictionary of Mālikī jurists.[25]

22 'Abd al-Raḥmān al-Jabartī, *'Ajā'ib al-āthār fi'l-tarājim wa'l-akhbār* (4 vols., Cairo: Bulaq, 1880). It was translated as Thomas Philipp; Moshe Perlmann, 'Abd al-Raḥmān al-Jabartī's History of Egypt: *'Ajā'ib al-thar fī 'l-Tarājim wa 'l-Akhbār* (Stuttgart: Franz Steiner Verlag, 1994).

23 On Ahmad Baba, see Hunwick, *Arabic Literature of Africa*, IV: 17–31; Brockelman, *Geschichte der Arabischen Literatur* II: 618; Supplementbänden II: 715–16; Mahmoud A. Zouber, *Ahmad Baba (1556–1627). Sa vie et son œuvre* (Paris: Maisonneuve et Larose, 1977); John Hunwick, 'Ahmad Baba and the Moroccan invasion of the Sudan (1591),' *Journal of the Historical Society of Nigeria*, 2, 1, 1962, 311–28; John Hunwick, 'A New Source for the study of Ahmad Baba al-Timbukti (1556–1627)', *Bulletin of the School of Oriental and African Studies*, 27, 1964, 568–93; Mohamed Zaouit, 'Mi'raj as-su'ud et les Ajwiba: Deux consultations juridiques d'Ahmad Baba de Tombouctou relatives à l'esclavage des Noirs au Bilad al-Sudan au XVIème et début du XVIIe siècle: édition critique et analyse historique', PhD diss., Université de Paris 1, 1997; ISESCO, *Ahmad Baba al-Timbukti: Buhuth al-nadwa allati 'aqadatha ISESCO bi-munāsabat murūr arba'a qurūn wa niṣf 'aā wilādatihi*, Actes du colloque organisé par l'ISESCO quatre siècles et demi après la naissance de Ahmed Baba (Marrakesh: ISESCO, 1993); M.A. Cherbonneau, 'Essai sur la littérature arabe au Soudan d'après le Tekmilet ed-Dibaje d'Ahmed Baba le Tombouctien', *Annales de la Société archéologique de Constantine*, ii, 1854–55, 1–42; Tim Cleaveland, 'Ahmed Baba and His Islamic Critique of Slavery in the Maghreb', *Journal of North African Studies*, 20, 1, 2015, 42.

24 Paulo F. de Moraes Farias, 'Ahmad Baba', *Encyclopaedia of Islam III* (Leiden: E.J. Brill, 2007).

25 Titled *Nayl al-Ibtihāj fi Taṭrīz al-Dibāj*, it was written as a supplement to *Al-Dibāj al-Mudhahhab fi ma'rifat a'yān 'Ulamā' al-madhhab* by Ibrahim b. Ali b. Farhun. See John Hunwick, *Arabic Literature of Africa*, IV, 23.

It is also well known that Sufi orders played a major role in Islamic education and intellectual production in sub-Saharan Africa.[26] Yet there is a perception that the Sufi orders were a gift to black Africa from the Middle East and North Africa. This story, according to Zachary Wright,[27] is incomplete. Instead, 'Black African scholars had long been involved in articulating the constituent elements of the *Ṭarīqa Muḥammadiyya* phenomenon that the Tijāniyya drew upon so heavily'.[28] In fact, 'Abd al-'Azīz al-Dabbāgh, an important source for the *Ṭarīqa Muḥammadiyya*'s emphasis on direct contact with the Prophet Muḥammad[29] and whose teaching exerted considerable influence on Shaykh Aḥmad al-Tijānī, studied with a Borno scholar named 'Abdallah al-Barnāwī.[30] The same cliché is true for Salafiyya/Wahhābiyya doctrines, which are assumed to have been brought to Africa by returning pilgrims. Chanfi Ahmed demonstrates that scholars from West Africa have helped the nascent regime of Ibn Sa'ud in the field of teaching and preaching in Saudi Arabia but also outside Saudi Arabia and were instrumental in the development of Wahhābī theology (chapter 4 of this volume).[31]

Beyond the Orality/Textuality Dichotomy

By documenting the literary cultures of Africa through the study of manuscripts and biographies of prominent Muslim scholars, pioneers in the field of Islamic scholarship in sub-Saharan Africa have refuted the notion that Africa had no written literary tradition prior to European colonial rule. In the process, however, they have failed to clarify the ways in which orality and textuality interact in the

[26] Rudolph Ware; Zachary Wright; Amir Syed, *Jihad of the Pen Sufi Scholars of Africa in Translation* (Beirut: Oxford University Press, 2018) 11.

[27] See Wright, 'African Roots', chapter 1 of this volume. See also Wright, *Realizing Islam: The Tijaniyya in North Africa and the Eighteenth-Century Muslim World* (Chapel Hill: University of North Carolina Press, 2020), in which he fully develops the argument.

[28] Wright, 'African Roots'.

[29] Wright, 'African Roots'.

[30] 'Abd al-'Azīz al-Dabbāgh is reported by his student and compiler of his thoughts Al-Lamāṭī (1679–1743) to have said: 'Sayyidi 'Abd Allah al-Barnāwī remained with me. He guided me, directed me and strengthened me, and the fear in my heart ... was removed.' See Aḥmad b.al-Mubārak Al-Lamāṭī, *Pure Gold from the Words of Sayyidī 'Abd al-Aziz*, translated by John O'Kane and Bernd Radtke with notes and an outline (Leiden: Brill, 2007) 133.

[31] See also Chanfi Ahmed, *West African 'ulamā' and Salafism in Mecca and Medina: Jawāb al-Ifrīqī – The Response of the African* (Leiden: Brill, 2015); Chanfi Ahmed, *AfroMecca in History. African Societies, Anti-Black Racism, and Teaching in al-Haram Mosque in Mecca* (Newcastle: Cambridge Scholars, 2019).

transmission of knowledge. As documented in many chapters in this volume, orality has always been central in this tradition and, for that matter, Islamic epistemology. Lidwien Kapteijns and Alessandra Vianello (chapter 14) document very well the ways in which Somali Sufi Shaykhs in Brava composed religious didactic poems orally or in writing. Yunus Kumek (chapter 9) shows that in the everyday life of Egyptians, the Qur'ān is performed orally. In his analysis of the traditions of oral commentary and teaching in the Islamic sciences, especially philosophy and Sufism, Oludamini Ogunnaike (chapter 6) demonstrates that there can be significant creative intellectual activity that does not necessarily leave behind written traces.

Unlike the modern context where students learn much from reading books alone in their rooms, the direct oral transmission of knowledge from master to students had always been deemed the most reliable form of transmission in Islam,[32] as it had been in most traditional African cultures as well. Simply put, African Muslims had a deep and intimate knowledge of the relative strengths and drawbacks of both oral and written expression and knowledge transmission and intentionally used each – and often both simultaneously – when necessary or advantageous. Thus, the orality/textuality dichotomy which continues to be a trope in this field is misleading. Islamic scholarship in particular has embraced both oral and written transmission and merged the two in some ways, presenting an important and direct challenge to the teleological process of development from orality to literacy that is often taken for granted in the West.

The abovementioned Shaykh Ibrahim Niasse is one of the most prolific and influential Sufi authors of the twentieth century. He wrote abundantly in all fields of knowledge. Yet, the most lasting impact of his teaching was conducted orally. He conducted exegesis of the Qur'ān in Arabic for his Arabic-speaking disciples, some of whom were Arabs and other non-Senegalese West Africans, and in Wolof for his Senegambian disciples. Both exegeses were recorded and circulated widely among his disciples.[33] It was only in 2010, thirty-five years after his passing, that his Arabic *tafsīr* was transcribed and started circulating in printed form.[34]

32 See Gregor Schoeler, *The Oral and the Written in Early Islam* (London and New York: Routledge, 2006) 45; Chase Robinson, *Islamic Historiography* (Cambridge: Cambridge University Press, 2003) 145.

33 For the oral *tafsīr* in Wolof, see Ibrahim Niasse, *Traduction et interprétation du Saint Coran en Wolof 1950–1960* (New York: Sall Family Publishers, 1998) 30 cassettes, with a preface by Ibrahim Mahmoud Diop. It is also now on YouTube. See https://www.youtube.com/user/CheckhIbrahimNiass. Accessed March 2020.

34 Ibrahim Niasse, *Fī Riyāḍ al-Tafsīr li'l-Qur'ān al-Karīm* (Vols. 1–6) (M. Ibn al-Shaykh ʿAbdullāh, Ed.).

Nigerian disciples of his who listened to the *tafsīr* either in Arabic or Wolof taught it in turn orally in Hausa when they returned to their home country.[35]

On a related note, the workshop addressed the ways in which orality has regained momentum with the spread of the new technologies of information. The affordability of cellphones and internet connection and the availability of social media such as YouTube, WhatsApp, and Facebook is transforming the transmission of Islamic knowledge and the modalities of spiritual cultivation in a fundamental way and significantly expanding the reach of the teaching of West African scholars. Students enrolled in modern urban schools are using social media apps, Skype for example, to simultaneously study a traditional Islamic curriculum with a teacher based in rural areas. Teachers based in Africa are offering online classes to students residing hundreds if not thousands of kilometres away on a regular basis covering a substantial amount of material. The process of spiritual initiation or *tarbiya*, which typically required bodily encounters betweeen the master and the disciple, now takes place via social media apps. This dynamic and adaptation of the traditional system of Islamic education demonstrates that it is not dying out with increased globalization, but is rather absorbing features of the new technological era to increase its reach and allow its students to participate in both arenas. De Diego González (chapter 8) shows how the current generation of Tijānī shaykhs, and especially Shaykh Muhammad Mahi Cisse, whose following includes Muslims from not just Africa, but also America and Asia, uses these media to connect and answer the questions of his disciples.

'Ajamī as Vehicle of Transmission of Sophisticated Knowledge

The spread of Islam paved the way for the development of *'Ajamī* – the use of Arabic script to transcribe African languages. There is virtually no region that has been under Islamic influence that has not adopted the Arabic alphabet for transcribing local languages. Current research on the African manuscript heritage attests to the usage of the Arabic script in eighty languages and in all parts of Africa.[36] It is well documented that literate Africans have written in *'Ajamī*

[35] Andrea Brigaglia, 'Learning, Gnosis and Exegesis: Public Tafsīr and Sufi Revival in the City of Kano (Northern Nigeria), 1950–1970', *Die Welt des Islams*, 49, 2009, 334–66.

[36] Meikal Mumin, 'The Arabic Script in Africa: Understudied Literacy', in Meikal Mumin; Kees Versteegh, *The Arabic Script in Africa. Studies in the Use of a Writing System* (Boston and Leiden: Brill, 2014) 41–76; Mahmud Hamu, *Al-kashf 'an al-makhṭūṭāt al-'arabiyya wa al-maktūbāt bil-ḥarf al-'arabī fi minṭaqat al-Ṣāḥil al-Ifrīqī*, Timbuktu, undated and unpublished manuscript. I am grateful to Andrea Brigaglia for supplying me with a copy of this manuscript.

to explain complex notions of Islamic theology to the masses of Africans who knew no Arabic. Most of the *'Ajamī* literature addresses very old manuscripts and almost treats *'Ajamī* as a thing of the past. However, in many areas *'Ajamī* is still very much a living tradition that people at various intellectual levels use to transmit information of all types.[37] A new body of sophisticated *'Ajamī* writings is challenging the idea that the main goal of *'Ajamī* was to transmit basic knowledge. This body of writings includes elaborate poetry, exegesis of the Qur'ān, and theology that together articulate sophisticated knowledge intended for an erudite audience. A close examination of this body of *'Ajamī* writings challenges the assumption of a language hierarchy that informs most of the study of *'Ajamī* in Africa.

As noted, Shaykh Ibrahim Niasse produced an exegesis of the Qur'ān in both Arabic and Wolof in an equal degree of lexical and epistemological sophistication. By no means was the Arabic exegesis more sophisticated than the Wolof one. Some of the *'Ajamī* exegeses of the Qur'ān were delivered only orally. But others were produced in written form and destined for a learned audience. Such is the case of the exegesis of Muhammad Dem, a Murid scholar entitled *mawrid al-ḍama'ān fī tafsīr al-Qur'ān* ('Springs of the Thirsty. A Qur'ānic Exegesis').[38]

Islamic Scholarship in Africa and the Social Sciences Debates

In the debate among social scientists about the production of knowledge on Africa, Islamic scholarship has for a long time been completely ignored among Europhone intellectuals.[39] The Council for the Development of Social Science Research in Africa (CODESRIA), a leading pan-Africanist consortium founded in 1973, took it from the ghetto into the major debates.[40] Indeed, at the turn of the twenty-first century, CODESRIA commissioned a working paper aimed at

37 Fallou Ngom, *Muslims Beyond the Arab World: The Odyssey of Ajami and the Muridiyya* (New York: Oxford University Press, 2016).

38 See Jeremy Dell, 'Unbraiding the Qur'an: Wolofal and the *Tafsīr* Tradition of Senegambia', *Islamic Africa,* 9, 2018, 55–76.

39 The phrase 'Europhone' was coined by Kwame Appiah to refer to intellectuals trained in European languages and especially French, English, and Portuguese in sub-Saharan Africa. See Kwame Anthony Appiah, *In My Father's House: Africa in the Philosophy of Culture* (London: Methuen, 1992) 4. 'Non Europhone' refers to those scholars who use African languages as a medium of knowledge transmission. See Ousmane Kane, *Non-Europhone Intellectuals* (Dakar: CODESRIA, 2012).

40 For more on CODESRIA's role in promoting the social sciences in Africa, see the conclusion of this volume by Ebrima Sall entitled 'The Study of Islamic Scholarship and the Social Sciences in Africa: Bridging Knowledge Divides, Reframing Narratives'.

setting a research agenda bringing Islamic scholarship in Africa into the debate among social scientists about knowledge production in Africa. Published initially in French as 'Intellectuels non europhones', it was translated and published in Arabic, English, and Spanish.[41] CODESRIA subsequently partnered with the Human Sciences Research Council of South Africa and the University of Cape Town to sponsor the collective volume *The Meanings of Timbuktu*, which brought African Islamic erudition to the attention of African social scientists. To ensure wide dissemination, the volume was also published in French.[42]

A few groundbreaking studies with considerable theoretical sophistication were accomplished by intellectual historians of Islam in Africa.[43] Yet the majority of scholars in the field of Islamic scholarship failed to put the study of Islamic scholarship in Africa in conversation with cutting-edge debate in the social sciences. In that respect, Dahlia Gubara remarks that 'the lack of attention to concepts mars many of their approaches, and the absence of a sustained analysis of the guiding proposition that "Africa" could or should be integrated through texts, libraries, and above all the Arabic language, into a domain defined as "Islamic", does little to subvert disciplinary thinking'. Reading intelligently al-Jabartī's *'Ajā'ib al-āthār*, she shows for example that 'instead of the singular all-encompassing modern designation "black", there existed a variegated palette of skin-colours – aṣmar, aswad, abyaḍ, aḥmar, qamḥī, etc. Similarly, in place of the distinct category of African, there existed an assortment of identity-markers (zanj, sūdān, aḥbāsh, nūba, barābirah, takārnah, etc.) partaking of a different geographical imaginary that is reflected in the organization of al-Azhar itself.' 'The very search for Africans in al-Jabartī,' she argues, 'is contingent upon the presence of a unitary "Africa" (black or not), which

[41] Ousmane Kane, *Intellectuels non Europhones* (Dakar: CODESRIA, 2003), translated in English as *Non Europhone Intellectuals* (Dakar: CODESRIA, 2012); in Arabic as *Al-muthaqqafūn al-ifriqiyyūn al-mutaḥaddithūn bi-lughāt ghayr urūbiyya* (Cairo: Center for Arab Studies, 2005), and in Spanish as *Africa y la produccion intellectual no eurofona. Introduccion al conocimento islamico al sur del Sahara* (Madrid: Oozebap, 2011).

[42] Shamil Jeppie; Souleymane Bachir Diagne (eds.), *Tombouctou: Pour une histoire de l'érudition en Afrique de l'Ouest*, trans. Ousmane Kane (Dakar and Cape Town: CODESRIA and Human Sciences Research Council, 2012).

[43] To cite some of them: Rudolph Ware, *The Walking Qu'ran. Islamic Knowledge, the Body, and History in West Africa, 1000CE–present* (Chapel Hill: University of North Carolina Press, 2014); Louis Brenner, *Controlling Knowledge: Religion, Power and Schooling in a West African Muslim Society* (London: Hurst, 2000); Bruce S. Hall, *A History of Race in Muslim West Africa, 1600–1960* (Cambridge: Cambridge University Press, 2011); Sean Hanretta; *Islam and Social Change in Africa* (New York: Cambridge University Press, 2009).

does not exist in the *ʿAjāʾib* quite simply because there was no place for a continentalist vision in al-Jabartī's worldview.'[44]

Road Map

This volume is organized in one general introduction, four parts, and a general conclusion. Each of the four parts is preceded by an introduction presenting the articles in that part and the ways in which they serve the general topic of the book, which is to present new and exciting work in the field and to chart new directions in the study of Islamic scholarship.

Part I, 'History, Movement and Islamic scholarship', introduced by Zachary Wright, comprises four articles. The African presence in centres of learning and pilgrimage, including many prominent teachers, is documented with Zachary Wright's 'The African Roots of a Global Eighteenth-Century Islamic Scholarly Renewal', Dahlia Gubara's 'Muhammad Al-Kashnāwī and the Everyday Life of the Occult', and Chanfi Ahmed's 'African Community and African *'Ulamā'* in Mecca'. Ousmane Kane's 'Transformation of Pilgrimage in West Africa' shows how the pilgrimage tradition which for centuries was linked to intellectual pursuits became divorced from erudition, and linked to trade and tourism.

Entitled 'Textuality, Orality, and Islamic Scholarship', Part II, introduced by Oludamini Ogunnaike, includes five chapters. Some of these address major intellectual contributions by West African scholars, including Mami's *Kitāb al-bādiya*, Dan Tafa's many works on philosophical Sufism in the Sokoto Caliphate, and 'Umar Tāl's *Kitāb al-Rimāḥ*. Other chapters demonstrate that textuality had never been divorced from orality and address the specific advantages of both orality and textuality and how they are strategically employed in the transmission of knowledge and the performance of spirituality. De Diego González shows that orality has regained momentum with the use of information and communications technology (ICT) to transmit knowledge, especially esoteric knowledge. Yunus Kumek's chapter on the Qur'ānic performance in Egypt also shows how spirituality and the reading of the Qur'ān in particular contributes to the peace, serenity, and tranquillity of Egyptian populations.

Part III, introduced by Britta Frede, is entitled 'Islamic Education'. All four chapters in this part address the ways in which Islamic education has been transformed in West and East Africa. Caitlyn Bolton's 'Modernizing the Madrasa: Islamic Education, Development, and Tradition in Zanzibar' and Laura Cochrane's

[44] See Gubara, 'Al-Azhar and the Orders of Knowledge', 242; same author, 'Al-Azhar in the Bibliographic Imagination', *Journal of Arabic Studies*, 2012; and same author, 'Revisiting Race and Slavery Through Abd al-Rahman al-Jabarti's 'Ajā'ib al-āthār', *Comparative Study of South Asia, Africa and the Middle East*, 38, 2, 2018, 230–45.

'A New *Daara*: Integrating Qur'ānic, Agricultural and Trade Education in a Community Setting' look at how development concerns are reconfiguring the curriculum of Islamic education in Senegal and Zanzibar, while Britta Frede, who focuses on women's education in Mauritania, traces similar transformations. Finally, Hannah Hoechner's chapter documents how the demand for Islamic education by Senegalese immigrants in the United States has contributed to the emergence in the home country of a new type of school in Senegal that is both Islamic and international in outlook.

Part IV, entitled '*'Ajamī*, Knowledge Transmission, and Spirituality', deals with the role of African languages in the production of Islamic knowledge. Introduced by Jeremy Aaron Dell, and focusing on the writings of Sufi scholars of the 'Alawiyya and the Qādiriyya in East Africa, or the Murīdiyya in West Africa, these chapters offer a fascinating window into the elaborate devotional poetry produced in *'Ajamī*. Lidwien Kapteijns and Alessandra Vianello's 'Bringing *'Ilm* to the Common People: Sufi Vernacular Poetry and Islamic Education in Brava, c. 1890–1959', Khadim Ndiaye's 'A Senegalese Sufi saint and *'Ajamī* poet: Sëriñ Moor Kayre (1874–1951)' and Abdulkadir Hashim's 'Praise and Prestige: Significance of Elegiac Poetry among Muslim Intellectuals on the Late Twentieth Century Kenya Coast' all contribute to that effort. Hashim's article shows notably that the composition of elaborate Swahili poetry in the Arabic script, as testified notably by the globetrotter Ibn Battuta who visited the Swahili Coast in the fourteenth century, spans a period of at least eight centuries.

Last but not least, the general conclusion is authored by Ebrima Sall, who served twenty-five years in CODESRIA, directing various research programmes and also heading the organization for eight years. It was under his leadership of CODESRIA that Islamic scholarship in Africa became a priority in the research agenda of the Council. Entitled 'The Study of Islamic Scholarship and the Social Sciences in Africa: Bridging Knowledge Divides, Reframing Narratives', the conclusion reflects on the ways in which debates in the social sciences and post-colonial and decolonial studies can be enriched by close attention to the study of Islamic erudition.

PART I

HISTORY, MOVEMENT, AND ISLAMIC SCHOLARSHIP

Introduction

Zachary Wright

Islamic learning in Africa has always been in fruitful dialogue with broader developments in Islamic intellectual history elsewhere in the world. African Muslims travelled or migrated to the Middle East and other places in the Muslim world. Arabs and others visited or came to live in Africa. Africans read the literatures of Muslims around the globe, and sometimes studied under the great scholars of their time in Cairo and the like. So too did non-Africans read the works of African Muslim scholars, and apprentice themselves to them when given the chance. Historical dynamism, travel, and circulation have been consistent themes of African Islamic intellectual history.

This story is important because understandings of African Muslim societies often privilege the reading of local contexts in preference to global exchanges. Of course, local contexts, in Africa and elsewhere, ultimately remain indispensable for understanding the reception and performance of Muslim identities. But sometimes the artificial circumscription of African places returns us unwittingly to older colonial mentalities of an *Islam Noir*: a 'black Islam' that, unlike its Arab counterpart, was thought to be illiterate, superstitious, static, and servile. It is thus important to recognize African Islam as scripturally informed, unbound by place, responsive to racial stereotypes, adaptive to changing pedagogical priorities, and often self-perceived as authoritative.

It is related, by way of example, that the formative black African (*sūdānī*) scholar of Timbuktu, the fifteenth-century Muḥammad al-Kābarī, was once slandered by a Moroccan scholar jealous of the Timbuktu scholar's renown, and called '*al-Kāfirī*' (infidel) instead of al-Kābarī. According to al-Saʿdī's *Tārīkh al-sūdān*, God punished the Moroccan man for his affront against one of God's saints, afflicting him with leprosy. The man became desperate and consulted a soothsayer who advised him to eat the heart of a young boy to cure himself. This he did, and for this lapse into the ways of infidels, God caused him to die in a 'most pitiable condition'.[1] From the perspective of some West African intellectuals,

[1] 'Abd al-Raḥmān al-Saʿdī, *Tārīkh al-sūdān*, in John Hunwick, *Timbuktu and the Songhay Empire* (Leiden: Brill, 2003) 69–70.

then, Arabs or others disrespected the scholarly credentials and sainthood of black African Muslims at their own peril.

Zachary Wright's 'The African Roots of a Global Eighteenth-Century Islamic Scholarly Renewal' highlights the importance of African scholars in articulating the central ideas debated at the dawn of the modern era in the Muslim world. Recent research has redeemed the intellectual vibrancy of this period, and suggested that ideas on legal theory, *ḥadīth*, Sufism, and esotericism equalled or even transcended earlier articulations. African Muslim scholars sometimes preceded their Arab and Indian counterparts in these articulations, other times they were present in Cairo or Medina at the time of development of these ideas, and still other times they corresponded with the key interlocutors of these scholarly networks. This chapter uses the background of West African participation in discourses of global Islamic scholarly exchange to reflect on the spread of the Tijāniyya Sufi order in the region. While founded in North Africa with little direct connection to West African scholars, many Muslims south of the Sahara readily accepted the Tijāniyya because they had prefigured the main ideas of 'Muḥammadan Sufism' (*Ṭarīqa Muḥammadiyya*), independent scholarly reasoning (*ijtihād*), and saintly authority that Aḥmad al-Tijānī (d. 1815, Fez) himself articulated.

In 'Muhammad al-Kashnāwī and the Everyday Life of the Occult', Dahlia Gubara provides a valuable case study of a notable Central African scholar in the early eighteenth century. After accomplishing the pilgrimage to Arabia, al-Kashnāwī settled in Cairo. There he had a wide intellectual influence, most particularly on an Egyptian scholar who would later produce arguably the most important text of eighteenth-century Egypt: al-Jabartī's 'History of Egypt' (*'Ajā'ib al-athār*). Gubara shows how 'modern reconfigurations' concerning the Islamic esoteric or talismanic tradition serve to marginalize the intellectual contributions of scholars like al-Kashnāwī. But in his time, al-Kashnāwī was appreciated for his broader scholarly expertise in theology, Islamic law, and mysticism, as well as in esotericism. His fascinating work, *al-Durr al-manẓūm*, is a commentary of one of the Islamic literary tradition's most difficult works, Fakhr al-Dīn al-Rāzī's (d. 1209) *al-Sirr al-maktūm*. It was begun in response to the request of al-Kashnāwī's Arab student in Mecca. Aside from clarification of al-Rāzī's lengthy philosophical and esoteric mediations, al-Kashnāwī makes several important additions that underscore the originality of his work. The book also contains useful historical information about eighteenth-century scholarly networks, summarizes the esoteric scientific understandings of the day, and reflects on the occult practices of a variety of religions.

Chanfi Ahmed shows in 'African Community and African *'ulamā'* in Mecca' that some African scholars have made names for themselves in the highest echelons of the Saudi clerical establishment. While pejorative Saudi stereotypes of Africans residing in the Hijaz do persist, many Saudi citizens push back against the structural marginalization of those of African descent in contemporary Saudi society. And in a country styling itself as the bastion of pure Islam, several Afro-Saudi scholars have insisted on their unique positionality for the desired spread of Islam on the African continent: a claim that no doubt ensures their reputational as well as their financial well-being. Overall, Chanfi's chapter demonstrates that African scholars were not limited in their global influence to traditional juristic (*madhhab*) or Sufi (*ṭarīqa*) networks. Even if they traded their traditional African clothes for the uniforms of contemporary Arab Salafism, African intellectuals inscribed themselves into the centres of the modern Wahhābī reform movement and expanded its reach far beyond the Arab Gulf.

Ousmane Kane's 'The Transformation of the Pilgrimage Tradition in West Africa' tracks how changes in the pilgrimage tradition became divorced from intellectual pursuits. Unlike in the pre-modern period when pilgrimage was closely linked to scholarship, it has become linked more to tourism in the contemporary world. African *ḥujjāj* now return from the pilgrimage with bags full of gifts from Mecca and other global cities visited en route, influencing dress styles in their places of origin. New technologies permit increasing numbers of people, including women, to make this prestigious journey. While nation-state restrictions on visas and the length of stay no longer permit substantive knowledge exchanges while on pilgrimage, African Muslims have responded by applying for separate student visas to study in the Muslim world, or to organize their own pious visitations (*ziyāra*) to centres of scholarship in West Africa. Some of these gatherings of African Muslims, to celebrate the birthday of the Prophet Muḥammad for example, are today almost as large as the *Ḥajj* itself, with millions of people coming to hear lectures, buy books, and exchange knowledge. African Muslims are not only some of the *Ḥajj*'s most enthusiastic participants, they also build on the pilgrimage tradition to inspire large-scale regional movements and exchanges of people and knowledge for religious purposes.

This section on the 'History, Movement, and Islamic Scholarship' thus speaks to the exchange of ideas, people, representations, and pedagogies in ways that highlight the adaptability, ingenuity, and authority of African Muslim subjects. While African Muslim identities must also be understood with reference to local contexts and discourses specific to bounded African places, such local conversations are inevitably shaped by global conversations. African Muslims have always been active participants in trans-regional exchanges associated with the global Muslim world.

CHAPTER 1

The African Roots of a Global Eighteenth-Century Islamic Scholarly Renewal

Zachary Wright

Islam noir, the notion that 'black' Muslims inherently practise a different (less orthodox, less scriptural, less warlike) form of Islam than their Arab coreligionists, cannot be fully destabilized without a deeper intellectual history of African Muslim scholarship. Many African and Islamic Studies researchers continue to ignore black Muslim scholars as constitutive participants in global Islamic discourses. Failing to insert a global Islamic perspective, appropriately historicized, persistently localizes and trivializes African Muslim scholarship inconsonant to the ways African Muslim scholars see themselves.

The current academic excitement surrounding African *'Ajamī* literatures, for example, ignores the high probability that a greater percentage of Islamic scholarly production in Senegal, for example, happens in Arabic versus Wolofal, than does Arabic versus Persian in Iran, or Arabic versus Urdu in Pakistan. Islamic scholarship among West African Muslims is arguably more Arabicized than any other non-Arab Muslim population. As Ousmane Kane has observed, 'Islam and the Arabic language are no more foreign in Africa than they are in Syria, Lebanon, Palestine, and Iraq … Arabic is by far the most widely spoken African language.'[1] The translation and articulation of Islamic identity in local African languages remain important, especially for a non-scholarly audience, but this process is no more pronounced in West Africa than is Muslim scholars' use of Arabic vernaculars to explain Islamic learning in Egypt, Morocco, or other Arabic-speaking countries. Another example of the misleading localization of African Islam would be studies of Islamic talismanic sciences in African Muslim societies that very seldom take up the challenge of comparing such practices to similar 'occult' expressions in Arab, Turkish, or Iranian societies. The enduring strength

[1] Ousmane Kane, *Beyond Timbuktu: An Intellectual History of Muslim West Africa* (Cambridge, MA: Harvard University Press, 2016) 207–8.

of shaykh–disciple relationships in many African Muslim communities can also be misinterpreted: my earlier work on the community of Shaykh Ibrahim Niasse demonstrated that such practices were in fact at the core of classical Islamic pedagogical techniques throughout the Muslim world.[2] The disciple's willing submission to his shaykh was an attempt to fully actualize Islamic identity; it did not invoke some sort of African authoritarianism said to define '*Islam noir*'.

Like other stories of Islamic intellectual history since the spread of Islam in Africa, the dramatic scholarly activity of the eighteenth century involved Sudanic Africa in significant ways. Many have readily observed, of course, that the nineteenth century witnessed a flurry of Sufi activity on the African continent, with a number of 'reformist' Sufi orders expanding the social involvement of clerical communities and even engaging in jihād against the perceived injustices of local rulers and encroaching colonial interests. From 'Uthmān ibn Fūdī of the Qādiriyya in Nigeria, to 'Umar al-Fūtī Tāl of the Tijāniyya in Senegal and Mali, to Muḥammad al-Sanūsī of Sanūsiyya-Shādhiliyya in Libya, to Muḥammad 'Abdallāh al-Ḥasan of the Ṣāliḥiyya-Shādhiliyya in Somalia, activists were connected through global networks of teacher–student relationships that had culminated in the eighteenth century and which shared lines of knowledge transmission and similar (though not identical) perspectives on Sufism. But eighteenth-century scholarly revival is often narrated as emerging from the Hijaz and Cairo, with resonance on the peripheries of the Muslim world. Like so many other stories of Islamic intellectual history, Africa appears as the receiver of external trends, not as the constitutive interlocutor with these trends. Returning to such narratives is essential for locating African Muslim scholars in global intellectual exchanges, and thus for decentring the lingering racialization of African Islam.

This paper argues that sub-Saharan African scholars were active participants in a sphere of scholarship linking West Africa with Morocco and Egypt, one that dated back at least to the sixteenth century. While John Hunwick, Stefan Reichmuth and others have earlier highlighted such remarkable exchanges, I go further here in suggesting that sub-Saharan Africa was a determinative source for the emergence of an eighteenth-century scholarly revival centred on the idea of the *Ṭarīqa Muḥammadiyya*. Thus, the reception of new, ostensibly 'foreign' Sufi orders – most notably the Tijāniyya – cannot be explained by a supposed racialized pre-disposition of 'black' sub-Saharan Africans to follow the lead of 'white' North Africans. Rather, black African scholars had long been involved in articulating the constituent elements of the *Ṭarīqa Muḥammadiyya* phenomenon that the Tijāniyya drew upon so heavily.

[2] Zachary Wright, *Living Knowledge in West African Islam: the Sufi Community of Ibrāhīm Niasse* (Leiden: Brill, 2015) 32–3.

The *Ṭarīqa Muḥammadiyya* refers to the increasing tendency of Sufi intellectuals in the eighteenth century to invoke a pre-eminent 'Muḥammadan' Sufi path that 1) bound aspirants to following the behavioural ideal of the Prophet, 2) stressed the Sufi's worldly involvement, and 3) held the promise of the aspirant's direct connection to the enduring spirituality of the Prophet Muḥammad through the practice of 'prayer on the Prophet' (*ṣalāt ʿalā al-nabī*). The combination of these ideas often led *Ṭarīqa Muḥammadiyya* scholars to criticize excessive veneration for a particular school of law (*madhhab*), to temper some of the perceived excesses of 'popular Islam' (including fascination with esoteric sciences such as talismans and geomancy), and to articulate remarkable claims of spiritual authority. Nonetheless, none of these notions – by themselves – were particularly new in the intellectual history of Sufism.[3] And as an idea rather than a movement, various Sufi communities forwarded their own interpretations of the 'Muḥammadan Way'.[4] But the fact remains that the eighteenth-century flourishing of Sufism usually invoked a pre-eminent *Ṭarīqa Muḥammadiyya* with a relatively standard set of practices and doctrines. Scholars in sub-Saharan Africa were leading proponents of these ideas from at least the sixteenth century, and they may have influenced their Arab counterparts in the Middle East.

This chapter draws upon source materials that reference Islamic scholarly exchanges between North and sub- (or perhaps trans-) Saharan Africa prior to the nineteenth century. Primary centres of scholarship include Timbuktu, Fez, Kanem-Bornu, and Cairo. Leaving aside the more impressionistic glosses that can be found elsewhere, I am more interested in evidence of the particular ideas that were common to the eighteenth and nineteenth century spread of *Ṭarīqa Muḥammadiyya* movements, ostensibly from the Middle East and North Africa to sub-Saharan Africa. This exploration is part of a larger historical inquiry into the origins of the Tijāniyya, probably Africa's most popular Sufi order since the nineteenth century. I thus include reference to specific Tijānī invocations of this earlier trans-Saharan intellectual history, as a means to better understand the Tijāniyya's rapid spread south of the Maghreb. A summarized version of this research has been included in the first chapter of my recent monograph of the Tijāniyya,[5] but this paper broadens the analysis of intellectual exchange between sub-Saharan Africa and the Middle East and North Africa.

[3] R.S. O'Fahey; Bernd Radtke, 'Neo-Sufism Reconsidered', *Islam*, 70, 1993, 52–87; Bernd Radtke, 'Sufism in the 18th Century: an attempt at a provisional appraisal', *Die Welt des Islams*, 36, 3, 1996, 326–64.

[4] John Voll, 'Neo-Sufism: Reconsidered Again', *Canadian Journal of African Studies*, 42, 2/3, 2008, 314–30; Zachary Wright, *Realizing Islam: the Tijāniyya in North Africa and the Eighteenth-Century Muslim World* (Chapel Hill, NC: University of North Carolina Press, 2020) 6–7, 48–52.

[5] Wright, *Realizing Islam*, 24–30.

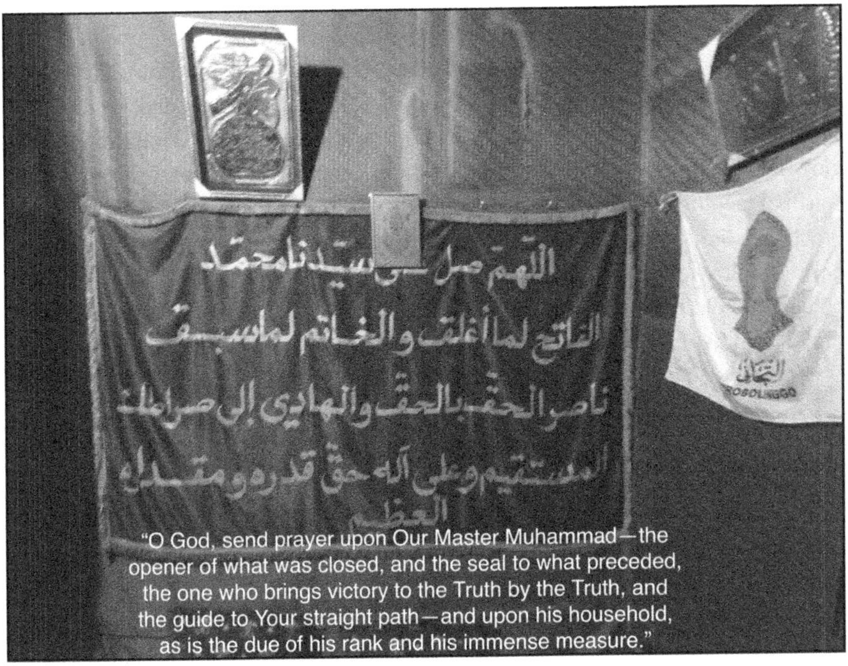

Fig. 1.1 The *Ṣalāt al-fātiḥ* (the prayer of opening) displayed on the wall of the room in which Aḥmad al-Tijani performed spiritual retreat in Boussemghoun, Algeria in the 1880s (Credit: Ousmane Oumar Kane)

Muḥammad al-Bakrī and the Scholars of Timbuktu

The Egyptian Muḥammad b. ʿAlī al-Bakrī (d. 1585) was a shaykh at Al-Azhar and one of the most renowned scholars of sixteenth-century Egypt. He is celebrated within the Tijāniyya as the source for the legendary prayer on the Prophet Muḥammad, *Ṣalāt al-fātiḥ* (the prayer of opening – see Figure 1.1),[6] which later became a pillar of Tijānī litanies. Al-Bakrī was so named because his family claimed descent from the Prophet's companion Abū Bakr Siddīq. His grandfather originally hailed from the Fayyum oasis in the Egyptian desert. He was extremely wealthy, and his father was the first to perform the pilgrimage rituals while being carried in a palanquin. 'Abd al-Wahhāb al-Shaʿrānī (1493–1565) referred to al-Bakrī as the 'reviver' (*mujaddid*) of the sacred law, and esteemed his famous collection of Sufi prayers, the *ḥizb al-bakrī*.[7]

[6] This illustration shows the *Ṣalāt al-fātiḥ* displayed in the wall of the room in which Aḥmad al-Tijānī performed spiritual retreat in Boussemghoun, Algeria in the 1880s.

[7] Michael Winter, *Society and Religion in Early Ottoman Egypt: Studies in the Writings of ʿAbd al-Wahhāb al-Shaʿrānī* (New Brunswick, NJ: Transaction Publishers, 2009) 170.

Interestingly enough, Muḥammad al-Bakrī also makes an appearance in chronicles of Timbuktu. He is described in ʻAbd al-Rahmān al-Saʻdī's *Taʾrīkh al-Sūdān* in several places as 'the friend of God' (*walī Allāh*) and 'axial saint' (*quṭb*) of his time 'who had great affection for the scholars of Timbuktu'.[8] This glowing description led Nehemia Levtzion to conclude 'The Bakri shaykhs were spiritual mentors of the scholars of Timbuktu, who were themselves [like al-Bakrī] practising Sufis without an affiliation to a brotherhood.'[9] While al-Bakrī apparently did provide a close spiritual mentorship for several scholars of Timbuktu, he clearly held their scholarly credentials as equal to his own. He thus addressed the Timbuktu *ḥadīth* scholar and jurist, Aḥmad b. Aḥmad b. ʻUmar Aqīt in verse:

> I swear by God that I am true to you, with love for you unchanged,
> affection likewise true.
> The sweetness of our days together I recall, those times our talk
> was grave and deep.[10]

Al-Bakrī was one of many Arab scholars that Timbuktu pilgrims visited in Egypt on their way to Mecca in the sixteenth century. For his part, al-Bakrī attested to the sainthood of Timbuktu scholars, especially of the line of ʻUmar Aqīt. Some of these latter scholars spent time in Egypt studying with al-Bakrī, such as ʻUmar Aqīt's grandson Abu Bakr (d. 1583), 'who remained particularly close to the father of honor Muḥammad al-Bakrī, from whom he derived blessing, and on whose teachings he made notes'.[11]

Aside from the practice of Sufism disconnected from a formalized Sufi brotherhood,[12] al-Bakrī evidently shared several characteristics with the scholars of Timbuktu. Al-Bakrī emphasized the Sufi's involvement in society, the study of the law unbound by one *madhhab*, and the propensity for direct spiritual unveiling, particularly in relationship to the spirituality of the Prophet. Al-Bakrī was a gifted poet and accomplished mystic, who apparently preceded Aḥmad Sirhindi (d. 1624) in qualifying Ibn al-ʻArabī's concept of *waḥdat al-wujūd*: 'The unity

[8] John Hunwick, *Timbuktu and the Songhay Empire: al-Saʻadī's Taʾrīkh al-Sūdān down to 1613 and other contemporary documents* (Leiden: Brill, 2003) 43, 87.

[9] Nehemia Levtzion, 'Eighteenth Century Sufi Brotherhoods: Structural, Organizational and Ritual Changes', in Peter Riddell; Tony Street (eds.), *Islam: Essays on Scripture, thought and society: a festschrift in honour of Anthony Johns* (New York: Brill, 1997) 154.

[10] Hunwick, *Timbuktu and the Songhay Empire*, 47.

[11] Hunwick, *Timbuktu and the Songhay Empire*, 61.

[12] This may have been the case of most Sufi practitioners prior to the eighteenth century, such as al-Ghazālī and al-Suyūṭī. See Levtzion, 'Eighteenth Century Sufi Brotherhoods', 147–60.

is experiential, not ontological.'[13] Nonetheless, he was well regarded by Ibn al-ʿArabī's primary popularizer ʿAbd al-Wahhāb al-Shaʿrānī, who apparently shared with al-Bakrī a nominal association with the Shādhiliyya.

Despite al-Bakrī's affiliation to the Shāfiʿī *madhhab*, the scholars of Timbuktu perceived him as sympathetic to their Mālikī expertise. The *Taʾrīkh al-Sūdān* has al-Bakrī appearing in a spiritual vision to bless the young Timbuktu scholar ʿUryān al-Raʾs' study of the key Mālikī text, al-Qayrawānī's *al-Risāla*:

> Sidi Muḥammad al-Bakrī came across him [al-Raʾs] sitting at the door of the Sankore mosque in the early afternoon … The divinely favored shaykh stopped beside him and inquired what the book was in his hand, and was told it was the *Risāla*. Stretching out his blessed hand the Shaykh asked to see it, and after examining it for a while, gave it back to him saying, 'May God bring blessing upon you through it,' and continued on his way.[14]

The text goes on to suggest that al-Bakrī was a regular visitor to other scholars of Timbuktu, despite his physical presence in Egypt.

According to Levtzion, a later generation of Timbuktu scholars, represented by the famous Aḥmad Bābā, began to favour Egyptian scholarship over their Moroccan counterparts for the latter's exclusive interest in Mālikī texts.[15] While al-Suyūṭī's writings were no doubt influential in Timbuktu, the more sustained contact with al-Bakrī may have been the more direct scholarly exchange with Egypt from the sixteenth century that influenced Bābā's criticism of Morocco. Moreover, the scholars of Timbuktu had other subsequent contacts with (non-Mālikī) Arab scholars of note. A certain Ahmad Bābā (different from the original) from Timbuktu met the Syrian Naqshbandī Shaykh 'Abd al-Ghanī al-Nābulusī in Medina in 1694, and at the Timbuktu scholar's request composed a commentary on the versified rendition of Muḥammad b. Yūsuf al-Sanūsī's (d. 1490) *ʿAqīda al-ṣughra* by the Timbuktu student of the original Aḥmad Bābā, Muḥammad Baghrūʿu.[16] The contact between Ahmad 'al-Timbuktī' and Nabulusī is significant, as the latter's ideas on the *Ṭarīqa Muḥammadiyya*, transmitted through a

[13] Khaled El-Rouayheb, *Islamic Intellectual History in the Seventeenth Century: Scholarly Currents in the Ottoman Empire and the Maghreb* (New York: Cambridge University Press, 2015) 244.

[14] Hunwick, *Timbuktu and the Songhay Empire*, 76.

[15] Nehemia Levtzion, 'Islam in the Bilad al-Sudan to 1800', in R. Pouwels; N. Levtzion (eds.), *History of Islam in Africa* (Athens, OH: Ohio University Press, 2000) 72.

[16] Al-Nabulusī named this work *al-Laṭāʾif al-unsiyya ʿalā naẓm al-ʿaqīda al-sanūsiyya*. See Stefan Reichmuth, 'Islamic Education in Sub-Saharan Africa', in R. Pouwels and N. Levtzion (eds.), *History of Islam in Africa*, 428.

book on the subject and through his Khalwatī student Muṣṭafa al-Bakrī (d. 1749), helped define eighteenth-century articulations of the concept.[17]

While Timbuktu's scholarly exchanges with al-Bakrī are of note, the Sufi credentials of this Egyptian notable deserve emphasis. Despite his great wealth and expertise in Islamic law, he had a reputation for spiritual unveiling (*kashf*) that resonated in Timbuktu. The ability to 'see' God, the Prophet Muḥammad, and absent saints were all miracles of wide circulation in Timbuktu. Yaḥyā al-Tadilisī, for example, used to see the Prophet Muḥammad every night, until he was deprived of it on account of questionable business practices.[18] Al-Bakrī attested to the aforementioned ʿUryān al-Raʾs' ability to see God, even if the vision had temporarily confused his mind: 'He has seen a sight that cannot be endured. The final outcome of it will be good for him.'[19]

Tijānī sources also reference the saintly unveiling of Muḥammad al-Bakrī, namely as the source for the central Tijānī prayer, *ṣalāt al-fātiḥ*. Here is Aḥmad al-Tijānī's testimony to al-Bakrī and the *ṣalāt al-fātiḥ* as related in ʿAlī Harāzim's (d. 1802) *Jawāhir al-Maʿānī*:

> I occupied myself with the remembrance of *ṣalāt al-fātiḥ limā ughliq* upon returning from *Ḥajj* until I reached Tlemcen, because of what I perceived of its bounty. Namely, that one recitation is worth six hundred thousand prayers (of blessing on the Prophet), as is related in *Wardat al-Juyūb*.[20] The author of the *Wardat* mentions that its author, Sīdī Muḥammad al-Bakrī al-Ṣiddīqī, lived in Egypt and was an axial saint (*quṭb*), may God be pleased with him. He said, 'Whoever recites it one time and does not enter Paradise, let him arrest its author in the presence of God.' I continued to recite it until I traveled from Tlemcen to Abī Samghūn. Then I saw a prayer equivalent to seventy thousand times of *Dalāʾil al-khayrāt*[21] and I

[17] For al-Nabulusī's influential work on the subject, see ʿAbd al-Ghānī al-Nabulusī, *al-Ḥadīqa al-Nadiyya Sharḥ al-Ṭarīqa al-Muḥammadiyya wa l-Sayra al-Aḥmadiyya* (Beirut: Dār al-Kutub al-ʿIlmiyya, 2011).

[18] Levtzion, 'Islam in the Bilad al-Sudan', 73. Levtzion is here quoting from the *Taʾrīkh al-fattāsh*.

[19] Hunwick, *Timbuktu and the Songhay Empire*, 76.

[20] I believe this is a reference to ʿUmar b. ʿAbd al-ʿAzīz al-Jazūlī, *Wardat al-juyūb fī ṣalāt ʿalā l-ḥabīb*, a text available for download online from https://www.wdl.org/ar/item/11234/. Accessed 30 November 2016, originally sourced from the Library of Congress. The final pages reference the date of compilation as 1146 AH (1733 CE), although the final number of the date (6) is difficult to make out. The *ṣalāt al-fātiḥ* appears as the twenty-fourth of roughly forty prayers compiled in this manuscript, page 76. There is no mention in this copy of the manuscript of the benefit of different prayers included in the text, as evidently was the case for the copy al-Tijānī possessed. This manuscript may in fact be the first textual reference to *ṣalāt al-fātiḥ*.

[21] The famous collection of prayers on the Prophet authored by the North African

> left aside *al-Fātih limā ughliq* ... But then the Prophet commanded me to return to *Ṣalāt al-fātiḥ limā ughliq* ... and he informed me that one recitation of it was equivalent to all the glorifications ever uttered in creation, and all remembrances and all supplications, large or small, and of the Qur'ān six thousand times, since it (the Qur'ān) is among the remembrances.[22]

While al-Bakrī's prayer was apparently known before the emergence of the Tijāniyya, it was no doubt the Prophet's testimony of its merit to al-Tijānī that popularized it. Indeed, al-Tijānī goes on to assert the divine provenance of the prayer:

> The Prophet informed me that it was not the authorship of al-Bakrī. He devoted himself to God for a long time, asking that he be graced with a prayer upon the Prophet that contained the reward of all other prayers (upon the Prophet), and that was the secret of all prayers. And he persisted in his request for a long time. Then God answered his supplication, and an angel came to him with this prayer written on a sheet of light.[23]

The Tijāniyya thus claimed to have accessed the most treasured inheritance that al-Bakrī had left. The Prophet's appearance to al-Tijānī rescued *ṣalāt al-fātiḥ* from relative obscurity and purported to tell the real story of an exceedingly valuable prayer. Indeed, al-Bakrī seems to have kept *ṣalāt al-fātiḥ* more or less hidden during his lifetime. If he taught it to the scholars of Timbuktu, they neglected to pass it on themselves, and its mention is absent from biographical dictionaries of the period. The Tijāniyya's investiture of a prayer linked to al-Bakrī as the best of all prayers must have struck a chord with West African Muslim scholars who remembered the mutual affection between al-Bakrī and the scholars of Timbuktu.

Sub-Saharan Scholars in Egypt and the Hijaz

There is no doubt that Egypt in the eighteenth century, as earlier, was one of the great centres of Islamic learning. The revival of the Khalwatiyya in Egypt, which in the eighteenth century 'spread like a brush fire',[24] certainly influenced Sufi activism in sub-Saharan Africa. Aḥmad al-Tijānī was notably initiated into the Khalwatiyya at the hands of the Iraqi scholar Maḥmūd al-Kurdī. Al-Tijānī's relationship with Kurdī involved him in Middle Eastern networks of Sufi-scholarly exchange that involved sub-Saharan Africa long before the spread of the Tijāniyya south of the Sahara.

Shādhilī Sufi Muḥammad al-Jazūlī (d. 1465).

22 ʿAlī Ḥarāzim al-Barāda, *Jawāhir al-Maʿānī* (Beirut: Dār ak-fikr, 2001) 100.

23 Al-Barāda, *Jawāhir al-maʿānī*, 101.

24 Levtzion, 'Eighteenth Century Sufi Brotherhoods', 150.

Sub-Saharan African scholars were long present in Egypt, and the Middle East more generally, as both teachers and students. By the eighteenth century, three out of Azhar's twenty-five student dormitories were dedicated to students from central or western Africa. Students from the Maghreb had one dormitory.[25] Prominent African scholars resident in the Middle East for the period included Muḥammad al-Kashnāwī (d. 1741, Cairo), a mysterious 'Shaykh al-Barnāwī' (alive late eighteenth century, Cairo), and Ṣāliḥ al-Fullānī (d. 1803, Medina). The establishment of African scholars in Cairo is further attested by more quotidian mention in nineteenth-century Egyptian records. 'Umar Muḥammad al-Burnāwī al-Takrūrī (d. 1824, Cairo) died leaving a slave-girl and an extensive library that included a Qur'ān, the prayer-poem *Dalā'il al-khayrāt*, a commentary on the Mālikī legal text *Mukhtaṣar al-Khalīl*, several collections of Prophetic narrations, and books on 'spiritualism' (*rūḥaniyāt*).[26] An 1848 Cairo census mentions a certain 'Abdallah al-Dakrūrī (Takrūrī), 'a mufti and student at al-Azhar' who owned his own house in the city.[27] Travelling scholars from sub-Saharan Africa also frequently appeared in Egyptian *ijāza* literature, from al-Suyūṭī to Murtaḍā al-Zabīdī. Among al-Zabīdī's visiting students in Cairo from the Western Sudan, for example, were several direct students of Mukhtār al-Kuntī (d. 1811), with whom the later Tijāniyya would have close (if not always congenial) interactions, and Jibrīl b. 'Umar, the teacher of 'Uthmān b. Fūdī in central Sudan.[28] But it is the resident African scholars that deserve further mention for their more sustained dialogue with eighteenth-century intellectual developments in the Middle East.

The central Sudanic scholar Muḥammad al-Kashnāwī became well known in Egypt as the teacher of Ḥasan al-Jabartī, the father of the famous Egyptian historian 'Abd al-Raḥmān al-Jabartī, and as the author of an important treatise on the esoteric sciences: *al-Durr al-manẓūm wa khulāsat al-sirr al-maktūm fī l-siḥr*

[25] Dahlia Gubara, 'Al-Azhar and the Orders of Knowledge', PhD diss., Department of History, Columbia University, 2014, 229–30.

[26] Terence Walz, 'Trans-Saharan Migration and the Colonial Gaze: The Nigerians in Egypt', *Alif: Journal of Comparative Poetics*, 26, 2006, 94–118, 102.

[27] Terence Walz, 'Sudanese, Habasha, Takarna, and Barabira: Trans-Saharan Africans in Cairo as Shown in the 1848 Census', in Terence Walz; Kenneth M. Cuno (eds.), *Race and Slavery in the Middle East: Histories of Trans-Saharan Africans in 19th-Century Egypt, Sudan, and the Ottoman Mediterranean* (Cairo: American University in Cairo Press, 2011) 55. Walz reminds us that names such as Takrūrī or Burnāwī in Egyptian sources are sometimes misleading. Takrūrī, for example, could have included Bornu, Wadai, and Darfur, as well as the lands of Western African traditionally associated with the ancient kingdom of Takrūr.

[28] Stefan Reichmuth, *The World of Murtaḍa al-Zabīdī* (Cambridge: Gibb Memorial Trust, 2009) 190–4.

wa l-ṭalāsim wa l-nujūm.[29] While certainly known as an esotericist in Egypt, he boasted a comprehensive scholarly training before leaving Katsina sometime before 1730. Among his teachers were Muḥammad al-Walī al-Burnāwī and possibly Muḥammad Fūdī, the father of ʿUthmān b. Fudī.[30] Al-Walī (flourished late seventeenth century) was among the most famous scholars of Kanem-Bornu. Aside from his writings on ʻAshʻarī theology, his legal opinions prohibiting smoking made him one of the few Mālikī scholars of his age to take such a stance.[31] Indeed, al-Walī's prohibition may have signalled a shift against tobacco in sub-Saharan Africa, still largely tolerated in the eighteenth-century Middle East, that endeared the Tijāniyya to the region. Al-Nabulusī, for example, argued against the prohibition of smoking.[32] Al-Jabartī's description of the Egyptian Khalwatī Sufi and Mālikī jurist, ʿAlī al-Saʿīdī al-ʿAdawī (d. 1775), thus highlights the aversion of some of his peers for al-ʿAdawī's campaigns against smoking.[33] Al-Walī's moral rigour also characterized Kashnāwī's writings, as it did later Ṭarīqa Muḥammadiyya movements like the Tijāniyya.

Al-Kashnāwī's disposition towards the esoteric sciences appears to resonate with later Tijānī articulations:[34] he accepted their role in the actualization of religious knowledge, but he cautioned against their misuse. Al-Kashnāwī was hesitant to teach students his esoteric knowledge, having been warned previously:

> If I reached the countries of the East and especially the Ḥaramayn, I should not reveal to any of their inhabitants that I know something of those letter-based sciences, and what resembles them of the sand-based sciences, on account of their prevalent uses in these countries for causing corruption, tribulations and dissension [among people] in plain sight of those of discerning minds.[35]

29 An important summary of Kashnāwī's life and work can be found in chapter four of Dahlia Gubara's fascinating dissertation, 'Al-Azhar and the Orders of Knowledge'. Subsequent information on Kashnāwī is borrowed from Gubara's research.

30 Gubara, 'Al-Azhar and the Orders of Knowledge', 259–60.

31 According to Van Dalen, 'By the end of the seventeenth century, most jurists in the centers of the Middle East as well as the Maghreb, and certainly most Mālikī jurists, had come to the conclusion that smoking tobacco was allowed.' See Dorrit Van Dalen, *Doubt, Scholarship and Society in 17th-Century Central Sudanic Africa* (Leiden: Brill, 2016) 166.

32 Elizabeth Sirriyeh, *Sufi Visionary of Ottoman Damascus: ʿAbd al-Ghanī al-Nābulusī, 1641–1731* (New York: Routledge, 2011) 7.

33 Al-Jabartī, *History of Egypt*, I: 697.

34 For more on the esoteric sciences in the Tijāniyya, see Zachary Wright, 'Secrets on the Muhammadan Way: Transmission of the Esoteric Sciences in 18th century scholarly networks', *Islamic Africa*, 9, 1, 2018, 77–105.

35 Al-Kashnāwī, *Durr al-manẓūm*; cited in Gubara, 'Al-Azhar and the Orders of Knowledge', 319.

Al-Kashnāwī's book is not merely a collection of esoteric sciences, but a moral pronouncement on the 'virtues and misuses of the secret sciences'.[36] He laid out twelve preconditions for practising such secrets, ranging from initiation, concealment, seriousness of need, to the fear of God.[37] This was no doubt important advice: by the eighteenth century, the esoteric sciences were studied throughout Egypt by 'leading members of the establishment'.[38] The appearance of a sub-Saharan African scholar in Cairo as a foremost teacher and moral guide to the use of esoteric sciences in Cairo demonstrates that Africans in the Middle East were not peripheral to the intellectual debates of their age.

Another central Sudanic scholar appears prominently in the scholarly exchanges surrounding the circle of Muḥammad al-Ḥifnī (d. 1767), the Shaykh al-Azhar and the leading Khalwatī Shaykh of Egypt in the eighteenth century. Several accounts of Moroccan scholars of the period mention studying with a 'Shaykh al-Burnāwī' in Egypt, along with a standard caste of Middle Eastern Khalwatī shaykhs such as al-Ḥifnī, Kurdī and Muḥammad al-Sammān (d. 1775, Medina). The renowned 'Quṭb of Fes',[39] Aḥmad al-Ṣaqillī (d. 1764), may have been the first to bring the Khalwatiyya to Morocco following his initiation at the hands of al-Ḥifnī in 1745. Several of al-Ṣaqillī's students accompanied him, or followed him later. In Egypt, they visited and 'took from' al-Burnāwī. Al-Burnāwī's Moroccan student-guests thus included al-Ṣaqillī's students ʿAbd al-Majīd b. ʿAlī al-Zubādī (d. 1750) and ʿAbd al-Wahhāb al-Tāzī (d. 1791).[40] Al-Tāzī was also the student of ʿAbd al-ʿAzīz al-Dabbāgh (d. 1719, Fez), an important source for the *Ṭarīqa Muḥammadiyya*'s emphasis on direct contact with the Prophet Muḥammad and who also had a teacher from Bornu (see below). Al-Tāzī was moreover the teacher of Aḥmad b. Idrīs,[41] who along with al-Tijānī was a primary spokesman for the *Ṭarīqa Muḥammadiyya* concept by the early nineteenth century. While such scholarly exchanges tell us little about the actual teaching of this Shaykh al-Burnāwī in eighteenth-century Cairo, it is clear that a sub-Saharan African scholar was at the centre of Egypt's most important Sufi revival of the century.

[36] Gubara, 'Al-Azhar and the Orders of Knowledge', 323.

[37] Gubara, 'Al-Azhar and the Orders of Knowledge', 330–3.

[38] Gubara, 'Al-Azhar and the Orders of Knowledge', 247–8.

[39] According to Kattānī's *Salwat al-anfās*, al-Tijānī once remarked of Ṣaqillī: 'There is no axial saint buried within the walls of Fez except our master Aḥmad al-Ṣaqillī.' See Muḥammad b. Jaʿfar b. Idrīs al-Kattānī, *Salwat al-anfās wa muḥādathat al-akyās* (Rabat: Dār al-amān, 2014), I: 180.

[40] Al-Kattānī, *Salwat*, II: 264–5; III: 69.

[41] R.S. O'Fahey, *Enigmatic Saint: Ahmad ibn Idris and the Idrisi tradition* (Evanston: Northwestern University Press, 1990) 40–2. O'Fahey, perhaps lacking direct access to al-Kattānī's *Salwat*, appears to confuse the Cairo-based Burnāwī with ʿAbdallāh al-Burnāwī, the teacher of al-Dabbāgh.

The Khalwatiyya's presence among African scholars in the Middle East, as well as in Central Sudan with Jibrīl b. ʿUmar and in Morocco with al-Ṣaqillī, no doubt opened audiences to the similar teachings of the Tijāniyya a generation or so later.

Ṣāliḥ al-Fullānī, a Fulani scholar from Futa Jallon (modern-day Guinea), came to reside in Medina with a wide reputation for Islamic scholarship. A later Indian scholar, Muḥammad ʿAẓīmābādī (d. 1905), referred to al-Fullānī as the scholarly renewer (*mujaddid*) of his age,[42] and his legacy has been variously appropriated by India's *Ahl al-Ḥadīth* movement as well as Arab Salafism. But al-Fullānī was also a *ḥadīth* teacher of Muḥammad al-Ḥāfiẓ al-Shinqīṭī (d. 1830), the student of al-Tijānī and famous propagator of the Tijāniyya into the Sahara, as well as the Moroccan Tijānī scholar Ḥamdūn b. al-Ḥājj (d. 1857).[43] Al-Fullānī was also an associate of the Khalwatī Shaykh in Medina, Muḥammad al-Sammān.[44] While several of al-Fullānī's students no doubt rejected the Sufi orders and the *madhāhib* along with their teacher's stance against 'following the schools of law with zeal and narrow-mindedness',[45] others remained defenders of such institutions. Al-Fullānī's Mauritanian student *imām* ʿAbd al-Raḥmān b. Aḥmad al-Shinqīṭī (d. 1809) established himself in Morocco as a prominent Mālikī jurist and later accepted the Tijāniyya, confirming al-Tijānī's scholarly credentials to countrymen like Muḥammad al-Ḥāfiẓ. 'By God,' *Imām* ʿAbd al-Raḥmān swore of al-Tijānī, 'there is no one more knowledgeable on the face of the earth than him.'[46] Indeed, al-Fullānī's argument for *ijtihād* by reading established textual sources (*naṣṣ*) in dialogue with scholarly opinion was similar to al-Tijānī's own legal methodology, although al-Tijānī himself otherwise remained a practising Mālikī.[47] Although al-Fullānī remains an example, for many, of a West African 'Salafī' in Arabia, he exemplifies the ability of African scholars to situate themselves at the centre of *ijtihād* and *ḥadīth* renewal networks that were in fact closely related to Ṭarīqa Muḥammadiyya revivalism. Rather than reading Fullānī's stance on *ijtihād* as

42 Chanfi Ahmed, *West African 'Ulamā' and Salafism in Mecca and Medina: Jawāb al-Ifrīqī – the Response of the African* (Leiden: Brill, 2015) 92.

43 Ahmed, *West African 'Ulamā'*, 95.

44 Ahmed, *West African 'Ulamā'*, 96, claims that he was 'introduced to the Sammāniyya Ṭarīqa and maybe to other turuq, though he was not formally initiated into a Sufi order'.

45 This phrase appears in the subtitle of al-Fullānī's most important work, *Īqāẓ himam ūlī l-abṣār*. See Hunwick, 'Ṣāliḥ al-Fullānī: The Career and Teachings of a West African ʿĀlim in Medina', in A.H. Green (ed.), *In Quest of an Islamic Humanism* (Cairo: American University in Cairo Press, 1984), 139–54; Ahmed, *West African 'Ulamā'*, 94.

46 Al-Kattānī, *Salwat*, III: 469–70.

47 Ahmed, *West African 'Ulamā'*, 95. For al-Tijānī's discussion of the centrality of *naṣṣ* in legal opinions, see Wright, *Realizing Islam*, 58–9.

evidence of his influence by Salafī-Wahhabism, he in fact evidences a critical West African engagement with the *madhāhib* that dates at least back to Aḥmad Baba and the scholars of Timbuktu. As mentioned above, Baba similarly criticized his Moroccan counterparts for their excessive attachment to the Mālikī school.

Black African Scholars in Fez

The *Kitāb al-ibrīz* contains an intriguing account of a Central African shaykh in the Sufi training of ʿAbd al-ʿAzīz al-Dabbāgh, whose imprint on Sufism in eighteenth-century Morocco cannot be overestimated.

> I sent out for the shrine of Sayyid Abd-Allah al-Tawudi and when I reached Jisa gate [of Fez], behold there was a black man outside the gate. He began to stare at me, and I said to myself: 'What can this man want?' … When I came near him, he took hold of my hand and greeted me … With his words, by God, he removed my burden from me. I knew then he was one of the friends and knowers of God the Sublime. He said his name was ʿAbdallah al-Burnāwī, that he was from Bornu and that he'd come to Fez to see me.[48]

Al-Burnāwī stayed with al-Dabbāgh for five months, undertaking his spiritual training: 'The reason for his staying with me was to protect me from the darkness entering into me during the illumination I experienced.' Among al-Burnāwī's tests was to change his shape into that of a beautiful woman to tempt al-Dabbāgh: 'I wanted to test you because I know how fond of women are the sharīfs.' Finally al-Dabbāgh experienced the vision of the Prophet Muḥammad, after which time al-Burnāwī returned to his own country, saying:

> O Sayyid 'Abd al-Aziz, before today I was afraid for your sake. But today since God the Sublime, through his mercy, has united you with the lord of creation – God's blessing and peace upon him – my heart feels safe and my mind is assured. I therefore leave you in the hands of God the mighty and glorious.[49]

Despite his departure, al-Dabbāgh remained in spiritual contact with al-Burnāwī and was divinely informed on the day Burnāwī died, saying, 'When Sayyid 'Abd Allah al-Burnawi died, I inherited the secrets he possessed.'[50]

The formative training of Morocco's most influential Sufi of the early eighteenth century was thus undertaken by a mysterious black man who came to Fez for no other reason than to train the next axial saint. This story is paraphrased in

[48] Al-Lamāṭī, *Pure Gold from the Words of Sayyidī ʿAbd al-Aziz*, translated by John O'Kane and Bernd Radtke with notes and an outline (Leiden: Brill, 2007) 132–3.
[49] Al-Lamāṭī, *Pure Gold*, 133.
[50] Al-Lamāṭī, *Pure Gold*, 135.

the nineteenth-century encyclopedia of Moroccan scholars, al-Kattānī's *Salwat al-anfās*, where al-Burnāwī is credited with al-Dabbāgh's illumination and is himself referred to as the axial saint (*quṭb*) of his age.[51] Of course this was not the first reference to sub-Saharan African scholars in Morocco, and Ahmad Bābā's appearance in Marrakesh has been well documented. But black African scholars were present in Morocco much earlier. Ibn al-ʿArabī (d. 1240) makes reference, for example, to an earlier saint of Fez, named ʿAbdallah al-Ḥabashī ('the Ethiopian').[52] Aḥmad al-Tijānī similarly spoke of the high spiritual station of another Fez resident, Abū Yuʿzī al-Hazmīrī (d. 1177), described in al-Kattānī's *Salwat* as 'al-Ḥabashī'.[53] The overall conclusion here seems to be that sub-Saharan African scholars appeared early in North Africa both as students and teachers, and kept a close eye on North African scholarly and spiritual developments, especially in Fez, the so-called 'Baghdad of the Maghreb'.

Analysis of the Sudanese travelling scholar Aḥmad al-Yamānī (d. 1712, Fez) provides more details of the close scholarly relationship between sub-Saharan Africa and Morocco in the seventeenth and early eighteenth centuries.[54] Al-Yamānī was also the close disciple of ʿAbdallāh b. ʿAbd al-ʿAzīz al-Burnāwī, whom he first encountered in Bornu, and had undoubtedly spent more time with him than had al-Dabbāgh. In any case, it is likely that al-Dabbāgh's encounter with al-Burnāwī in the early eighteenth century refers to his visionary contact with al-Burnāwī's spiritual presence beyond the grave, as the central African saint had died in a Tuareg raid in 1677.[55] Al-Yamānī, following the earlier Arabic hagiography of al-Burnāwī called *Rīḥān al-qulūb,* referred to al-Burnāwī as 'the master of his time' (*ṣāḥib waqtihi*) and the 'wonder of his age'.[56] The *Rīḥān al-qulūb* relates of al-Burnāwī that he was sometimes in a state of spiritual ecstasy (*majdhūb*), but nonetheless the 'pole of the Sufi way' (*quṭb al-ṭarīqa*). He was also an accomplished scholar of the exoteric sciences: he had knowledge of theology, Qur'ān exegesis, and linguistics. He had a photographic memory, taught the *Alfiyya* of Ibn Mālik, and 'gave commentary on the Qur'ān like the exegesis of the great

[51] Al-Kattānī, *Salwat*, II, 284.

[52] Al-Kattānī, *Salwat*, III, 314.

[53] Al-Kattānī, *Salwat*, I, 236–7.

[54] Al-Yamānī was an ascription of lineage, not birth, as he was apparently born near Sinnar in modern-day Sudan. See H.T. Norris, *Sufi Mystics of the Niger Desert* (Oxford: Clarendon Press, 1990) 1.

[55] Hamid Bobboyi, 'Shaykh Abd Allah al-Barnawi and the world of Fes Sufism: some preliminary observations', in Fès Faculté des Lettres et des Sciences Humaines (ed.), *Fès et l'Afrique: relations économiques, culturelles et spirituelles* (Rabat: Institut des Études Africaines, 1995) 115–24.

[56] Al-Kattānī, *Salwat*, II: 480.

scholars'.[57] Al-Burnāwī claimed nonetheless that all his knowledge was a result of his friendship with God, saying: 'God does not make a saint (publicly) manifest, except that He supports him with knowledge.' Al-Burnāwī's portrait thus emerges here in more detail than in the *Ibrīz*. Taken as a whole, this African intellectual appeared in Fez as an eminent scholar-saint who emphasized the scholar's direct connection to the Prophet Muḥammad, the importance of Sufi training under a shaykh, and the balance between Sufism and the sacred law.

But al-Yamānī had more to say about African scholarship than his testimony of al-Burnāwī. Al-Yamānī came to Fez from East Africa across the Sahel. According to al-Kattānī, 'He spent a long time in the land of the blacks (*bilād al-sūdān*).' Aside from al-Burnāwī, he studied with other African scholars, such as 'Aḥmad al-Tārikay ('the Tuareg'), from the town of Agades (Adkaz), allegedly of the Suhrawardiyya Sufi order.[58] This is no doubt a reference to al-Yamānī's contact with the legacy of Sidi Maḥmūd al-Baghdādī, the alleged axial saint of his age,[59] who may have been the first to introduce a Sufi order in black Africa. According to H.T. Norris, the Maḥmūdiyya Sufi order was probably a combination of the Suhrawardiyya and Khalwatiyya (and perhaps Qādiriyya) Sufi orders, but came to be identified with 'an original Muḥammadiyya ṭarīqa, a theory in vogue at a much later date'.[60] The sixteenth-century Sufi Sidi Maḥmūd's teachings were collected by a Tuareg scholar 'Aḥmad b. 'Uways in the book *al-Qudwā*, written between 1670 and 1680. This author was likely the same Aḥmad that served as al-Yamānī's teacher in Agades. Here is the *Qudwā*'s description of the pre-eminent *Ṭarīqa Maḥmūdiyya*:

> The meaning of *Ahl al-Ṭarīqa al-Mahmudiyya* is 'those who call upon the people of Allah to a clarity of vision.' A clarity of vision and of awareness is the gift which

[57] Muḥammad b. al-Ṭayyib al-Qādirī, *Mawsū'at a'lām al-maghrib ma'hu Tadhkirat al-muḥsinīn bi-wifayāt al-a'yān wa ḥawādith al-sinīn li 'Abd al-Kabīr al-Fāsī wa al-A'lām bi-man ghabar min ahl al-qarn al-ḥādī 'ashar*, ed. Muḥammad Ḥajjī and Aḥmad al-Tawfīq (Rabat: Dār al-Gharb al-Islāmī, 2008), IV: 1593–7.

[58] Al-Kattānī, *Salwat*, II: 478–9.

[59] This was according to Muḥammad Bello b. 'Uthmān b. Fūdī, and also in 'Aḥmad b. 'Uways's *Qudwā*. See Norris, *Sufi Mystics*, 129.

[60] Norris, *Sufi Mystics*, 76. According to Triaud, this order was sometimes also remembered in Aïr as the 'Baghdadiyya'. See Jean-Louis Triaud, 'Hommes de religion et confréries islamiques dans une société en crise, l'Aïr aux XIXe et XXe siècles: le cas de las Khalwatiyya', *Cahiers d'Études Africaines*, 23, 1983, 239–80. An intriguing reference in the *Qudwā* to a 'Muḥammad al-Shannawi' (perhaps Ahmad al-Shinnāwī? See Norris, *Sufi Mystics*, 66), may indicate the later Maḥmūdiyya's connection with the Middle Eastern Shaṭṭariyya tradition as transmitted from Muḥammad al-Ghawth by Ahmad al-Shinnawi to Ibrahim Kurani in Medina in the seventeenth century.

> was brought by him [the Prophet]–the blessing and peace of Allah be upon him–to teach mankind about Allah. It was his *sunna* and the word of his Lord. As for the Ṭarīqa of Sidi Mahmud, it is the original path and the other paths have borrowed from it. It is the way of the sons of the world to come, in canonic law, in mystical discipline, and in ultimate truth. All else is but the following of a wayward fancy.[61]

Interesting here is the notion that the pre-eminent, original Sufi order would teach the knowledge of God as a gift from the Prophet. There is no specific mention that the Prophet Muḥammad appeared to Sidi Maḥmūd to teach him the *Ṭarīqa Maḥmūdiyya*, but the *Qudwā* has Sidi Maḥmūd specifying that the Sufi circles of remembrance in the 'western lands' (thus those of Sidi Maḥmūd) were 'organized and made ready by the Prophet'.[62]

According to Norris, al-Yamānī likely brought a copy of the *Qudwa* with him to Fez after studying it in Agades.[63] If so, the idea of a transcendent *Ṭarīqa Muḥammadiyya* that defined the purest form of Sufism, as a gift from the Prophet, had a resonance in sub-Saharan Africa prior to its popularization in Fez prior to ʿAbd al-ʿAzīz al-Dabbāgh and ʿAḥmad al-Tijānī.[64] Moreover, the *Ṭarīqa Maḥmūdiyya* was not the only sub-Saharan African-based Sufi order to make an appearance in Fez. There was later a *muqaddam* of the Kuntiyya-Qādiriyya from Mukhtār Kūntī (d. 1811) based in Fez, a certain Sharīf Muḥammad b. al-Hādi al-Dabbāgh (d. 1867).[65] Whatever the case, it is clear that the notion of a pre-eminent *Ṭarīqa Muḥammadiyya* linking followers to the Prophet Muḥammad was already well established in sub-Saharan Africa prior to the eighteenth century.

While al-Tijānī had no known scholarly links connecting him to al-Burnāwī, al-Dabbāgh, or al-Yamānī, their ideas had clearly come to permeate Fez by the time of al-Tijānī's establishment in Fez in 1798. Students regularly asked al-Tijānī about various statements of al-Dabbāgh in *al-Ibrīz*. The grandson of al-Dabbāgh, ʿUmar b. Muḥammad b. ʿAbd al-ʿAzīz, reportedly recognized in al-Tijānī the saint who could train him in divine gnosis (*maʿrifa*), and subsequently entered Tijāniyya. A letter to ʿUmar from al-Tijānī praises his grandfather (al-Dabbāgh) as 'the arrived axial saint and the perfect succor (*ghawth*)'.[66] As al-Dabbāgh's example indicates, the scholarly atmosphere of eighteenth-century Fez was infused

61 Norris, *Sufi Mystics*, 70.
62 Norris, *Sufi Mystics*, 66.
63 Norris, *Sufi Mystics*, 7.
64 The notion of the *Ṭarīqa Muḥammadiyya* had in fact appeared in Morocco in the sixteenth century with the teachings of Muḥammad al-Ghazwānī of the Jazūliyya-Shādhiliyya. See Vincent Cornell, *Realm of the Saint: Power and Authority in Moroccan Sufism* (Austin, TX: University of Texas Press, 1998) 219.
65 Al-Kattānī, *Salwat al-anfās*, I, 404.
66 Aḥmad Sukayrij, *Kashf al-ḥijāb*, ed. Rāḍī Kanūn (Rabat: Dār al-Amān, 2012) 630.

with references to Islamic scholarship south of Morocco. Biographical collections from the period present no fewer than nineteen separate Saharan scholars, with the designation 'al-Shinqīṭī', residing in Morocco.[67] Al-Tijānī himself only left Fez in the later years of his life to visit the Saharan oasis town of Tuwat, where he exchanged knowledge with scholars there, perhaps of the Kuntī-Qādiriyya scholarly lineage, originating further south, which was pronounced in the town by the late eighteenth century.[68] If such references were lost on later generations of Moroccans, sub-Saharan Islamic scholarship certainly remembered its long-standing dialogue with Moroccan intellectual history.

Conclusion

The reception of Aḥmad al-Tijānī's *Ṭarīqa Muḥammadiyya* in sub-Saharan Africa drew on a long legacy of scholarly interaction between sub-Saharan Africa and the Middle East/North Africa. Constituent elements of eighteenth-century scholarly renewal, such as *ijtihād* outside of the *madhāhib*, claims of saintly authority, critical exploration of the esoteric sciences, emphasis on invoking blessing on the Prophet, and the notion of a transcendent 'Muḥammadan Way', were all present in the *Bilād al-Sūdān* prior to the spread of the Tijāniyya in the nineteenth century. Perhaps most importantly, African Muslims had prior exposure to the notion of visionary experience. Aside from the previous examples cited above, the late seventeenth-century Fulani scholar and warrior Nāṣir al-Dīn was said to be in the constant presence of Khiḍr (the immortal guide of Moses). The later Mauritanian Shaykh Muḥammad al-Yadālī (d. 1750) reflected on Nāṣir al-Dīn's example in concluding:

> The pure lights in the saints are only due to the illumination of the Prophethood bestowed on them. The 'real presence' of Muḥammad may be likened to that of the moon ... just as the sun's light continues both by night and by day, so the lights of the Messenger of God remain in saints after him ... as it has been permitted to the Prophet to recount the unknown and the unseen, so it is permitted to the saints; since what is possible as a prophetic miracle (*muʿjiza*) is also possible as a saintly miracle (*karāma*).[69]

[67] Muḥammad b. al-Ṭayyib al-Qādirī, *Mawsūʿat aʿlām al-maghrib maʿhu Tadhkirat al-muḥsinīn bi-wifayāt al-aʿyān wa ḥawādith al-sinīn li ʿAbd al-Kabīr al-Fāsī wa al-Aʿlām bi-man ghabar min ahl al-qarn al-ḥādī ʿashar*, eds. Muḥammad Ḥajjī; Aḥmad al-Tawfīq (Rabat: Dār al-Gharb al-Islāmī, 2008) V. 10, 3706–7.

[68] Reichmuth, *The World of Murtaḍa al-Zabīdī*, 190–1.

[69] H.T. Norris, 'Znāga Islam during the Seventeenth and Eighteenth Centuries', *Bulletin of the School of Oriental and African Studies* 32, 3, 1969, 509–10.

In receiving the light of the Prophet Muḥammad, saints thus appeared in Africa as illumined beacons of knowledge in direct contact with the 'real presence' of the Prophet. Such scholars were recipients of special knowledge from visionary experience. Aḥmad al-Tijānī's notion of his own *Ṭarīqa Muḥammadiyya* propagated by visionary exemplars thus resonated with pre-existing concepts in sub-Saharan Africa; it did not occasion significant doctrinal changes. Though Tijānī sources list exclusively Middle East and North African scholarly influences for al-Tijānī himself, Sudanic scholars such as al-Yadālī, al-Kashnāwī, al-Burnāwī, and al-Fullānī may have done as much to prepare the formation and reception of the Tijāniyya as al-Tijānī's more direct Middle Eastern connections to *Ṭarīqa Muḥammadiyya* networks.

The notion of the *Ṭarīqa Muḥammadiyya*, especially when conflated with the discredited term of 'Neo-Sufism', often suggests the Sufi's inclination towards worldly involvement and social activism. The idea that the saint would be involved in his or her society is of course not new to the eighteenth century. But there is no doubt that Sufi activism in the eighteenth and nineteenth centuries translated into popular social movements and even political action. Moroccan elites of the early nineteenth century were thus not surprisingly impressed with news of Sufi scholars taking direct political action in Sudanic Africa. The Moroccan Sultan Mawlay Sulayman, perhaps himself a disciple of al-Tijānī,[70] wrote a letter to congratulate ʿUthmān b. Fūdī on the establishment of the Sokoto Caliphate:

> After greetings, a letter has reached us informing us of your disposition, of your words, and of your works, it is right that we should be your friends and a party to your cause. This news of you we received from a certain chief in your parts. He has told us of your character in his letter. He has told us that you are a defender of the faith of God. He has told us how you are steadfast in the cause of religion, that you are ruling in the right way and are preventing evil customs so that many people are entering the true faith and a multitude of Muslims are coming to you from all parts. He tells us that you are of perfect character, that you are settling the affairs of many people in your great kindness. May you find all happiness from God. May God bless you and protect you from all evil and establish your power.[71]

[70] Sukayrij, *Kashf al-ḥijāb*, 742–54. Sukayrij's assertion is disputed by Mohamed El-Mansour, *Morocco in the Reign of Mawlay Sulayman* (London: Middle East and North African Studies Press, 1990) 161–2.

[71] Hamid Bobboyi, 'Scholars and scholarship in the relations between the Maghreb and the Central Bilad al-Sudan during the pre-colonial period', in Helen Lauer; Kofi Anyidoho (eds.), *Reclaiming the Human Sciences and Humanities through African Perspectives, Volume I* (Ghana: Sub-Saharan Publishers, 2012) 760. The source for Mawlay Sulayman's information was apparently Ibn Fūdī's acquaintance Muḥammad Bakirī b. Adal.

Mawlay Sulayman's letter recognizes Ibn Fūdī's Sufi realization (disposition, character), his scholarship (words, steadfastness in the cause of religion) and just sovereignty (works, defender of the faith). The sultan's minister, Muḥammad al-Kansūsī, would make a similar observation of the West African Tijānī scholar-activist ʿUmar Tāl:

> Our ears have been delighted by this good news about you and your majesty, good news which when heard makes people happy, and whenever a Muslim hears it he is cured of his envy and raises his voice and is filled with joy and praise … In truth this is a glory for the Muslim nation, a victory through a road that had previously been blocked, it is a joy for the saints of God who repeat it standing and sitting. I pray that the swords of truth will strike the foreheads and cheeks of the evil people. When the news became public knowledge and we got details from all sources, it became necessary for us to come to your doorway with this congratulation.[72]

Of course, al-Kansūsī is here speaking to a fellow Tijānī disciple, but such sentiments clearly represent a shared scholarly heritage and activist stance, informed by the *Ṭarīqa Muḥammadiyya* Sufi renewal of the late eighteenth century, and shared between North and Sudanic Africa.

The sentiments of Moroccan notables like Mawlay Sulayman and Muḥammad al-Kansūsī demonstrate a marked admiration for the intellectual and social achievements of African Muslim scholars south of the Sahara. This chapter has made the case that many Arab and even Indian intellectuals in the eighteenth century shared such admiration for African scholarship, largely because they had first-hand experience of African Muslim scholars as both teachers and students. The ready adoption and articulation of eighteenth-century intellectual trends in black Africa, such as the *Ṭarīqa Muḥammadiyya* of Aḥmad al-Tijānī, represent not simply the region's reception of global Islamic currents. From Timbuktu's dialogue with Muḥammad al-Bakrī, to al-Kashnāwī's pietistic systemization of the esoteric sciences, to al-Burnāwī's training of al-Dabbāgh in experiencing the direct encounter with the Prophet Muḥammad, African scholars were as much at the centre of the *Ṭarīqa Muḥammadiyya* as were the scholars of Cairo and the Hijaz.

[72] Al-Kansūsī to ʿUmar Tāl, letter dated 1860; cited in David Robinson, 'Failed Islamic States in Senegambia: Umar Tal', *Pluralism and Adaptation in the Islamic Practice of Senegal and Ghana*, online http://aodl.org/islamicpluralism/failedislamicstates/essays/43-1A9-F/#jump. Accessed 4 January 2018.

CHAPTER 2

Muḥammad al-Kashnāwī and the Everyday Life of the Occult

Dahlia E.M. Gubara

Sometime before 1730, a scholar left his native Katsina (in today's Northern Nigeria) to embark on the pilgrimage and fulfil the ethical injunction of seeking knowledge. He sojourned in the Holy Cities and then in Cairo where he taught as a guest of the shaykh of an East African student lodge at the illustrious mosque-seminary al-Azhar, in whose home he died in 1741. The shaykh's son, 'Abd al-Raḥmān al-Jabartī, would later write what was to become one of the most renowned historical works of Ottoman Egypt wherein the name of his father's visitor, Muḥammad b. Muḥammad al-Kashnāwī al-Sudānī al-Danrankāwī al-Mālikī al-Ash'arī – the 'unequaled *imām*', 'broad sea of learning … and treasury of mystical graces' – was forever immortalized.[1]

Despite such acclaim, al-Kashnāwī has received little to no critical attention in the scholarship. This chapter is an attempt in that direction. It follows two separate but related threads of analysis. It locates al-Kashnāwī within the broader historical and conceptual frameworks of the scholarly field 'Islam in Africa', where a binary logic has tended to oppose Arab to African and occult science to other forms of knowledge. These dualities have largely defined how the author and his work have been apprehended. The chapter then moves to a close reading of al-Kashnāwī's main work on the 'secret sciences', *al-Durr al-manẓūm wa khulāṣat al-sirr al-maktūm fī 'ilm al-ṭalāsim wa'l-nujūm*. Read in juxtaposition to al-Kashnāwī's own words, the historiography's analytical frames quickly give way to reveal an altogether different epistemic configuration where modern racial categories were inoperative, where knowledge was understood as an organic indivisible whole – and where, crucially, disciplines of knowledge were intricately bound to disciplines of the self and the everyday life of their practitioners.

[1] 'Abd al-Raḥmān al-Jabartī, *'Ajā'ib al-āthār* (Cairo: Bulaq, 1880), I:159/260. All translations are adapted from Thomas Philipp and Moshe Perlmann (eds. trans.), *'Abd al-Raḥmān al-Jabartī's History of Egypt* (Stuttgart: Franz Steiner Verlag, 1994). References are given in the text for both the Arabic and English editions respectively.

* * *

Information on al-Kashnāwī's early years is hazy, and little can be glimpsed from the biographical dictionaries.[2] While the date of his birth is unknown, it is generally accepted that he was born in Katsina, and most probably (given the affiliative *nisba*, al-Danrankāwī) in Kurmin Dan Ranko, a Katsinan town noted for its scholarship. An extended province of Hausaland, Katsina had from the late seventeenth century onwards reached a zenith of power that was at once political, economic, and scholarly, attracting students and visitors from all corners of the continent and beyond. It is in this world that al-Kashnāwī had been nurtured, as he completed studies in the classical disciplines: Qur'ān, *ḥadīth*, theology, *fiqh*. He would also have been introduced, if in a less systematic fashion, to other subjects: literary and linguistic, historical, mathematical, philosophical, medical and astronomical, including of course the esoteric and occult sciences in which he would come to develop a profound interest, as well as *taṣawwuf* more broadly.

In his necrology, al-Jabartī explicitly names five scholars who appear to have been formative in al-Kashnāwī's education: 'He studied in his homeland with the *shaykh* and *imām* Muḥammad ibn Sulaymān ibn Muḥammad al-Nawālī al-Birnāwī al-Baghiramāwī, the master and Shaykh Muḥammad al-Bindū, the perfect Shaykh Hāshim, and Shaykh Muḥammad Fūdū, which means "the great" [*al-kabīr*].' When recounting his travels, al-Jabartī further lists a Shaykh Muḥammad Kr'k with whom al-Kashnāwī spent five months studying 'many aspects of the secret sciences and geomancy'. Together, they read Maḥmūd al-Kurdī's *Kitāb al-wālīyah*, 'a great and highly respected book on geomancy', as well as 'al-Rajrājī and some books on arithmetic'.[3]

Al-Kashnāwī's teachers in Katsina and the surrounding region were established authorities in multiple fields of scholarship. With Muḥammad Fūdū,[4] al-Kashnāwī studied syntax and grammar as well as poetry, becoming, according to al-Jabartī, so '[p]roficient in these subjects that his *shaykh* used to call

[2] See entries in: Khayr al-dīn al-Ziriklī, *Al-A'lām: Qāmus tarājim li-ashhur al-rijāl wa al-nisā min al-'arab wa al-musta'ribīn wa al-mustashriqīn* (Beirut: Dar al-'ilm lil-malayīn, 1990); 'Umar Riḍā Kahhāla, *Mu 'jam al-mu'allifīn* (Beirut: Dār ihyā al-turāth al-'arabī, 1958); Carl Brockelmann, *Geschichte der Arabischen Litteratur* (Leiden: Brill, 1943–49).

[3] 'Abd al-Raḥmān al-Jabartī, *'Ajā'ib al-āthār*, I:159/260.

[4] A.D.H. Bivar and Mervyn Hiskett have suggested that 'this Fūdū is the father of Usuman dan Fodio', which, if correct, would tie al-Kashnāwī to this 'celebrated reformer' and his family. ('The Arabic Literature of Nigeria to 1804: a provisional account', *BSOAS*, xxv, 1962, 5, 136). Muḥammad Makhlūf has him as 'al-Shaykh Muḥammad Jūdū'. (*Shajarat al-nūr al-zakīyya fī ṭabaqāt al-Mālikīyya* [Cairo: 1349/1930–1] 337).

him "Sibawayh", [and] connoisseur of prosimetric verse [*maqāmāt*]'.[5] About Shaykh Hāshim we know little beyond the fact that he was connected to another influential scholar from the region, al-Ṭāhir b. Ibrāhīm al-Fallātī al-Barnāwī, who composed (among other works) a versified treatise on the diagnosis and treatment of haemorrhoids.[6] What al-Kashnāwī studied with Muḥammad al-Nawālī (or al-Wālī) is not made explicit, but this famous scholar's primary interests were in theology, linguistics, and jurisprudence.[7] In contrast to al-Wālī, biographical information on al-Bindū is extremely sparse, but he too seems to have had a great influence on his student's all-round training. According to al-Jabartī:

> With Shaykh Muḥammad al-Bindū, [al-Kashnāwī] studied the art of magic squares, arithmetic, and chronology in the style of the Maghrebian path (of Sufism), mastering esoteric disciplines of all kinds, literal and numerological, as well as mathematical and calendrical devices. He benefitted greatly from him. As [al-Kashnāwī] said, 'I read with him *uṣūl* and topics of rhetoric, eloquence, and logic, the *Alfīya* of al-ʿIrāqī and al-Sanūsī's six (works) on (theological) doctrine in their entirety'. He studied [with al-Bindū] the text of al-Bukhārī: three quarters of the *Mukhtaṣar* of Khalīl, from the beginning of the chapter on sales to the end of the chapter on contracts for delivery with prepayment, and from the beginning of the chapter on rent to the end of the book; about a third of *Kitāb mulakhkhaṣ al-maqāṣid,* which is a book on *kalām* by Ibn Zikrī, a contemporary of Shaykh al-Sanūsī, in 1,500 verses of poetry, together with most of the books he composed; and other works. As he said, 'I learned from him much that was wonderful and useful – amazing stories, reports, anecdotes, and knowledge of the (*ḥadīth*) transmitters, their classes, and ranks.' He mentioned this in the list of his *shaykhs*.[8]

Al-Kashnāwī's education in Africa clearly partook of a broad and deep tradition of scholarship, connecting him to various important intellectual currents of the time, with echoes far and wide reverberating well into the nineteenth century, as attested by his Cairene biographer. Evident too is the seamless integration in this scholarly horizon of the different domains of knowledge. No strict differentiation appears to be made between what we would separate as esoteric and exoteric

5 ʿAbd al-Raḥmān al-Jabartī, *ʿAjāʾib al-āthār*, I:159/260.

6 See A.D.H. Bivar; Mervyn Hiskett, 'The Arabic Literature', 137–9; Mohammad Belo, *Infāq al-maysūr fī tārīkh Bilād al-Takrūr,* ed. Bahija Chadli (Rabat: Mohammed V University Publications of the Institute of African Studies, 1996) 61–2.

7 See John O. Hunwick (ed.), *Arabic Literature of Africa: Volume II, The Writings of Central Sudanic Africa* (Leiden: E.J. Brill, 1995) 34; A.D.H. Bivar; Mervyn Hiskett, 'The Arabic Literature' *n.* 2, 136; Louis Brenner, 'Three Fulbe Scholars in Borno', *The Maghreb Review,* 10:4–6, 1985, 107–13.

8 ʿAbd al-Raḥmān al-Jabartī, *ʿAjāʾib al-āthār*, I:159/260.

disciplines, or indeed between what we would now identify as 'religious' and 'secular' knowledge. Geomancy, magic, mathematical and calendrical devices are mentioned in the same breath as syntax, logic, transmission of traditions, eloquence and jurisprudence.

Such scholastic polymathesis is further reflected in al-Kashnāwī's own writings, most of which seem to have been penned during his travels. To date, eight works in total have been identified, but there may have been others, if we are to go by al-Kashnāwī's words as relayed by al-Jabartī:

> [Al-Kashnāwī] possessed great energy and a genuine desire to acquire the knowledge on which the understanding of books depends. He used to say, 'One of the ways in which God bestowed favor upon me was that I never read anything in a loaned book. The least I did when I wanted to read a book which I did not own was to copy its text, leaving space between the lines to write whatever comment I wanted, or for the remarks of my *shaykh* when he was teaching it. When I was more ambitious, I would copy out the commentary and gloss also.'[9]

Makhlūf alludes to something similar in his biographical dictionary of Mālikī scholars, when describing al-Kashnāwī as having 'had a long hand in most sciences and complete knowledge of the subtleties of secrets and illuminations'.[10] Two of the eight cited works, the travelogue and compendium of authorities, are lost.[11] The remaining works are: *Bulūgh al-arab min kalām al-ʿarab* – a work on Arabic grammar; *Bughyat al-mawālī fī tarjamat Muḥammad al-Wālī* – a biography of Muḥammad al-Wālī; *Manḥ al-quddūs* – a didactic poem on logic drawn from *Mukhtaṣar al-Sanūsī*, on which al-Kashnāwī then wrote an extensive commentary entitled *Izālat al-'ubūs 'an wajh Manḥ al-quddūs*; and three major treatises on the esoteric sciences, *Durar al-yawāqīt fī 'ilm al-ḥurūf wa al-asmā'* – a commentary on al-Jurjānī's *Kitāb al-durr wa'l-tiryāq fī 'ilm al-awfāq*; *Bahjat al-āfāq wa īḍāḥ al-lubs wa'l-ighlāq fī 'ilm al-hurūf wa'l-awfāq* – a numerological work on the science of magic squares; and finally, *al-Durr al-manẓūm wa khulāṣat al-sirr al-maktūm fī 'ilm al-ṭalāsim wa'l-nujūm* – an abridged commentary dealing with three domains of the 'secret sciences' (*al-ʿulūm al-sirriya*), to which I return in detail below.

[9] ʿAbd al-Raḥmān al-Jabartī, *ʿAjā'ib al-āthār*, I:159/260.

[10] Muḥammad Makhlūf, *Shajarat al-nūr al-zakīyya fī ṭabaqāt al-Mālikiyya* (Cairo: 1349/1930–1) 337.

[11] A manuscript entitled *Al-Taḥrīrāt al-rā'iqah* (concerning the Prophet's state and his deeds after death) does not appear in al-Jabartī's listing nor in the other Arabic dictionaries but is reported in Brockelmann who gives *Rabīʿ* I 1156 AH, two years after al-Kashnāwī's death, as the date of composition. If this is indeed so, then the attribution to al-Kashnāwī cannot be precise (*GAL* S II:484; *ALA* II:38–9).

An accomplished student and scholar already, al-Kashnāwī set out on the *Ḥajj*. After sojourning some time in the Hijaz, he moved to Cairo where he secured lodgings in the immediate vicinity of al-Azhar and set about writing. In the short space of less than four years he completed *al-Durr al-manẓūm* and wrote *Bahjat al-āfāq, Bulūgh al-arab* and *Durar al-yawāqīt*.

Al-Kashnāwī never returned to Katsina but died sometime in 1741–2 (1154 AH) in Ḥasan al-Jabartī's home. He bequeathed his manuscripts to his friend and host, who oversaw the management of his estate and presided over his funeral. He was buried in Cairo's *Bustān al-ʿUlamāʾ* in *al-Mujāwirīn*, a cemetery reserved for the most dignified of scholars, his gravestone 'inscribed with his name and the date of his death'.[12]

* * *

In the Spring of 2009, I set out in search of the textual remnants of al-Kashnāwī's polyvalent career at the al-Azhar Library in Cairo. I was after two manuscripts on the occult sciences in particular, *Bahjat al-āfāq* and *al-Durr al-manẓūm*, which were listed in the library's catalogue (under the category for divination, *ḥarf wa raml*) but which I was prevented from viewing. Further inquiries revealed that the al-Azhar library administration had instituted a ban – when exactly is unclear – on all manuscripts under this classification on account of their 'dangerous nature'. Declining to comment on juridical matters of *ḥalāl*, *ḥarām*, or *makrūh* with respect to the occult, al-Azhar library officials repeatedly affirmed that the reason for the ban was the interest of the general public (*al-maslaḥa al-ʿāmma*) and its protection from harmful acts. The decision was thus necessitated by al-Azhar's putative mission to 'lead Muslims and serve religion'. The fact that major figures in the institution's pre-modern annals (including presiding Rectors, such as the celebrated Shaykh Aḥmad al-Damanhūrī, 1769–78) penned important works in these sciences was explained away in terms that echo modern spatio-temporal constructs: it had been a dark age of decline (*inḥiṭāṭ*).

The irony is that one could readily purchase copies of occult works for a modest price in the very shadow of al-Azhar's walls. *Darb al-Atrāk*, as the main street linking a labyrinth of dense alleyways just behind al-Azhar is still commonly known, was and remains a buzzing entrepôt of commercial and residential activity. In previous centuries it was the residential quarter for many Azhari scholars – in fact, it was there that al-Kashnāwī finally settled upon his arrival from the Hijaz. It was also in *Darb al-Atrāk* that the main market for books and writing equipment, historically known as *al-warrāqah*, was located. Sources from the

[12] ʿAbd al-Raḥmān al-Jabartī, *ʿAjāʾib al-āthār*, I:160/262.

period provide fascinating sketches of scholars and students who supplemented their living by copying manuscripts that they then sold at the market, and of merchants who traded books from the different corners of the Muslim world in its alleyways. Later, at the turn of the twentieth century, the American protestant missionary, Samuel Zwemer, would describe the scene in his widely read 1929 travelogue, *Across the World of Islam*, as follows:

> In Cairo, tourists seldom wander to what we call 'Pasternoster Row,' the booksellers' quarters. Here, near the Azhar University, piled high, you may see huge parcels of Arabic books addressed to Kordofan, Timbuktu, Cape Town, Zanzibar, Sierra Leone, Mombasa, and Madagascar. Islam pours out literature and extends the area of Arabic literates every year …[13]

As Terence Walz notes, Zwemer, who was concerned above all with the spread of nationalist 'Muḥammadan ideas' in the colonies, was also interested in what he considered the 'animist' basis of Islam, which he perceived as a barrier to spreading a rational Christian faith and salvation through the Gospel. He authored a number of mostly polemical tracts on the topic and never failed to point out that in this very presence of al-Azhar, sellers of amulets, aphrodisiacs, and charms abounded and that, in fact, 'some of [al-Azhar's] professors and many students promote the industry. A favourite among those printed by the thousands and sent from Cairo to North Africa, Central Africa, and the Near East is "The Amulet of the Seven Covenants of Solomon".'[14]

In 2009, the scene, while certainly less exoticized than Zwemer's portrayal, was not all too dissimilar. The book market continues to dominate the landscape of the neighbourhood and one still finds students and scholars parlaying in the many coffee shops or selling their textual wares in makeshift stalls of various sizes and specializations. And sometimes, amongst their bundles, one finds an array of books on all aspects of the occult, old and new. In fact, it was here that I finally obtained, for a very reasonable sum, a copy of *al-Durr al-manẓūm*, a 1961 Muṣṭafa al-Bābī al-Ḥalabī print edition on which this study is based. The vendor, himself a student at al-Azhar and novice occultist, was in turn connected to an extensive network of other teachers, students, and masters to whom he happily introduced me in the months to come.

* * *

[13] Cited in Terence Walz, 'Trans-Saharan Migration and the Colonial Gaze: The Nigerians in Egypt', *Alif*, 26, 2006, 114.

[14] Walz, 'Trans-Saharan Migration', 110.

Scholarly discussions of the occult in the Islamic tradition, and of al-Kashnāwī in particular, have tended to uncritically assume modern configurations of the concepts of religion, science and magic, as well as history, geography and race. Involving on the one hand, particular framings of occult knowledge and practices, and on the other a presumed 'syncretic African Islam', they have largely pre-scripted the sparse treatment that al-Kashnāwī has received in the existing historiography, which is explicitly calibrated to his *Africanness* and his interest in the occult. Both independent and interlaced, these clusters determine his place in the literature as one marked by a dual marginalization: that of Africa from Islam's central (Arab) heartland, and of 'magic' from the orthodox (proper) realms of scholarship.

The dichotomy between magic or religious superstition and science proper is foundational to modernity. Katharine Park and Lorraine Daston show how potently seductive the story of the scientific revolution, and 'its drama of worlds destroyed and reconstructed', remains. Despite the plethora of deconstructive critiques levied against it, it retains its 'hold, even on those who have contributed to its unravelling'. This, in large part, is because the story of the scientific revolution is quite simply a good story, involving the 'inevitable rise to domination of the West, whose cultural superiority is inferred from its cultivation of the values of inquiry that, unfettered by religion or tradition, produce the sixteenth and seventeenth century 'breakthrough to modern science'.[15] And yet, it was always well known that many of the story's chief protagonists were implicated in various aspects of occult and/or religious thought and practices.[16] The larger and obvious lesson to be drawn from this point then, is that conceptions of what is 'real' as opposed to 'occult' science are placated *ex post facto* by the contemporary scholar on what was in fact a much more fluid web of scientific practices and beliefs.

As critical scholarship has shown, there is a certain magic to modernity itself, which lies in the very interplay between 'concealment' (exclusion) and 'revelation' (inclusion), and the many illusions it conjures up.[17] In short, magic, like science, *belongs* to modernity: as concepts, both are abstractions which supplement one another and are rendered real (or unreal) by the discursive and contextual spaces within which they are produced. Read in this way, the tale of the scientific revolution is 'also a myth about the origins and nature of modernity'. It

15 Katharine Park and Lorraine Daston, 'Introduction: The Age of the New', in Park and Daston (eds.), *The Cambridge History of Science, Vol. 3: Early Modern Science* (Cambridge: Cambridge University Press, 2013) 15.

16 Examples are too numerous to recount, but perhaps the most telling is that of Sir Isaac Newton, in whose very person 'modern Western science' was born.

17 See Brigit Meyer; Peter Pels (eds.), *Magic and Modernity: Interfaces of Revelation and Concealment* (Stanford: Stanford University Press, 2003).

both teleologically flattens European history and is productive of another 'mist-shrouded entity, the modern mind',[18] defined in direct opposition to a 'primitive' one (in the first instance medieval, but also rural and non-European – worlds captured mainly by anthropological inquiry). This paradigm too has undergone repeated critiques. Yet, much like the meta-narrative of the 'scientific revolution', the basic discursive parameters of early anthropology, which lent magic its conceptual vocabularies, stubbornly endure. Having seeped into other disciplines and knowledges, they conspicuously animate discussions of the occult and reify the *subjects* of the historical saga to be told: the Arab, the African, and the European (but also, the scientist, the magician, the orthodox scholar, the superstitious peasant, etc.).

The second web of constraints that weighs upon any lucid approach to al-Kashnāwī is the heavy baggage of the field of study variously known as 'Islam in Africa', 'African Islam', etc. Though it is often made to go back to Arab geographers of the classical period, this is evidently an anachronism, for these authors had neither a formulated conception of Islam nor Africa, let alone of their conjugation. More relevant are the writings of European explorers, missionaries, colonial officers, and scholars that, in aggregate, assembled what Valentin Mudimbe (echoing Edward Said) has described as the 'colonial library', through which Africa was 'invented' as a coherent geographical space where competing *external* monotheisms penetrated the fabric of traditional, primitive, pagan *host* societies.

More than anyone else perhaps, it was John Spencer Trimingham, Church Missionary Society representative and pioneer scholar of the study of Islam in Africa, who provided the conceptual parameters of the field: the dialectic of Islamization and Africanization, in which the former provides structure and the latter content. Trimingham's proscriptions were clearly shaped by the juxtaposition of anthropological understandings of 'African religion and society' and Orientalist conceptions of Islam. The two frames organize his assorted writings on the subject, culminating in the instrumental synthesis, *The Influence of Islam upon Africa*, published in London in 1968.

The kernel of Trimingham's topography is the existence of an indigenous African substratum (delineated through geographic, linguistic and racial criteria) underneath the forceful weight of a globalizing (Islamic) superstructure. It is this logic that sustains his history of Islam's 'penetration' into 'African societies' and its introduction of *universalist* concepts (monotheism, religion, ideology, etc.) into *particularist* (animistic) settings. The accommodation of Islam as the 'religion of the elite', and Arabic as its linguistic corollary (the so-called 'Latin of Africa') is precisely framed as a 'compromise' between these two strata.[19] Accordingly,

[18] Park and Daston, 'Introduction: The Age of the New', 15.

[19] John Spencer Trimingham, *The Influence of Islam Upon Africa* (London: Longmans,

African societies are only *nominally* Muslim, local factors having determined the *syncretic character* of the religion. *Ergo*, Islam in Africa must be understood as a unique phenomenon to be studied according to its own internal logics, structures and forms, amongst which is its characteristic marginality.

The most enduring effect of this framework's corroboration of an insider/outsider, centre/periphery logic has been the idea that the superficiality of Islamization in Africa allowed for the continued flourishing of an indigenous attachment to the occult despite any professed doctrinal opposition. This in part helps to explain why al-Kashnāwī's writings have received very little direct or critical attention in their own terms.[20]

It is precisely the internalization of these two conceptual strands of the modern order of knowledge (magic/science and Arab/African) by the colonial-national elite that permitted the reframing of al-Azhar's role as a standard of *rational* religion against magical superstition, and a beacon of Islam-proper amongst the improperly Islamized primitives everywhere (and especially in Africa). In contrast, al-Jabartī's chronicle is simply teeming with accounts of colourful magicians and mystics who were often also adroit scholars of *fiqh*, *ḥadīth,* and theology, as well as a broad segment of respected practitioners, many of them notable names in the annals of Azhari historiography, of what were then known as the '*gharīb* sciences'. These men (and sometimes women) formed worlds of shared scholarly interests and personal networks enlivened by the intellectual, social and economic prospects that these studies afforded at the time. Together, they produced hundreds of manuscripts on a startling array of subjects and crafts, revealing an everyday life of the occult within a socially and morally embedded regime of knowledge-making that encompassed the 'mundanely mystical', the 'rationally philosophical', and the downright 'pantheistic'.[21]

* * *

Al-Durr al-manẓūm is an abridged commentary of the famous astrological treatise attributed to Fakhr al-Dīn al-Rāzī (d. 1209), *al-Sirr al-maktūm fī mukhāṭabāt al-nujūm*.[22] It is devoted to three overlying spheres of the occult sciences: *siḥr*

1968) 11–12. See also John O. Hunwick, 'West Africa and the Arabic Language', *Sudanic Africa,* 15, 2004, 133–44.

20 Louis Brenner's 'Three Fulbe Scholars in Borno' is a notable exception. H.I. Gwarzo provides a rather brief discussion of al-Kashnāwī's theory of chronograms that barely skirts the question of the occult beyond quoting al-Kashnāwī on the esoteric properties of numbers ('The Theory of Chronograms', 116–23).

21 Wael B. Hallaq, 'What is Shari'a?' *Yearbook of Islamic and Middle Eastern Law*, 2005–2006, 12 (Leiden: Brill Academic Publishers, 2007) 156.

22 *Al-Durr al-manẓūm wa khulāṣat al-sirr al-maktūm fī 'l-siḥr wa'l-ṭalāsim wa'l-nujūm.*

(magic, conditioned by *ʿilm al-nujūm wa ʾl-tanajjum* [astrology] more largely); *ʿilm al-ṭalāsim* (talismanology); and *al-nīrandj* (a Persian term denoting magic that is also used for prestidigitation, fakery, and the creation of illusions). The extended prolegomena outlines the contents of the book and anchors the more technical chapters which follow into a larger worldview. It is in these sections that the author justifies his venture most explicitly and orients the reader in approaching the work. It is also here that al-Kashnāwī speaks of his pilgrimage and the immediate context of the book's composition.

Owing to the aforementioned historiographical biases, these prefatory passages have been read as evoking the author's racial and scholarly estrangement from the heartland of Arab orthodoxy, and confirming the special affinity between 'African Muslims' and the occult.[23] However, on closer reading, the text paints a rather different picture, where the norms of an anachronistic orthodoxy (both religious and scientific) are provincialized, and the occult, the superstitious and the charismatic are normalized.

Al-Durr al-manẓūm opens, in formulaic fashion, by bestowing thanks to God for its author's safe and privileged arrival to the Ḥaramāyn:

> In the name of God, the Beneficent, the Merciful, may His prayers be upon our master Muḥammad and upon his family and companions: Oh Allāh, gratitude is due only to You, and reliance, only upon You. You are the Sufficient, the Forgiver of my deficiencies in fulfilling my duty to thank You. I take refuge in You and repent for my knowledge, for none can forgive sins but You. None but You can provide for me, preserve my interests or assist me in times of hardship and ease: to You is gratitude in the beginning and the end.[24]

Al-Kashnāwī then proceeds to describe God by the miracle of His celestial creations: 'I bear witness that You are the Creator of the celestial universes and what they contain of planets ... and the two earths and what they contain of lands, meadows and seas ...'[25]

In the next segment, he continues to express gratitude even as he describes his providential journey to the Hijaz, and the opportunity it conferred to visit God's House and his Prophet. The experience of the *Ḥajj* is expressed here not simply as

---

Various manuscript and printed editions exist in Cairo and elsewhere. The version used here is Mustafa al-Babi al-Halabi (Cairo: 1381/1961).

[23] See for instance Stefan Reichmuth, 'Autobiographical Writing and Islamic Consciousness in the Arabic Literature of Nigeria', in János Riesz; Ulla Schild, *Autobiographical Genres in Africa* (Berlin: Dietrich Reimer Verlag, 1996) 179–89; and the collection of articles in *Kano Studies, New Series 2/2* (1981).

[24] Muḥammad al-Kashnāwī, *al-Durr al-manẓūm*, 3.

[25] Muḥammad al-Kashnāwī, *al-Durr al-manẓūm*, 3.

the fulfilment of a normative obligation, but as a spiritual gratification, which the author duly accentuates along with the power of God's hidden Hand in directing all his affairs: 'When the Deliverer of destiny and sempiternal will delivered me, and the Usher of divine mercy ushered me to visit His good Prophet … and to perform the pilgrimage of His holy sanctified House, I stayed there for some time and grew through these prayers … [I duly] thank Him, the Gracious, for variegating an arboretum for me. A slight utterance [*sha'rat lisānan*] indeed given that greatest of graces that He has bestowed upon me …'[26]

Thanks were indeed owed, for the journey across the African continent to the Hijaz was a long and arduous one, replete with perils of all kinds: from natural disasters, disease and pestilence to acts of larceny and highway robbery.[27] Indeed so severe was the situation that West African scholars, beginning in the seventeenth century, would reinterpret the force of the juridical requirement to perform the pilgrimage, taking advantage of the wide construal margin proffered by the Qur'ānic concept of *istiṭā'ah* (capability). Ostensibly then, al-Kashnāwī could have foregone the pilgrimage altogether. Instead, he chose to shoulder the physical and financial burden and embarked on a journey from which he would not return.

Having eventually crossed the Red Sea, his first destination was Medina. More than a stop along the way, the visit to the Prophet's city was highly commended by tradition. For Mālikīs such as al-Kashnāwī, it would have comprised a normative pillar of the *Ḥajj* owing to *Imām* Mālik b. Anas' association with the town. Al-Kashnāwī thus expresses his sense of relief and joy at having reached the virtuous abode: 'I arrived at *al-Madīna*, may God increase her light and perfect the conditions of her inhabitants. And this was on Tuesday, the twelfth night of *Jumāda I* of the months of the year 1141 of the Prophet's *hijra* … And so, my visit preceded my pilgrimage, and I sojourned there, blessed and pleased for a little less than three months.'[28]

We do not know how al-Kashnāwī spent his time in the city, but we have a good sense of the vivacious intellectual world that animated the Medinan and Meccan milieus of the time.[29] This eighteenth-century world connected seekers of

[26] Muḥammad al-Kashnāwī, *al-Durr al-manẓūm*, 3.

[27] See al-Naqar, *The Pilgrimage Tradition in West Africa: An Historical Study with Special Reference to the Nineteenth Century* (Khartoum: Khartoum University Press, 1972) 94.

[28] Muḥammad al-Kashnāwī, *al-Durr al-manẓūm*, 4.

[29] The significance of the Ḥaramāyn network is associated mainly with the work of John Voll. For a recent, decentralizing account of these scholarly constellations, see Ahmad S. Dallal, *Islam Without Europe: Traditions of Reform in Eighteenth-Century Islamic Thought* (Chapel Hill: University of North Carolina Press, 2018).

knowledge in broad networks stretching from Morocco and West Africa, through Egypt and the Mashriq, to the Indian subcontinent and beyond. Characterized by a strong revivalist current, it combined diverse schools of thought, so that the margins of anything we might strictly call *orthodoxy* appear nebulous at best. The spectrum of scholars included at one extreme, a figure such as the young Muḥammad b. ʿAbd al-Wahhāb, and at the other, miracle-working Sufi peripatetics – with the likes of Muḥammad b. ʿAbd al-Karīm al-Sammān, who advocated a balanced method of existential spiritual illumination with scriptural observance, somewhere in the middle.

From Medina, al-Kashnāwī tells us, he headed to Mecca, 'the happiest of trails for one hoping to attain the pleasure of his Lord in his life and religion'.[30] At this point, he begins to weave an explanation, abounding with fortuitous encounters, of the circumstances that prompted his desire to write *al-Durr*. The work was written, he explains, at the behest of a Meccan notable, Ismāʿīl b. Hamza al-Duḥaydiḥ, to whom he had been introduced by a fellow pilgrim:

> In Mecca ... I came upon a veritable friend, the righteous and sincere, of pure descent and noble distinction, our brother in God the Exalted, Shaykh Yūnus b. Muḥammad al-Sūdānī al-Ḥawsāwī al-Kanāwī who sojourns in God's land ... He wanted me to meet with [al-Duḥaydiḥ] and to relate to him something of what I know of the secret sciences. [Al-Kanāwī] pursued me on this matter with plentiful exaggerated laudation [of al-Duḥaydiḥ], his pleasing dispositions and graceful virtues, until he had me lean towards appreciating him for it is normal to love those who are loved by one's companions, and '*it may be that you hate something that is good for you*' [Qur'ān 2:216].[31]

Al-Kashnāwī repeats more than once that it was only at al-Kanāwī's continual insistence that he grudgingly agreed to meet with al-Duḥaydiḥ. Al-Kashnāwī frames his uncertainty in broad terms along what he viewed as the unethical treatment by the people of the Hijaz of others in their midst:

> I was suspicious of him because I find that in most cases in these lands, they don't like anyone, especially if he be of our people the Sudanese [*min jinsunā al-sūdāniyīn*], unless they seek to benefit from him without any true affection or care. And when they attain what they want from him, they abandon him. He becomes to them like a thing discarded, as though they never knew or befriended him.[32]

[30] Muḥammad al-Kashnāwī, *al-Durr al-manẓūm*, 4.
[31] Muḥammad al-Kashnāwī, *al-Durr al-manẓūm*, 4.
[32] Muḥammad al-Kashnāwī, *al-Durr al-manẓūm*, 4–5.

This passage has been read as evidence of racialist thinking, implying a systematic contempt on the part of 'Arabs' towards 'black Africans': 'In these remarks al-Kašnâwî, apart from his nostalgia, shows a clear sense of being *differentiated by his African social habits* from the *Arabs* among whom he lived.'[33] This analysis wildly overstates the reference to '*jinsunā al-Sūdāniyyīn*', anachronistically imposing modern conceptual grammars.[34] Instead, I would like to suggest that what is undeniably palpable here is rather a note of relief at having fears of abandonment and destitution assuaged. Such alienation of the pilgrim-*mujāwir* cannot be solely reduced to being an 'outsider in a foreign land' (especially in a space theoretically conceived as God's sanctuary [*ḥaram*]). Denoting the intense sacrifice and hardship which the devoted servant endures for the sake of God's pleasure, the trope of exile is an essential quality in the idea of *ṭalab al-ʿilm*: it emanates from the scholar's acute awareness of being in a perpetual quest for learning and to the pious conviction that ultimately *all* humans are guests in this world, especially the pilgrim. Any sense of exile that al-Kashnāwī may have felt would thus have been part and parcel of the condition of *mujāwara* writ large – and what is longed for is partly one's 'real' home, but especially a *spiritual* home. Such yearnings reverberate through al-Kashnāwī's own words and are most perceptible in poignant verses he penned – epitomizing a journey, both mystical and actual, in the typically self-deprecating tone of one who seeks to settle one's worldly soul in knowing anticipation that its true enlightenment and emancipation is in the World to come – with which al-Jabartī chooses to conclude his necrology:

> I sought a domicile in every land, but I found no domicile
> for me on earth.
> I followed my ambitions, and they enslaved me; had I been
> content, I would have been free.[35]

The connections between exile, *mujāwara*, pilgrimage and *ṭalab al-ʿilm* are further marked in the formulaic nature of the text's prolegomena. Always critical statements of intended beginnings, it flags authorship, piety, eloquence as well as the contents and aims of the text to come. In the case of *al-Durr*, it evokes from the onset a mantra of thanksgiving accompanied by enunciations that it is God alone who determines one's affairs. Indeed, this opening discourse of gratitude and acceptance of one's predicament resounds throughout the entirety of the work.

A second explanation which the author gives for his reluctance to pursue al-Duḥaydiḥ's proposal concerns the acceptability of the occult in Meccan society of that time. Al-Kashnāwī relates that he had been advised by friends that he

33 Stefan Reichmuth, 'Autobiographical Writing', 182. Emphasis added.
34 See Dahlia E.M. Gubara, 'Revisiting Race and Slavery', 2018.
35 ʿAbd al-Raḥmān al-Jabartī, *ʿAjāʾib al-āthār*, I:160/262.

must not boast of his involvements in the occult sciences while on his travels, 'on account of their prevalent uses in these lands [*al-bilād al-mashriqīyah* and especially the Ḥaramāyn] for causing corruption, tribulations and dissension in plain sight of those of discerning minds'.[36] The occult sciences were thus not peripheral but rather prevalent in the most 'central' of Islamic heartlands. Moreover, the passage makes clear that (like the al-Azhar today) the primary concern remains the *uses* to which occult knowledge might be put. Rather than any condemnation of the esoteric *tout court*, what was feared was its potential for causing corruption and discord.

It is as a form of protection (both to himself and the world around him) then, that al-Kashnāwī was counselled to conceal what he knew of the concealed, so to speak. The occult, like other sciences in the tradition, entails a requisite disposition on the part of its practitioners, hence al-Kashnāwī's considered exposition of his Meccan courtier's *ethical* qualities, tallying with his evaluation, later in the text, of the *virtues* and *misuses* of the secret sciences. Indeed, it is on account of said qualities that al-Kashnāwī and al-Duḥāydiḥ are able to develop an intimate and profound friendship in the course of their studies of the occult.[37]

Turning his attention to his *raison d'écrire*, al-Kashnāwī writes:

> We remained in this state of reading … books on magic squares, illusion and several other registers, until one day amidst our discussions, the conversation turned to the book *al-Sirr al-maktūm* and its compilation of many astrological, talismanic and magical benefits. From this I understood a desire on [al-Duḥāydiḥ's] part to study the aforementioned book, which was in my possession. I brought it to him, he immediately wrote it down and we began reading it together.[38]

He explains that the introduction to *al-Sirr* was long and complicated, expounding various points of natural philosophy (*al-ʿulūm al-ajnabīya al-ṭabīʿīya*) and others that in al-Kashnāwī's estimation were not geared towards the novice. This prompted him to produce an abridged commentary: 'So, I began to summarize the text … and when I wrote some folios or more, I gave [al-Duḥāydiḥ] that précis.

[36] Muḥammad al-Kashnāwī, *al-Durr al-manẓūm*, 4.

[37] '[A]ll the while I was examining his loyalty, the sincerity of his friendship and other things of his condition, one after the other until it became as clear to me as daylight that the man is all that Shaykh Yūnus had described him to be and more, for his qualities were immeasurable … I found him of highest ability [*qadran*] amongst those of his times, the widest of chest, most bountiful of forbearance [*ḥilm*] and mind, the most robust in chivalry, the most exquisite of dispositions, the deepest in glory and the most loyal to his promises.' (Muḥammad al-Kashnāwī, *al-Durr al-manẓūm*, 5).

[38] Muḥammad al-Kashnāwī, *al-Durr al-manẓūm*, 5.

He examined it in depth and was pleased with the manner and course that I presented because it eased matters for him greatly by simplifying the benefits to be attained and summarizing key arguments so that they may be better understood.'[39] Al-Kashnāwī describes his method as above all a practical one, driven by the needs of his student (and presumably patron at this stage), a point he emphasizes throughout (with phrases such as: 'this was his demand', or 'his soul yearned for this').[40] The manoeuvre repeatedly underscores the pragmatic and didactic dimension of the work, imparting a sense of how embedded these sciences were in the everyday life of students, scholars and practitioners.

Al-Kashnāwī states that he exerted 'great effort and mental energy to collate the different statements [in the book] and organize them by their resembling characters, each corresponding to an overarching heading, and to elucidate meanings that often read like riddles', until finally there emerged a text that 'was free of the stresses of eloquence and the monotony of verbosity'. The original text, we are told, was great and well known, but had become like 'a broken necklace whose beads were now scattered'. Through abridgement and revision, the new edition made the contents, course and concerns of the text more easily accessible to every seeker without 'blurring thought or causing confusion'.[41]

These passages are clearly intended to convey a faithfulness to the original. At the same time however, al-Kashnāwī is keen to underline *his own authorship*: 'but with all this [restructuring]', he tells us, 'this book of ours is not devoid of good additions and notifications that cannot be ignored and are required by the beginner but also useful to the expert'. 'For this reason,' he concludes, 'I named it "*al-Durr al manẓūm wa khulāṣat al-sirr al-maktūm*" [The Ordered Pearls and the Summa of "*al-Sirr al-maktūm*" – the Hidden Secret] and I organized it into an introduction, a conclusion and five chapters, and have enumerated its subject matter for those who wish to understand its contents as a whole.'[42]

Less linear than its author would suggest, *al-Durr* is not so evidently easy to navigate, and it is certainly not free of repetitions. It is structured through overlapping sections with an extended introduction that addresses the place of the occult within a broader discussion of the virtues of knowledge. The three fields of the occult (astral magic, talismanology, and *nīrandj*), though treated separately, are all calibrated to the determination of the nature and characteristics of the spheres (*al-kawākib*) and their earthly active vectors (*al-qawābil al-arḍiyya al-munfa'ila*). Under each heading he provides a definition of terms and of the main aims of the science in question with brief sketches of debates concerning

39 Muḥammad al-Kashnāwī, *al-Durr al-manẓūm*, 6.
40 Muḥammad al-Kashnāwī, *al-Durr al-manẓūm*, 6.
41 Muḥammad al-Kashnāwī, *al-Durr al-manẓūm*, 6.
42 Muḥammad al-Kashnāwī, *al-Durr al-manẓūm*, 6.

the locations and influence of the planets as played out in the tradition. His own position, interwoven in his discussion of talismanology, is squarely among those who do not dispute the influence of the stars but consider it an extension of God's omnipotence.[43]

Subsequent chapters elaborate on various dimensions of the three fields. For example, under *siḥr*, al-Kashnāwī delineates four major schools (*madhāhib*) and engages judgements concerning the teaching and application of this knowledge. Here he draws a distinction between magic that is 'true' (*ḥaqīqī*) and that which is 'un-true' (*ghayr ḥaqīqī*), relying instead on forms of illusion and prestidigitation.[44] The different methods for marshalling the former in the four schools are further elaborated. Thus, we learn, amongst other things, that the Indian method (*ṭarīqat ahl al-Hind*) was based in the first instance on the purification of the soul and the suspension of illusion; the Nabatean method (*al-Nabṭ*) revolved principally around the invitation and supplication of the planets; the Greek (*al-Yūnān*) entailed the subjugation of the planetary spirits by way of fasting and sacrifices; and the way of the Hebrews, the Copts, and the Arabs (*al-ʿibrānīya, al-qibāṭ wa'l-ʿarab*) amalgamated the above three and was for al-Kashnāwī the superior method.[45]

Throughout these sections, and especially when outlining the properties and astral influences of the zodiacal signs (*al-burūj*), al-Kashnāwī displays knowledge of scientific and cosmological theories prevailing over the centuries in all of the Islamic, Christian and Jewish traditions, as well as their precursors in classical antiquity. And often, he engages these various strands in a critical fashion. Under the discussion of talismanology, he provides a dazzling list of the many functions to which talismanic seals may be put, their correspondence to each of the seven planets, their known natures, and methods for their subjugation. Encompassing almost all aspects of quotidian human life, these sections read very much like a step-by-step manual, and for al-Kashnāwī they categorically affirm the premise that for 'every earthly movement or part, there is a guiding [planetary] spirit [*rūḥan mudabbira*]'. This claim is repeated at various points throughout the book, and if taken in conjunction with the all-encompassing applications of the practice, is indicative of the *everyday life of the occult* as a vital component of knowledge writ large. Thus, in expounding the ideals of absolute knowledge (*al-ʿilm al-muṭlaq*), al-Kashnāwī reiterates the basic principle of the convergence of belief, knowledge and practice, where knowledge (both semantically and symbolically) represented ontological and epistemological frames that point invariably to agency in speech and thought, as well as belief and action.

[43] Muḥammad al-Kashnāwī, *al-Durr al-manẓūm*, 83.
[44] Muḥammad al-Kashnāwī, *al-Durr al-manẓūm*, 19.
[45] Muḥammad al-Kashnāwī, *al-Durr al-manẓūm*, 19–35.

In his discussion of the virtues of knowledge and the conditions incumbent upon its practitioners, al-Kashnāwī begins by contrasting 'absolute science' to 'absolute ignorance'. 'Know,' he affirms, 'that science and wisdom [*al-ʿilm wa'l-ḥikmah*] cleanse souls from the filth of vile natures just as soap cleans clothes.' And he proceeds to explain, drawing mainly on classical Greek sources, that the essence of knowledge is to grasp what changes, not that which is static. He quotes Socrates as proclaiming: 'is alive not he who indulges in appetites and kills the soul by plunging it in immediate desires; alive is he who knows of the extinguished desires of the past, and becomes certain that what will come next is like the past in its ephemerality'. Building on dichotomies contrasting knowledge and habit, the spiritual and the bodily/natural, al-Kashnāwī thus develops a notion of the live, enlightened soul as one that gets beyond its immediate existence to embrace wisdom (*ḥikma*) of a deeper, more enduring and more powerful nature.[46]

Having demonstrated the virtue of knowledge in general, al-Kashnāwī delves into the details of the virtues of the secret sciences in particular. 'This knowledge,' he begins, 'is of the most delectable and most noble of sciences because it provides the secrets of the other/higher and nether/lower world, because it makes one an observer of, and converser with, the planetary spirits [*al-rūḥāniyyāt*]. Indeed, it causes one to become so mixed with them as if [he were] one with them.'[47] At a more concrete level, he outlines five basic virtues of the secret sciences, to which he adduces examples and references, often classical but also sometimes Islamic: it allows its practitioners to cure difficult diseases that medical doctors cannot; it lets one vanquish one's adversaries without going to war; it can give tidings of events before they occur; it may save the oppressed from the clutches of tyranny; and finally, its permits the observation and manipulation of things from afar.[48] However, the achievement of such objectives (detailed in the sections devoted to each branch of the three subfields) is provisional upon an entire series of conditions borne by the practitioner, which are then outlined in great detail, first for the secret sciences as a whole and in general, and then, for each subfield more specifically.

The general requisites are fascinating, as they provide for the type of ethical subjects, character traits and embodied practices that al-Kashnāwī envisioned as the human, personal, and relational horizon upon which his scholarship depended. He outlines twelve 'absolute, general and comprehensive conditions' (upon which he later elaborates).

The first condition is that the practitioner be 'absolutely certain and determined in the completion of the work, because whosoever does such a work while

[46] Muḥammad al-Kashnāwī, *al-Durr al-manẓūm*, 11–13.
[47] Muḥammad al-Kashnāwī, *al-Durr al-manẓūm*, 13.
[48] Muḥammad al-Kashnāwī, *al-Durr al-manẓūm*, 13–15.

harboring doubts will not benefit from it'. The logic is straightforward: since spirits only answer when one wholeheartedly believes in them, soul power (*al-quwwah al-nafsānīyah*) is crucial to the work and is compromised by scepticism. A subsequent warning explains that this prerequisite is confirmed by both reason and transmitted knowledge (*al-'aql wa'l-naql*), and two further authoritative *ḥadīths* are cited (including the commonly known '*innamā 'l-a'mālu bi'l-niyyāt*').[49]

The second condition echoes the first, stipulating 'persistence ... and the avoidance of boredom and weariness', emphasized by quotes attributed to Aristotle and other proverbial wisdoms.[50]

The third is the by now familiar vow of secrecy and silence (*al-kitmān*): 'the scholars and sages have agreed that one of the conditions of these sciences is *al-kitmān* for it is done in an empty place [*fī mawḍi'in khālī*], where no one can see the practitioner, who in turn may not say to anyone "I did this, and I didn't do this, and such and such was done to so and so".' Again, the point is accentuated by classical references mobilized to explain why, and it has to do with some form of *maṣlaḥah*, the concern that said knowledge falls into the wrong hands – of those full of 'conceit, pride, and who are driven by concerns of achieving flattery and power, or who would use it to further vile ends in this World, with disregard for the Next'.[51]

This leads to the fourth condition, piety and devotion (*al-ṭaqwah*): 'and in piety is included the consumption of what is *ḥālal*, avoidance of doing harm to others, restraint from falsehood, slander and self-aggrandizement, adherence to sincerity, the giving of friendly advice to common folk and elite alike, and regarding both [groups] with mercy, compassion, and sympathy'. 'This is why,' he adds, 'the *Imām* al-Rāzī originally said, "all scholars and sages agreed that, concerning the practitioner of this science, the more he seeks and approaches the good, the more successful his work will be, for whosoever fears God, then everything becomes subservient and obedient to him".'[52]

The ensuing two conditions involve the objectives and frequency of employing the occult: it should not be overused (since calling on the planetary spirits too often diminishes potency) nor employed for petty goals (for which other means can be called upon).[53]

[49] Muḥammad al-Kashnāwī, *al-Durr al-manẓūm*, 35–6.
[50] Muḥammad al-Kashnāwī, *al-Durr al-manẓūm*, 36.
[51] Muḥammad al-Kashnāwī, *al-Durr al-manẓūm*, 36–7.
[52] Muḥammad al-Kashnāwī, *al-Durr al-manẓūm*, 37.
[53] Muḥammad al-Kashnāwī, *al-Durr al-manẓūm*, 37–8.

The seventh condition concerns the 'soul' of the practitioner, which must be a 'live soul, not a dead one', as per the aforementioned definition attributed to Socrates presumably.[54]

The next three conditions return to procedural matters concerning the efficiency of the practice: it obliges the full description (*tashkhīṣ*) of the person on which the art is to have an effect, including a full physiognomic depiction, and not just naming; and one must remember by heart the words by which one calls upon the spirits, rather than have them written on a piece of paper or a board.[55]

The eleventh condition evokes the need for a licence (*ijāza*) from a shaykh authorizing the transmission and practice of the science: 'it is learned and earned by obtention from shaykhs in the same manner as a (political) pledge [*bayʿah*] or the instruction or inspiration [*talqīn*] of the Sufis'. To emphasize this relational and experiential dimension, al-Kashnāwī furthermore cautions that 'whoever learns this science without obtaining such an *ijāza* is like the child without a father to whom he can relate and from whom he may be instructed'.[56]

Finally, the last condition is also the most obviously technical: a basic knowledge of astronomical observation (*al-raṣd*) is essential. And, indeed, much of the subsequent lessons he then elucidates involve the effect of celestial forces.[57]

These then are only the most general criteria for practical and scholarly engagements in the secret sciences – others are included specifically for more precise fields (often involving such things as calibrated periods of fasting, sacrifices and other ritual commitments, among others).

Coming full circle, *al-Durr* ends by insisting on the supreme virtue and potency of the greatest talismanic seal (*al-khātim al-akbar*), of which all others are approximations, and the means and prayers by which to benefit from its blessing with God's will. Thus, providing a certain symmetry with the text's prolegomena which established the cosmological proofs for the existence of the two worlds (the celestial and the material) and their correlation as a reflection of God's Wisdom and Ability. With this, al-Kashnāwī subordinates the book and its contents to God's final and only true Magnificence, seeking His forgiveness and bestowing the commended prayers on the Prophet Muḥammad, His Messenger and Servant.[58]

* * *

[54] Muḥammad al-Kashnāwī, *al-Durr al-manẓūm*, 38.
[55] Muḥammad al-Kashnāwī, *al-Durr al-manẓūm*, 38–9.
[56] Muḥammad al-Kashnāwī, *al-Durr al-manẓūm*, 39.
[57] Muḥammad al-Kashnāwī, *al-Durr al-manẓūm*, 39.
[58] Muḥammad al-Kashnāwī, *al-Durr al-manẓūm*, 229–30.

In conclusion, rather than conforming to the conventional contours delineated by the dualities of Africa/Islam, centre/periphery, occult/science, orthodox/heterodox, my reading of al-Kashnāwī's text reveals instead a thoroughly integrated world of scholarship, where so-called Africans and Arabs (and many others) rubbed shoulders continuously, and where the domains of the occult were not barricaded from other sciences, but rather partook in a wider epistemic cosmos grounded in what we could call an *embodied ethics of learning*. Indeed, what is most striking is the extent to which al-Kashnāwī's framing of his work resembles the epistemic contours of many other disciplines, fields, and texts in the tradition at the time. Knowledge here is understood first and foremost as an everyday *lived* practice. Its seeker displays an almost physical proximity to the subject matter. Its focus is on ends and outcomes, not just its truth. Its transmission is articulated to a relational, interpersonal system of validation intended to guarantee its integrity.

Al-Kashnāwī's text certainly bespeaks of an 'esoteric episteme', to borrow Louis Brenner's phrase,[59] but there was nothing African or especially unique about it. Its parameters extended to a larger edifice of knowledge production and transmission wherein the occult, rational and transmitted sciences seamlessly cohabited – and in that respect, the adjective 'esoteric' is perhaps even redundant. Crucially, this episteme hinges in its entirety, whether it relates to the occult or otherwise, on the constant ethical fashioning of the self, and how to practice this or that science as a faithful subject living the good life. This is also a direct result of the fact that these knowledges, all of them, from formal jurisprudence to talismanology, were discursive practices, organically rooted in a moral community and embedded in a thoroughly textualized world.

[59] Louis Brenner, *Controlling Knowledge: Religion, Power and Schooling in a West African Muslim Society* (Bloomington: Indiana University Press, 2001) 7.

CHAPTER 3

The African Community and African *'Ulamā'* in Mecca: Al-Jāmī and Muḥammad Surūr al-Ṣabbān (twentieth century)

Chanfi Ahmed

الخلافة في قريش والحكم في الآنصار والدعوة في الحبشة
والجهاد والهجرة في المسلمين

'Al-khilāfa fī Quraish wa al-ḥukm fī al-anṣār wa al-da'wah fī al-Ḥabasha wa al-jīhād wa al-hijra fī al-muslimīn' [*The Khilāfa (political authority) is the business of Quraish; judicature is that of the Anṣār; the propagation of Islam (da'wa) is that of the Ethiopians (and by extension black Africans), jihād and hijra is that of all Muslims.*] (Ḥadīth)

This chapter examines first, the specific history of the African community of Mecca, and second, more generally that of Hijaz, the south-westerly region of the Arabian Peninsula where the two holy cities Mecca and Medina are located. Consequently, the two parts of the chapter are titled 'MeccAfrica from below' (the microview) and 'MeccAfrica from above' (the macroview).

MeccAfrica from below concerns the history of Africans in Mecca from the nineteenth century till the creation of Saudi Arabia in the twentieth century, and specifically until the period of the economic boom brought about by the unprecedented rise in the price of oil in the 1970s. Paradoxically, while the majority of Saudis became increasingly wealthy, the material situation of Saudis of African ancestry stagnated. In addition to not being able to land well-paying jobs, banks denied them the kind of credit they gave others to set up businesses, and they faced increasing discrimination from both the political authorities and non-Africans. Of course, we observe this same pattern of anti-black racism in Western societies. Wherever it occurs, such anti-black racism not only undermines the humanity of black people, it also reproduces poverty in their midst and consolidates racial prejudice that assumes that black populations are poor because they are less intelligent than others. Such vicious cycles unfortunately and unjustly legitimize structural and systemic anti-black racism everywhere.

The chapter examines how such racial discrimination operates in the daily life of one district of Mecca where the majority of the inhabitants are African. Besides uncovering the history of a forgotten African diaspora, this chapter shows how despite the centuries-old presence of Africans in Mecca and the great contributions they have made to all aspects of society, and despite the precepts of Islam that reject racial discrimination, nonetheless the political authorities and non-Africans in Mecca have continued to discriminate against Africans there.

The chapter also discusses the divisions running through the African communities. It uses sociologist Norbert Elias' concepts of the established person and the outsider to illustrate this phenomenon. Here, the Salafī *'ulamā'* of African origins and those who evolved around them represent the established persons, whereas the majority of Africans who were not Salafī *'ulamā'* but rather Sūfī from the Qādiriyya and the Tijāniyya, represent the outsiders.

The chapter's second part, on MeccAfrica from above, presents the biographical itinerary of Al-Jāmī and Muḥammad Surūr al-Ṣabbān, two twentieth-century Saudi personalities of African origin who made significant contributions to the religious, cultural, educational, political, and economic life of Saudi Arabia, both in the country's founding days and well beyond. Even if their contributions were exceptional, they were far from the only ones. Other Saudi personalities of African origin made equally remarkable contributions to their country.

Al-Jāmī was a student and disciple of various African *'ulamā'* who were well known in Saudi Arabia, among them the Malian ʿAbdu al-Raḥmān Yūsuf al-Ifrīqī (1908–57), the Mauritanian Muḥammad al-Amīn al-Shinqīṭī (1907–73), and the Malian Ḥammād al-Anṣārī (1925–97); they came to Saudi Arabia in the 1920s, 1940s, and 1950s respectively.[1] Over time, these African elites who had once occupied important positions in the Saudi state disappeared completely. This suggests that the positions that the Saudi political authorities granted to these few personalities of African origin were not granted out of sympathy, nor out of a sense of justice, let alone respect for merit and talent, nor as a result of a policy of minority integration, but simply and only because these individuals were essential to and

[1] On the history of these African ʿulamāʾ and their great contribution in the teaching and the propagation of Wahhābī-Salafism both inside and outside of Saudi Arabia in the Saudi nascent state, see Ahmed Chanfi, *West African ʿulamāʾ and Salafism in Mecca and Medina: Jawāb al-Ifrīqī – The Response of the African* (Leiden: Brill, 2015) and Ahmed Chanfi, *AfroMecca in History. African Societies, Anti-Black Racism, and Teaching in al-Haram Mosque in Mecca* (Newcastle upon Tyne: Cambridge Scholars Publishing, 2019).

irreplaceable in the nascent state. As soon as non-African Saudis had the skills to perform those tasks, they replaced the African Saudi elites. This explains why today there are no longer *'Ulamā'*, politicians, and businessmen of African origins in Saudi Arabia like ʿAbdu al-Raḥmān Yūsuf al-Ifrīqī, Al-Jāmī, or Muḥammad Surūr al-Ṣabbān – with the single exception of Shaykh ʿĀdil al-Kalbānī whom the Saudi king appointed in 2009 as the first black *imām* of the al-Ḥaram mosque in Mecca. Yet even in ʿĀdil al-Kalbānī's case, he stayed in this position for only one month, the rumour being that particular prominent Saudi personalities, including members of the royal family, could not tolerate a black man in such a prominent position, and successfully pressured the king to end his tenure. ʿĀdil al-Kalbānī returned to Riyadh where, instead of resuming his duties as *imām* of the King Khalid mosque, he became the *imām* of the al-Muḥaysin mosque in the Ishbiliyā district, north-east of Riyadh.

MeccAfrica from Below: The History of the African Diaspora in the Hijaz, Particularly in Mecca (Nineteenth to Twentieth Centuries)

Although the presence of the African diaspora in the Hijaz dates to the emergence of Islam, the African diaspora of the nineteenth and twentieth centuries consisted of *ḥujjāj* (pilgrims) who came and stayed, along with their descendants and the descendants of former slaves. These, however, represent the minority within the African diaspora of Mecca. Beginning in 1930, trade in slaves declined significantly. This decline was caused partly by the controls the English imposed on methods of transporting slaves, and partly by the advent of the motor car, which now transported the pilgrims between Jedda, Mecca, and Medina, replacing camels and their African slave attendants. Slavery had not yet ended. However, international pressure against the practice in Saudi Arabia increased, and the Saudi government began to take appropriate measures in this direction. It was only thirty years later on 6 November 1962 that Faisal, vice king of the Hijaz, published his ten known reforms, the tenth completely abolishing slavery.

From the nineteenth century until the early 1970s and specifically before the enormous increase in wealth that the country experienced in response to the exceptional rise in oil prices, the majority of Africans lived in the Misfala neighbourhood of Mecca and in Jarwal, in short in the southern part of the city, as C. Snouck-Hurgronje, alias ʿAbd al-Ghaffār, already observed in 1884–85.[2] The best known of the African ethnic groups of Mecca (and Saudi Arabia as a whole) were the Hausa, the Fallāta or Fulani (also called Fulbe or Peul), and the

[2] C. Snouck-Hurgronje, *Mekka in the latter part of the 19th century. Daily life, customs and learning. The Moslims of the East-Indian-Archipelago* (Leyden: E.J. Brill Ltd; and London: Lucaz and Co., 1931) 5–6.

Bornawī (from Borno's region in Nigeria). But all West Africans were known as Takrūrī or Takrūnī (pl. Takkāra, Takārira or Takārina or Takarna). Among the best-known social characteristics of these African groups, Snouck-Hurgronje[3] briefly describes the music and dance that they performed for their own entertainment on Thursdays and Fridays. One of their dances was the Mizmār, a folk dance which still exists today and is the most popular one among the men of Mecca (and the Hijaz) of all social and ethnic backgrounds – in short, not only of Africans. Burckhardt, Hurgronje, and Burton, the three well-known Westerners who visited Mecca in the nineteenth century and later wrote about their experiences in their books, repeatedly mention the presence of the black African communities in Mecca. Unlike Burckhardt, the other two evoke the black people in inhumane and degrading terms, although Burton was by far the more disgusting in his descriptions. Yet though Burton spoke about black people in inhumane terms, he also spoke about all other non-European people in racist terms. For example, when he compared the supposed avarice of the Meccans and Medinans to that of the European Jews, he wrote: 'The Madani are, like the Meccans, a curious mixture of generosity and meanness of profuseness and penuriousness. But the former quality is the result of ostentation; the latter is a characteristic of the Semitic race, long ago made familiar to Europe by the Hebrew.'[4]

In short, the black people of Mecca (and of Saudi Arabia as a whole) are either from West Africa and are known by the names Takkārā, Takārira, Takārina, or Takarna (sing. Takrūrī)[5] or are the descendants of African slaves called *muwallidūn* (lit. the natives of the country, sing. *muwallad*), or came from the Horn of Africa and were known as Aḥbāsh (sing. Ḥabashī).[6]

[3] Snouck-Hurgronje, *Mekka in the latter part of the 19th century.*

[4] Richard Burton, *Personal Narrative of a Piligramage to Mecca and Medina* (Leipzig: Bernhard Tauchnitz, 1874, vol. II) 167.

[5] 'The name Takārir, also Takarna is often heard in the Holy places of Islam and the Middle Eastern world in general. Like the terms Jāwa or Shanāqita, it is in fact a generic term conveniently used to describe a group of people whose relationship is mainly geographical. The Jāwah are all Muslims of the Malay race of south-east Asia; the Shanāqita come from the western Sahara; the Takārir are all West African Muslims', and 'The appellation is not derogatory in any sense – many are proud of it for it is the reflection of the identity of Muslim West Africa in the world of Islam' in Umar Al-Naqar, *The Pilgrimage Tradition in West Africa: An Historical Study with Special Reference to the Nineteenth Century* (Khartoum: Khartoum University Press, 1972) 3–5.

[6] Snouck-Hurgronje was not interested in this category of the population of Mecca, for the simple reason that he had a colonial mission consisting of writing – for the government of his country, Holland – a report on the lives of the Jāwa (those who originated from Java in Indonesia, sing. Jāwī) who were at that time Dutch colonial

More fully than did Hurgronje, in his 1829 book *Travel in Arabia* John Lewis Burckhardt (Johann Ludwig Burckhardt or Jean Louis Burckhardt alias Shaykh Ibrahim Ibn ʿAbdallāh) described Misfala in Mecca, Medina, and Jedda in response to his stay there between September 1814 and April 1815. Misfala, the southern part of the city of Mecca, was certainly very close to the al-Ḥaram mosque, but because of the seasonal flooding and the large transient population, it was also the least comfortable place to live in Mecca. It was the neighbourhood where poor Bedouins, Yemenis, Indians, Jawas, and especially black Africans lived. The pilgrims from Jeddah and other parts of the coast entered and left Mecca largely by Misfala. The northern part consisted mainly of Muʿalla (where the main cemetery of the city called Jannat al-muʿalla was to be found) whose rainfall, especially during flood season, poured down to the lower region of Misfala, causing damage to the al-Ḥaram mosque and to the entire Misfala neighbourhood.

In contrast to Hurgronje, Burckhardt evokes the black communities of Mecca many times in his book and does so in more humane (if not positive) terms than the Dutchman, who writes only of the 'important' personalities of Mecca (mainly of Yemeni origin). Each of these two travellers had intimate knowledge of the black communities: Burckhardt was accompanied by a black slave throughout his journey, and Hurgronje (disguised as a Muslim) lived in Mecca with an Ethiopian concubine. Burckhardt wrote that the neighbourhood of Misfala included on its margins a market named Sūq al-sūghayyir around which were huts and other modest shelters inhabited by Bedouins from southern Arabia. They sold charcoal and products like coffee (brought from Mokha), cereal, raisins, etc. Poor Indian and African pilgrims also lived here. African men tended to work as porters and sold firewood gathered in the mountains around Misfala. They also worked in the construction of houses. In fact, notes Burckhardt, they had a monopoly on building houses and selling firewood not only in Misfala but throughout Mecca. As for the African women, the modest among them sold *bouza* (*boozeh* or *boozah*), a fermented drink made from sorghum grain.[7] Burckhardt mentions other nationalities who lived in Misfala, both pilgrims who wanted to return to their home countries

subjects. This was also the reason why he reserved the fourth and final chapter of his book – Snouck-Hurgronje, *Mekka in the Latter Part of the 19th century* – for the Jâwah (Jāwa).

[7] *Bouza* is an indigenous drink of Nubia and the Sudan but is now brewed in Egypt by expatriate Nubians. It is a drink of the poorer classes, according to Lane (1860), who report that 'Boozeh or boozah which is an intoxicating liquor made from barley-bread, crumbled, mixed with water, strained and left to ferment, is commonly drunk by the boatmen of the Nile, and by other persons of the lower orders.' In Ian Spencer, *A History of Beer and Brewing* (Cambridge: The Royal Society of Chemistry, 2003) 46.

and pilgrims who had decided to become permanent residents in Mecca. There were also Maghrebians and people originating from Suleymanye (that is to say the people of Afghanistan, Kandahar, Kashmir and other people originating from Indus, among whom are often found Indians). But the majority of the inhabitants of Misfala were black Africans, followed by Indians and Yemenis. Burckhardt, the European who knew Mecca better than anyone else of his time, estimated the entire population of Mecca to be between 25,000 and 30,000 inhabitants, plus 3,000 or 4,000 Ethiopian slaves. The latter, in addition to other black slaves and blacks who were not slaves (Hurgronje does not specify their number), made blacks an important segment of the city's population.

The Builders of Mud Houses[8]

Having briefly glimpsed the history of black Africans of Mecca and its region by relying in part on descriptions of travellers such as Burckhardt, Burton, and Hurgronje (respectively from the early, mid-, and late nineteenth centuries), we turn now to look at these Africans of Mecca and its environs in the twentieth and twenty-first centuries.

As in earlier times, one of the sectors where black Africans of the Hijaz had the monopoly for centuries was home building. They built houses for the rich and not so rich, and earned enough money from these activities to enjoy the respect due to manual tradesmen. However, in light of the wealth that oil brought to the Saudis, the income and the prestige of African builders of traditional-style houses decreased significantly after the 1970s. Now houses were being built with a lot of concrete and other modern materials, not as before with clay, an art in which Africans were the masters in the region.

In many of my discussions with black Africans of Mecca, they complained of discrimination, racism, and marginalization against them by the Meccan Arabs and especially by the political authorities of the city. Some said that this phenomenon has worsened since the period of '*ṭafra*' (lit. time of economic boom). '*Zaman al-ṭafra*' or '*ʿahd al-ṭafra*' is the expression that Saudis use to describe the period that followed the oil boom and the unprecedented wealth that Saudi Arabia had begun to amass.

[8] In the traditional society of Mecca and the Hijaz, the house builder was called *muʿallim* (master / pl. *muʿallimūn*).

Life in 'African ghettos' in Mecca

Shāriʿ al-Manṣūr in Mecca: Mecca, the capital of Nigeria

In an internet chat forum, someone wrote an acerbic critique of the black Africans of Mecca.[9] Much of the content has long been familiar to me. Now in written form, this criticism tells us much about the discrimination that black Africans are subject to in Mecca, in the Hijaz, and in Saudi Arabia as a whole. Indeed, the text contains many racist stereotypes that are often made against black Africans everywhere, not just in Saudi Arabia.

The title of the text is: *Makka al-mukarrama ʿāṣimat Nayjīryā / Mecca, the capital of Nigeria*. The writer begins his attack like this:

> Yes, it is true … and we cannot escape the truth … Some African tribes (*qabāʾil Ifrīqiyya*) impose their laws on Mecca without any problem. What hurts the most is that they took Mecca as their capital forever. They took Mecca just like that, simply by making it their capital by their demographic importance, increasingly Takrūrī (*takrana fī takrana*). These tribes perform their African activities as if they were in Nigeria. It is true that they are Muslims, but they completely mock the laws of the State! Of course, we do not deny the efforts of the *al-Jawāzāt* (the border and immigration police) especially the almost daily control campaigns it conducts within these communities. But these campaigns of control fail to produce a good effect within these black Africans, while they are effective within the communities originating from Egypt, Indonesia, Pakistan, Afghanistan and India. Now, this situation of the Africans has become so normal that it seems that the country belongs to them. They have no fear of the Border and Immigration Police (*al-Jawāzāt*). On the contrary, the police are now afraid of them. For, it often happens that these Africans beat and mistreat the police … Concerning African women, they are hardy and persevering. Some of them remained in Mecca, while others moved to Jeddah because earning a living there is easier for them than in Mecca! I could hardly believe it when I was told that Africans in Mecca occupy the traffic lights. Beggars and hawkers among them monopolize the traffic lights and ask money from drivers. They also dominate the neighborhoods in which they circulate perpetually to sell their products, which are either stolen, or expired, or simply manufactured by them … As for their women, who are more hard working and more robust, they take advantage of this situation much more than the men. But the way in which they make their living is partly licit and partly illicit. After searching every day in public bins, they head for the private homes of Saudis to clean and other such work. Others specialize in stealing and witchcraft … As

[9] http://aljsad.org/forum9/thread19866/. Accessed January 2010.

> for areas inhabited by Africans, they are very dangerous neighborhoods. They are dangerous especially for non-Africans who venture there.
>
> If it turns out that the non-African visitor has links with the state, his day will be a black day (*fa sayakūn yawmuhu aswad*). If someone goes to Jedda, he will see that there are many Africans who managed to secure a shelter and food. As for African women, they carry out two kinds of work: the sale of fireworks throughout the corniche and prostitution. If we return to Mecca to consider Africans again, we find that in the al-Ḥaram's Mosque, they also engage in small pious activities that bring them money. For example, they reserve to themselves the places closest to the *imām*, those close to the *ka'ba*, etc. They try to offer these places to visitors. After the prayer, they offer them *Zamzam* water; they seek their shoes, etc. Visitors offer them some money for these apparently selfless good manners. But some offer them large sums of money that can go up to 200 riyals. These are for these Africans large sums of money unimaginable for them. However, the important business (*al-tijārat al-umm*) for these Africans is washing cars. They gather in a public place and wash cars of people in exchange for money. Some Saudis help some Africans to regularize their residence status and then open official places to wash cars and this work will be assured by these Africans. Some Saudis after helping Africans to regularize their residency status hire them as drivers and as bodyguards. They use their muscular bodies for their security. Dear readers, this is however a drop in the ocean. For, I am not talking about their criminal acts in the animal market. Here, some Saudis had their hands or feet cut off by the clumsy knives of these Africans. We do not mention here, in addition, their practices of witchcraft and their management of bedroom apartments for prostitution.[10]

The text elicited many responses; the majority of the respondents agreed with its sentiments. However, one person wrote about this question from a more human perspective. This respondent, named 'Abdallah Mar'ī b. Maḥfūẓ, wrote in the newspaper *al-Madīna* an article entitled 'The Marginalized in the Society in the Region of Mecca'.[11] The author begins his article by stating a truth. He writes:

> These marginalized people did not put themselves in a situation of misery; it is not they who refuse to improve their situation and integrate into the Saudi society. Marginalized people living in slums actually want to live a dignified life away from discrimination and deprivation of basic human rights which would demonstrate their presence in society and not their quasi-disappearance [in] this society. Those interested in this issue of marginalized people in the Saudi society can also

[10] http://aljsad.org/forum9/thread19866/. Accessed January 2010.

[11] *'Al-muhammashūn fī mujtama' manṭiqat makka al-mukarrama'.*

read some aspects of this phenomenon in some novels of Saudi writers such as Fahd al-ʿAtīq (Kāʾin muʾajjal), ʿAbduh Khāl, Rajāʾ ʿĀlim, etc.'[12]

The letter's author urges readers to differentiate between Africans who have been in the country for forty years (that is to say, the period in which Saudi Arabia was not yet a rich country) and those who came more recently with a work visa or for *Ḥajj* or *ʿumra* and remained in the country without a residence permit and without a job. The author also shows his disappointment vis-à-vis the lack of concern of international organizations about the fate of more than two million marginalized Africans of Mecca and its neighbouring region and other minorities like the *Burmāwīyyūn* (Rohinga) and Baluchis. The author continues by saying that certainly in the 1970s these communities (*al-jāliyāt*) were able to remain faithful to the traditions and customs of their country of origin, but reminds his readers that this is no longer the case for those of the second and third generations who were born and raised in Saudi Arabia. They have adopted the customs and traditions of other Saudis and are fully integrated into the Saudi social fabric. The great love these communities have for Saudi Arabia, the land of the two holy cities of Islam, contributed much to their integration. The author mentions the example of young people with whom he was at school and with whom he played in Mecca, his hometown. They were the young Africans of the Shāriʿ al-Manṣūr neighbourhood, the young Baluchis of al-Shashta neighbourhood, and the young Burmawiyyūn of Qūz al-Nakāsa district. The author estimated the number of these young people who have Saudi citizenship at about 350,000, whereas their parents number about 70,000.

Dukan Kida and *Shāriʿ al-Manṣūr* in Mecca

Dukan Kida in Hausa means 'the great and long house'. For thirty years or so, the term designated a large building that was on Shāriʿ al-Manṣūr Street. This is what the building (and the place around it) was named first by Hausa speakers and then by others. The seven-storey building, which was the tallest and largest one built at that time in that street, belonged to Shaykh ʿAqīl al-Sayyid. This latter installed here, among other things, the Baqqāla ʿAqīl, a large food store widely known in Mecca. Today, many buildings larger than the one of Shaykh ʿAqīl al-Sayyid have been built on this street. The street is named after prince Manṣūr b. Abd al-ʿAzīz, who in the 1970s was the defence minister of Saudi Arabia. The prince had built there a palace that still exists today.

The quarter *Shāriʿ al-Manṣūr* is best known for the presence of a large number of African people. Among them, we find those who have acquired Saudi citizenship, those who have a residence permit according to the *kafāla* system, and

[12] *Al-Madīna* (newspaper), 22 April 2005, 18.

unlawful residents. Africans have lived for centuries in various districts of the city of Mecca. They started to settle in this street fify years ago and have now become the majority community in this district.

Before the oil boom of the 1970s, many of the Africans of Mecca lived in the Misfala neighbourhood, especially around the two areas called Zango Malla Mūsā and *Dahlat al-Wilāya*, which are now close to the Burj al-misfala (al-misfala Bridge). In Misfala, alongside the Africans, lived also the Jāwī (people from Java) and by extension those of South-east Asian origin. But they too left Misfala when it became gentrified and thus expensive, and settled elsewhere in Mecca. However, memories of the two communities remain in Misfala. There are, for example, the *Ḥārat al-Jāwī* (the Jāwī quarter), although there are no more Jāwī, and Zongo Malla Mūsā with its Hausa street (Shāriʿ al-Hausa), although there are no more Hausa there.

On this street of Shāriʿ al-Manṣūr and around the Baqqāla ʿAqīl, one can find the largest African market of Mecca, which Africans call the Sūq Dukan kida. The critics of Africans named it the Sūq al-ḥarāmiyya (market of the thieves), thus implying that items sold in this market are stolen. This market is very well known both in West Africa and in Mecca, so that if someone takes a taxi anywhere in Mecca (and even in Jeddah) and asks to be brought to the Sūq Dukan kida, the taxi driver will know right away where the place is located. The Ramadan and *Ḥajj* period are the two exceptions in which the market is filled daily by a majority of Africans. The rest of the year, the market is open every day after the dawn prayer (*ṣalāt al-fajr*) until ten in the morning and after afternoon prayer ʿAṣr (until sunset). The market is more crowded on Fridays, both by Africans and members of other communities of Mecca. People sell everything in this market: electronic products, building materials, car parts, fabrics, and African and Saudi clothes. Over time, it has become the largest market in Mecca. But because the majority of people who frequent it are blacks of African origin, and due to the racial prejudices of many Arabs against black people, countless rumours have circulated about illegal acts allegedly committed by Africans in this market. Indeed, stealing, the sales of drugs, and even prostitution happen in this market. But it happens elsewhere in Mecca and other cities in Saudi Arabia too, for especially if someone does not have a residence and work permit, the chance is high that they will revert to illegal means to earn money to survive. But when this situation concerns black people, the reports about it are disproportionately exaggerated. In addition, rumours circulate about weird things believed to happen in this market, things such as magic rituals, murder, prostitution, the sale of illicit drugs, sexual orgies, and various allegedly strange 'Sufi practices'. What these rumours have in common is that they all exemplify racist stereotypes about black people. Here too, therefore, the black person is made to embody and reflect the deep fears and unconscious desires of many non-black peoples. But despite all that, the Africans of Mecca still love their city.

Within these black African communities, some personalities become well known for their various contributions in Mecca and beyond. In the twentieth century, Muḥammad Amān al-Jāmī and Muḥammad Surūr al-Ṣabbān are particularly well known. The first came as a pilgrim, intending to remain in Mecca to study after the pilgrimage, where he spent time in the traditional study circles of the *al-Ḥaram* Mosque and in the *Madrasa Dār al-ḥadīth* of Mecca. After a while, he left to continue his studies in Riyadh before settling permanently in Medina. He is one of a group of persons whom the Saudis condescendingly refer to as *baqāya al-Ḥajj* (lit. the remains of the *Ḥajj*). This category forms the majority of black Africans in Mecca and the Hijaz. As for Muḥammad Surūr al-Ṣabbān, he represents the second category of black Africans in Mecca (and Hijaz), namely the descendants of slaves called *muwalladūn* (lit. native of the country).

MeccAfrica from Above

Muḥammad Amān al-Jāmī

The following information on al-Jāmī was collected from various sources. Notable among them are biographical notes incorporated in his own and other scholars' writings, including some of his students, particularly a'Abd al-Qādir al-Fullānī (originating from West Africa) who wrote four articles in the Kuwaiti newspaper *al-Ṣafā* (2013) on the life of his Shaykh al-Jāmī.

After completing the study of the Qur'ān, al-Jāmī started to learn the Shāfi'ī fiqh, the *madhhab* of the majority of Muslims in Ethiopia and East Africa more broadly. In particular he learned the elementary books of *fiqh* called *mukhtaṣarāt*. First, he began to learn Arabic with Shaykh Muḥammad Amīn al-Harārī in his own village. Subsequently, he travelled to another village in search of knowledge, as was the custom in Islamic tradition. There he met a man who would become his closest friend and travelling companion, Shaykh 'Abdu al-Karīm, with whom he migrated later to Saudi Arabia.

Indeed, a few years later, the two men decided to go to Mecca to perform the pilgrimage and continue their Islamic studies. They left Ethiopia for Aseb, and from there took a boat to Mocca (Yemen). They subsequently travelled on foot first to Hudayda and then to Mecca. While in Ethiopia, the two students did not know much about the Salafī-Wahhābī doctrine. It was only at Hudayda that people had warned them of the 'danger' of this doctrine which they believed to be extremist and intolerant.

The Training of al-Jāmī in Saudi Arabia

After completing the *Ḥajj* in 1369/1949, al-Jāmī began to study in the various *ḥalaqāt* (study circles) of the al-Ḥaram Mosque in Mecca. It seems that al-Jāmī understood how to promote his career and to network with influential people, just as junior scholars do in the Western academy. Thus, he grew close to Shaykh 'Abd al-'Azīz Ibn Bāz, who at the time was a rising religious authority of Saudi Arabia. The latter, having noticed al-Jāmī's potential as a talented and promising Salafī and an important *'alim* in the making, later brought him to Riyadh where Al-Jāmī attended and became a teacher at the *Ma'had al-riyāḍ al-'ilmī.*[13] In Riyadh, he grew close to the Grand Mufti of that time, Shaykh Muḥammad b. Ibrāhīm, whose mosque was the meeting point for junior as well as well-established *'ulamā'* from Najd and elsewhere. In this Ma'had, al-Jāmī met students who later became well-known *'ulamā'* of the country, especially in the 1970s. These included Shaykh 'Abd al-Muḥsin al-'Abbādī who served as Vice President of the Islamic University of Medina in the 1970s. He also met and was taught by the following *'Ulamā'*, who later became his mentors: Mufti Shaykh Muḥammad b. Ibrāhīm, the deputy and future successor to Shaykh Ibn Bāz, Shaykh Muḥammad al-Amīn al-Shinqīṭī (from Mauritania), Shaykh 'Abd al-Raḥmān al-ifrīqī and Shaykh Ḥammād al-Anṣārī (both from Mali), and Shaykh 'Abd al-Rāziq 'Afīfī (from Egypt). The latter greatly influenced al-Jāmī's teaching and preaching methods.[14] After completing his 'secondary' education in Ma'had al-riyāḍ al-'ilmī, al-Jāmī continued his graduate studies at the Faculty of Islamic Law (Kuliyyat al-Sharī'a) and graduated in 1380/1960. He then studied in the Dār al-'ulūm in Cairo and joined the University of Punjab in Pakistan in 1974 where he got a master's degree and, later, a doctorate.

Al-Jāmī became an official teacher in the state system when he was appointed at the *Ma'had al-'ilmī* of Ṣāmit in the Jāzān region in the south. He was then appointed professor in the Islamic University of Medina, where he rose through the ranks until he became the first director of the Faculty of the Sciences of Ḥadīth

[13] The *Ma'had al-riyāḍ al-'ilmī* was the first state institution of Islamic education to train teachers and *Quḍḍāt* (sing. *Qāḍḍī*/Islamic judge). On this institution, see Chanfi, *West African 'ulamā' and Salafism in Mecca and Medina*, 9–10, 43–4, 52–3, 112–14, and 182–3.

[14] Shaykh 'Abd al-Rāziq 'Afīfī was of Egyptian origin. He was once chairman of the Anṣār al-*Sunna* al-Muḥammadiya movement before immigrating to Saudi Arabia in about 1950 after being invited by the then king of Saudi Arabia, 'Abd al-'Azīz Ibn Sa'ūd. He was a teacher at *Ma'had al-riyāḍ al-'ilmī* before passing through all the ranks and becoming a member of the Council of higher *'ulamā'* of the country (*Hay'a Kibār al-'ulamā'*) and secretary general of this Council, a position he held until his death in 1993.

and director of the *ʿAqīda* doctoral studies programme. It was his main mentor, Shaykh Ibn Bāz, who recommended him for all these appointments. Al-Jāmī taught various disciplines in addition to the *ʿaqīda* or *tawḥīd* (the Salafī-Wahhābī doctrine of the oneness of God). He and Shaykh Ḥammād al-Anṣārī were the only non-Najdī *ʻulamāʼ* who taught the *ʿaqīda* or *tawḥīd*. As the heart of Wahhabism, the teaching of the *ʿaqīda* has been the monopoly of teachers and professors from the Najd (a region in central Arabia), the birthplace of Wahhabism. This shows the symbiosis that had long existed between al-Jāmī and the Salafī-Wahhābī milieu of Saudi Arabia.

Al-Jāmī left behind him disciples who continued his *daʿwa*. Among them were Shaykh Rabīʾ b. Hādī al-Madkhalī, Shaykh Zayd b. Hādī Madkhalī, Shaykh Nāṣir Faqīhī, a teacher at the Prophet Mosque, Shaykh Muḥammad b. Ḥammūd al-Wālī, teacher at the Prophet Mosque and once Deputy Rector of the Islamic University of Medina, and Shaykh Bakr b. ʿAbdallah Abū Zayd, who was once a member of the Saudi Council of Higher *ʻulamāʼ* (*Hayʾa Kibār al-ʻulamāʼ*).

Al-Jāmī wrote mostly 'pamphlets' of *daʿwa*, the majority of which have been collected in a book entitled *Aḍwāʾ ʿalā ṭarīq ad-daʿwa ilā al-islām* ('Lighting the Road of the Islamic daʿwa')[15]. Four chapters of this book give us a clear idea of his Salafiyya-Wahhābiyya doctrine: the first is *Manzilat al-Sunna fī al-tashrīʿ al-islāmī* ('The Place of the *Sunna* in Islamic *Sharīʿa*'); the second 'Defending the Sunna' (*al-muḥaẓara al-difāʿiyya ʿan al-Sunna al-Muḥammadiyya*); the third 'Reason and Scriptural Evidence by Ibn Rushd' (*al-ʿAql wa al-Naql ʿinda Ibn Rush*), and the fourth 'The History of Islam in Africa' (*Al-Islām fī Ifrīqyā ʿabra al-tārīkh*).These four chapters will be the focus of our discussion in the following section).

1) *Manzilat al-Sunna fī al-tashrīʿ al-islāmī* ('The Place of the *Sunna* in Islamic *Sharīʿa*', published in 1988)

This is a booklet of sixty-four pages. In the introduction, al-Jāmī writes: 'The messages revealed by God and entrusted to the prophets that He has chosen from all other humans, are the link between heaven and earth. All these revealed messages were all identical (*muttaḥida uṣūluhā*) since their first appeal was 'Serve God: you have no god other than Him.'[16] These messages, however, were different from each other regarding their law and method. This is because every prophet was sent to his community with a message in the language of his community. This situation remained so for a long time until God decided to send Muḥammad as

[15] Muḥammad Amān al-Jāmī, *Aḍwāʾ ʿalā ṭarīq ad-daʿwa ilā al-islām* Riyadh, *al-Riʾāsa al-ʿāmma li idārāt al-buḥūth al-ʿilmiyya wa al-iftāʾ wa ad-daʿwa wa al-irshād* (1404/1984), 304.

[16] The Qur'ān, 7:59.

the last Prophet.[17] He also gave him his last book, the Qur'ān, which He described as follows: 'A book which falsehood cannot touch from any angle.'[18] A Book that God has entrusted Himself to defend and protect, as He rightly says in the Qur'ān: 'We have sent down the Qur'ān Ourselves and We Ourselves will guard it.'[19] Then al-Jāmī continues by saying that if believing in the prophecy of Muḥammad is a fundamental basis of the Islamic faith, believing in his *Sunna* is an inseparable part of the Islamic faith because Muḥammad authored the *Sunna*. It is in this sense, according to al-Jāmī, that Ibn al-Qayyim (*al-Imām* Ibn al-Qayyim, as al-Jāmī called him) has defined what the faith is. According to Ibn al-Qayyim, this faith is a reality based on knowledge of the Prophet's message that the Muslim must believe in his heart, confirm by his words, apply the lessons of the message, and call others to do the same as much as possible (*al-da'wa 'ilayhi bi ḥasb al-imkān*). Thus, according to Ibn al-Qayyim, to follow the teachings of the Prophet's message in a total way is the meaning of the true faith.

Therefore, after the introduction, al-Jāmī begins to treat the subject of his book by the classical Islamic method. He defines the *Sunna* semantically (*al-Sunna lughatan*) and afterwards according to *sharī'a* (*al-Sunna shar'an*). First, he explains the meaning of *manzila*. He writes that *manzila* is the status, the rank occupied by something or someone in any hierarchy. Here it means the status and rank occupied by the *Sunna* in Islamic law. Indeed, in this area, the *Sunna* alone is enough to make a law or to explain a law established by a Qur'ānic text.

Thus, according to al-Jāmī, semantically *Sunna* means the way, regardless of whether the way is good or bad. Al-Jāmī remains a *muḥaddith* in all his manner of argument. Thus, to explain better the semantic meaning of *Sunna*, whether defined as good or bad, he uses the following *ḥadīth*: 'Whoever builds a track will have the reward of his work and the reward of the one who follows this way; and that until Doomsday. Whoever built a wrong path, will bear the fault and the fault of the one who follows this way, and that until the Last Judgment.'[20]

Now, concerning the meaning of the *Sunna* in Islamic law (*ma'nā al-sunna shar'an*), al-Jāmī ensures that *'ulamā'* specialists of the *sharī'a* (*'ulamā' al sharī'a*) do not differ on this point but if they do, it would be only on the appearance of the word and not on the content (*ikhtilāfan lafẓiyyan lā jawhāriyyan*).

[17] Al-Jāmī; *Aḍwā' 'alā ṭarīq ad-da'wa ilā al-islām*, 6.

[18] The Qur'ān, 41, 42.

[19] The Qur'ān, 15:9.

[20] '*Man sanna sunnatan ḥasanatan falahu ajruhā wa ajru man 'amila bihā ilā yawmi al-qiyāma, wa man sanna sunnatan sayyi'atan falahu wizruhā wa wizru man 'amala bihā ilā yawmi al-qiyāma*' in Musnad Aḥmad (4/357, 359, 360, 361); *Ṣaḥīḥ Muslim: al-zakāt, bāb al-ḥathth 'alā al-ṣadaqa (2/705), al-'ilm, bāb man sanna sunnatan ḥasanatan aw sayyi'atan* (4/2059).

Thus, the *'ulamā' of al-uṣūl*, according al-Jāmī, called every word, every action, and every decision of the Prophet *Sunna.* Sometimes they also used the term to describe the actions of companions of the Prophet such as Abū Bakr and 'Uthmān, referring to their action of collecting the different parts of the Qur'ān into one corpus. And this is also the opinion of some members of the *Ahl al-Ḥadīth.*

For *fuqahā* (scholars of classical Islamic law) *Sunna* is when one performs a religious act that is neither obligatory nor essential (*fī ghayr wujūb aw luzūm*). One of the known terms used by *fuqahā* to define the concept of *Sunna* is the following: '*Sunna* is the action whose doer is rewarded by God, and he who did not do it is not punished by God.'[21]

For the *'ulamā'* specialists of *ḥadīth, Sunna* is the opposite of *bid'ah.* In addition, for them the *Sunna* also means the qualities of the Prophet, his character, and his conduct or his biography (*sīrah*). Moreover, according to al-Jāmī, the words of Khadīja comforting Muḥammad, her husband in the following *ḥadīth* illustrate that better: 'No! God will not let you ever fall in misfortune. You are attached to your extended family; you support the weak; you welcome well the stranger; you support the poor; you help others in their times of crisis.'

According to al-Jāmī, the *Sunna* is so important that it is almost equivalent to the Qur'ān. As he wrote, the '*Sunna* is the full brother of the Qur'ān', that is to say, they are both from the same origin. *Sunna* is an inseparable part of the revelation (*al-sunna mina al-waḥy*), as indicated in the following verse: 'Muḥammad was not misguided; what he says does not come by his mere inclination, but rather a revelation from God.'[22] To show that the *Sunna* is also a revelation as he said (*al-sunna ṣinw al-Qur'ān wa huwa waḥyun mithluhu*) and the inseparable companion of the Qur'ān and that many Qur'ānic verses cannot be understood without the *Sunna*, al-Jāmī reminds us of the following *ḥadīth* of the Prophet: 'I was given the Qur'ān with what it is similar to him.'[23]

2) 'Defending the Sunna' (*al-muḥāẓara al-difā'iyya 'an al-Sunna al-Muḥammadiyya*)

This chapter is mainly a response to a lecture delivered by the Sudanese Sūfī intellectual Maḥmūd Ṭāha that al-Jāmī attended by chance in the town of 'Atbara in the Sudan in 1963. After listening to the opinions of Maḥmūd Ṭāha and discussing them with him, al-Jāmī had requested the opportunity to debate publicly with Ṭāha, but the latter flatly refused. Considering his ideas to be atheistic, al-Jāmī then organized a lecture to refute Maḥmūd Ṭāha's ideas.

21 *'Anna al-sunna mā yuthābu fā'iluhu wa lā yu'āqabu tārikuhu'.*

22 The Qur'ān, 53:2, 3, 4.

23 *'Alā wa innī ūtiytu al-Qur'ān wa mithlahu ma'hu'* (Aḥmad 4/131); Abū Dāwūd: al-sunna, bāb luzūm al-sunna (5/11).

He wrote that the most dangerous idea he had heard from Maḥmūd Ṭāha was that a human being can by his own moral strength and goodness elevate himself to a divine status in which he could say: *Ana huwa* (I am Him i.e., God). Al-Jāmī argued that this idea is the cornerstone of Maḥmūd Ṭāha's propaganda. Maḥmūd Ṭāha, he claims, 'exempts' everyone from the divine obligations, obligations such as following the commands and avoiding prohibitions. The second most dangerous idea of Maḥmūd Ṭāha, according to al-Jāmī, is that the learned elites chosen by God (*al-khawāṣ al-ʿārifīn*) are exempt from prayer (*ṣalāt*). However, according to al-Jāmī, these so-called learned elites are, in reality, ignorant people. The third of Maḥmūd Ṭāha's positions that al-Jāmī considered to be dangerous concerns *zakāt* (obligatory charity). According to Maḥmūd Ṭāha, the *zakāt* no longer conforms to the needs of our modern era. It was certainly a smart institution in early Islam, but is now completely outdated. Instead, he said, in our modern era the *zakāt* should correspond to the level of the true meaning of Islam, that is of social justice (*al-ʿadāla al-ishtirākiyya*). By this he meant private property should be abolished and that the earth and all its products must belong to everybody. Al-Jāmī insists that what is problematic about Maḥmūd Ṭāha is that he does not distinguish between what belongs to the realm of the human order (*al-awḍāʾ al-bashariyya*) and what belongs to the realm of the divine order (*al-manhaj al-samāwī*). This latter is established by God in this world for humans to live their lives in accordance with the injunctions of the divine order during the whole life. This divine order, according to al-Jāmī, remains unchanged throughout life, regardless of time and space. Al-Jāmī then further severely criticizes Maḥmūd Ṭāha's other ideas, speaking about the irrelevance of the *zakāt* in our modern world in the following terms: Maḥmūd Ṭāha argued that supporting the obligation of *zakāt* in our modern world amounts to legitimizing private property. However, the central objective of Maḥmūd Ṭāha is to abolish the latter. He identifies this objective with socialist justice (*al-ʿadāla al-ishtirākiyya*), which, according to him, is the meaning of Islam. Al-Jāmī objected that private property is natural and a necessary fact that cannot be escaped.

Regarding Maḥmūd Ṭāha's claim that the Prophet never gave *zakāt*, and that therefore *zakāt* is not a requirement, al-Jāmī conceded that this was true, but the reason was that the Prophet was poor. What he earned annually never reached the *nisāb* or minimum amount that a Muslim must have before being obliged to give *zakāt*. Because the Prophet was no longer working as a merchant, he lived from his share of the booty given to him after each battle. Moreover, God forbade the Prophet and his family (Āl baytīhi) to take *zakāt*. Maybe, al-Jāmī said, the reason is that if the Prophet and his family were allowed to take *zakāt*, *zakāt* would seem to be established for his personal economic gain. Another reason could be that the Prophet and his family took one-fifth of the booty after every battle, as prescribed.

What scriptural evidence (*al-nuṣūṣ*) did Maḥmūd Ṭāha use to make his case? And how did al-Jāmī reply to the charges? Maḥmūd Ṭāha relies first on the following verse: 'They ask you again what they should give as alms, say: give what you can spare.'[24] Maḥmūd Ṭāha argues that the content of this verse was never implemented but it does not matter because the meaning of the verse is just a call to socialist justice (*al-ʿadāla al-ishtirākiyya*). However, the true meaning of the verse, al-Jāmī argues, is that if you want to give alms, you must give the superfluity of what you need, you and those in your care.

'We shall be sure to guide to Our ways those who strive hard for Our cause.'[25] According to Maḥmūd Ṭāha, this verse means that the human being, by his spiritual effort and obedience to the injunctions of God, can communicate with God without intermediaries. Al-Jāmī considers this explanation to be one of the aberrations of the Sufis (*shaṭaḥāt al-Sufiyya*) and the heretics (*zanādiqa*). Maḥmūd Ṭāha's ideas, al-Jāmī argues, are not as new and original as Ṭāha presents them to his disciples. He actually borrowed them from the known classical works of the *mutakallimūn* and *zanādiqa*. For al-Jāmī, the meaning of the verse is that God will guide on the right path those who fear God and strive to understand and follow his commands. Al-Jāmī also mentions two other Qur'ānic verses which he alleges Maḥmūd Ṭāha had explained inadequately because his explanation rests on the Sufi contrast distinguishing *ẓāhir* (literal and apparent) and *bātin* (deep and hidden) explanations. Al-Jāmī refutes also the comments by Ṭāha on some *ḥadīths*. Most of these *ḥadīths*, according al-Jāmī, are weak (*ḍaʿīf*). In addition, they are interpreted by Maḥmūd Ṭāha in a partisan manner and often under the Sufi binomial *ẓāhir*/*bātin*.

3) 'Reason and Scriptural Evidence' by Ibn Rushd (*al-ʿAql wa al-Naql ʿinda Ibn Rushd*):

This lecture could also be called 'Ibn Rushd through the Eyes of Twentieth-Century Salafism'. At first glance, it seems surprising that an uncompromising Salafī like al-Jāmī could lecture on the philosopher Ibn Rushd. However, he did not willingly deliver the lecture, but felt obliged to do so. As he states in the introduction, the Saudi government asked the Islamic University of Medina to send a representative to a festival in Morocco on Ibn Rushd, probably in 1976. The university authorities designated al-Jāmī to represent them.

In the introduction to his lecture, al-Jāmī prefaces the biography of Ibn Rushd by saying:

> Before addressing the position of Ibn Rushd on the relationship between reason and scriptural proof, we should first say something about the person of Ibn Rushd,

[24] The Qur'ān 2:219: '*Yasʾalūnaka mādhā yunfiqūn, qul al-ʿafw*'.

[25] The Qur'ān 29:69: '*Wa al-ladhīna jāhadū fīnā lanahdiyannahum subulanā*'.

> his life, and his philosophy. All this in order to know the circumstances in which he grew up to become one of the Great teachers of philosophy. This will also allow us to understand why he had been the subject of so much repression, violence, wandering and sometimes accusation of atheism and heresy 'zandaqa.'

He writes that Ibn Rushd first learned the Islamic sciences in his hometown Qurṭuba (Andalusia) with his father, who then was among the *'ulamā'* and judges (*quḍāt*) of the city. Ibn Rushd was very young when he began to study the law (*sharīʿa*), medicine, and metaphysical sciences (*al-ʿulūm al-māwarāʾiyya*). What surprised many of his contemporaries was that they did not know exactly how Ibn Rushd had learned philosophy and other metaphysical sciences. Who was his teacher in this discipline? Some argued that the famous philosopher Ibn Bāja (Avempace) was his teacher. However, historical facts do not support this narrative because Ibn Bāja died in 1138 when Ibn Rushd was only twelve years old – too young to learn philosophy. Others think that the great philosopher Ibn Tufail was his teacher. However, history teaches us that Ibn Tufail knew Ibn Rushd only by name and after the latter had become famous. He met him only once and only for a very short time. In fact, al-Jāmī continues, it would be fair to say that Ibn Rushd had no philosophy teachers, and that he was self-taught by reading the books of Aristotle. Indeed, one can easily see the influence of Aristotle in his books. In any case, al-Jāmī said, Ibn Rushd was a great philosopher. But was he an inconsistent philosopher, as some believe? Was he a philosopher whose thought embraces philosophy and religion together, as is evident in some of his writings? Was he *ashʿarī*? Or was he not affiliated with any theological school? Such questions arise because of his ambiguous positions, al-Jāmī writes, because Ibn Rushd showed that ostensibly he followed the views of the majority, but that in reality he was in another world, that of the elites (*ʿālam al-khawāṣ*). These elites claimed to understand the texts of the *sharīʿa* in an elitist manner (*fahman khāṣ*), different from that of the majority of Muslims (*jumhūr*). This position implies that the elite (*al-khawāṣ*) have to tolerate the views of the majority of Muslims (*jumhūr*) but must not share them. They should have their own opinions. If in such discussions, the *'ulamā'* are often seen as the elites (*al-khawāṣ*) versus *jumhūr* (the majority of Muslims, that is to say the rest of the Muslims who are not *'Ulamā'*), Ibn Rushd pushes the distinction of *khawāṣ* (elites) further. The *khawāṣ*, he said, are a superior group of *'ulamā'* who are to be found first above the *jumhūr* and then above the majority of *'ulamā'*. These *khawāṣ* are the *'ulamā'* specialists of Kalām (speculative theology of Islam) whom he calls *jadaliyyūn* (sing. Jadali), which means disputants. The latter, according to al-Jāmī, like to discuss and interpret the scriptural texts of plural meaning (*mā tashābaha mina al-nuṣūṣ*) in order to create conflict (*ibtighāʾal-fitna*).

Ibn Rushd, according to al-Jāmī, is a very elusive personality. Sometimes we see him as a specialist in Islamic law (*fiqh*) who even, in some places, praises the Salafī school of law (*madhhab al-Salaf*) because it does not interpret scriptural texts but follows the apparent meaning (*ẓāhir*) in accordance with what God wanted. But sometimes we see the same Ibn Rushd slide down the slope (*inzalaqa*) of philosophers, as is the case in his book *Manāhij al-adilla*, in which he writes: *'Al-'aql al-ṣarīḥ lā yukhālif al-naql al-ṣaḥīḥ*/ 'A clear reason never contradicts an authentic scriptural text.' Then al-Jāmī begins to explain and define the meaning of '*'aql*' and that of '*naql*'. He first cites the text, '*al-'aql al-ṣarīḥ lā yukhālif al-naql al-ṣaḥīḥ* / A clear reason never contradicts an authentic scriptural text.' This text is almost identical to the following well-known one of Ibn Taymiyya: '*al-ma'qūl al-ṣarīḥ lā yukhālif al-manqūl al-ṣaḥīḥ*.' Ibn Taymiyya, in addition, wrote a book on this subject entitled '*Muwāfaqat ṣarīḥ al-ma'qūl li ṣaḥīḥ al-manqūl*' or Correspondence between what is in the realm of the reason with what is in the realm of the scriptural text.

Al-Jāmī continues:

> This quote must be central to our discussions. It should also be the rule from which we start our discussions ... If the reason is the one that has brought us to know God and his Prophet, so any rejection by the reason of what is prescribed by the Qur'ān of God and the *Sunna* of the Prophet on the pretext that this prescribed thing in question would be contrary to the reason, such a rejection would be contrary to the reason.

Al-Jāmī then begins the definition of *'aql* (reason) in the conventional manner. He writes: '*al-'aql nūrun rūḥānī tudriku bihi al-nafsu al-umūr al-ḍarūriyya wa al-fiṭriyya* / The reason is a divine light by which the soul perceives the essential and natural things'.

Ibn Rushd, according to al-Jāmī, gives the impression of following the Salafī position on the issue of the relationship between *'aql* and *naql*, but in reality his position is different. In fact, he shares the position of *'ulamā'* experts of *kalām*. He disagrees with them only in the way in which they teach and practise their doctrine. Thus, he sometimes criticizes their way of interpreting scriptural texts (*nuṣūṣ al-kitāb wa al-Sunna*) and he said that their interpretation of these texts has negatively affected the *sharī'a*. However, Ibn Rushd, according to al-Jāmī, is not, in fact, against the interpretation (*ta'wīl*) as such, but only against the fact that the *'ulamā' al-kalām* taught the interpretation (*ta'wīl*) to the majority of Muslims (*al-jumhūr* or *al-'āmma*/*al-'awām*). Therefore, Ibn Rushd is for the interpretation (*ta'wīl*), provided that it remains only within the circle of the *'ulamā'* and is not taught to the majority of Muslims (*jumhūr al-muslimīn*), because these latter are *ḥarfiyyūn*, i.e. they are accustomed to following the scriptures literally. Al-Jāmī writes that this ambiguous position (*ghayr wāḍiḥ*) of Ibn Rushd in his philosophy and religious doctrine is called *al-tawfīq* (conciliation) between philosophy and *sharīʿa* (*bayn al-falsafa wa al-sharīʿa*) and between wisdom and religion (*bayna al-ḥikma wa al-sharīʿa*). Thus, al-Jāmī said, Ibn Rushd criticized *Imām* al-Ghazālī for exposing doctrinal positions to the majority of Muslims (*al-ʿawām/ al-jumhūr*) when they would normally be reserved only for the elite (*al-khawāṣ*).

Falsafat Ibn Rushd (The Philosophy of Ibn Rushd)

Al-Jāmī reaffirms that Ibn Rushd was certainly a great philosopher, but also someone who had hidden his true doctrine and in doing so had confused many people (*bāṭiniyyi ghāmiḍ*). Al-Jāmī suggests that perhaps Ibn Rushd was perceived as holding an ambiguous stance toward religious doctrine because of the repression to which the sultan of the Almohad Dynasty (*al-muwaḥḥidūn*), al-Manṣūr b. Abū Yaʿqūb, had subjected him. The sultan burned Ibn Rushd's philosophy books and accused him of being atheist (*mulḥid*). Among the oft-cited reasons for these repressions were that one day before the governor of *Qurtuba* (Cordoba) he had denied the historical existence of *Qawm ʿĀd* (people of ʿĀd) mentioned in the Qurʾān. But despite all this, al-Jāmī stresses that anyone who had read Ibn Rushd remarked on the depth of his philosophical thought and especially his effort to 'link philosophy to *sharīʿa*' (*rabṭ al-falsafa bi al-sharīʿa*). According to al-Jāmī, Ibn Rushd had criticized the Ashāʿira, the Muʿtazila and the Māturīdiyya quite heavily. He felt that each of these groups had tried to ensure that the scriptural texts were in conformity with its views. This is why Ibn Rushd chose a philosophical and doctrinal viewpoint of his own. Yet according to al-Jāmī, this perspective was false. His subsequent ideas, said al-Jāmī, show that he was in error. For example, he said that if someone found verses in the Qurʾān that seem to contradict the philosophical theses, he should explain them in a 'popular way' (*yajib tafsīruhā tafsīran shaʿbiyyan*) because each verse has two meanings, the literal and popular one (*ḥarfiyyun shaʿbī*), and the spiritual and elitist one (*rūḥiyyun khāṣṣ*). The first is for the people; the second for the philosophers. Just as the prophets of God receive their message to convey it to the people, so too philosophers, who are the prophets of the class of the scholars, receive their message to transmit it to the scholars. Thus, religion and science must go hand in hand, and *'ulamā'* should unite Philosophy and *sharīʿa* together. He said, 'The truth can not be contrary to another truth but is in conformity with other truth and strengthens this latter as evidence.'[26] According to Ibn Rushd, the *'ulamā'* of *sharīʿa* are part of the people (*al-ʿawām, al-jumhūr*) and those who deserve to be called *'ulamā'* are only the philosophers whom he sometimes calls *ḥukamā* (sages). Of course, al-Jāmī condemns these philosophical positions of Ibn Rushd.

26 '*al-ḥaqq lā yuḍād al-ḥaqq bal yuwāfiqhu wa yashhad lahu*', al-Jāmī; *Aḍwāʾ ʿalā ṭarīq ad-daʿwa ilā al-islām*, 143.

4) 'The History of Islam in Africa' (*Al-Islām fī Ifrīqyā ʿabra al-tārīkh*)

In this text, al-Jāmī explains that the spread of Islam in Africa happened as follows: First, there was the time of the first *Hijra* in Ethiopia by the group of Muslims from Mecca led by Jaʿfar b. Abū Ṭālib and welcomed by Najjāshī (Negus Ashama ibn Abjar), the king of Ethiopia at the time. The Prophet Muḥammad, of course, ordered the *Hijra*. However, after the group of Jaʿfar b. Abū Ṭālib had left Ethiopia to return to the Hijaz, a long absence of Islam on the continent ensued, until ʿUthmān became *Khalīfa*. From that point, the very beginning of the expansion phase of Islam began in North Africa through military expeditions. The most famous of these expeditions was the conquest of Tunisia known as the *ghazwat al-ʿabādala* in reference to the seven leaders of the expedition, all named ʿAbdallah. This is what al-Jāmī called the first phase of the expansion of Islam in Africa. Islam then spread throughout Africa. This is what al-Jāmī called the second phase of the expansion of Islam in Africa. According to al-Jāmi, the second phase of the expansion of Islam in Africa was that the *daʿwa* during this time was not at all organized and carried out by well-trained missionaries of Islam (*duʿāt*) and *'ulamā'* who were able to distinguish the original (*al-aṣīl*) from the intruder (*al-dakhīl*) in Islam. The missionaries of Islam (*duʿāt*) of this period consisted of the Arab traders and Sufi guides.

In East Africa, Arab traders travelled to Ethiopia, Sudan, Somalia, Kenya, Tanzania, for the purpose of trade, but they simultaneously brought with them their religion. As they were either totally untrained or not well trained in the Islamic sciences, even if their *da'wa* was sincere, it was nevertheless mixed with some Arabian Peninsula non-Islamic traditions which they viewed as Islamic. In this regard al-Jāmī wrote, Africans generally considered everything the Arab taught them about Islam to be true by the mere fact that it came from the community of the Prophet. Thus, Africans trusted everything that these Arab traders told them. They did not take into account the amateur nature of their *daʿwa*. However, al-Jāmī added, we should remember that these traders were sincere and wanted good for Africans.

The second category of the first missionaries of Islam (*duʿāt*) in Africa are the so-called Sufi guides (*al-mashāʾikh al-mutaṣawwifa*) who spread their doctrines in East and West Africa. These people, according to al-Jāmī, brought everything to Africa except the true Islam of Muḥammad, despite the widely held view that they were the real disseminators of Islam in Africa.

Al-Jāmī said he wanted to establish the truth on this point by writing, 'It is true that the Sufi guides (*al-mashāʾikh al-ṣūfiyya*) deployed much effort to spread their message in Africa but what they called the people to was not the real Islam. Many of them knew that, even if some of them did not know it and thought they were working for the true Islam.'

The third and final phase of the spread of Islam in Africa is that of correcting the way in which Africans understood Islam. According to al-Jāmī, the creation of the Islamic University of Medina was a significant step in that direction. It trained missionaries in a communal programme and sent them back to their home countries to spread Salafī Islam. Al-Jāmī therefore praised the cooperation established for this purpose between the Islamic University of Medina and *Idārat al-buḥūth al-ʿilmiyya wa al-iftā wa al-daʿwa wa al-irshād* (known simply by *Dār al-iftā*/Office of fatwās). The Saudi religious authorities decided that at the end of each academic year the Islamic University of Medina would submit to the Dār al-iftā in Riyadh, under the leadership of the Mufti of Saudi Arabia, the list of graduates deemed qualified to be appointed as missionaries (*dāʿīn mabʿūth*).

The World Islamic League (*Rābiṭa al-ʿālam al-islāmī*) had established the same kind of cooperative arrangement with the Islamic University of Medina, though the missionaries supported by the *Dār al-iftā* were better funded than those supported by the *Rābiṭa*. This division of labour between the three institutions to support the *daʿwa* in Africa continues to this day.

Al-Jāmī noted that the history of Africa has already experienced reformist missionaries (*duʿāt muṣliḥūn*). Among them, he mentions ʿUthmān Dan Fodio, whom he calls '*al-mujāhid al-ʿālim al-salafī*'. He also recommended that anyone who wanted to know about Dan Fodio and his method of *daʿwa* should read Dan Fodio's writings. The most important of them, he said, is *Sirāj al-ikhwān fī ahamm mā yuḥtāj ilayhi fī hādhā al-zamān* (Shedding Light to the brothers on what is needed for our time).

The second of these former local missionaries is Shaykh Muḥammad ʿAbdallah al-Mālī al-Madanī (Ag Maḥmūd).[27] Al-Jāmī recalls that this Shaykh lived in Medina for a long time and was *Imām* of the Prophet Mosque at the beginning of the rule of King ʿAbd al-ʿAzīz. Following his tenure there, he travelled to India, Sanaa (Yemen), and Ethiopia before returning to Mali, and he stayed there till his death. In all the countries he visited, alongside his activities as a trader he led *daʿwa* activities in which he preached and taught the Salafī doctrine in mosques and schools (*madāris*). Those *daʿwa* activities in Mali lasted from 1938 until his death in 1953.

The third local *dāʿī* of the past, according to al-Jāmī, was Shaykh Ṭāhir al-Jazāʾirī who wrote extensively on the *ʿaqīda* salafiyya. Al-Jāmī recalled that this work of Salafī *daʿwa* that these Africans had already carried out in the past in the continent shows a long history of Salafism in Africa.

[27] For more on this Shaykh, see Chanfi Ahmed, *West African 'Ulamā' and Salafism in Mecca and Medina: Jawāb al-Ifrīqī – The Response of the African* (Leiden: Brill, 2015) 8, 94.

Regarding the missionaries of Islam (*du'āt*) in Africa today, al-Jāmī gives them the following four pieces of advice:

1) The missionary of Islam (*dā'īya*) should be someone with a strong and true *'aqīda*.
2) He should have a good knowledge of religion and a clear vision.
3) He should avoid deception.
4) He should be patient and avoid difficulties. For the *da'wa* is a long-term work.

Al-Jāmī then compares the work of Christian missionaries (*al-mubashshirūn*) with that of the missionaries of Islam (*du'āt*). He considers that the first ones, despite the erroneous nature of their mission, are very organized, very resistant to challenges, and sacrificial. Regarding the missionaries of Islam, he says that despite the truth of their mission, they lack seriousness and organization. This he attributes first to the fact that they consider their *da'wa* work (Islamic missions) as a secondary activity alongside their professional activities, which they consider to be their priority. The *da'wa* is conducted as a secondary activity.

By arguing in this way, al-Jāmī positioned himself against the historical tradition of *da'wa* in Islam, because in Islam *da'wa* had been conducted as a secondary activity. The *dā'ī* (missionary of Islam) first led commercial activities or other professional activities and only then preached his religion to others in a variety of ways. Unlike with Christian missionaries, in the history of Sunni Islam there had never really existed full-time professional Muslim missionaries. So the latter tended to have other primary occupations by which they sustained themselves and gained entry into communities.

Al-Jāmī and the al-Jāmiyya Movement in Saudi Arabia

The name of Shaykh Muḥammad 'Alī Amīn al-Jāmī and al-Jāmiyya, the Salafī current of Islam he represented, became more present in the media and discussions in Saudi Arabia after the first Gulf War (2 August 1990 to 28 February 1991). Shaykh al-Jāmī and his followers, such as Rabī' al-Madkhalī and Muqbil b. Hādī al-Wādī'ī (a Yemenite) and others, launched their offensive against the Ṣaḥwa Islamist movement in a public space to defend the Saudi government, the royal family, the Council of Higher *'Ulamā'*, and the decisions they were taking, particularly the presence of US forces on Saudi territory. One argument that followers of al-Jāmī had advanced was the *ḥadīth* of the Prophet, according to which it is prohibited to 'come out against the ruler' (*al-khurūj 'alā al-ḥākim*), i.e. to rise up against the ruler, unless he had professed or practised impiety openly and publicly (*kufrun bawwāḥ*). The Jamistes criticize the followers of the Ṣaḥwa movement on many questions, such as their *'aqīda*, which they considered not to be quite Salafī; their almost exclusive interest in political issues to the detriment of *ʿilm* (knowledge of classical Islamic religious texts); their partisan or factionalist character (*ḥizbiyya*); their *bidʿa* methods of *daʿwa*, such as summer camps (*mukhayyamāt al- ṣayfiyya*), Islamic songs, etc. Similarly, in order to avoid *fitna* (chaos) among Muslims, they categorically reject any jihād, except when decreed by the legitimate ruler. This kind of loyalty to the political power and attachment to the status quo was advocated before al-Jāmī by Saudi Salafī *'ulamā'* of West African origin, such as ʿAbd al-Raḥmān al-Ifrīqī and Muḥammad al-Amīn al-Shinqīṭī, who both taught al-Jāmī. All were followers of the *Ahl al-Ḥadīth* Salafī movement, and all came to Mecca first to perform the *Ḥajj*.

Al-Ḥarakiyyūn al-islāmiyyūn against the Jāmiyya

Al-Jāmī and his followers understood Salafism as the practice and way that the first three generations of Muslims understood Islam. They therefore did not compromise on this principle, especially regarding the obedience due to the political authorities (*ulī al- ʾamr*). On this point, al-Jāmī constantly reminded others of what he thought was a cornerstone of the Salafī tradition: one owes obedience to the Muslim holder of political authority (*ulī al- ʾamr*) as long as that person does not openly and knowingly commit impiety in full sight of everyone (*kufrun bawwāḥ*). The *'ulamā'* must provide advice to the holder of political authority, but must do so discreetly. For this reason, al-Jāmī had supported fully and unrestrictedly the regime of the Saudi kingdom and stood against any opinion or political activity that could be interpreted as opposition to the regime. He labelled that *ḥizbiyya* (relative to political party/*ḥizb*) which, according to him, was contrary to Salafī Islam. Thus, the targets of al-Jāmī's attack were the Egyptian Muslim Brotherhood and its affiliates, especially those residing in Saudi Arabia. Al-Jāmī heavily criticized the doctrine of the writings of the two main leaders of the Muslim Brothers, Ḥasan al-Bannā and Sayyid Quṭb. Thus, the Muslim Brothers and other Islamists, including politicized Salafī (*salafiyyūn ḥarakiyyūn*) such as Surūrī and other Saḥwā, Salafī takfirist, violent Salafī, etc., all made al-Jāmī their principal enemy. All those who identified with traditional Salafism – that is to say, those who were pietistic, apolitical, and quietist – were called partisans of al-Jāmī (or *jāmiyyūn*).

In addition to al-Jāmī, other famous people from the black community had lived in Mecca and the Hijaz in the twentieth century. One of them was Muḥammad Surūr al-Ṣabbān.

Muḥammad Surūr al-Ṣabbān (1898–1971)

Muḥammad Surūr al-Ṣabbān was the most prominent among the Hijaz elites of his time. His contribution was outstanding in civil society activities as well as in those of the nascent Saudi state. He was, in some way, the founding father of the intellectual and cultural renaissance of Hijaz, and of Saudi Arabia as a whole. He had stimulated literary production by encouraging writers and by creating the first publishing house in the country. He was a man of letters and a philanthropist who supported literary production, a rich businessperson and a politician. He was the first Minister of Economy and Finance of Saudi Arabia and the first secretary general of the World Islamic League (*Rābiṭa al ʿĀlam al-Islāmī*), of which he was a founding member.

Muḥammad Surūr al-Ṣabbān was born in 1316/1898 in the town of al-Qunfudha in the Hijaz, a town where his father worked as a merchant before going to settle with his family first in Jeddah and then in Mecca. The young Muḥammad got only a basic education in the schools of Jeddah and Mecca. There, as he himself wrote, he learned 'to read, write, count and read the Qurʾān according to its specific rules (*tajwīd*)'.[28] From al-Qunfudha (Qunfodah), his family arrived in Jedda in 1902. Then between 1911 and 1912, the family left Jeddah to settle in Mecca. Muḥammad entered the Madrasa of Shaykh Khayyāṭ and also daily helped his father in his workshop. His father bought and sold goods wholesale. However, the aspect of business in which the father earned the most money was trade in animal skins (cows, sheeps, goats, etc.).

He bought animal skins from all over the Hijaz, treated them, then sold them on the spot or exported them for sale abroad (to Yemen, Egypt, etc.). Although he had received only an elementary education, Muḥammad Surūr al-Ṣabbān was an autodidact. He read the classics of the Islamic religion and of Arabic literature as well as the classics in the history of Islam and the Muslim world. He also read a great deal of the foreign literature that had been translated into Arabic at that time. From his youth, his experience trading with his father fostered his interest in economics and finance, and he had therefore also read the literature on economics and finance available in Arabic. Though he was well equipped to build a personal fortune, Muḥammad Surūr al-Ṣabbān chose instead to put his wealth and skills to the service of Hijaz and of his country, Saudi Arabia. In the cultural and social domains, he began by editing and publishing classic books in Islam at his own expense. In 1935, he founded the Sharikat al-ʿarabiyya li al-ṭabʿ wa al-nashr (Arabic House for Editing and Publishing). He also authored three books himself. The first was titled *Adab al-ḥijāz aw ṣafḥatun fikriyya min adab al-nāshi ʾa al-ḥijāziyya shiʿran wa nathran* (1925). In the second, *Al-Maʿraḍ* (1926), he summarized the ideas and literary trends of a new generation of writers in the Hijaz. In the third, *Khawāṭir muṣarraḥa* (1926), he gathered together ideas on language and literature of the Hijaz in prose and poetry.

[28] Muḥammad Surūr al-Ṣabbān, *Adab al-ḥijāz: ṣafḥatun fikriyya min adab al-nāshiʾa al-ḥijāziyya shiʿran wa nathran* (Jeddah: *Dār al-Iṣfahānī*, 3rd edition, 1383/1963) 144.

He opened two public libraries, one in Jeddah and one in Mecca, and in so doing laid the foundation of modern cultural activity of the Hijaz or Saudi Arabia more broadly. What is true about his pioneering work in the cultural realm is equally true of his contributions in the social, political, and economic realms. In 1934, he established the Foundation of Relief and Charity (*Jamʿiyya al-isʿāf al-khayrī*), a charitable social organization whose core agenda was to provide medical care to the needy. In 1935, he started a fundraising initiative for Palestinians named *Jamʿiyya Qirsh Falasṭīn*, and in 1937, he founded the Committee for the Defence of Palestine (*Lajnat al-Difāʿ ʿan Falasṭīn*).

Regarding economic development, he was among the earliest founders of modern economic activities in Saudi Arabia. He established several companies, some belonging to him and his family and others to the state. These companies include: *Sharikat al-falāḥ li al-sayyārāt* (a company for the import and sale of cars); *al-Sharika al-ʿarabiyya li al-tawfīr wa al-iqtiṣād* (a savings and loan company); *al-Sharika al-ʿarabiyya li al-ṣādirāt* (an export company); *Sharikat milḥ wa kahrabāʾ jāzān* (a salt and electricity company based in Jazan); *al-Sharika al-ʿarabiyya li al-ṭabʿ wa al-nashr* (the aforementioned editing and publishing company); *Sharika al-zahrāʾ li al-ʿimāra* (the Zahra Construction Company); and *Sharika Muṣḥaf Makka* (the company he founded in Mecca for editing and publishing the Qurʾān).

His commitment to politics and the state is well known. In 1917, at the age of eighteen, during the reign of Sharīf Ḥusayn in the Hijaz he was appointed to the city of Mecca administration. He then became its general secretary (*raʾīs kitāb*). After the fall of Sharīf Ḥusayn, King ʿAbd al-ʿAzīz b. Saʿūd maintained him in the same role after having him detained in prison for a while with some of the elite of the Hijaz. In 1924, he was unanimously elected as secretary general of the General Assembly of Mecca (*al-majlis al-ahlī*). For political reasons, he was arrested on 22 July 1927 and sent to prison in Riyadh, where he remained for almost two years. After his release, he worked in his private businesses until 1931, then returned to the affairs of the state. That year, he was appointed as an official in the finance ministry. There, he rose through the ranks by successfully taking on various functions until he became finance minister when Saʿūd b. ʿAbd Al-ʿAzīz became king. He succeeded Shaykh ʿAbdallah Sulaymān who was in charge of state finances. When Faiṣal succeeded Saʿūd as King of Saudi Arabia, Muḥammad Surūr Ṣabbān was appointed as the first secretary general of the Muslim World League (Rābiṭa al-ʿālam al-islāmī), as one of the founding members.

Relationships between 'Established' and 'Outsider' Members of the African Community of Mecca

In considering the question of the relationship between established and outsider members of the African community in Mecca, I have been inspired by the German Jewish sociologist Norbert Elias' terms. He observed how the mechanics of exclusion operated in the German society of his time, a mechanics of exclusion which the Nazi regime pushed to its most extreme form in the slaughter of innocents in concentration camps and the systematic robbing of their assets. Elias had the experience of being a member of a minority and stigmatized group, but also felt fully integrated into the culture and political destiny of the majority that stigmatized him. Elias defended Germany, his country, as a soldier during the First World War, but was forced to leave the same country to save his life shortly before the Second World War. The origin of Elias' sociological theory of the relationships between 'established' and 'outsiders' lies in a study he conducted in the late 1950s in a suburb of Leicester in England on two groups of the working class, that is people of the same social class.[29] However, the former inhabitants, the 'established', strove to distinguish themselves from the newcomers, the 'outsiders'. The dominant group (the former inhabitants/established) reproduced its domination by excluding the 'outsiders' from the places of decision and power (councils, churches, clubs, etc.). It used a variety of means such as rumour, gossip and other prejudices to reinforce the positive image it had of itself and the negative image that it had of the newcomers. Beyond this specific case, Elias intended to show how his model could help to explain a variety of configurations showing all kinds of social inequalities and discriminations. How can this theory help to clarify the relationship which existed (and still exists to some extent) between the African elites of Mecca (*'ulamā'* and politicians) and the Africans of *Shāri' al-Manṣūr*? Of course, Elias' theory does not fit the Meccan context entirely. That is why I refer to it as a starting point to explain my case and, consequently, to extend the theory to other cases. Apart from the presence of the essential category of 'established' and 'outsiders', my case does not resemble that of Elias. In my case, the 'established' did not live in the same neighbourhood (here *Shāri' al-Manṣūr*) as the 'outsiders'. They were elites who enjoyed the privileges of the Saudi state like all the other elites of the country. In fact, a gap separated the 'established' from the 'outsiders' of *Shāri' al-Manṣūr*. The two groups did not share the same politico-religious ideology. The 'established' supported and propagated Salafism-Wahhabism, while the majority of the Africans of *Shārī' al-Manṣūr* were West Africans who followed the Tijāniyya and Qādiriyya Sufi *ṭarīqas*.

The ties between the 'established' Africans and the other Africans of Mecca were minimal. Indeed, these ties were limited only by the courses that these

[29] Norbert Elias, *The Established and the Outsiders* (London: Sage Publications, 1965).

'established' Africans gave at the *al-Ḥaram* Mosque, courses that the outsider-Africans followed as free listeners and not as regular students. Thus, the physical link of living in the same neighbourhood or of having a teacher/pupil or Shaykh/disciple relationship did not exist. However, the emotional link based on the fact that 'established' and 'outsiders' originated in sub-Saharan Africa did exist.

Conclusion

The black populations of Mecca are composed mainly of descendants of pilgrims (*baqāya al-Ḥajj*), most of whom arrived in Mecca during the period from the beginnings of the colonization of Africa to the post-Second World War era. The second group (smaller than the first) consists of the descendants of former slaves. Each of the two groups can be recognized by their family names. The first group has 'African names', which in reality are often *nisba* (adjective of relationship designating the origins of something or someone) such as al-Hausāwī (of Hausaland), *al-Burnāwī* (of Borno in Nigeria), and *al-Sūmālī* (of Somalia). The second category has Arabic names, often those of their former masters, for example al-Ḥarbī, al-Kalbānī, etc. Sometimes they simply bear the name of al-Muwallad (lit. the native), which means that before the emancipation of the father or the grandfather, their surname was that of the master.

Within all of these black populations, who were predominantly very poor and very marginalized, we find a small elite that miraculously survived and succeeded. The two personalities presented above are part of this elite. Yet they are part of a generation which lived during the first half of the twentieth century. From this period onward, corresponding to the beginnings of the regime of Āl Saʿūd, black people disappeared almost entirely from social, political, economic, and cultural view, except in football (soccer).

Until the early 1970s, the material situation of these populations did not differ much from that of the rest of the population of Mecca. But from this period, known by Saudis as 'the period of abundance' (*zaman al-ṭafra*), the standard of living of the black populations remained stagnant, while that of the other populations rose every day, thanks to the oil money which black populations could not access. Thus, it can be said that the black populations of Mecca (and of all Saudi Arabia) are the ones who have been left behind by the Āl Saʿūd regime.

Yet, as the history of Ṣabbān and al-Jāmī shows, the African communities of Mecca and of Saudi Arabia as a whole have also contributed to the establishment of the Saudi regime from the very beginning. After being the minister of finance of King Saʿūd b. ʿAbd al-ʿAzīz, Ṣabbān became secretary general of the newly created World Islamic League (*Rābiṭa al-ʿālam al-islāmī*) under the leadership of King Fayṣal b. ʿAbd al-ʿAzīz, the successor of Saʿūd. Ṣabbān was the main engine behind the creation of this institution. The *Rābiṭa* (founded in 1962) and the Islamic University of Medina (founded in 1961) had the following two political missions: 1) to use Pan-Islamism to oppose Nasser's Pan-Arabism and the Baathism of the Iraqi and Syrian regimes; 2) to propagate the *Salafī-Wahhābī* version of Islam in the world, especially in Africa. Ṣabbān, the secretary general of *Rābiṭa*, played an important role not only in the *Rābiṭa*, but also in the Islamic University of Medina, especially in the organization of joint *daʿwa* missions between the two institutions abroad, particularly in sub-Saharan Africa. Al-Jāmī actively participated in virtually every mission sent to Africa at the time.

The proceedings of the conferences that al-Jāmī often held to mark these occasions were published in small books and then in a single book. These texts that I have consulted and analysed focus on three types of themes: 1) those related to what is permissible (*ḥalāl*) and what is defended (*ḥarām*) in Islamic rituals; 2) themes relating to the misdeeds of communism and the regimes, which claimed it, particularly in Africa; and 3) themes on the misdeeds of colonialism and the disastrous consequences it left behind after independence. His critical speech against the Muslim Brotherhood (*Ikhwān al-muslimūn*) and its well-known leaders such as Ḥasan al-Bannā, Sayyid Quṭb, and Muḥammad al-Ghazzālī, his criticisms of the Ṣaḥwa movement in Saudi Arabia, and his full support for the ruling family of Saudi Arabia and the Council of the *'ulamā'* of the country, all this appeared late in the 1990s, especially after the first Gulf War.

All these religious and political questions left the African communities of Mecca indifferent. Not having benefited from the oil wealth, as other Saudi communities had, especially during the *ṭafra* period (the 1970s), the members of these communities lived hand to mouth from whatever they traded at their markets, particularly the Dukan Kida market, from *Ḥajj*-related activities, and from trade with family members who remained in Africa.

CHAPTER 4

The Transformation of the Pilgrimage Tradition in West Africa

Ousmane Oumar Kane

There is large consensus in Islamic historiography that the Greater Pilgrimage to Mecca, the *Ḥajj*,[1] was institutionalized in the ninth year of the Islamic calendar.[2] It takes place every year in the first half of the Muslim month of *dhil Ḥijja*, culminating in the station at Mount Arafat on the tenth day of that month. Since then, Muslims from all over the world have travelled to the Holy Lands to fulfil this religious obligation, which is incumbent on all Muslims who can afford it. The *Ḥajj* is the opportunity for the atonement of all past sins. It is unique among the great religious pilgrimages for its doctrinal centrality, geographic focus, historical continuity and size, and global coverage.[3] Alongside, and often associated with the *Ḥajj*, is the tradition of *ziyāra* or pious visitation in special mosques or mausoleums of Muslim holy people. The most important mausoleum for Muslims is that of the Prophet Muḥammad located in Medina, about four hundred kilometres from Mecca. Although not part of the ritual of the *Ḥajj*, the trip to Medina is made by pilgrims performing the Greater Pilgrimage or the Lesser Pilgrimage to Mecca (*'umra*). In Medina, pilgrims visit the mausoleums of the Prophet, his

[1] Several important academic studies of the *Ḥajj* have appeared in Western languages in the last hundred years or so. Notable among them are M. Gaudefroy-Demombynes, *Le pèlerinage à la Mecque* (Paris: Geuthner, 1923); F.E. Peters, *The Hajj. The Muslim Pilgrimages to Mecca and the Holy Places* (Princeton, NJ: Princeton University Press, 1994); R. Blanchi, *Guests of God. Pilgrimage and Politics in the Islamic World* (New York: Oxford University Press, 2004); Eric Tagliacozzo; Shawkat M. Toorawa (eds.), *The Hajj. Pilgrimage in Islam* (Cambridge: Cambridge University Press, 2016); Babak Rahimi; Payman Eshaghi (eds.), *Muslim Pilgrimage in the Modern World* (Chapel Hill: The University of North Carolina Press, 2019).

[2] Khadim Mbacké, *Le pèlerinage aux lieux saints de l'islam. Participation sénégalaise 1886–1986* (Dakar: Presses universitaires de Dakar, 2004) 14.

[3] Robert Bianchi, 'Ḥajj', in *The Oxford Encyclopedia of the Islamic World. Oxford Islamic Studies Online*, http://www.oxfordislamicstudies.com/article/opr/t236/e0289. Accessed 18 March 2019.

companions, members of his family, and Muslim martyrs and some historical sites of great significance for the early Muslim community such as Mount Uhud and the Mosque of Two *Qiblas*.

Visitations (*ziyāra*) also take place to the mausoleums of Shiite *imāms* or Sufi shaykhs in Fez,[4] Cairo,[5] Ajmer Sharif,[6] and Touba.[7] For a long time, the *Ḥajj* was linked to the tradition of study (*riḥla*), as most pilgrims were scholars who spent time in centres of learning along the way to and in the Holy Lands to study, acquire books, and seek scholarly credentials.[8]

Like elsewhere in the Muslim world,[9] religious travel in West Africa was motivated by those very three reasons. The first was to perform the Greater (or Lesser) Pilgrimage to the Holy Lands and the second was to visit the shrines of holy Islamic figures. Last but not least, the third type of travel, which could be combined with either of the first two, was the search for esoteric and exoteric knowledge, which is typically sanctioned by the award of an authorization to transmit that knowledge (*ijāza*). In the twentieth century, a combination of factors contributed to radically transform the nature of and participation in the pilgrimage in West Africa, the Holy Lands, and for that matter, globally. In the process, I will argue, the pilgrimage tradition became divorced from intellectual pursuits and linked instead to tourism and trade. Understanding the transformation of the pilgrimage tradition in West Africa is therefore central to understanding the transformation of Islamic scholarship in twentieth-century Africa. Geopolitical change and technological progress played an important role in this transformation. Before the twentieth century, pilgrims travelled by foot and/or on camel between West Africa and the Holy Lands. The trip lasted a minimum of two years each way and

4 Fawzi Skali, *Saints et Sanctuaires de Fez* (Rabat: Marsam, 2007).

5 Michael Gilsenan, *Saint and Sufi in Modern Egypt: An Essay in the Sociology of Religion* (Oxford: Clarendon Press, 1973).

6 See for example P.M. Currie, *The Shrine and Cult of Mu'īn al-Dīn Chistī of Ajmer* (Oxford: Oxford University Press, 1989).

7 Cheikh Guèye, *Touba: La capitale des mourides* (Paris: Karthala, 2002).

8 Dale F. Eickelman; James Piscatori, *Muslim Travellers: Pilgrimage, Migration, and the Religious Imagination* (Berkeley: University of California Press, 1990).

9 For example, scholarship on Islamic education in Asia has revealed that students travelled across continents in the search for knowledge long before the current era of globalization. See Brannon D. Ingram, *Revival from Below: The Deoband Movement and Global Islam* (Oakland: The University of California Press, 2018) 8; Farish A. Noor; Yoginder Sikand; Martin van Bruinessen, 'Behind the Walls: Re-Appraising the Role and Importance of Madrasas in the World Today', in Farish A. Noor; Yoginder Sikand; Martin van Bruinessen (eds.), *The Madrasa in Asia: Political Activism and Transnational Linkages* (Amsterdam: Amsterdam University Press, 2008).

a round trip lasting ten years was not uncommon. The journey from Mecca to Medina took a minimum of one week. The travel by camel of the 100 kilometres separating Mecca from Jeddah, where pilgrims travelling by boat landed, lasted two days.[10] Now, West African pilgrims, and indeed the majority of pilgrims from the 168 countries participating in the *Ḥajj*, can fly the same day from their country to the Holy Lands, and comfortable and affordable buses cover the distance from Mecca to Medina in four hours and from Jeddah to Mecca in one hour. For centuries prior to the rise of the nation states, many pilgrims travelled without identification or vaccination against the deadly diseases that decimated them. In the course of the twentieth century, several international agreements between Saudi Arabia and countries sending pilgrims ensured the acquisition of adequate documentation and vaccination prior to travel to the Holy Lands. This considerably reduced the disappearance and death toll due to diseases among pilgrims. Before the twentieth century, travel within the Arabian Peninsula was unsafe, as was trans-Saharan travel. Bedouins routinely looted pilgrim caravans. In the twentieth century, with the consolidation of the state of Saudi Arabia, the insecurity was eradicated and pilgrims travelled safely from one part of the Holy Lands to the other. A related development to the increased security is the modification of the gender distribution of the pilgrims. Indeed, until the mid-twentieth century, virtually all West African pilgrims were male. Now female pilgrims are equal in number to their male counterparts, and some years outnumber them.[11] Until the mid-twentieth century, the Holy Mosques of Mecca and Medina could host only a few thousand worshippers. In the last four decades, tens of billions of dollars have been invested by Saudi Arabia to considerably expand the hosting infrastructure of these sacred sites. In West Africa, most of the funding for pilgrimage was raised locally until the 1960s. At the turn of the twenty-first century, a sizable West African Muslim diaspora settled in the West. This diaspora opened new routes by investing abundant material resources in maintaining and creating ties between their homeland centres of pilgrimage, the Muslim Holy Lands, North Africa, and their Western host societies. Until recently, the travel of pilgrims culminated in the Holy Lands. Now, in one trip, many pilgrims can perform pilgrimage in holy sites in North Africa on their way to or from Mecca, and they can include other global

[10] Timothy P. Barnard, 'The Hajj, Islam, and Power among the Bugis in Early Colonial Riau', in Eric Tagliacozzo (ed.), *South East Asia and the Middle East. Islam, Movement and the Longue Durée* (Stanford, CA: Stanford University Press, 2009) 65–82, 73.

[11] For West Africa, see Mbacké, *Le pèlerinage aux lieux saints de l'islam*, 363. Bianchi demonstrates that globally the growth of the *Ḥajj* has been accompanied by a steady rise in the proportion of women pilgrims. Bianchi, *Guests of God, Pilgrimage and Politics in the Islamic World* (Oxford: Oxford University Press, 2004) 68.

cities such as Dubai, Shanghai, and Beijing in their trip. Last but not least, the overwhelming majority of West African pilgrims were motivated by the search for knowledge and scholarly credentials prior to the twentieth century. Now, this peripatetic tradition has completely disappeared, partly due to the rise of nation states with an effective control of their borders. These Arab states of North Africa and the Gulf do give student visas and scholarships to support studies of Muslims from all over the world, as they give tourist visas for pilgrims. But these are two completely different processes involving different categories of people. Prior to the twentieth century, the pilgrimage was the main source of supply of scholarly works. Students/pilgrims would buy or beg for manuscripts or spend time copying them. Their bags were full of books when they returned home. Now, many of those books are available for free download from some Islamic websites and can be accessed anywhere in the world or purchased in bookstores in any country in the Muslim world. Books no longer figure prominently among items brought back by pilgrims. Instead, the pilgrimage has become the main source of supply for video clips of the Holy Lands. All pilgrims have smartphones and use them to capture video clips of each moment during the pilgrimage. They share these videoclips via WhatsApp with friends from all over the world. They also bring huge bottles of water from the well of Zemzem, offered graciously in the Holy Lands (3.7 million gallons were offered in 2018),[12] as well as fashionable clothing from the Holy Lands. In fact, the widespread popularity of Arab clothing in many areas of West Africa is linked directly to the explosion in the number of pilgrims from the region. As more and more people travelled to pilgrimage sites in North Africa and Saudi Arabia, and as China became involved in producing these clothes at more affordable prices, they became increasingly popular in West Africa, whether those who wear them have gone on pilgrimage or not.

In what follows, I will discuss how the West African pilgrimage tradition to the Muslim Holy Lands and to North Africa was transformed. Next, I will analyse the emergence of new sites of pilgrimage in West Africa that parallel in scope the pilgrimage of the Holy Lands. I will also discuss the role that the West African diaspora played in connecting them. By exploring these transformations, I will illustrate the connections between the rise of the nation state in the Muslim world, globalization, the transformation of material culture, and intellectual history.

[12] Learn Religions, 'Hajj Statistics: How the Needs of 2 Million Pilgrims Are Met', Hajj Pilgrimage Statistics, 22 June 2018, https://www.learnreligions.com/hajj-by-the-numbers-2004319. Accessed February 2020.

From Foot and Camelback to Air Travel: The Transformation of the West African Pilgrimage to Mecca

African Muslims have been performing the pilgrimage to Mecca for centuries, but the history of the pilgrimage before the nineteenth century is poorly documented. The majority of the sources are unpublished travelogues. Learned pilgrims wrote travel narratives, but these exist in manuscript form and were never published due to the lack of printing technology in West Africa before European colonialism. The most solid evidence available prior to the twentieth century concerns royal pilgrimage. By the eleventh century, a few West African kings had converted to Islam. The earliest recorded royal conversion to Islam is that of War Jabi, the king of Takrūr, a kingdom in present-day northern Senegal. It was in 1040 that War Jabi converted to Islam and his people along with him. It was followed by the conversion of the king of Manding in 1050, and the Sayfawa ruler of the kingdom of Kanem Borno in 1085. Mention of Takrūrī or Barnāwī (in reference to Takrūr and Borno) in Arab writings suggests that pilgrims from these regions were well known in the Holy Lands in the thirteenth century. Several other kings converted subsequently and many of them performed the pilgrimage to Mecca.

Renowned Arab and African authors[13] have written on the royal African pilgrimage, including Al-'Umarī (d. 1349) in his book entitled *Pathways of Vision in the Realms of the Metropolises* (*Masālik al-abṣār fī mamālik al-amṣār*, in Arabic), Ibn Khaldūn (d. 1406) in his *Prolegomena* (*Kitāb al-'ibar*, in Arabic), Al-Maqrīzī, in his work entitled *Moulded Gold on those Kings who Made the Pilgrimage* (*al-Dhahab al-Masbūk fi dhikr man ḥajja min al-Mulūk*, in Arabic), a chapter of which deals with the kings of Takrur, Ibn Battuta in his Journey (*Riḥla* in Arabic), and the famous seventeeth-century Timbuktu Chronicles. Two such royal pilgrimages have been abundantly chronicled. The first is that of Mali's emperor Mansa Musa. In the year 1324, Mansa Musa stayed three days in Egypt. He arrived in Cairo during the rule of Mamluk ruler Al-Nasir b. Qala'un on his way to Mecca. He distributed so much gold that his passage was recorded in great detail by Egyptian and other historians.[14] He brought books of Mālikī jurisprudence to Mali and attracted Muslim scholars to his kingdom as well.

Kanem Borno had a long history of royal pilgrimage. According to the *Dīwān of the Sultans of Borno* by Idriss Aloma, twenty kings of the Sayfawa dynasty

[13] On these authors, see Nehemia Levtzion; J.F.P. Hopkins, *Corpus of Early Arabic Sources for West African History* (Princeton, NJ: Markus Wiener Publishers, 2011).

[14] Ralph Austen, *TransSaharan Africa in World History* (Oxford: Oxford University Press, 2010) 23. Indeed, a picture of Mansa Musa is featured in the Catalan Atlas of 1375 drawn by Abraham Cresques, one of the first maps providing serious information about Africa to Europeans.

who ruled Kanem Borno from the eleventh to the nineteenth century performed the pilgrimage to Mecca.[15] Another pilgrimage worthy of note is that of Askiya Muḥammad of Songhay in 1497. He met the Abbassid *Khalīfa* in Cairo, who appointed him *Khalīfa* for the *Bilād al-Sudān* (Land of Black people), which referred to sub-Saharan Africa.

There were two main precolonial pilgrimage routes from West Africa. The first was from Mali through Niger, north-eastern Nigeria, Chad, Sudan and through the Red Sea to the Arabian Peninsula. Most West African pilgrims took that route because of the availability of wells and grazing land for the animals of the caravan. The other was the route through Mauritania, Morocco, and ultimately Egypt. It offered the possibility of spending time in prestigious centres of learning in North Africa such as Shinqīṭ, Fez, Tlemcen, Tunis, Kairouan, and Cairo.[16] West African pilgrims also took other trade routes or minor or temporary pilgrimage routes.

Unlike North African states, which provided care and assistance to pilgrims (including sending a *maḥmal*, a regular dispatching of gifts, organizing an institutionalized caravan led by an *Amir al-Ḥajj*), there was no institutionalized pilgrimage in precolonial West African states. But West African pilgrims could join some of the caravans departing from North Africa to the *Ḥajj*.

Aside from the recorded royal pilgrimages, we know very little about the pilgrimage tradition before the nineteenth century.

At the turn of the twentieth century, another drive toward Mecca took place. Called the '*hijra* doctrine' by Sudanese Historian Al-Naqar, this movement was prompted by the colonial expansion of the late nineteenth century.[17] Europeans who had settled in the West African Atlantic Coast since the sixteenth century occupied only 10 per cent of its landmass until the late nineteenth century. Between the Berlin conference convened in 1884–5 by the European colonial powers and 1905, they conquered the remaining 90 per cent of the African continent. Many African Muslims who did not want to live under non-Muslim rule fled to the Holy Lands. The learned among them played an important role in the consolidation of

[15] See Taqī al-Dīn Aḥmad al-Maqrīzi, Kitāb al-Mawā'iẓ wa 'itibār in Nehemia Levtzion; J.F.P. Hopkins, *Corpus*, 353. In the mid-thirteenth century, a school had already been established in Cairo for the benefit of Borno students through an endowment given by Borno merchants/pilgrims to the qadi 'Alām al-Dīn Ibn Rashīq named after the School (Madrasat Ibn Rashīq).

[16] Khadim Mbacké, *Le Pèlerinage Aux Lieux Saints De L'Islam : Participation Sénégalaise, 1886–1986* (Dakar, Senegal: Presses Universitaires De Dakar, 2004) 170–1.

[17] See Umar al-Naqar, *The Pilgrimage Tradition in West Africa: An Historical Study with Special Reference to the Nineteenth Century* (Khartoum: Khartoum University Press, 1972).

the rule of King 'Abd al-Azīz, the founder of the kingdom of Saudi Arabia, in the field of preaching and teaching both inside and outside Saudi Arabia.[18]

Although the pilgrimage is of utmost ritual importance for Muslims, only a small number of West African Muslims (or for that matter of all Muslims) performed the pilgrimage prior to the mid-twentieth century. Until the mid-1950s, the total number of pilgrims rarely exceeded 100,000, which means that about 0.2 per cent of the Muslim global population would expect to complete this fifth pillar of Islam. At the beginning of the twenty-first century, the number of pilgrims exceeded 2 million, reaching 3.1 million in 2012, including 1.7 million international pilgrims and 1.4 million Saudis.[19] This is still a tiny percentage of the Muslim global population, now approaching 1.8 billion. But the number grew by a factor of thirty in just a few decades. Given the huge logistical challenge of hosting so many people in pilgrimage sites, the Saudi state, upon the recommendation of the Organization of the Islamic Conference dated 1987, fixed a quota of pilgrims at one thousand pilgrims per one million of the populations of the states sending pilgrims.

One of the conditions of the pilgrimage is that candidates must be able to afford to perform the pilgrimage. But even those who could afford it were dissuaded because the trip entailed many risks, especially insecurity in the regions traversed by pilgrims and diseases. For several centuries, the Sharifians were custodians of the two Holy Mosques of Mecca and Medina. To reach the Holy Mosques, pilgrims had to travel through territories governed by tribal leaders who considered themselves absolute lords of their territories and exacted duties upon goods carried through them.[20] To ensure the safety of pilgrims, duties were paid to the leaders of those tribes. Those duties were a budgeted part of the Ottoman government's *Ḥajj* expenses when the Hijaz was under Ottoman rule. Its distribution, however, was all but transparent. The local government official in charge of the supervision of the pilgrimage (*Amir al-Ḥajj*) and the caravan commanders routinely withheld some of the monies destined to tribal leaders. They made generous payments to the most powerful and aggressive tribes and very little or nothing to weak tribes. In this context, tribes asserted their own terrifying credibility vis-à-vis the government to maintain their position versus other rivals as *Ḥajj* protector. Attacks against caravans were commonplace. Very often pilgrims were looted and sometimes killed by Bedouins. For this reason, the majority of

[18] Chanfi Ahmad, *West African 'Ulamā' and Salafism in Mecca and Madina* (Leiden and Boston: E.J. Brill, 2015).

[19] Andy Sambidge, 'Hajj Pilgrims Total 3.1m, Says Saudi Arabia', *Arabian Business*, 26 June 2017, https://www.arabianbusiness.com/hajj-pilgrims-total-3-1m-says-saudi-arabia-477638.html. Accessed June 2019.

[20] Information in this paragraph relies on Peters, *The Hajj*, 160.

pilgrims travelled in large groups and were armed to defend themselves if needed. Thus, many were dissuaded from travelling for several centuries.

Diseases were also a major issue. Pandemics like cholera decimated pilgrims. In 1865, 15,000 out of 90,000 pilgrims died in Mecca.[21] In addition to these risks, shared equally by all pilgrims, West Africans were exposed to another risk: kidnapping and enslavement. Given the old racial prejudice against black people in the region, the kidnapping and enslaving of black people was commonplace, taking place not just on the way to the Holy cities, but in Mecca and Medina themselves until the twentieth century.[22] Among the members of the African diaspora in the area, quite a few are descendants of enslaved African pilgrims.

Several developments in the early twentieth century changed the ability of West Africans to travel. The first was European colonial rule, which considerably limited the geographic mobility of colonial subjects. All candidates to the colonially sponsored pilgrimage had to seek a travel permit. Colonial masters sponsored pilgrimage most of the time for their loyal subjects, who travelled by boat to the Holy Lands. The second development was the subjugation of the Holy Mosques by the dynasty of Āl-Saʻūd. They established their authority over the entire peninsula and were able to significantly improve the security situation.

After World War Two, dozens of Muslim-majority countries became independent from European colonial rule. Taking the pilgrimage very seriously, they created an official body to organize the pilgrimage staffed by learned scholars and a medical team. This body takes care of all the needs of pilgrims, from visas to vaccinations, to escorting them throughout the trip until the return home, to teaching them how to perform the rituals of the pilgrimage.

Finally, a series of conferences contributed to improving the overall conditions of the pilgrimage, including the conference of Paris of 1930 in which sending countries signed agreements that contributed significantly to improving the conditions.[23] According to the agreements, all countries would inform the Alexandria Office of the Pilgrimage of the approximate number of their pilgrims and their itinerary at least two months before the pilgrimage. All sending countries would ensure that candidates for pilgrimage would be vaccinated against cholera and smallpox. They would deliver proper pilgrimage photo ID to candidates after establishing that they possessed a round trip ticket to the pilgrimage. They would also ensure that sending countries would pay all duties due to countries through which pilgrims transited no later than three months after the pilgrimage and, finally, all travellers possessing a passport and going to the Hijaz during the period

21 M.N. Pearson, 'The Indian Ocean and the Red Sea', in Levtzion; Pouwels (eds.), *The History of Islam in Africa* (Athens, OH: Ohio University Press, 2000) 37–59.

22 Mbacké, *Le pèlerinage aux lieux saints de l'islam*, 28.

23 Information in this paragraph relies on Mbacké, *Le pèlerinage*, 219.

of the pilgrimage would be treated decently as pilgrims whose security would be assured by the political authorities of the Hijaz.

Additionally, travel agents typically supply their pilgrims with several forms of identification. These commonly include an ID with their visa number and the addresses of their residence in Mecca and Medina, a scarf with the name of their travel agents, and finally bracelets with tracking devices, similar to those of prisoners, which allow the travel agents to locate them in the Holy Lands in case they are ever separated from the group.

At the turn of the twenty-first century, new developments contributed to transforming the pilgrimage even further. The oil wealth provided huge resources to Saudi Arabia. Hundreds of billions of dollars were invested in the pilgrimage industry. Since 1950, one hundred billion dollars has been invested in the expansion of the Mosque of Mecca. By 2017, it had become the largest mosque in the world, capable of hosting 1.5 million worshippers. It is being further expanded to host a total of 2.2 million pilgrims.[24] Before the expansion of the Mosque, all rituals were performed at ground level. Another two levels have been built so now pilgrims can perform the main rituals, that is the circumambulation of the Kaaba and the hurried walk between the Mounts of Ṣafā and Marwa, in the surroundings of the Mosque of the Kaaba. Likewise, in neighbouring Mina, where the lapidation of Satan is performed, the ritual can be accomplished on three levels. The ritual of the Great Pilgrimage culminates at the Mount of Arafat where all pilgrims spend the day. When I performed the pilgrimage for the first time in 1982, Arafat and Mina were in a desert where all pilgrims built a tent for one day with very poor materials and dismantled them at the end of the day. Now, they have been completely transformed. Forty-five thousand permanent tents in concrete have been established with air conditioning, toilets and showers. Pilgrims bring their own portable mats and can stay the whole day comfortably.[25] Housing is also organized in quarters for each nationality. All the 168 countries and territories sending pilgrims have their own quarters.

Another development is the growth of the religious tourism industry both in the Holy Lands and in the host country. In the vicinity of the Holy Lands, in both Mecca and Medina, hundreds of huge hotels and apartments have been built to accommodate pilgrims, from modest rooms to five-star hotels. The cost of the room or suite varies according to the period and standing of the hotels. During the *Ḥajj* or the last ten days of the month of Ramadan, a suite close to the Holy Mosque of Mecca costs several thousand dollars a night. But there is affordable

[24] Ali Daye, 'Grand Mosque Expansion Highlights Growth of Saudi Arabian Tourism', https://blog.realestate.cornell.edu/2018/03/21/grandmosqueexpansion/. Accessed March 2018.

[25] Learn Religions, 'Hajj Statistics'.

housing for all pilgrims. These are typically farther from the Mosque and rooms are shared by up to six or seven people.

In sending countries, various strategies have contributed to making the pilgrimage accessible to more people. Typically, most people who travel from West Africa to the Holy Lands are offered the trip by relatives or other philanthropists. But many official institutions budget some tickets for their employees and selection is made by an annual lottery. In Africa as well as in the diaspora, there are many associations set up to sponsor the pilgrimage not just to Mecca but also to North Africa, especially the city of Fez where the founder of the Tijāniyya Sufi order, Aḥmad al-Tijānī, is buried. This leads me to discuss a second major site of West African pilgrimage.

From the Pilgrimage of Scholars to the Pilgrimage of Lay People: The Transformation of the West African Tijānī Pilgrimage to North Africa

The Tijāniyya[26] takes its name from its founder, Ahmad b. Muḥammad b. al-Mukhtār al-Tijānī, born in 1739 in Aynoumadi, southern Algeria, where he received most of his education. An exceptionally gifted student, he memorized the Holy Qur'ān at the age of seven and then proceeded to study the main subjects of Islamic knowledge, including the exegesis of the Qur'ān (*tafsīr*), Islamic jurisprudence (*fiqh*), Prophetic traditions (*ḥadīth*), the art of Qur'ānic recitation (*tajwīd*), Arabic literature, etc.[27] He received part of his education, and notably his formation in the Prophetic tradition, in Fez, Morocco. He also developed a great interest in Sufism (*taṣawwuf*) and studied with major Sufi shaykhs of eighteenth-century Morocco.[28] In his youth, Aḥmad al-Tijānī was initiated in several Sufi orders including the Wazzāniyya, the Nāsiriyya, the Shādhiliyya and the Khalwatiyya. He travelled widely in North Africa and Asia to perform the pilgrimage, seek knowledge, and connect with major Sufi teachers.

The year 1784 CE is a landmark in the history of the Tijāniyya. It was in that year that Aḥmad al-Tijānī saw the Prophet not in a dream, but in reality while

[26] For more on the ideology and spread of the Tijāniyya, see Jamil Abun-Nasr, *The Tijaniyya: A Sufi Order in the Modern World* (London and New York: Oxford University Press, 1965); Jean-Louis Triaud; David Robinson (eds.), *La Tijaniyya. Une confrérie musulmane à la conquête de l'Afrique* (Paris: Karthala, 2000); Zachary Wright, *Realizing Islam: The Tijaniyya in North Africa and the Eighteenth-Century Muslim World* (Chapel Hill: University of North Carolina Press, 2020).

[27] Zachary Valentine Wright, *On the Path of the Prophet. Shaykh Ahmed al-Tijani and the Tariqa Muhammadiyya* (Atlanta, GA: The African American Islamic Institute, 2005) 25.

[28] Wright, *On the Path of the Prophet.*

performing spiritual retreat in Boussemghoun, Algeria. The Prophet informed him that he was the seal of all saints and instructed him to create his own Sufi order of the Tijāniyya, which he did. In the following decade, the Tijāniyya *tariqa* started to spread in Algeria. Due to persecution from Ottoman authorities who

Fig. 4.1 Quote from Ibn Al-ʿĀshir Al-Andalusi engraved on a stone at the entrance to the *zāwiya* of Boussemghoun (Credit: Ousmane Oumar Kane)

ruled Algeria then, Aḥmad al-Tijānī left his natal town of Aynoumadi, Algeria to settle in Fez in 1798. He was welcomed by the ruling Sultan Mawlay Suleymān (1766–1822) who offered him a house in Fez, which still attracts pilgrims. In addition, the sultan invited him to join the council of scholars of the court. At his death in 1815, he was buried in the *zāwiya* that he built in Fez.

In the course of the nineteenth and twentieth centuries, the Tijāniyya spread to become a major articulation of global Islam. Its following in the world runs in the tens of millions, and at least 90 per cent of them are from sub-Saharan Africa and its diaspora in the West. Tijānī followers in West Africa have made a huge contribution to its development. They have built schools, lodges (Sufi *zāwiyas*) and initiated tens of millions of people in Africa. But it is not just in numbers that sub-Saharan Africans dominate the Tijāniyya. It is also in intellectual production. As demonstrated in this volume by Farah al-Sharif on 'Umar Tāl (chapter 7) and Antonio de Diego González on Ibrahim Niasse and his community (chapter 8), some of the major doctrinal elaboration of the Tijāniyya was the work of West African Tijānīs.[29] Tijānīs on both shores of the Sahara have endeavoured to maintain close ties through epistolary exchanges, poems praising each other, and of course through pilgrimage from West Africa to Tijāniyya holy sites as well as travel from North to West Africa.

The pilgrimage from West Africa to Fez is as old as the Tijāniyya itself. It has waxed and waned, involved many categories of people with various motivations, but has remained a link between Tijānīs of North and West Africa for almost two hundred years. In the nineteenth and first half of the twentieth centuries, it was mostly scholars who performed the pilgrimage to Fez. The first is the Mauritanian Idaw 'Alī scholar Muḥāmmad al-Hāfiẓ (d. 1830),[30] who was initiated into the Tijāniyya by Aḥmad al-Tijānī himself. Most Senegambian chains of transmission to the Tijāniyya are traced to Muḥāmmad al-Hāfiẓ. Throughout the nineteenth century, it was mainly the religious elites who performed the pilgrimage to Fez.

29 To cite a few, Al-hajj 'Umar Tāl's *Kitāb Rimāh al-ḥizb al-rahīm 'ala nuḥur ḥizb al-rājīm* is the second most important book clarifying the doctrines of the Tijāniyya which is published in the margins of the *Jawāhir al-ma'āni* of 'Alī Ḥarāzim. The next most influential book is Ibrahim Niasse's *Kāshif al-albās 'an faydāt al-khatm abī 'Abbas* the magnum opus of Ibrahim, one of the most influential Sufi authors in the twentieth century. His brother Muhammad Niasse also authored a most influential defence of the Tijāniyya *ṭarīqa Al-Juyūsh al-ṭulla' bi murhafāt al-quṭṭa' 'alā ibn Mayāba akh- tanaṭṭu'*. In Nigeria, Ibrāhīm Sālih Ḥusseinī, whose authorship includes over a hundred books, authored two books in defence of the *ṭarīqa Tijāniyya (al-Takfīr* and *al-Mughīr)*. See Ousmane Kane, *Muslim Modernity in Postcolonial Nigeria* (Leiden: E.J. Brill, 2003).

30 Jilali El Adnani, 'Entre visite et pèlerinage: le cas des pèlerins oust-africains à la zâwiya Tijâniyya de Fès', *Al-Maghrib al-Ifrîqî*, 6, 2005, 7–37, 9.

Abdoulaye Niasse, the founder of the Niasse branch of the Tijāniyya, went to Fez in 1909 where he received the *ijāza muṭlaqa* (full permission to initiate and appoint deputies of the Tijāniyya). For Tijānī scholars, the pilgrimage to Fez was a means to seek blessing at the shrine of the founder of the Tijāniyya and the opportunity to accumulate prestigious chains of transmission that linked them directly to the Tijānī establishment in Fez.

After the consolidation of French colonial rule, Tijānī leaders, some of whom were involved in anticolonial activities, renounced armed resistance and pledged loyalty to the French with whom they collaborated for most of colonial rule.[31] In the process of the consolidation of their rule, the French found it beneficial to cooperate with the Muslim clerisy and particularly the Tijānī communities. Because they were literate in Arabic, Muslim leaders served in the colonial bureaucracy as teachers, interpreters, and judges in Muslim tribunals. They engaged in the colonial economy by cultivating cash crops. They urged their followers to abide by colonial laws, to pay taxes, and to be loyal to the French colonial state. But as proven by surveillance files on most Tijānī leaders, the French never trusted them entirely. One of the greatest fears of European colonial powers throughout their rule was Pan-Islamism (i.e., a large transnational coalition of African Muslims against colonial rule). To exorcise that fear, they restricted the movement of colonial subjects between North and West Africa. The French monitored the movement of African pilgrims to North Africa and the Hijaz closely. But nevertheless, among those Muslims allowed by the French colonial government to perform the pilgrimage, Tijānīs figure prominently. The Senegalese pilgrims received the highest quota of pilgrimages to Mecca and Fez in the 1950s.[32] Of the 553 pilgrims returning to Senegal from Mecca, 313, more than half of them, stopped in Fez[33] to perform the pilgrimage.

Towards the end of colonial rule, the restrictions on travel between North and West Africa were lifted. By the time of independence, pilgrims no longer needed the permission of colonial authorities to travel between these two regions. In addition, postcolonial states of North and West Africa endeavoured to strengthen their cooperation. Morocco maintained diplomatic relations with African governments but it also maintained parallel diplomacy with Sufi leaders and particularly prominent Tijānī shaykhs. Because Morocco sheltered Aḥmad al-Tijānī when he fled his country, the Tijāniyya has been an important component of Moroccan diplomacy

31 David Robinson, *Paths of Accommodation: Muslim Societies and French Colonial Authorities in Senegal and Mauritania 1880–1920* (Athens, OH: Ohio University Press, 2000).

32 El Adnani, 'Entre visite et pèlerinage', 11.

33 Oumar Kane, 'Les relations entre la communauté tijane du Sénégal et la zawiya de Fèz', *Annales de la Faculté de Lettres et des Sciences Humaines*, 24, 1994, 49–68, 65.

towards West Africa. All three kings who ruled postcolonial Morocco (Mohamed V, Hassan II, and Muhammad VI) committed to maintain those ties. In addition to supporting the *zāwiya* of Fez, the Moroccan kings provided generous assistance to the building or renovation of major mosques in Senegal (for example, the Great Mosque of Dakar, the Great Mosque of Medina Baye in Kaolack, and the Great Mosque of Tivaouane). They invited and offered five-star hospitality to Senegalese Tijānī leaders to spend Ramadan in Rabat as guests of the king every year; provided healthcare to all major Tijānī leaders in the best Moroccan hospitals; and offered numerous scholarships directly to Tijānī shaykhs who sent their children and disciples to study in Moroccan universities, particularly the ancient Qarawiyyīn college. Consequently, since independence, thousands of West African students have studied in Morocco. In 1985, the Kingdom of Morocco convened a major conference on Sufism in Fez and invited hundreds of Tijānī leaders to attend. After the conference a league of *'ulamā'* of Morocco and Senegal was established and the Tijānī shaykh Ibrahim Mahmood Diop was appointed and served as secretary general until his death in 2014. It was at the suggestion of Diop that the king opened an Institut d'Etudes Africaines of the Université Mohamed V at Rabat, which is producing high-quality research on trans-Saharan connections.

It was in the early 1960s that the first full packages for the pilgrimage to Fez were organized. Built by the Chantiers de l'Atlantique in Saint-Nazaire and inaugurated in 1962 by French President General de Gaulle, the French boat *Ancerville* provided regular chartered trips of Tijānī pilgrims from Dakar to Casablanca. The trip was considerably shorter than the journey by camel, lasting only six days each way. In this period, pilgrimage and trade went hand in hand. Many pilgrims seized the opportunity of the pilgrimage to purchase goods in Morocco destined to be resold back home. The cost of the trip was relatively affordable and there was no weight limitation for the pilgrims. Pilgrims/merchants could bring as many commodities as they wanted. In 1973, the boat *Ancerville* was sold to the Chinese and renamed the *Minghua*.[34] In the 1970s, the boat service tended to be replaced by air travel. Not only was the airfare higher than the boat fare, but airlines gave passengers a limited luggage allowance and charged a high fee for excess luggage. This caused the number of travellers to drop significantly from the mid-1970s through the 1990s.[35] During this period, most pilgrims travelled individually or as a part of small groups led by a Tijānī shaykh.

At the beginning of the twenty-first century, the rise of the tourism industry in West Africa revived the full package options. Several companies offered

[34] The source for the information about the *Ancerville/Minghua* in this paragraph is https://fr.wikipedia.org/wiki/Ancerville_(paquebot). Accessed September 2020.

[35] Nazarena Lanza, 'Péleriner, faire du commerce et visiter les lieux saints. Le tourisme religieux sénégalais au Maroc', *L'année du Maghreb*, 11, 2014, 157–71.

affordable full packages in Senegal. The Moroccan airline, Royal Air Maroc, operates two daily flights to Casablanca from Dakar and all these flights include pilgrims to Fez.[36] In addition, some tour operators offer packages combining visits to Tijāniyya sites and major tourism destinations in Morocco such as Casablanca, Rabat and Marrakesh. In Rabat, frequently visited sites include the Tour Hassan, the Mausoleum of King Mohamed V and King Hasan II, but also the shrines of Sīdī Arabī b. Sāyiḥ (1813–91), a prominent figure of the Moroccan branch of the Tijāniyya. In the old city of Marrakesh, founded by the Almohad dynasty, are found the shrines of prominent Tijānī shaykhs such as Ahmed Skirej Ayāshi and Sidi Mohamed Kensoussi.[37]

Most organized group visits tend to take place during major Tijānī or Muslim festivals. Among the religious celebrations, the night that Shaykh Aḥmad al-Tijānī saw the Prophet in Boussemghoun, known as *Leylat al-Katmiyya*, attracts large numbers of pilgrims from Africa and its diaspora. Likewise, the birthday of the Prophet Muḥammad is celebrated twice. The first celebration coincides with his birthday and the second one week after. This enables Tijānīs who cannot attend the first celebration for any reason to pay their *ziyāra* to the saint.

Another celebration is the twenty-seventh day of the month of Rajab, which coincides with the nocturnal ascension of the Prophet Muḥammad (*Leylat al-isrā wal mirāj*). Finally, the last ten days of the Muslim month of Ramadan is another period of visits by very large groups to Fez. Some groups of up to 300 people visit major Tijānī sites in Morocco and Algeria. Some of them stay in Fez on their way to or from the Hijaz where they perform the lesser Muslim pilgrimage (*'umra*).

The growth of the West African diaspora in the West is another factor that stimulated the growth of the religious tourism industry in North Africa. In the postcolonial period, West Africa experienced a huge labour emigration. Some migrated within West Africa to more affluent countries such as Côte d'Ivoire. From the 1980s large contingents were migrating to Asia, Europe, and the Americas. Towards the turn of the twenty-first century, sizable West African communities were found all over the world, from Tokyo to Melbourne, from Turin to Buenos Aires, from Paris to New York. The remittances of this diaspora are estimated at billions of dollars and have made a great impact on West African development.[38] Members of this diaspora contributed to the growth of religious tourism in their home countries by offering full pilgrimage packages to Mecca

[36] Oumar Kane, 'Relations entre la communauté tijane', 68.

[37] Mohammad al-Mansour al-Mohieddine Tidjani, *Ahmad Tidjani et ses valeureux compagnons* (Paris: Albustane, 2015) 392–8.

[38] Ousmane Kane, *The Homeland is the Arena. Religion, Transnationalism and the Integration of Senegalese Muslims in America* (New York: Oxford University Press, 2011).

or Fez to their parents. Fez is now the site of a permanent settlement of the West Africa diaspora[39] which offers hospitality services to pilgrims.

But the diaspora did more than that. They purchased buildings to establish mosques that operated also as Sufi lodges where Sufi rituals were performed regularly in Western Europe and the US. They also organized group trips to main Tijānī centres in West and North Africa. Many would combine the two pilgrimages together. They would leave Italy or New York for Senegal with Royal Air Maroc, transit in Morocco for a few days to perform a pious visit in Fez and continue to Kaolack or Tivaouane to attend a major celebration, usually the celebration of the birthday of the Prophet Muḥammad. Politicians have also become major players in this religious tourism industry. In order to build political support, prominent politicians offer full packages to notables of their constituencies. Several institutions also offer trips to active or retired members.[40]

The stay in Fez is a period of intense spirituality. Pilgrims devote most of their time to praying in the *zāwiya*. Some of the pilgrims are hosted in the *zāwiya*, others in nearby hotels such as 'Hotel Tombouctou', 'Hotel Tidjani' or pilgrim residences not far from the *zāwiya*. A Tijānī shaykh from Senegal, Mansour Barro, purchased a four-storey building in front of the *zāwiya* of Fez which offers very affordable meals and accommodation to pilgrims. There are also VIP packages offering a stay in five-star hotels in Fez, such as the Royal Mirage; a regular bus service is organized from the hotel to the *zāwiya* where pilgrims attend the five daily Muslim prayers, the Tijānī collective ritual of *waẓīfa*, recite the Qur'ān and make invocations.

Descendants of Shaykh al-Tijānī are usually seated in the mosque where pilgrims can come and greet them, seek their blessing and give them donations. Sometimes pilgrims expose their concerns to them and ask that they mobilize the *baraka* (spiritual blessing or power) of their ancestor on their behalf in order to fulfil their wishes. Sometimes pilgrims wish to acquire additional and more prestigious chains of affiliation to the Tijāniyya and request that the custodians of the shrine renew their affiliation to the Tijāniyya. But Fez, where Shaykh Aḥmad al-Tijānī was buried, is not the only Tijāniyya site of pilgrimage. At his death in 1815, one of his closest disciples, 'Alī Tamāsīnī , assumed the leadership of the Tijāniyya and returned to Algeria with part of the family of Aḥmad al-Tijānī. There, they established several major *zāwiyas*, of which three attract huge numbers of pilgrims, those of Tamacine, Aynoumadi, and Bussemghoun.

[39] Johara Berriane, 'Intégration symbolique à Fès et encrages sur l'ailleurs: les Africains sub-sahariens et leur rapport à la zawiya d'Ahmad al-Tijani', *L'Annéee du Maghreb*, 11, 2, 2014, 142; Johara Berriane, *Ahmed al-Tijani de Fez. Un sanctuaire soufi aux connections transnationales* (Paris: L'Harmattan, 2015).

[40] Lanza, 'Péleriner', 161.

Pilgrimage to the Tijāniyya Sites in Algeria

The Algerian branch of the Tijāniyya strived to cultivate its own direct ties with Tijānīs in West Africa through correspondence or regular tours in West Africa. Some Algerian descendants of al-Tijānī settled in other African countries. One such Algerian is Muḥammad al-Habīb al-Tijānī (d. 1984), a great-grandson of Aḥmad al-Tijānī, who settled in Senegal in the 1950s. He married three daughters of the most prominent Senegalese Tijānī shaykhs. Muḥammad al-Habīb was honoured by other Senegalese Tijānī communities, and particularly the Tijānīs of Medina Gounass, who offered him a big residence in Pikine Senegal, which became his base and where he lived until his death. When he died, it was the Pointe de Sangomar, the personal aircraft of Abdou Diouf, the then-president of Senegal, which repatriated his corpse to Aynoumadi in Algeria, accompanied by the most prominent Senegalese Muslim dignitaries. This alerted the Algerian government to the important political weight of the Tijāniyya in West Africa and led to the revision of the reorientation of the Algerian government's attitude towards the Tijāniyya.[41] In 1987, the Algerian government under Chadli Benjedid sponsored a major conference on Sufism and invited hundreds of Tijānī leaders to attend. The goal might have been to influence West African diplomacy in favour of the Algerian position in the Western Saharan conflict, putting them on the side opposing the Moroccan government, and indeed, they seem to have succeeded. This and other diplomatic incentives seem to have affected the Senegalese decision to vote in favour of the autonomy of the Western Sahara.

After the arrival of President Bouteflika in power, the relations between the Algerian government and the Tijāniyya leadership in Aynoumadi improved considerably and the Algerian government is very supportive of the *ziyāra* in Tijānī sites in Algeria. The descendants of Muḥammad al-Habīb al-Tijānī based in Dakar serve as a link between the Algerian base of the Tijāniyya and Senegambian Tijānīs. In collaboration with local Tijānī shaykhs and the Algerian embassy in Dakar, every year they organize a trip involving hundreds of pilgrims mainly to Algeria, but also Morocco. During the whole trip, pilgrims are hosted in *zāwiyas* and the homes of Tijānī families and provided with food.

[41] The FLN, which ruled Algeria after independence, was very close to Ibn Badis and the Salafī movement. Deep doctrinal and political differences set the Salafī-oriented Algerians against the Tijāniyya. They charged the Tijāniyya establishment in Algeria with collaboration with the French colonial authorities and, along the same lines as their Salafī allies, they criticized the veneration of Sufi saints and other Sufi rituals. In addition, the postcolonial Algerian government implemented a socialist development plan, expropriating large latifundia, of which Tijānī were victims.

The Rise to Prominence of West African Pilgrimage Sites

In West Africa itself, several sites of religious pilgrimage are now drawing crowds from all over Africa and the African diaspora. Some of these religious gatherings parallel in scope the great Muslim pilgrimage in the Holy Lands. The largest such gatherings happen during Rabī' al-Awwal, the third month of the Islamic calendar in which the Prophet Muḥammad was born.[42] Hundreds of thousands of people head to major religious cities to celebrate the event. In religious cities like Tivaouane or Medina Baye in Senegal, thousands of people meet every night from the beginning of the month to recite poems in praise of the Prophet and especially the poem named 'Mantle' or Bourda,[43] composed by Sharaf al-Dīn al-Būṣīrī al-Sanhajī (d. 1296). Al-Būṣīrī, so the story goes, suffered a stroke and became paralysed. One night, he dreamed the Prophet Muḥammad covered his paralysed side with a mantle. Awake, he found himself miraculously cured. As a token of his gratitude for the miraculous prophetic intervention, al-Būṣīrī composed this poem, which was the most celebrated of all the panegyrics of the Prophet. The celebration culminates in the night of the twelfth of Rabī' al-Awwal when men and women wear their most beautiful African clothes; for the majority, these will be new clothes. They spend the whole night awake, reciting the Qur'ān and panegyrics of the Prophet. Many will compose new poems in praise of the Prophet, and other Muslim saints. Renowned speakers give lectures centred on the biography (*sīra*) of the Prophet.

In the last few years, the celebration of the *mawlid* has also included organizing academic conferences, in which prominent scholars address issues of concern for Muslims in the world, development, diplomacy; they offer Sufism as a solution to the contemporary problems of Muslims. In the aftermath of 11 September, when Islam became associated with terrorism, many such *mawlid* lectures tend to highlight the role of Sufism in fostering peace as opposed to Wahhabism or Salafism, which they charge as nurturing terrorism and violence. Such academic conferences are celebrated throughout West Africa and the Maghreb.

Because Muslims typically name their children one week after their birth, which is the opportunity for great celebration, the celebration of the Prophet Muḥammad's birth is extended to the seventh day after his birth, considered as the day of naming ceremony (*tasmiya* in Arabic). Many communities celebrate

42 The twelfth Rabī' al-Awwal is the accepted date among most of the Sunni scholars, while Shi'a scholars regard seventeenth Rabī' al-Awwal as the accepted date.

43 The full title is 'al-Kawākib al-durriyya fi madḥ khayr al-bariya' (The Shining Planets or the Eulogy of the best of All creatures). For the full text of the poem and the Arabic translation, see Hamza Boubakeur (trans.) Al-Burda. *Le Manteau. Poème consacré au Prophète de l'islam* (Monteuil: Imprimerie TIPE, 1980).

the day of naming as intensely as the day of the *mawlid* itself. There are other special events centred on the life of West African saints that also draw huge crowds. In Senegambia, the Sufi order of the Murīdiyya organizes a festival every year called Grand Magal de Touba, which is the largest celebration, religious or secular, in Senegal and which has now become one of the most popular pilgrimages in the world. In Wolof, Magal means celebration, and the Great Magal of Touba originates in a request by Amadu Bamba in which he asked that his followers celebrate the anniversary of his exile to Gabon by the French. In the last years three million people had participated in the Magal (one million pilgrims and two million local inhabitants of Touba). The large number of pilgrims in Touba during the Grand Magal demands a huge degree of organization and logistical management. The human and material resources mobilized by the Senegalese state, the Murid Sufi order hierarchy, and the inhabitants of Touba is huge. The police and fire department of the Senegalese state are fully deployed to provide security on the roads and within Touba itself. Murid associations (called *dā'iras*) are responsible for maintaining different pilgrimage sites within Touba itself and for feeding pilgrims.

The Tijāniyya Sufi order also organizes celebrations in West Africa in addition to the *mawlid*. The largest such celebration which parallels in scope the Magal is the annual celebration of the birthday of Shaykh Ibrahim Niasse. Although it is celebrated in many African countries where the Shaykh's disciples reside, the biggest celebration takes place annually in Nigeria, where the number of his disciples runs in the millions. In 2014, the celebration took place in Gombe. According to estimates, there were more than three million people participating in the Greater Pilgrimage to Mecca. All these events celebrated in West Africa are also replicated among the West African diaspora.

Conclusion

I have analysed the transformation of the tradition of Muslim pilgrimage in West Africa and argued that West African Muslims have been performing the pilgrimage to Mecca for a millennium. The spread of Sufi orders from the Maghreb, and especially the Tijāniyya, created new pilgrimage sites in North Africa. Prior to the twentieth century, the trip was long and unsafe. Many would never return home. The majority of pilgrims were students in search of knowledge or scholarly credentials. They spent time along the way or at the pilgrimage sites to study.[44]

[44] Dahlia El-Tayeb Gubara, 'Al-Azhar and the Orders of Knowledge', PhD diss., Department of History, Columbia University, 2014, Chapter 4, which is centred on the biography of Muhammad al-Kashnāwī, a renowned African scholar who left his home from Katsina in present-day Northern Nigeria to perform the *Ḥajj*, spend time

When West Africa fell under European colonial domination in the twentieth century, restrictions were imposed on the travel of citizens by the colonial state which closely monitored the pilgrimage. It determined quotas of Africans allowed to go to the *Ḥajj*. Only 'loyal colonial subjects' were permitted to travel in the colonially sponsored pilgrimage. But the trip was shorter; the roundtrip travel to Mecca lasted between three and six months because pilgrims would sojourn in centres of learning in North Africa and Egypt on their way to the Holy Lands to study. Some of them travelling through Morocco could include a stop in Tangiers and performed the pilgrimage to Fez. It was also safer, as pilgrims possessed proper documentation. They were assisted in the Holy Lands by the colonial consulates based in Jeddah or Riyadh.

It is important to note, however, that many West African pilgrims continued to travel to Mecca overland according to the old pattern of step migration. They created more or less permanent settlements along pilgrimage routes, and especially in Chad and the Sudan. As shown by the works of Birks, Works and Yamba, most of them ended up becoming labour migrants. Only a tiny minority ultimately reached Mecca,[45] unlike those pilgrims who travelled by boat under the auspices of the colonially sponsored pilgrimage.

In the late twentieth century, the nature of and participation in the pilgrimage and conditions of pilgrimage were radically transformed. The Saudi state invested a lot of money to expand hosting infrastructure and to ensure pilgrimage safety. The number of pilgrims multiplied exponentially.

Technological development has now made air travel virtually the only means of travel either to North Africa or the Holy Lands, and many pilgrims are able to visit sites in North Africa and Saudi Arabia in a few days. The shifts in pilgrimage have contributed to fragmenting the pilgrimage tradition and eliminating the itinerant scholar tradition.

Previously scholars and students would visit many of the holy sites along the way to or from the Holy Lands, but now they can simply skip most of these sites by taking a plane. Consequently, the more regional pilgrimages have become separated from the *Ḥajj* pilgrimage tradition. However, pilgrims include many students who go to Morocco, Algeria and Saudi Arabia for studies and take

---

in centres of learning along the way and, in the Holy Lands, learn from and interact with scholars from other regions.

45 J.S. Birks, *Across the Savannas to Mecca. The Overland Pilgrimage Route from West Africa to Mecca* (London: Frank Cass, 1978); John A. Works, *Pilgrims in a Strange Land. Hausa Communities in Chad* (New York: Columbia University Press, 1992); C. Yamba Bawa, *Permanent Pilgrims: The Role of Pilgrimage in the Lives of West African Muslims in Sudan* (Edinburgh: Edinburgh University Press for the International African Institute, London, 1995).

advantage of their position to make pilgrimages. Whereas before, scholars took advantage of the *Ḥajj* to pursue studies, now students take advantage of their international studies to pursue pilgrimages. West African women pilgrims now often outnumber men.[46] Pilgrims also include many young people. The most radical transformation, however, is the emergence of new pilgrimage sites in West Africa that parallel the Holy Lands in Mecca.

As a central pillar of Islam, the *Ḥajj* is one of the best-known and popular pilgrimage traditions in the world, easily recognized and familiar to Muslims and non-Muslims alike. West African participation in this massive global tradition is as old in the region as Islam itself. It has constituted a central feature in the development and flourishing of Islam in West Africa. It has also historically been linked to other important sites and traditions of pilgrimage from the Atlantic coast to the Holy Lands in present-day Saudi Arabia. Modern geopolitical, technological, and economic changes have quite revolutionized practically every aspect of this tradition. As more people and different types of people have engaged in pilgrimage, the nature and purpose of the pilgrimage, the physical conditions of pilgrimage, and many other factors have changed dramatically. So has its effect on the practice of Islam, and especially on Islamic erudition in West Africa, and for that matter, other parts of the Muslim world. This chapter, which is part of a larger project, seeks to document and analyse the current state of affairs in ways that have previously been impossible – both in terms of new ways of observing and documenting the experiences of pilgrimage, but also these new and innovative aspects of the pilgrimage tradition itself. Understanding the importance and the experience of pilgrimage traditions is of critical importance in West Africa, but a deep understanding of the changing nature of pilgrimage in this region could also put us at the cutting edge of understanding the changing nature of one of the most important Islamic rituals, and how this affects Islamic intellectual history on a global scale.

[46] Mbacké, *Le pèlerinage aux lieux saints de l'islam.*

PART II

TEXTUALITY, ORALITY, AND ISLAMIC SCHOLARSHIP

Introduction

Oludamini Ogunnaike

Issues of orality and textuality have been of central concern to the academic study of Islam in Africa from its origins in the accounts of colonial officials, orientalists, and Africanists. On the one hand, the pervasive Hegelian racial mythologies of *Islam noir* divided the continent into a 'white' region north of the Sahara of textuality and written history, and a 'black' sub-Saharan region of 'orality'. Well into the twentieth and twenty-first centuries, some Africanists spoke of sub-Saharan African intellectual traditions as being 'oral' and 'having no written legacy',[1] while some of the scholarship that sought to correct this error by focusing on the written traditions of Islamic learning in sub-Saharan Africa – what Ousmane Kane has dubbed 'Timbuktu studies'[2] – neglected the importance of orality in cultures of Islamic learning both on the continent and abroad, subtly equating intellectual activity with literary production. More recent works on Islamic epistemology and pedagogy in Africa[3] have emphasized the importance of personal transmission and non-discursive practices of the cultivation of *adab* in Islamic learning, emphasizing that performative and oral dimensions of texts – the way in which they are memorized, recited, held and used – tell us just as much, if not more, about the traditions in which they operate, as do their written content. As Walter Ong argued in his famous *Orality and Literacy*, writing allows for a kind of separation of knowledge, knower, and the known difficult to conceive of in an oral culture,[4] and it is precisely this kind of separation between knowledge and

1 For example, J.E. Wiredu, 'How not to compare African traditional thought with Western thought', *Transition* 75/76, 1997, 320–7.

2 Ousmane Kane, *Beyond Timbuktu. An Intellectual History of Muslim West Africa* (Cambridge, MA: Harvard University Press, 2016) 18.

3 Rudolph Ware, *The Walking Qur'ān: Islamic Education, Embodied Knowledge, and History in West Africa* (Chapel Hill: University of North Carolina Press, 2014); Zachary Wright, *Living Knowledge in West African Islam: The Sufi Community of Ibrāhīm Niasse* (Boston: Brill, 2015); Robert Launay (ed.), *Islamic Education in Africa: Writing Boards and Blackboards* (Bloomington: Indiana University Press, 2016).

4 Walter Ong, *Orality and Literacy* (New York: Routledge, 2013) 45–6.

knower that traditional Islamic pedagogies and epistemologies sought to prevent. However, as Ruth Finnegan's work demonstrates, orality and literacy are not two distinct and opposing 'things', but rather operate as mutually influential poles of a continuum, especially in the case of Islamic literatures.[5] The entries in this section each develop new, nuanced approaches to this theme of orality and textuality, challenging many other schemas and much of the received wisdom about Islamic scholarship in Africa in exciting ways.

Ismail Warscheid's '"Those Who Represent the Sovereign in his Absence": Muslim Scholarship and the Question of Legal Authority in the Pre-Modern Sahara' explores the debates surrounding the application of Islamic Law in nomadic, Saharan contexts, specifically those contexts in which there is no legitimate Islamic ruler (*imām*) to appoint judges and enforce their rulings. Challenging long-standing academic assumptions of a divide between rural and urban societies in North and West Africa, Warscheid demonstrates that these eighteenth- and nineteenth-century Saharan scholars conceptualized their rulings as a kind of '"cosmopolitan vernacular": a localized understanding of transcendent legal norms and models'. The legal literature produced by these scholars is thus more than a source of cultural and social history, but a kind of snapshot of a dynamic intellectual tradition in action – as these scholars creatively adapt and apply Islamic legal theories and norms developed in and for urban settings to environments with radically different socio-political institutions, geographies, and material conditions. The examination of this literature reveals a 'kind of circularity' in which the contemporary local contexts are examined from the 'external' perspective of the norms of canonical literature of post-classical Mālikī *fiqh*, which emerged in the past from 'non-local' places, but which is read, interpreted, and applied in a local context, 'on the spot'.

This fascinating dynamic can be seen in the debates surrounding the legal problem of the application of Islamic law outside or on the fringes of the official state authority. The general solution, to have local councils of elites (*jamā'a*) who are 'powerful enough to prevent disorder' stand in place of the sultan, created its own novel and complex debates on the nature of this alliance between judges and local councils. This legal literature provides a glimpse of the process of the creation of new juridical and political institutions and notions of authority through its written traces, which reveal much about the 'unwritten' rules, dynamics, and forces that shaped the development of these societies and, 'closing the circle', the evolution of the legal tradition from which this literature itself emerges.

Oludamini Ogunnaike's entry, 'Philosophical Sufism in the Sokoto Caliphate: The Case of Shaykh Dan Tafa', explores the oeuvre of 'Abd al-Qādir ibn Muṣṭafā

[5] Ruth Finnegan, *Literacy and Orality: Studies in the Technologies of Communication* (London: Callender Press, 2014) 307.

('Dan Tafa') (d. 1864), the grandson of the founder of the Sokoto Caliphate, Shehu Usman dan Fodio. Focusing on Dan Tafa's works of philosophical Sufism and two unique works Dan Tafa wrote on his own intellectual pursuits, Ogunnaike examines the evidence in these texts for the existence of a hitherto unexplored tradition of Islamic philosophy (*falsafa*) in the region, and sheds light on the underexamined tradition of *Akbarī* (Ibn 'Arabī-derived) philosophical Sufism in West Africa. This challenges the long-held notions about the history of Islamic philosophy and philosophical Sufism, namely that the former died out in Western Islamic lands in the twelfth century, and that the latter was not present or prominent in sub-Saharan Africa, and especially not amongst the reformist movements of the eighteenth and nineteenth centuries, of which the leaders of the Sokoto jihād are paradigmatic. However, Dan Tafa wrote a commentary on 'abd al-Karīm al-Jīlī's magnum opus of philosophical Sufism, *al-Insān al-Kāmil*, which he claims to have studied with his uncle Muḥammad Sanbu, who studied it with his father, Usman dan Fodio. Since neither Sanbu nor dan Fodio left behind works on al-Jīlī, this highlights the importance of these kinds of intellectual activity and scholarship that leave behind little or no written traces.

Moreover, in a poem categorizing and describing the various sciences he mastered, Dan Tafa describes three of the six categories of these sciences as 'sciences for which there are neither written texts nor rational proofs' and whose 'elaborated exposition has been forbidden', and in another work he vows to 'keep secret what I possess of the sciences of the spiritual realities and secrets, and to conceal my works regarding these. This is because these sciences are an exalted class of sciences for the spiritually elite and are only designated for those who are spiritually prepared from among the People of God' – posing significant challenges to the traditional, text-based methods of scholars of Islamic intellectual history. When it comes to such intellectual traditions, the absence of written evidence is far from the evidence of absence. Ogunnaike's article concludes with translations of two of Dan Tafa's works, which, in addition to illustrating Dan Tafa's creative adaptations of *Akbarī* philosophical Sufism and philosophy, have a dense and allusive style which suggests that they were meant to be studied with the oral commentary of the author. In fact in one of these commentaries, Dan Tafa himself writes, 'I have made this commentary very condensed as a precaution against unwanted incursion and dissension (*fitna*)' – emphasizing the implicit oral dimensions of these written texts, which somewhat paradoxically, allusively describe forms of knowledge 'for which there are no written texts'.

Furthermore, scholarly work on figures like Dan Tafa should hopefully finally lay to rest the still-prevalent schemas in which the 'legal/traditional' (*naqlī*), the 'rational' ('*aqlī*), and the 'mystical' (*kashfī/ladunī*) are conceived as being opposed to or incompatible with each other, and in which 'rational' logicians, jurists, or historians can't be 'mystics', and *sharī'a*-emphasizing reformers shouldn't be reading Ibn 'Arabī. The empirical evidence suggests the very opposite, and such categorizations tell us more about contemporary conceptions of the 'legal/scriptural', 'rational', and 'mystical' than their supposed counterparts in contexts such as the Sokoto Caliphate. It is likely that Dan Tafa met the subject of the next article, al-ḥājj 'Umar Tal, who died in the same year (1864) and who spent significant time in the court and company of Muḥammad Bello (Dan Tafa's uncle, teacher, and second sultan of the Sokoto Caliphate), on his way back from his pilgrimage.

Farah el-Sharif's chapter '"If all the Legal Schools were to Disappear": 'Umar Tāl's Approach to Jurisprudence in *Kitāb al-Rimāḥ*' highlights an important feature of 'Umar Tal's legal thought that directly challenges received notions that associate anti-*madhhabism* with reformist, Salafī movements and traditionalist Sufism with adherence to a *madhhab*. As el-Sharif demonstrates, 'Umar Tal, like 'Abd al-'Azīz al-Dabbāgh, Aḥmad ibn Idrīs (d. 1837) and Aḥmad al-Tijānī, and even Ibn 'Arabī before him, had a different conception of the methods and sources of *fiqh al-ṭarīqa* than the standard Mālikī or other *madhhabs*. Due to the direct access to the spiritual reality (*ḥaqīqa*) or person (*dhāt*) of the Prophet, which certain Sufis claimed, these encounters with the ever-present Prophet constituted a new source of juridical rulings for Tal. However, this did not lead to an abandonment of the whole structure and tradition of Mālikī fiqh, but rather created a 'vertical' dimension that allowed for direct Prophetic interventions in addition to the standard 'horizontal', historical constructions of juridical rulings based on established legal precedents and procedures.

Moreover, in his magnum opus, *al-Rimāḥ*, Tal describes *fiqh* as a means to an end, namely, *ma'rifa,* the direct encounter with the reality of the Prophet, and access to the deeper or inner meanings of the Qu'rān. So while Salafī reformers advocated cutting through accumulated legal traditions to go back to the Qur'ān and the *Sunna* to derive legal rulings directly from them, Tal emphasizes that the Qur'ān and Prophet are the source of all of the different opinions and procedures of the different *madhhabs*, and advocates going back to this source by following the Tijānī *ṭarīqa*, which promises direct access to the spiritual reality of the Prophet, from whom these legal rulings can be directly derived. For Tāl, this direct spiritual, oral, and even embodied contact with the Prophet supersedes, but does not destroy, the textual, oral, and embodied transmissions from legal scholars, which have a role to play in helping the aspirant attain this direct connection with the Prophet.

This is analogous to the Tijānī conception that Aḥmad al-Tijānī's initiation at the hands of the Prophet in a waking visionary encounter superseded the other chains of Sufi initiation and spiritual and scholarly transmission he had already received, which, from a certain point of view, helped him to attain this close relationship to the Prophet in the first place. The analysis of these complex dynamics forces us to rethink the nature of the relationship between Sufism and *fiqh*, and the characterization of nineteenth-century reform movements, given the central importance of the direct spiritual, personal, and 'oral'/embodied encounters with the spiritual reality of the Prophet, the source of spiritual instruction and legal rulings.

De Diego González's fascinating article takes up the phenomenon of 'e-Sufism', particularly the use of virtual and social media by the *Fayḍa*, a popular Tijānī movement founded by Shaykh Ibrahim Niasse (d. 1975) that spread rapidly through sub-Saharan Africa and abroad in the second half of the twentieth century. De Diego González traces the genealogy of the movement's relationship to mass media technologies, describing the founder's early adoption of the 'new media' of his time such as radio and audiocassettes to the use of WhatsApp, Facebook, and YouTube by the founder's grandchildren and successors. De Diego González argues that the new media of the twenty-first century has come to constitute a new kind of 'orality', in which the *baraka* and *ḥaḍra* (presence) of a Sufi master is contained in audiocassettes and YouTube clips or communicated via Skype or a phone call more directly than in the written transcriptions of their words. The case of the late Ustadh Barham Diop (d. 2014), Ibrahim Niasse's personal secretary and close confidant, is particularly instructive. While regarded as one of the foremost scholars of the *Fayḍa*, Barham Diop left behind very few works; rather, the legacy of his scholarship is captured in the audio and video recordings of his classes in which he lectured on contemporary issues and commented upon the Qur'ān, classic works of Sufism, such as Ibn 'Aṭā Allāh's *Ḥikam*, and especially the poetry and prose works of his teacher, Shaykh Ibrahim Niasse. Interestingly, some of these lectures have been transcribed and translated and now circulate in both written and audio forms, much like Ibrahim Niasse's complete Qu'rānic exegesis, *Fī Riyāḍ al-Tafsīr*.

While the use of mass and new media are usually associated with Salafī reformist movements, and several scholars have noted the similarities in the implicit 'democratizing' structure of these technologies and Salafī epistemologies in which anyone can have access to anything, de Diego González illustrates that these technologies are taken up in a different way in Sufi paradigms, in which they extend the presence (*ḥaḍra*) of the spiritual master, paralleling older Sufi notions of the metaphysical omnipresence of the Prophet and great shaykh, and the 'democratization' of *ma'rifa* (direct, experiential knowledge of God) that is one of the features of the *Fayḍa* movement. Social media platforms such as Facebook have also become an important site of these hybrid oral–textual discourses in which videos of classes, sermons, or recitations of poetry are posted online, commented upon in a unique textual idiom (involving emojis and the unique discourse of text messaging). These technologies have also reshaped the space in which these traditions operate, as de Diego González notes that such virtual content is often most used and driven by those at the physical periphery – those distant from the centres of Dakar and Medina Baye in Senegal. The periphery of the physical becomes, in a sense, the centre of the virtual.

The dynamics and debates about the merits and effects of the traditional forms of orality and textuality and their new, virtual counterparts are most clearly seen in the debates surrounding *tarbiya*, or spiritual training – the process by which disciples are brought to *ma'rifa* – which is the defining feature of the *Fayḍa* movement. Traditionally this was achieved through oral instruction by a qualified master (*shaykh al-murabbī*), the performance of ritual exercises under his or her direct supervision, and spending time in the physical company of the living example of this master. With the advent of new technologies, however, some disciples, especially those outside of Senegal, choose to undergo *tarbiya* virtually – via Skype or phone – connecting with masters located at the order's centre instead of their local representatives. This practice has been hotly debated amongst the *Fayḍa* movement, revealing different conceptions of the nature of the process of *tarbiya* itself.

These forms of new and social media are usually associated with the virtual domain of simulacra *à la* Baudrillard, which eclipses and replaces reality and the possibility of real knowledge by erasing the difference between representation and reality. The migration and adaptation of discourses and practices oriented towards *ma'rifa* – direct, unmediated, existential knowledge of the Real (*al-Ḥaqq*) – into this realm of the virtual is a fascinating, complex, and theoretically rich process which, as de Diego González' article shows, not only changes Sufi discourses and practices and our understanding of them, but could also change the dynamics of 'the virtual' and our understanding of it. What happens when a paradigm of ontological knowledge (*ma'rifa*, which is described as both the knowledge of being and the being of knowledge, as the site where both knowledge and being converge) enters a domain characterized by the de-ontologizing of knowledge? What is the relationship between the erasure of the difference between the Real (*al-Ḥaqq*) and its 'representations' of *ayāt* or *tajallīyāt* (signs or Divine self-disclosures, meaning, all created things) in the Sufi experience of *fanā'* (annihilation, described as the doorway to *ma'rifa*) and the erasure of difference between the reality and representations in the postmodern experience of 'simulation'? It is to be hoped that this article will be among the first of many others in this new and fertile field.

Yunus Kumek's article, 'The Sacred Text in Egypt's Popular Culture', also takes up the use of new technologies to examine the role they play in mediating Qur'ānic text and recitation in the construction of a sacred space of tranquillity or '*sakīna*' in contemporary Cairo. Like de Diego González, Kumek argues that these new media technologies provide 'new vehicles' for concepts and practices with a long history in the Islamic tradition. In this rich ethnography, Kumek examines the conceptions and practices surrounding engagement with the Qur'ān and '*sakīna*' among residents of Madinat Naṣr in Cairo. The Qur'ān itself straddles the continuum from orality to textuality – understood to have been revealed orally, as a recitation (indeed Qur'ān can mean 'recitation' in Arabic) its verses allude to its textual form, especially the separated letters (*al-ḥurūf al-muqaṭṭa'āt*) that begin several of its chapters (such letters only come into being through textuality – purely oral languages have phonemes, not letters). Kumek documents the various ritual, oral, and textual (usually all three simultaneously) engagements with the Qur'ān in public and private spaces to construct a phenomenology of the experience of *sakīna* and how it conditions the experiences of 'poverty and fear' in contemporary Cairo. These engagements (playing mp3s, listening to the radio, reciting the Qur'ān at home or in prayer in a mosque, etc.) are analysed as a kind of 'embodiment' of the Qur'ān in Egyptian popular culture that can create the sacred space of *sakīna* not only in mosques, but also in cars, homes, coffee shops, and even interpersonal relationships, revealing the importance and even centrality of the Qur'ān to the contemporary Cairene soundscape and cultural space.

In summary, each of these papers opens up exciting new directions in the study of Islam not only in Africa, but throughout the world. New perspectives on the study of Saharan legal literature reveal the ways in which legal literature can be used to understand not only the contexts they describe and from which they emerge, but also the dynamics and mechanisms of these legal traditions themselves. New avenues of research in the intellectual history of Islamic West Africa invite us not only to consider the presence and importance of traditions of philosophical Sufism and Islamic philosophy therein, but also the relationship between philosophical Sufism and eighteenth- and nineteenth-century reform movements, and, more generally, the distinction between intellectual activity and literary production and the existence and importance of Islamic sciences and forms of knowledge that leave behind few, if any, written traces. New perspectives on the anti-*madhhabism* of nineteenth-century reform movements invite us to reconsider the relationship between *fiqh* and Sufism and to more carefully consider the radical reformations of Islamic traditions made possible by the phenomenon of 'direct contact' with the Prophet.

New perspectives on the complex dynamics surrounding and resulting from the migration of Sufi discourse and practice from people and texts, to audiocassettes and radio, to videotapes, to digital and social media invite us to reconsider the nature of these 'new forms of textuality and orality', their relationships to older forms of textuality and orality, as well as the convergence of contemporary 'traditional' Sufi epistemes with 'postmodern' technologies. Finally, new perspectives on popular engagements with the Qur'ān invite us to consider the way in which the Qur'ān, in both its oral and textual presences, is used to construct and maintain adaptive, sacred spaces (*sakīna*) in contemporary Egyptian culture and environments. By taking novel perspectives on Islamic scholarship in Africa, the studies in this part invite us to extend their insights and new avenues of inquiry beyond these particular, local contexts to establishing new directions in the study of Islam, Africa, and knowledge in a global context.

CHAPTER 5

'Those Who Represent the Sovereign in his Absence': Muslim Scholarship and the Question of Legal Authority in the Pre-Modern Sahara (Southern Algeria, Mauritania, Mali), 1750–1850

Ismail Warscheid

In one of his legal opinions (*fatwā*, pl. *fatāwā*), Muḥammad b. ʿAbd al-Raḥmān al-Tinilānī (d. 1233/1817–18), a Muslim scholar from the oases of Tuwāt in present-day southern Algeria, compares the work of *qāḍīs* and muftis in his region with legal practice in Fez, which was then one of the most prominent centres of Islamic learning in Western Africa:

> There is no difference in the nature of legal decisions issued in our country and those issued in Fes. The principles of the sharia do not vary when countries change and differences between them become apparent. This is because the message of our Prophet, peace and blessings be upon him, is of universal validity, directed to all of humanity and to any place in the world.[1]

Al-Tinilānī's fatwā emphasizes the claim of Islamic law to be universal and, furthermore, insists on a fundamental equality between all Muslims with regard to their duties and rights. His conception of what I would call an Islamic legal space is nonetheless a hierarchical one. The mufti implicitly distinguishes between a centre and a periphery. His fatwā refers to the city of Fez as the natural environment for the application of Islamic religious and legal norms. Like many of his contemporaries, al-Tinilānī identifies these norms as being inherent to settled urban life (*ḥaḍāra*). However, he maintains that they are transferable to any

[1] '*Lā farqa fī hadhā bayna kawn al-taḥākum bi-bilādinā aw bi-Fās li-anna aḥkām al-sharʿ lā tabdilu bi-tabaddul al-bilād wa-ikhtilāfihā li-anna risāla nabiyinā ṣallā Allāh ʿalayhi wa-sallam ʿāma fī jamīʿ al-nās wa-fī kulli'l-bilād*': M. al-Balbālī and A. al-Balbālī, *al-Ghuniyat al-muqtaṣid al-sāʾil fī-mā waqaʿa fī Tuwāt min al-qaḍāyā wa-l-masāʾil* (Lemtarfa, MS *khizāna* Lemtarfa collection): f. 635.

geographical and social context, since they emanate from a divine revelation. Seen from this vantage, his position – and the very existence of his fatwā – challenges the long-standing tradition of Western scholarship to postulate a 'great divide' separating rural and urban societies in North and West Africa.[2]

A few decades later, another Saharan jurist, Muḥammad al-Māmī (d. 1282/1865–6), a nomad from the Tiris region in present-day northern Mauritania, provides a fairly different account on the relationship between Islamic legal scholarship as a part of 'urban civilization' (*'umrān*) and the 'nomad way of life' (*badāwa*), to speak in Khaldunian terms.[3] In his *Book of the Desert* (*Kitāb al-Bādiya*), he writes:

> It appeared to our scholars [...] that there are many questions peculiar to the inhabitants of the desert (*masā'il ahl al-bādiya al-khāṣa bihim*) on which no one has made authoritative statements [literally: no one has spoken] and on which no writings (*muṣannaf*) exist ... This is because legal literature originates from cities (*madīniyya*). However, urban people in general speak of their own affairs or, at most, on questions they have in common with us. They are silent about topics proper to the people of the desert. This is either because they cannot imagine these questions within their living conditions or because of the prohibition on them to speak about custom (*'urf*) that is not the custom of their region. Therefore, if we submit to them our questions, we have to make them ask us about our customs. However, [their silence is also due to the fact] that they have no interest in [our affairs], since urban civilization (*tamaddun*) is obligatory for them and nomadism considered as something reprehensible (*tabaddī manhī 'anhu*).[4]

[2] Especially with regard to the pre-modern period, Islamic legal traditions and institutions are generally thought to have had little impact on rural contexts where different types of customary law are supposed to have regulated most forms of social interaction. It might be useful to remember that the model of a great divide found one of its most elaborate, and also most uncompromising, expressions in Ernest Gellner's work on the Maghreb, mainly his *Saints of the Atlas* (Chicago: Chicago University Press, 1969) and *Muslim Society* (Cambridge: Cambridge University Press, 1981). Drawing on French colonial sociology, David Hume's *Natural History of Religion* and Ibn Khaldūn's theory of civilization, Gellner depicts normative order in North Africa as having been constantly shaped by the antagonism between a state-controlled urban Islam and a more or less autonomous rural environment where, instead of literate legal specialists, charismatic saints and tribal councils were the main actors of social regulation and, instead of the *sharī'a*, custom law the main, if not the only, source of legislation.

[3] Abdesselam Cheddadi, *Ibn Khaldûn: l'homme et le théoricien de la civilization* (Paris: Gallimard, 2006).

[4] al-Shaykh Muḥammad al-Māmī al-Bukhārī al-Bārikī, *Kitāb al-Bādiya wa nuṣūṣ ukhrā* (Rabat: Centre d'études sahariennes, 2014) 175.

It was both the absence of authoritative legal works dealing with the specific concerns of Saharan nomadic people and the ambition to contribute as a scholar from the 'Land in-between' (*bilād al-fiṭra*) to the juristic debates of his time that seem to have motivated al-Māmī to write one of the most original contributions to Islamic legal thought in pre-modern West Africa. In his book, which has only recently been edited, al-Māmī not only discusses the implementation of the *sharī'a* in Bedouin society. He also addresses one of the main epistemological issues within Muslim jurisprudence during the postclassical period, namely the relationship between independent legal reasoning (*ijtihād*) and commitment to established school doctrine (*taqlīd*).[5] It is precisely al-Māmī's Saharan background that allows him to connect the two themes: since many legal cases (*nāzila*, pl. *nawāzil*) and questions (*mas'ala*, pl. *masā'il*) pertaining to life in the desert have not received appropriate treatment in the urban-shaped literature of the *malikı* school, local jurists in their functions as muftis and *qāḍīs* are forced to find their own answers. They thus engage in a form of legal positivism for which Muḥammad al-Māmī intends to construct a doctrinal framework centred around what Sherman Jackson has called the '*ijtihād* of the *muqallid*-jurisconsult', that is the procedure of extrapolation from authoritative school texts (*takhrīj*) and the 'pondering' of legal opinions (*tarjīḥ*).[6]

The positions defended by Muḥammad b. ʿAbd al-Raḥmān al-Tinilānī and his Mauritanian colleague Muḥammad al-Māmī regarding the transposition of the *sharī'a* from urban to rural contexts perfectly summarizes the hermeneutical challenge that was posed to Muslim scholars by the large-scale diffusion of Islamic literate culture in the pre-modern Sahara. From the sixteenth century onwards, in what are today Algeria, Mauritania, and Mali, the multiplication of places of religious learning, controlled by saintly and scholarly lineages, fostered the diffusion of Islamic law in both sedentary and nomadic contexts. Forms of social ordering were progressively refashioned through the encounter between the customary institutions of local groups and two instances of normative regulation that had hitherto been limited to urban contexts: Islamic jurisdiction (*al-shar'*) and notarial certification (*tawthīq*). However, as al-Māmī rightly stresses in his *Kitāb al-Bādiya*, the social environment in which the agents of these institutions had to

[5] Ismail Warscheid, 'Le *Livre du désert*: la vision du monde d'un lettré musulman de l'Ouest saharien au XIXe siècle', *Annales: Histoire, Sciences Sociales* 73, 2, 2018, 359–84. See also Mohammed Fadel, 'The Social Logic of *taqlīd* and the Rise of the *Mukhtaṣar*', *Islamic Law and Society*, 3, 2, 1996, 193–233; Wael Hallaq, *Authority, Continuity and Change in Islamic Law* (Cambridge: Cambridge University Press, 2004); Sherman Jackson, *Islamic Law and the State: The Constitutional Jurisprudence of Shihāb al-Dīn al-Qarāfī* (Leiden: Brill, 1996).

[6] Jackson, *Islamic Law*, 94.

work were different from that of their urban counterparts. Muslim judges, muftis, and notaries were to operate in areas beyond direct state control, whose inhabitants governed themselves through institutions based on community autonomy, lineage structure, and clan solidarity (*ʿaṣabiya*). Furthermore, they had to face a situation of 'weak' legal pluralism:[7] jurisdictional authority had to be shared with other normative institutions outside the *sharīʿa* system, commonly referred to as 'custom law'.[8] In short, Islamic cultural and legal models had to be considerably reinterpreted in order to accommodate the particularities of local contexts.

The process of creative appropriation and adaptation of Islamic law in its *mālikī* version eventually led to the constitution of a regional tradition of legal thought. It leaves us with a rich literary heritage which comes in the form of biographical dictionaries, commentaries (*sharḥ*, pl. *shurūḥ*), treatises such as the *Kitāb al-Bādiya*, and, most importantly, hundreds of comprehensive collections of legal opinions (*nawāzil*; *ajwiba*).[9] In these fatwā collections – the most ancient known dates back to the end of the seventeenth century and is attributed to the Chinguetti scholar Ibn al-Aʿmash (d. 1107/1695–6) – the integration of Islamic law within the local cultural milieu is most perceptible. While perpetuating the classical tradition of legal consultation (*iftāʾ*),[10] these collections allow us indeed to reconstruct not only the development of an intellectual tradition that linked scholarly circles from the southern Maghreb to the edge of the Sahel, but also the multiple ways in which local populations made use of *sharʿī* institutions and devices.

[7] Lauren Benton, *Law and Colonial Cultures: Legal Regimes in World History 1400–1900* (Cambridge: Cambridge University Press, 2002) 11.

[8] Ismail Warscheid, *Droit musulman et société au Sahara prémoderne : la justice islamique dans les oasis du Grand Touat (Sud algérien) XVIIe–XIXe siècles* (Leiden: Brill, 2017) 185–207.

[9] Chouki El Hamel, *La vie intellectuelle islamique dans le Sahel ouest-africain, XVIe–XIXe siècles: une étude sociale de l'enseignement islamique en Mauritanie et au nord du Mali, XVIe–XIXe siècles, et trad. annotée de 'Fatḥ al-šakūr' d'al-Bartīlī al-Walātī (mort en 1805)* (Paris: l'Harmattan, 2002); John O. Hunwick, *Arabic Literature of Africa Volume 4: The Writings of Western Sudanic Africa* (Leiden: Brill, 2003); Rainer Osswald, *Schichtengesellschaft und islamisches Recht : die Zawāyā und Krieger der Westsahara im Spiegel von Rechtsgutachten des 16.–19. Jahrhundert* (Wiesbaden: Harrasowitz Verlag, 1993); Ulrich Rebstock, *Maurische Literaturgeschichte*, 3 vols. (Würzburg: Ergon, 2001); Charles Stewart, *Arabic Literature of Africa Volume 5: the Writings of Mauritania and the Western Sahara*, 2 vols. (Leiden: Brill, 2016); Ismail Warscheid, 'Entre mémoire lettrée et vécu institutionnel: la compilation de nawāzil dans le grand Touat (Algérie) aux XVIIIe et XIXe siècles', *Studia Islamica* 108, 2 (2013) 214–54.

[10] Muhammad Khalid Masud; Brinkley Messick; David Powers (eds.), *Islamic Legal Interpretations: Muftis and their Fatwas* (Harvard: Harvard University Press, 1996).

Recent research has demonstrated the relevance of this literature as a source for the region's social and cultural history.[11] Relying on fatwās and other legal texts, Ghislaine Lydon's study of trans-Saharan trade networks in the nineteenth century has stressed the importance of Muslim jurists as 'legal service providers' in developing normative structures across the great desert that provided 'a semblance of social and economic order'.[12] My exploration of Islamic legal institutions in eighteenth-century Tuwāt, which is based on the examination of five local *nawāzil* collections, concurs with Lydon's observations. Islamic courts were able to operate without state support by integrating community institutions within their organizational framework.[13] In his pioneering study on the social history of Timbuktu, published in 1983, Elias Saad had already observed a similar pattern of governance, though he did not make use of legal sources.[14] Lastly, Bruce Hall has shown the impact of the writings of Saharan jurists such as Ibn al-Aʿmash or the late Kunta scholar Bāy al-Kuntī (d. 1929) on the evolution of inter-ethnic relations in the Niger Belt in the long term.[15]

However, there is more to it. As a literary genre, fatwā collections, like any other type of legal writing, are foremost normative texts. When discussing local issues, the intention of jurists is not so much to preserve the cultural memory of their communities as to think of these issues as a normative problem that, at one moment, has come up either as a case (*rafaʿat al-nāzila*) or as a generic question (*masʾala*). In other words, when using legal texts as a historical source, we must imperatively take into account their technical aspects. A kind of circularity is observable in how Saharan jurists reflect on their environment. Local issues are examined with the help of legal models and concepts derived from the authoritative literature of the *fiqh* and the *mālikī* school in particular. Although most of these works must be considered 'external' and relate to past times, their referential use is, however, embedded in local contexts. Textual comprehension and interpretation emerge, so to say, 'here and now'. In this respect, the juristic debates

[11] Bruce Hall, *A History of Race in Muslim West Africa: 1600–1960* (Cambridge: Cambridge University Press, 2011); Ghislaine Lydon, *On Trans-Saharan Trails: Islamic Law, Trade Networks, and Cross-Cultural Exchange in Nineteenth Century Western Africa* (Cambridge: Cambridge University Press, 2009); Rainer Osswald, *Sklavenhandel und Sklavenleben zwischen Senegal und Atlas* (Wiesbaden: Ergon Verlag, 2016); Judith Scheele, *Smugglers and Saints of the Sahara: Regional Connectivity in the Twentieth Century* (Cambridge: Cambridge University Press, 2012); Ismail Warscheid, *Droit musulman.*

[12] Lydon, *On Trans-Saharan trails*, 275.

[13] Warscheid, *Droit musulman.*

[14] Elias N. Saad, *A Social History of Timbuktu* (Cambridge: Cambridge University Press, 1983).

[15] Hall, *A History.*

about the local application of legal norms and procedures are tantamount to the gradual formation of a regional tradition of legal reasoning that situates itself in the wider context of postclassical Malikism. The main result is what I would call, transposing Sheldon Pollock's philological concept, the emergence of 'a cosmopolitan vernacular': a localized understanding of transcendent legal norms and models.[16] This chapter explores some aspects of this process. I first expose how scholars from the oases of Tuwāt relied on local governance structures to ensure the implementation of legal decisions during the eighteenth and the early nineteenth centuries. Then I turn to the conception of political authority to be found in al-Māmī's *Kitāb al-Bādiya*.

Community Structures and Islamic Law in Eighteenth-century Tuwāt

The creation of any legal institution necessarily entails claims of legitimacy and sovereignty. In the case of Islam, the existence of qāḍī courts, assisted by trained muftis, guarantees the application of the sacred law in society and, thereby, not only confers legitimacy to its political and legal institutions, but also ensures its place within the *dār al-islām*, the part of the world where *sharīʿa* law is observed. According to classical Muslim political thought, the implementation of God's law (*iqāmat al-sharʿ*), through the appointment and the supervision of judges, are among the most prominent duties of the *imām*, the legitimate political ruler in Islam.[17] But then a question arises: what about those regions that are situated outside or at the margins of the Islamic state, yet inhabited by Muslim populations practising their religion? Shall they invariably be assigned to the status of communities that are deprived of the foundational attachment to a legitimate Islamic ruler (*bilād al-sāʾiba*), which sustains integration into the global Muslim community (*Umma*)?[18] Or can such political and legal legitimacy also exist without the patronage of the *imām*? These are classic problems of Islamic jurisprudence, though they have not yet received much attention from legal historians. In the political context of the pre-modern Sahara, such debates were of utmost importance. They led to the development of a constitutional doctrine that tried to

[16] Sheldon Pollock, 'A New Philology: From Norm-Bound Practice to Practice-Bound Norm in Kannada Intellectual History', in Jean-Luc Chevillard (ed.), *South-Indian Horizons: Felicitation Volume for François Gros* (Pondichéry: Institut Français de Pondichéry/Ecole Française d'Extrême-Orient, 2004) 400–1.

[17] See Emile Tyan, *Histoire de l'organisation judiciaire en pays d'Islam* (Leiden: Brill, 1960).

[18] Houari Touati, 'Le prince et la bête : enquête sur une métaphore pastorale', *Studia Islamica*, 83, 1996, 101–19.

counterbalance the absence of direct administrative state control by endorsing the power of local community institutions in legal and political matters.[19]

Since the Saadian conquest of the Songhay Empire at the end of the sixteenth century, many parts of the western and central Sahara formally recognized the Moroccan sultan as the legitimate *imām*. However, the allegiance of nomadic groups and oasis dwellers to the sultan was scarcely equivalent to state-controlled administration, as this may have been the case of the coastal regions of Western Morocco (*al-Gharb*). On the contrary, even in areas such as the oases of Tuwāt, where agents sent by the Moroccan state (*makhzan*) regularly levied taxes and whose most influential *qāḍīs* were nominated by the sultan, local communities remained autonomous in dealing with internal affairs. Indeed, official appointments of judges (*tawliya*) seem to have rather been intended to consecrate the judicial activities of established local scholarly families (*dār*, *bayt*)[20] to which all *makhzan*-invested judges belonged. Thus the Moroccan state did not interfere with the self-government of the oases and, rather than exercising direct control, sought to establish alliances with the local notability, mainly in order to ensure tax payments.[21] From a local point of view, the authority of the sultan was perceived as being distant and fragile, often threatening and even unjust at times given the extreme violence that characterized tax collection expeditions (*ḥarka*). Therefore, if local populations were to adopt the institutions and symbols of an Islamic polity, their scholars had to find ways to do so without the presence of the sultan.

In the case of Tuwāt, local jurists adopted a legal solution developed by medieval Mālikī scholars such as Abū ʿImrān al-Fāsī (d. 430/1039) that considers the 'community of the faithful' (*jamāʿat al-muslimīn*) to be the legitimate representative of the *imām* in his absence (*man qāma bi-maqām al-imām fī ghiyābihi*). Commenting on the nomination of local judges, the eighteenth-century mufti Muḥammad al-ʿĀlim al-Zajlāwī summarizes the theory as follows:

19 Some preliminary studies have been realised on the topic. See Rahal Boubrik, 'Les fuqahâ' du prince et le prince des fuqahâ': discours politique des hommes de religion au pays maure (Mauritanie, XVIIe–XIXe siècle)', *Afrique et histoire* 7, 1 (2009) 153–72; Abdel Wedoud Ould Cheikh, 'Théologie du désordre : Islam, ordre et désordre au Sahara', *L'année du Maghreb*, 7, 2011, 61–77; Warscheid, *Droit musulman*, 158–84.

20 Cf. Houari Touati, 'Les héritiers: anthropologie des Maisons de sciences maghrébines aux XIe /XVIIe et XIIe /XVIIIe siècles', in Hassan Elboudrari (ed.), *Modes de transmission de la culture religieuse en Islam* (Le Caire: Publications de l'IFAO, 1993) 65–92.

21 Ismail Warscheid, 'Les Jours du Makhzen: levée d'impôt et relations communautaires dans les oasis du Touat (Sud algérien), 1700–1850', *Revue d'histoire du XIXe siècle*, 59, 2019, 31–48.

> Concerning the question of the appointment of a judge by the community (*jamāʿa*), who is then competent in all domains that fall within the area of responsibility of the qāḍī, Shaykh Sālim has reported the principle according to which in regions situated outside the authority of the legitimate ruler (*imām*) the local virtuous people must take his place. In the same way, al-Nafrāwī wrote in his commentary on the *Risāla*: usually, it is the sovereign or his local representative, under the condition that he is a man of integrity, who appoints the *qāḍīs*. In the absence of these two authorities, it falls to the Muslim community to proceed to nominations, as well as it is its duty to exercise the other prerogatives of the legitimate ruler.[22]

The abstract wording of the fatwā should not mislead us. The expression *jamāʿat al-muslimīn* refers to the most important political institution in rural North Africa, namely the council of the notables of a given community (*jamāʿa*), may it be a village or a nomadic group. The powers accorded to the *jamāʿa* were not limited to the appointment of judges. Since qāḍī courts did not exist in all parts of the region, Tuwātī jurists conceded the *jamāʿa* council to act in such cases as their substitute in all administrative matters. These included the management of *ḥubus*/*waqf* endowments, the appointment of trustees for orphans and other legally incapable persons (*maḥjūr*), the enforcement of subsistence payments (*nafaqa*) for women from their husbands or even pronouncement of divorce on grounds of harm (*ḍarar*).[23] Moreover, they acknowledged the right of the *jamāʿa* to supervise the exploitation of collective natural resources, mainly the irrigation system in the oases, to regulate the expansion of private propriety (*milk*) over unoccupied land (*mawwāt*) and to control operations of 'vivification' (*iḥyāʾ*). Thus, it is hardly surprising that in cases of litigation between individuals and community councils, the latter's the authority was generally enforced. Abū'l-Anwār al-Tinilānī, a scholar from the Tidikelt region in southern Tuwāt, rejects for example in one of his fatwās the complaint of a man who contested the concession of a *mawwāt* plot to another person by the *jamāʿa* of his village many years earlier, pretending that the land belonged to his ancestors. In his fatwā, the mufti argues that the decision of the *jamāʿa* had created a legal fact that is now binding.[24]

The strong support given to the *jamāʿa* reflects an enduring political alliance between 'maraboutic' families (*mrābṭīn*), to which most scholars belonged, and 'secular' notable families, mainly the powerful *shurafāʾ* lineages, who were heavily involved in caravan trade between Morocco and the Niger Bend. Both groups closely cooperated in the administration of public affairs, as illustrates the narrative by the eighteenth-century mufti ʿAbd al-Raḥmān al-Tinilānī (d. 1189/1775)

[22] al-Balbālī, *Ghuniya*, 616.

[23] Warscheid, *Droit musulman*, 173–9.

[24] Muḥammad al-Zajlāwī, *Nawāzil*, Lemtarfa Library MS, 87.

of a lawsuit that took place in the small village of Zaouiet Kounta situated in the south of Tuwāt:

> Mawlāy Zayn and Ubba Ḥammū b. ʿAbd al-Raḥmān have been appointed legal representatives (*wakīl*) in the presence and with the approval of the mentioned council [the jamāʿa of Zaouiet Kounta] and its *qāḍī* al-Sayyid Muḥammad b. ʿAbd al-Muʾmin. They then proceeded to the deduction of his expenses (*muḥāsaba*) from the father's inheritance. At the end of the process, the elder brother asked me in presence of the council, its doyen (*kabīr*) Mawlāy ʿAbd al-Raḥmān b. ʿAlī, and the aforementioned *qāḍī*, whether Mawlāy al-ʿArabī's claims against him have now been fulfilled. I answered him that such is indeed the case and that the act is enforceable and irrevocable.[25]

The consequences of the alliance between Muslim legal scholars and those who held 'worldly power' (*ṣāḥib al-jāh*) in their communities were twofold: on the one hand, religious and legal legitimacy was conferred to the oligarchic order that prevailed in most oasis regions in pre-modern North and West Africa where political power at the local level was distributed among members of competing lineages. Furthermore, the interventions of these elites in order to provide a minimum of public order were converted into legal actions in accordance with *sharīʿa* norms. On the other hand, by recognizing customary institutions such as the *jamāʿa*, Muslim scholars could recline upon them in legal procedures. As the example quoted above illustrates, *qāḍīs* and muftis worked hand in hand with community councils.

The *nawāzil* compilations from Tuwāt, furthermore, inform us that members of *jamāʿa* councils also served as professional witnesses (*shuhūd*) and legal experts (*ʿurrāf*). In this case again, local jurists strove to provide a legal justification for the social fact of collaboration between religious and 'secular' elites. The *fiqh* prescribes that any testimony to be thoroughly valid must be given by an individual recognized as a person of integrity (*ʿadl*). However, the criteria to assess such integrity are defined according to values and norms associated with urban society. Therefore, the question of whether such integrity (*ʿadāla*) may exist in rural areas has been one of the most controversial debates in North African Malikism.[26] Most jurists, those of Tuwāt included, took a sceptical attitude towards the matter, deploring the 'corruptness' (*fasād*) and 'ignorance' (*jahl*) of many professional witnesses.[27] Nonetheless, community life could not do without the existence of a body of reliable *shuhūd* who ensured the legal validity of transactions and judicial

[25] al-Balbālī, *Ghuniya*, 236.

[26] Cf. Jacques Berque, *Ulémas, fondateurs, insurgés du Maghreb* (Paris: Sindbad, 1982) 215–17.

[27] Warscheid, *Droit musulman*, 175–9.

procedures.[28] How did the jurists from Tuwāt then resolve this dilemma? They did so in a quite pragmatic manner by stipulating that 'in those areas where it is impossible to find upright witnesses, the testimony of those who are among the most virtuous (*afḍal*) of their respective community will be accepted'.[29] Despite the abstract wording, the argument is straightforward: the establishment of legal facts is incumbent on local notables (*aʿyān*), since Muslim scholars hardly expected to find such virtuousness among subaltern groups.[30]

Thus, the accreditation of community councils and their members confirmed and sustained the local political and social order as the backbone of *sharʿī* legal practice. In effect, the implementation of *sharīʿa* law in the oases of Tuwāt rested entirely upon village communities and their leading figures, as illustrates the following request for a fatwā (*istiftāʾ*) addressed to ʿAbd al-Raḥmān al-Jantūrī (d. 1160/1747), a scholar from the Gourara region. We learn from it that the notables (*aʿyān*) of the oasis of Tinerkouk had once gathered to create a weekly market. During their deliberations, a *qāḍī* was appointed as the only person entitled to settle future disputes concerning transactions concluded on the market. It was further agreed that litigants had the right to submit copies of rulings issued by the qāḍī to ʿAbd al-Raḥmān al-Jantūrī for verification.[31] Seen from this vantage, the doctrinal reasoning in which Tuwātī jurists engaged appears as a decisive element in local judicial institution building. In this contribution, I can only offer a glimpse of the complexity of this process. Much more needs to be said, since the authority of the *jamāʿa* was not always unchallenged. Not every villager felt compelled to submit to community decisions and the recourse to Islamic courts and legal specialists could also be intended to oppose such decisions.[32] Likewise, the cooperation between jurists and village councils was often fraught with tensions. The few examples presented here nonetheless indicate that the analogy drawn between the *jamāʿa* council and the community of Muslims provided the theoretical foundation upon which Islamic legal institutions could be built within a pluricentric political system.

[28] On these aspects, see also Christian Müller, *Der Kadi und seine Zeugen: Studie der mamlukischen Ḥaram-Dokumente aus Jerusalem* (Wiesbaden: Harrasowitz, 2013).

[29] al-Balbālī, *Ghuniya*, 670.

[30] On traditional social hierarchies in Saharan societies, see Remco Ensel, *Saint and Servants in Southern Morocco* (Leiden: Brill, 1999); Urs Peter Ruf, *Ending Slavery: Hierarchy, Dependency, and Gender in Central Mauritania* (Bielefeld: Transcript Verlag, 1999); Marielle Villasante-de Beauvais (ed.), *Groupes serviles au Sahara: approche comparative à partir du cas des arabophones de Mauritanie* (Paris: Éd. du CNRS, 2000).

[31] ʿAbd al-Raḥmān al-Jantūrī, *Nawāzil*, Badriane Library MS, 166.

[32] Warscheid, *Droit musulman*, 117–27.

The 'Land in-between' (*bilād al-fitra*)

Let us now turn to Muḥammad al-Māmī's *Kitāb al-Bādiya*. Scholars have already highlighted the singularity of the work within the history of Muslim scholarship in Western Africa.[33] However, it still awaits an in-depth study that fully explores the legal doctrines developed by its author. This is deplorable, for the *Kitāb al-Bādiya* is one of the most original contributions by a Saharan scholar to the development of Islamic legal thought in the postclassical age. Unfortunately, a detailed discussion of the work is beyond the scope of this paper. Therefore, I will concentrate on how Muḥammad al-Māmī deals with the question of legitimate political power as a prerequisite for the existence of Islamic legal institutions.

As mentioned above, the author of the *Kitāb al-Bādiya* was a nineteenth-century nomadic scholar, Sufi, and saint who spent most of his life as a member of the Ahl Bārik Allāh 'maraboutic' tribe (*zawāya*)[34] in the region of Tiris in northern Mauritania, where his tomb is still known as a pilgrimage site (*qabruhu yuzār*).[35] Like many other Saharan scholars, Muḥammad al-Māmī received his initial training from his close relatives, but acquired most of his knowledge as an autodidact through the collection and reading of books.[36] Even though al-Māmī travelled extensively in present-day Mauritania and Senegal, there is no indication that he received teaching certificates (*ijāza*, pl. *āt*) from local scholars, nor that he visited other parts of North and West Africa or the Middle East in order to 'seek knowledge' (*riḥla li-ṭalab al-ʿilm*) from distinguished authorities of his time.[37] Conversely, according to the editors of the *Kitāb al-Bādiya*, he attracted numerous disciples among his kin, as well as from other nomadic groups of the region. Even the name of a member of the Kunta confederation is mentioned in this context.[38] What is more important for our purpose here is that he was a prolific writer, acclaimed for both his legal works and his poetry, some of which is composed in the local Hassāniya dialect.[39] His talents as a poet also served his work as a jurist, since many of his poems deal with legal questions. Furthermore, he versified the standard reference book of the Mālikī school in his time, the *Mukhtaṣar* of Khalīl b. Isḥāq (d. 776/1374), which was widely read in the region.

33 Boubrik, 'Les fuqahâ' du prince'; Ould Cheikh, 'Théologie'.

34 Cf. Charles Stewart, *Islam and Social Order in Mauritania: A Case Study from the 19th Century* (Oxford: Clarendon Press, 1973).

35 al-Māmī, *Kitāb*, 9. For al-Māmī's biography, see also Ould Cheikh, 'Théologie'.

36 al-Māmī, *Kitāb*, 24–5.

37 Houari Touati, *Entre Dieu et les hommes : lettrés, saints et sorciers au Maghreb 17e siècle* (Paris: Ed. de l'EHESS, 1994) 31–4.

38 al-Māmī, *Kitāb*, 30.

39 al-Māmī, *Kitāb*, 27.

The *Kitāb al-Bādiya* is undoubtedly al-Māmī's *opus magnum*. In his introduction (*muqaddima*), the author qualifies it as a *majmū'*, a compilation, since it contains a series of letters dealing with the local application of *shar'ī* norms. The editors of the text presume that al-Māmī decided to compile these letters shortly after finishing his versification of the *Mukhtaṣar* around 1236/1820. Both works appear indeed quite complementary with regard to al-Māmī's profile as a legal scholar. The versification of the *Mukhtaṣar* illustrates a firm commitment to post-classical *mālikī* doctrine, which is also expressed in some of his poems.[40] But such commitment does not preclude an active endeavour to 'catch the *fiqh*, since otherwise it will slip from hands'.[41] This is to say that the different letters, assembled into four chapters (*tamliya*), contain a thorough examination of the possibilities to maintain legal structures based on *mālikī* law in the nomadic context of the western Sahara, while at the same time engaging in a reflection on norm creation under the regime of *taqlīd*.[42] In short, the *Kitāb al-Bādiya* represents a genuine attempt to discuss local legal practice from the perspective of legal hermeneutics (*uṣūl al-fiqh*).

According to Muḥammad al-Māmī, the western Sahara, being inhabited by nomadic people, must be seen as a 'Land in-between' (*bilād al-fitra*), a kind of no man's land situated between the Kingdom of Morocco and the Islamic states of the Sahel.[43] By this, al-Māmī refers to both a geographical space and a legal category subsuming the local modalities of *shar'ī* norm application. Its characteristics are defined in relation to the spatial and political distance separating them from urban centres. Rural dwellers who live close to cities have to submit to the decisions of urban legal institutions, since these can be still applied there.[44] In those areas, however, 'that are not attained by such decisions, nor are governed by a ruler (*za'īm*)',[45] the implementation of *shar'ī* norms is subjected to peculiar conditions that al-Māmī purports to expose. They represent a separate category, the world of the Bedouins (*al-bādiya*) as opposed to urban settled life (*al-ḥaḍāra*). Muḥammad al-Māmī not only considers the existence of a legitimate Islamic ruler as relevant for the application of Islamic law. He further takes into account the particularities of Bedouin life, which leads him to distinguish between two different regimes of legal practice. If one may say so, Ibn Khaldūn's civilizational theory is translated into the language of *fiqh*, though al-Māmī makes no direct allusion to

[40] al-Māmī, *Kitāb*, 26.
[41] al-Māmī, *Kitāb*, 128.
[42] See Jackson, *Islamic Law*.
[43] On the conception of the western Sahara as an intermediary space, see also Ould Cheikh, 'Théologie'.
[44] al-Māmī, *Kitāb*, 177.
[45] al-Māmī, *Kitāb*.

the author of the *Muqaddima*. Discussing the *shar'ī* norm of 'covering the private parts of the body' (*sitr al-'awra*) and, more generally, the question of male/female segregation, Muḥammad al-Māmī argues, for example, that its full application is virtually impossible given the mobile lifestyle of pastoral groups.[46] The absolute obligation of such groups to constantly move between different places creates an imperative need (*ḍarūra*) that may partially suspend the strict prohibition of any direct male–female interaction outside marriage and close kin relations. The author compares this kind of justified departure from established school doctrine due to social necessities with similar regulations in urban contexts concerning the hammam as a public institution, which makes it possible for townspeople to perform their ritual ablutions without being obliged to leave the city.

Like the scholars from Tuwāt, Muḥammad al-Māmī thus takes the absence of a legitimate Islamic ruler (*imām*) as the starting point for his analysis. However, his discussion of the relation between political authority and legal order addresses a question that is lacking in the fatwā compilations from Tuwāt, namely the question of Islamic penal law. For al-Māmī, the existence or absence of a political actor who imposes the implementation of Qur'ānic punishments (*iqāmat al-ḥudūd*) is the main criterion for evaluating its legitimacy in Islamic terms.[47] This actor can be either a single ruler or the *jamā'a* council. Consider the following passage where Muḥammad al-Māmī discusses different types of political entities to be found in areas that are outside the scope of cities' authority:

> If someone [from the inhabitants of these areas] seizes power (*yataghallab*), obedience (*ṭā'a*) to him is mandatory, even if he is a slave (*'abd*). Al-Nawāwī quotes in his *Minhaj* the Prophetic saying, 'Listen and obey even if he is a black slave (*'abdan ḥabashiyan*)' ... as for those [areas] where no such self-proclaimed ruler exists, their inhabitants are the people of the intermediate land situated between the two Imāmic states (*imāmayn*). Therefore, the application of Qur'ānic punishments (*iqāmat al-ḥadd*) is dependent on the emergence of such a ruler (*illā ba'da naṣabihi*), if there is no notable council, which is powerful enough to prevent disorder (*fitna*)[48], like the Ahl Būṣayba or the people of Fes. In what concerns those [areas] ruled by a leader (*za'īm*) such as Aḥmad Lobbo, the Almāmī Abū Bakr[49] or by a notable council powerful enough to prevent disorder, their legal decisions (*aḥkām*) are to be regarded as identical to those issued by the legitimate

[46] al-Māmī, *Kitāb*, 219.

[47] On Islamic penal law, see Rudolph Peters, *Crime and Punishment in Islamic Law: Theory and Practice from the Sixteenth to the Twenty-First Century* (Cambridge: Cambridge University Press, 2005).

[48] Literally: 'with which no disorder has to be feared'.

[49] Although his identity is not clear, Abū Bakr was probably a local leader within the Islamic state created by Almāmī 'Abd al-Qādir (d. 1207/1797–8) in Futa Tooro.

> ruler (*imām*), notwithstanding if [their inhabitants] are nomads or sedentary people (*sawāʾ kānū ahl bādiya aw ḥāḍira*); and I personally saw the Almāmī Abū Bakr implementing the Qur'ānic punishments.[50]

The quotation integrates the *jamāʿa* doctrine in a much more complex vision of legal order in the pre-modern Sahara and its political foundations. It connects the analysis of social relations within nomadic societies to the historical circumstances in which Muḥammad al-Māmī writes. The author indeed mentions two major events of the eighteenth and nineteenth centuries: the formation of the so-called 'emirates' in present-day Mauritania[51] and the West African jihād movements.[52]

Both elements, the social structure and its historical manifestation, are discussed simultaneously. On the one hand, Muḥammad al-Māmī recognizes the decentralized character of political authority in pre-modern Saharan societies, where community decisions regularly encountered the resistance of individuals pursuing their interests. The condition imposed on the *jamāʿa* to be 'powerful enough to prevent disorder' perfectly summarizes the type of social negotiation in which community councils such as those in Tuwāt had to engage in order to enforce legal decisions. On the other hand, Muḥammad al-Māmī resigns himself to the 'right of the strongest', which, in his view, is at the origin of the emergence of personal power. Our author clearly alludes to the figure of the emir that appeared within the Western Saharan 'warrior' groups (*ḥassan*) from the end of the seventeenth century onwards.[53] Confronted with this new political configuration, Muḥammad al-Māmī adopts a pragmatic approach: although the seizure of power by the leaders of the Ḥassān has no legal foundation, as the term *mutaghallib* indicates, it has to be accepted, and may even serve as the institutional basis for the establishment of an Islamic legal order. I would indeed argue that al-Māmī's emphasis on the Qur'ānic punishments (*ḥudūd*) must primarily be understood here as a symbol for the rule of law.

The two primary forms of politic authority to be found in the early nineteenth-century Sahara, the oligarchic rule of community notables and the personal rule based on 'force' (*jāh*),[54] are thus presented as a framework for the implementation of Islamic law, as long as political actors are willing and have the power

[50] al-Māmī, *Kitāb*, 177.

[51] Pierre Bonte, *L'émirat de l'Adrar mauritanien: Ḫarîm, compétition et protection dans une société tribale saharienne* (Paris: Karthala, 2008).

[52] David Robinson, *The Holy War of Umar Tal: The West Sudan in the Mid-Nineteenth Century* (Oxford: Clarendon Press, 1985).

[53] Osswald, *Schichtengesellschaft*.

[54] For a sociological study of these mechanisms, see Robert Montagne, *Les Berbères et le Makhzen dans le Sud marocain: essai sur la transformation politique des Berbères sédentaires (groupe chleuh)* (Paris: Alcan, 1930).

to do so. Such a position was, of course, fairly consensual among eighteenth- and nineteenth-century Saharan scholars. However, Muḥammad al-Māmī adds another layer to the classical argument, according to which the prevention of disorder (*fitna*) is one of the most important objectives of political authority. By presenting the movements launched by the contemporary jihād leaders as an alternative to the rule of the *imām*, he reminds us of the persisting – and somehow utopian – aspirations of Saharan and Sahelian scholars towards the construction of a 'truly' Islamic polity. Muḥammad al-Māmī's note about his encounter with the Almāmī Abū Bakr seems highly significant in this regard, since it reflects the great appeal of the jihāds to literate Muslim circles in the area.[55] One should probably add that the surname (*laqab*) 'al-Māmī' pays tribute to Almāmī ʿAbd al-Qādir (d. 1207/1797–8) the jihād leader in Futa Tooro.[56] Nevertheless, the urban ethos of Islamic culture is also implicitly reintroduced through the mention of the *jamāʿa* of Fez as an example of a community with sufficient power to maintain an Islamic legal order. The argument further suggests that Muḥammad al-Māmī must have had considerable knowledge of political life in pre-modern Morocco, which was indeed shaped by a latent antagonism between the scholarly milieu of Fez, jealous of its autonomy, and the Alawite Sultan.[57]

Conclusion

Muḥammad al-Māmī's *Kitāb al-Bādiya* and the fatwā collections from Tuwāt reflect both the sophistication of juristic debates among pre-modern Saharan scholars and their embeddedness in local contexts. They document the emergence of creative forms of legal reasoning, dealing with the social and political realities of life in the desert. As such, they forcefully illustrate the relevance of Saharan legal literature for research on the history of Muslim societies in pre-modern West Africa, which, until quite recently, tended to disregard the fundamental importance of Islamic law, focusing almost exclusively on the analysis of Sufi brotherhood networks, charismatic sainthood, and mechanisms of social mediation.

[55] On this point, see also David Robinson, 'The Islamic Revolution of Futa Toro', *The International Journal of African Historical Studies* 8, 2, 1975, 185–221.

[56] Al-Māmī, *Kitāb*, 23.

[57] Jacques Berque, *Ulémas.*

CHAPTER 6

Philosophical Sufism in the Sokoto Caliphate: The Case of Shaykh Dan Tafa[1]

Oludamini Ogunnaike

إني وإن لم ألحق بركاتهم　　لمكثر في ذكره ومطول
ومردد في ذكرهم متمتع　　منه وحثو الركاب وأجفلوا
حسبي وإن خلفت فردا بعدهم　　أني بهم متوسل متطفل

And if their baraka I've not achieved
I'll mention it at length and frequently
There's joy in 'membering them repeatedly
It spurs the rider on and gives him speed
If after them, I'm left alone, enough for me
Is that I cling to them dependently
– Shaykh Dan Tafa[2]

Introduction

Two major theses, now mostly discredited, have implicitly structured the study of Islam in Africa in the nineteenth and twentieth centuries. The first is the thesis of decline, specifically intellectual decline from the so-called golden age of sophisticated and creative medieval philosophical, scientific, and metaphysical thinkers such as al-Farābī, Ibn Sīnā, al-Ghazālī, Fakhr al-Dīn al-Rāzī, Ibn Rushd, Ibn 'Arabī, and Jalāl al-Dīn Rūmī to a simpler, pietistic, anti-rational 'mystical', magical, and legalistic intellectual activity of the sixteenth century

[1] This article is dedicated to Shaykh Muhammad Shareef who first brought Dan Tafa's works to my attention and whose painstaking efforts to study, collect, transcribe, and translate Dan Tafa's works and transmit his legacy is the foundation of the present work and the source of much of its substance.

[2] This appears to be a poem by Dan Tafa, which he used to conclude a commentary on one of his own poems.

onwards.[3] Characteristic of this thesis is the assertion that Islamic philosophy ended (or ended in the Islamic West) with Ibn Rushd (d. 1198) (an assertion which, ironically, many twentieth-century Arab intellectuals adopted on the basis of these European sources) being eclipsed by dogmatic philosophy (*kalām*) and the mysticism of Sufism (*taṣawwuf*). In reality, the disciplines of *falsafa* (philosophy), *kalām* (theology), and *taṣawwuf* (Sufism) each took up theoretical discussions and arguments that would be considered 'philosophical' by almost any measure, and by the thirteenth century onwards, these disciplines had significantly interpenetrated each other.

More recently, this thesis has been updated to acknowledge the thriving traditions of *falsafa* in the Ottoman and Persianate Islamic lands after Ibn Rushd, and the significant philosophical activity of certain works of logic, theology, and Sufism in the Islamic West. However, it is still generally believed that *falsafa*, as an independent discipline, more or less died out in the Maghreb, sub-Saharan Africa, and the Arab heartlands by the thirteenth century.[4] Furthermore, while

[3] See Marshall G.S. Hodgson, *Rethinking World History: Essays on Europe, Islam, and World History* (New York: Cambridge University Press, 1993); Bernard Lewis, *What Went Wrong? Western Impact and Middle Eastern Response* (New York: Oxford University Press, 2002); *Islam and the West* (New York: Oxford University Press, 1993); and A.J. Arberry, *Sufism, an Account of the Mystics of Islam* (London: Allen & Unwin, 1950). For a critique of these positions, see the Introduction of Khaled el-Rouayheb's *Islamic Intellectual History in the Seventeenth Century: Scholarly Currents in the Ottoman Empire and the Maghreb* (New York: Cambridge University Press, 2015).

[4] For example, the online West African Manuscripts archive (www.westafricanmanuscripts.org, accessed 14 July 2017) lists six works of 'philosophy' (three of which are logic primers) in contrast to 1,364 works of 'theology' and 2,319 works of 'Sufism'. Oliver Leaman's *An Introduction to Classical Islamic Philosophy* says, 'The death of Averroes saw the end of Peripatetic (*falsafa*) thought in the Islamic world for many centuries, until its rediscovery during the Islamic Renaissance or Naḥda of the nineteenth century' (Leaman, *An Introduction to Classical Islamic Philosophy* (Cambridge: Cambridge University Press, 2001) 28) and Nasr's *Islamic Philosophy From its Origin to the Present* explains, 'After Ibn Rushd, Islamic philosophy began to wane in the Maghreb but did not disappear completely. 'Abd al-Ḥaqq ibn Sab'īn (d. 669/1270) wrote a number of important treatises based on the doctrine of *waḥdat al-wujūd* (the transcendent unity of being), and the Tunisian 'Abd al-Raḥmān ibn Khaldūn (d. 780/1379) developed a philosophy of history in his *al-Muqaddimah* ('Prolegomena'). The most important of these later figures from the Maghreb, however, was Muḥyī al-Dīn ibn 'Arabī (d. 638/1240), expositor of Sufi metaphysics. Although not a philosopher in the sense of *faylasūf*, he is one of the greatest expositors of mystical philosophy in any time and clime, and he exercised a profound influence on Sufism as well as later Islamic philosophy. Although Islamic philosophy in the Maghreb seems to have come suddenly to an end, philosophical thought did

the study of and works on logic and philosophical theology in the Maghreb are beginning to receive the scholarly attention they deserve,[5] the tradition of theoretical or philosophical Sufism is also supposed to have more or less migrated east in the thirteenth century along with figures such as Ibn 'Arabī (d. 1240) and Ibn Sab'īn (d. 1271).[6]

The second structuring thesis, *Islam noir*, posited a racial and geographic divide between the 'pristine' Arab, rational, militant Islam of North Africa and the Middle East, and the magical, mystical, more peaceful 'black Islam' in which illiterate sub-Saharan Africans worshipped wonder-working marabouts.[7] While the theses of decline and *Islam noir* have been widely discredited, one of their corollaries remains: the assumption of the absence of noteworthy philosophical activity in Islamic sub-Saharan Africa before the postcolonial period. While this is more of an unstated assumption than a specific hypothesis, it has created an unfortunate lacuna in which scholars of Islamic intellectual history have by and large neglected sub-Saharan Africa, while scholars of Islam in Africa (most of whom were trained as historians) have largely neglected the philosophical dimensions of the works of sub-Saharan African scholars, focusing instead on their historical writings and socio-historical contexts. This has meant that the philosophical

not disappear completely but took refuge mostly in philosophical Sufism and philosophical theology as we see also in much of the rest of the Arab world. This later phase has hardly ever been treated in general histories of philosophy but needs to be studied.' (S.H. Nasr, *Islamic Philosophy From its Origin to the Present, Philosophy in the Land of Prophecy* (Albany: SUNY Press, 2006) 115.)

[5] For example, see El-Rouayheb's *Islamic Intellectual History in the Seventeenth Century*.

[6] For two different perspectives on 'philosophical Sufism', see M. Rustom, 'Philosophical Sufism', in C. Taylor; L.X. López-Farjeat (eds.), *The Routledge Companion to Islamic Philosophy* (New York: Routledge, 2016) 399–411; and A. Akasoy, 'What is Philosophical Sufism?', in P. Adamson (ed.), *In the Age of Averroes* (London: Warburg Institute, 2011) 229–49. For the purposes of this chapter, we define philosophical Sufism as the discursive tradition of intellectual exposition of the doctrines and practices of Sufism that relies on philosophical terminology and arguments, and not only on appeals to the authority of tradition or mystical experience. While North and West African Sufism have received some scholarly attention, with a few exceptions, there is remarkably little scholarship on philosophical Sufism in the region (excluding Egypt) after the thirteenth century, especially in comparison to the central and eastern lands of Islam. In fact, some studies have even concluded that the Islamic literature of West Africa has 'no philosophical depth'. See Abdul-Samad Abdullah, 'Arabic Poetry in West Africa: An Assessment of the Panegyric and Elegy Genres in Arabic Poetry of the 19th and 20th Centuries in Senegal and Nigeria', *Journal of Arabic Literature*, 35, 3, 2004, 368–90.

[7] Vincent Monteil, *L'islam Noir* (Paris: Seuil, 1964).

dimensions of the works of figures such as Shaykh Dan Tafa, the current focus of this study, have lain in obscurity despite the fact that Dan Tafa and his works have been known to the West since the German explorer Heinrich Barth met with him in the nineteenth century.[8]

In this chapter, I hope to contribute to filling in this gap by evaluating some of Shaykh Dan Tafa's works and their ramifications for our understanding of the history of *falsafa* and philosophical Sufism in West Africa, and the role of these two traditions in the intellectual history of the region.

Brief Biography

'Abd al-Qādir ibn Muṣṭafā al-Turūdī (d. 1864/1280), better known as Dan Tafa,[9] was born on the nineteenth of Dhu'l-Qa'da 1804/1218 in Fankaaji, a village in what is today Northern Nigeria, but was then part of the Hausa city-state of Gobir. Dan Tafa was born in the middle of the *hijra* (migration) that marked the beginning of the Sokoto Caliphate into one of the most-renowned families of West African Islamic scholarship and politics, the Fulani clan of 'Uthmān dan Fodio (d. 1817). As his name indicates, Dan Tafa was the son of Muṣṭafā ibn Muḥammad (d. 1845/1261), known as Mallam Tafa, and Khadīja (d. 1856), the oldest daughter of 'Uthmān dan Fodio (d. 1817). Like her younger sister and student, Nana Asma'u, Khadīja was an accomplished scholar in her own right, translating the famous Mālikī *fiqh* text, the *Mukhtaṣar* of al-Khalīl, into Fulfuude. Khadīja, who was also known for her sanctity and spiritual attainment, was the daughter of 'Uthmān dan Fodio's wife 'Ā'isha, known as *Iyya Garka*, a woman renowned for her piety and knowledge.

Mallam Tafa was a scribe and advisor of 'Uthmān dan Fodio and was educated by the Shehu's younger brother 'Abdullah dan Fodio in several Islamic sciences and was considered one of the senior scholars of 'Uthmān dan Fodio's clan and new political order. Mallam Tafa was given a plot of land and was encouraged to set up his own school by Muḥammad Bello, the son and successor of 'Uthmān dan

[8] Barth records that Dan Tafa was described to him as 'The most learned of the present generation of the inhabitants of Sokoto' (John Hunwick; Sean O'Fahey, *The Arabic Literature of Africa: Vol. 2 The Writings of Central Sudanic Africa* (Leiden: Brill, 1995) 221). The one notable exception to this oversight has been Shaykh Muhammad Shareef of the Sankore Institute, who studied the works of Dan Tafa with the latter's descendants and has collected and digitized the manuscripts and created the critical editions of the texts of Dan Tafa cited in this chapter. This chapter would not have been possible without the pioneering work, assistance, and advice of Muhammad Shareef.

[9] Hausa for 'ibn Muṣṭafā'.

Fodio, in Salame, a few miles north of Sokoto. Before Mallam Tafa died and was buried in Wurno (next to his friend Muḥammad Bello) in 1845, he named his son, Shaykh Dan Tafa, as his successor in governing Salame and running its school.

Dan Tafa was born shortly after the Fodiawa clan left Degel[10] the migration that marked the beginning of dan Fodio's jihād and the Sokoto Caliphate. In fact, 'Uthmān dan Fodio had his community halt their emigration for a few days so that his daughter Khadīja could safely give birth to Dan Tafa.[11] As such, Dan Tafa was considered a child of the *hijra* and the Sokoto reform movement, being born at its very inception. Shaykh Dan Tafa's education began with his parents, as he writes in *Tarjuma ba'ḍ 'ulamā' al-zamān*, a biography of his teachers:

> Now, as for my father, Muṣṭafā ibn Muḥammad, it was with him that I read most of what I transmitted and it was from him that I took most of what I studied. Rather, it was under his guidance that I excelled and became distinguished in knowledge. It was through his grace that I was able to awake and attain the fragrance of erudition.[12]

When Dan Tafa was fifteen, he began his spiritual training under the guidance of his maternal uncle, Muḥammad Sanbu (d. 1826),[13] for whom he would retain a lifelong devotion. As Dan Tafa writes in his *Bayān al-Ta'abbudāt*:

[10] The *hijra* dan Fodio and his community began when they left Degel on Thursday the 12th of Dhu'l-Qa'ada 1218 AH. They halted at Fankaaji on Tuesday the 17th, and Dan Tafa was born on the 19th of the same month.

[11] J. Boyd, *The Caliph's Sister: Nana Asma'u (1793–1865): Teacher, Poet, and Islamic Leader* (London: Frank Cass, 1989) 12.

[12] *Tarjuma ba'ḍ al-'ulamā' al-zamān* ... Muhammad Shareef (trans. and ed.) (Maiurno, Sudan: Sankore Institute of Islamic-African Studies International, 2010) 8.

[13] The *Infāq al-Maysūr* of Muḥammad Bello ('Uthmān dan Fodio's son and successor) describes Sanbu in the following terms: 'Among those necessary to mention from the children of the *Shehu*, was Muḥammad Sanbu. He is an erudite scholar who has successfully joined together the sciences of the *sharī'a* and the *haqīqa*. He is a genuine master of the science of spiritual purification. However, it is his custom to remain isolated from people, for sometimes he is in a state of spiritual constriction and sometimes in a state of spiritual expansion.' To which Dan Tafa adds the following description, 'He was our shaykh and spiritual master, the right acting scholar, the upright sage and knower by God. He had an immense station in sainthood (*wilāya*), a well-established footing in direct knowledge of God, and a genuine spiritual state in the realm of sincerity (*ṣiddīqiyya*). He was the spiritual pole of the circle of reliance upon God. He possessed authentic spiritual unveiling and profound spiritual states, where he himself mentioned in some of his works that he was given the miracle of walking upon the surface of water, the ability to fly in the air and that he had witnessed the fabled land of Sesame and had entered its realm. The knowers of Allah say that this fabled land can only be entered by one who has attained the station of forty (*maqām'l-arba'īn*), a spiritual station which is

> The first time I began to follow him [Muḥammad Sanbu] and became acquainted with him from the perspective of the spiritual path was in the year 1234 AH (circa 1819 CE), about two years after the death of Shehu 'Uthmān. At that time, I was fifteen years old. The time between this first encounter and my attaining the level of spiritual mastery (*tashyīkh*) was three years only. From that moment, he continued to show me his spiritual states and directed me with the subtlety of his teachings, until I eventually became completely guided on the spiritual path and was able to be acquainted with all the customs of the divine realities (*rusūm al-haqā'iq*). And there occurred as a result, amazing matters about which I will not speak here. So have a good opinion or do not even ask about the affair. Then he ordered me after that to place myself in the service of the outward sciences and to be preoccupied with reading the books of those topics, because at that time his spiritual state was that he could not endure intermixing with people for long periods. Consequently, I continued to study with him the esoteric sciences of the spiritual path and divine realities as we did in the beginning. However, I would study other sciences with others as well.[14]

Dan Tafa also mentions his uncle and master first in his biography of his teachers, praising his high spiritual station and states and outlining the texts he studied with him:

> As for Shaykh Muḥammad Sanbu, I took from him the path of *taṣawwuf*, and transmitted from him some of the books of the Folk [the Sufis] as well as their wisdom, after he had taken this from his father, Shaykh 'Uthmān; like the *Ḥikam* [of Ibn 'Aṭā' Allāh al-Iskandarī], and the *Insān al-Kāmil* [of 'Abd al-Karīm al-Jīlī], and others as well as the states of the spiritual path. I kept company with him often and became completely inundated by him.[15]

This passage indicates that not only did Dan Tafa study al-Jīlī's magnum opus of *Akbarī* philosophical Sufism (on which he wrote several commentaries), but that his teacher had studied the same work with Shaykh 'Uthmān dan Fodio as well.

---

well known with the People of God. Once he said about himself that his capacity to enter this mystical land flowed from the station of supreme sanctity (*maqām al-ghawthiyya*), although he later discounted these words during his states of spiritual sobriety. This is an immense spiritual station, which is essential to recognize for this shaykh, because these instances were well known and witnessed outwardly upon him by every possessor of knowledge (*ma'rifa*) who knew him.' quoted in *Tarjuma ba'ḍ al-'ulamā' al-zamān* by Muhammad Shareef (trans. and ed.) (Maiurno, Sudan: Sankore Institute of Islamic-African Studies International, 2010), 5–7. Translation modified by author based on Arabic original.

14 *Bayān al-Ta'abbudāt*, 2–3. Translation modified by author based on Arabic original.

15 *Tarjuma ba'ḍ al-'ulamā' al-zamān*, 8.

Dan Tafa was also a pupil of his maternal uncles Muḥammad Bello and Muḥammad al-Bukharī, studying works of Sufism, poetry, the science of letters, medicine, and other disciplines with the former and grammar and the linguistic sciences with the latter.[16] He also studied logic, rhetoric, and jurisprudence (*uṣūl al-fiqh*) with Gidado ibn Aḥmad ibn Ghārī, poetry, prosody and the 'sciences of the ancients'[17] with Shaykh Mudi ibn Laima, and received various Sufi litanies and prayers from Muḥammad Yero ibn Ghārī.[18]

In short, Dan Tafa was raised in the extraordinary milieu of the founding and early years of the Sokoto Caliphate in which 'Uthmān dan Fodio was able to attract and train a significant cohort of scholars highly trained in various Islamic sciences. As a result, his grandson, Dan Tafa, was exposed to virtually all of the Islamic sciences transmitted in West Africa at the time, from medicine, mathematics, astronomy, geography, and history, to the sciences of the Arabic language, jurisprudence, prophetic traditions, and Qur'anic interpretation, to logic, theology, philosophy, Sufism, and the occult science of letters (*'ilm al-ḥurūf*) amongst others.

Relatively little is known about Shaykh Dan Tafa's life. We know he married two wives, both named Fāṭima (one of whom was the daughter of Muḥammad Bello) and had nine sons and two daughters with them.[19] We also know that

[16] Dan Tafa writes, 'As for Muḥammad Bello, his brother, I studied with him the *al-Jawhar al-Maknūn* [of al-Akhḍarī], some of the poets, some of the teachings of the People of *taṣawwuf*, some of the books on the fundamental principles of medicine and other than that. As for Muḥammad al-Bukharī, I took from him the linguistic sciences and grammar, like *al-'Imrīṭiyya*, *al-Mulḥa*, *al-Qaṭr* and *al-Khulāṣa* and he benefited me in many areas.' quoted in *Tarjuma ba'd al-'ulamā' al-zamān*, Muhammad Shareef (trans. and ed.) (Maiurno, Sudan: Sankore Institute of Islamic-African Studies International, 2010) 10. Translation modified by author based on Arabic original.

[17] *'ulūm al-awā'il*: medicine, physiognomy, arithmetic, astronomy, geography, magic squares, the science of letters, geomancy, and others.

[18] Dan Tafa writes, 'As for Shaykh Gidado, I studied with him the *al-Kawkab al-Sāṭi'* [of al-Subkī] and the *al-Niqāya* [of al-Suyūṭī] along with their commentaries, as well as the *al-Sullam al-Murawnaq* [of al-Akhḍarī] in the science of logic, the *al-Kifāya* of Ibn Malik, and one of his own works called *Kāshif al-Af'āl* in the science of metaphors, maxims and proverbs (*amthāl*); and other than that. As for Shaykh Mudi, I studied with him the *al-Rimāza* in the science of prosody (*'arūḍ*). As for Muḥammad Yero, I took from him some of the litanies (*awrād*) and spiritual exercises (*waẓā'if*). In short, I took transmission, learned and studied from the best scholars of my time.' quoted in *Tarjuma ba'ḍ al-'ulamā' al-zamān*, Muhammad Shareef (trans. and ed.) (Maiurno, Sudan: Sankore Institute of Islamic-African Studies International, 2010) 10–11. Translation modified by author based on Arabic original.

[19] Hunwick records his wives' names as Khadīja bint Muḥammad Bello and Hushi, but Muhammad Shareef reports, on the authority of his descendants, that Dan Tafa's

he never held (and seemed to never have vied for) a high political office in the caliphate,[20] merely succeeding his father in governing the town of Salame and running its school, which became highly regarded during his lifetime. However, Dan Tafa does seem to have been an important advisor of the amirs, wazirs, and sultans of the Sokoto Caliphate, as well as being widely regarded as its foremost scholar. The German explorer Heinrich Barth, who met him in 1853, described him as 'the most learned of the present generations of the inhabitants of Sokoto ... On whose stores of knowledge I drew eagerly.'[21] Dan Tafa died in 1864 at the age of sixty and was buried next to his mother behind the school where he studied and taught for so many years.[22]

wives were both named Fāṭima. See Hunwick; O'Fahey, *The Arabic Literature of Africa: Vol. 2*, 221 and Muhammad Shareef, 'Ilaawat'l-Muttaalib Fee Shukr'l-Waahib al-Mufeeda'l-Mawaahib' (Sankore Institute of Islamic-African Studies International, 2013), 15, https://siiasi.org/shaykh-dan-tafa/shukrl-waahib/.

20 According to an oral tradition recorded by Murray Last in his book, *The Sokoto Caliphate*, Dan Tafa became close friends with Aḥmad ibn Abī Bakr Atiku, the son of the third sultan of Sokoto. Aḥmad promised to make Dan Tafa his wazir if he ever became sultan, but 'Abd al-Qādir ibn Gidado, the then-wazir of the fourth sultan of Sokoto ('Alī Babba ibn Bello), wanted his own son, Ibrāhīm Khalīlu, to become wazir after him. So when 'Abd al-Qādir ibn Gidado got wind of Dan Tafa's arrangement with Aḥmad, he refused to support the latter's bid to become sultan unless he rescinded his offer to Dan Tafa and promised to make Ibrāhīm Khalīlu ibn 'Abd al-Qādir his wazir instead. Aḥmad agreed and with ibn Gidado's backing, became the next sultan after the death of Sultan 'Alī Babba ibn Bello. 'Abd al-Qādir ibn Gidado served as wazir under the new sultan, Aḥmad ibn Abī Bakr Atiku, for only forty days, whereupon he died. Upon 'Abd al-Qādir's death, Sultan Aḥmad honoured his promise to the late wazir and appointed Ibrāhīm Khalīlu to his late father's post. Dan Tafa seems to have not contested this change of fortune. See Murray Last, *The Sokoto Caliphate* (New York: Humanities Press, 1967) 162–5.

21 Heinrich Barth, *Travels and Discoveries in North and Central Africa* (London, 1858) vol. iv, 101. Barth also wrote, describing his encounter with Dan Tafa, 'and here I first made the acquaintance of the learned Abd e-Kadar dan Tafa, whom I was most anxious to see, in order to obtain from him some historical information ... He paid me a visit in the evening, and furnished me immediately with some positive data with regard to the history of the dynasty of the Asaki, or Askia, the ruler of Songhay, which he had perfectly, in his head, and which were of the greatest importance in giving me an insight into the historical relation of the western countries of their regions with that of Central Negroland.' A.H.H. Kirk-Greene, *Barth's Travels in Nigeria* (Oxford: Oxford University Press, 1962) 260.

22 M. Shareef, 'The Life of Shaykh Dan Tafa: The life and times of one of Africa's leading scholars and statesmen and a history of the intellectual traditions that produced him' (Maiurno, Sudan: Sankore Institute of Islamic-African Studies, n.d.) 49.

Works

Fortunately, we do know more about Shaykh Dan Tafa's works of which Hunwick records 72 titles (including works of poetry, although some of these are duplicates) and the Sankore Institute lists 44.[23] These works can roughly be grouped into seven categories: elegies/biographies, history, natural sciences, jurisprudence and teaching texts, philosophy (*ḥikma*), theoretical Sufism and theology, and practical Sufism.[24] Dan Tafa is best known in the secondary literature for his historical and legal works, especially the *Rawḍāt al-Afkār* ('Gardens of Thoughts') and the *Mawṣūfat al-Sūdān* ('Description of the Sudan'), which is a translation and augmentation of a Fulfuude poem of Nana Asmā'u describing the jihād of dan Fodio and events up to the date of its writing in 1842. The *Rawḍāt al-Afkār* describes the various states of Western and Central Sudan in the period leading up to dan Fodio's 1804 jihād, the jihād and the establishment of the Sokoto Caliphate, and various events therein until the writing of the work in 1824. Interestingly, the work dates years from 1804 onwards in terms of years after 'Uthmān dan Fodio's *hijra*.[25]

This article is primarily concerned with the last three categories (philosophy, theoretical Sufism and theology, and practical Sufism), but before we delve into these treatises and poems that constitute these categories, it is useful to consider how Shaykh Dan Tafa himself understood and categorized his diverse intellectual pursuits. For this, we turn to two truly remarkable and unique works of his that give an overview of his entire intellectual career: the *Shukr al-Wāhib al-Mufīḍ lil-Mawāhib* ('Thanking the Giver for the Overflow of the Gifts') and the '*Uhūd wa Mawāthīq* ('Oaths and Promises'). These two short works broadly outline the various branches of Islamic learning Dan Tafa had mastered, as well as his categorization of and approach to them.

Shukr al-Wāhib

According to the author, this poem of 67 lines was written to 'thank the Giver for the overflow of the gifts for which we were singled out with respect to sciences. This is in order to fulfill the obligatory right of giving thanks to Him, not for fame

[23] Shareef, 'The Life of Shaykh Dan Tafa'.

[24] These categories are largely heuristic, as some works of philosophy could also be classified as 'natural science', and many works of 'theoretical Sufism' contain practical advice and directions or could be classified as theology or philosophy.

[25] See Hunwick; O'Fahey, *The Arabic Literature of Africa: Vol. 2*, 228; and *Rawdat al-Afkaar: The Sweet Meadows of Contemplation*, Muhammad Shareef (ed. and trans.) (Maiurno, Sudan: Sankore Institute of Islamic-African Studies International, 1991) 18.

or in order to boast of them, but rather out of desire for increase in them by means of it [giving thanks].'[26] The work is divided into six sections describing six types of knowledge/sciences acquired by the author and how he acquired them.

The first section describes the 'Sciences of the Sharī'a' which the author lists as linguistic sciences (morphology, grammar, and rhetoric), principles of jurisprudence (*uṣūl al-fiqh*) and theology (*kalām*), jurisprudence (*fiqh*), the Prophetic tradition (*Sunna*-[*ḥadīth*]), Qur'anic exegesis (*tafsīr*), other transmitted sciences (*dirāya*), as well as the Sufism of character development (*taṣawwuf al-takhalluq*).[27] He describes acquiring these sciences through transmission (*naql*), oral transmission (*sam'*), study (*ta'rīf*), memorization (*hifẓ*), and diligence (*'ināya*).

The second section describes 'the sciences of the ancients (*'ulūm al-awā'il*) which he received by transmission (*naql*) and other means'. He lists these sciences as medicine, arithmetic, logic, the wisdom (*ḥikma*) of the stars (astrology) and physics, the science of magic squares and letters, various forms of divination.[28] He explains that he acquired some of these sciences by assiduously studying these texts on his own and others by transmission, studying texts with masters of these sciences.

The third section describes 'the sciences/knowledge of realities' (*'ulūm al-ḥaqā'iq*) which the author lists as the knowledge (*'ilm*) of Divinity and essences, attributes, and the Divine Essence, the knowledge of manifestation of the Divine Names and Qualities, the knowledge of the Mother of the Book, the knowledge of the spirits and the *malakūt* (unseen, formal, level of reality), and that of the Spirit of spirits and the *jabarūt* (unseen, supraformal, level of reality). He explains that he received these sciences or knowledge with 'the help of the Real', and that they are based on 'realization (*taḥqīq*) and spiritual elevation (*taraqqī*)'. He also

26 *Shukr al-Wāhib al-Mufīḍ lil-Mawāhib,* Muhammad Shareef (ed. and trans.) (Maiurno, Sudan: Sankore Institute of Islamic-African Studies International, 2013) 5–6.

27 A reference to the tradition 'become characterized by the character traits of God' (*takhalluq bi akhlāq Allāh*). In his *Fatḥ al-Baṣā'ir*, 'Uthmān dan Fodio (the author's grandfather) divides Sufism into two kinds of parts: the ethical Sufism of character refinement (*taṣawwuf al-takhalluq*), which he identifies with the writings and ascetic traditions of al-Ghazālī and al-Muḥasibī, and metaphysical Sufism of realization (*taḥaqquq*), which he identifies with Abu'l-Ḥasan al-Shādhilī. A similar division is also found in the *qawā'id al-taṣawwuf* of Aḥmad Zarrūq. See *Fatḥ al-baṣā'ir litaḥqīq Waḍ' 'ulūm al-bawāṭin wa'l-ẓawāhir*, Muhammad Shareef (ed. and trans.) (Maiurno, Sudan: Sankore Institute of Islamic-African Studies International, 1996) 11.

28 Including *khaṭṭ al-raml* (geomancy), and the *ziyārij*, circular divination tables, the most famous of which is attributed to the Marrakeshī Sufi as-Sabtī, and is described in detail by ibn Khaldūn in his *Muqaddima*.

mentions that he has 'transmitted texts regarding the methods [of these sciences] from reliable authorities'.

The fourth section describes 'the sciences/knowledge of the saints (*awliyā'*), which are the sciences/knowledge of secrets/mysteries, from the Sufi path'. He describes them as 'sciences/knowledges for which there are neither written texts nor rational proofs' and whose 'elaborated exposition has been forbidden' so he 'must only mention them by allusion'. He then lists a number of symbolic names drawn from the Qur'ān, *ḥadīth*, and Sufi texts such as 'divine attraction', 'annihilation', 'the tablet and the *nūn*', 'the pen', 'the shadow', 'the griffon', 'white pearl', 'the throne and the footstool', 'the lote tree', etc. The author describes being granted perfect comprehension in these sciences by God and that their understanding comes from the direct experience (*dhawq*) of spiritual wayfaring (*sulūk*) and divine attraction (*jadhb*).

The fifth section describes 'the sciences/knowledge of secrets/mysteries from outside of the Sufi path'. Again these 'secrets' are only alluded to by symbolic titles such as the knowledge of 'the place of ascent of the luminous elements', 'the Holy Divine Sea of Jesus', and 'the living water of the spring of Khiḍr', as well as the 'knowledge of the letters at the opening of Qur'anic chapters', and 'the knowledge of the letters of His Tremendous Name'. These sciences/knowledges are described as being bestowed on the author by 'The Wise, the Opener'.

The sixth and final section describes 'the sciences/knowledge of secrets/mysteries that I have received from the sciences/knowledge of the greatest unveiling, which none but us have a chance of obtaining, and which none will disclose except for the Muḥammadan Seal, who is the Mahdi, peace be upon him'.[29] As with the other 'sciences of secrets', these knowledges are alluded to by symbolic titles such as 'the knowledge of the manifestation of the night and the day', 'the sciences of the Throne', 'the universal circumference' as well as some more familiar titles such as 'the meanings of the Hidden Greatest Name', and the 'knowledge of the possessors of might (*ūlū-l'aẓm*)',[30] and 'the knowledge of the additions to the

[29] This statement of personal superiority perhaps should be taken with a grain of salt as the claims are often explained by Sufis as coming from a state of annihilation in a given spiritual reality, such as when Ḥallāj famously uttered, 'I am the Real.' Dan Tafa himself records (see note 13) that his master, Muḥammad Sanbu, made claims of being the supreme saint of his time (*al-ghawth*), but retracted these when he returned to states of spiritual sobriety. It is also notable that the author identifies the Muḥammadan Seal of Ibn 'Arabi's hagiology as the Mahdi. Tijānīs claim that Aḥmad al-Tijānī is Muḥammadan Seal, and various other Sufi masters from the thirteenth century onwards (including Ibn 'Arabi) have claimed this title of supreme sanctity for themselves.

[30] Generally understood to be the Prophets Noah, Abraham, Moses, Jesus, and the Prophet Muḥammad.

sciences of the Prophets'.[31] At least one of these sciences is described as being attained in 'a true vision during sleep, without any difficulty'.[32]

The six-part schema is illuminating for a number of reasons, the first of which is that the author doesn't follow the standard '*aqlī*/*naqlī* (rational/transmitted) division of the Islamic sciences, but instead divides the sciences based on their origins: the sciences unique to Islam, the sciences of the ancients taken up by Islamic scholars, the sciences/knowledge of spiritual realities and those of the saints derived from the path of the Sufis, those derived from outside the path of the Sufis, and finally, those derived from the 'greatest unveiling'. The first two categories are described as being acquired through textual study, the third through spiritual realization, the fourth through spiritual wayfaring and attraction, the fifth through Divine bestowal, and the sixth through true visions during dreams.

The first four categories are relatively straightforward, but the description of a whole category of knowledge of secrets coming from 'outside the way of the Sufis' (which is also distinct from the occult sciences of the second category) indicates that the author is using the term Sufism (*taṣawwuf*) in a way more precise than contemporary parlance, which as Carl Ernst has noted, tends to use 'Sufism' as a catch-all term for certain contemporary orientations towards certain ethical and metaphysical elements of the Islamic tradition and against Salafism.[33] For example, although their works have been subsumed into the broader category of 'Sufism', Andalusian mystics such as Ibn Masarra and Ibn Barrajān did not consider themselves 'Sufis' but rather 'contemplatives' (*mu'tabirūn*).[34] Similarly, Ibn 'Arabi reserved the term 'Sufi' for a kind of intermediate saint, preferring the terms such as 'verifier' (*muḥaqqiq*) or 'Muḥammadan' (*muḥammadī*) for those like him. Parallels can also be found in the works of Ibn Turkah and other 'lettrists' who distinguished Sufism from these kabbalistic sciences and mysteries, arguing that the latter went beyond and encompassed the former.[35] Furthermore, the last three

31 Perhaps a reference to the structuring concept of Ibn 'Arabi's *Fuṣūṣ al-Ḥikam*, and the Sufi doctrine of the saintly inheritance of sanctity and knowledge from particular prophets, each Sufi saint being described as being 'on the foot' of a particular prophet.

32 For a more detailed discussion of this work, see the commentary by Muhammad Shareef entitled "Ilaawat'l-Muttaalib Fee Shukr'l-Waahib al-Mufeeda'l-Mawaahib', Sankore Institute of Islamic-African Studies International, 2013, https://siiasi.org/shaykh-dan-tafa/shukrl-waahib/

33 See Carl Ernst, 'Between Orientalism and Fundamentalism: Problematizing the Teaching of Sufism', in Brannon Wheeler (ed.), *Teaching Islam* (Oxford: Oxford University Press, 2002) 108–23.

34 See Yousef Casewit, *The mystics of al-Andalus. Ibn Barrajan and Islamic thought in the twelfth century* (Cambridge: Cambridge University Press, 2017).

35 See M. Melvin-Koushki, 'The Quest for a Universal Science: The Occult Philosophy

categories of Dan Tafa's work are distinguished from the first three in that they are designated as secrets/mysteries (*asrār*) which the author states must and cannot be expressed through ordinary discursive means or rational proofs. Nevertheless, Dan Tafa does discuss some of these secrets in his other works, especially his *'Uhūd wa mawāthīq* ('Oaths and Promises'), which further outlines his approach to these secrets and other forms of knowledge.

'Uhūd wa mawāthīq

In this short treatise written in 1272 AH/1855–6, Dan Tafa outlines a series of oaths he has taken 'at the hand of the greatest *Nāmūs* and the most noble teacher' (probably a reference to the archangel Jibrīl and/or the Prophet) which he has recorded to 'remind himself of them' and tell others who wish to follow him in taking these oaths, described as 'part of the Muḥammadan character and angelic virtues'.[36] Ahmad Kani describes this work as being 'an apologia ... to his critics among the orthodox scholars who viewed philosophy with skepticism'.[37] This

of Ṣā'in al-Dīn Turka Iṣfahānī (1369–1432) and Intellectual Millenarianism in Early Timurid Iran', PhD diss., Yale University, 2012.

[36] The first oath of this text reads, 'I have taken upon myself an oath and covenant to spread the wing of mercy to all things in creation; and to view them with the same eye which the Real viewed them when He desired to create them. In this, I desire all good and sympathy for them; and to extend affection and kindness to all of them; regardless of whether they be believers, disbelievers, righteous, sinful, human, jinn, animals, plants, stones or mere clods of dirt. To this extent, I have made it obligatory to daily make an all-embracing supplication for the good of the whole of creation by saying: "Oh God be merciful to the whole of Your creation and suffice them where they are incapable." I say this three times every day and intend by it to fulfill this oath with the duty of holding back evil from them to the best of my ability.' *'Uhūd wa mawāthīq*, Muhammad Shareef (trans. and ed.) (Maiurno, Sudan: Sankore Institute of Islamic-African Studies International, 2016) 4. Translation modified by author based on Arabic original. Amongst other similar ethical oaths of this sort are: 'I have taken an oath and covenant that I will not contend with anyone in a way in which that person may dislike, even when the bad character of that person requires me to. For, there is clear discourtesy and harm in contending with others in ways that are disliked. This oath is extremely difficult, so may God assist us in its fulfillment by His benevolence and kindness.' And 'I have taken an oath and a covenant that I will not take honor in any thing of excellence or lineage or worldly accidents or otherworldly actions, but rather my taking honor will only be in what I have of knowledge of the Real (*ma'rifa al-Ḥaqq*) and companionship with His Messenger and nothing else. So I ask God to aid me in this by His kindness, for He has power over whatever He wills.' (*'Uhūd wa mawāthīq* trans. and ed. by Muhammad Shareef, 5.)

[37] Quoted in Hunwick; O'Fahey, *The Arabic Literature of Africa: Vol. 2*, 230. However, the work also consists of several oaths of an ethical nature such as 'I have taken an

may very well be the case, as several of the twenty-one oaths that comprise this work concern his practice and teaching of philosophy (*falsafa*), occult sciences, and secrets (*asrār*) and are somewhat defensive and apologetic in nature. For example, Dan Tafa writes:

> I have taken an oath and covenant not to call anyone from the people to what I have acquired from philosophy (*falsafa*) and the sciences of the ancients; even though I took these sciences in a sound manner, rejecting the erroneous perspectives within them. Along with that, I will not teach these sciences to anyone in order that they may not be led astray; and errors will thus revert back to me, may God protect me. On the contrary, I will call them to sound knowledge (*ma'rifa*), the Qur'an, the *Sunna*, jurisprudence and Sufism.

and

> I have taken an oath and covenant not to utilize anything from the sciences of differentiation, spells, incantations, charms, and the subjugation of jinn for either advantage or protection. On the contrary, I have abandoned these all together, even though I acquired and mastered the essentials of these sciences.
>
> I have taken an oath and covenant in line with the above vow, not to implement anything from the science of letters and names, in a way which could cause harm to Muslims. However, when it can bring benefit to me, I will utilize it on the condition of it being appropriate for attracting benefit or for defense.

and

> I have taken an oath and covenant not to search into the unseen by means of divination, soothsaying, astrology, or any of the baseless occult sciences. Yet, apart from these sciences, I have obtained knowledge of the unseen by means of the true dream. For nothing has occurred in these times except that I have seen it effortlessly in my dream before it actually occurred.
>
> I have taken an oath and covenant to keep secret what I possess of the sciences of the spiritual realities and secrets, and to conceal my works regarding these. This is because these sciences are an exalted class of sciences for the spiritually elite and are only designated for those who are spiritually prepared from among the People of God.

Perhaps most tellingly, the second oath reads:

---

oath and covenant not to dishonor anyone among the Muslims whoever he/she may be; and even if they exhibited intense enmity towards me. I have taken an oath and covenant not to be arrogant, not to be oppressive, and not to act haughty in order to safeguard myself with the eternal veil of God as a protection.'

> I have taken an oath of covenant to construct my doctrine upon the verses of the Qur'an and not upon rational proofs or theological opinions. In this position I am a follower (*muqallid*) and the source of my following is the infallible Qur'an.[38] If I were asked, for example, for the evidence of the temporal creation of the cosmos, I would not answer with: 'The temporal creation (*ḥudūth*) of the requisite accidents (*al-a'rāḍ al-mustalzama*) is due to the temporal creation of the essential entities (*al-'ayān*).' Nor would I [answer with something] other than this from theological perspectives. Rather, I would say: 'God says: '*God is the Creator of everything*.'' For there is no evidence for me other than that. Therefore, I would explain this evidence from God having absolute certainty in the reality of the Qur'an and no other; since I have seen that the rational evidence in no way leads to the direct knowledge (*ma'rifa*) of God. The evidences of reason are limited to establishing the existence of an incomprehensible deity and that Its attributes are such and such. But the evidences of reason cannot fathom in any way Its essential reality. As for the Qur'an, it emerged from presence of God by means of Jibrīl to His messenger Muḥammad; and that is a matter which is decisive. So realize that.[39]

While this last oath represents a position common in the school of Ibn 'Arabi[40] (and was also held by the great Ash'arī theologian, Fakhr al-Dīn al-Rāzī at the

[38] Probably a reference to 'Uthmān dan Fodio's refutation of the widely-held theological opinion (of al-Sanūsī's massively influential *Umm al-Barāhīn*) that equated belief with rational proof of the essential matters of *'aqīda* (doctrinal creed), and inversely, equated *taqlīd* (typically, a negatively-charged term) with the inability to provide rational proof and unbelief. In his *Ḥiṣn al-Afhām*, dan Fodio defends *taqlīd* in belief, explaining its necessity for the commoner and scholar alike, and drawing on Sufi critiques (such as those mentioned here) of the capacity of rational proofs to lead to knowledge of God. (B. Fodiye, *Ḥiṣn al-Afhām min Juyūsh al-Awhām*, F.R. al-Ṣiddīqī (ed. and trans.) Kano: Quality Press, 1989.)

[39] This does not imply any contradiction between the proofs of reason and the authority of the Qur'ān for Dan Tafa, as another oath reads, 'I have taken an oath and a covenant to weigh all of my understanding with the verses of the Qu'rān and *ḥadīth*, and I have been given a special capacity in this, so that I understand nothing save that its origin in the Qur'an and *ḥadīth* is also clear to me. Whoever doubts this, then let him try me (*falyajribbahu 'alayya*).' (*al-'Uhūd wa Mawāthīq*, 5). Amongst other oaths in this work, the author also promises not to reveal 'the knowledge of secrets by which God established this Sokoto government. The authority in the government is not befitting to anyone in this community except for the one whom this secret has become an established fact. For this secret moves freely among them as it wishes, so realize that.'

[40] Similarly, Ibn 'Arabi wrote, 'By God, were it not for the Sharī'a brought by the divine report-giving, no one would know God! If we had remained with our rational proofs – which, in the opinion of the rational thinkers, establish knowledge of God's Essence, showing that "He is not like this" and "not like that" – no created thing

end of his life[41]) the work does seem to be written for an audience somewhat hostile to philosophy, occult sciences, and the 'sciences of the ancients', but may also be a sincere expression of the author's approach to these traditions. Perhaps Dan Tafa really did refuse to teach anyone philosophy (*falsafa*) because he feared leading them into error, or perhaps his milieu was so hostile to philosophy and the sciences of the ancients that he had to make these oaths public.[42] However, the fact that he composed works on these topics, in verse, indicates that he may very well have taught these sciences to others, perhaps before taking this oath. In any event, the fact that he wrote down such an oath is compelling evidence that he did in fact study works of *falsafa*.[43]

---

would ever have loved God. But the tongues of the religions gave a divine report saying that "He is like this" and "He is like that", mentioning affairs which outwardly contradict rational proofs. He made us love Him through these positive attributes.' (Quoted in W. Chittick, *The Sufi Path of Knowledge: Ibn al-'Arabi's Metaphysics of Imagination* (Albany: SUNY Press, 1989) 180.)

Moreover on the eternity of the world, Chittick explains, 'By having recourse to the fixity of entities (*al-'ayān*) in the divine knowledge, Ibn 'Arabî is able to say that the dispute between theologians and philosophers over the eternity of the world goes back to their perception of the entities. Those who maintain that the world is eternal have understood that "the Real is never qualified by first not seeing the cosmos, then seeing it. On the contrary, He never ceases seeing it." Those who maintain that the world is qualified by new arrival (*hudûth*) "consider the existence of the cosmos in relation to its own entity", which is nonexistent. Hence they understand that it must have come into existence (Ibn 'Arabî, *al-Futûhât*, 1911 edition, 2:666.35).' William Chittick, 'Ibn Arabi', in Edward N. Zalta (ed.), *The Stanford Encyclopedia of Philosophy*, Spring 2014, http://plato.stanford.edu/archives/spr2014/entries/ibn-arabi/. Dan Tafa appears to be alluding to this latter point.

41 In his last testament, Al-Rāzī wrote, 'I tried the methods of *kalām* and *falsafa*, and I did not find in them the profit which I found in the great Qur'an; for it calls to ascribing all greatness and majesty to God, and prevents from delving deeply into the preoccupation with objections and contradictions. This is so only because of our knowledge that human minds come to nothing and fade away in these treacherous defiles and hidden ways.' Quoted in Ayman Shihadeh, *The Teleological Ethics of Fakhr al-Dīn al-Rāzī* (Boston: Brill, 2006), 201.

42 Given 'Uthmān dan Fodio's condemnation of the occult sciences in some of his writings (despite what seems like the widespread teaching and practice of these sciences amongst the scholars of his family), it seems probable that these disciplines would be controversial in the Sokoto Caliphate. See Last, *The Sokoto Caliphate*, 208.

43 Moreover, the fact that he calls this discipline *falsafa* and not *ḥikma* is significant, since the former was used to refer to Hellenistic and Avicennan traditions, while the latter had a wider scope including works of Sufism, philosophical theology, and more mystical philosophical traditions (such as al-Suhrawardī's).

Works of *Falsafa*

Hunwick's catalogue lists several works of philosophy by Dan Tafa, including a *manẓuma* or introductory poem to the science of philosophy (*ḥikma*), as well as *al-Futūḥāt al-Rabbāniyya* ('The Divine Openings'), a work which Kani characterizes as 'a critical reception of the materialists', naturalists', and physicists' perception of life ... matters relating to the transient nature of the world, the existence or non-existence of the spirit, and the nature of celestial spheres are critically examined in this work'.[44] The Sankore Institute also has what appears to be an incomplete copy of Dan Tafa's *Kulliyāt al-'ālam al-sitta* ('Universals of the Six Worlds'), a brief but dense philosophical poem about the origins, development, resurrection, and end of the body, soul, and spirit, as well as a discussion of *hyle* (prime matter).[45] These works are quite different from theological works that incorporate philosophical arguments and terminology, and may indicate the presence of a heretofore unexplored tradition of *falsafa* in West Africa through the nineteenth century. The vocabulary and structure of these works indicate that they may be derived from or at least influenced by Athīr al-dīn Abharī's (d. 1265) *Hidāyat al-ḥikma*,[46] which Maghrebi scholars such as Abū Sālim al-'Ayyashī (d. 1679) studied in Medina with the great Kurdish scholar and defender of Ibn 'Arabī, Ibrāhīm Kūrānī (d. 1690).[47] This work or others like it may have made their way from the Hijaz to the Sokoto Caliphate with scholars returning from

[44] Quoted in Hunwick; O'Fahey, *The Arabic Literature of Africa: Vol. 2*, 222. I have as yet been unable to obtain a copy of this work.

[45] Interestingly, Dan Tafa appears to identify *hyle* with the *'ayān al-thābita* (fixed entities) of the *Akbarī* tradition. Ibn 'Arabi makes a similar identification writing, 'God is identical with the existence of the things, but He is not identical with the things. The entities of the existent things are a "hyle" for the things, or they are their "spirits"' (*Sufi Path of Knowledge*, 89). See the appendix at the end of this chapter for an original translation of this work of Dan Tafa's.

[46] See Andreas Lammer, 'Eternity and Origination in the Works of Sayf al-Dīn al-Āmidī and Athīr al-Dīn al-Abharī: Two Discussions from the Seventh/Thirteenth Century', *The Muslim World* 107, 3, 2017, 432–81. And Nicholas Heer, 'Al-Abhari and al-Maybudi on God's Existence: A Translation of a Part of al-Maybudi's Commentary on al-Abhari's Hidayat al-Hikmah', 2009, http://faculty.washington.edu/heer/abhari-sep.pdf. Abharī's introductory work on logic, *Kitāb al-Isaghūjī fī Manṭiq* (a commentary on Porphyry's *Isagoge*), was known and studied in the region, especially in the form of its versification by the Algerian 'abd al-Raḥmān al-Akhḍarī (d. 1575), *al-Sullam al-murawnaq fī 'ilm al-manṭiq* ('The Ornamented Ladder in the Science of Logic'), which Dan Tafa studied with Shaykh Gidadu.

[47] El-Rouayheb, *Islamic Intellectual History in the Seventeenth Century*, 51, 254. Al-'Ayyāshī also apparently studied the Illuminationist philosopher Suhrawardī's (d. 1191) *Ḥikmat al-Ishrāq* with al-Kūrānī.

ḥajj such as al-ḥājj 'Umar Tāl, or they may have come from Moroccan, or more likely, Egyptian sources (given the long-standing networks of trade and scholarship connecting Egypt to local centres of learning such as Kanem-Borno, Agadez, Katsina and Kano). For example, Jibrīl ibn 'Umar, one of 'Uthmān dan Fodio's teachers, studied and received an *ijāza* from the famous Cairo-based scholar, Murtaḍā al-Zabīdī (d. 1791).[48] However, further research is needed to verify these speculations as to which texts of *falsafa* Dan Tafa studied, with whom, and from where they came.

Works of Philosophical Sufism

Closely related to these works of *falsafa* are Dan Tafa's works of theoretical or philosophical Sufism, a term which the author does not use himself, but which has been used, in one form or another, by its proponents and detractors since the thirteenth century to distinguish the tradition of theoretical, philosophical exposition of Sufi doctrine from the more practical works on Sufi method, ethics, and hagiography.[49] In the tradition of Ibn 'Arabi, these works often involve sophisticated discussions and arguments that critically engage with the philosophical and theological traditions. As in the writings of Ibn 'Arabi, Qunawī, and Jīlī (all of whom Dan Tafa quotes in these works), these works of Dan Tafa's draw on the concepts, vocabulary, and arguments of *falsafa,* including the natural and occult sciences. For example, Dan Tafa's *Muqaddima fī'l-'ilm al-marā'ī wa ta'bīr* presents an introduction to the science of dreams and their interpretation from the perspective of both natural philosophy and philosophical Sufism, which contains interesting arguments about the relationship between spirit (*rūḥ*), soul (*nafs*), and body (*jasad*).[50] Similarly, his *Naẓm al-qawānīn al-wujūd* ('Poem

[48] Stefan Reichmuth, *Murtaḍa al-Zabīdī (1732–1791): Life, Networks, and Writings* (Oxford: Gibb Memorial Press, 2009) 64, 90.

[49] A variant of the term 'philosophical Sufism' (*taṣawwuf al-falāsifa* – literally 'the Sufism of the philosophers') was used pejoratively by Ibn Taymiyya, Ibn Qayyim al-Jawzī and others to criticize figures such as Ibn Sab'īn, Qunawī and the *Akbarī* school, and Ibn 'Arabi (although to a lesser extent) whose ideas and methods they found dangerously erroneous, identifying these errors as importations from Hellenic philosophy. Taking their cue from Ibn Taymiyya, this term is also used by contemporary opponents of the school of Ibn 'Arabi to contrast it with so-called 'Sunni Sufism' or even 'Salafī Sufism' – forms of Sufism they find more tolerable. See A. Knysh, *Ibn 'Arabi in the Later Islamic Traditions: The Making of a Polemical Image in Medieval Islam* (Albany: SUNY Press, 1999).

[50] For example, in this work, Dan Tafa argues that the soul does not leave the body during sleep, as certain other thinkers had claimed, but rather encompasses the body, and is encompassed by the spirit (*al-rūḥ*). According to Dan Tafa, the soul's

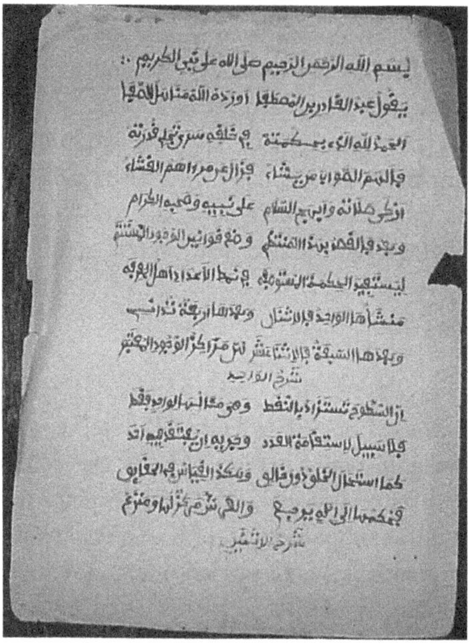

Figure 6.1 Dan Tafa's 'Origin of Existents', Folio 1 of *Nasab al-mawjūdāt*, archive of Shakyh Bello ibn Abd'r-Raazqid ibn Uthman ibn Shakyh Abd'l-Qaadir Dan Tafa (Credit: Muhammad Shareef)

of the Rules of Existence') presents a Pythagorean description of the unfolding of various levels of existence according to the numbers 1, 2, 3, 4, 7, and 12, while his *Nasab al-mawjūdāt* ('Origin of Existents', see Figure 6.1) describes the origin of each existent thing in terms of its essence, its attributes, its governing principle (*nāmūs*), and its nature.[51] These are the theoretical perspectives underlying several of the occult sciences, as Dan Tafa explains in his *Kashf al-Kunūz wa Ḥall al-Rumūz* ('Unveiling of the Treasuries and Solving of the Mysteries', which could be considered a work of *falsafa* and/or the natural/occult sciences of the ancients) in which he explains the cosmological and metaphysical symbolism and spiritual/astrological realities represented in various *jadwals*, or talismanic charts/diagrams.[52]

This category of Dan Tafa's writings shows the substantial influence of 'Abd al-Karīm al-Jīlī, especially his *al-Insān al-Kāmil* ('The Perfect Man'). In fact, perhaps Dan Tafa's earliest work, the *Manẓuma Iṣtilaḥāt al-Ṣūfiya* (composed

apparent dwelling in the body is the result of its focus on or regard (*naẓar*) towards the body during the waking state, and thus during the state of veridical dreams, the soul or spirit turns its focus from the body towards the angelic world of dominion (*ālam al-malākūt*). *al-Muqaddima fī ʿilm al-marāʾī wa l-taʿbīr* (Maiurno, Sudan: Sankore Institute) 3. Similar notions can be found in earlier Sufi literature, such as Ibn 'Aṭā Llāh's ḥikam #246, 'The cosmos envelops you in respect to your corporeal nature, but it does not do so in respect to the immutability of your spiritual nature.' V. Danner, *The Book of Wisdom* (New York: Paulist Press, 1978) 107.

51 Discussions similar to these two works can be found throughout Ibn 'Arabi's *Futūḥāt al-Makkīya*, see W. Chittick, *Self-Disclosure of God* (Albany: SUNY Press, 1998).

52 B. Muṣṭafā, 'abd al-Qādir (Dan Tafa), *Kashf al-Kunūz wa Ḥall al-Rumūz*, Muhammad Shareef (ed.) (Maiurno, Sudan: Sankore Institute of Islamic-African Studies International, n. d.).

in 1821, when the author was just 17 lunar years old), summarizes the technical vocabulary and concepts of Jīlī's magnum opus. As Dan Tafa writes in his *al-Kashf wa'l-Bayān limā ashkala min Kitāb al-Insān* ('Unveiling and Clarification of what is Confusing in the Book of [the Universal] Man'):

> I took this book [Jīlī's *al-Insān al-Kāmil*] by means of transmission from my spiritual master, the righteous teacher, the ascetic sage and Knower by God, my maternal uncle, Muḥammad Sanbu. And in turn, he took it by means of transmission from his father, Shehu 'Uthmān dan Fodio, may God have mercy on both of them. Due to his frequent study of the issues of the book, he benefited me incredibly greatly. Then, I myself began a deep study of the text repeatedly until I completely possessed it, realized it and extracted from it innumerous rare extractions. Among them was a poem which I composed regarding the technical vocabulary of the book based upon its chapters, composed in thirty verses. I then composed a commentary upon this poem with reliable teachings. Among these works of mine extracted from this book is a poem I composed which was like an introduction to the study of the text, which I lost many years ago. Among them also was a small tract that I composed in about three folios in which I assembled much benefit. And there were other works of mine as well. God gave me openings in this book, which He had not given to others. Rather, I do not know anyone in these times, after my abovementioned spiritual master, who had uncovered the secrets with which I had become acquainted from studying this book.[53]

This short poem and its commentary discuss the nature of the Divine Essence, Attributes, Qualities, Names, and the technical meaning of other Qur'ānic terminologies such as the 'Throne', 'Footstool', 'the Two Feet', 'the Pen', 'the Tablet', 'the Lote Tree', etc.

al-Kashf wa'l-Bayān limā ashkala min Kitāb al-Insān presents a more in-depth discussion of thirteen problematic or difficult topics from Jīlī's work: 1) God's existentiation of the cosmos from Himself like ice from water; 2) Divine Oneness in the multiplicity of manifestation likened to waves of the ocean; 3) The identity of the will of creatures with the Divine Will and their differentiation; 4) How the Real's knowledge of Its own unknowability does not limit Its knowledge; 5) The Qur'ānic request and unique kingdom and power granted to the Prophet Solomon ; 6) The relationships between the Divine Throne, the Divine Tablet, and the Universal Soul; 7) The universal and the particular in Divine Knowledge; 8) The nature and cessation of Hellfire; 9) The pleasures experienced in hell by its denizens; 10) The return of everything to its Divine Origin, particularly Iblīs and

[53] B. Muṣṭafā, 'abd al-Qādir (Dan Tafa), *al-Kashf wa'l-Bayān limā ashkala min Kitāb al-Insān*, Muhammad Shareef (ed.) (Maiurno, Sudan: Sankore Institute of Islamic-African Studies International, 2010) 4.

the people of hell; 11) The position of the Prophets Noah, John, and Jesus in the heavenly spheres; 12) The sphere of the fixed stars in Ibn 'Arabi's cosmology; 13) The worship and felicity and punishment of the infidel in view of their origin from and return to God.[54]

Hunwick lists several other works in this category including *Ḥaḍrat al-Hāhūt wa wāḥidiyya al-Lāhūt* ('The Presence of the Level of Divine Ipseity and the Oneness of the Level of Divinity'), whose title shows the clear influence of the terminology of Ibn 'Arabi and Jīlī, and a work entitled *Maqāmāt al-anbiyā'* ('Stations of the Prophets'), which he describes as an 'expansion of an earlier work on the same subject which the author claims was based on divine inspiration not transmitted knowledge'.[55] Hunwick also lists treatises on 'The Superiority of Men to Angels' and a commentary on al-Ghazālī's famous statement on 'the best of all possible worlds'.

Works of Practical Sufism

Several of Dan Tafa's works on Sufism include or are entirely focused on its practical dimension. Among these works are his *Kashf al-ghiṭā' wa'l-rayb fī dhikr anwā' mafātiḥ al-ghayb* ('Removal of the Veil and Doubt by the Mention of the Kinds of Keys to the Unseen'), which briefly describes six keys or methods to obtaining knowledge of the unseen utilized by six different classes of people: 1) the Luminous Key for the worshippers of God and the prophets; 2) the Spiritual Key for the people of spiritual exercises; 3) the Astral Key for the astrologers and astronomers; 4) the Imaginal Key for the possessor of true dreams; 5) the Ideal/Archetypal Key for the people of benefits (*fawā'id*); and 6) the Auditory Key for the people of God.[56] Similarly, Dan Tafa's *Ma'rifat al-Ḥaqq* ('Knowledge of the Real') describes eight doors to the existential/direct knowledge of the Real: 1) Primordial Human nature/innate disposition (*fiṭra*); 2) Reports (*khabr*); 3) Rational reflection (*naẓar*); 4) Contemplation of Divine Majesty (*Jalāl*); 5) Contemplation of Divine Beauty (*Jamāl*); 6) The Qur'ān; 7) Prophetic tradition (*ḥadīth*); and 8) the spiritual states of direct experience (*al-aḥwāl al-dhawqiya*). This work is a commentary upon a well-known Fulfuude poem of Shaykh 'Uthmān dan Fodio.[57]

[54] See the appendix to this chapter for an original translation of certain sections of this work.

[55] Hunwick; O'Fahey, *The Arabic Literature of Africa: Vol. 2*, 224.

[56] B. Muṣṭafā, 'abd al-Qādir (Dan Tafa), *Kashf al-ghitā' wa'l-rayb fī dhikr anwā' mafātiḥ al-ghayb*, Muhammad Shareef (ed.) (Maiurno, Sudan: Sankore Institute of Islamic-African Studies International, 2010).

[57] B. Muṣṭafā, 'abd al-Qādir (Dan Tafa), *Ma'rifat al-Ḥaqq*, Muhammad Shareef (ed.) (Maiurno, Sudan: Sankore Institute of Islamic-African Studies International, 2003).

This indicates the derivation of some Arabic texts from *'Ajamī* ones, in contrast to the commonly assumed direction of knowledge and literature from Arabic to *'Ajamī*.

Perhaps most interesting of the works of this category is Dan Tafa's *'Ibādāt Shaykh Muḥammad Sanbu* or *Bayān al-ta'abbudāt* ('The Worship of Shaykh Muḥammad Sanbu' or the 'Clarification of Worship'), which describes the spiritual practices and method of his own shaykh and uncle (and presumably his as well). This work was inspired by a dream in which the then-deceased Muḥammad Sanbu instructed the author to explain his method of worship. Amongst other things, this method is distinguished by the centrality of true dreams, the concealing of miracles and spiritual states, and asceticism and solitude, and offers a uniquely precise and detailed account of the spiritual methods and perspectives of some of the founders of the Sokoto Caliphate. This work also contains an illuminating discussion of certain technical terms of Sufi vocabulary.

Conclusion

As the works above demonstrate, the early Sokoto Caliphate was host to traditions of *falsafa / ḥikma* (philosophy) and philosophical Sufism, which were often combined with traditions of the natural and occult sciences. It is clear that not only Dan Tafa, but also Muḥammad Sanbu, Shaykh 'Uthmān dan Fodio and others were well versed in the philosophical Sufism of Jīlī and perhaps in the traditions of Avicennan philosophy through the medium of Abharī's summation. Dan Tafa's works testify to the vitality and integration of these various disciplines in the early years of the Caliphate, although his work 'Oaths and Promises' may indicate a somewhat hostile environment to some of them. Most of Dan Tafa's works are characterized by a density and concision that seems to necessitate an oral commentary. The wit and rhetorical force of the rhyming couplets in his poetic works cited above and in the appendix is also quite striking and, unfortunately, beyond my skill to capture in translation.[58] This may be a regional style (from the eighteenth century onwards, West Africa witnessed an explosion of summary versifications and dense, didactic texts and commentaries in fields such as *fiqh* and *'ilm al-tawḥīd / kalām*), or it may indicate that these texts were meant to be taught with an oral commentary, or it may indicate a degree of hostility or mistrust in his milieu towards some of the topics dealt with in these dense treatises, or perhaps this style is meant to protect these works from the unworthy or unqualified. All of these factors probably exerted an influence, to one degree or another, on his distinct style. As Dan Tafa himself wrote at the end of his commentary upon his own

[58] I have tried my best to approximate this notable aspect of Dan Tafa's literary style in the poetic epigram to this chapter.

poem on technical Sufi vocabulary (*iṣṭilaḥāt*), 'I have made this commentary very condensed as a precaution against unwanted incursion and dissension (*fitna*).'[59]

This fact underscores the importance of orality in knowledge transmission in the Islamic sciences. Perhaps because of the publish-or-perish paradigm in which we operate, there is a tendency in contemporary scholarship to assume the equivalency of literary production and creative intellectual activity.[60] However, as the traditions of oral commentary and teaching in the Islamic sciences, especially philosophy and Sufism, demonstrate, there can be significant, creative intellectual activity that does not necessarily leave behind written traces.[61] Recall that Dan Tafa vowed in a written oath to 'keep secret what I possess of the sciences of the spiritual realities and secrets, and to conceal my works regarding these. This is because these sciences are an exalted class of sciences for the spiritually elite and are only designated for those who are spiritually prepared from among the People of God', and that his teacher, Muḥammad Sanbu, left behind almost no written works aside from a few poems. When it comes to these traditions, the absence of written evidence is far from the evidence of absence. Thus, Dan Tafa's few written works and mentions of his studies of *falsafa* may just be the tip of the iceberg of a much deeper tradition of Islamic philosophy in the region.

[59] B. Muṣṭafā, 'abd al-Qādir (Dan Tafa), *Manẓuma Iṣtilaḥāt al-Ṣūfiya*, Muhammad Shareef (ed.) (Maiurno, Sudan: Sankore Institute of Islamic-African Studies International, 2006), 6. This is something of a tradition in Islamic philosophy and philosophical Sufism as Seyyed Hossein Nasr notes, 'In order to avoid the criticism and condemnation of certain exoteric *'Ulamā'* and also the uneducated who might misconstrue their teachings, most philosophers couched their ideas in deliberately difficult language whose meaning they then taught orally to their chosen students. Although there are exceptions in this matter, as one sees in the case of Mulla Sadra, the majority of the masters of Islamic philosophy practised this art of dissimulation through a deliberately complicated language, the key to whose understanding remained in the hands of those well acquainted with the oral tradition which alone could elucidate the meaning or the levels of meaning of the technical vocabulary (*al-isṭilāhāt*). That is why books such as the whole class of *al-Istilāhāt al-sūfiyya* by 'Abd al-Razzāq Kashani and others, *al-Ta'rifat* by Sayyid Sharif al-Jurjani, *Kashshāf isṭilāhāt al-funūn* by al-Tuhawī, and other works on terminology have been so important in the history of Sufism and Islamic philosophy.' S.H. Nasr, 'Oral Transmission and the Book in Islamic Education: The Spoken and the Written Word', *Journal of Islamic Studies* 3,1, 1992, 3.

[60] We even commonly speak of knowledge 'production', a conceptualization quite alien to Dan Tafa's epistemology in which knowledge is not 'produced', but rather 'transmitted' or 'unveiled'.

[61] This is by no means limited to Islamic philosophy, as many of the founders of major schools of ancient philosophy such as Socrates, Diogenes the Cynic, Pyrrho, and Carneades left behind no writings.

Or it may not; more research must be conducted to determine the exact content and sources of Shaykh Dan Tafa's works, and whether he was a lone exceptional figure or if he was a part of a larger network of scholars studying and producing works not only of logic and jurisprudence but also of philosophy and philosophical Sufism. If so, this could radically alter our understanding of the intellectual landscape of precolonial Islamic West Africa, as well as developing our understanding of the history and spread of Islamic philosophy and philosophical Sufism. While much more work remains to be done, Dan Tafa's oeuvre does clearly demonstrate the presence of philosophical Sufism in the region, the importance of al-Jīlī in transmitting the *Akbarī* tradition in West Africa, and they may indicate a heretofore unexplored tradition of *falsafa* in the region. I hope further study of Dan Tafa and figures like him will also shed light on the philosophical texts that were studied and transmitted in the Islamic West during the period in which this tradition was long supposed to have died out (fourteenth to nineteenth centuries).

Appendix: Selected Translations of Dan Tafa's Works

The Unveiling and Clarification of What is Difficult in the Book of the Perfect Man

On God's Knowledge:

The Fourth Issue: 'Is God's knowledge limited by the fact that He knows that He is unknowable?'

Among the difficult topics of this book is his statement in the 25th chapter on Perfection (*Kamāl*): 'For He, may He be exalted, perceives His quiddity (*māhiyyatihi*) while He perceives that it is not perceived, for if it has no limit from His perspective and from the perspective of other than Him, then this limitlessness of His in His Essence, may He be exalted, is that it is not perceived, and so it has no limit from His perspective.'

In this, the difficulty is apparent in its negation of perception from the perspective of God, because God, transcendent and exalted, encompasses all things, the eternal and the created as he explained in his statement 'He perceives it', but then he undercuts this by saying, 'it has no limit from His perspective nor from the perspective of other than Him'.[62] This is due to the absence of limitations of His Perfections while distinguishing, in general and in application, between the encompassing of knowledge and the absence of limitations of the Divine Perfections. This is the site of the difficulties of his statement, so understand, and

[62] The classical definition of knowledge is the 'encompassing of the known by the knower', which would be impossible for something with no limits. Hence the unlimited is equivalent to the unknowable.

prior to that, of the differences and difficulties in the books of the theologians. Al-Sanūsī asserted the limitation of the Divine Perfections with regards to His Knowledge [i.e. The perfection of Divine Knowledge is limited in that it cannot know the Divine Essence, which is absolutely unknowable]. However, It [the Divine Essence] has no limit from the perspective of our knowledge, due to the necessity of the comprehensiveness of [Its] knowledge, and this is the correct way, so understand and God facilitate your guidance.[63]

The Seventh Issue: 'The Particular and Universal in God's Knowledge'

Among the difficult topics in this book is his statement in the 52nd chapter: 'So know, may God grant us and you success, that the Real, it is not possible for It to be understood comprehensively or exhaustively, ever, neither the eternal nor the temporally created [aspects of It]. As for the eternal, this is because His Essence does not fall under the purview of an attribute of His Attributes, namely, knowledge. So it [knowledge] does not encompass It [the Essence]. The existence of the universal in the particular does not necessarily follow from this, and God is exalted above the universal and the particular, so knowledge cannot exhaust It [the Essence] in any sense.'[64] – to the end of his statement.

The essence of the difficulty in this is its assertion of the absence of the encompassing of knowledge of the essence of the existent thing.

The like of this has been introduced earlier along with the explanation of the disagreement amongst the theologians on this point, although the correct

[63] I believe Dan Tafa is arguing here that any statement we make about the Divine Essence's knowledge of Itself is necessarily part of our knowledge of It, which is limited because it cannot encompass the Divine Essence. So even our assertion that Divine Knowledge encompasses the Divine Essence or not, is to limit It according to our knowledge, which cannot encompass it. We cannot speak from the perspective of the Divine Essence, so the best thing is to assert the absolute limitlessness of It and Its Knowledge from our perspective. Ibn 'Arabi's statement at the end of the *Fuṣūṣ* provides a different perspective on this problem that I believe is relevant here: 'But the Absolute Divinity is not encompassed because it is identical with things and with Itself. You don't say that a thing encompasses itself or doesn't encompass itself, so understand!' (Faṣṣ Muḥammad, *Fuṣūṣ al-ḥikam Li Shaykh al-Akbar Muḥyī al-Dīn ibn 'Arabī, ed. Abū al-'Ala Affīfī* (Beirut: Dār al-kutub al-'Arabī, 2002) 226).

[64] The assertion here seems to be that since God is neither a universal nor a particular, He can neither be known as a universal nor as a particular, and so He cannot be known. It could also be a rejection of a perspective that describes the Essence as universal and Divine Knowledge as a particular. Moreover, since the Real is the essence of everything, that means the essences of particular things cannot be known – a seeming refutation of God's knowledge of particulars – a celebrated debate between the philosophers, theologians, and Sufis. Dan Tafa's response, building on the earlier issue, is that God knows everything with Self-Knowledge.

approach is the limitlessness of the comprehensiveness of knowledge, so know this. This issue is like the problems in the issues of theology (*kalām*) and Sufism (*taṣawwuf*). And I have not found a satisfactory explanation [in any other work], so whoever finds it, let him attribute it to this place and not conceal the fact that I called for the necessity of the particular and the universal being included in the knowledge of Itself/the Essence. But, in the first place, the absence of the applicability of the universal and particular is not necessary for Itself/the Essence. This is because knowledge is not among the transitive attributes, such that the inclusion of itself requires a [separate] locus under its own rule, like the attribute of power, for example, for it requires in the inclusion of itself, a locus because it is a transitive attribute. So understand! May God facilitate our guidance and yours.[65]

On Eschatology:

The Eighth Issue: 'The Nature and Cessation of Hellfire'

Among the difficult topics in this book is his saying in the 58th chapter in mentioning the Fire: 'The portion related to him by His name *al-Qāhir* (The Dominant), is that from which the Fire was created, and this is from a secret of the manifestation of His Name, *al-Ghāfir* (the Forgiving). So its people [of the fire] rely upon this to provide them good in the afterlife, as the Prophet narrated about the fire, 'that *al-Jabbār* (the Compeller) will put His foot in it [the Fire] and it will say, "enough, enough". Then the *Jirjīr*[66] tree will sprout in it.' He also says the same chapter in the final section: 'So know that *al-Jabbār* (the Compeller), whenever it manifests to them, is from the perspective of the Divine Power, it reveals to them the appropriateness which is the cause of connection in everything. So the foot of compulsion is placed on the Fire, and then comes the statement of the Most High, and He says about that, "Enough, enough". This speech is the state of the essence under the dominion of Glory, by this expression he means, "so it ceases". Then He says, 'Know that since the Fire is not original in existence, it disappears in the end. The secret of this is that the attribute from which it was created is preceded

65 It seems that Dan Tafa is arguing that since the attribute of Knowledge does not leave an effect upon the object of knowledge, it does not require a separate entity or locus to exercise itself (self-knowledge is not like self-power or control because knowledge can know itself whereas power must have an effect on something else), then the Real knows Itself fully with this kind of self-knowledge which includes both the universal and the particular, because these are not other than the Real, which is the very Essence of both, although the Real is not limited by either category.

66 Its name is similar to that of the watercress (*jirjīr* or *jarjarīr*) mentioned in other *ḥadīths* about the cessation of Hellfire.

[by something else], and the statement, "My mercy precedes my wrath" attests to that.' – to the end of his statement.[67]

There has been a lot of talk disparaging what is mentioned here, so he said in the last section of the chapter mentioned (the 58th): 'Know that the Fire is as mentioned' then he said in the last section of the chapter mentioned (the 58th): 'Know that the Fire, since its affair is an accident in existence, its disappearance is permissible and [this is true of everything] except for impossibilities. It [The Fire] disappears only when the burning leaves it, and with the leaving of the burning, the angels of the Fire leave, and with their leaving, the angels of bliss return, and so with the arrival of the angels of bliss, the *Jirjīr* tree sprouts in it. It [the tree] is green, and green is the most beautiful/best color of paradise. So what was Hell is reversed to become blissful.' – to the end of his statement.

The essence of the problem in this is obvious in its assertion of the lifting of burning and punishment from the people of the Fire without restriction because it is the fire of disobedience. This is different from what is known from the Book and the *Sunna* about the eternity of the punishment of the disbelievers, [which is] like the eternity of the bliss of the believers. However, I solve this problem with his statement in the chapter about the level of the disbelievers, 'Then God, Most High, created the gate of this level of disbelief and idolatry (*shirk*) as He said, *Truly the disbelievers among the People of the Book and the idolaters are in the fire of Hell, abiding therein; it is they who are the worst of creation* (98:6), *and [the Fire] will say, "Is there more?"* (50:30) without ending.' So this text of his, may God be pleased with him, is useful for its preceding assertion about the fire of disobedience.[68] So with this you can bring his view into line with that of the people of the *Sunna*.

[67] This references a *ḥadīth* from Bukhārī which reads, 'As for the Fire, it will not be filled till God puts His Foot over it whereupon it will say, "Enough, Enough". At that time it will be filled, and its different parts will come closer to each other; and God will not wrong any of His created beings. As regards Paradise, God will create a new creation to fill it with.' Book 65, *ḥadīth* 4850.

[68] Although Dan Tafa is somewhat circumspect here, he appears to be alluding to the Qur'ānic passage, '*As for those who are wretched, they shall be in the Fire, wherein shall be for them groaning and wailing, abiding therein as long as the heavens and the earth endure, save as thy Lord wills. Surely thy Lord does whatever He wills. And as for those who are felicitous, they shall be in the Garden, abiding therein as long as the heavens and the earth endure, save as thy Lord wills – a gift unfailing*' (11:106–8). The key qualification 'as long as the heavens and the earth endure' seems to imply a kind of end or cessation to the Fire, as Dan Tafa explains in the following sections.

The Ninth Issue: 'The pleasure of the people of the Fire'

Among the difficult topics in this book is his statement in the chapter mentioned above (the 58th): 'Truly, for some of the people of the Fire, there is a pleasure which they enjoy in it.' So that he mentions that it is joined with some of the people of the Fire. He said, 'I saw the Garden given to them as a replacement [for the Fire], but they hated it.' And he also mentioned, 'truly, some of the people of the Fire perceive some things among the Divine Realities that other than them amongst the believers do not perceive.'

The answer to what he mentioned about the pleasure of the people of the Fire and their realization of Divine Realities is familiar to us and it is an existential matter of spiritual realities. As for me, God informed me of the meaning of that, but it is not proper to unveil the like of that because it would lead to the rending of the people's veils, and so we keep silent about it, so understand! May God facilitate our guidance.

The Tenth Issue: 'On the salvation of Iblīs'

Among the difficult topics of this book is his statement in the 59th chapter in mentioning the affair of Iblis in His saying, '*Indeed, My curse is upon you until the Day of Judgement*' (38:78) and his saying, '*until the Day of Judgement*' is a limit. So when the Day of Judgement has passed, then there is no curse because of the lifting of the ruling of natural darkness on the Day of Judgement. And we have already explained what is meant by the Day of Judgement in the final chapter of this book. So Iblis is not cursed, which is to say that he was only expelled from the [Divine] Presence before the Day of Judgement because of what his origin required of him. It is only the obstacles of nature which prevent the spirit from realizing the Divine realities, but after that, the natural elements are themselves among the perfections, and so then there is no curse, but rather pure nearness. So at that time, Iblis will return to what he had with God of Divine Nearness, and that is after the cessation of Hell, because everything that God created must return to what it was in this origin from which it was separated, so understand!'

The reason for the problem in this statement is obvious from its positing the return of Iblis to what he had with God of Divine nearness. Felicity is not fitting for Iblis then because we assert the perpetuity of his wretchedness and torment because he is a wretched, accursed *kāfir*, far from the mercy of God as is known in the religion by necessity. So I say that this statement is deeply problematic for those who have no realization among the people of the transmitted sciences because they do not accept its interpretation. But as for the verifiers/realizers there is no problem for them because they know that for every existent there is a known, specified level with God, from which it is created and to which it returns. So this level (*rutba*), if it is among the loci of Divine Beauty, its possessor is destined for felicity in its existence, and if it is among the loci of Divine Majesty, its possessor is sentenced to wretchedness. Then when the wheel turns for this creation with the manifestation of the matter in full swing, and with the realization of the realities, each reality among the realities of existents returns to the level which it had with God, and that is the Divine nearness mentioned [above]. And in this, Iblis is no different from others, and a disbeliever is no different from a believer. However, the return of believers is by way of the Beauty from which they were created, and it is this which necessitates their felicity; while the return of the disbelievers is by way of the Majesty from which they were created, and it is this which necessitates their wretchedness, expulsion, and Divine Nearness. Each of the two parties is fixed when they return to Him. He says, '*To Him are you returned*' (29:21). Were this nearness not established for the people of the Fire in the afterlife, then the speech of the Real would not be fulfilled concerning them, and Its response to them as [is stated] in the verses of the Qur'ān, which are addressed to the people of the Garden and their speech as well as to the people of the Fire and their speech. However, the Real addresses each in accordance with what is required of its station and its reality. So He says to the people of the Garden, '*Peace be unto you, you have done well [so enter it to abide*]' (39:73), and He says to the people of the Fire, '*Begone therein [and speak not to Me]*' (23:108).[69] So let us halt this discussion at this point since there is no way to reveal this secret. So understand! The people of misery are only veiled in the afterlife from direct witnessing, not from the witnessing of nearness and discourse.

So when you realize [the meaning of] the preceding sentence, the difficulties will be unravelled for you all at once, unless you are constrained by the fetters of your thinking and veiled by the force of your blind imitation. So if you are like that, then know that there is no way for you [to realize] these realities, so remain in the company of your thought, and stay in the place of your reason, for that is safer for you.

Introductory Poem on the Universals of the Six Worlds

In the Name of God, the Merciful, the Compassionate
  Prayers and peace upon he after whom there is no prophet

Praise be to God who has established
  The rules of existence and taught us … [illegible]
The purest of his prayers upon the people of perfection

[69] This entire passage, through its vocabulary, also implicitly alludes to the discussion of the afterlife at the end of Surah Hūd (11:103–19).

Muḥammad and the prophets and 'the Men' (*al-rijāl*)[70]
And so, the Intellect holds what grants
Since each known object by its judgement … [illegible]
The men of old did not cease
To work towards its perfection by state (*ḥāl*)
And how not? Since it is that which roams free
After this body … [illegible]
This is a poem, a wonderful recital
Of the wisdom entrusted to the intellect [illegible …]

In exile it is thrown down so that it descends
into the form of the body, by ordainment [illegible …]
To its separation from limitations
That drag it down into the troubles of fate

On the Soul and the Intellect:

The soul is that which is in man of thoughts/spirit (*ma'ānin*)
And the intellect is that which by it collects the sweetness of understanding (*bayān*)
Its origin is from the world of spirits
It was deposited into the forms of the human figures
The natural elements come together
In the world of the spheres in an aspect/mode (*al-ḥaythiya*)
It is, when life is gone,
Transferred, as it is not dead
Here it manages alone
As in the first affair, so take instruction!

On the Body (*jism*) and body (*badan*):

The body is composed of compounded natures
And it is returning back to them
It is composed of particular elements
Created, made, particularly for it
And they, that is, the above-mentioned elements
Are composed of natures which are formless
And this is prime matter and it is a fixed entity (*'ayn thābit*)
From it, the varieties of existence are established

[70] This term does not refer to gender, but rather to spiritual attainment and maturity.

On the Body's Share of Life:

The life of this body is from warmth
    It does not remain for its essence is its evaporation
It boils up in infants, what for youth –
    What does not oppose the multitude of flame
Without it, in manifestation in youth
    And in old age, the body of this gate
[In it] appears an inward/contained coolness
    So the inward/contained heat is weakened
And illnesses become plentiful in the wounds
    Of the body, then death approaches
Until when the heat comes to its end
    And its life is ended by its death

On the Soul's Share of Life:

Its share is from the glance/consideration of the spirit
    Reflecting/corresponding to the formal structure (*al-haykal al-ṣurī*) [the body]
It [the soul] is its [the body's] management and governance
    And it makes it [the soul/life] visible and witnessed
Until when the warmth is gone
    It is raised and separated from its abode

On the *Barzakh* and the Afterlife:

The spirit in these two, its governance is apparent
    Its site is elevated and its manner pure
The sweetness of knowledges and perfections
    And the curse of imperfection and foulness of state
Here are so many possessors of might and primordial nature (*fiṭra*)
    But the thinking of the ignorant about it is spoiled.

On the Development of the Intellect:

The development of intellects is by firm patience
    Its striving in actions … [illegible]
It brings news of all matters,
    And seeks to clarify what is required and what is supererogatory for them
And it holds your soul back from its lusts
    And eliminates aggression to prevent injuries

And silence and reflection and contentment
    And spiritual retreats of the aspirant for relaxation

On the Development of Souls:

The development of souls is through humility
    From elevation due to rank
Restraining yourself from harming, and love of poverty
    And holding yourself back from the prestige of pride
And the exile of the soul and asceticism
    And sadness and generosity and restraint

On the Development of Spirits:

The development of spirits is through ignoring
    And your refusal of the known is through inattention
Your taking knowledge is equivalent to
    its absence and opposition and adversary

The Journey of the Soul after Death:

Its journey is in accordance with its state
    Of its lacking the necessary or its perfection
So its lack is its painful punishment
    and its perfection, its eternal bliss

The Journey of the Body after Death:

Its journey is its return to its origin
    Its return is also to its folk
Its determination is erased in that state
    Due to its loss of [both] lack and perfection

On the Resurrection of the Spirit:

The resurrection of the spirits is their dispersal/unfolding
    Seeking the centre that contains their final resting place
The problems of the forms of the body
    Are the supports for calling on the Name

On the Resurrection of the Body:

Its resurrection is apparent in/by the spirit
    It takes form in the spiritual world
It tastes the pleasures of the spirit
    In accordance with its spiritual perfection

On Prime Matter:

The [prime] matter is the fixed entities
  Before their attributes are qualified by existence

And the continuous rain (*dīma*) is like the soul, from it arises
  Warmth with coolness, and they spread
And so follows wetness and dryness
  And the rest of four basic elements
Then appear the spheres and the planets
  Orbiting them, and likewise the fixed stars
The motions perpetually traverse the spheres
  Running with darkness and illuminating the kingdom (*al-mulk*)
Then from them appear the engendered beings [the kingdoms]
  Which are multiple and composite
Like the mineral, plant, and animal [kingdoms]
  They differ in their governing principle
From which they become hot and dry [fire], cold and wet [water]
  And the inverse of these concomitants occurs [hot and wet (air), cold and dry (earth)]
In accordance with natural transformation
  At the places of land and sea
As for animals, their nature is different
  As we mentioned, they have a difficult journey, so understand!
And likewise, the mineral kingdom and that
  Has been clearly established, O keen one.
Then the plant kingdom, its nature and governing principles
  Are different, as [its members] change position
Among it [the plant kingdom] are food, and medicine, and the like
  And heat and cold and the coming of their opposites …

[The manuscript ends here, but the lack of typical closing formulae indicates that either this work or this copy are incomplete]

CHAPTER 7

'If all the Legal Schools were to Disappear': ʿUmar Tāl's Approach to Jurisprudence in *Kitāb al-Rimāḥ*[1]

Farah El-Sharif

Al-Ḥājj ʿUmar b. Sa'īd al-Fūtī Tāl (1796–1864) was among the most prominent West African scholarly figures in the nineteenth century. His magnum opus, the *Kitāb Rimāḥ Ḥizb al-Raḥīm 'alā Nuḥūr Ḥizb al-Rajīm* ('The book of the spears of the league of Allah the Merciful against the necks of the league of Satan the accursed'), is considered one of the most important – yet understudied – works of the nineteenth century in the Muslim world.[2] According to Louis Brenner, *al-Rimāḥ* is arguably 'the most widely disseminated text by any nineteenth-century West African author'.[3] The work is normally printed on the margins

[1] I wish to thank Professor Ousmane Kane of Harvard University for providing helpful feedback on earlier versions of this chapter and for enabling me to participate in the New Directions in the Study of Islamic Scholarship in Africa workshop. I am grateful to the expert insights and scholarship of Professor Zachary Wright on the Tijāniyya, without whom my research would fall short. I would also like to thank my colleague and friend, Professor Oludamini Ogunnaike, for helping me hone my argument of *taḥqīq* over *taqlīd*, and suggesting I look into *fiqh* of Ibn 'Arabi.

[2] This topic is the author of this chapter's PhD dissertation in progress. For more scholarship on the contents of the *Rimāḥ*, see Bernd Radtke, 'Studies on the Sources of Kitāb Rimāḥ Hizb al-Rahīm by Hajj Umar', *Sudanic Africa*, 6, 1995, 73–113; John Hunwick, 'An Introduction to the Tijānī Path: Translations of the Chapter Headings of al-Rimah', *Islam et Sociétés au sud du Sahara*, 6, 1992, 17–32; Sa'īd Bousbina, 'Un siècle de savoir islamique en Afrique de L'Ouest, 1820–1920. Analyse et commentaire de la littérature de la confrérie Tijāniyya à travers les œuvres D'al-Hajj Umar', PhD diss., Université de Paris, Panthéon-Sorbonne, 1996; and Saïd Bousbina, 'Les mérites de la Tijāniyya d'après 'Rimah' d'Al-Hajj Umar', *Islam et sociétés au Sud du Sahara*, 3, 1989, 253–60.

[3] Louis Brenner, *Controlling Knowledge: Power, Religion and Schooling in a West African Muslim Society* (London: Hurst, 2002) 136.

of the major work of 'Ali Ḥarāzim's *Jawāhir al-Ma'ānī*.[4] After leading armed anticolonial resistance against the French, Al-Ḥājj 'Umar formed a state in 1860 which, although short-lived, was one of the largest ever seen in the Western Bilad al-Sudan. More academic attention has been paid to Tāl's political life[5] rather than his writings and intellectual stances, at least in the European-language literature. The fascination with Tāl as a warrior and not as a serious scholar is perhaps due to the Western academic tendency to view African and Islamic studies through separate lenses. In *Jihad of the Pen: the Ṣūfī Literature of West Africa*, Zachary Wright remarks that 'the near absence of their [Ṣūfī *'ulamā'* from West Africa] authorial voices leaves a void at what should be the heart of an intellectual history'.[6] Focusing on the intersection of the Sufism and Islamic law in the *Kitāb al-Rimāḥ*, this chapter is motivated by the effort to bring Tāl's contributions to the fore of modern Islamic intellectual history. *Kitāb al-Rimāḥ* is normally classified as a 'Sufi' text. In it, however, Tāl discusses a range of topics from *fiqh* to theology and cites more than 650 direct quotes from over 100 sources. Almost half of the quotes come from 'Abd al-Wahhāb al-Sha'rānī (d. 1565), whose seminal work, *Al-Mizān al-Kubrā* ('The Supreme Scale'), compares the rulings of all four Sunni schools as if they were a single school.

The erudition and mobility of Tāl, no doubt propelled by the edicts of the modern Sufi order, the Tījāniyya, which stressed the importance of the attainment of knowledge, exacerbated his scholastic rigour and his ability to memorize and transcribe a large corpus of oral and written sources. Backed up by an overwhelming plethora of quotes, one can say that *al-Rimāḥ* offers a succinct worldview and is a thorough corpus for belief and worship from a rich array of sources from the Islamic intellectual tradition. In addition, it is a reformist text par excellence. Through Tāl's critical insights and scathing adages, *al-Rimāḥ* holds the effect of rousing the reader from a complacent slumber and succeeds in awakening the mind to introspect. The name itself, *al-Rimāḥ* ('The Spears') for the text is appropriate, as it is full of unapologetic attacks against the thought and beliefs of

4 'Alī Harāzim Al-Barrāda, *Jawāhir al-ma'ānī wa-bulūgh al-amānī fī fayḍ Saydī Abī l-'Abbās al-Tijānī* (Beirut: Dār al-Fikr, 2001).

5 See David Robinson, *The Holy War of Umar Tal* (Oxford: Clarendon Press, 1985); Fernand Dumont, *L'Anti-Sultan, ou al-Hajj Umar du Fouta* (Dakar and Abidjan: Nouvelles éditions africaines, 1974); John Willis, *In the Path of Allah, the Passion of al-Hajj 'Umar: An Essay into the Nature of Charisma in Islam* (London: Frank Cass, 1989); Madina Ly-Tall, *Un Islam militant en Afrique de l'Ouest au XIXe siècle: la Tijāniyya de Saïku Umar Futiyu contre les pouvoirs traditionnels et la puissance coloniale* (Paris: L'Harmattan, 1991).

6 Rudolph T. Ware; Zachary Wright; Amir Syed, *Jihad of the Pen: Sufi Scholars of Africa in Translation* (Cairo: American University in Cairo Press, 2018) 1.

erroneous 'fools'. Tāl uses the third person throughout the text – 'informing *them* that ... telling *them* that ...' – which signifies his aim towards corrective guidance.

Most studies on any form of modern Islamic reformist thought usually begin with the eighteenth-century Wahhābī movement as the beginning of a 'fundamentalist mode of Islam'.[7] Ahmad Dallal critiques conventional approaches to studies of Islamic modernism[8] as ones that tend to create an 'intellectual cohesion' among the revivalist thinkers of the mid-eighteenth and nineteenth centuries as members of the same 'intellectual family tree'.[9] In Dallal's view, the normative associations that are usually made when describing Islamic reformers often resemble these descriptors:

> The need to return to the Qur'ān and *Sunna*, return to origins, revival of *ijtihād* (scholarly interpretation of the Law) and *ḥadīth* studies, rejection of innovation and imitation (*taqlıd*) in matters of law, and rejection of the excesses of Sufism.[10]

This chapter is motivated by a rejection of the above cohesive consensus on Islamic reform and seeks to move away from making blanket claims about associations usually made with Sufism and Islamic law in the nineteenth century, one of which is that debates over *taqlīd* are tied to legal matters outside the purview of the 'non-rational' realm of mysticism. Rather than 'quoting isolated ideas out of their general ideological context',[11] I show that compartmentalizing works associated with Sufism into insular categories due to their 'mystical' (i.e. 'non-rational') representation risks the emergence of blind spots in understanding the mystic's overarching spiritual, legal and intellectual project. Islamic intellectual historians of the modern period would be amiss not to place Tāl within the ranks of the leading revivalist thinkers in the nineteenth century.

The Features of Tāl's Liminal Anti-*Madhhabism*

From the fifteenth to the nineteenth centuries in North and West Africa, from Aḥmad Zarrūq (d. 1493) to Ahmad ibn Idrīs (d. 1837), we find many debates on

[7] Wilfred Cantwell Smith, *Islam in Modern History* (Princeton: Princeton University Press, 1977) 24.

[8] The term 'modernism' itself is a contested one, but I use it here to simply connote what the *Oxford Encyclopedia of Islam* describes as a thought movement that advocates a 'flexible, continuous reinterpretation of Islam'.

[9] H.A.R. Gibb, *Modern Trends in Islam* (Chicago: Chicago University Press, 1947) 27–8.

[10] Ahmad Dallal, 'The Origins and Objectives of Islamic Revivalist Thought (1750–1850)', *Journal of the American Oriental Society*, 113, 3, 1993, 341–59, 341.

[11] Dallal, 'The Origins and Objectives', 358.

efforts to define the balance between *ṭarīqa* and *sharīʿa*, and attempts to promote a 'juridical Sufism' that emphasizes the importance of jurisprudence and critiques the excesses of certain Sufi practices. Under competition from epistemic and reformist contenders from colonial and intra-Muslim forces, Tāl articulates an intervention to this debate in a pronounced and forceful way, indicating that the stakes for this debate have become heightened. Of particular significance is his opinion on the issue of adhering to the authority of a single *madhhab*.

Chapter 8 of *al-Rimāḥ*, entitled 'informing them that God did not oblige one to follow a specific school from the schools of the *mujtahidīn*',[12] is the focal topic of this chapter. The chapter is directed against 'those who are misled to believe that whoever goes against the ruling of one of the four *imāms* disobeys God and that this act is enough to cast him out of the entire *madhhab*'.[13] Tāl's criticism of the *madhāhib* is therefore not absolute, rather, indicates that it is directed against a trend of *'ulamā'* who upheld the view that one must follow a single *madhhab* and stick to it unquestioningly, lest they incur God's wrath. Tāl decries this claim as erroneous, citing that even the caliph 'Umar b. al-Khaṭṭāb himself was never content with his own rulings on legal matters. The issue of *taqlīd* (justified conformity) is central to understanding his grievance against following a *madhhab.* Tāl criticizes trends among certain followers of legal schools, who follow an *imām*'s opinion even though that ruling may be wrong in their own judgment.[14] He does not cast blame on the *imāms* of the four legal schools, but rather on their followers who take their word as infallible and akin to the word of God.[15] Instead, Tāl advises believing men and women to hold fast to the 'sharīʿa *muḥammadiyya*', strictly follow and know the Qur'ān and *Sunna* to the best of their abilities[16] and exert themselves in the path of knowledge and at the feet of living *'ulamā'* who embody the Muḥammadan reality, rather than 'the books of dead men', lest they 'drown in a sea of ignorance and darkness'.[17] 'There is no one more ignorant than those who claim that soundness is circumscribed in the understanding of a singly one *imām*',[18] he adds.

Tāl makes a clear link between the unifying authority of the Prophet Muḥammad and the field of jurisprudence to reject the singular emphasis on the authority of legal schools:

[12] ʿUmar Tāl, *Kitāb Rimāḥ Ḥizb al-Rahīm ʿAla Nuḥūr Ḥizb al-Rajīm* (Beirut: Dār al-Fikr, 1981) 69.

[13] *Rimāh*, 69.

[14] *Rimāh.*

[15] *Rimāh*, 77.

[16] *Rimāh*, 83.

[17] *Rimāh*, 86.

[18] *Rimāh.*

> Know that the *sharī'a* that Prophet Muḥammad brought was without division among people ... how can the *imāms* cause disunity among Muslims knowing that judgment belongs to God alone and that there is no path to finding his judgment except through the Book which he sent down and the *Sunna* of the Prophet?[19]

In the tenth section of the book, entitled 'The Saint for whom the door of Truth has been opened is not tied to any particular doctrine among the legal doctrines of the independent jurists', Tāl quotes al-Sha'rānī (d. 1565) in a parable comparing the gnostic and *muqallid* (the conformist), and likening the gnostic to one who enters a house in broad daylight and sees its contents, whereas the *muqallid* stands outside the house and listens to a group of people who describe to him the interior of the house. Next, he says that if two gnostics enter the same house and debate its contents, they would definitely come to agreement on what they both see, whereas if two *muqallids* debate the contents of the house, they would not be able to do so with certainty, adding: 'this is why two gnostics have never disagreed about their knowledge of Allah Exalted is He'.[20]

This position is not unique within the context of its time period, nor is it surprising in mystical approaches to Islamic law. It is reminiscent of that of his contemporary Aḥmad ibn Idrīs al-Fāsi (d. 1837), the great mystic who was dubbed '*Muḥyī al-Sunna*' (the reviver of the *Sunna*) and underwent self-exile from his native Fez to the Arabian Peninsula in order to dwell among the exoteric community of 'Abd al-Wahhāb (d. 1792), despite their staunchly diverging positions on Sufism. Both Ibn Idrīs and 'Abdul Wahhāb converged on one key point, however, which was the impetus for Ibn Idrīs to immigrate: their rejection of the *taqlīd* of one *imām* of the four Sunni legal schools and the act of following a single school exclusively. But the length of Tāl's argument, backed up by quotes from figureheads such as *Imām* Mālik (d. 795), al-Qarāfī (d. 1285), Ibn 'Arafa (d. 1401), Ibn Juzayy (d. 1357), al-Dasūqī (d. 1296), al-Damīrī (d. 1405) and many others, points to the substantial effort to discredit exoteric scholars and cast them into the camp of those who break with the consensus approach of past scholars in the Islamic intellectual tradition on this particular matter.

In the eighth chapter of his work, Tāl names three types of students of knowledge: those who pursue the opinions and narrations of the *fuqahā'* without knowing the Qur'ān and the *Sunna*; secondly, those who do focus on the Qur'ān and the *Sunna* without consulting the *'ulamā'* and their opinions and opt for a return to consulting 'rulings during the time of the Prophet only'[21] (an obvious nod to Wahhabism); and lastly, those who he dubs people of 'light and *taḥqīq*

[19] *Rimāh*, 67–8
[20] *Rimāh*, 97.
[21] *Rimāh*.

(realization), who, with the guidance of gnostics, no door can ever be shut for them'.[22] It is through this framework that Ibn Idrīs' and Tāl's anti-Maddhabism poses criticism towards the anti-*taqlīd* of 'Abd al-Wahhāb, the doyen of Salafism. Even though, contrary to conventional assumptions as circulated in secondary sources on Salafism, 'Abd al-Wahhāb barely devotes any of his writings to an elaborate rejection of *taqlīd* in favour of *ijtihād* (scholarly interpretation of the Law).[23] Tāl's criticism of a certain class of exoteric legal scholars is undoubtedly undergirded by political motivations, but it is ultimately an attack on their perceived lack of attaining *ma'rifa* (gnosis) through the aid of a living shaykh. For adherents of the Wahhābī movement, this cannot be possible because of their vehement stance against external forms of Sufism. *Kitāb al-Rimāḥ* therefore offers a differing understanding of Islamic reformist thought in which legal and mystical epistemology are not mutually exclusive spheres. For Tāl, the goal of *taḥqīq*[24] (verification) supersedes the exoteric *taqlīd* conformity of earthly *'ulamā'*: knowing God is the all-encompassing goal, which de facto subsumes the obtainment of superior legal knowledge via one's living *shuyūkh*, the embodiments of the *ḥaqīqa Muḥammadiya* (the Muḥammadan reality). In this sense, Tāl's rhetoric gestures to the point that all Muslims must naturally adhere or conform to the authority of God and the Prophet, so he is in effect calling for *ṭaqlīd*, but a *taqlīd* of the Muḥammadan reality. After all, the linguistic meaning of the term *ṭaqlīd*, of wearing, being clad with or putting on, closely describes the way in which gnostics come to know this *ḥaqīqa* in Tāl's overarching project. His exoteric 'anti-*ṭaqlīd*' project, therefore, can be seen in fact as a project of *ṭaqlīd* of the Muḥammadan reality.

As previously mentioned, regarding Sufism as the arbiter of all knowledge is not a wholly new approach by mystics. One of Islam's greatest mystics, Muhyīddīn Ibn 'Arabī (d. 1240), whom Tāl quotes heavily, is similarly sceptical of what he called 'books of opinions', meaning the works of *fiqh*. James Morris relates the following translation from the *Futūḥāt*:

> Most people's intellects are veiled by their thoughts and fall short of perceiving this (reality), because of their lack of spiritual purification (*tajrīd*) ... so whoever God grants its understanding will recognize it and distinguish it from the rest. For that is the True Knowledge.[25]

[22] *Rimāh.*

[23] Dallal, 'The Origins and Objectives', 350.

[24] Khaled El-Rouayheb suggests that the features of emphasis on *ṭaḥqīq* doctrinally can be traced back to the seventeeth century. See Khaled El-Rouayheb, *Islamic Intellectual History in the Seventeenth Century: Scholarly Currents in the Ottoman Empire and the Maghreb* (New York: Cambridge University Press, 2015) 235–56.

[25] James Morris, 'Ibn 'Arabi's "Esotericism": The Problem of Spiritual Authority',

In the introduction to *The Exoteric Ahmad Ibn Idrīs*, Radtke, O'Fahey and O'Kane cite al-Lamatī's relation of the words of al-Dabbāgh in *al-Ibrīz*, which is also cited in the opening of Tāl's tenth chapter, and make a similar point:

> If all the legal schools were to disappear – because of direct contact with the Prophet – the gnostic would be able to restore the whole of *sharīʿa* ... knowledge of this kind is far superior to that of an ordinary theologian and jurist. From the vantage point of the fanatic factionalism of the schools of jurisprudence, this obviously appears absurd, since the activity of the schools is based on fallible human understanding.[26]

Without expounding on the methodology and meanings of the Sufi teachings mentioned above, for great gnostics like Tāl and Ibn ʿArabi, knowledge, whether mystical or legal, can only be obtained directly from the perpetual, experiential knowledge of God and the Prophet rather than from the 'books of dead men'. In the Tījāni methodology, the complete shaykh – by virtue of his lofty *maqām* (station) and closeness to the 'living Prophet' – enables the *murīd* (Sufi follower) to follow acts governed by *sharīʿa* in a confirmed, assured way. The sphere of *fiqh* thus becomes a means to an end (*maʿrifa*), rather than an end in and of itself. In *al-Rimāḥ*, it is evident that *fiqh* as a discipline and field of knowledge remains central but is subsumed under the holistic, superior authority of the gnostics by virtue of their Prophetic inheritance.

While the aims of *sharīʿa* remain central to this pursuit, Tāl warns that the field of *fiqh*, when studied alone, can present a veil to the seeker of knowledge. In chapter 4 of the *Rimāḥ*, partially entitled 'regarding some of the veils which prevent people from recognizing the friends of God', he names 'contemporaneousness'[27] as one of the veils and remarks: 'no one is more inflicted with this veil than the *fuqahāʾ* (jurists) that remain stuck on the sciences of *furūʿ* (branches), which categorically is called '*fiqh*'.' He also calls jurists *ahl ʿilm al-ẓāhir* (the people of exoteric knowledge) and *ahl al-inkār* (the deniers) in multiple instances.

Prophetic 'Open Source'

In an essay on Neo-Sufism in the *New Cambridge History of Islam*, Bruce Lawrence suggests that the single most important question that demarcates Sufi

---

Studia Islamica, 71, 1990, 37–64, 41.

26 Bernd Radtke; John O'Kane; Knut S. Vikor; R.S. O'Fahey, *The Exoteric Aḥmad Ibn Idrīs: A Sufi's Critique of the Madhāhib and the Wahhābīs: Four Arabic Texts with Translation and Commentary* (Leiden: Brill, 2000) 18.

27 Denying a saint based on the fact that he/she could not possibly live in the same time as the denier.

from non-Sufi Muslims is whether the Prophet Muḥammad is alive or dead.[28] Lawrence asserts that Sufis of all generations have held this view that the Prophet is living, yet, I argue, what distinguishes the nineteenth century is that it is a time that witnessed a more explicit, and more openly public, awareness of the Prophet as the crucial, 'living' link among Sufi-oriented intellectuals. This more public awareness naturally incited increased criticism from anti-Sufi detractors. Yet the figure of the Prophet, in the work of Tāl and others, possesses a timeless omniscience. Intercession with the Prophet is certainly not a new idea, with the origins of documenting this experience able to be traced in the works of past mystics such as Ibn 'Arabi, al-Ṣuyūṭī and others. Jonathan Brown briefly treats the question of *kashf* (unveiling) via visions as a means of attaining legal knowledge in his seminal work on *ḥadīth*.[29]

Tāl's text is undergirded by the doctrinal belief that the Prophet's physical death in 632 CE did not – at least for some eighteenth-century mystics like Tījāni – signify the end of a direct juridical access to legal knowledge. Zachary Wright describes the Tījāni epistemology and the centrality of the Prophet Muḥammad's spiritual reality:

> By the late eighteenth century Sufi *shaykhs* began to be seen, increasingly, as the living personification of the Prophet Muḥammad's spiritual reality (*ḥaqīqa muḥammadiyya*), itself symbolizing true knowledge of God. The highest Sufi authorities maintained direct contact with the Prophet Muḥammad's enduring bodily presence (*dhāt*), receiving both religious and worldly guidance.[30]

It is due to figures like Tāl, Uthmān b. Fūdi (d. 1817) and others, that the feature of seeing the Prophet in a waking state (*yaqaẓatan lā manāman*[31]) became normative in eighteenth- and early nineteenth-century West African and Moroccan Sufism. After all, Prophetic access is the basis on which the Tijāniyya was founded, and continues to be a source of ongoing legal and mystical guidance beginning with its founder Aḥmad al-Tijānī (d. 1815) and subsequent leaders and followers of the *ṭarīqa* to this very day. Allegorically speaking, for Tāl the *Sunna* can therefore be seen as a perpetual 'open source'; for some, open, in the sense that it is a perpetually open door to accessing prophetic knowledge.

[28] Lawrence Bruce, 'Sufism and Neo-Sufism', in Michael Cook (ed.), *The New Cambridge History of Islam* (Cambridge: Cambridge University Press, 2009) 355–84, 355.

[29] Jonathan Brown, *Hadith: Muhammad's Legacy in the Medieval and Modern World* (Oxford: Oneworld Publications, 2009) 110.

[30] Zachary Wright, *Living Knowledge in West African Islam: the Sufi Community of Ibrahim Niasse* (Leiden and Boston: Brill, 2015), 58.

[31] Zachary Wright, *Realizing Islam: The Tijaniyya in North Africa and the Eighteenth-Century Muslim World* (Chapel Hill: University of North Carolina Press, 2020) 128.

Such claims have been met with controversy and are naturally an inflammatory point of contention among critics of Sufism and *ṭuruq*. Questions of accessibility, elitism and the theme of secrecy come to the fore when discussing the mystical experience of seeing the Prophet in a waking state, but the *Jawāhir* – the Tijāniyya's seminal text – glosses over this experience matter of factly. Similar illuminations appear in the work of great mystics such as Al-Dabbāgh (d. 1719) and Aḥmad ibn Idrīs (d. 1837). The *ṭarīqa* Tijāniyya is especially unique in the issue of Prophetic accessibility because it derives its exclusivity and central doctrine from the fact that Aḥmad al-Tījāni is claimed to have received direct sanction to start the *ṭarīqa* from the Prophet himself.[32] Through that, al-Tījāni claimed the ranks of *quṭb-al-aqṭāb* (the pole of poles) and *khatm al-wilāya al-muḥammādiyya* (the seal of Muḥammadan inheritance), which implies that no one would achieve the same rank after him. The centrality of the Prophet's accessibility as central to Tāl's construction of a doctrine in the *Rimāḥ* cannot be understated.

Tāl cites Aḥmad Zarrūq (d. 1493) in his *Qawāʿid*: 'do not follow except the *maʿṣūm* (the immaculate one) i.e. the Prophet'. Tāl devotes an entire section[33] to the issue of seeing the Prophet in a waking state. He heavily cites the works of sixteenth-century Egyptian scholars 'Abd al-Wahhāb al-Sha'rānī and Jalāluddīn al-Suyūṭi's (d. 1505) who both emphasized the centrality of the Muḥammadan Path with its intensified devotion to the Prophet as the ultimate guide and shaykh, wrote against those who deny the possibility of witnessing the Prophet in a waking state, sought to revive understandings of the *sharīʿa* that were not bogged down by exotericism and egoism, and also wrote treatises challenging the authority of sultans and princes who are perceived to be oppressive and unjust. For example, he cites Suyūṭi's *Tanwīr Al-Ḥalak fi Imkān Ru'yat al-Nabī wal-Malak* ('Illuminating the eyes with the possibility of seeing the Prophet and the angels') and from *al-Ibrīz* he narrates the entirety of *Dīwān al-Awliyā'* ('the assembly of God's friends') as further proof. In addition to citing the Qur'ān and *Sunna* on the validity of seeing the Prophet in a waking state, he ends the section with the following culmination:

[32] Radtke et al., *The Exoteric Aḥmad Ibn Idrīs*, 66.

[33] Chapter 31 is entitled: 'informing them that the friends of God see the Prophet may God bless him and grant him peace in a waking state, and that he may, God bless him and grant him peace, attend any assembly or place he wishes in body and soul and acts as he wishes and travels wherever he desires in all regions of the earth and in the Divine realm (*malakūt*) in the form in which he was before his death, without any change, but hidden from sight just as the angels are, despite their being alive corporeally; and [informing them that] if God wills that a servant should see [the Prophet] He lifts the veil from His servant and he sees the Prophet in his actual form.'

> You will come to see clearly that the meeting of … Shaykh Aḥmad al-Tijānī with our Master the Prophet of God (was) in a waking not sleeping state. Only ignorant, stupid, envious, accursed seekers would deny this, and none can Guide them except he who God wills to guide.[34]

For the Tijānīs, seeing the Prophet in a waking state is not simply a matter of mystical ascension, but is rather a proof for the ultimate authority of God and his prophet, the shaykh and his guided followers.

By emphasizing connection to the living Prophet, Tāl reconstitutes the hierarchy of authority in the disclosure of knowledge. While doing this, he does not insinuate a sense of secrecy to preserve these mystical disclosures, quite the contrary; he constructs a doctrine derived from them. He does so at a time when aphorisms such as 'he who does not have a shaykh, the devil becomes his shaykh' and the practice of finding a *shaykh wāṣil*, one who can help link wayfarers to God through a verified mystical chain, was being challenged, but still held traces of normativity. Tāl goes on to blame a person's defunct free will and shortcomings as the primary hindrance for not being able to comprehend or believe such a claim throughout his text. The effects of *al-Rimāḥ* on its readership, therefore, has a more tangible impact than the words of Dabbāgh or Ibn Idrīs; his text does not mince its words as an open invitation to take the *ṭarīqa* as a means of salvation and obtaining closeness to the Prophet. For mystics of the eighteenth and nineteenth centuries and in the major Sufi texts mentioned in this paper, none of the authors prescribes a *ṭarīqa* as a clearly outlined methodology as does the *Rimāḥ*.

Superior Knowledge

In a poem, Tāl cites the risks associated with the path of knowledge: vanity, or hesitancy in acquiring knowledge, procreating, talking too much and loving the world.[35] He warns of those who claim to spread *fiqh* but are not truly *fuqahā'*

[34] *Rimāḥ*, 459. For more works that mention seeing the Prophet in a waking state, see *Bughyat al-Mustafīd fī-Sharḥ Munyat al-Murīd* by Shaykh Muḥammad al-ʿArabī b. al-Sā'īḥ (d. 1892), *Imām* Suyūti's sixteenth-century work, *Al-Iʿlām b. Ḥukm ʿIsā ʿalayhi as-salam* ('Informing People on the Status of Isa God's Peace be Upon him'), where he details that one of the key *karāmāt* of the *awliyā'* is the ability to see the Prophet ﷺ in a waking state and taking from him knowledge and inductions, this is confirmed by the likes of Al-Qarāfī, Al-Ghazāli, Abu Bakr Ibn ʿArabī, Al-Bayhaqī and Al-Laqqānī. This *ḥadīth* is often cited as proof of this phenomenon: 'Mūsā is alive in his grave praying upright' and another *ḥadīth*: 'the Prophets are alive in their graves praying'.

[35] *Kitāb al-Rimāḥ*, 92.

(knowledgeable),[36] signalling towards an important insight into Tāl's methodology: the mystic, in the eyes of Tāl, possesses superior power over the exotericist in his or her ability to access the Prophet as a living guide and as a source of knowledge 'regarding all questions to do with delivering legal judgments'.[37] I propose that in the mystic's view, the concept of *Sunna* is not simply tied to normative practice and the dominant methodology of deriving laws from *ḥadīth*, but can instead be approached as an esoterically oriented epistemology.[38] For Tijānī and his followers then, *Sunna* signifies a rather different thing than it does for the likes of Ibn Taymiyya (d. 1328) or 'Abd al-Wahhāb.[39] This is epitomized by the consideration that, for the mystics, their approach to *Sunna* possesses the power to verify and confirm ambiguous legal questions directly from 'the source' himself, which transcends the limits of the physical world, and even has the ability to introduce new ones. This claim to a higher authority, however, did not escape the criticism of various Muslim scholars throughout history. For example, the al-Azhar educated Ḥasan Al-'Aṭṭār (d. 1835) reproached Ibn Idrīs for claiming to maintain direct verbal contact with the Prophet.[40] In addition, in his *al-Ṭarīqa al-muḥamadiyya wa-al sīra al-aḥmadiyya*, the sixteenth-century Ottoman theologian al-Birkāwī (d. 1573) explicitly criticized how certain Sufis in his time claimed direct contact with the Prophet.

Tāl, aware that the trope of direct contact with the Prophet is met with ambivalence among laity and scholars alike, attributes this to limitations in cognitive and spiritual aptitude, accessibility and the 'fallibility of human understanding'.[41] He does not directly indicate that not all Muslims are able to acquire this state, let alone are required by law to believe in its possibility. In their 'Neo-Sufism Reconsidered', Radtke and O'Fahey elucidate this very point as a key source of conflict between jurists and mystics that arose in early Islam.[42] Juxtaposing Ibn

36 *Kitāb al-Rimāḥ*, 90.

37 *Kitāb al-Rimāḥ*.

38 Mouhamadou Cissé dubs this approach 'juridico-mystique' in his PhD dissertation. See Mouhamadou Alpha Cissé, 'El Hadji Omar Foutiyou Tall, une Grande Figure de la Tijāniyya en Afrique Occidentale au XIXème siècle: Pensée juridico-mystique à travers "Rimah"', PhD diss., Université Cheikh Anta Diop de Dakar, 2011.

39 The consensus on the definition of '*Sunna*' emerged in the era of *Imām* Shāfiʿi, who created the association between the Prophet's actions and speech with the science of *ḥadīth* as a source of the law. For more on the origins of *Sunna*, see the introduction to Daniel W. Brown, *Rethinking Tradition in Modern Islamic Thought* (Cambridge: Cambridge University Press, 1999).

40 Radtke et al., *The Exoteric Ahmad Ibn Idris*, 19.

41 Radtke et al., *The Exoteric Ahmad Ibn Idris*, 18.

42 R.S. O'Fahey; Bernd Radtke, 'Neo-Sufism Reconsidered', *Der Islam* 70, 1, 1993, 52–87, 61.

Idrīs and Ibn Taymiyya, it is conferred that both would agree that knowledge is valid insofar as this knowledge comes from God; but 'the fundamental difference between the two men is that for the latter, revelation is closed, for the former, it is not'.[43]

The Tijāniyya and the Mālikī School

Concerning the accessibility of the Prophet and asking him questions on legal matters and verifying the weak *ḥadīths*, there is no indication in *al-Rimāḥ* that Tāl regards this as a replacement for the historical evidence of traditional *fiqh* and *ḥadīth* sciences. Throughout *al-Rimāḥ*, Tāl cites *ḥadīth* with their proper historical chains, and when he references the Prophet in a waking state, he only cites the visions of Aḥmad al-Tījāni who in the *Jawāhir* in numerous places simply says '*qāla lī rasūl Allāh*' ('the Prophet of God told me …'). Today, one would be hard pressed to find the position of Tāl on the authority of *madhāhib* widespread among neo-traditionalist and Sufi practitioners, and most adherents of the Tijāniyya order and Muslims in West and North Africa follow the Mālikī school of law. It is possible to consider, however, that the Mālikī school may possess unique flexible features in that, as Zachary Wright notes, 'it laid particular emphasis on learning in the presence of teachers rather than texts'.[44] Sufism in West Africa, Wright asserts, 'drew on the legacy of bodily mimesis and the scholarly-ascetic ideal in the Mālikī *fiqh* tradition, [it] also challenged the juristic tradition'.[45] Such a flexibility in interpreting the legal canon, I argue, stems from the Tijāniyya's emphasis on experiential *ma'rifa* before all else. Similar stances can be found in more contemporary manifestations of Tījāni practice, even among its professedly Mālikī adherents.[46]

The renowned Shaykh Ibrahim Niasse (d. 1975), who is considered one of the most important Tījāni figures and revivalist Muslim scholars of the twentieth century, was known to have said: 'we are Mālikīs but we are not *mamālīk* (slaves) of *Imām* Mālik'.[47] According to Wright, Shaykh Ibrahim Niasse's position on the *madhāhib* is that the strict following of one of the four *imāms* blindly can shield someone from benefiting from a living shaykh, since most people cannot master all four legal schools and their rulings.[48] The issue of *qabd* (folding one's arms to

[43] O'Fahey; Radtke, 'Neo-Sufism Reconsidered', 61.
[44] Wright, *Living Knowledge in West African Islam*, 34.
[45] Wright, *Living Knowledge in West African Islam*, 39.
[46] Though Aḥmad al-Tijānī himself was Mālikī, he also went against certain Mālikī practices in preference of those perceived to be closer to the *Sunna*.
[47] Well-known oral tradition of Shaykh Ibrahim Niasse.
[48] Wright, *Living Knowledge in West African Islam*, 224.

the chest in prayer) is one such example. Zachary Wright relates the fascinating timeline of how Ibrahim Niasse broke the custom of praying as most Mālikīs do, in *sadl* (with one's hands folded against the sides) due to seeing a vision in which the Prophet instructed him to pray in *qabd* instead of *sadl*.[49] It bears to mention that *Kitāb al-Rimāḥ* of 'Umar Tāl is one of the three most referenced sources in Ibrahim Niasse's own magnum opus, *Kāshif al-Ilbās*, which was written in 1931.[50]

Conclusion

In the *Principles of Sufism* of Aḥmad Zarrūq, he writes: 'he who maintains that "a Sufi has no legal school" is wrong, except in the sense that the Sufi chooses from each school what is best as a proof, a goal, a precaution, or something else, which will lead him to a spiritual state; otherwise, Junayd was a Thawrī, al-Shiblī a Mālikī, al-Jurayrī a Ḥanafī and Muḥāsibī a Shāfi'ī, and these men are leaders and pillars of the path'.[51] Tāl's views on *fiqh* in the *Rimāḥ* align with this statement. 'Forgoing all the legal schools is what is forbidden. But leaving the opinions of some of them is alright ... for all the schools of the *ummah* are valid paths for the believers and not only one of them.'[52] A later Tijānī text, *Bughyat al-Mustafīd li Sharḥ Munyāt al-Murīd* by Muḥammad al-'Arabī b. al-Sā'īḥ (d. 1892) corroborates this point, citing an oral narration by al-Ghazālī (d. 1111) who,

> after tasting *taṣawwuf* said: 'we wasted our life in falsehood', i.e. in the study among *ahl al-jadal* (the people of disputation) ... but the truth is, Ghazālī said this during a state of gnosis drunkenness because the study of *fiqh* is not falsehood, rather, it is the principal of the way, and it is incumbent upon the people of the way for all their actions and stillness to be based on the Qur'ān and the *Sunna*, and that cannot be known except by sailing in the sciences of *tafsīr* and *ḥadīth* ... so the goal of the Sufi, then, is to have his or her actions backed up by his or her own knowledge (*'ālimun bī 'ilmihī*), no more, no less.[53]

Clearly, Tāl's scathing critique of the *fuqahā'* is motivated by certain manifestations of what he perceived to be singularly exoteric knowledge-seeking

[49] Wright, *Living Knowledge in West African Islam*.

[50] Zachary Wright, 'The Kāshif al-Ibās of Shaykh Ibrahim Niasse: Analysis of the Text', *Islamic Africa* 1, 1, 2010, 109–23, 115.

[51] Ahmad Zarruq, '*Qawāid at-Taṣawwuf, Principles of Sufism*: an Annotated Translation with Introduction', trans. Zaineb Istrabadi, PhD diss., Indiana University, 1987, 84.

[52] *Kitāb al-Rimāḥ*, 74.

[53] Muḥammad al-'Arabī b. al-Sā'īḥ, *Bughyāt al-Mustafīd li Sharḥ Munyāt al-Murīd* (Rabat: al-Ma'ārif al-Jadīda, 2017) 61.

prevalent in his time. But *al-Rimāḥ*'s forceful disparagement of exoteric *taqlīd* takes previous debates on Sufism and Islamic law to another level of analysis, previously ignored in studies on Islamic modernism and reform emerging from nineteenth-century West Africa. It is a critique of exoteric *taqlīd*, but its ultimate aim is experiencing *taḥqīq* within the Muḥammadan reality. Quoting Khaled-El Rouyaheb, Zachary Wright reminds us of the often neglected dichotomy that '*Ijtihād* was not always the only solution to "blind imitation" (*taqlīd*): "verification" (*taḥqīq*) could also be a relevant exercise.'[54] Though the critique of the authority of the legal schools has today been normatively paired with Salafī ideology, Tāl's text and the many sage interlocutors he cites therein complicates this narrative: Sufi *'ulamā'* also questioned the prevalence of *taqlīd*, but to them, 'a return to the Qur'ān and *Sunna* only' meant something rather different to them from the likes of Abdul Wahhāb and his adherents. For Sufis like Tāl, 'Qur'ān and *Sunna*' is rather an invitation for re-centring the authority of gnosticism, and the experiential *dhawq* (taste) of knowing God as the highest goal for knowledge-seeking. It regards the attainment of knowledge not as a path of prestige or worldly gain, but a tenacious path of sincerity, humility and acting upon what one knows to be true through experience, not via intellectualism alone.

Yet, texts alone cannot give a complete picture of how certain contentions manifest in reality. In order to understand the issue of Tāl's approach to *taqlīd* more effectively, further research needs to be done in order to test how his views on *fiqh* 'translated' in a practical way into his social milieu. As a political and religious leader, how did he adjudicate among his community? Seeing as he founded a warrior state, how, if at all, did his writings apply to the legal institutions, courts or rulings that emerged under his rule? Such questions will surely aid in gaining a clearer understanding of the practical manifestations of the anti-*taqlīd* debate in nineteenth-century Senegambia and beyond.

Suffice it to say for the purposes of this chapter that, for the Tijāniyya, the centrality of the Prophet is not simply a methodology but a complete *weltanshauung*. With the experiential knowledge of God at its epicentre, *al-Rimāḥ* points to a mystically invigorated epistemology for approaching *sharī'a*. For Tāl, the *sharī'a* is known through the *taqlīd* of a living shaykh in possession of direct access to the Prophet; the ongoing, living embodiment of the *Sunna* itself.

Perhaps the views of Ibn Idrīs and Tāl on the link between Sufism and jurisprudence offer a potential point of dialogue with adherents of the Salafī movement today. Proponents of 'traditional Islam' today, who vehemently champion the validity of Sufism and *taqlīd* as their signifying marker, can no longer fully reject those they deem as 'bad' Salafīs due to their rejection of the *madhāhib*

[54] Zachary Wright, *Realizing Islam*, 49, quoting El-Rouayheb, *Islamic Intellectual History*, 358.

(many of whom practice manifestations of esotericism, or Sufism with a small 's', and many of whom are in actuality proponents of *taqlīd* of the school of *Imām* ibn Ḥanbal).[55] At the very least, *al-Rimāḥ* invites purveyors of intellectual history to complicate the narrative of modern Islamic reform, and challenges us not to accept the reductive classifiers and wholesale descriptors in the contentions between Sufism and Salafism. At most, the *Rimāḥ* invites readers to re-centre this text into its rightful place as an important contribution to modern Islamic intellectual and legal history.

[55] On the work of the late contemporary Syrian scholar who was known for his polemical writings against those who reject the following of a *madhhab*: Farah El-Sharif, 'The Rhetoric of Twentieth-century Damascene Anti-Salafism', *Contemporary Levant*, 5, 2, 2020, 113–25.

CHAPTER 8

A New African Orality? Tijānī Sufism, Sacred Knowledge, and the ICTs in Post-Truth Times[1]

Antonio de Diego González

West Africa is a space of paradoxes. Not even the most traditional Sufis can resist information and communication technologies (ICT). Nowadays they carry the *tasbīḥ* (prayer beads) in one hand and, in the other, a mobile phone or an iPad of the latest generation, to help them transmit ancient knowledge. From this it seems that sacred knowledge (*ma'rifa*) and technology are compatible since they make life easier for the Muslim community, as Ibrahim Niasse (1900–75) already pointed out in the 1950s.[2]

Shaykh Ibrahim has been a well-authorized voice. He himself founded the *Fayḍa* community in 1929, reviving Tijānī Sufism in West Africa, and adapting it to current times,[3] while maintaining a great respect for the traditional episteme. Niasse not only lived during the beginnings of the technological revolution, but he also authorized the use of microphones, speakers, and recordings for the purpose

[1] I would like to thank Ousmane Kane (Harvard University), Zachary Wright (Northwestern University), Lidwien Kapteijns (Wellesley College), Yunus Kumek (SUNY Buffalo), and Oludamini Ogunnaike (College of William and Mary) for their feedback on earlier versions of this chapter. Secondly, I thank the generosity and cooperation of the Tijānī *Fayḍa* communities in West Africa and the diaspora where I conducted fieldwork from 2013 to 2016. Finally, I thank Sara El Azrak for translating this paper into English.

[2] Ibrahim Niasse, *Al-Ḥujja al-bāligha fī kawn idhā'at alqurān sā'i'gha* (Dakar: Muḥammad al-Ma'mūn b. Ibrahim Niasse, 1988).

[3] Antonio de Diego González, *Ley y Gnosis. Historia Intelectual de la ṭarīqa Tijāniyya* (Granada: Editorial Universidad de Granada, 2020); Joseph Hill, 'Divine Knowledge and Islamic Authority: Religious Specialization among Disciples of Baay Ñas', PhD diss. in Anthropology, New Haven: Yale University, 2007; Rudiger Seeseman, *The Divine Flood: Ibrahim Niasse and the Roots of a Twentieth-century Sufi Revival* (Oxford: Oxford University Press, 2011); Zachary Wright, *Pearls from the Divine Flood* (Atlanta: FaydaBooks, 2015), revised 2nd edition.

Fig. 8.1 Shaykh Mahi Cisse (Credit: Klinfos.com)

of helping Muslims in their *dīn*.[4] He was also a strong advocate of contemporaneity, which did not prevent him from being one of the greatest mystics of the twentieth century, and keeping Sufism in balance with Islamic law (*sharīʿa*).

His children and grandchildren have followed this same path. Today, it is not uncommon to see his grandson Shaykh Mahi Cisse [figure 8.1] in Medina Baye – the spiritual city founded by Shaykh Ibrahim in Senegal – using several mobile phones to answer questions from his disciples based in Singapore or in the United States through WhatsApp or Facebook. A Malaysian disciple told me once in Medina Baye:

> Shaykh Mahi never leaves his phones. You know that you can always call him to ask any question, especially concerning matters of *maʿrifa* (gnosis). When I call

[4] Niasse, *Al-Ḥujja al-bāligha*, 54–6.

> him and he cannot not answer my call immediately, he returns me call later. He does never neglect us; he is always with us. His voice always cheers you up, it is full of *baraka*.[5]

This testimony is illustrative of many things. The interviewee not only expresses how a Sufi master uses technology, but at the same time he emphasizes the transmission of *baraka* (subtle and beneficial energy) through the voice of the shaykh. Traditionally, the *baraka* was obtained in the presence of shaykhs and holy people, but today, as the testimony of this informant suggests, it can be conveyed through a telephone conversation. The physical presence of yesteryear is replaced by today's digital presence. A call, a video, or a recording on YouTube can be very beneficial for the disciple who is in search of knowledge and for the shaykh who is imparting it. Information and communication technologies (ICT) have brought together traditional and contemporary models, but maintaining an important element: orality.

Orality is one of the markers of Islamic identity. It is both complex and rich – beyond the clichés imposed by orientalism, anthropology, and the colonial and modern Arab intellectuals[6] – in the case of Africa it constitutes one of the primary sources for the study of African intellectual history. If we fail to take orality into account, we lose essential speeches, very valuable traditions and, above all, precision in the speech that is transmitted generation after generation.

Without the Eurocentric and modern prejudice towards orality, the Islamic episteme showed its two faces: on the one hand, its written side, and on the other, its oral and aural dimensions. African Muslims, like so many others, created a whole lived knowledge that made memorization and orality its most recognizable sign.[7] Precisely, Ware explains that it was not only African Muslims that used orality, but also non-African Muslims. The Prophet Muḥammad himself received the revelation orally.[8] Corporeality, orality, and aurality have been central in the Islamic epistemological model since the birth of Islam. Islamic knowledge often goes beyond the limits of rationality and the mental arena in order to enter into other spaces, creating an 'epistemology of *living knowledge*' where the oral, corporeal, and aural dimensions have fundamental values.[9] Therefore, it is not

[5] An interview with a Malaysian disciple of Mahi Cisse. Medina Baye, July 2016.

[6] Ousmane Kane, *Beyond Timbuktu. An Intellectual History of Muslim West Africa* (Cambridge: Harvard University Press, 2016) 23–4.

[7] Wright, *Pearls from the Divine Flood*; Rudolph T. Ware, III, *The Walking Qur'an: Islamic Education, Embodied Knowledge, and History in West Africa* (Chapel Hill: University of North Carolina Press, 2014).

[8] Ware, *The Walking Qur'an*, 25–9.

[9] Wright, *Pearls from the Divine Flood*, 15–16.

surprising that Niasse did not have any problems in recognizing the value of technology and did not consider it to be an innovation (*bid'a*).

As pointed out by Cemil Aydin, the Islamic world has been a complex and diverse space because in the nineteenth century, it began to change with the emergence of pan-Islamic and modernist positions.[10] The Islamic modernism of the nineteenth century attacked the traditional episteme, accusing it of being lagging and superstitious, while being protected by European colonialism; European colonialism demonized the vision of a *living knowledge* compared to the rational and illustrated knowledge to foster a 'return to the true Islam'.[11] It was leaving aside the orality, the *baraka*, and the *ḥaḍra* (presence), which were replaced by textual literalism, the imitation of European modernity and political action.

This proposal derives from Eurocentric modernity. The same one that had racialized Muslims now offered them a tool to dominate the narrative and to adapt it to the ongoing historical progress. Also, European philologists had been doing this since the sixteenth century, starting with European colonial expansion. Walter Mignolo in his book *The Darker Side of the Renaissance* mentions that European modernity produced the ontologization of the written Western language above any other system that does not belong to this civilization. A question was raised as to the legitimacy, and even the existence – as pointed out by Mignolo – of any other intellectual manifestation outside the West.[12] The objective standard, scientific and Eurocentric – prepared by the thinkers of Modernity – was the pattern in which the rest of cultures and their practices were measured. This way, categories such as orality or corporeality were condemned to oblivion by stripping them from their ontological or historical value.[13]

Africa got to know these policies of modernity twice over. It wasn't just reduced to an abstract and unitary entity and therefore excluded from the global history following the opinions of the Hegelian philosophy of history,[14] but the modernist Islamic authors also vehemently attacked the Sufis and African

[10] Cemil Aydin, *The Idea of the Muslim World: A Global Intellectual History* (Cambridge: Harvard University Press, 2017) 6–8.

[11] Aydin, *The Idea of the Muslim World*, 82–3; Antonio de Diego González, 'El juego geopolítico de Marruecos y Arabia Saudí en África Occidental', *Araucaria Revista Iberoamericana de Filosofía, Política, Humanidades y Relaciones Internacionales*, 21, 41, 2019, 415–38.

[12] W.D. Mignolo, *The Darker Side of The Renaissance: Literacy, Territoriality and Colonization* (Ann Arbor: University of Michigan Press, 1995).

[13] Anibal Quijano, 'Coloniality and modernity/rationality', *Cultural Studies*, 21, 2–3, 2007, 168.

[14] Georg Wilhelm Friedrich Hegel, *Lectures on the Philosophy of World History: Volume I: Manuscripts of the Introduction and the Lectures of 1822–1823*, P. Hogdson (ed. & trans.) (Oxford: Oxford University Press, 2011) 196–8.

traditionalists[15] without recognizing their role in the Islamic world. Some historical narratives have constructed the image of a wild, tribal, irrational, syncretic, and chiefly oral Africa without taking into account the true sense of its orality. One of the highest authorities on the subject, Ruth Finnegan, affirms that there is often a confusion between the oral, unwritten, and written dimensions through which Africa has chosen to manifest itself.[16] Traditionally we are led to believe that what is written is something imperative and fundamental, as explained,[17] for the creation of a cultural literature. At the same time, possessing literature has always been considered a mark of the distinctive cultural level of a people[18] and of epistemic complexity.[19] But, according to Finnegan, orality can generate literatures as complex as written ones can be; it is only necessary to rethink some assumed concepts such as originality or continuity.

Eurocentric philology has imposed that, in order to have a written text, there must be an original canon from which to make copies, making it a certified version with a special ontological consideration. Finnegan points out that in oral literature there is also a text that does not have a reason to be original, but which is represented in a performance with its unique characteristics and its own orality.[20] The performance that connects with the *living knowledge* is where the value of this practice dwells. The oral is legitimized in the tradition that has had tools to justify it since early Islam.[21] Knowledge passes aurally from master to disciple, and the latest receives permission (*ijāza*) to continue transmitting and updating it.[22] A possessor of knowledge acts as a guarantor of it, but also as the link in a chain (*isnād*) that verifies and legitimizes his status. This is the Islamic premodern example, but each culture has its own procedures for the verification and legitimation of knowledge. West African Muslims assumed that part of this epistemic paradigm to consolidate their position as intellectual authorities in the Islamic world.

All over the world, and particularly in Africa, ICTs are still academically questioned as to how to treat written knowledge when it is placed in opposition to what

15 Antonio de Diego González, 'Identidad y modelos de pensamiento en África', PhD diss. in Philosophy, Universidad de Sevilla, 2016, 225.

16 Ruth Finnegan, *Oral Literature in Africa* (Cambridge: Open Book Publishers, 2012).

17 Mignolo, *The Darker Side of The Renaissance*, 46–7.

18 Finnegan, *Oral Literature in Africa*, 6.

19 Daniella Merolla, 'Introduction: Orality and technauriture of African literatures', *Tydskrif vir letterkunde*, 51,1, 2014, 80–90.

20 Finnegan, *Oral Literature in Africa*, 13.

21 Gregor Schoeler, *The Genesis of Literature in Islam. From Aural to Read* (Cairo: The American University in Cairo Press, 2009).

22 Ware, *The Walking Qur'an*, 55; Schoeler, *The Genesis of Literature in Islam*, 122–3.

has been called traditional orality.[23] YouTube, Facebook, Skype, or WhatsApp are channels through which large amounts of information are transmitted instantly, in a way that is similar to the way we used to use analogical audio tapes or DVDs. That is why it is not surprising that this reconfiguration of orality is conveying a new challenge at the time of the post-truth.[24] And, of course, it makes specialists raise a question that is difficult to answer: is this the classical African orality or has a new one just emerged?

The theme proposed in this chapter is highly complex to deal with, but it fits very well in a book that addresses these features. Orality has always been an identity marker of African intellectual history. A large part of its production and its subsequent oblivion spring from it. Certainly, it is not about speaking of orality in Africa, which is a widely discussed topic and by various authors. But this chapter attempts to answer the question as to whether there has been a new African orality based on ICT or if it remains the same orality with some dressings. To illustrate this question, I will analyse the ways in which ICT impacted Tijānī Sufism from the second half of the twentieth century.

This Sufi community – as we have already seen – is not unaware of the transformations of the contemporary world. It has adopted new discursive styles[25] and technologies to reach out to a wider audience using both African languages (Wolof, Hausa, Pulaar) and European languages (French, English). I was able to document different cases during the drafting of my thesis, and the fieldwork that I carried out in Senegal, Mauritania, the United States, and Europe. This chapter draws from these experiences and theorization surrounding them to illustrate the intersections between orality, ICT, sacred knowledge, and Sufism in times where the post-truth and Baudrillard's *simulacra* constitute the epistemological norm.

[23] Carmen Pérez-Sabater, 'The Linguistics of Social Networking: A Study of Writing Conventions on Facebook', *Linguistik Online*, 56, 6, 2012, 81–93.

[24] Post-truth is an epistemic concept in which truth works based on emotivity instead of consensus (metaphysical or logical). This concept is linked to the concept of 'simulacra' by the French philosopher Jean Baudrillard (*Simulacres et Simulation* (Paris: Éditions Galilée, 1981)), in which the truth does not correspond with his metaphysical/logical correlate – for example, as it works in classical Islamic thought – but with a purely emotive and deontologized reading by the subject. In our context, religious post-truth is deeply connected with religious populism and it threatens other epistemic manifestations that are not linked with the main discourse where populism is dominating. Antonio de Diego González, *Populismo Islámico* (Córdoba: Almuzara, 2020).

[25] Joseph Hill, '"Baay is the spiritual leader of the rappers": performing Islamic reasoning in Senegalese Sufi hip-hop', *Contemporary Islam*, 10, 2, 2016, 267–87.

From the Oral to the Written Word: the Recordings of Ibrahim Niasse

I heard the voice of Ibrahim Niasse for the first time in May 2014 while I was conducting fieldwork in Maʿaṭā Maūlāna, Mauritania. After the ʿ*asr* prayer, a kid from the town told me that it was time to listen to the '*tafsīr* of the Shaykh'. Surprised, I asked, 'Which shaykh?' 'What other shaykh can it be?' he said, surprised by my question. 'Of course Shaykh Ibrahim [Niasse].'

I must have had a remarkable expression on my face, knowing that Shaykh Ibrahim had died thirty-nine years ago. The boy held me by my hand and led me onto an esplanade where there was a Mauritanian *khayma* (tribal tent) and all the people gathered around a rickety boombox whose sound was amplified by a microphone. The voice in Arabic of Shaykh Ibrahim sounded from the speaker, explaining *sūra Maryam* of the Qur'ān. At the end of the meeting of *tafsīr*, they explained to me that the cassette recording was one of the greatest treasures of the town, just like ancient manuscripts. And they highlighted the *great baraka* that the experience of hearing the *tafsīr* in the mouth of the shaykh represented.[26]

This small anecdote shows the value that *technauriture* has among the Mauritanian disciples of Shaykh Ibrahim Niasse. Technology allows anyone to take part in a past performance and enjoy the benefits that traditional epistemology associates to such performance, as happened in his grandson Shaykh Mahi's previous case. The *baraka* in contemporary times can also be stored in cassettes. Some time later, once in Medina Baye, a grandson of Ibrahim Niasse gave me a USB key with five gigabytes of digitalized recordings of his grandfather, including two copies of the *tafsīr*, one in Wolof and another one in Arabic – precisely the one I had heard in Mauritania.

The *tafsīr* of Ibrahim Niasse has a very interesting history. We can find it nowadays in oral format (analogical, digital, and living performances) and also in a written one (transcribed and translated). We must make clear that it is not simply a typical book or a recording, but it is an answer to the complex attitude of contemporary *technauriture* where orality has an impact on the subject producing situations of virtuality.[27] For the followers of *Fayḍa,* Shaykh Ibrahim is the one who speaks, not a machine or a simple recording. The presence (*ḥaḍra*) of the shaykh is real at that moment, that is why the boy insisted on taking me to the session of *tafsīr* with urgency, in order for me to benefit from the knowledge and *baraka* of the shaykh.

There are two recordings of the oral version: the first one in Wolof, and the second in classical Arabic. Both were recorded during the month of Ramadan

[26] Notes of fieldwork in Maʿaṭā Maūlāna, May–June 2014.

[27] Merolla, 'Introduction: Orality and Technauriture of African Literatures', 80–90.

between the 1950s and 1960s,[28] in sessions of approximately an hour or an hour and a half. Shaykh Ibrahim offered two types of *tafsīr*. Carried out in classical Arabic in accordance with Islamic tradition, the first is thorough. It was destined for his most erudite disciples, using clarity and a formal language. The second one is in Wolof, starting with a Qur'ānic verse followed by a long explanation that was directed at a local audience. Its content becomes more symbolic and accessible for that audience. Some recordings do not follow a temporal continuity and are of poor quality, as some fragments cannot be heard clearly. The Arabic version lasts 22 hours and 16 minutes, whereas the Wolof one lasts 16 hours and 16 minutes.

As Ousmane Kane explains, Shaykh Ibrahim conducted oral *tafsīr* drawing inspiration from the traditional model learned from his family, and introducing some innovations.[29] Andrea Brigaglia refers to it as a supra-commentary (*ta'wīl*) of the classical *tafsīr* of Jalālayn, which is the main text used by Niasse to interpret the Qur'ān.[30] The comments also articulate reflections on metaphysical and cosmological issues[31] that are deeper and more suggestive than those accomplished by his contemporaries. The version in Wolof, in my opinion, is a little more spontaneous than the Arabic one, which in turn is more rigidly rhetorical. In the Wolof version, the musicality of the Wolof poetry is used more often. The Wolof one is also governed by the principle of solidarity with the public, something that requires more effort to be appreciated in its Arabic version because it needs a higher cultural level of the audience. Niasse's emotional involvement in his *tafsīr*, however, is very similar in both versions, trying not to show excessive involvement, but giving it slightly metaphysical flavours.[32] This shows that the Islamic tradition is not broken at any time, at least on the formal level.

Of the two recordings, the first to appear was the Wolof version in 1998.[33] Sponsored by the Sall family, it was released on cassette tapes in New York

28 Brigaglia points out that the Arabic version of Shaykh Ibrahim's *tafsīr* was recorded between 1963 and 1964 during fifty-six sessions in the month of Ramadan. Andrea Brigaglia, 'Two Exegetical Works from Twentieth-Century West Africa: Shaykh Abu Bakr Gumi's Radd al-adhhān and Shaykh Ibrahim Niasse's Fī riyāḍ al-tafsīr', *Journal of Qur'anic Studies*, 15, 3, 2013, 253–66.

29 Kane, *Beyond Timbuktu*, 80.

30 Brigaglia, 'Two Exegetical Works from Twentieth-Century West Africa', 258; Niasse, Ibrahim, *In the Meadows of Tafsīr for the Noble Qurān*, trans. Moctar Ba (Atlanta: FaydaBooks, 2014) 36.

31 Andrea Brigaglia, 'The Radio Kaduna tafsir (1978–1992) and the construction of public images of Muslim scholars in the Nigerian media', *Journal for Islamic Studies*, 27, 1, 2007, 173–210, 335.

32 Brigaglia, 'Two Exegetical Works from Twentieth-Century West Africa', 258.

33 John Hunwick et al., *Arabic literature of Africa Vol. 4: Writings of Western Sudanic Africa* (Leiden: Brill, 2003) 198; Kane, *Beyond Timbuktu*, 80.

with an introduction by Shaykh Barham Diop which was also oral in prologue form. It has recently been uploaded online at Archive.org[34] and to the YouTube channel titled *Mady Barham*.[35] The second one, the Arabic version, has not been published. There are some fragments on YouTube on the CheckhIbrahimNiass channel,[36] but the most interesting part of this recording is its transcription and publication in Arabic, a language very well known by many followers of Shaykh Niasse.

The transcription of the *tafsīr*[37] in Arabic was carried out by Muḥammad wuld 'Abdallāh (b. 1942), a *muqaddam* of Shaykh Ibrahim, under the title of *Fī Ryaḍ al-tafsīr li al-Qurān al-Karīm* ('In the Gardens of the Exegesis of the Noble Qur'ān') in six volumes. According to the biography by Baye wuld Hayba attached to the English edition of *tafsīr*, it took thirty-six years for the renowned and erudite scholar to complete the work, which was published in 2010.[38] Very carefully from a philological point of view, this edition includes not only the text of the *tafsīr*, but all the full sources and citations made by Niasse during the sessions. The text transliterates very faithfully the sessions and complements them with a valuable and critical apparatus of notes. This is a well-done adaptation of orality. One can listen to the recording while reading the text without finding any noticeable difference. The first volume of the Arabic transcription by Muḥammad wuld 'Abdallāh was translated into English by Moctar Boubakar M. Ba and published by Faydabooks. The translation of subsequent volumes in English is scheduled to be completed in the next few years. However, the general view among the disciples of the *Fayḍa*, the *talibé Baye*, is that it is much more beneficial to listen to the shaykh in the recording than to read him in the book. 'In written form there is a lack of his presence and his deep voice … the Shaykh is missing,' said a *talibé* in Medina Baye to me, being really convinced.[39]

The remaining African disciples of Shaykh Ibrahim did not need a transcription or written translation of his *tafsīr* because they have commented on it in oral sessions in their own languages. This constitutes a case of epistemic dynamism, favouring performance over textual fidelity. The most significant case is that of Ṭāhir Bauchi (b. 1927). He is the most famous *mufassir* among the disciples of Niasse due to his expressive richness.[40] As Shaykh Kano explained on the

[34] https://archive.org/details/Baye-tafsir. Accessed 11 June 2017.

[35] https://www.youtube.com/user/madybi2/videos. Accessed 11 June 2017.

[36] https://www.youtube.com/user/CheckhIbrahimNiass. Accessed 11 June 2017.

[37] Ibrahim Niasse, *Fī Riyād al-tafsīr li al-Qur'ān al-Karīm*, Muḥammad wuld 'Abdallāh (ed.) (Lemden, Mauritania: Shaykh Muḥammad wuld 'Abdallāh Publisher, 2010).

[38] Niasse, *In the Meadows of Tafsīr*, 31.

[39] Notes of fieldwork in Medina Baye, July 2016.

[40] De Diego González, *Ley y Gnosis*, 130.

YouTube channel platform Fathu Gado, one finds almost all the *tafsīr* conducted in Hausa by Bauchi and based on the *tafsīr* in Wolof by Shaykh Ibrahim, which Bauchi attended as a student in Senegal.[41] Bauchi conducts the exegesis of the Qur'ān each Ramadan in front of his disciples, who are fascinated by him. Andrea Brigaglia has noticed the political courage that these performances inspired in Nigeria during the years of war between Wahhabism and Sufism.[42]

The USB key that the grandson of Ibrahim Niasse gave me also included various recordings of *waxtane* (the Wolof term for speeches) on different occasions (*gamou*, Islamic festivities, classes). This grandson of Shaykh Ibrahim insisted that this material is more valuable than all the books that I already possessed, and that the Arabic exegesis of Shaykh Ibrahim was more 'refined' and interesting than that in Wolof.[43] These recordings are a unique and very valuable material to understand not only the legal or academic facet of Niasse, but also his connection to and charismatic appeal vis-à-vis his disciples. The recordings have been zealously preserved by his relatives, only recently being digitized and made available to the disciples of the *ṭarīqa*. Some of them are available in the portal Archive.org under the title of *Gamou et discours of Cheikh Ibrahima*.[44] Most of them are in Wolof – 'erudite Wolof', as my Senegalese informants pointed out to distinguish Wolof spoken in the Saloum from the one spoken in Dakar – and deal with sensitive esoteric aspects and internal recommendations that the *ṭarīqa* etiquette imposes can only be discussed with initiates. Most remain unpublished, though Zachary Wright has translated three of them: 'The eternal Islam'; 'The inheritance of the Prophet'; 'May Allah give us to Allah'.[45]

Analogical recordings represent the first intersection between recording technology and Sufism. Niasse allowed the audio recordings, taking a big step forward. The central idea of these recordings is not knowledge itself, but the awareness of being co-participants in the presence of the shaykh even through low-quality audio tracks. The *baraka* coming from the voice of the shaykh being transmitted in these recordings is the essential element, being immortalized for coming generations. The disciples revive the old schemes in every audition. Even if they are not fully aware of the meaning conveyed by these recordings, it is an experience to enjoy every time. Orality is the lived presence, something beyond writing, it is like being with the shaykh, listening to him and not simply reading him. For this reason, the experience of orality in the community of the *Fayḍa* has been very fruitful. Something similar happened to one of Niasse's favourite

[41] http://www.youtube.com/watch?v=NZJLpPHqvHw. Accessed 11 June 2017.
[42] Brigaglia, 'The Radio Kaduna tafsir'.
[43] Interview with Mahi b. Makky Ibrahim Niasse, Medina Baye, July 2016.
[44] https://archive.org/details/GamousBaye. Accessed 11 June 2017.
[45] Wright, *Pearls from the Divine Flood*, 83–110.

disciples, *Ustadh* Barham Diop, who became a shaykh with an immense and indispensable oral corpus of the contemporary Tijāniyya, unknown outside the Wolof-speaking community.

The Shaykh and His Recordings: the Audiovisual Corpus of Barham Diop

The second generation of the *Fayḍa* did not only keep the audio recordings, but added video shortly after the death of Niasse. Thirty years have passed from VHS to YouTube, a time in which the Tijāniyya was able to adapt itself to the new times. Video became the preferred format of the *talibé Baye*. They could now enjoy the presence of the shaykh, apart from listening to him. The component of presence is fundamental in Sufism, because it involves co-partnership between the disciple and his teacher. The one who sees something participates in that moment and, of course, obtains the *baraka*. The shaykh used to be available to the disciple whenever the last one needed him, the only thing he had to do was rewind the tape. And from all the Tijānī shaykhs that have been recorded when giving a class, there is one who stands out above all: Barham Diop.

Barham Maḥmud Diop (1932–2014) has been, for many years, the indefatigable secretary of Shaykh Ibrahim. After his death, Barham Diop became one of the most esteemed advisers of King Hassan II of Morocco – who called him 'the walking library'. He became the secretary of the Council of Ulema of Morocco and Senegal, attending regularly the Ramadan lectures (*Durūs ḥasaniyya*) held in Rabat during the month of Ramadan.[46] What distinguishes him from many Tijānī shaykhs is that Diop, like Shaykh Ibrahim himself, made it clear that the *Fayḍa* was neither a local product nor a project anchored in the past. He considered it to be the best choice between modernity and tradition.[47] Contrary to what might be expected, Barham Diop wrote very little. But he delivered hundreds of lectures in Wolof, many of them during his trips to Tijānī communities in Europe and all of them have been recorded both in audio and video. He treats topics like gnosis (*ma'rifa*) or the doctrines of the Tijāniyya *ṭarīqa*, but also current social issues such as pacifism and social rights,[48] social development,[49] or Islamic law and modern life.[50]

These lectures were recorded by his disciples in a near professional way and are generally of good quality. As Ousmane Kane remarks, many of them were sponsored by members of the diaspora community who, in turn, gained prestige

[46] https://www.youtube.com/watch?v=xGnlUbcmA3U. Accessed 11 June 2017.
[47] De Diego González, *Ley y Gnosis*, 407–8.
[48] Conference in Madrid (Spain), 16 July 2011, private recording accessed 12 June 2017.
[49] Conference in Bilbao (Spain), 25 June 2011, private recording accessed 15 June 2017.
[50] Conference in Paris (France), 9 July 2011, private recording accessed 12 June 2017.

in their countries of origin for serving their shaykh (*khidma*).[51] Some examples of these recordings are found in the Mady Barhama[52] channel on the YouTube platform, others (the audio recordings mainly) are located on the Archive.org portal.[53] The latest comprise a corpus of eighty-five lectures of the *waxtane* genre. In addition, there is a collection of recordings of his talks in the European meetings of *Ansaroudine*, the international association of *talibé Baye*,[54] from 2011 to 2014. Apart from these, Diop had recorded documents of enormous value for the study of the community of the *Fayḍa*: his own commentaries on all the main works of Ibrahim Niasse. Very valuable, these should be regarded as primary sources because they include direct comments by Shaykh Ibrahim Niasse that Diop, who was close to him, reported. Notable among them, for example, are Diop's commentary on *Ruḥ al-Adab*[55] or *Kāshif al-Albās*,[56] two major works of Shaykh Niasse. On audio there are commentaries by Diop on the extensive collections of Niasse's poetry. The availability of these works in written format is essential for the study of *Fayḍa* as a religious phenomenon of the twentieth century. For this reason, it is essential to review and revalue the corpus.

In all this audio-visual corpus, there is a revitalization and amplification of orality because the shaykh is being seen and felt as a lived presence. This is very important in the diaspora since it allows an interaction with the teacher, even without having him physically present. Unlike the early recordings of Ibrahim Niasse, the production of Diop is destined for the Wolof-speaking diaspora in Europe and the United States, a population that needs to remember not only its origins but also its *maḥabba* (love) for the shaykh. It was no longer necessary to go to Senegal to receive the teachings because technology had made it much simpler. Moreover, this form kept all the traditional identity and epistemological markers. The example of Barham Diop and the digital orality, as described above,

[51] Ousmane Kane, *The Homeland is the Arena. Religion, Transnationalism and the Integration of Senegalese Muslims in America* (New York: Oxford University Press, 2011) 164.

[52] https://www.youtube.com/user/madybi2. Accessed 12 June 2017.

[53] https://archive.org/details/ChIbDiop. Accessed 15 June 2017.

[54] De Diego González, *Ley y Gnosis*, 407.

[55] https://www.youtube.com/watch?v=9sOugTJ6Kds. Accessed 15 June 2017. For an English translation of the work, see Ibrahim Niasse, *The Spirit of Good Morals* (Atlanta: FaydaBooks, 2016).

[56] https://www.youtube.com/watch?v=IGrVnAB2Ymk. Accessed 15 June 2017. For an English translation of the work, see Ibrahim Niasse, *The Removal of Confusion Concerning the Flood of the Saintly Seal Ahmad al-Tijani: A Translation of Kashif al-ilbas an fayda al-khatm abi 'abbas*, translated by Zachary Wright, Muhtar Holland and Abdullahi Okene with forewords by Sayyid Ali Cisse, Shaykh Tijani Cisse, Shaykh Hassan Cisse (Louisville, KY: Fons Vitae, 2010).

can be extrapolated to any of the popular members of the second generation of the *Fayḍa*,[57] such as Ḥassan Cisse,[58] Shaykh Tijānī Cisse,[59] Ḥājj al-Mishry,[60] or Shaykh wuld Khayri,[61] among others. Their recordings are all very popular and, as I have noticed during my fieldwork, are constantly being used by the disciples, especially in the diaspora.

Until the appearance of *streaming* videos, the communities had these recordings on CD or DVD to listen to what the teacher had said in other communities in the diaspora. The rise of YouTube in 2005 accelerated this process because all the communities uploaded videos or audios of their recordings. At that time, the shaykhs regained the primacy of orality over written texts. This type of format constitutes not only the reaffirmation of orality as an element of transmission in a traditional context, but also the democratization of knowledge (*'ilm*) through these recordings. It implies a second moment in the intersectionality between technology and Sufism. In a rudimentary way, the virtuality and the co-presence of the shaykh were implemented, which was no longer reduced to a private sphere and personal transmission.

YouTube was a great element in favour of the Tijāniyya *ṭarīqa* because it democratized and made accessible its teachings to many people who would not have had access to them otherwise due to their geographical location or their lack of connections with the *ṭarīqa* itself. Interestingly, this practice is well accepted within the *ṭarīqa*, even the low use of these technologies is rather criticized by some shaykhs and *muqaddams* like Shaykh al-Hājj al-Mishry. His opinion is that in the Tijāniyya they should be used as much as in other *ṭarīqas* like the Ḥaqqani's Naqshbandiyya or Bentounes' 'Alawiyya.[62] In fact, much of the current success of the Tijāniyya in Europe or the United States is due to this phenomenon, coupled with its virality in social networks. This has generated a new way of understanding both the Tijāniyya *ṭarīqa* and the traditional shaykh–disciple relationship, after the emergence of social networks.

[57] De Diego González, *Ley y Gnosis*, 406–23.

[58] Hassan Cisse in Nigeria, https://www.youtube.com/watch?v=qlAqXEjDlTg. Accessed 15 June 2017.

[59] Shaykh Tidiane Cisse in Benin and Togo, https://youtu.be/UfudRd8colc. Accessed 15 June 2017.

[60] https://www.youtube.com/watch?v=ReDCSmaolXE. Accessed 15 June 2017.

[61] https://www.youtube.com/watch?v=mVqzsb2KM94. Accessed 15 June 2017.

[62] Interview with al-Ḥājj 'Abdallāh w. Muḥammad Mishry, Medina Baye (Senegal), December 2016.

Sufism 2.0: the Shaykh and the Social Network

Of all technological revolutions, none can be compared to the one produced by social networks. The emergence of Facebook, Twitter, Instagram and Snapchat has changed the social identities and epistemological perceptions[63] of contemporary societies, including those based on traditional epistemologies. Sufis have undergone these processes taking a real advantage of this great revolution in order to permanently amalgamate traditional knowledge with new technologies.[64] This has not only generated important sociological changes within the *ṭarīqa*, but also epistemological changes, since it does not renounce the transmission of the sacred knowledge (*ma'rifa*) through platforms that are precisely living forms of deontologizing narratives and knowledge.[65] At the same time, a new generation of disciples is increasingly aware of the fact that the presence of a teacher is not necessary to develop spirituality.

Social networks act as agglutinative of social relations and as an immediate transmitter of information. As soon as the information is processed, it is launched and can become viral, that is to say, it is spread massively through the internet. There is no time to reflect on it. Knowledge is reduced to a photo plus a text of no more than a thousand words or a video of a few minutes. In many cases, a link with a canonical PDF text is enough to generate a reverie in the collective imagination. And the mass use of the recordings that we described in the previous section needs to be added to this too. The co-presence of the recording becomes a diffuse shadow in the imaginary of the members of a social network, because the social network tends to lower the burden of truth, when understood from an ontological level, of the sent message.

In the specific case of the Tijānīs, this change has been driven by those living on the periphery. American, European, or Asian disciples have pushed a whole campaign in order to spread through social networks. Diverse *muqaddam*, with any amount of computer skills, spread and teach through the internet attracting a diverse audience. The most interesting thing is that they formally use techniques similar to those used in Africa making orality in the discourse predominate. There may be texts, but they are written in a fully oral record because Facebook conversations are more oral than written. The narrative model used by these *muqaddam* resembles the African ones both in aesthetics and in procedures, something of

[63] Lisa Dawley, 'Social network knowledge construction: emerging virtual world pedagogy', *On the Horizon*, 17, 2, 2019, 113.

[64] Carl Ernst, 'Situating Sufism and Yoga', *Journal of the Royal Asiatic Society*, 15, 1, 2005, 15–43; Shelina Janmohamed, *Generation M: Young Muslims changing the World* (London: I.B. Tauris, 2016) 85–91.

[65] Baudrillard, *Simulacres et Simulation*.

which they are proud.[66] They address issues of etiquette (*adab*) of the *ṭarīqa*, knowledge (*ma'rifa*) or actuality and always from the immediacy, a clear sign of these social networks, and especially from their interaction with the public. This interaction was already developed, in a first phase, in the Yahoo mailing list *Tijāniyya*.[67]

In recent years, Facebook has become one of the most important places to appreciate these phenomena. For example, the page *Tijani Ṭarīqah*[68] is one of several examples of Tijānī online communities with a predominantly Anglophone and Western audience, reaching 20,817 followers. Its basic structure consists of posting a text with a photo, with the intention of drawing the attention of the public. Their material is typically drawn from classical books of the Tijāniyya or extracted from oral sources and altruistically translated by members of the *ṭarīqa*. The translations of the texts, however, are not signed and no one regulates the quality or veracity of the text. This is one of the most negative aspects of this type of group, since it exposes a very sensitive knowledge of the *ṭarīqa* to the public without subjecting it to the verification procedure (*taḥqīq*). In fact, pro bono translations can lead to an underlying ideologization or to a personal interpretation of texts.

Another of Facebook's best-known groups is *Mady Barhama Niasse*.[69] This group has 94,640 followers, and although Senegalese in origin, it has recruited membership from different countries. This group posts, above all, videos of shaykhs of the *ṭarīqa*. The visual component is very strong and it has a large file, which it shares with its aforementioned YouTube channel. This group is fully oral and there are hardly any written elements. Unlike *Tijānī Ṭariqa*, there are no doctrinal or personal opinions, and the only thing that is posted are authorized videos of shaykhs of the *ṭarīqa*. It is a group that nurtures a great number of followers of the Tijāniyya in order to viralize contents referred back to it. There are many other pages similar to these two, where a high level of content is produced daily. For example, in Ramadan 2017, Facebook Live, Facebook's online streaming tool, broadcast the live *tafsīr* sessions performed by Shaykh Māḥy b. Ibrahim Niasse on the Kossy TV page.[70] Usually, these videos of the *ṭarīqa* are broadcast by its followers either via Facebook Live or Snapchat in social events (*gamou*, conferences, etc.), giving a component of collective participation and immediacy.

If Facebook groups are important, we could say much or more of individual profiles. There is a new generation of *muqaddams* who act publicly in front of a

[66] Interview with Shaykh Muḥammad Abdullahi, email, May 2017.

[67] https://groups.yahoo.com/neo/groups/qutbulmakhtum. Accessed 15 June 2017.

[68] https://www.facebook.com/Tijanitariqah. Accessed 15 June 2017.

[69] https://www.facebook.com/MadyBayeNiass. Accessed 15 June 2017.

[70] https://www.facebook.com/KOSSY-TV-1758686851041722. Accessed 15 June 2017.

diverse audience because they are aware of the situation in the global arena. In fact, that is something that can be observed. On the one hand, shaykhs and African scholars traditionally transmit using their classical rhetoric, and they worry mainly about traditional epistemological questions. Thus, they always quote and do not go too far in the speech, they maintain a tone of authority[71] and some distance with the public. On the other hand, *muqaddams* in the diaspora act as transmitters of Tijānī discourse using new strategies and discourses. They bind together thousands of followers and have made of Facebook a space of public communication and diffusion of the Tijāniyya.

With great charisma, they are able to treat current issues, finding space for *ma'rifa* in public. These Facebook profiles are not scholars as such, they are social enablers and *influencers*, since their mission is to diffuse elements, but in a different way from traditional shaykhs. Often, they use short texts that are almost oral, with a great expressive force that includes the dialogue with other users, users who, on the other hand, feel less inhibited about expressing themselves than in traditional disciple–teacher social relationships. They exert so much influence that they have revived narratives and practices in a peripheral world where the shaykh is not present at all and where the virtualization of the practice is greater.

Epilogue: Sacred Knowledge and Virtuality in Post-truth

In the last five years, a boom in what I have called *e-Sufism* or Electronic Sufism can be observed among Tijānīs communities. *E-Sufism* manifests itself through a virtualization and *simulation* of the spiritual practice in a way similar to that described by Baudrillard.[72] This is reduced to a relationship of the disciple with a famous shaykh without full physical contact, but also happens in an epistemic sphere. Relationships and transmissions are reduced to electronic communications, in addition to some punctual visits to the shaykh. In this way, the practices are also virtual and the disciple does not have a full epistemic experience of the Sufi practice, since his experience is reduced to what he captures by himself, lacking the component of the physical transmission and its associated codes (gazes, gestures, etc.). Obviously, this practice usually occurs in the periphery where the shaykh is not present, virtualizing itself through the ICTs (social networks such as WhatsApp, Skype, Instagram, etc.). On many occasions, the disciple develops

71 A good example of this is the statement of Abdel-Malik Niasse, son of Shaykh Ibrahim, in full controversy with a *muqaddam* who overstepped his functions in September 2016. The video uploaded to the YouTube platform went viral on Facebook in a few hours among all the community of the *Fayḍa*, https://www.youtube.com/watch?v=d6hbgaejQbE. Accessed 15 June 2017.

72 Baudrillard, *Simulacres et Simulation.*

an idealized love, *maḥabba*, mediated by virtuality (*e-maḥabba*), the acquisition of knowledge (*'ilm)* often online (*e-learning*), and it can even achieve on the spiritual level a spiritual training that is aloof and that takes place through the internet (*e-tarbiya*). Finally, the real experience becomes virtual, generating its own epistemological status.

Many of these digital *Murids* end up visiting the shaykh in his own physical space, while others do not, despite obtaining permits that accredit them as *muqaddam*. The controversy is served in these circles. Some disciples defend themselves by saying: 'My relationship with the shaykh is pure love, I need nothing more than a call to know about him',[73] to which other disciples respond, 'It is impossible to be [Tijānī] from the *Fayḍa* without visiting Medina Baye. You do not realize what it is to be a disciple of your shaykh until you come here.'[74] In *e-Sufism* one of the central components is orality. It represents an ontological legitimacy of the discourse, as it was in recordings, to hear the shaykh, having a transmission of the shaykh himself even in an epistemic *simulation*. Of all these practices, the most paradigmatic example is the *e-tarbiya*.

I heard a definition of this concept three years ago among Tijānī communities of the diaspora. These are usually related to a shaykh outside the community, specifically in the case of the *Fayḍa*, who is usually affiliated with the e-family. The internal structures of the group, or their own experience, generate an identification with this figure as a 'transmitter of knowledge'. So, when the time comes for spiritual initiation or *tarbiya*,[75] they decide to do it online rather than with a *muqaddam* in their area. This is because who better than Cisse, prioritising his surname and lineage over the real *mahabba* that the disciple may have for him, can make the spiritual opening come sooner and in a better way?[76]

The traditional and physical *tarbiya* is performed as an initiatory experience in which, beyond the scholastic classifications, a desire to know God[77] is emphasized and in which the role of the shaykh consists of helping the disciple. My informants during my fieldwork pointed out that the *tarbiya* according to the Niassene model must take place in an environment of proximity to and daily interactions with the shaykh of *tarbiya* or the *murabbī*. Therefore a physical coexistence is required, which provides a model of behaviour and gnosis to the disciple, a kind of lived teaching. That is the basis of an experience which makes you know God.[78]

[73] Interview with an American disciple of Mahi Cisse, Atlanta, November 2013.
[74] Interview with a British disciple of Shaykh Tijānī Cisse, Medina Baye, July 2016.
[75] Seesemann, *The Divine Flood*, 71–9; Wright, *Pearls from the Divine Flood*, 145–8.
[76] Interview with an American disciple of Mahi Cisse, Atlanta, November 2013.
[77] Wright, *Pearls from the Divine Flood*, 147.
[78] De Diego González, *Ley y Gnosis*, 176–9.

It is paradoxical that *e-tarbiya* questions the epistemic mechanisms of Sufism and the *tarbiya* itself, since they demand a certain presence of the *murabbī* to carry out the process, that is to constitute a relationship that helps the disciple to make the journey, in which the physical *baraka* is a fundamental component. In this way, the physical presence makes it possible for the shaykh to accompany the disciple in the *tarbiya* process. However, in *e-tarbiya*, the bodily experience is replaced by a virtual one and the central component of coexistence and the experience of the gnostic as everyday life is lost. There is a long tradition in the Islamic world in which corporeality is fundamental, it represents its own imaginary.[79] The gaze, the saliva, the breath, etc. are elements that intercede and interfere in the transmission of knowledge (*'ilm*) and sacred knowledge (*ma'rifa*), and this disappears in the virtual experience. Moreover, the sense of tranquillity in the presence (*ḥaḍra*) of the shaykh is fundamental during the *tarbiya* phase. A French informant told me:

> By virtualizing the *tarbiya* you lose the knowledge transmitted by the shaykh, you lose a special connection with the *himma* of the shaykh and you become more dispersed. It's not the same as when he is in front of you. When you are in it [presential *tarbiya*] nothing disconnects you from him.[80]

This French *talibé*, who had experienced an *e-tarbiya* and later finished his experience on a traditional *tarbiya*, made it clear. Another informant told me that 'online *tarbiya* is only for pragmatic people and for those who know that the *murabbi* is truthful, that he is one of those you know'.[81] Because the symbolic readings of everyday life are another element that generates this climate in which the gnosis transmission is possible, the disciple becomes conscious of a mystical level from a reality lived physically.

But in the *e-tarbiya* – as one informant pointed out – everything is diluted in a virtual and *simulacra* experience where everything is volatile. 'Something important is lost', a *talibé* detractor of the *e-tarbiya* informed me, 'if you are not physically with your shaykh.'[82] While supporters admit that it is a 'mystical' subject and that 'the shaykh knows things that others do not know, even through Skype'.[83] It should be noted that among Tijānīs, this is a very disputed issue that has both supporters and detractors in equal parts since it affects a central aspect of the doctrine. However, they concur on the traditional vision: the word of the

[79] Scott A. Kluge, *Sufis and Saints' Bodies: Mysticism, Corporeality, and Sacred Power in Islam* (Chapel Hill: University of North Carolina Press, 2007).
[80] Interview with a French disciple of Mahi Cisse, Paris, April 2015.
[81] Interview with a British disciple of Mahi Cisse, Granada, May 2014.
[82] Interview with a Mauritanian disciple of Ḥājj al-Mishry, Ma'ta Maulana, May 2014.
[83] Interview with an American disciple of Mahi Cisse, Atlanta, November 2013.

shaykh and the lived experience, in their oral, aural, and corporeal facets, of the disciple are worth more than a thousand books written on *ma'rifa*.[84] So, we can appreciate a sacrifice of the praxis and *habitus* of traditional Sufism.

The oral, once again, re-emerges over any other epistemological marker in the experience of Sufism. But one more step has been taken. Not only the co-presence that existed on the recordings is required, but an interaction with the shaykh is needed, and – ultimately – the construction of reality where all this process unfolds depends on the disciple. ICTs mediate and relativize reality, a reality that, to produce transmission, needs to be ontologized. Sacred knowledge (*ma'rifa*) demands the transmission of a 'real truth', something that virtuality and epistemic *simulation* cannot achieve at all. Thus, the experience of the real is redefined with respect to what is written in books and what teachers report. And there is the challenge for the Tijānīs, when trying to solve the epistemological problems derived from these experiences with the ICTs.

The Tijānīs show, nowadays, a very changing reality at an epistemological level. Technology mediatizes not only their personal identities but also community identities. The publicity given by social networks makes Sufism, to paraphrase Carl Ernst, to be not only for Muslims,[85] nor the Tijāniyya for Tijānīs who grew up in the epistemic structures of *ṭarīqa*. Thus, it expands more easily in more complex contexts and in post-truth times, and this has produced a profound deontologization of knowledge,[86] an age where feelings and subjectivities prevail over the experience of the metaphysical grounds. This is paradoxical for a type of knowledge, as it is the *ma'rifa* that demands the reality (*ḥaqīqa*) of the experience.

Our era of post-truth, heiress of postmodernity, is characterized by placing narratives between the borders of reality and fiction, playing with the enormous capacity of viralization of these. Absolute and ontological knowledge appears, in these days, as impossible. And yet, supported by their mechanisms, the Tijānīs launch messages with gnostic and absolute content, accepting and defying – in a paradoxical way – the norms of contemporary communication. The ICTs, and their enormous volumes of information, present a challenge to a classical epistemology based on personal transmission where the oral, the aural, and the corporeal have a great weight, because the message is considered sacred and real ontologically. This encompasses not only the imaginary, but also the physical. Although Eurocentric modernity wanted to reduce knowledge to a mere written and closed corpus, the knowledge of Sufism is a truly living knowledge.

All this work on the analysis of the three phases of ICTs in Tijāniyya, from the time of its first recordings to the introduction of social networks, leads us to note

[84] Interview with al-Ḥājj Abdallah w. Muḥammad Mishry, Córdoba, April 2014.

[85] Ernst, 'Situating Sufism and Yoga', 205.

[86] Baudrillard, *Simulacres et Simulation*.

that the answer to the question of whether a new orality has been generated based on ICTs is highly ambiguous and paradoxical, as the issue is in itself. In my opinion, based on all that I have shown, African orality is the same, although many new mechanisms of technology have been introduced, changing many aspects from an epistemological level. Thus, as a partial conclusion, due to the absence of a deeper exploration of the topic, I would like to point out four characteristics that can serve as approximations to the difficult question posed in the introduction.

First, it must be pointed out that the classical orality of Islam in Africa remains operative, invigorated, and retains most of its elements, symbolic meanings, and traditional markers. The episteme of African Islam defends and protects the mechanisms of legitimation[87] not only from an epistemological level but from the experimental one. Similarly, there is an entire tradition associated with the esoteric value of the shaykh's word, such as the example of the recording of *tafsīr* in Mauritania. Therefore, it is improbable that this orality will devalue at least in these communities.

In this way, and secondly, this traditional orality, first adapted in analogical media, has been amplified and revalued thanks to the appearance of video recordings and streaming platforms. Shaykhs are still 'talking' in front of the production of 'written' material, as in the example of video recordings of shaykhs and scholars. The globalization of ICTs has affected disciples more than teachers. Disciples of diaspora or non-African Tijānī communities have taken orality as one of their discourse markers, integrating it into their own episteme.

Thirdly, the greatest changes in orality have occurred with the introduction of social networks, the viralization of content, and the environment of the past in recent years. These have affected epistemological aspects of orality as the experience of the oral that has passed from the physical to the virtual plane. It is paradoxical that narratives with an ontological value as large as *ma'rifa* coexist in environments where the value of the others is not clear. For many disciples, there is a loss of value in the mechanisms of verification (*taḥqiq*) and corporality, although the immediacy and the massive diffusion prevail.

Finally, the *ṭarīqa* Tijāniyya has not yet developed concrete epistemic strategies to rethink all these changes in order to transmit it to the disciples. While this occurs, and as it is often the case in Islam, normativity is intimately linked to the personal experience of both the *muqaddam* and the disciple. This is something that denotes the enormous plasticity of *ṭarīqa*.

[87] Ware, *The Walking Qur'an*, 55.

CHAPTER 9

The Sacred Text in Egypt's Popular Culture: the Qur'ānic Sounds, the Meanings and Formation of *Sakīna* (Sacred Space) in Traditions of Poverty and Fear

Yunus Kumek

This chapter deals with the presence and culture of the Qur'ān in Egyptian everyday life including its presence in media, mosques and homes. Based on my fieldwork in Nasr City, Cairo, I discuss the culture of the Qur'ān in the everyday experience of Egyptian Muslims through the behaviour which encloses them in a sacred space, *sakīna*. The effects of this sacred space form religious sentiments about the challenges of poverty and fear. *Sakīna* creates a centre of religiosity that is omnipresent in Egypt. The chapter also asks whether the technology of the recent period affects the religiosity of Egyptians and concludes that the technology merely provides new vehicles for thoughts and feelings that have not changed substantially since long ago.

Egypt is notable for its ancient history and the diversity of its peoples. Due to the fecundity of the Nile River, Egypt has always been densely populated.[1] It has been a critical land for settlement by different empires and religious movements such as Judaism, Christianity and Islam.[2] Before the introduction of Islam in Egypt, the country was part of the Byzantine or Eastern Roman Empire. Egyptians met with Islam when Caliph 'Umar (579–644 AD) sent 'Amr Ibn al-Āṣ (585–664 AD) to introduce it to Egypt. 'Umar and 'Amr Ibn al-Āṣ were the immediate companions (*ṣaḥāba*) of the Prophet Muḥammad. When the Prophet passed away, the expansion of Islam continued very rapidly through his immediate companions.

[1] C.F. Petry, *The Cambridge History of Egypt* (Cambridge: Cambridge University Press, 2008) 2–3.

[2] Kelly Bulkeley, *Dreaming in the World's Religions: A Comparative History* (New York: New York University Press, 2008) 169–210.

Over the years and centuries, as Islam was introduced to Egyptians, the dominant language became Arabic in colloquial and formal communication. There has been a long-standing discussion of the ethnic identity of Egyptians: are they originally Coptic, or Arabs, or Africans? The identity of Egyptians is rooted in the conceptualization of culture as something fluid and it is a contingent process.[3] However, in the discourses of my interlocutors in Cairo or elsewhere in Egypt, the answer may not be as simple as predicted in our identity discussions.

This chapter discusses the role of the Qur'ān in the everyday experience of Egyptian Muslims through behaviour enclosing them in sacred space, *sakīna*. The phenomenological approach relates to the experience of reading or hearing the Qur'ān and the feeling that each person has in their sacred space. The effects of this sacred space form religious sentiments towards the challenges of poverty and fear. This creates a centre of religiosity that is omnipresent in Egypt.

The Field Experience

During several extended stays between 2006 and 2011 in Cairo and Alexandria, I was able to experience the culture of Islam on the streets, in mosques and in homes of Madinat Nasr, or Nasr City as it is known by its popular Western name. In my fieldwork, I concentrated on two mosque communities in Nasr City next to the International Garden (Hadiqatul Dawliya). These mosques were Masjid Al-Lìbi and Mousa Ibn Naseer. Madinat Nasr was a middle class populated town. Due to its proximity to Al-Azhar, the great and historical Islamic university, the town had a number of international students and teachers. I used a mixed methodology in acquiring my data through participant observation, ethnography, and interviews.

In Cairo, one can vividly observe the diverse behaviours in this densely populated city: people walking, sellers on the street trying to clean the dust from their shelves, taxis and cars honking at each other. Dust and sand were very common in daily life in Cairo due to the surrounding desert. One can see the sand on the streets and in the areas of worship. There was a rush hour early in the morning, and an increased, moving human population. In the morning, street cars sold special Egyptian breakfasts, *fūl*, with a variety of side dishes: mint, parsley, hot sauce, tomato and pitta bread. Amidst the rank smell of garbage on the streets and of the animals, dogs and cats, it was difficult to keep sand out of one's eyes and off one's body, but there was also warm social interaction via the Egyptian colloquial dialect of *ammiyya*. Egyptian falafel or *tāmiya* – fast foods and cheap meals – were available at any time, twenty-four hours a day.

[3] Nicola Pratt, 'Identity, Culture and Democratization: The Case of Egypt', *New Political Science*, 27, 1, 2005, 73–90.

Alexandria (Iskandariyah) was a completely different city, with its moist breezes from the Mediterranean Sea. At night, walking on the Corniche was part of the tradition of hanging out at night. The Corniche was the seashore and waterfront, the major corridor of traffic and lights. One could see thousands of people walking, driving or riding in horse-drawn carts. In the inner city of Iskandariyah, tasty round sweet treats, *luqmat al-qadi*, were sold by the street food carts, with the sound of chatter around them.

There have been numerous previous studies of religion in Egypt. One of the earliest and most renowned was the vivid, rich and monumental description of daily life and popular culture in Egypt by Edward William Lane.[4] His chapter on religion and law is especially impressive. He describes the daily religious rituals in detail. There are also some contemporary works understanding the religiosity through different discourses. Some focus on the content dynamics of sermons listened to on audio players by Egyptians.[5] Charles Hirschkind[6] analysed how listening to sermons engaged Egyptian Muslims, invoking ethical sensibilities. One can see how the accessible and commonly used cassettes of sermons could kindle religious sentiments in Egypt. Saba Mahmoud[7] engages with Egyptian women in her fieldwork to disclose the politics of piety through different representations of rituals or religiosity.[8] Similarly to my study, the anthropologist John Bowen asserts the importance of understanding the lenses of sacred texts in doing anthropology.[9] In the present study, I seek to examine the relationship between the agency of the Muslim sacred text, the Qur'ān,[10] and the orthodoxy and ortho-

[4] William Edward Lane, *An Account of the Manners and Customs of the Modern Egyptians: written in Egypt during the years 1833–1835* (London: Ward and Lock, 1890).

[5] Charles Hirschkind, *The Ethical Soundscape: Cassette Sermons and Islamic Counterpublics* (New York: Columbia University Press, 2006) 114–30.

[6] Hirschkind, *The Ethical Soundscape.*

[7] Saba Mahmood, 'Rehearsed Spontaneity and the Conventionality of Ritual: Disciplines of "Salat"', *American Ethnologist*, 28, 4, 2001, 827–53; Saba Mahmood, *Politics of Piety: The Islamic Revival and the Feminist Subject* (Princeton, NJ: Princeton University Press, 2011).

[8] Clifford Geertz, *Local Knowledge: Further Essays in Interpretive Anthropology* (New York: Basic Books, 1983) 219; Talal Asad, *Genealogies of Religion: Discipline and Reasons of Power in Christianity and Islam* (Baltimore and London: Johns Hopkins University Press, 1993) 29–51.

[9] John Bowen, *A New Anthropology of Islam* (New York: Cambridge University Press, 2012).

[10] Webb Keane, *Christian Moderns: Freedom and Fetish in The Mission Encounter* (Berkeley: University of California Press, 2007) 125–6; Webb Keane, 'Self-Interpretation, Agency and the objects of Anthropology: Reflections on a genealogy', *Comparative Studies in Society and History*, 45, 2, 2003, 222–48.

praxy of happiness, poverty and fear in the daily life of Egyptian Muslims in a mosque community in the town of Madinat Nasr. I use the terms orthodoxy and orthopraxy to mean common and established beliefs and practices.[11] As one of the vivid outcomes of this study, one can understand emerging notions around the Qur'ān's agency in establishing orthodoxy and orthopraxy in order to cope with the difficulties of poverty and fear in the daily lives of Egyptian Muslims.

The Qur'ān in Public Spaces

While engaging with my interlocutors in Nasr City, it was quite usual to observe the presence of the Qur'ān in public life. It was an everyday practice for common Egyptians to carry a Qur'ān in their shirt pocket or on the dashboard of their vehicle. In taxis, it was common to see drivers listening to the Qur'ān on separate radio channels or from cassette tapes instead of listening to the news or music. Listening to the Qur'ān was much engraved in Egyptian Muslim culture and was available through a number of media.

Egypt was mentioned in the Qur'ān in five places. The Arabic name for Egypt is Miṣr, or more colloquially, Maṣr. When a word is not conjugated according to Arabic grammar that word can be a proper name and/or it can be non-Arabic. There were four places in the Qur'ān where the non-conjugated word for Egypt (Miṣr) was mentioned. Egyptians were proud of their land being in the Qur'ān.

Sālih and Muḥsin were two of my participants. Sālih was getting close to sixty years of age. He was married and from Cairo. He did not have any children and was retired. He had worked for a company as an engineer. Sālih seemed not to make jokes as much as Muḥsin. Sālih used to often spend time with his brother in law, Muṣṭafā. Muṣṭafā was a pious man who used to go to mosque. Muṣṭafā used to go on pilgrimage to Saudi Arabia with his sister, Ṣālih's wife, almost every year. Muṣṭafā used to encourage Sālih to go to mosque with him. Sālih was much involved with politics at the level of following it through the news but not participating in any social or political movement. He liked to follow technological updates, and often used Twitter and Facebook.

Muḥsin was another married informant who lived in Alexandria and was from the same family. He had a son and a daughter and had been a manager in a company. He passed away recently when in his seventies. Muḥsin was an amazingly good-humoured character but did not have a close friend. Although he did not go to mosque much and used to make jokes with some religious sentiments, he seemed to sympathise with the pious.

[11] Nancy C. Ring, *Introduction to the Study of Religion* (New York: Orbis, 2007) 127.

Sālih, in a proud voice, said 'Yes, Egypt is in the Qur'ān'. The Qur'ān generally avoids specifically naming people or places. This helps the reader to connect with the text over generations regardless of time and place. The understanding is that even though historically, the verse can have a specific reason (*sabab nuzūl*) to be revealed, the teachings of the verses are still applied at any time and place, eternal and permanent. As it is very rare for a proper name to be mentioned, the exegetical scholars often assert that the specific person or place mentioned has a special significance.

In daily life, people commonly used expressions or prayers from the Qur'ān. For example, it was common to see the prayer from the Qur'ān (43:13) '*Subḥāna al-ladhī sakhkhara lanā hādhā wa mā kunnā lahu muqrinīn*' on apartment elevators in Egypt, while the same chapter from the Qur'ān was broadcast in the elevator, triggered by photoelectric sensors as people entered. Initially, the automated Qur'ānic recitation startled an outsider like me. The above-mentioned prayer is elaborated in the Qur'ān (43:12 and 13):

> God is the One who has created all opposites. And God is the One who has provided for you all those transportation vehicles and animals to ride on. In order that you might gain mastery over them, and that, whenever you have mastered them, you might remember your Sustainer's blessings and say: 'Limitless in God's glory and God has made all this subservient to our use. Without God's grace and favor, we would not have been able to attain to it.'[12]

The wording of the verses suggests it covers all transportation vehicles such as cars, planes, trains, ships, elevators, indeed any vehicle that transports humans, goods and animals. The purpose of reciting this verse was to be thankful for all bounties that God provides. Saying these prayers from the Qur'ān and following the practices of the Prophet Muḥammad transformed daily, routine habits into a form of worship. These habits can include eating, riding, relieving yourself in the bathroom, and even sexual intimacy. It meant that the person fulfilled their human needs through the act of pleasing and thanking God by remembering through reading prayers during, before and after these actions. The certainty in belief was that the person not only enjoyed the goods but also attained reward in the afterlife because of their remembrance of God. According to the Egyptians, this practice was inherited from the Prophet Muḥammad (*ḥadīth).* The prophet recited this phrase from the Qur'ān to thank God for the blessing of transportation. Egyptians emulated him as their role model.

For Egyptians in Nasr City, religious education started during the early years of school. The children acquired the Islamic values found in the Qur'ān and in

[12] Muhammad Asad, *The Message of the Qur'ān: Translated and explained* (Al-Andalus: Gibraltar, 1980) 689–90.

the practices of the Prophet Muḥammad. Among the teachings of the Qur'ān that *imāms* inculcated in Egyptians was setting a goal in life, not being pessimistic, but being active in intention and good deeds. According to my informants, there were different notions in the Qur'ān that portrayed an ideal human being through living in the present, remembering the past and getting prepared for the future. In the Qur'ān, living a goal-oriented life was very important. Goal-oriented life started with the intentions for today and tomorrow. Pessimism, hopelessness, laziness were some traits that were criticized in the Qur'ānic teachings as instilled by Satan. According to the Qur'ān, every day was a new day, a new creation of God, and a new opportunity to gain momentum in the world and after death. The Qur'ān discoursed regularly about this dynamism in natural events and in human psychology. Some of the verses on the universe and natural events read as follows, as adapted from SInternational (the Qur'ān, 35:27–8).[13]

> Do you not see that God sends down rain from the sky, and we produce with it fruits of varying colours? And in the mountains are the pathways, white and red, of different colours and [some] completely black. And similarly, there are various of colours among people, moving creatures and cattle. Only scholars who have knowledge appreciate, respect and truthfully fear from God among His servants. Indeed, God is Mighty, Forgiving.[14]

According to Egyptians, the Qur'ān seemed to require an animated psychological analysis of the self and gave the solutions to problems of the self through goal setting. Real examples were presented from history, animals, and natural events. According to the Qur'ān, spiritual freshness was very important. There were numerous verses that focused on spiritual death rather than physical death. Some interpretations of these verses can cause physical death.

In the Qur'ānic discussions, spiritual death occurred in the 'self' (*nafs*). It can be a death of self, for example, 'not caring', or being in a 'heedless' (*ghaflah*) state, or normalising something unethical so that it becomes ethical. Lying, cheating, or physical harming such as killing became normal for the dead self:[15]

> For [thus it is:] the blind and the seeing are not equal; (35, 20) nor are the depths of darkness and the light; (35, 21) nor the [cooling] shade and the scorching heat: (35, 22) and neither are equal the living and the dead [of heart]. Behold, [O Muḥammad] God can make hear whomever He wills, whereas thou canst not make hear such as are [dead of heart like the dead] in their graves: (35, 23) thou art nothing but a warner.

[13] SInternational, *The Qur'ān* (Jeddah: Abul-Qasim Publishing House, 1997) 427–8.
[14] Author's translation.
[15] Adapted from Asad, *The Message of the Qur'ān*, 616.

In the town of Madinat Nasr in Masjid al-Lìbi mosque, I used to participate in morning prayers. The *imām* was called Ahmad and was in his thirties, always smiling, very friendly and active. He used to do supererogatory/optional fasting on Mondays and Thursdays and seemed to enjoy teaching a lot. This mosque was next to Al-Azhar, of which *Imām* Ahmad was a graduate. Al-Azhar was a benchmark and famous historical institution in Islamic and regular sciences in Egypt. The campus was spread out among towns all across the country. Most of the *imāms* and religious scholars seemed to have some affiliation with Al-Azhar. The university attracted a lot of international students from all Muslim countries who wanted to study the Islamic sciences, the Qur'ān and other areas such as *ḥadīth*, history and law. It was therefore very common to encounter international students in daily Egyptian life. The town of Mahalla, located north of Cairo, also had many international students. A lot of them were studying and at the same time working in the local stores.

Most of those students appeared to be passionate to learn. They wanted to learn Islamic studies from the highest Islamic educational institute, Al-Azhar. Some enjoyed learning with its challenges. Some of them had already been offered positions in their home countries before they finished their studies. However, some of the international students seemed to lose their initial zeal for learning either due to the difficulty of the courses or the length of the study. These international students engaged in daily trading activities while maintaining their student status in the country.

Learning and education were of critical importance in Egyptian life. In my dialogue with my interviewees, Egyptians positioned themselves as the intellectuals of the Arabs. In the morning rush hour, the pious recited Qur'ānic verses, while the mind was fresh, listening to the Qur'ān on public media. After the early morning (*fajr*) prayer, the devout immediately recited their daily portion of the Qur'ān. Some of them memorized the Qur'ān at that time. Some of them practised by looking over and reviewing their previously memorized parts. The tradition in the mosques was that after the early morning, people formed Qur'ān circles (*halaqa*) to recite the Qur'ān and tried to finish some portion of it daily. The attendees rotated different sections of the Qur'ān among the members in the circle. The reading circle groups were led by the *imām* of the mosque. Depending on the mosque, some morning mosque groups completed the entire Qur'ān in a month, some in two months or more. To keep those attending the mosque awake and alert in the early morning recitations between 5.00 a.m. and 6.30 a.m., light snacks with coffee/tea were available on tables in the mosque. Afterwards, people went to their homes to get ready to go to work. Some took a small nap if they still had time before going to work.

It emerged that the Qur'ān was forming a sacred space (*sakīna*) around listeners. This space pervaded the mood and spiritual sense of listeners, who related many of the passages to personal experiences even when they were not able to translate them literally. Sometimes they were, and sometimes they were not, able to identify the names of chapters recited from the Qur'ān. Yet, they firmly believed that listening to the chapters of the Qur'ān had a purifying effect. This Qur'ānic space, or *sakīna,* enclosed the listener and all those present sharing the experience. One can argue how the specific ethnographic context of the Qur'ān can help us form ideas about 'local agency'[16] in the case of Egyptian Muslims. Agency through the Qur'ān can be deeply rooted with self-consciousness and individual self-transformation. Agency can be the *sakīna* that was formed with the recitation of the Qur'ān. *Sakīna* in Keane's argument[17] was a vehicle to transform the self in the religious experience of the Egyptian Muslim.

Muslim Egyptians in the Mosque Community of Madinat Nasr

There were two major orientations toward religiosity in the mosque communities in proximity to Hadiqatul Dawliya (the International Garden). The devout ones, mostly literally and sincerely, tried to implement the teachings of the religion. In this group, there were two further divisions: the devout with and without political agendas. My ethnographic study focused on the devout ones without any political interests or agendas. The members of this group appeared to be happy with what they were practising in their social and religious environments, especially after prayers, chatting in the social areas of the mosque. Their motivation was to please God. According to them, Muslims were going through trials and tribulations because they were not sincerely following the original teachings of Islam and the *Sunna* of the Prophet. The closed and active social religious environments provided a sense of meaning for their life and afterlife. They seemed to seldom watch TV, follow Twitter or Facebook. This group seemed to have committed themselves to following the teachings of Islam with piety in order to please God. They were trying to stay away from issues related to politics. They did not follow daily news and events about politics or Muslims. This minimised their disturbance emotionally and spiritually by any type of fear, or a negative and pessimistic outlook on life.

The non-devout were not religious and were critical of those who were devout. This group readily criticized the practising devout ones. My definition of the 'devout' here are those who were demanding literal and sincere following of the teachings of Islam: in the dress code, having a beard as the part of the *Sunna* (following the practice of the Prophet Muḥammad), going to mosque often, and being involved with social religious activities through practising the teachings of

[16] Keane, *Christian Moderns*, 125–6.

[17] Keane, *Christian Moderns*.

Islam 'commanding right and forbidding wrong' (*amr bil-ma'rūf wa nahy 'an al-munkar*). Some of the members of the non-devout group criticised the practising devout ones. In the non-devout group, some only prayed the annual prayers of celebration ('*īd* pl. *a'yād*), some only prayed the weekly required prayer (*jumu'a*) and some prayed five times daily. Rather than going to mosque, they preferred to pray in their homes. Their spouses wore headscarves. These Egyptians were closely following current events and news. Some of them were using Facebook. Some of them seemed angry and critical of the problems in the world about Muslim discourses. Occasionally, they blamed the devout Egyptians as the source of some of their problems. The non-devout group seemed to liberally and personally interpret the legal teachings and disagreed with some of the interpretations presented by the legal scholars.

There were also members who seemed to be in transition mode between the two groups. This transitioning group experienced the confidence and spiritual determination of the devout ones. They often wanted to belong and identify with the devout ones. Yet, when they were angry about following certain religious legal rulings, they aspired to side with the less religious groups such as the non-devout group categorized above. I especially observed this tendency among female Egyptian Muslims in Madinat Nasr. Among my partakers, these women appeared to follow the religion and be pious and spiritual. At the same time, they vocally criticised some of the legal rulings of the religion. Some of those women attributed their outburst to the patriarchal dominance of religious scholars or husbands.

Intriguingly, *Imām* Shāfi'ī, a famous ninth-century legal jurist, who lived the final years of his life in Egypt and died in Cairo,[18] acknowledged and applauded this 'toughness' of Egyptian Muslim women. 'Toughness' here represents a form of bravery in a positive sense. It is being spiritual, vocal, and critical. During my discourses with some of the female interviewees, the implicit and sometimes explicit demonization of men (mostly husbands) came up in the conversations. However, when the object of discussion was their brothers and sons, they were in a more neutral tone or praise mode. It was apparent that Egyptian women were very capable of interpreting the Qur'ān in their daily, social or family-related conflicts to support their stance, especially in the understanding of gender relations and roles. According to Tarek Masoud,[19] the Egyptian women were often qualified for leadership positions due to their understanding of the religion and the Qur'ān. He argued for the need to empower Arab women by using Qur'ānic arguments.

[18] John Esposito (ed.), *Oxford Encyclopedia of Islam* (Oxford: Oxford University Press, 2009) 107.

[19] Tarek Masoud, 'Using the Qur'ān to Empower Arab Women? Theory and Experimental Evidence from Egypt', *Comparative Political Studies*, 49, 12, 2016, 1555–98.

On the other hand, Paul Anderson[20] presented the concept of devoutness with 'piety'. According to him, piety came about through listening to and reciting the Qur'ān not through the self as worship. Practising piety was also a means of benefiting others. Piety,[21] he argues:

> is constituted through transaction and exchange rather than through individual worship. Second, it directs attention to the ideology of language in Egyptian piety movements, whereby ethical communities form around and through the efficacy of the Qur'ān and language that recalls the example of Prophet Muḥammad. Third, it reflects the way in which urban piety movements in Egypt constitute themselves in conscious opposition to a notion of secularism (*'almana*) which is associated with a commodity economy of goods, words and images experienced as morally and socially corrosive.

Virtue is through social manners and interaction (*mu'āmalāt*) rather than self-discipline or worship (*'ibāda*).[22] Similarly, my finding was that piety or happiness for Egyptians resided in listening to the Qur'ān and emulating the Prophet Muḥammad. However, the ethnographic data suggested that the individual was not able to fully implement the exercise of benefiting others (*mu'āmalāt*) unless self-happiness or discipline were achieved. I therefore did not observe or focus much on verbal religious discourses through formal sermons. Rather, by focusing on the self, an implicit way of happiness or piety in the lives of Egyptian Muslims was demonstrated mainly through worship or listening to the recitation of the Qur'ān. In other words, it appeared that Egyptians have a personal preference for the direct and immediate textual effect of the Qur'ān on themselves compared to the vehicle of a human delivering the same message in a formal sermon.

The Qur'ān's Textual Effect

The Qur'ān was revealed in Arabic. Anglophone Westerners and some modern Egyptians regard its translation into English as merely an attempt to render its meaning. Muslims consider only the Arabic revelation as the Qur'ān, the word of God – Allah. Although translations can give close and intended meanings of the original revelation of the Qur'ān in Arabic, there is consensus among the Islamic scholars that these translations are not the original revelation. Some emphasize that with everyday translations, the translator makes choices amidst myriad possibilities and these choices are human choices, not God's. Therefore, to emphasise

[20] Paul Anderson, 'The Piety of the Gift: Selfhood and Sociality in the Egyptian Mosque Movement', *Anthropological Theory*, 11, 1, 2011, 3–21.

[21] Anderson, 'The Piety of the Gift'.

[22] Anderson, 'The Piety of the Gift'.

this, some of the translations are presented in their title pages as translations or interpretations of the meanings of the Qur'ān. They are not the Qur'ān itself.

It is not uncommon for a person in Madinat Nasr to arrange their daily activities around the Qur'ān. As soon as they open their eyes in the morning, they can say while still in the bed, 'Thanks be to God who resurrected me after my death (sleep) and we will return to Him.' This phrase is an instruction from the Prophet Muḥammad (*ḥadīth*). Then, while still in the bed, reading the talismanic[23] chapters of the Qur'ān (chapters 112–14) is another common practice. The Qur'ān has 114 chapters, 6,236 verses and approximately 600 pages. There are different partitions in the Qur'ān, which make it easy for people to read the Qur'ān regularly.

For example, approximately every twenty pages is called *juz'* (a section). A Muslim who likes to finish the entire Qur'ān in a month can read one section daily. This makes it possible to recite during the holy month of Ramadan (*tarāwīḥ*) at the rate of one *juz'* per day. The Qur'ān has a critical presence in the life of Egyptian Muslims in the town of Madinat Nasr.

Daily interaction with the Qur'ān is done for a variety of reasons. In their daily discourses, Muslims read and recite the Qur'ān during the five prayer periods. Most Egyptian Muslims in Nasr City read the Qur'ān in remembrance of God. Some read or recite it to gain the blessing of the sacred text from God. They also attempt to apply the meaning of the text to their personal lives. These behaviours are appropriate ones for followers of the faith and confer orthodoxy upon them.

Sufis are considered to be the mystics of Islam. A few members of the researched mosque communities seemed to follow Sufi teachings. Sufis give importance to the mystical understandings of the text besides its literal meanings. For the Sufis, the Qur'ān has a critical and unique place in personal practice. Some of the Sufis in these communities did not seem to look at any text or utter any word until they had looked at the text of the Qur'ān or recited loudly the wordings of the Qur'ān. This was an effort to have the blessing of the day with the Qur'ān. They wanted to put something 'in their eye, ear or mouth' related to the text of the Qur'ān at the beginning of the day. Some even did not want to eat or drink anything until they read a portion from the Qur'ān. They wanted to get the blessing of the words of God by prioritizing the Qur'ān in their daily schedule.

While Sufis have this mystical understanding, other members in the mosque community tend to treat reading the Qur'ān in their mornings in a similar fashion to those Christians who read the Bible in the morning upon rising. Members very commonly used the Qur'ān to spiritually relieve personal tension. Although most of them cannot fully comprehend Qur'ānic Arabic, reading and listening to it and understanding as much as possible gave them peace and tranquillity. Their firm

[23] They are called *mu'awwadhatān* (protective) in Arabic because of the talismanic virtues.

and certain belief was that the Qur'ān is God's word even though they cannot understand it. This therapeutic effect can also sometimes be called remembrances, or *dhikr* in Arabic. Some Egyptians tried to understand the meanings of the Qur'ān and tended to connect these meanings with the sound of recitation. One of my informants reminded me about the fourth caliph 'Alī, 'If you want to talk to God, pray. If you want God to talk to you, then read the Qur'ān.' In this way, there was a lot of personal dialogue between the individual and God via the holy text.

It was an established custom among my interviewees to read a regular daily portion from the Qur'ān (*wird*). They took the advice and practices of Prophet Muḥammad very seriously. He suggested in the traditions (*ḥadīth*) that a Muslim should at least read the entire Qur'ān monthly. More than one month without such a recitation can disconnect the person from the Qur'ān. With this understanding since the time of the Prophet, there have been people like *Imām* Abū Ḥanīfah reading the entire Qur'ān daily and some like *Imām* Shāfi'ī[24] completing the Qur'ān every three days. It was suggested that those who memorize the Qur'ān read it completely at least every six to seven days. For the lay person, who cannot find the time to complete the duty of reading the Qur'ān in their routine schedule, the month of Ramadan was a unique opportunity to read the full Qur'ān in thirty days in congregational prayer in the mosque. It is an established practice among the devout Muslims during Ramadan to pray together in the nights of fasting and read and listen to a *juz'* behind an *imām* (*tarāwīḥ*) in the mosque.

Sakīna: Personal Sacred Space

Personal sacred space is important to focus, discharge, relieve and maintain the state of peace and tranquillity for Muslims in Madinat Nasr. The concept of *sakīna* can be the experience or emotional state of the person in peace, tranquillity, and spiritual empowerment. My quest has been to understand if these moments are bound to time and/or space.

One of the emerging phenomena has been personal sacred space within public sacred spaces. For example, people used to go to mosque, a sacred space referred by all Muslims. A person in this mosque community habitually preferred a specific spot in the mosque due to their level of concentration, or due to their experience of *sakīna* in that spot. Some of the informants knew from experience that the physical locations where people prayed and meditated can encourage the good.

Once someone starts praying they do not want to leave that physical space because of the build-up of sacredness through prayer and recitation of the Qur'ān in that spot. The feeling of *sakīna* cannot be immediate. The recitation of the

[24] Esposito, *Oxford Encyclopedia of Islam*, 107.

Qur'ān in the public space is thought of as a powerful trigger of *sakīna*. The devout can also seek it in the nearby mosques. *Sakīna*'s power on believers also expresses itself in appropriate behaviours in the mosque, a place for prayer. Sabri, one of my informants, mentions the *ḥadīth* from the Prophet Muḥammad that 'if a person wants to visit a place from paradise in this world they should visit a mosque'. In Islamic legal teachings, a person cannot sell or buy in the mosque. One cannot visit the mosque with bad odours on one's person. Other mosque etiquettes include not shouting, keeping silent, always being engaged in the moments of silence, reflection, recitation and listening to the Qur'ān, teaching and learning. The notion is that sacred spaces like mosques are designed for people to spiritually discharge themselves. Another informant, Yasin, says that:

> When I wake up in the morning I do not talk or eat till I go to morning (*fajr*) prayer. I pray at the mosque or I pray at home. After I pray the morning prayer I remain in my same spot where I prayed till the sunrise then I pray again. Prophet Muḥammad *SAW* (Peace Be Upon Him) says, whoever prays the morning prayer remains at the same spot, engaging in the remembrance of Allah *SWT* (the Most Glorified, the Most High) through recitation of the Qur'ān, and other means of remembrance of Allah *SWT*, *dhikr*, then this person can get the reward of going to pilgrimage three times.

Naila, sister of Sālih, used to constantly pray the morning prayer at home and remain in her spot till sunrise because of this teaching. Naila was divorced and had three children. She did not have a college education and only completed middle school. Naila was not religious until middle age, but she had a transformation in her practice of religiosity.

It seemed that people experienced the moments of *sakīna* in their personal sacred space formed by recitation of the Qur'ān. Some of the participants expressed *sakīna* as tranquillity in their hearts and minds. Some described it as sweetness on the tongue, others as a 'positive motivational energy'. One of the Sufi participants, Ahmad, a lover of *Imām* Shafi'i, mentioned prayer as possibly leading to an epiphany, a kind of culmination of spiritual feelings:

> The reality and goal of life is to 'hunt' (detect) those moments of tranquility (*sakīna*). These are the moments of intimacy with God. These are the moments that a person does not want to end. These are the moments that you want to prolong as long as possible. You don't want to go back to the bitterness of life and bitterness of people, screams, curses, and bad spiritual and physical smells. Your rank is elevated to angelic status. So, don't leave it and hold it with your teeth (symbolically meaning tight).

Some expressed the fulfilling sentiment of pleasing God by reciting the sacred text. This fulfilment of joy emerged as Yasin said: 'I did not waste my time. At least, I did something for my afterlife.' Yasin was an interesting character. He was a teacher in his forties and liked to travel. According to him, the notion of tranquillity, *sakīna*, filled the heart and mind because of the satisfaction of preparing for an unknown, death. As he said, 'by reciting or listening to the Qur'ān, I am illuminating my grave and my journey after death'. He mentioned that 'the nights are dark, to be illuminated with the light of the recitation of the Qur'ān'.

In Egypt, there is a special printed Qur'ān in the markets to encourage people to wake up in the middle of the night and read the Qur'ān in solitude and privacy while everyone is sleeping. This recitation of the Qur'ān in prayers (*salah*) at night is called *tahajjud* or *qiyāmul layl*. These specially printed Qur'āns are called '*tahajjud*' Qur'āns and their bigger and more readable pages are designed to encourage people to read. *Tahajjud* prayers are performed at home. People form this sacred space by reciting and listening to the Qur'ān in their homes. Naila had a dedicated place and a prayer rug at home when she recited the Qur'ān. While I was staying in a room adjacent to her house, I used to hear late in the night, around 3.00 a.m., that she used to cry during her *tahajjud* prayers.

The transition stages from these *sakīna* moments to painful moments of life were gradual for my discussants. A person in a *sakīna* state through recitation of the Qur'ān can store positive energy. As this energy decreases with the minute details and stresses of life, it vanishes, and a negative state can overcome the person. The solution in that case is to again engage with reciting and listening to the Qur'ān to build more energy to cope with the problems. There were members who treated the regulatory five times a day of prayer as a means to store this lost energy against the frictions of life.

A person during these five daily prayers engages with the recitation of the Qur'ān, with sacred soothing sounds, meanings, praises of God, discharges of repentance, physical movements of humbleness, and rationalizing meanings of the Qur'ān to cope with fears and injustices. After finishing it, the person gains momentum to go forward on their spiritual journey. Some of the Egyptian Muslims such as Sabri call this gain and loss cycle the real meaning of struggle (jihād). It continues until one dies. When the person meets with God after death, God informs them of the result of this lifelong struggle. The reward of absolute and unending real tranquillity, *sakīna*, comes with the real union with God. The punishment is separation from God.

When the individual associates with the Qur'ān in a public space, then this space becomes a private space. Cars provide important sacred spaces for Muslims in Madinat Nasr. The physical presence of the Qur'ān and listening to the Qur'ān in the car while driving produces the spiritual sacred space for silence, meditation and reflection. I observed that some of the Egyptians preferred to stay in their cars to form this sacred space instead of standing outside and hanging out with their friends. Their preference was to listen to the Qur'ān from the radio or to read the

Qur'ān in their car. Two of my informants, Tanar and Hamid, said that 'the best place for me is reading the Qur'ān in the car. When I go home or go to mosque everyone wants to talk to you, a lot of disturbance.' They used to park their cars either on the street next to their homes or the mosque and stayed inside their cars and read the Qur'ān.

It is noteworthy to see the convergence of the notion of *sakīna* with Asad's[25] arguments when he attempts to challenge Geertz[26] about the universal definition of religion. The concept of *sakīna* implies a flexible sacred space and time with a discursive process. In contrast to Geertz's definition of religion as an anthropological category, formation of *sakīna* goes far beyond both a simple nominalism and a representation of symbols.[27] Revisiting the argument of agency of *sakīna*, is the agency of *sakīna* in opposition to 'structure' and 'culture'? Or as Turner says:[28]

> While one religion prevails, social and cultural structures seem immutable. But structures, and the symbols which manifest them, do break up and crumble. What often persists is communitas, no longer normative or ideological, but waiting to be given new form by a new religion.

Communitas is a platform that takes the community of the Qur'ān to the shared and common experience of *sakīna*. Communitas of *sakīna* brings everyone to an equal and accessible level. Is the formation of *sakīna* a challenge to the normative experiences of rituals? One experiences the essence of the rituals during engagement with them. The ritual of engagement with the Qur'ān produces *sakīna* as one of the essential fruits of this ritual. In addition, it does not seem that *sakīna* is a 'self-interpretation'[29] but an empirical experience of the sacred space. This demonstrable sacred space emerges as one engages oneself with the Qur'ān either through reading or listening.

Engagement through the scriptures can be in various modalities. One can observe *sakīna* in various modalities, in a public space such as on the streets, in a taxicab or in a religious building such as in a mosque or at home. Streets or taxicabs can be examples of generalized public spaces and mosques can be the specific public spaces. *Sakīna* finds itself complete in masjid or prayer circles. In a literate society, people have their own multiple modalities as they are in the states of *sakīna*. It is interesting to observe how *sakīna* can transfer and transform

[25] Asad, *Genealogies of Religion*, 29–51.
[26] Geertz, *Local Knowledge*, 219.
[27] Asad, *Genealogies of Religion*, 29–51.
[28] Victor Turner, 'The Center Out There: Pilgrim's Goal', *History of Religions*, 12, 1973, 202.
[29] Keane, *Self-Interpretation, Agency and the Objects*, 222–48.

the self in different venues. Totalizing the whole life experience through different modalities, these *sakīna* moments can take over the individual's agency. Anything or everything that the person does can be interpreted through genres. Within this, *sakīna* is the product of the medium of the Qur'ān.

Sakīna can also be substantially observed in familial relationships at home. The love of God through the Qur'ān in a family can form *sakīna*. If there is no *sakīna* in a family, it can lead to divorce. Therefore, the Qur'ān suggests the formation of *sakīna* creates an ideal familial relationship: 'Among his wonders is this: God created for you mates out of your own kind, so that you might incline toward them, and God engenders love and tenderness between you' (The Qur'ān, 30:21). Couples complement each other with love and caring for each other through the formation of *sakīna*.

The phenomenological approach relates to the experience of reading or hearing the Qur'ān and the feeling that one has in one's sacred space.

Happiness and Poverty

This chapter suggests that there were still substantial levels of poverty in Egypt at the beginning of the millennium, as depicted in Unni Wikan's[30] considerable ethnographic work on poverty between the years 1969 and the 1980s in the streets of Cairo. In my visits and stays in Cairo, I witnessed similar sights to those illustrated by Wikan. Beggars, street sellers, unhygienic conditions, and overcrowded transportations were some of the venues where one could encounter the meagre economic conditions of daily life. In contrast to Wikan, my quest was to explore how the Egyptians affected by these conditions use religiosity, especially the scripture of the Qur'ān, as an avenue to maintain happiness in their daily lives.

As I routinely wandered the streets of Cairo, the effect of religion in an Egyptian's daily life was evident through the Islamic language and dress and people's attachment to listening to various reciters of the Qur'ān. Asim, one of my interviewees, mentioned the importance of creating a sacred space for oneself and one's family. Asim was an *imām*, the lead clergy in one of the mosques. He was in his forties and married. He wanted me to rationalize how people can define what 'backwards' or a 'backward approach to life and its problems' was; that was, moving from the Qur'ān to life rather than from life to the Qur'ān. He emphasized that a space not protected from the evil or the influence of unknown spiritual distractions can change a person's mood and make them unhappy. To achieve this, one of the ways to promote sacred space and sacred time was to embellish the daily activities around the Qur'ān. Replacing listening to music with the

[30] Unni Wikan, 'Living Conditions among Cairo's Poor: A View from Below', *Middle East Journal*, 1985, 7–26.

beautiful Qur'ān recitation was a simple and practical way of implementing this goal according to him. Although people may have been disturbed by different personal, family and social conflicts, they can gain some relief from and even ignore them while being focused on the recitation of the Qur'ān. In these engagements, they can move from the Qur'ān to life problems rather than approaching the Qur'ān from these problems.

It was my very common and vivid experiential discovery in Egypt that people listened to the Qur'ān in order to be happy and maintain this mood throughout the day. On the other hand, listening to music or any other human-created songs or rhythms, even religious hymns, helped people relieve their immediate stress but as soon as this human-made melody ended the sorrow and pain started again according to my interviewees. However, in my conversations with Egyptian informants they often claimed that the peaceful effect of the Qur'ān continued even if they stopped listening to it. They mentioned that music had a placebo effect whereas listening to the Qur'ān had spiritual effect that was more than that. This was mainly because these sounds were the words of God. As the Creator cannot be compared to the created, God's words superseded in all aspects the words of humans. Spiritually edifying music – Kavali, masses, chants – are never mere entertainment. However, there was a classification of religious and secular music as part of one's art and the Qur'ānic recitation as another separate art:[31]

> To label Qur'ānic recitation as music undermines the perfection and uniqueness of the text, trivializing its effect on listeners and reducing it to the status of entertainment.

When I visited some of the traditional Qur'ānic schools (madrasa), the young students immensely enjoyed memorizing the Qur'ān. It was not clear in the beginning if the students' enjoyment was through understanding the meaning of the words or through the Divine sounds or both. Some of the programmes at al-Azhar required the students to memorize the Qur'ān as a prerequisite for acceptance to the college. Before being admitted to some of the academic programmes in the Islamic sciences at al-Azhar, a student dedicated two to three years of his or her life solely to memorizing the Qur'ān. The programme was intense, with students spending six to eight hours daily memorizing the Arabic sacred text. The goal was to make the students internalize the sacred sounds and phrases and to equip them with critical thinking and analysis skills to use in their personal and academic lives.

The Qur'ān memorization teachers stationed themselves in classical sitting areas on the ground. They reviewed each student's memorization daily and

[31] Kristina Nelson, *The Art of Reciting the Qur'ān* (Cairo: American University Press in Cairo, 2001) xv.

dedicated all their life to this task. According to them, this was a very noble and pleasurable cause. It was interesting when one of the Qur'ān teachers said about their enjoyment while engaged in the Qur'ān recitation: 'If the kings knew of the pleasure that we experience, then they would leave their thrones and come, sit with us and try to take our positions.'

I tried to empathize with them, given our perception of norms and pleasures in the West. To understand my bafflement, it is important to look at their daily interactions. They seemed to be very content and serene in their daily transactions. They embodied their belief that the Qur'ān calmed them, gave them peace and tranquillity. It gave meaning to their lives, a purpose, and motivation toward the afterlife. It gave them hope and patience and made them self-accountable. Although they were in poor, underserved areas, they tried to maintain their Qur'ān recitation. The Qur'ān instructed them to behave with dignity, as for example, in the verse:

> An ignorant person would think them as financially self-sufficient because of their restraint and modesty, but you will know them from their noble character. They do not ask people. And whatever you spend of good, indeed, God knows it.[32]

These teachers seemed to exemplify the character of the above verses. The verses referred to a person who needed basic human survival items such as food, clothing, perhaps even shelter, but hid it from others. The Qur'ānic verses urged finding such dignified people and fulfilling their needs.

This did not mean that one did not see beggars on the streets of Egypt. Yet, for most Egyptians, begging seemed to be frowned upon. The Qur'ān's teachings provided the poor with a sense of self-worth. According to my interlocutors, the Qur'ān and the Prophet instructed believers to ask and beg only from God for any type of need. They tried to refrain from asking others even for their essential needs.

Attending live Qur'ānic recitations was an important recreational activity in Egypt. Egyptians would even drive hours to listen to a Qur'ān recitation from a good reciter in another city. For Egyptians, this habit was similar to going to a concert. Most of the time, these recitation sessions were in the mosques open to the public. Sometimes, there was also protocol-level representation from government officials and soldiers at these gatherings.

We can examine questions such as, 'How do Egyptians experience poverty? How do they handle it in daily life?' In our understanding of happiness, having a structured life, travelling, being successful, being promoted at one's job, and/or having a nice family are all elements of contentment. In Egypt, a person may

[32] Adapted from SInternational, The Qur'ān, 41; The Qur'ān, 2:273.

not have a tightly scheduled life, meetings with different people, promotion at their job or much travelling experience. This lifestyle seems to be uncomplicated, simple. For an Egyptian, the schedule mostly centres around the five prayer times of the Muslim ritual. In the mosques, there is especially increased attendance during the early morning prayer (*fajr*), which could be anytime between 5.00 a.m. and 6.30 a.m., and during the late-night prayer (*'ishā*), which can be anytime between 8.00 p.m. and 10.00 p.m. The Prophet Muḥammad strongly encouraged Muslims to make an effort to attend these early morning and late-night prayers if they were not able to attend the full five daily prayers in the mosque. Each prayer can take from four to ten minutes depending on the portion of the day and the person who is leading the prayer. *Imāms* in official mosques in Egypt are employed by the government.

Some of the big mosques are not located within immediate walking distance of residential areas. Their attendance may be as high when compared to the smaller mosques (*masjid*) in residential areas. Some of these praying accommodations (*muṣalla*) were converted from neighbourhood front stores or basements. Yet, people seemed to fill these smaller mosques often to pray five daily prayers in congregation. These worship areas, most of the time, did not have an official *imām* employed by the government. A qualified person, who memorized some portions of the Qur'ān and had knowledge of Islamic legal rulings, seemed to lead the prayers. The optional Qur'ān recitations occurred most of the time either before or after the prayer. Either people read their daily portion of the Qur'ān (*awrād*), or they made a reading circle and everyone read a portion of it as a collective reading. The *imāms* occasionally explained or gave a short lecture about the meaning of the verses that they read during the prayer or during the reading circles (*ḥalaqa*). There was often informal group discussion among the attendees during or after these Qur'ānic recitations. The discussion was accompanied by questions, personal stories, or jokes.

During my interviews, Sabri, who was an engineer and from a rural part of Egypt but lived in Alexandria, mentioned that in marital disputes it was common to recite the Qur'ān. To rid the house of evil thoughts or energy, people recited or played the Qur'ān recitation especially during potential familial troubles. The exterior or interior portion of the houses, or buildings, had the full, or portions of, the Qur'ān written on a tablet or piece of paper as protection from the evil eye and any type of evil occurrence. It was typical to see some of the coffee shop owners opening their stores in the mornings by playing the Qur'ān recitations. Sabri said 'There is a great respect for the Qur'ān. Even they open the coffee shops with the Qur'ān and they do other things later on … [giggles].' He meant that some of the events that take place in coffee shops may not be fully Islamic. Yet, they still opened the store with the recitation of the Qur'ān to receive blessings from God.

According to Egyptian Muslims in Nasr City, Qur'ānic methodology meant that the Qur'ān always presented the problems along with the solutions. Some of the solutions included awareness, ethics, spirituality, right intentions and rituals. The people who upheld these values were praised regardless of their historical era, membership, or gender. In my conversations with Egyptians, they cited historical illustrations from the Qur'ān. They mentioned the story of the sons of Adam as the first example on earth of an unjust killing. The Qur'ān contained animated illustrations of the followers of Moses experiencing immense oppression under the pharaoh, the disciples of Jesus following the 'truth' regardless of their small number and their fear of execution, and the companions of Muḥammad going through huge spiritual and ethical transformations from darkness to enlightenment. The Qur'ān praised the Jews, Christians, women, men, and even animals who were upholding the values of consciousness, ethics, spirituality, right intention and rituals.

Imām Asim asserted that the Qur'ān praised the wife of the pharaoh in Egypt because of her stance against injustices perpetuated by her husband, despite being afraid for her own life. Indeed, according to some narratives, her husband did kill her because of her stand for justice. The Qur'ān praised the sister of Moses in her wise and determined effort to help her baby brother be taken care of by her mother in Egypt. The Qur'ān praised Christian priests who were in sincere devotional prayers at night, crying in contemplation of creation and being in a state of spiritual consciousness. The Qur'ān praised the bird '*hud hud*' (hoopoe) for its arguments about divinity and perplexing King Solomon. Thus, from the perspective of my Egyptian informants, people obtained well-being, not through physical or socio-economic wellness, but rather through spirituality, ethics, and rituals. Listening to and reciting the Qur'ān was inculcating these values on a level beneath consciousness.

One of the common themes that emerged during my ethnographic research was the widespread optional (*nawāfil*) ritual of fasting. Fasting was a supplement to or enhancement of the Qur'ānic recitations. This is how *Imām* Ahmad in Cairo justified this ritual:

> As your physical body gets weaker with hunger through fasting, your spiritual body gets stronger. On the contrary, as your physical body gets stronger through overindulgence with eating your spiritual body gets weaker.

Imām Ahmad often used to do the optional fasts. He used to look pale and a little sleepy by the end of the day. He mentioned:

> The Prophet Muḥammad encourages Muslims to fast on Mondays and Thursdays. He also encourages them to fast in the middle three days of the month when the moon is in full phase.

In my observation, Egyptians appeared to enjoy undertaking the optional fasting in their daily lives. The fasting was without any food and drink from sunrise to sunset. It seemed that the fasting person went through the discipline of an inner struggle. However, the sentiment and intention of pleasing God and the exuberant experience of breaking the fast (*ifṭār*) fortified the members of the mosque with spiritual and rational fulfilment and satisfaction. *Imām* Ahmad said about the ritual of fasting:

> A Muslim motivates oneself that the goal and intention is really to please God and God will give the person the real reward of fasting, that is all physical and spiritual wealth and richness in the afterlife.

Given the widespread low economic status of many Egyptians, the fasting person seemed to find happiness not through physical means and material indulgence but in spiritual self-discipline. According to them, a person established a stronger connection with the Qur'ān through fasting. Different convoluted and intricate meanings of the Qur'ān revealed themselves to the fasting person. As a result, the Qur'ān was revealed to the Prophet Muḥammad in the month of fasting, Ramadan. A fasting person easily extracted the appropriate meanings from the Qur'ān according to their personal need to overcome tribulations and establish and sustain happiness.

Times of Fear

Many of my informants seemed to avoid political discussions. Some of them struggled to survive and focused on making a living. Chatting about the Qur'ān was relaxing and non-political despite the strong temptations to discuss the issues of the day. For them, power struggles in politics were a brief part of their informal chatting. The way to obtain real and substantial happiness was through listening to and reading the Qur'ān.

Muḥsin used to make jokes with some religious sentiments but seemed to sympathize with the pious. He used to joke sometimes about the 'great' religiosity of his son. His son, however, was a very dedicated practising man. He tried to perform all five prayers in the mosque and was involved in different religious activities through his mosque. He was constantly looking for ways to increase his religious understanding and ended up moving to Saudi Arabia.

Sālih had undergone multiple heart surgeries. Although he was not dedicated to practising his religion, he used to play the Qur'ān on his mp3 player all night. He used to sleep and wake up with the Qur'ān constantly playing in the background.

Muḥsin's family often complained about his lack of religiosity and persistently advised him to pray the five daily prayers. Although he did not fully practise his religion according to the Egyptian norms of religiosity, he was constantly listening to the Qur'ān. Similarly to Sālih, the Qur'ān played in the background while Muḥsin tried to sleep. Both of them listened to famous Egyptian reciters, such as Abdussamed and Minshawi, along with many others such as Muhammad Rifat.[33] Egyptian Qur'ān reciters have an established tradition, a permanent methodology of reciting the Qur'ān in a slow (*tartīl*) but rhythmic style, inspired by the meanings of the verses. It seems contradictory that the Egyptian Arabic dialect of these informants was close to the street language (*'ammi*). However, the Egyptian reciters were fully trained to recite the Qur'ān in its original language, *classical* Arabic.

While I was in the streets of Cairo and Alexandria, there were fears about demonstrations, possible military interventions, and a chaotic period during the expected change in the leadership of the country in June 2010. Although some people were closely following the news on TV and Twitter, personal lives on the streets continued in small shops, market places and mosques. Some Egyptians were coping with their fear of change by ignoring the news and listening to the literary and recitational melody of the Qur'ān. Listeners compared incidents in the Qur'ān with their current fear of either poverty or chaos. Some of the recitations reflected fear of political change and suggested that good and evil people and policies were part of God's plan. In this regard, some related the uncertainty of the current situation to chapter 29, verses 1–6 of the Qur'ān:

1. Alif, Lām, Mīm.
2. Do the people think that they will be left alone by saying simply 'We attained to the faith' and they will not be tested?
3. Yes, Indeed. We have certainly tested those before them, and God will surely make evident those who are truthful, and will surely make evident the liars.
4. Do those who do evil deeds think that they can escape from Us? What a bad judgment! Evil is that on which they base everything.
5. Whoever looks forward meeting with God, indeed, the scheduled time set by God is definitely approaching. And God is the All-Hearing, the All-Knowing.
6. And whoever puts an effort does so only for his own good. Indeed, God does not need anything and anyone; definitely, God is independent from all of the worlds, all of the creation.[34]

These verses focus on the concept of fear as part of the Divine way of testing people. There could be various reasons contributing to the different types of fear in an Egyptian's life. Some of them feared becoming poor. Some feared losing social status. Some, especially those dedicated to their religion, feared not using the time

[33] Abdullah Wan Hilmi Wan, 'Muhammad Rifat and His Reciting Records', *International Journal of Islamic Thought*, 2013, 74–81.

[34] My translation.

wisely as a preparation for the afterlife. Some feared being part of a political or group movement that meant they could be victimized in a witch hunt. Some were even afraid to practise their religion in order not to be labelled as 'extreme'. How could a non-complex minded, simple Egyptian handle all these different types of fear? In my ethnography, sometimes jokes, sometimes silence, sometimes daily non-purposeful chats, but, observably and mostly, listening to the recitation of the Qur'ān gave people solace, peace and hope to manage the stresses in life. As mentioned above, in chapter 29 of the Qur'ān, called the Chapter of the Spider, God talked of the reality and need for fear by different means in order to 'elevate' people's status next to God and filter their spiritual and transcendent ranks; these were 'tests being the process of separating coal from diamond where the main element for both is carbon'.[35] The Qur'ān instructed that if a person abstained from daily routine activities due to fear then that person could fail in other aspects of life. According to the Egyptians' understanding of the Qur'ān, the real source of fear had to be singular and should only be from God. The other types of fear existed as a test but once a person was distracted, misplaced their main objective, and deviated from their ethical and belief values, then that could be the sign of failing. Fear did not have to make a person leave their belief, nor make them abandon the daily practice of prayers, nor deter them from doing good. However, according to the Egyptians in Nasr City, the Qur'ān accepted and recognized that humans experience fear in many situations. For example, Moses in Egypt feared Pharaoh although Moses was one of the elect individuals who was close to God. He said (The Qur'ān, 28:33) 'my Lord … I fear that they will kill me' and (The Qur'ān, 28:34) 'I fear that they will deny me'. Moses realized this fear in himself and asked God for a remedy.

Poststructuralism, Phenomenology and Embodiment

Egyptian religiosity formed a crucial part of the flow of daily life for Muslims. This pious religious animation gave meaning and sense to the person. The Qur'ān was a paramount agent to construct this animation. In Egyptian daily life, an implicit way of happiness or piety was created through listening to the recitation of the Qur'ān. Muslims supplemented this passive relation with the Qur'ān by attending their mosque and engaging in other activities inside the mosque. Egyptians in the researched mosque communities often seemed to deal with the problems related to poverty through the Qur'ānic text rather than activism, in contrast to some other traditions or religions.[36]

[35] Said Nursi, *The Collection of Light (Nursi),* translated by S. Vahide, Ihlas Nur Publication, 1993, 622.

[36] Christopher Duncan, 'Catholicism, Poverty and the Pursuit of Happiness', *Journal*

One can always argue about the methodology of anthropology in ethnographic studies. How can the observation of a particular community at a specific time be extended to the general? One can question the methodology of transferring the data from specificity into generalizability.

In this regard, it is important to reflect on the whole popular culture of the Qur'ān in the other communities of Egypt. This is particularly important when considering very different lifestyles due to socio-economic, ethnic and gender-related cultures and practices in Egypt. It is important to identify the nature of popular culture of Egyptians in relation to the Qur'ān in these wide-ranging variations. It is similarly essential to understand in this relationship what remains over the decades and becomes permanent and what is temporal, reflecting only specific behaviour and the context of the time, place and people.

The fieldwork of Saba Mahmood on the female mosque communities in Egypt[37] emphasizes the notions of poststructuralism as formality, disparate structures of authority, models of the self, disciplinary practice, and codified behaviour. This chapter has purposefully tried to avoid discussing Egyptian or world politics, and institutional power relations focusing on gender.[38]

Similarly to Mahmoud's[39] case in poststructuralism,[40] Islamic knowledge as a mode of conduct as well as a set of principles sometimes appears to be the source of experience. For example, to the casual listener, the sound of the Qur'ānic recitation was melodious. However, knowing the science behind the rhythmic recitation of the Qur'ān made it a unique phenomenon,[41] not just nice musical sounds. The Qur'ān has a divine therapeutic effect on the soul and heart. Particularly when the Qur'ān was properly recited in accordance with the subtleties of the articulation (*tajwīd*) rules, it had a powerful effect.[42] Listening through electronic devices rather than traditional live experiences increased its accessibility.

Another example of the poststructural case was that the robust knowledge and belief in God among the Egyptian Muslims made them regard the sacred text as a vital beneficial force. They mentioned this treatment in some of the Sufi contexts as '*adab,*' which is the notion of acknowledging respect for the sacred text due

of Poverty, 12, 1, 2008, 49–76.

37 Mahmood, *Politics of Piety.*

38 Marilyn Booth, 'Islamic Politics, Street Literature, and John Stuart Mill: Composing Gendered Ideals in 1990s Egypt', *Feminist Studies*, 39, 3, 2013, 596–627.

39 Mahmoud, *Politics of Piety.*

40 Sindre Bangstad, 'Saba Mahmood and Anthropological Feminism After Virtue', *Theory, Culture & Society*, 28, 3, 2011, 28–54.

41 Kristina Nelson, *The Art of Reciting the Qur'ān*, xv.

42 Annette Wilke; Oliver Moebus, *Sound and Communication* (Berlin: Walter de Gruyter GmbH, 2011) 344.

to its divine source. During my observations and conversations with the Egyptian Muslims in the Nasr City mosque community, the type of respectful (*adab*) behaviour seemed to build up in stages. First came fully accepting that the Qur'ān was from God, 'Creator of all the heavens and earth' (*Rab al-ālamīn*). Subsequently, there came firmly believing that the Qur'ān did not change, was still authentic, and it was not going to change till the 'end of days' (*Yawm al-qiyāmah*). There was an assurance in the Qur'ān by God: 'We revealed this book and we are going to protect it' (15:9). There was a certitude that God would protect the authenticity of the Qur'ān. The Qur'ān was not going to face human alterations when compared to previous sacred books sent by God. This knowledge of and trust in the validity of the Qur'ān made the Egyptian Muslims handle the text in a very 'receptive' way.

Contrary to Saba Mahmoud's[43] case, there were avenues that paralleled the phenomenology in attaining spiritual states such as *sakīna* through the means of the text, space, and other tools. In this regard, direct experience preceded the knowledge. Deductive experience led to the inductive engagements. For example, mosques were formally designated 'sacred spaces' in Egyptian Islamic life. In this case, knowing did not precede the experience but experience or indulgence preceded knowing. For example, the habit of reading the Qur'ān in public space suggested the private sacred space for the person. Egyptian Muslims tended to form those informal sacred spaces through the recitation of and listening to the Qur'ān. As already mentioned, these flexible sacred spaces were formed at any time and any place, at a mosque, at home during prayer and sleeping, in a coffee shop, in a car, in an elevator. When a person was in these sacred spaces, the peculiarities were the sentiments and thoughts of tranquillity, relief, coping with fear and poverty, happiness, moments of joy, meaning for life and physical and spiritual satisfaction.

The phenomenological approach relates to the experience of reading or hearing the Qur'ān and the feeling that one has in one's sacred space. One can call this *sakīna* as an experience. One may also call this a psychic state.

In this regard, the mixed approach of both phenomenology and poststructuralism was an indispensable model of a reciprocal relationship between the sender and receiver. We can call this mixed approach the embodiment of the Qur'ān[44] through *sakīna*. One can see this reciprocal or embodied relationship in that Egyptians move from the Qur'ān to life problems rather than from these problems to approach the Qur'ān. When a sender sends a message in different frequencies

[43] Mahmoud, *Politics of Piety*.

[44] Rudolph T. Ware III, *The Walking Qur'an: Islamic Education, Embodied Knowledge, and History in West Africa* (Chapel Hill: University of North Carolina Press, 2014).

or wavelengths, if the receiver is not tuned accordingly, then it will not receive the message. Therefore, the Egyptian Muslims revered the Qur'ān in a very personal and spiritual way as if the Qur'ān was not revealed to the Prophet Muḥammad but to themselves, as the poet Iqbal's father advised his son.[45] Egyptian Muslims sometimes utilized the sacred as a tool to attain ethical and moral standards similar to the nuances observed by Saba Mahmoud in her understanding of the five daily prayers among Egyptian women in Cairo.[46] The formation of sacred space, *sakīna*, beyond specific venues, rather than considering it as a 'conventional ritual',[47] was present. *Sakīna* has been far more than a simple nominalism and representation of symbols among Egyptian Muslims.[48] Perhaps, *sakīna* was a therapeutic spiritual experience through the agency of the Qur'ān during the period when conditions of life deteriorated for Egyptians. It did not support pessimism and feebleness but sustained dignity, self-happiness and flexibility. While one can methodologically observe the binary opposition of structuralism, one can also realize how this ethnographic data can fit within the framework of phenomenology. The embodiment of the Qur'ān via sacred space or *sakīna* in the popular culture of Egypt can be viewed through poststructural and phenomenological approaches.

One can view the *sakīna* as the temporal or purposeful engagement of talismanic effects, but relating *sakīna* to mere talismanic effects can be reductionist. Alternatively, *sakīna* can fit better in the anthropological embodiment of the Qur'ān through recitation or listening as a permanent and substantial pillar of the virtual space.[49] In other words, the Qur'ānic *sakīna* can be appropriate in the embodiment paradigm of culture and the self.

[45] Z. Anjum, *Iqbal: the Life of a Poet, Philosopher, and Politician* (India: Random House, 2015).

[46] Mahmood, *Politics of Piety*.

[47] Mahmood, *Politics of Piety*.

[48] Asad, *Genealogies of Religion*, 29–51.

[49] T.J. Csordas, 'Embodiment as a Paradigm for Anthropology', *Ethos*, 18, 1, 1990, 5–47.

PART III

ISLAMIC EDUCATION

Introduction

Britta Frede

Islamic knowledge (*'ilm*) and its transmission refer to long-standing traditions that have changed over time within and between different strands of Islamic thinking. Some examples of these strands of Islamic thinking are Sufis with a focus on spiritual practice often combined with an emphasis on textual knowledge. Further, there are Islamic scholars who stress the importance of *fiqh* (jurisprudence), *ḥadīth* (traditions of the prophet), or philosophy. Finally, more recently, there are Salafī-oriented scholars with their neglect of tradition (*taqlīd*) and attempted return to the early Islamic period (*salaf aṣ-ṣāliḥ*) while frequently giving substantial weight to the Ḥanbalī *madhhab* (school of law). These strands have evolved into trans-local networks from an early point in history, fostered through teacher–student relations that developed within institutions of knowledge transmission: mosques, fortifications including mosques and schools, Qur'ānic schools, colleges teaching various disciplines of Islamic knowledge, Sufi lodges (*zāwiya*) often including schools as well, or more recently, Islamic institutes or Islamic universities.

Various doctrines and institutions have developed different conceptions of Islamic knowledge and sometimes even different hierarchies between the disciplines for its transmission. Furthermore, periods of exclusive initiation into knowledge alternate throughout Islamic history with periods of popular dissemination of Islamic knowledge to vast parts of the Muslim populace, giving rise to transformations concerning the performance of authority,[1] modes of knowledge transmissions,[2] and finally, the composition of the textual repertoire building the

[1] Marc Gaborieau; Malika Zeghal, 'Autoritiés religieuses en Islam', *Archives des sciences sociale des religions*, 49, 125, 2004, 5–21; Masooda Bano (ed.), *Modern Islamic Authority and Social Change. Vol 1: Evolving Debates in the Muslim-Majority Countries* (Edinburgh: Edinburgh University Press, 2018).

[2] E.g. Rudolph T. Ware III, *The Walking Qur'an. Islamic Education, Embodied Knowledge, and History in West Africa* (Chapel Hill: University of North Carolina Press, 2014); Rüdiger Seesemann, 'Epistemology or Ideology? Toward a Relational Perspective on Islamic Knowledge in Africa', *Journal of African Religions*, 6, 2, 2018, 232–68.

corpus of knowledge.[3] Nevertheless, no matter how much these conceptions may vary, to attach great importance on seeking and transmitting religious knowledge is one of the shared duties and a central element of all Islamic strands of doctrine and practice.[4] This has led to the development of various kinds of institutions dedicated to religious knowledge transmission. The oldest institution in this context might be the mosque.[5]

Three outstanding Medieval institutions of higher education can be found in Africa that enfolded a transregional scholarly influence: al-Qarawiyyīn (founded 859) in Fez (Morocco), al-Azhar (founded 988) in Cairo (Egypt), and az-Zaitūna (built around 856 as a mosque, which during the thirteenth and fifteenth centuries expanded to an institution for higher education) in Tunis (Tunisia). These institutions attracted students and scholars from all parts of Islamicate Africa and contributed substantially to the dissemination of variations of Islamic doctrine and spiritual practice. Such exchange has not been a one-way project transmitting knowledge from 'centres' of learning in North Africa to the Sahara and beyond but was and is going on in all networked directions. As much as texts, pedagogies, doctrines and ideas had been imported, *ʿulamāʾ* (pl. Islamic scholars) of Saharan and sub-Saharan origin have substantially contributed to the development of Islamic education in the North, i.e. at al-Azhar in Egypt.[6] Nevertheless, the transmission of knowledge was not always formally institutionalized, as learning circles in the mosque that address a broader public might vary in their content and level of knowledge transmission. Furthermore, private learning circles were a widespread practice for knowledge transmission and a quite common practice in most parts of Africa until today. Such semi-informal modes of learning, mostly decentralized and uncontrolled by government institutions or institutionalized clergies, offer a broad spectrum of knowledge transmission and diverse strategies of scoping with the different audiences.

Transregional transmission of knowledge was further guaranteed by the travelling practice as pilgrimage, be it to Mecca (*ḥajj*, *ʿumra*) or to other places of

[3] E.g. Brinkley Messick, *The Calligraphic State. Textual Domination and History in a Muslim Society* (Berkeley: University of California Press, 1993); Stefan Reichmuth, *Islamische Bildung und soziale Integration in Illorin (Nigeria) seit ca 1800* (Münster: LIT Verlag, 1998); Zachary Valentine Wright, *Living Knowledge in West African Islam: The Sufi Community of Ibrahim Niasse* (Leiden: Brill, 2015).

[4] Franz Rosenthal, *Knowledge Triumphant. The Concept of Knowledge in Medieval Islam* (Brill: Leiden, 1970) 334–5.

[5] George Makdisi, *The Rise of Colleges: Institutions of Learning in Islam and the West* (Edinburgh: Edinburgh University Press, 1981) 10.

[6] Benaouda Bensaid; Tarek Ladjal, 'The Struggle of Traditional Religious Education in West Africa: The Case of Mahdara in Mauritania', *Journal of Ethnic and Cultural Studies*, 6, 1, 2019, 152–61, 152–3.

veneration (*ziyāra*), or just simply travel for studying (*riḥla*) from the early beginning of Islamic history.[7] Therefore, a transregional exchange of knowledge and its methodologies of transmission have been facilitated by such institutions of mobility long before technical innovations throughout the nineteenth and twentieth centuries transformed the ways and speeds of communication and transport. However, colonial modernity fostered, in some regions, more institutionalized versions of travelling as with the example of *ziyāra* within West and North African Tijāniyya,[8] and transformed older forms of travelling, such as that of the *ḥajj*.[9]

Technical innovations and a new order of political hegemonies have not only contributed to innovations within institutions of knowledge transmission, but they also encountered other regimes of knowledge production and transmission that provoked a rethinking and reformation of Muslim institutions of knowledge transmission. A renowned example is the reform of the al-Azhar in Cairo,[10] or the innovations by Ahmadiyya mission schools throughout Africa,[11] or the efforts of colonial administrations in cooperation with local Islamic scholars to motivate Muslim parents to allow their kids to be educated in integrated schools.[12] In more contemporary times, this encountering and its innovations continued, especially with the rise of Islamic and Christian schools provoked by the privatization of education since the 1990s throughout Africa.[13]

The four chapters collected within Part III all deal with knowledge transmission in contemporary African Muslim communities. As achieving Islamic knowledge is perceived as closely connected to piety within Muslim practice, the transmission of religious knowledge within Islam is not exclusively directed to children,

7 E.g. Henri Touati, *Islam and Travel in the Middle Ages*, trans. Lydia G. Cochrane (Chicago: University of Chicago Press, 2010).

8 Rüdiger Seesemann, 'Ziyāra: Funktionen und Bedeutungen in der Tiǧānīya (Westafrika)', *Der Islam*, 83, 1, 2006, 158–70.

9 Umar Ryad (ed.), *The Hajj and Europe in the Age of Empire* (Leiden: Brill, 2017).

10 E.g. Malika Zeghal, 'The "Recentering" of Religious Knowledge and Discourse: The Case of al-Azhar, Radical Islam, and the State (1952–94)', in Robert Hefner and Muhammad Qasim Zaman (eds.), *Schooling Islam: The Culture and Politics of Modern Muslim Education* (Princeton, NJ: Princeton University Press, 2007) 107–30; Wulf Frauen, *Backfire on the State? Eine Analyse zu den langfristigen Konsequenzen der Reform der Al-Azhar (1961, 1994)* (München: AVM, 2013).

11 E.g. David E. Skinner, 'Conversion to Islam and the Promotion of "Modern" Islamic Schools in Ghana', *Journal of Religion in Africa*, 43, 4, 2013, 426–50.

12 E.g. Louis Brenner, *Controlling Knowledge. Religion, Power, and Schooling in a West African Muslim Society* (London: Hurst, 2000).

13 E.g. Hansjörg Dilger; Dorothea Schulz, 'Politics of Religious Schooling: Christian and Muslim Engagement with Education in Africa: Introduction', *Journal of Religion in Africa*, 43, 4, 2013, 365–78.

but to adults as well. Islamic knowledge transmission is contributing to identity making, be it to educate the good citizen, the good Muslim, or just the member of a certain Muslim community. Institutions of Islamic knowledge transmission compete with other educational institutions; they can create alternative spaces within society or contribute to a greater national belonging. These institutions can focus on religious issues only or integrate non-religious knowledge as well. They adapt in creative ways to the societal demands of their community. Further, they relate to ideas and concepts that turn out to be influential within their communities, be it images of progress and development (Bolton), the work ethics of a certain Sufi movement (Cochrane), a concept of national identity embedded in notions of Islamic authenticity (Frede), or cosmopolitanism (Hoechner).

Bolton studies religious knowledge transmission in Zanzibar and emphasizes that the institution introduced into the local education market as madrasa already constitutes a reformed institution. The contemporary Zanzibari madrasa differs tremendously from its namesake in the medieval Middle East as an institution for advanced Islamic learning. Rather, the madrasa as educational institution introduced in colonial Zanzibar constituted a school for young pupils to memorize the Qur'ān and was an addition to government schools attended before or after class. While the madrasa was first introduced to substitute governmental schools with proper religious education, the contemporary madrasa adapts much more so as to even offer 'marketable skills'[14] by introducing secular subjects within the curriculum of the madrasa or focusing on pre-school education with a broad range of secular subjects taught beside basic religious education. Alongside institutions for children, even a madrasa for women appears as a more institutionalized form of mosque learning circles. What is most interesting in these three examples Bolton discusses in her chapter, is that all three institutions present themselves as contributing to the national project by fostering progress and development. We see that institutions of religious knowledge transmission in Islam engage not only with government schools and their curriculum and teaching methodologies but also with ideological national discourses, such as the Zanzibari emphasis on development and progress. However, the meaning of such terms becomes obviously transformed by religious interpretations that add spiritual dimensions to the material and technological understandings, as it is propagated within global programmes of development that might contribute to frame and form such national narratives as witnessed in Zanzibar's public self-perception as a nation that needs development and progress.

Cochrane's chapter deals with Sufi institutions of knowledge transmission in Senegal (the *daara)* run by the Murīdiyya. These institutions as well adapt to

[14] Roman Loimeier, *Between Social Skills and Marketable Skills: The Politics of Islamic Education in 20th Century Zanzibar* (Leiden: Brill, 2009).

political frameworks and discourses. However, rather than contributing to a great national project, this example focuses more on a holistic well-being. In reference to the educational doctrine of the Murīdiyya's founder Amadu Bamba, spiritual education in these institutions is combined with practical knowledge. Agriculture and trade are the non-religious subjects taught in these institutions. Work is perceived as central for service to God and thus the faith motivates participation in work for the community. Cochrane illustrates how environmental and economic crises have had an effect on curriculums and the development of an inclusive education within the Murid *daara* in the late 1800s, the 1980s and in the years after the global economic recession of 2007–11. Drawing on local knowledge, philosophies and religious tradition, the community successfully faced economic and environmental challenges. Bringing together various social strata, the Murīdiyya popularized Islamic knowledge and spiritual education with great success. In combination with the emphasis on community work, the Murīdiyya have embraced a great number of followers and attracted economic gain due to peanut agriculture. The revival of community work aims at reviving the Murīdiyya while bringing prosperity back to the region.

The individual quest for religious knowledge is present in most African Muslim communities. The longing for an authentic self, well embedded within its religious belief while coping with the challenges of contemporary life, social change, economic struggle, and, sometimes, political power imbalance, is a phenomenon that can be found in most African Muslim settings. Frede sketches traditional institutions for knowledge transmission among adult women in contemporary urban Mauritania. By concentrating on the development of the *maḥḍara* in Nouakchott, her chapter demonstrates that traditional institutions are flexible and cope in creative ways with social transformations, responding to the need of the community they serve. While the *maḥḍara* is considered in Mauritania as an important part of national cultural heritage, giving proof to the authentic Islamic tradition of its people, the institution still adapts to government schools, their pedagogical methodologies, and knowledge conceptions that indicate epistemological changes. Such shifts in epistemology can, in the long run, have tremendous impacts on knowledge production itself by introducing new approaches to text.[15] However, the Mauritanian *maḥḍara* still holds on to their classical body of locally produced text that has been established as curriculum within the last centuries.

Hoechner's chapter looks instead not at the national interplay of Islamic education and state schools but at the relationality of Muslims in the diaspora and their home regions. By focusing on the children and youth of Senegalese migrants in the USA, she sheds light on a more or less neglected aspect within the literature

[15] E.g. Aria Narkissa, 'An Epistemic Shift in Islamic Law. Educational Reform at al-Azhar and Dār al-ʿUlūm', *Islamic Law and Society*, 21, 3, 2014, 209–51.

on the transformation of Islamic education. This perspective offers a fresh look at educational reform within faith-based institutions that calls to be explored in deeper ways. While migratory parents might have economic and/or moral ambitions guiding their decisions to send children back to Senegal for religious education, the Senegalese educational institutions also have to respond to the needs of this new clientele, which arrives with a habitus that differs substantially from children who have grown up in Senegal. As Hoechner hints at in her conclusion, such a response is not only visible through the foundation of new educational institutions that bridge the diverting lifeworld of the migrant siblings, but even the use of new technological opportunities like social media, which allows an outreach of Senegalese *ʿulamāʾ* into the homes of Senegalese migrants in the US. One might ask what kind of effect the intertwining of migrant communities and Senegalese home communities has in the processes of Islamic identity building.

CHAPTER 10

Modernizing the Madrasa: Islamic Education, Development, and Tradition in Zanzibar

Caitlyn Bolton

'Some people are so afraid to develop children spiritually', explained a teacher trainer at the Aga Khan Foundation's Madrasa Pre-School programme in Zanzibar. 'It means to be kind, not rude, not to take others' things, to respect others,' she continued. 'They think maybe we are teaching them to be terrorists, but it is not true.' The Madrasa Pre-School programme is one initiative among many by Islamic organizations in Zanzibar that seek to redraw the boundaries of religious and secular educational structures, recasting 'secular' subjects as part of Islamic knowledge and the madrasa as a site of knowledge and learning more broadly. These programmes are in direct contrast to British colonial education reforms that introduced public government schooling in the hope of displacing local Qur'ānic schools, which they deemed as antiquated, unhygienic, and 'deadening' to the intellect. As with petitioning parent associations in the 1920s, contemporary religious educators are put in a position where they must push back against dominant portrayals that homogenize their schools and present them as purveyors of 'backwardness', instead emphasizing the relevance of Islamic education to personal and societal progress.

'Madrasas' enter contemporary Euro-American media and political discourse as a space of the past, of entombed tradition antagonistic to modernity, and at its most extreme, as 'breeding grounds for terrorists'.[1] This portrayal of Islamic schools has a lengthy history. British colonial officials in Zanzibar in the early twentieth century, for example, regarded Islamic schools as a 'block to progress',[2] and made every effort to close them down in favour of their own schools. Yet despite this representation as having 'existed for centuries'[3] just as they are,

[1] Ebrahim Moosa, *What Is a Madrasa?* (Chapel Hill: University of North Carolina Press, 2015) 2.
[2] Zanzibar National Archives (ZNA) BA6/3.
[3] Zanzibar National Archives (ZNA) BA6/3.

Islamic knowledge transmission in Zanzibar has taken many forms, shifted over time, and been indelibly affected by dominant ideologies of imperial and global processes. Reflecting this, and quite the opposite of these prevalent portrayals, the work of some contemporary madrasas in Zanzibar is embedded within a global discourse of 'development/progress' (*maendeleo*) – even if reworking the concept by rejecting a sacred/secular divide, expanding it to include 'development for the afterlife', and understanding social and economic progress within the 'complete system' (*mfumo mzima*) of Islam. Examining the shifting forms of a site identified with 'tradition', even by many Muslims, questions popular understandings of a concept often associated with rigidity and the past, while locating the madrasa as a site that is fluid, historically contextualized, and embedded within popular ideologies and concepts.

Islamic Education in Nineteenth- and Twentieth-Century Zanzibar: Orality, Literacy, and *Ustaarabu*

The contemporary setting of Islamic education in Zanzibar is woven together by layers of migratory webs of scholars, merchants and sultans across the Indian Ocean, and in particular from the Arabian Peninsula. But despite this deep historical connection to the Arab Islamic world, Islamic learning in Zanzibar was not always Arab-centric or characterized by universal Arabic literacy. Before the introduction of the Arabic printing press in Zanzibar in the nineteenth century alongside the establishment of Omani Arab rule,[4] foundational Islamic learning was transmitted largely by oral Swahili religious traditions with only semi-literacy in Arabic texts.[5] As with other specialized tradecrafts, advanced religious learning was considered a vocation and was fulfilled by only a few descent groups who possessed the additional written Arabic resources.[6] Such individuals provided key social functions in their communities, arbitrating on property rights, town commerce, marriage and divorce, war, and relations with overseas commercial clients.[7] They were called *walimu* (educated ones, teachers) and were part of the

[4] Amal N. Ghazal, *Islamic Reform and Arab Nationalism: Expanding the Crescent from the Mediterranean to the Indian Ocean (1880s–1930s)* (New York: Routledge, 2010) 16.

[5] Anne K. Bang, *Sufis and Scholars of the Sea: Family Networks in East Africa, 1860–1925* (New York: Routledge, 2003) 128.

[6] Randall L. Pouwels, *Horn and Crescent: Cultural Change and Traditional Islam on the East African Coast, 800–1900* (Cambridge: Cambridge University Press, 1987) 87.

[7] Pouwels, *Horn and Crescent*, 94–5.

waungwana, those exhibiting the distinguishing standards of coastal urban civilization – *uungwana.*[8]

This equilibrium between local and imported Islamic influences changed in the nineteenth century as the ideal of civilized lifestyle became increasingly associated with Arab traits. *Ustaarabu* – a Swahili word derived from the Arabic *ista'araba*, meaning to become Arab-like – began to eclipse *uungwana* to express 'civilization'. This was due to the rapid acceleration of trade with Oman and the transfer of the capital of the Omani sultanate to Zanzibar in the 1830s, that later became an independent Arab sultanate. While religious authority over the integration of new Muslims had previously been the prerogative of the *waungwana*, the new sultanate sought to bring all Muslims under a more institutionalized religious authority, creating a corps of Islamic officials dispatched to local communities.[9] Where beforehand, Islamic knowledge had significantly been transmitted orally and in Swahili, there emerged in the 1860s and 1870s a new cadre of scholars who had been trained in Arabic, often in Arabia.[10]

This new class of *'ulamā'* promoted a more literate Islamic learning as they had extensive ties across the Arabic-speaking Muslim world, many travelling to Cairo, the Hijaz, and familial homelands in Oman and Hadramaut for pilgrimage and to study with learned masters to obtain *ijāza*s (licences to teach certain texts). Many of the most influential of this new class of scholars in the late nineteenth and early twentieth centuries were part of the 'Alawiyya Sufi *tarīqa* originating from Hadramaut, and came to dominate the religious leadership in Zanzibar, including the position of chief qāḍī (judge). Such scholars, and in particular Sayyid Ahmad Ibn Sumayt and Shaykh Abdallah Bā Kathīr, increasingly came to define the content and scope of Islamic education in the twentieth century.

The more literate, and Arabic-centric, Islamic education guided by this new class of scholars took place in local Qur'ān schools, called *chuo,* pl. *vyuo* (Swahili) or *kuttāb*, pl. *katātīb* (Arabic). Parents would send their children to a local teacher from the age of six until nine or ten, after which boys would be initiated into the vocational arts of their fathers, with some continuing on to the advanced Islamic sciences.[11] The teachers (*mwalimu*, pl. *walimu*) would not get paid a salary, but rather a small entrance fee (*ufito*, literally the 'cane' for disciplining) of two to three rupees, and as the student reached milestones in memorizing the Qur'ān. Students also recompensed their teachers in the form of labour in his fields or around the house, including laundry, cooking and cleaning. Students

[8] Laura Fair, *Pastimes and Politics: Culture, Community, and Identity in Post-Abolition Urban Zanzibar, 1890–1945* (Athens, Ohio: Ohio University Press, 2001) 43.

[9] Bang, *Sufis and Scholars*, 127.

[10] Bang, *Sufis and Scholars*, 128.

[11] Pouwels, *Horn and Crescent*, 80.

would progress according to their own pace rather than a standard timeline, first memorizing the Qur'ān, followed by more advanced Arabic texts in jurisprudence imported from Cairo.[12]

This instructional system exhibited certain key features, many of which are echoed in nearby regions given the transnational nature of Arabic Islamic learning at the time. For one, teaching was guided not by a formal syllabus or learning schedule for the entire class, but rather each student 'would proceed to the next step in learning as soon as he had mastered the last'.[13] With individual writing tablets, as compared to a government school's singular class blackboard,[14] students could progress on their own learning schedule in a direct and personal relation to their teacher-master. In fact, the very name *kuttāb* is likely a plural of the word *kātib*, meaning writer or scribe – so students would not be attending a *kuttāb* as a place, but rather the learned individuals present. It is also reflective of the centrality of literate learning that the name itself refers to writing. This closeness or *ṣuḥba* between student and educator[15] was also exhibited by, for more advanced students, the *ijāza* – a certificate detailing that one has mastered a specific text as learned from a particular scholar, and is licensed to teach it. One graduated not from an institution, but mastered individual texts under a scholar's guidance, extending the genealogical chain of personal knowledge transmission one link further. Many Zanzibaris of Hadrami descent would travel to Hadramaut in modern-day Yemen to obtain *ijāza*s, as the personal knowledge transmission from a well-known scholar was just as important as the textual content.[16]

A second key element of this instructional system was its focus on memorization (*dhakara*) and repetition (*takrār*) of textual sources – what later colonial officials, and some Islamic reformers, would deride as 'rote' learning and 'parrot talk'. As described in other scholarship on Islamic educational practices in other sites, the goal was not to 'educate' in the broader sense of the term, but rather 'to provide at proper moments the written and spoken word of the Quran', inculcating a 'directness of the relationship with Allah through the Word'.[17] This required training (*riyāḍa)* that was not 'parrot talk' but 'a thoroughgoing process

[12] Roman Loimeier, *Between Social Skills and Marketable Skills: The Politics of Islamic Education in 20th Century Zanzibar* (Leiden: Brill, 2009) 166.

[13] Loimeier, *Between Social Skills and Marketable Skills*, 172.

[14] As in Yemen, see Brinkley Messick, *The Calligraphic State: Textual Domination and History in a Muslim Society* (Berkeley: University of California Press, 1992) 105.

[15] Jonathan Porter Berkey, *The Transmission of Knowledge in Medieval Cairo: A Social History of Islamic Education* (Princeton, NJ: Princeton University Press, 1992) 34.

[16] Bang, *Sufis and Scholars*, 113.

[17] Timothy Mitchell, *Colonising Egypt* (Berkeley: University of California Press, 1991) 87.

of subjecting the self to repeated exercises that shape and form the soul' until it became 'second nature'[18] – what Foucault calls 'care of the self', meaning technologies that permit individuals to transform themselves in order to attain a certain state. Messick, writing of Qur'ānic schools in Yemen, notes the root of the Arabic word for 'physical maturity' (*bulūgh*) as coming from the same root as 'eloquence/rhetoric' (*balāgha*), such that maturity entails the 'capacity to articulate the word'.[19] The training provided in Qur'ān schools 'ideally culminated in an individual who had embodied, and was capable of appropriately reproducing, the interrelated forms of both texts and behaviour'.[20] This created human 'bodies of knowledge', literally 'walking Qur'āns', as Ware describes in the case of Senegambia.[21]

These interrelated forms of texts and behaviour prompt a third key feature of this educational paradigm, namely the interrelatedness of knowledge (*'ilm)*, faith (*īmān*) and action (*'amal*). Classical Muslim scholars defined knowledge more broadly than that which simply pertains to acquired learning, the intellect or cognition. They also included intuitive kinds of knowledge pertaining to the heart and soul – where knowledge is 'a light thrust by God into the heart', or 'the arrival of the soul at the meaning of a thing'.[22] Nūr al-Dīn al-Sālimī, an Omani religious scholar turned to by Zanzibari Muslims at the turn of the twentieth century, defined knowledge as 'the achievement of the heart, just as insight (*baṣr*) is the achievement of the eye that sees'.[23] In this context, faith (*īmān*) does not mean assent to propositional statements that may or may not be based on objective fact, including blind adherence to received tradition – but can itself constitute a kind of knowledge. Knowledge (*'ilm*) and faith (*īmān*) are often equated in the Qur'ān, whereas unbelief (*kufr*) is a result of lack of knowledge, or ignorance (*jahl*), of God.[24] Further, religious or mystical kinds of studies, for example of dream interpretation, were considered among the '*sciences* of religious law'.[25] All sciences

[18] Wael B. Hallaq, *The Impossible State: Islam, Politics, and Modernity's Moral Predicament* (New York: Columbia University Press, 2014) 132.

[19] Messick, *Calligraphic State*, 79.

[20] Messick, *Calligraphic State*, 79.

[21] Rudolph T. Ware, *The Walking Qur'ān: Islamic Education, Embodied Knowledge, and History in West Africa* (Chapel Hill: University of North Carolina Press, 2014).

[22] *Ḥadīth* cited in Franz Rosenthal, *Knowledge Triumphant: The Concept of Knowledge in Medieval Islam* (Leiden: Brill, 1970) 68, 61.

[23] *'al-'ilm darak al-qalb mithlu al-baṣr yakūn darak al-'ayn 'aynd al-naẓr'*, Al-Sālimī, Nūr al-Dīn. *Jawhar al-niẓām fī 'ilmayy al-adyān wa-l-aḥkām*, Abū Isḥāq Aṭfiyyash; Ibrāhīm al-'Ibrī (eds.) 11th ed. (n.p., 1989) 3.

[24] Rosenthal, *Knowledge Triumphant*, 101.

[25] Ibn Khaldūn, cited in Amira Mittermaier, *Dreams That Matter: Egyptian Landscapes of the Imagination* (Berkeley: University of California Press, 2011) 58.

(*'ulūm*), including 'religious' sciences, are interdependent and part of knowledge (*'ilm*) more generally, which ultimately comes from God.[26]

Students in the Qur'ān schools increased their knowledge/faith through memorization, repetition and embodiment of the divine word, not simply for knowledge's sake but with the aim of producing particular behaviour in society. In education, knowledge (*'ilm*) was paired with action (*'amal*), and in fact preceded it.[27] The goal of Islamic education in Zanzibar in this period was not only to produce a knowledgeable Muslim, but also to produce a good person – with manners (*adabu*), moral conduct and self-restraint (*heshima*), and 'sound judgment' (*akili*) based on one's knowledge of the Qur'ān.[28] An *adīb* was not only a well-mannered person, but also an educated person, with the causative verb of the same root in Arabic (*addaba*) meaning 'to educate'.[29] Education, on the whole, was for the cultivation within children of *utu*, meaning both 'humanity' and the more normative 'goodness' in Swahili.[30] *Utu* mediates between 'an inner (possibly religiously inspired) motivating force for action, the *imāni* (good faith) within the individual, and the subsequent outer sphere of social recognition expressed through *heshima* (respect)',[31] linking the personal and the social. The Qur'ānic school simultaneously shaped knowledge, faith and action, within the context of a personal relationship with a scholar-master, progressing through an ocean of knowledge and interpretation according to one's own individual pace.

The Reordering of Knowledge in Colonial Zanzibar: Progress, Syllabus and Citizen

The colonial project in Zanzibar had significant implications for Islamic educational practices – for its direct effect on Islamic schools, its ideologies about the purpose of education, and as it crafted its own Islamic curriculum for government schools. Public schooling was introduced in Zanzibar first for Arab boys when the Arab sultan imported teachers in 1905 from Egypt, and was supervised by the British colonial Department of Education beginning in 1907.[32] The primary aim

[26] Rosenthal, *Knowledge Triumphant*, 44, 29.

[27] Rosenthal, *Knowledge Triumphant*, 246.

[28] Benyan S. Turki, 'British Policy and Education in Zanzibar, 1890–1945', PhD diss., University of Exeter, 1987, 89.

[29] Messick, *Calligraphic State*, 77.

[30] Kai Kresse, *Philosophising in Mombasa: Knowledge, Islam and Intellectual Practice on the Swahili Coast* (Edinburgh: Edinburgh University Press, 2007) 172.

[31] Kresse, *Philosophising in Mombasa*, 148.

[32] Ghazal, *Islamic Reform and Arab Nationalism*, 110.

of the colonial educational system was to produce 'useful and loyal citizens'[33] who could contribute to the material progress of the colony. In particular, colonial officials were eager to make the colony self-sustaining and provide a ready labour supply on clove plantations, having formally ended slavery in 1897.[34] Yet colonial officials faced a significant problem: students did not attend. Enrolment stayed low, as most families preferred to continue within the educational paradigm of the Qur'ānic school. To lure students to their classrooms, the director of education paired with local Islamic leaders to devise an Islamic studies class with its own syllabus and materials in Swahili translation. In the process, they not only objectified Islam as a codified school discipline that needed to be studied and tested through exams, they also prompted reforms within some of the Qur'ānic schools themselves. Such schools began to focus increasingly on 'marketable skills' and introduced some 'secular' subjects alongside the traditional Qur'ān recitation and memorization.[35]

The 'chief aim of the government in education', wrote the director of education in 1927, was 'to fit the young men of Zanzibar to be useful and loyal citizens'.[36] For Indian and elite Arab students, 'useful' meant the ability to populate clerical posts or to work in civil service or business.[37] Yet for 'native' African students, 'useful' meant working in agriculture, particularly on the islands' clove plantations. The British had justified their incursion into Zanzibar as an attempt to abolish the slave trade, yet when faced with the cheap labour needs of the islands' clove plantations they became concerned with 'how to formally end slavery while continuing to bind "freed" slaves to the land and their former masters'.[38] The slave emancipation decree in 1897 was therefore written in the most restrictive way possible, including onerous conditions for a slave to win his freedom.

Beginning in the 1920s, as schools opened to non-Arabs and the medium of instruction was shifted from Arabic to Swahili, the Department of Education increasingly took on the mantel of creating workers content in agricultural labour, drawing upon educational theories from the American South. In the wake of emancipation and the labour needs of Southern cotton plantations, Booker T. Washington and the Tuskegee Institute's 'compromise' (as W.E.B. DuBois called it) was to promote 'industrial education' for American blacks, teaching the

[33] ZNA AB1/390.

[34] William Cunningham Bissell, *Urban Design, Chaos, and Colonial Power in Zanzibar* (Bloomington: Indiana University Press, 2010) 97.

[35] Loimeier, *Between Social Skills and Marketable Skills*, 172.

[36] ZNA AB1/390.

[37] Bang, *Sufis and Scholars*, 175.

[38] Bissell, *Urban Design*, 97–8.

'dignity of labor' while also neatly promising to mitigate their political activism.[39] A Tuskegee focus on 'industrial education' had already been imported to Africa at the turn of the century, as German colonial officials sought to grow American cotton in Togo and 'reproduce the New South of cotton and coercion in Africa'.[40] This educational philosophy was brought to East Africa through the 1924 visit of the Phelps-Stokes Commission, an American organization established to recommend policy for the education of African Americans – and further reinforced in a 1934 visit to schools in the American South by Zanzibar's chief inspector of schools and his wife, the headmistress of the Government Girls' School.[41] This educational programme aimed to 'make those of the future generation, more efficient, healthier and happier in the same sort of life as their fathers' – namely, in agriculture.[42] Successive education reforms until independence stressed the need for more and more 'practical' education, lamenting the 'problem of what to do with these people who no longer desire to follow the occupations of their fathers' after receiving an 'academic' education.[43]

Colonial 'practical' education was aimed toward creating 'useful and loyal citizens' who could provide for the agricultural labour needs of the post-emancipation clove plantation colony and contribute to economic progress, yet this does not mean that 'morality' was absent from colonial education. Moral concerns were indeed prominent in the construction of curriculum, resulting in the inclusion of sports as an alternative to other physical 'vices', Boy Scouts for 'character training', as well as the employ of military drill instructors to ensure the height of discipline in schools.[44] Yet the moral virtues chiefly promoted in this training – including discipline, thrift, and cleanliness – were those most in service of the economic and technical progress of the colony, producing thrifty and disciplined workers in administrative service or on clove plantations. Even government girls' education, which started in the 1920s and most overtly focused on moral concerns including respectability (*heshima*), hygiene, and mothercraft, was seen as valuable to the colony only insofar as proper care of families helped improve the productivity of men.[45]

[39] Andrew Zimmerman, *Alabama in Africa: Booker T. Washington, the German Empire, and the Globalization of the New South* (Princeton, NJ: Princeton University Press, 2012) 22, 44.

[40] Zimmerman, *Alabama in Africa*, 22.

[41] ZNA BA6/6.

[42] Emphasis in original, ZNA BA6/4.

[43] ZNA BA6/4.

[44] Corrie Decker, 'Investing in Ideas: Girls' Education in Colonial Zanzibar', PhD diss., University of California Berkeley, 2007, 59.

[45] Decker, 'Investing in Ideas', 19.

The main problem for the colonial department of education, however, was that students simply did not attend their schools – preferring instead to continue at the Qur'ānic schools. This was baffling to colonial officials, who called the Qur'ān schools 'deadening to potential intellect', and simply a 'survival of a social and religious system of many centuries'.[46] The British Resident wrote, 'From the modern educational point of view, they are of no great value ... but as a means of mental development or of attaining modern knowledge of science, they are useless.'[47] One official described the education as 'the parrot-like repetition of the Koran in a foreign tongue, which even the teacher does not understand'.[48] Another wrote in a report that the schools have 'an atmosphere the effect of which is indisputably harmful'. The boys are 'put into an unventilated room' where the teacher does 'not bother about cleanliness'. They are taught 'the Arabic alphabet which is presented to him in a dry and uninteresting way' and the teacher 'uses his stick so frequently that it puts the boys in a constant state of fear'. Rather than paying a regular salary, the 'pupils do almost all the domestic work at their teacher's house', including washing, cleaning clothes, cooking and gathering wood.[49]

Despite colonial officials' disdain for the local Islamic school system, they realized that the only way to increase attendance in their schools was to include Arabic and religious training. As the director of education later wrote in a confidential missive about this inclusion: 'The truth is that Arabic is taught for no other reason than to please the Arab parents and to induce them to send their boys to school.'[50] This new strategy was initiated by the new director of education, William Hendry, who convened a commission in 1924 to introduce an Islamic curriculum of Arabic and Qur'ānic studies. The British Resident had given permission despite his preference to the opposite, saying: 'I do not wish to make the Arabs suspicious of our methods and I think it well to go slowly in any matters in which Koran teaching is concerned.'[51] The commission included all four leading *kadhis* (Islamic judges, from qāḍī [Arabic]) of Zanzibar Town including Ibn Sumayt, who were reformist-oriented and influenced by Islamic modernist movements from Egypt where 'education was viewed not only as a path to closer knowledge of God, but also as a greater social good'.[52] These reformist-oriented *kadhis* were open to other classes alongside religious instruction, as well as instruction in Swahili to promote

[46] Cited in Loimeier, *Between Social Skills and Marketable Skills*, 244–5.

[47] Cited in Loimeier, *Between Social Skills and Marketable Skills*, 246.

[48] William Harold Ingrams, *Zanzibar, Its History and Its People* (London: H.F. & G. Witherby, 1931) 433.

[49] ZNA AB1/390.

[50] ZNA AB1/390.

[51] ZNA AB1/390.

[52] Bang, *Sufis and Scholars*, 186.

comprehension of religious subjects. The final curriculum thus entailed primary instruction in Swahili rather than Arabic, and Arabic instruction only insofar as it enabled students to read selected passages from the Qur'ān. Since no textbooks on Islamic subjects existed in Swahili, they commissioned the translation of an introductory treatise on Islamic subjects from Hadramaut (*al-Risālat al-Jam'iya*), and the publication of a compilation of Qur'ānic verses alongside Swahili translation and explanation (*Aya Zilizochaguliwa*). They turned the 'ocean of knowledge' and interpretation that had characterized Islamic education into a confined syllabus, with success judged not by religious scholars in a personal relationship but by the standards of the 'Cambridge Overseas Examination'.[53]

This refashioning of Islamic education in the space of the new government schools also paralleled changes within some of the Qur'ānic schools themselves. A new class of Islamic schools emerged that were increasingly called madrasa (pl. *madāris*), a term which in Arabic classically referred to an Islamic institution of higher learning focused on jurisprudence and often situated within a mosque complex. These schools were more formalized, with entrance fees, primers and class blackboards.[54] They used a syllabus, progressed in synchronized and standardized learning units, and instead of a circle (*ḥalqa)* they sat in rows (*ṣufūf*).[55] And some, like Madrasat An-Nūr which was founded by the family of Ibn Sumayt's protégé Bā Kathīr, have expanded today to teach mathematics, computing and English alongside Qur'ānic memorization and recitation.

This new kind of madrasa, no longer an institution of advanced Islamic learning but one for small children to learn Arabic and memorize the Qur'ān, was (and still is) attended daily by children along with the government schools, which are called in Swahili *shule* or *skuli* after the German and English terms for 'school'. These madrasas were not directly created by colonial officials, who indeed long retained the hope that Islamic schools would disappear altogether, but rather were the products of local Muslim leaders influenced by the trends of pan-Arabism and Islamic modernism, some of whom were among the *kadhis* who helped draft the Islamic curriculum for the 1920s' colonial education reform. When they finally accepted that Islamic schools would not disappear, colonial officials did attempt to influence the kind of instruction within them 'by attempting very gradually, and without advertising the fact, to bring the native mallams [teachers] into headquarters for occasional training'[56] – including the creation of the Muslim Academy to train Qur'ān school teachers. Yet even in the late 1950s, just years

[53] Loimeier, *Between Social Skills and Marketable Skills*, 337.
[54] Loimeier, *Between Social Skills and Marketable Skills*, 172.
[55] Loimeier, *Between Social Skills and Marketable Skills*, 172.
[56] ZNA AB1/390.

before independence, they were reluctant to issue diplomas to its 'graduates', a word which appeared in quotation marks in internal colonial correspondence.

Rather than stamping out independent Islamic education, colonial interventions in Zanzibari education encouraged the creation of a dual interdependent system, where Islamic education became increasingly 'reformed' and ordered to mirror colonial educational paradigms. Today, this dual system endures and has perhaps become even more entrenched as government schooling takes place now in two shifts (morning and afternoon) with students attending madrasa during the opposite shift to make up an entire school day.

Contemporary Madrasas, History and Progress/Development (*Maendeleo*)

Contemporary madrasas in Zanzibar, rather than being static holdouts of the past in a changing world, are reflective of these various historical influences. For example, 'rote' memorization of the Qur'ān in Arabic remains a main function of madrasa education, yet often each Arabic phrase is followed by a 'rote' recitation of the translation into Swahili, showing a concern for understanding and translation advocated by both colonial reforms and Islamic modernists. The three contemporary madrasas described below evidence this hybridity of historical influences and the shifting meanings of madrasa education, yet further, they also frame their work as contributing to the very process that colonial officials said that they 'blocked': progress and development.

While with deeper roots, the concept of progress and later, development and modernization, was a central ideological justification and frame for colonialism. In the colonial archives in Zanzibar, progress can 'inevitably be slow', 'impressive', 'speedy', or 'impeded' – but the concept of progress is ever-present. It was a linear concept, with stages that social scientists were keen to identify – whether from 'Savagery to Civilization'[57] or from 'Traditional Societies to Mass Consumption'[58] – stages that always culminated in Europe and later, America. This linearity is preserved in development discourse today in the language of 'first' and 'third' world, and when Africa is described as having 'leapfrogged' over certain technological stages, for example in the widespread use of cellular technology without having first fully established telephone land-line infrastructure. It is also chiefly measured by economic indicators and technological advances,

[57] Edward Tylor, *Primitive Culture: Researches into the Development of Mythology, Philosophy, Religion, Art, and Custom* (New York: Harper & Row, 1958).

[58] Walt Whitman Rostow, 'The Five Stages of Growth – A Summary', in *The Stages of Economic Growth: A Non-Communist Manifesto* (Cambridge: Cambridge University Press, 1960).

while religion is often seen by development programmes as either irrelevant or an obstacle to modernization.[59]

Whether viewed as the panacea for third-world problems or an instrument of neocolonialism, development has become a hegemonic concept in East Africa, permeating all levels of society, even personally – such that a married man with a house and children could be described as having 'attained development' (*umepata maendeleo*).[60] Zanzibari newspapers regularly label Zanzibar as a third-world country (*nchi ya dunia ya tatu*) or among the developing nations (*nchi zinizoendelea*), and they describe the importance of nearly every new government policy in terms of its contribution to development, whether related to tourism, banking, or education. As such an overarching concept, it can be seen how it might enter the discourse of many social institutions, including madrasas.

However, the adoption of a colonial or global ideology does not necessitate that it remain the same, and indeed the concept of progress/development employed by these madrasas is one in which religion is vitally central. The following three examples of contemporary madrasas in Zanzibar show how the contours of madrasa education are fluid and vitally shaped by historical influences. Today this includes framing their instruction as contributing to 'progress/development' (*maendeleo*), even if they rework the concept by rejecting a sacred/secular divide, expanding it to include 'development for the afterlife', and understanding social and economic progress within the 'complete system' (*mfumo mzima*) of Islam.

Computers and Qur'ān: Madrasat An-Nūr

Ustadh Khalid, headmaster of the largest madrasa in Zanzibar within which a quarter of the children in Zanzibar Town have studied,[61] spoke of one of his brightest students who was already teaching madrasa classes by the time he finished secondary school. Salmin received a scholarship to study Arabic in Saudi Arabia, but also an opportunity to study Engineering at the University of Dar es Salaam. He sought the advice of Ustadh Khalid, who himself had studied in Saudi Arabia. 'Go to the University of Dar es Salaam', he replied. 'If you go there you will become an engineer and come help society. In our society the level of Islamic studies is enough.' Years later he is now a manager in a prominent government office. 'Now if he had gone to study Arabic', Ustadh Khalid explained, 'he'd have returned and sat in a *kanzu* [long Islamic robe], not helping society.'

[59] Gerrie Ter Haar; Stephen Ellis, 'The Role of Religion in Development: Towards a New Relationship between the European Union and Africa', *The European Journal of Development Research*, 18, 3, 2006, 351–67.

[60] James Howard Smith, *Bewitching Development: Witchcraft and the Reinvention of Development in Neoliberal Kenya* (Chicago: University of Chicago Press, 2008) 6.

[61] Loimeier, *Between Social Skills and Marketable Skills*, 516.

Madrasat An-Nūr, or as it is commonly called Kwa Bā Kathīri (Bā Kathīr's place), is the most prominent of Zanzibar's madrasas, linked to the influential Bā Kathīr family which has been transmitting Islamic knowledge since the early twentieth century in Zanzibar and has ties to the great regional centres of Islamic learning in Lamu and Hadramaut. Abdallāh Bā Kathīr arrived in Zanzibar in 1892 after travelling throughout Mecca, Medina and Hadramaut to learn from scholars, having obtained thirty-five *ijāza*s in Hadramaut alone.[62] He began teaching at the central Gofu mosque in Stone Town, soon after expanding his classes by teaching in his nearby home, what was called Madrasat Bā Kathīr. He taught *fiqh, tafsīr*, Arabic language and grammar along a regular syllabus, producing the most prominent scholars and *kadhis* (judges) of Zanzibar – such that one student called him the 'Scholar of Scholars'.[63] Advanced classes took place around a 'long table covered with voluminous works of reference'[64] across different schools of law and philosophical traditions, within which they would research topics and discuss them, employing a 'non-sectarian approach to religious learning'.[65] Upon his death in 1925 his classes were taken over by his son Abūbakar and his students, with the present building founded in 1967 by his grandson and expanded in 1993 to accommodate more students, using Saudi and Pakistani funding.[66]

Madrasat An-Nūr began teaching 'secular studies' (*masomo ya sekula*) in 2000, as they noticed that some of their older students were not coming to madrasa during times of school exams or to receive tutoring on school subjects. 'We included secular studies to help our students achieve and do well in their secular studies at school', Ustadh Khalid explained. During the week, students study religious subjects in either the morning or afternoon shift according to when they attend school, and on the weekend have the additional subjects of computers, English and maths. English and maths follow the curriculum from school, and indeed the children are placed in grades that mirror those in government schools even for their religious studies. Computer class teaches how to use Word and Excel software, and is taught by the abovementioned Salmin who volunteers on the weekend. But it is not just in the maths curriculum that Madrasat An-Nūr mirrors government schooling, as they have also instituted written exams even for religious subjects. As Ustadh Khalid explained: 'We came from the order of the

62 Jean-Claude Penrad, 'Madrassat Al-Nur. Une École Coranique de La Ville de Pierre et Son Shaykh', in Colette Le Cour Grandmaison; Ariel Crozon (eds.), *Zanzibar Aujourd'hui*, 307–20 (Paris: Éditions Karthala, 1998) 312.

63 Ali Muhsin Al-Barwani, *Conflicts and Harmony in Zanzibar: Memoirs* (Dubai: n.p., 1997) 22.

64 Al-Barwani, *Conflicts and Harmony*, 23.

65 Bang, *Sufis and Scholars*, 148.

66 Loimeier, *Between Social Skills and Marketable Skills*, 515.

past (*nidhamu ya zamani*), with all students together [in one room] … and came to the system of classes (*madarasa*).'

The headmaster sees their curriculum as contributing to Zanzibar's development through its support of secular studies along with religious studies' ability to decrease immoral behaviour that impedes development. 'Now here if you look you will see how Madrasat An-Nūr has a syllabus (*silibasi*) that helps society … there are so many doctors now who have come from Madrasat An-Nūr,' Ustadh Khalid continued – one of whom is now his supervisor and the chairman of the madrasa, an economist who is also currently vice chancellor at nearby Sumait University. 'You can't bring development (*maendeleo*) except through science and technology (*sayansi na teknolojia*), and technology and science are obtainable through education. Religion (*dini*) encourages the search for knowledge, and not just studying religion alone but also secular studies,' Ustadh Khalid explained. The search for knowledge is obligatory (*fardhi*), yet it is divided into two kinds: *farḍ 'ayn*, which is obligatory for everyone and includes religious studies, and *farḍ kifāya*, what is communally obligatory but only a sufficient few need to undertake it. For example, a society needs doctors, engineers, pilots, architects, and other professions, but not all need to study medicine, only a number sufficient to meet society's medical needs.

Religious studies are obligatory for all, Ustadh Khalid says, because they 'build faith (*imani*) which helps to build good character/behavior (*tabia*)'. This has personal benefits, yet its prime benefit is social: 'When a person who has a good character goes into society he is helping to drive society' by, for example, handling their job well and with good character, including not taking bribes or engaging in corruption that impedes development. Salmin, the volunteer computer teacher, expanded saying that 'all knowledge comes from God because we believe that God created everything', but biology and geography do not say what is good and bad. Religion 'equips a child to be good in society'. Seeing someone in need of help in the street, he explained, if he were without religion he would think 'this person got there because of his own stupidity … but if I had religion I would receive the faith to be able to help him'. For Salmin, worldly studies (*masomo ya dunia*) may enable you to help others but primarily it is to advance personally and economically by ensuring a good income. Religion 'builds a person individually, his values so that he is truthful, trustworthy, and loves to do work' that then translates into broader society so that 'we help each other, respect each other, and sit well together as a community'.

All knowledge fits within what they both describe as the 'complete system/order for life' (*mfumo/utaratibu mzima wa maisha*) that is the 'definition' of Islam. Social problems arise when economic and technological development is not matched by religious and moral development: 'from a religious perspective we are developed maybe thirty years back,' Salmin explained, as now there is television but children unthinkingly imitate what they see on it. 'Technologically we are moving, but morally we are going down' (*kitechnology tunaenda lakini kii-madili tunashuka*), he said. The prime culprits, he says, are technology, globalization (including tourism), and a foreign idea of 'freedom' (*uhuru*) that encourages youth to shirk the authority of their parents and elders.

In teaching 'secular studies' in madrasa, Madrasat An-Nūr is truly a complement and mirror to the government schools that it splits the day with, as these schools still teach an Islamic studies class determined by the government as was instituted during the colonial era and continued by the postcolonial state. Madrasat An-Nūr has deep roots in the past, and its various iterations – from one classroom of students progressing independently in a direct relationship with a scholar-master, to a segmented learning environment ordered by grades, exams and syllabi – reflects how a prominent madrasa has changed according to dominant ideologies and practices. Now it views its work as contributing to 'development', with its teaching of secular studies and commitment to advancing the spiritual and moral development of society alongside the technical and economic, as long as that development is understood within the complete system of Islam (*mfumo mzima wa Uislamu*).

Modernizing the Madrasa: The Aga Khan Foundation's Madrasa Pre-School

They said, 'Let us find a way to modernize this madrasa,' Zanzibar's academic director explained in an interview, narrating the beginnings of the Madrasa Early Childhood Development Programme in East Africa. The programme began in 1986 after Muslim residents in Mombasa, Kenya asked the Aga Khan during a visit to address the problem of their children falling behind in schools. After conducting a study, they determined that this could best be done through a quality pre-school education – a programme which now numbers schools in the hundreds throughout Kenya, Uganda and Tanzania.[67] It is administered by the Aga Khan Foundation (AKF), an international development agency under the Aga Khan Development Network (AKDN). As a development agency founded by an Islamic religious leader and operating within a Muslim community, the AKF and its Madrasa Pre-School are oriented toward both 'development' and Islamic education. The programme sees itself as countering the secularization and fragmentation of learning that occurred during colonialism by utilizing an 'integrated curriculum' that contributes to the 'spiritual development' of children, while also revealing itself as a product of many of those same reforms through its ordering of the classroom with a syllabus and its denigration of rote learning.

[67] Judith Evans; Kathy Bartlett, *The Madrasa Early Childhood Programme: 25 Years of Experience* (Geneva: Aga Khan Development Network, 2008) 6.

'In its basic meaning,' the Madrasa Pre-School curriculum states, 'a madrasa is a place where one studies.'[68] The AKF defines the madrasa classically and etymologically as a place of learning more broadly, despite its association with strictly religious study both locally and in the wider non-Arabic-speaking Muslim world. The curriculum cites an example of an eleventh-century madrasa that taught 'religion, the sciences, public administration and governance' together, and perhaps overstating the extent of instruction beyond religious subjects, writes that it was 'at the time of British colonial rule' that madrasas 'began to focus more exclusively on a narrower set of religious subjects, leaving instruction in more general areas to government schools'.[69] They position the development of their own curriculum in direct contrast to the colonial delimiting of Islamic education to religious studies classes, writing: the 'premise of the curriculum was that Islam is a way of life, not an additional subject in the syllabus'.[70] The Madrasa Pre-School is, they conclude, among the latest in the 'evolving role of madrasas and education in Muslim societies' that fits the 'twenty-first century'.[71]

It is within this context that they articulate their 'integrated approach' to education, where the 'teaching of Islam is integrated into all aspects of the pre-school experience' including 'the integration of Islam with secular education'.[72] There is a specific period within their daily timetable for direct religious instruction, covering *qirā'a* (Arabic reading), *tawḥid* (the oneness of God), *'ibāda* (prayer rituals and pillars of Islam), *sīra* (the life history of the Prophet), and *akhlāq* and *ḥadīth* (ethics through the sayings/stories from the Prophet). But the other subjects – including language and literacy, mathematics, creative arts, health education, initiative and social relations, interacting with the environment, music, and physical movement – are to be taught within a frame of Islamic 'culture'. While the curriculum does not give direct suggestions for accomplishing this under the sections for each of the other class subjects, teachers are nonetheless encouraged to be 'incorporating Islamic motifs and patterns, narratives from the Qur'ān, as well as adab –the rules of etiquette, courtesy and cleanliness rooted in East African culture', so that they 'are woven into the curriculum'.[73] For example, the Zanzibar academic director sang a song that students are taught when learning numbers: 'Number one, Allah is one. Number two, two rakat of Fajri. Number three, three rakat of Maghrabi. Number four, four rakat of Isha ...' Students are taught the

[68] Aga Khan Foundation (AKF), *The Madrasa Pre-School Curriculum* (Kampala: Madrasa Resource Centre, Uganda, 2009) 7.

[69] AKF, *Madrasa Pre-School Curriculum*, 7.

[70] Evans; Bartlett, *Madrasa Early Childhood Programme*, 18.

[71] AKF, *Madrasa Pre-School Curriculum*, 7.

[72] AKF, *Madrasa Pre-School Curriculum*, 58–9.

[73] AKF, *Madrasa Pre-School Curriculum*, 5.

numbers at the same time that they are taught the number of prayer cycles (*rak'āt*) to be said at each prayer time (dawn, sunset, afternoon, etc.).

In addition to an Islamic framing for all learning, the programme echoes earlier iterations of Islamic knowledge transmission in seeking to create goodness (*utu*), manners (*adabu*) and moral/ethical action (*akhlāq*). While they encourage 'the integration of ethical values' throughout 'the daily timetable',[74] this is specifically to be accomplished during the *akhlāq and ḥadīth* section of the Islamic studies period of the day. Children are presented with *ḥadīth* (sayings/stories from the Prophet) and *du'ās* (prayers) that 'are relevant for common situations (sharing, being kind, being honest)' and are encouraged to practise them throughout the day. To help students remember them, children are given 'plenty of opportunities to recite rhymes based on *ḥadīths* and du'ās' and even to 'draw pictures related to *ḥadīths* and du'ās'.[75] To further embody these principles, children are to 'make up stories about sharing, being kind, honest, trustworthy and tolerant' and to 'practice through activities such as songs, stories, and role-playing'.[76] Bi Sultana, a veteran teacher trainer of the organization, refers to this as the 'spiritual development' of children, which she feels is misunderstood by outsiders. She reflected: 'some people are so afraid to develop children spiritually ... At the children's level, it means to be kind, not rude, not to take others' things, to respect others. There is no harm in that! They think maybe we are teaching them to be terrorists, but it is not true.'

While seeking to reverse the fragmentation of knowledge that occurred during colonial educational reforms, particularly the delimiting of Islamic knowledge to one class subject, the Madrasa Pre-School is at the same time reflective of those reforms in other ways. Rather than being structured by individual rhythms and the call of the *adhān,* the daily timetable is broken down into the minutes of each day, defined by a clear syllabus. This, according to the AKF curriculum, helps 'children learn important social habits like timeliness and punctuality and begin to learn the concepts of efficiency and time management'.[77] Bi Sultana emphasized that 'here we don't teach by memorizing but by active learning, we don't force them to memorize', an approach that is markedly different from 'traditional "chalk and talk" exercises that produce empty repetition',[78] what colonial officials denigrated as 'rote' learning. While colonial officials wrote that Qur'ānic schools taught the Arabic alphabet 'in a dry and uninteresting way',[79] children in

[74] AKF, *Madrasa Pre-School Curriculum*, 66.
[75] AKF, *Madrasa Pre-School Curriculum*, 66.
[76] AKF, *Madrasa Pre-School Curriculum*, 66.
[77] AKF, *Madrasa Pre-School Curriculum*, 61.
[78] Evans; Bartlett, *Madrasa Early Childhood Programme*, 20.
[79] ZNA AB1/390.

the Madrasa Pre-School should be 'having fun with Arabic language', including playing with puzzles from Arabic letters or 'printing, painting over or tracing over Arabic letters'.[80]

Further, echoing the educational orientation toward 'progress' instituted during the colonial era, AKF sees their educational programme as being an important vector for the progress and development of the community. As the programme director said, 'we have been able to create a pathway that contributed to socio-economic problems. People who went through this programme now are serving as public health practitioners, teachers, and engineers.' In thirty years, the programme has oriented itself more toward framing their work as 'development' rather than 'Islamic education' due to funding concerns, with employees strategically describing the organization as 'secular' despite the heavy inclusion of Islam within its curriculum and teacher training. While, he reflects, it was important to 'start from existing institutions' as an 'entry point', now the name Madrasa has become an impediment when applying for development grants, as grant agencies assume that they provide only religious education instead of 'development'.

Development for the Afterlife: Madrasat Jihād An-Nafs

'You can't think that development (*maendeleo*) is building buildings only. Development is developing yourself for your afterlife (*jiendeleze wewe katika maisha yako ya baadaye*),' reflects Aisha, a founding member of a women's madrasa that meets at the edge of Zanzibar Town. Aisha is deeply involved in the economic development of the women around her: she leads a women's *Vicoba* group, a community banking or microfinance initiative that enables women to obtain occasional loans from a communal fund that each regularly contributes to. She has also, over the years, helped over fifty women find jobs as domestic servants – all while working as a domestic servant herself. That work is important for her, but not as important as the kind of development that she engages in at Madrasat Jihād An-Nafs: 'You can build up Zanzibar and change it. But you haven't developed Zanzibar, you have developed buildings ... development for the afterlife (*maendeleo ya ahera*) remains.'

While adult Islamic classes (*darsa*) are available in evenings at mosques, Madrasat Jihād An-Nafs as a women's Islamic education initiative is unique in having its own building, name and communal identity. It began as a small group of six women meeting in each other's homes, studying books of *ḥadīth* and *tafsīr* while reading *juz 'amma*, the thirtieth section of the Qur'ān that contains the shortest chapters and is often the first studied. In 2009, their organizer Zahra, with financial help from her husband, built the building that would house their

[80] AKF, *Madrasa Pre-School Curriculum*, 69.

madrasa, which meets daily during the hour before sunset prayers, drawing thirty to seventy women. It is led once a week by a guest lecturer, who speaks on issues such as education, caring for the sick, and Islamic burial laws, often intertwining practical issues such as cleaning a body for burial with meditations on how such situations spark reflection on one's own life – and death. In contrast to the packed rows during the guest lectures, the remaining days of the week are led by Zahra in a circle of women sitting together tightly, she tells them smiling, 'so that Satan cannot enter!' They read sections from a series of books in Swahili called *Darasa la Watu Wazima* (*Class for Adults*) published by the Islamic Propagation Centre based in Dar es Salaam, covering topics such as education, faith, the five pillars of Islam, family life, society, and Islamic history. Reading aloud is interspersed by questions to gauge understanding, Zahra's own explanations on the topic, and occasional extended reflections by other women in the group.

While rejecting a sacred/secular divide that views religion's relevance only to acts of worship, Madrasat Jihād An-Nafs works to educate women to battle with the 'self' so as to change character/behaviour (*tabia*) for a better life both here and beyond. 'Non-believers (*makafiri*) and even some Muslims, due to a narrow perspective on the meaning of religion that leads them to divide human life into two spheres, the life of religion (*dini*) and the life of the world (*dunia*), have also divided education into these two spheres', reads their study book.[81] But religious knowledge 'relates to daily life personally, with family, and socially', while at the same time the Qur'ān says that God taught Adam the 'names of all things', meaning 'all the fields of knowledge needed by humanity here in earth'.[82] Islam is an 'order or system of life (*utaratibu au mfumo wa maisha*)',[83] and as Zahra said in class, 'the Qur'ān is the book which is our guide (*mwongozo*)'. 'If I buy a fridge, or maybe a radio,' she continued, 'but I don't know how it works, I take the catalogue and read it. For everything you need the catalogue.' That is what the Qur'ān is, she says: everything is in the Qur'ān and everything comes from God, as 'there is no religion/world [divide] in Islam (*hamna dini na dunia katika Uislamu*)'.

Education, their study book reads, is defined as 'changes of character/behavior that come from knowledge (*mabadiliko ya tabia yanayotokana na ujuzu*)'.[84] Faith (*imani*), Zahra often insists in class, means 'good actions (*matendo mazuri*)' resulting from 'knowing in the heart with certainty (*kujua na uhakika moyoni*)'.

[81] Islamic Propagation Centre, *Lengo La Maisha Ya Mwanadamu (The Goal of Human Life)*. Vol. 1. *Darasa La Watu Wazima* (Dar es Salaam: Afroplus Industries (Ltd), 2003) 21.

[82] Islamic Propagation Centre, *Lengo La Maisha Ya Mwanadamu*, 21, 2.

[83] Islamic Propagation Centre, *Lengo La Maisha Ya Mwanadamu*, 34.

[84] Islamic Propagation Centre, *Lengo La Maisha Ya Mwanadamu*, 1.

This change of character and behaviour is accomplished through, as the madrasa's name indicates, *jihād an-nafs*: battling with the self. 'Jihād is what trains us, it is fighting with the self. At least it makes me progress developmentally for the afterlife (*inaniendeleza kimaendeleo kwenye ahera*),' Aisha explains. Jihād is not something for terrorists (*magaidi*), she continues, because 'we cannot fight because of Islam, people are mistaken. Now we do not fight wars, we fight to study. We study so that we understand, we must explain that now we are fighting for self-liberation (*tushajikomboa*).' *Jihād an-nafs* means to 'remove a person from a state of ignorance,' she says, to battle with the self until 'we are sated with the real food, this book'. It means fighting that 'internal voice (*sauti ndani*)' that wants to go to a 'disco' or does not want to be generous with others.

As an adult women's madrasa, Madrasat Jihād An-Nafs is a new kind of space in Zanzibar, although paralleled by the rise of women's mosque circles elsewhere.[85] Yet it nonetheless focuses on that change of character/behaviour (*tabia*) that has been central to other forms of Islamic and madrasa education, even if now understood as for 'development' for the afterlife.

Conclusion: Religion, Development, Tradition

Whether described as a 'block to progress' that has 'existed for centuries'[86] or as 'breeding grounds for terrorists',[87] popular Euro-American portrayals of madrasas share key features: that madrasas are preserved and static spaces of the past, stalwarts against modern times and antagonistic to 'progress'. Rather than such monoliths, institutions of Islamic education, as described in Zanzibar, have shifted and adjusted according to dominant historical ideologies, trends and influences. Technically, the 'madrasa' is, to some extent, already a modern institution insofar as it refers to elementary Islamic learning conducted in concert with government education since the early twentieth century, rather than a college of advanced Islamic studies to which the term referred in more classical eras.[88]

Today we can see this fluid engagement with dominant ideas as some Zanzibari madrasas frame their education in terms of contributing to progress/development (*maendeleo*), even if development is redefined to fit within the 'complete system'

[85] Mandana Limbert, *In the Time of Oil: Piety, Memory, and Social Life in an Omani Town* (Stanford, CA: Stanford University Press, 2010); Saba Mahmood, *Politics of Piety: The Islamic Revival and the Feminist Subject* (Princeton, NJ: Princeton University Press, 2011).

[86] ZNA BA6/3.

[87] Moosa, *What is a Madrasa?*, 2.

[88] George Makdisi, *The Rise of Colleges: Institutions of Learning in Islam and the West* (Edinburgh: Edinburgh University Press, 1981).

(*mfumo mzima*) that is Islam. This parallels what Deeb calls in another context a focus on both material and 'spiritual progress'.[89] In this perspective, believers should both welcome technological advancements while also increasing acts of piety so as to stem what is perceived as the 'emptiness of modernity as manifested in the West', including atheism, violence, consumerism, materialism, sexual promiscuity, an emphasis on the individual to the detriment of social relations, and the collapse of the family.[90] Progress, development and modernity in this context, rather than being distinct from or even opposed to religiosity, are fundamentally framed by religious narratives. Development/progress (*maendeleo*) is still centrally economic and technical, but this material progress is empty and morally suspect if not accompanied by spiritual progress that results in ethical behaviour writ large within society. This morality has concrete effects on material development, for example in countering corruption, but is not valued only for its contribution to material progress, such as creating thrifty disciplined workers within colonial educational structures. It is also about kindness, generosity, and other personal acts of piety that improve the spiritual life of the community.

This blending of sacred and secular, where religious organizations invoke the discourses of development and development organizations work within an Islamic framework, complicates the strict separation between material/spiritual, outer/inner, and West/East that Chatterjee argues is a central feature of postcolonial states.[91] While the West was more materially powerful in terms of science and technology, the East was spiritually superior – necessitating that postcolonial nations learn the 'superior techniques of organizing material life' from the West while also 'retaining and strengthening the distinctive spiritual essence of the national culture'.[92] The above Zanzibari organizations do express some of these concerns, for example Salmin's concern that youth are imitating Western culture because of media consumption. Yet religious 'tradition' in this context is not something that must be insulated and preserved from foreign corruption, it is an organizing framework through which material and spiritual progress can be pursued. Identifying something as a 'tradition' to be preserved, unadulterated and uncolonized, serves to freeze it at a moment in the past and isolate it from other spheres of modern life. Defining what was 'tradition' was indeed a central

[89] Lara Deeb, *An Enchanted Modern: Gender and Public Piety in Shi'i Lebanon* (Princeton, NJ: Princeton University Press, 2006).

[90] Deeb, *An Enchanted Modern,* 5, 24.

[91] Partha Chatterjee, *Nationalist Thought and the Colonial World* (London: Zed Books, 1986); 'Colonialism, Nationalism, and Colonialized Women: The Contest in India', *American Ethnologist*, 16, 4, 1989, 622–33.

[92] Chatterjee, 'Colonialism, Nationalism, and Colonialized Women', 623.

feature of colonial rule, whether to change it in the case of Indian widow burning[93] or to preserve 'native custom' in the form of tribal ruling structures and customary law.[94]

Examining closely a space that is identified with 'tradition' even by many Muslims challenges this predominant conception of tradition as unchanging in the face of modernity, as we see that 'traditional' Islamic education in Zanzibar has taken different forms. As a 'discursive tradition',[95] Islamic practice is constituted through a tradition of discourses and internal debates on what constitutes correct Islamic practice in changing times, referring to the precedent of the past while oriented toward an ideal future. The historical and current iterations of Islamic education in Zanzibar are an example of this discursive process and the ways in which it has changed within different eras, as Muslim teachers have sought to justify their positions on the place of Arabic literacy, rote memorization, Swahili translation for 'understanding', the inclusion of secular studies, and 'development' in the realm of Islamic knowledge transmission. Perhaps the key is not in 'modernizing the madrasa', but in recognizing that tradition is itself lived and evolving rather than a sealed storehouse of all that is uncorrupted yet outdated. In the case of Zanzibar, traditional learning has taken many forms – in Swahili and Arabic, oral and written, in circles and lines – and can continue to take new forms today.

[93] Chatterjee, 'Colonialism, Nationalism, and Colonialized Women', 623.

[94] Mahmood Mamdani, *Citizen and Subject: Contemporary Africa and the Legacy of Late Colonialism* (Princeton, NJ: Princeton University Press, 1996); *Define and Rule: Native as Political Identity* (Cambridge, MA: Harvard University Press, 2012).

[95] Talal Asad, 'The Idea of an Anthropology of Islam', *Occasional Papers Series* (Washington, DC: Center for Contemporary Arab Studies, Georgetown University, 1986).

CHAPTER 11

A New *Daara*: Integrating Qur'ānic, Agricultural, and Trade Education in a Community Setting[1]

Laura L. Cochrane

Mbakke Kajoor, in central Senegal's arid regions, is a historical site for the Murīdiyya, one of Senegal's most populous and influential Sufi orders. It was the home of the order's founder, Shaykh Amadu Bamba Mbakke, and the start of his educational and spiritual life's journey in the late nineteenth century. It is today the site of a new educational centre and *daara*, a spiritual community that echoes the Murīdiyya's origins. A focus on education and economic development motivates the leaders of this project. They designed their educational model using Bamba's teachings and religious traditions dating to earlier West African Islamic scholars, with the intent of addressing the local population's need for agricultural, professional, and spiritual training. The shaykh entrusted by the Murid *khalife général* to develop this space sees this combination of knowledges – Qur'ānic, agricultural, and trade – as a way to bring economic development to the area.

This essay argues that the new *daara* and educational centre has been successful thus far because it draws on a religious and cultural history that the region's population values. Using those religious and cultural teachings, it is creating an educational model that meets the current needs of that population. The new *daara*'s educational model promises to promote religious education, and also to bring professional and agricultural training to a region in need of it. By using cultural and religious traditions to address local needs, the project has the potential to attract regional participation as well as involvement from the larger national and global Murid network.

[1] The author extends her thanks to the residents of Yoff, Thiès, Louga, Ndem, and Mbakke Kajoor, particularly Sëriñ Babacar Mbow and Soxna Aïssa Cissé, whose welcome has shown extraordinary hospitality. She thanks Central Michigan University for its continued support of this ongoing research in Senegal; and Ousmane Kane, who created a new dialogue about Africa's Islamic intellectual heritage and made space for this essay.

The challenges the new *daara* face are steep: while local, they are tied to global issues. The 2007–11 global economic recession deepened the region's unemployment problems, increased food prices and reduced funding from international financial partners. Environmental shifts linked to global climate changes add to the effects of over a century of repeated droughts. Similar economic and environmental conditions have been historical backdrops for previous *daaras*, including Bamba's *daaras*. Difficult circumstances, specifically economic recessions and environmental catastrophes in the late 1800s and the 1970s, were motivations for developing new models of religious education. The Mbakke Kajoor project draws on these histories to address present-day educational, employment, and spiritual needs. It is creating a community-based educational centre to bring secular and religious education together, with the hope that it will serve the population's needs and revitalize the region.

This chapter starts with Mbakke Kajoor's religious history. It describes the context in which Bamba and his father emerged as educators and the Murīdiyya developed. This context includes French colonial occupation and the political and economic upheavals of the late nineteenth century. It also includes the significant religious teachings of both Bamba and his intellectual predecessors. The chapter then introduces Sëriñ Babacar Mbow and Soxna Aïssa Cissé,[2] a shaykh and his wife who established a *daara* in Ndem, a village two hours' drive west from Mbakke Kajoor. They are Baay Fall, a suborder of the Murīdiyya. Both Murid and Baay Fall traditions and teachings are therefore important to this story. They established the Ndem *daara* in the 1980s, a difficult time in Senegal with severe environmental and economic crises. In 2014, Sëriñ Babacar was entrusted with developing Mbakke Kajoor. He and his advisors planned the new *daara* using lessons learned from Ndem, plus new ideas to address the region's current needs.

The ethnographic research for this project is based on several semi-structured in-depth interviews in several towns (Yoff, Thiès, Louga, Ndem, and Mbakke Kajoor), and also a number of informal conversations about the Mbakke Kajoor project with residents of both Ndem and the Mbakke Kajoor construction site. My primary interviews for this chapter were with Soxna Aïssa Cissé, who emphasized the history of the site and its spiritual importance. I have conducted ethnographic research at the Ndem *daara* since 2009. In 2015, both Soxna Aïssa and Sëriñ Babacar invited me to follow the new *daara* in Mbakke Kajoor as part of my ongoing research in Senegal.

[2] Sëriñ and Soxna are earned honorific titles for men and women; they have both secular and religious connotations of respect. I use the names 'Sëriñ Babacar' and 'Soxna Aïssa' to index that respect, and also to follow the names used by their family and community.

Mbakke Kajoor and the origins of the Murīdiyya

Mbakke Kajoor is a town in the present-day region of Louga. It is near the site of Wolof monarch Lat Joor Joob's last battle against French colonial forces in 1886. A number of scholars point to Joob's death and the decline of the monarchy as marking the beginning of formal French colonialism in Senegal.[3] French economic occupation had begun decades earlier, however, with its increasing hold over the peanut cash crop and a railroad project that ensured French export of the crop out from the western-central regions of Senegal.[4] The resulting land exploitation left much of this area, referred to as the Peanut Basin, degraded. The French single-minded focus on the Peanut Basin required residents to reduce subsistence crops and replace them with peanuts. They were forced to abandon formerly successful strategies of rotating crops, using buffer zones for fields and letting fields lie fallow.[5] The land degradation left the area prone to steep agricultural and livestock loss, with a series of droughts that started in 1905 and that have recurred intermittently since. The 1968–74 drought was particularly devastating, with losses of both human lives and, in some regions, an estimated 90 per cent reduction in livestock.[6] These recurrent droughts have continued up to the present. And, each drought has compounded the land degradation over time. Mbakke Kajoor, then, is in a historically-rich and agriculturally-degraded region.

The holy site near the town of Mbakke Kajoor marks another important event in Senegal's late nineteenth-century history: the start of the Murīdiyya. Shaykh Momar Anta Sali Mbakke, a shaykh in the Qādirī Sufi order, started the *daara* in Mbakke Kajoor, moving his family to the centre of Wolof power when he became a qāḍī (judge) in the Islamic courts, and an advisor and primary judge for Lat Joor Joob. He became renowned as a teacher of science and Qur'ānic studies, attracting a number of students to the town. This focus on education had long been

3 John Glover, *Sufism and Jihad in Modern Senegal: The Murid Order* (Rochester, NY: University of Rochester Press, 2007) 80–1; James F. Searing, *'God Alone is King': Islam and Emancipation in Senegal. The Wolof Kingdoms of Kajoor; and Bawol, 1859–1914* (Portsmouth, NH: Heinemann, 2002) 60.

4 This is a gloss over a complex history: whether to allow the railroad or not was one part of an extended power struggle within the Wolof monarchy. For a complete history of these disputes that ultimately weakened the Wolof monarchy and led to the beginning of formal French colonial rule, see Germain Coly, *La Région de Thiès à Travers son Musée* (Thiès: Conseil Régional de Thiès, 1999); Glover, *Sufism and Jihad in Modern Senegal*; Searing, *'God Alone is King'*.

5 Adrian Adams; Jaabe So, *A Claim to Land by the River: A Household in Senegal 1720–1994* (Oxford: Oxford University Press, 1996).

6 Donal Cruise O'Brien, *Saints and Politicians: Essay on the Organisation of a Senegalese Peasant Society* (Cambridge: Cambridge University Press, 1975); Carol L. Rogers, 'Desertification', *Science News*, 112, 18, 1977, 282.

an important outreach of the Qādiriyya in West Africa. While the Qādiriyya had been popular in North Africa since the fifteenth century, Shaykh Sidi al-Mukhtār al-Kuntī (1729–1811), a member of a prominent scholarly family in Timbuktu, is given credit for organizing and popularizing it in West Africa.[7] Al-Kuntī's and others' scholarly teachings would become important later in the Murīdiyya, via the son of Shaykh Sali.

Shaykh Sali's son, who would inherit his father's love of teaching and learning, and become the founder of the Murid Sufi order, was Shaykh Amadu Bamba Mbakke (1853–1927). Bamba was therefore born into an intellectual and well-connected family. He was born in Mbakke Bawol, and started teaching in his father's *daara* in Mbakke Kajoor at a young age. Soxna Aïssa Cissé explained Bamba's early talent for teaching, using the honorific for Bamba, Sëriñ Touba.

> Sëriñ Touba would help his father's students, as he had a special aptitude for intellectual study from an early age. He was 29 years old when his father died, and he said he didn't want to be on Lat Joor's side. That is, he wanted to follow God, not a king. Sëriñ Touba received a vision from the Prophet Muḥammad, telling him to change education so that it was not only the Muslim sciences, but also focused on service and spirituality.[8]

In 1883, Bamba journeyed away from Mbakke Kajoor, first returning to Mbakke Bawol. After clashing with more conservative Muslim leaders there, he and his followers established a new *daara*, Daaru Salaam, close to Mbakke Bawol, where he started attracting a larger and larger number of disciples. This started a series of travels and new settlements, yet before leaving Mbakke Kajoor, he left his father's brother in charge of spiritual education there, and also asked one of his sons to stay in the town.[9]

While in Mbakke Kajoor and later in his own *daaras*, Bamba developed a new pedagogy that included three steps over a lifetime of study. The first was *ta'lim*, academic study of the Qur'ān and Islamic sciences. The second, *tarbiya*, was education of the soul. *Tarqiya*, the third, was intended for community leaders, moving

[7] Cheikh Anta Babou, 'Educating the Murid: Theory and Practices of Education in Amadu Bamba's Thought', *Journal of Religion in Africa*, 33, 3, 2003, 313; Abdal-Aziz Abdulla Batran, 'The Qadiriyya-Mukhtariyya Brotherhood in West Africa: The Concept of Tasawwuf in the Writings of Sidi al-Mukhtār al-Kuntī (1729–1811)', *Transafrican Journal of History*, 4, 1–2, 1974, 42; Glover, *Sufism and Jihad in Modern Senegal*, 86; Rudolph T. Ware III, *The Walking Qur'an: Islamic Education, Embodied Knowledge, and History in West Africa* (Chapel Hill: University of North Carolina Press, 2014) 154–8, 182–3.

[8] Soxna Aïssa Cissé, interview with author, 7 June 2015, Louga, Senegal.

[9] Glover, *Sufism and Jihad in Modern Senegal*, 88; Soxna Aïssa Cissé, interview with author, 7 June 2015, Louga, Senegal.

beyond material aspects of life. These three steps align with Sufi teachings; they also attend to both spiritual and outwardly social aspects of disciples' education and formation.[10] Bamba's teachings were modelled after those of renowned Sufi scholars. He paid particular attention to scholar Ibn Kaldun's (1332–1406) commentary on al-Ghazālī (1058–1111). Al-Ghazālī taught that Sufi adherents must not separate themselves from the world, but pair *sharī'a*, guidance on moral and ethical living, with their *tariqa*: their chosen spiritual path toward God.[11] Sufism in general, influenced by al-Ghazālī, is different in this respect from other mystical traditions that encourage seclusion from the social world. Living morally within the world aligned with al-Kuntī's teaching to wage jihād on one's soul, working to cleanse one's heart to become closer to God.

In addition to his three-step conception of education, Bamba created a learning community called a *daara tarbiya*, a *daara* with the goal of inclusive education of the soul, even for those who were not literate or of a clerical lineage. He saw the Sufi tradition of teacher (*murshid*) and disciple (*murīd*) relationship as a way to educate those without any previous education or literacy. The disciple both looks to the shaykh for a model of right living and behaviour, and learns service through serving the shaykh and the *daara* community.[12] This aligns with al-Kuntī's writings about the role of the shaykh and the disciple, which arises from disciples' need for a guide along this path. Al-Kuntī taught that the shaykh, or marabout, a French-derived North African term sometimes used interchangeably for shaykh in West and North Africa, was to be a role model for this way of living and spiritual path. As the disciple follows a chosen marabout, he or she emulates and follows the marabout's guidance toward deeper understanding of God. Disciples should not be expected to understand *ḥaqīqa*, the esoteric truths, al-Kuntī taught, without a shaykh's guidance. Spiritual guides are thus to be educators, both via direct teaching and via emulation of their social behaviour. Recognition of the marabout's authority is required, but the disciple can choose more than one marabout for spiritual guidance. This made the Qādiriyya different from other orders that demand exclusivity.[13] Bamba's use of this pedagogy allowed him to reach

[10] Cheikh Anta Babou, 'The al-Azhar School Network: A Murid Experiment in Islamic Modernism', in Robert Launay (ed.), *Islamic education in Africa. Writing boards and blackboards* (Bloomington: Indiana University Press, 2016) 176; Babou, 'Educating the Murid', 316; Ware, *The Walking Qur'an*, 182–4.

[11] Tanvir Anjum, 'Sufism in History and its Relationship with Power', *Islamic Studies*, 45, 2, 2006, 232.

[12] Ware, *The Walking Qur'an*, 184.

[13] Abdal-Aziz Batran, 'An Introductory Note on the Impact of Sidi al-Mukhtar al-Kunti (1728–1811) on West African Islam in the 18th and 19th Centuries', *Journal of the Historical Society of Nigeria*, 6, 4, 1973, 347; Batran, 'The Qadiriyya-Mukhtariyya Brotherhood in West Africa', 47–50.

the educated elite, but also offer spiritual education for the illiterate, including those of the slave castes in the Wolof kingdoms' caste system. In doing so, he and a number of other prominent shaykhs of the era, notably Tijāniyya leaders Shaykh al-Hajj Malik Sy and Shaykh Ibrahim Niasse, created a mass movement of Islamic education in Senegambia.[14]

Origins of the Baay Fall

While still in Mbakke Kajoor, Bamba met Shaykh Ibra Fall (1858–1930), who would become one of his most prominent and controversial disciples. Bamba often taught under a particular tree, called Guisguis Bamba. The site of the tree is now a pilgrimage site with a simple structure in which to pray and meditate, though the tree is no longer there. Soxna Aïssa continues the story, using 'Sëriñ Touba' as an honorific for Bamba.

> Shaykh Ibra Fall was in a royal family, and also had aptitude for intellectual study and could have been on the path to nobility. He left that life, though, in search of a spiritual guide. It was at the *guisguis* tree where Shaykh Ibra Fall met Sëriñ Touba and saw his light, even though no one else saw him illuminated. Shaykh Ibra Fall met Sëriñ Touba on the 4th day of Ramadan, and on the 20th day of Ramadan, he submitted his soul to Sëriñ Touba. The Angel Djibril [Gabriel] showed Shaykh Ibra Fall how to approach Sëriñ Touba. It was thus Shaykh Ibra Fall who taught the other disciples how to show deference to Sëriñ Touba.[15]

Another Baay Fall, Abdoulaye Ngom, told the story with slightly different details, but the same emphasis on mysticism and submission.

> [When Fall and Bamba met at Mbakke Kajoor], it was the first day of Muridism, it was the birth of Muridism, because of the *djebel* [Wolof, submission] made to Sëriñ Touba, and that's very important to Muridism. It's mystical, because Shaykh Ibra Fall already knew Sëriñ Touba in his head, but he found him at Mbakke Kajoor for the first time. That's why Mbakke Kajoor is very important in Muridism, because it was the place where Muridism was born. The others were students of Sëriñ Touba, but they had not yet made submission. Shaykh Ibra Fall was the first.[16]

The focus on submission as the start of the Murīdiyya is the recognition of Bamba as shaykh: this marks him as not only a teacher but a shaykh recognized for his

[14] Ware, *The Walking Qur'an*, 184–6.

[15] Soxna Aïssa Cissé, interview with author, 7 June 2015, Louga, Senegal, qtd. in Laura Cochrane, *Everyday Faith in Sufi Senegal* (New York and London: Routledge, 2017) 95.

[16] Abdoulaye Bamba Ngom, interview with author, 26 February 2016, Yoff, Senegal, qtd. in Cochrane, *Everyday Faith in Sufi Senegal*, 95.

baraka, his closeness with God and therefore someone to be followed. Al-Kuntī taught that disciples should acknowledge the shaykh's authority, and wholly obey his guidance, a teaching that Bamba adopted.[17] Submissiveness in this context is related to Sufism's goal of 'annihilation of self': giving up one's self on the lifelong path to achieve unity with God.[18] This is not giving up one's identity as a person, but creating one's identity as a spiritual person wholeheartedly following a religious path. Disciples thus carefully choose their marabout. Knowing who to show obeisance to, and how to show that deference, thus was so important that Fall received divine instruction: he was not only showing that submission, he was embodying it as a part of his own being and knowledge.

The teacher–disciple relationship between Bamba and Fall is often described as a joining of opposites. Fall is Lamp Fall, the illuminator, while Bamba is the one illuminated. Bamba is dressed in white robes in the only photograph of him in existence, a 1913 colonial portrait. Fall wears black robes in photographs depicting him and other disciples. Images of the two men on every surface imaginable throughout Senegal – on cars, buses, shops, murals, and icons displayed in taxis, t-shirts, and around one's neck – echo this black robe–white robe imagery. Bamba was an intellectual, a teacher whose writings and poetry are studied today and who lived out an example of pacifism during a tumultuous time in Senegal's history. Fall distinguished himself through scholarship: he authored books and was an intellectual in his own right. He is best known, however, for dedicating himself to labouring for Bamba, and thus showing his love for and submission to him. Other disciples did not agree with his extreme devotion shown through labour to the extent of neglecting intellectual study.[19]

Fall was not the only prominent disciple of Bamba. Bamba's younger brother, Shaykh Ibrahima Faty Mbakke (known as Maam Cerno, 1863–1943) was, according to the many accounts, Bamba's first disciple and supported Bamba's mission throughout his life. He also became a prominent and respected teacher with his own disciples.[20] Another disciple who studied under both Bamba and Sy was Ahmad Al-Kabir Mbaye, known as Maam Shaykh Mbaye (1864–1946), who was a less visible figure than Fall, but known for his intellect and knowledge.[21] A

[17] Babou, 'Educating the Murid', 312; Batran, 'An Introductory Note', 347.

[18] William. C. Chittick, *Sufism: A Beginner's Guide* (Oxford: Oneworld Publications, 2000) 9–15; Valerie J. Hoffman, 'Annihilation in the Messenger of God: The Development of a Sufi Practice', *International Journal of Middle Eastern Studies*, 31, 3, 1999, 351–4.

[19] Cheikh Anta Babou, *Fighting the Greater Jihad: Amadou Bamba and the Founding of Muridiyya of Senegal, 1853*–1913 (Athens: Ohio University Press, 2007) 64–5; Cruise O'Brien, *Saints and Politicians*, 50–1.

[20] Glover, *Sufism and Jihad in Modern Senegal*, 85–8.

[21] Mbaye became a renowned judge and scholar and eventually settled in Louga, the

Baay Fall interviewee explained that Mbaye and Fall had a 'sympathetic animosity'. He told me a proverb about the two to explain: Mbaye was a coin that is dropped in the sand. You can't see it, but it's still there and its value is still present. Fall was a coin that is dropped on a hard surface. It has the same value, but is much more visible.[22] Following Bamba's different disciples, there are many branches of the Murīdiyya, just as in other Sufi orders. The present-day story of Mbakke Kajoor, however, focuses on the Murīdiyya and its Baay Fall (Wolof, Father Fall) suborder.

Labouring for the Murid community is today celebrated in both the Murīdiyya at large and within the Baay Fall. Baay Falls model themselves after Fall's devotion to labour and Bamba's teaching about working for one's community. In many ways, they attract the same criticisms as Fall because of their practices. They consider labour a form of prayer: why should one stop to pray five times a day if one is already labouring/praying? Similarly, they do not fast during Ramadan, instead taking on the responsibility of preparing meals for pilgrims visiting holy sites so that the pilgrims can focus on fasting. In this same spirit, Baay Falls are often seen on city streets during Ramadan, giving out cups of coffee to people stuck in traffic at sundown, to help break the fast. While criticisms continue because of their departures from foundational practices of Islam, many other criticisms reflect on those who adopt the Baay Fall identity as an excuse to not take prayer seriously, and insistently beg for money without giving the money to the poor or to one's shaykh to be distributed. There is a gulf between these ostentatious displays and the Baay Falls who take Baay Fall principles seriously.

Bamba's teachings became the cornerstone of Murid and Baay Fall theology. First, similar to Al-Kuntī, Bamba taught submissiveness and acceptance of the authority of one's chosen shaykh as a spiritual guide.[23] This teaching is the reason that Fall's actions meant so much at the time, and continue to have meaning today. Second, also similarly to al-Kuntī's teachings, Bamba taught and modelled a pacifism that emphasized a jihād of the soul instead of military jihād.[24] Instead of military might, he taught that education was the better weapon against colonial and monarchical corruption.[25] His pacifist instruction and actions stood out in a time of colonial takeover and military resistance. He was not, though, the only

site of the interview in which he was mentioned. See also John Hunwick et al., *Arabic Literature of Africa Vol. 4: Writings of Western Sudanic Africa* (Leiden: Brill Academic Publishers, 2003) 455.

[22] Interviewee, interview with author, 7 June 2015, Louga, Senegal.

[23] Babou, 'Educating the Murid', 312.

[24] Christian Coulon, 'The Grand Magal in Touba: A Religious Festival of the Mouride Brotherhood of Senegal', *African Affairs*, 98, 391, 1999, 197.

[25] Babou, 'Educating the Murid', 311–12.

marabout who advocated for pacifism. Each marabout of the time faced difficult decisions to collaborate, or not, with the French, and whether to participate, or not, in warfare against the French or in other territorial battles between states.

A third teaching that can also be traced directly to his theological ancestors has to do with one's involvement in the world. As Bamba moved away from Mbakke Kajoor and attracted more and more disciples, he also taught the value of working for one's community rather than detachment from the world. He established a *daara*, an intentional spiritual community. *Daaras* continue today, in both rural and urban contexts. In urban areas, they are often study groups that meet regularly or schools for Qur'ānic study. In rural areas, *daara* residents live, work, and study together, under the spiritual direction of a marabout. To financially support his *daara*, Bamba set up a peanut plantation, tapping into the French colonial economy. A farm necessitates labour. In the *daara*, his disciples both laboured and received Qur'ānic education, no matter their own educational level or literacy. Both work and peanut agriculture, because of this history, became closely associated with the Murīdiyya, even while other Sufi shaykhs engaged in similar arrangements to support their communities.[26]

Educating people without elitism, devotion to one's shaykh, pacifism, and work are all themes that continue throughout the story of Mbakke Kajoor and the establishment of the Murīdiyya. This historical storyline and the emerging theology of the Murīdiyya and the Baay Fall suborder at the turn of the twentieth century is the backdrop and the foundation for the new project at Mbakke Kajoor.

Responding to a *Ndigal*

The call to revitalize the area around the pilgrimage site near the town of Mbakke Kajoor came in 2009. The *khalife général* of the Murīdiyya, Shaykh Sidi Moctar Mbakke, issued an *ndigal* to begin work there. A *ndigal* is a religious authority's directive, and has priority over even state laws and policies. Because of this potential for influence over their disciples, Murid leaders use it carefully.[27] When Shaykh Mbakke issued the *ndigal*, other construction projects that occupied Murid labour and resources were already underway, including a guesthouse in Touba, the Murid holy city. The project thus waited for its groundbreaking until January 2015. While he could have chosen any number of prominent marabouts to direct the revitalization, he gave the *ndigal* to Sëriñ Babacar Mbow, a Baay Fall

[26] Cruise O'Brien, *Saints and Politicians*, 60; Leonardo A. Villalón, *Islamic Society and State Power in Senegal: Disciples and Citizens in Fatick* (Cambridge: Cambridge University Press, 1995) 118.

[27] Searing, '*God Alone is King*', 133.

marabout who had started another project in the 1980s, a *daara* in Ndem, a village an hour's drive west of Mbakke Kajoor.

Ndem was already a village when Mbow and his wife, Soxna Aïssa Cissé, arrived there in the 1980s, but it was close to abandoned and the 1970s droughts had devastated it. They started a *daara* that is today partially funded by an artisanal centre. Over the past few decades, along with the artisanal centre, the *daara* has grown to include schools, a health centre, agriculture, and a garden to experiment with ways to grow produce in degraded soil. A borehole supplies clean drinking water sourced from groundwater. These projects employ and serve people from the fifteen villages that surround the *daara*. The *daara*'s residents and managers consider their local economic development to be spiritual, and modelled after Islamic principles, Bamba's teachings, and Fall's example. First, they interpret Islamic teachings on charity as reducing poverty through development work. Second, they see their *daara* as an emulation of Bamba's original *daara*: a place to support an impoverished population struggling against economic inequality and a degraded environment. Third, they are Baay Fall, so they consider their development work and constant labour a form of prayer and religious devotion.[28]

Sëriñ Babacar was assigned the *ndigal* to develop the site near Mbakke Kajoor in June 2014. As Fatou Diack, a resident of the Ndem *daara*, explained, when you receive an *ndigal*, you drop everything and you do it.[29] This meant that Sëriñ Babacar and Soxna Aïssa, along with a number of their adult children and Ndem *daara* residents, began plans to move to the new site in late 2014, and also began plans for the site, described below. The *ndigal*, however, was issued to the entire Murid community, not just Sëriñ Babacar. While residents of Ndem had an early view of the new project, other Murids were not as familiar. To raise awareness and recruit both the volunteers and the funds for the project, Sëriñ Babacar and a group of people from Ndem went on a mobilization tour in 2015, visiting major cities across Senegal.

I joined the tour, travelling with a group of people from Ndem, in June 2015 in Louga, a city in the northern part of central Senegal. The event included *sikkar*, a Sufi tradition of singing *dhikr*, the remembrance of God's names; speeches by local dignitaries; and informational videos about the project. The following morning, our group visited a grandson of Shaykh Ibra Fall. In a long discussion between Sëriñ Babacar, the shaykh, his accountant, and other dignitaries in the room, the shaykh offered enough money to buy 300 tons of cement for the project. Sëriñ

[28] Laura L. Cochrane, 'Religious Motivations for Local Economic Development in Senegal', *Africa Today*, 58, 4, 2012, 8; Laura L. Cochrane, 'Addressing Global Economic Inequalities in Local Ways in Senegal's Artisanal Workshops', *Economic Anthropology*, 2, 2015, 255.

[29] Fatou Diack, interview with author, 31 May 2015, Ndem, Senegal.

Babacar replied appreciatively. He suggested, though, that instead of giving the project cash, they could buy the cement and deliver it to the site, so that they could participate in the project, maybe bringing their own disciples to work. Involving people as well as asking for funds is an important strategy in developing Mbakke Kajoor. Encouraging participation in the project, not just giving funds, is intended to give the wider Murid community a sense of personal investment in the site: to see it as their own, not just a project by a small group of people.

From the start, a group of workers, along with Sëriñ Babacar and Soxna Aïssa, have lived at the construction site. The residences follow traditional construction of millet-straw walls and roofs. Concrete floors and reinforced roofs protect them from rainy season floods and pests. Their focus, in other words, has been on building the new centre, not their own homes. This group of workers, both men and women, provide the backbone of the project, and host other workers from around Senegal who come for weekend and sometimes longer work trips. The motivation of both the permanent work leaders and the visiting workers comes from following the *ndigal*, and also from Baay Fall and Murid philosophies of work. As one resident of Ndem, Fallou Fall, explained,

> Bamba said, 'When you work for me [Bamba], you work for the population.' You are born again when you work. Everything you do, you do for God. If you are a part of Muridism, you can start with Mbakke Kajoor, it's the door.[30]

Baay Falls take the idea of working for God through working for their community seriously. The Mbakke Kajoor project has already attracted enthusiastic work crews. They are motivated by belief that labouring for God and their community is a form of prayer, the belief that working to end poverty is work within the pillar of charity, the belief that a *ndigal* is to be followed, and a widespread belief that the religiously centred plan for Mbakke Kajoor will serve the communities around it.

These spiritual motivations for work are on display during a Baay Fall work project. The energy for work and, as one person working at Mbakke Kajoor described it, a 'joie de vivre' while working, is evidence of the commitment to work. One Baay Fall who lives in Mbakke Kajoor explained both the challenge and the motivation for the work.

> We are not many here – sometimes twenty, sometimes five. The work here is difficult. We are not masons here, but we need to learn and do masonry, for example. But with intention and heart, it's possible. God makes this possible.[31]

[30] Fallou Fall, interview with author, 31 May 2015, Ndem, Senegal.

[31] Interviewee, interview with author, 12 February 2016, Mbakke Kajoor, Senegal.

As he spoke, we watched a group of men construct the communal kitchen for the workers' residence area. The women who are in charge of preparing communal meals had asked for a more permanent kitchen that had a raised cement floor and cement block walls to keep sand and pests away from the food preparation. The work had just started that morning, and by mid-afternoon the floor was poured and the walls were rising at a fast pace. I commented that the work constructing the new kitchen was progressing quickly. The worker responded with the Wolof proverb, '*Mbolo mooy dolle*' (Union is strength). Coming together, in other words, makes difficult work possible.

A Philosophy of Integrated Education

Religious principles, the historical importance of the site, and a religious dictate are all motivations for the rehabilitation of the Mbakke Kajoor site. The vision is to establish an educational centre that joins Qur'ānic, trade, and agricultural education together. To do this, the project will have four centres.[32] The first, the Lieu de Ziarre, is the sacred site of the tree Guisguis Bamba, where Fall met Bamba. Ziarre comes from the Arabic *ziyāra*, a visit to a religious shrine. The second set of buildings is the Résidence Mame Cheikh Ibrahima Fall, where the visiting *khalife général* of the Baay Falls and other visiting shaykhs will lodge. The third, the Dahra Serigne Mame Mor Anta Sally Mbacké, will be the centre of Qur'ānic education and training in professional trades, and have lodging for students. The fourth, the Centre de Formation en Agro-Ecologie, will include spaces for hands-on training in animal husbandry and organic agriculture, plus lodging for students. There will be space for about one hundred students at a time. The managers of the project hope that the integrated educational goals of the site will continue to encourage participation not only in building the site, but also in its future training centres.

The threefold areas of education – Qur'ānic study, trades, and organic agriculture – address, in the project managers' minds, the needs of the region surrounding Mbakke Kajoor. As Soxna Aïssa described

> The responsibility has been given to Sëriñ Babacar to make this place alive again. You really see how this place is historically important to the world, as the birthplace of Muridism. In order to make this place alive, there's an element of education. There's a marriage of spiritual education and practical trades. For education,

[32] I have spelled the names of the four centres as they are presented on the brochure produced to advertise the building project. Because Wolof did not have a standard orthography until the 1970s, spelling of names, places, and terms are variable. Different spellings are not 'wrong', but instead acceptable variants.

> the context is Murid, but it is bigger than that. It's important for people to go back to the earth and to have a new relationship with agriculture.[33]

Religious study is the centrepiece of the project. As a holy site that has an historical connection to revitalizing spiritual education, this branch of the new educational centre will receive the most attention. Then, combining trades with Qur'ānic study is intended to train people in employable fields that support their communities, such as mechanical and sewing trades. Training in organic agriculture is intended to revitalize the environment. Taking Ndem's philosophy of total ecosystem change, rather than focusing on just one field or one crop, the new site already has plantings in the residence and common areas. These have changed the site from a sandy expanse to the start of a greener landscape. The need for holistic educational goals comes from the region's degraded landscape, unemployment, and economic challenges. It also comes from Senegal's sometimes-fraught relationship with religious education.

Education is a common theme in local economic development in Senegal. Ndem's education for grade school students is expressly designed so that families will be able to live in rural areas, and younger generations will have the education they need to contribute to their local economies. Many religious (and, in particular, Islamic) local organizations likewise focus on a number of concerns, such as village empowerment, small businesses,[34] health,[35] women's issues,[36] and agriculture.[37] Education is often an integral part of this work.[38] This concern with education comes from Senegal's state-wide struggle to increase access to

[33] Soxna Aïssa Cissé, interview with author, 7 June 2015, Louga, Senegal.

[34] Erin Augis, 'Aïcha's Sounith Hair Salon: Friendship, Profit, and Resistance in Dakar', *Islamic Africa*, 5, 2, 2014, 199–224; Cochrane, 'Religious Motivations'.

[35] Ellen E. Foley, *Your Pocket is What Cures You: The Politics of Health in Senegal* (New Brunswick: Rutgers University Press, 2010).

[36] Mara A. Leichtman, 'The Authentication of a Discursive Islam', in Mamadou Diouf; Mara Leichtman (eds.), *New Perspectives on Islam in Senegal: Conversion, Migration, Wealth, Power, and Femininity* (New York: Palgrave Macmillan, 2009) 111–38; Nadine Sieveking, 'We Don't Want Equality; We Want to Be Given Our Rights: Muslim Women Negotiating Global Development Concepts in Senegal', *Afrika Spectrum*, 42, 2007, 29–48.

[37] Cochrane, 'Religious Motivations'; Amy S. Patterson, 'The Dynamic Nature of Citizenship and Participation: Lessons from Three Rural Senegalese Case Studies', *Africa Today*, 46, 1, 1999; Donna L. Perry, 'Rural Weekly Markets and the Dynamics of Time, Space and Community in Senegal', *The Journal of Modern African Studies*, 38, 3, 2000.

[38] Augis, 'Aïcha's Sounith Hair Salon'; Leichtman, 'The Authentication of a Discursive Islam'; Rudolph T. Ware III, 'The Longue Durée of Quran Schooling, Society, and State in Senegambia', in Mamadou Diouf; Mara Leichtman (eds.), *New Perspectives*

schools. It also acknowledges the widespread sentiment that Qur'ānic education is of equal, if not greater, importance to secular education.

This attention to education is long-standing. The 1963 constitution guaranteed the right to public education for all, and allowed private schools to be accredited and operate under the authority of the state,[39] yet this does not mean that there is universal enrolment.[40] Families are often not able to afford the tuition and book fees to send their children to school, and many families prefer to enrol their children in Qur'ānic schools rather than secular primary schools. Qur'ānic schools in Senegal are not state-regulated and not state-funded, a debate in itself.[41] In 2002, the National Assembly introduced several changes to state education. It encouraged Qur'ānic schools to include secular subjects alongside religious education. For secular public schools, it included Islam in the curriculum and added instruction in national languages (Joola, Mandinka, Pulaar, Sereer, Soninke, and Wolof) in addition to French, Senegal's official language.[42] These changes did not end the most pressing part of the education debate, though. While few people dispute the importance of religious education, human rights abuses in poorly-run Qur'ānic schools – including malnutrition and violence against young Qur'ānic students, usually boys, and forcing them to beg in the streets intended as a lesson in humility – are the primary arguments for their regulation. In June 2016, President Macky Sall (2012–present) ordered arrests of corrupt instructors and removal of students from the streets and from abusive environments. This directive did not extend to regulating the schools themselves, but instead has increased action against abuses.[43]

---

on Islam in Senegal: Conversion, Migration, Wealth, Power, and Femininity (New York: Palgrave Macmillan, 2009) 21–50.

39 *Constitution du Sénégal de 1963,* 'Articles 21–23', http://www.gouv.sn/spip.php?article794. Accessed 15 March 2012.

40 The Global Partnership for Education, Senegal (http://www.globalpartnership.org/country/senegal, 2016), drawing on Senegalese national data, reported that 'gross enrollment rates went from 67.2% to 93%' between 2000 and 2013, yet schools across the country are variable in terms of access to educational resources and updated curricula, learning environments, and retention rates.

41 An interview with an *imām* in Thiès, El Hajj Barro N'Diéguéne, in 2011 (see fn.44) referenced this debate. He criticized those who open *daaras* without the ability or education to teach; he also criticized the lack of governmental support as the reason for *daaras* that lack adequate resources.

42 Penda Mbow, 'Secularism, Education, and Human Rights in Senegal', Institute for the Study of Islamic Thought in Africa Working Paper Series, Northwestern University, 2009, 3; Mariko Shiohata, 'Exploring the Literacy Environment: A Case Study from Senegal', *Comparative Education Review*, 54, 2, 2010, 248–9.

43 Human Rights Watch, Senegal, 'New Steps to Protect Talibés, Street Children',

While the debate over children's Qur'ānic education continues, *daaras* remain centres of Islamic learning and community, and Qur'ānic schools for both children and adults remain sought-after and largely positive learning environments. This brief overview, however, shows that Qur'ānic education, in the minds of many, is both important and in need of attention. As El Hajj Barro N'Diéguéne, an *imām* in Thiès, explained in an interview,

> We are a secular country. Public schools have civic education. But the students lack spiritual education. … True Islamic education is different. We who learn Islam, we are in the *daara*. An orphan is not a person who has lost his mother and his father. An orphan is he who has lost knowledge and a good education. Science without conscience, though, cannot work. You must have knowledge with conscience.[44]

His argument for a holistic education – knowledge must be paired with spirituality – is a common argument for combining secular and religious education. Xalima Sarr, the community leader who accompanied me to visit El Hajj Barro, agreed: he had also received his education in Qur'ānic schools, and credits them for introducing students to what they need:

> We must know ourselves: culture, language, history, everything. The students in *daaras* will become leaders. For example, in the market, they are the managers of workshops, of carpentry, of everything.[45]

Joining Qur'ānic and trade education is also a strategy in the Ndem and Mbakke Kajoor *daaras*. In developing their holistic philosophy of education, Ndem *daara*'s leaders and residents have established secular primary and secondary schools. They think of their artisanal workshops as professional education for adults, particularly for those without formal school training. Religious education, however, remains a priority. This includes Qur'ānic education and study groups, but also the everyday spiritual focus expected of a *daara*.

Making sure that the younger generation absorbs spiritual principles is a priority and a part of this daily education in Ndem's *daara*. For example, younger children pick up trash out of the sand, understanding that their care of the earth is their care for God's creation. They are also adept at showing respect to, and learning from, religious leaders. Soxna Aïssa Cissé pointed out that the *daara*'s children are free to run around and be a part of everything by design. As they grow up, they slowly take responsibility for different tasks and then for managing small projects. Young adults often direct and manage different projects in the *daara* and

---

28 July, https://www.hrw.org/news/2016/07/28/senegal-new-steps-protect-talibes-street-children. Accessed 24 August 2016.

44 El Hajj Barro N'Diéguéne, interview with author, 10 June 2011, Thiès, Senegal.

45 Xalima Sarr, interview with author, 10 June 2011, Thiès, Senegal.

the educational centre. She continued, describing the importance of education via the teachings of Bamba.

> And so education truly has a big role in Ndem, and in all the world. Because it's education that forms a being, that orients his spirit, and forms his heart and his soul. These are the things that form the very young. Sëriñ Touba said that the first seven years is like engraving on a stone. Then after those first years it's like throwing a stone in water. It ripples out within seconds. It's in infancy that you inscribe everything. So, the need for education is not for academic knowledge, what contributes to modern civilization is always more long-lasting than science, and always stronger. It's knowledge of which we speak. I'm talking about knowledge of relationships, things of life, things of mystery. … So, in Ndem we try to create an alternative life, to create a life which is, at its base, Baay Fall spirituality: the values of generosity, tolerance, patience, and work, the values that are fundamental to Islam, in a profound sense. By living with these values, we adapt to the situation of the Sahel. So, [we have] a difficult exterior situation, that is, a desert, few material resources, a population that for the most part is illiterate. … It's important to walk hand in hand, together, to become stronger together. And it's that for which the *daara* is important, it's spiritual education. We walk with God, to see reality.[46]

Soxna Aïssa did not discredit science here: scientific study and counsel from agricultural agents are both important aspects of Ndem's amelioration of their degraded environment. Instead, she placed greater significance on spiritual knowledge and developing human relationships. Ndem's projects engage a predominantly illiterate and economically impoverished population, in an environment degraded by drought and long-term land mismanagement. In response to these needs, Ndem's leaders have created a holistic perspective of education. It prioritizes religious study, yet also serves the needs of the region to develop sustainable agriculture and economically viable trades. It recognizes that people of all ages, not just children, are in need of these educational and economic opportunities. It was this holistic educational perspective that led them to focus the development of Mbakke Kajoor on education.

Using Tradition to Respond to Present-day Needs

The Mbakke Kajoor site is designed to be a space for Islamic education that addresses the particular needs of its locale. A number of challenges work against establishing such a centre in this region. These include degraded land ill-suited for agriculture, continued economic strains from the household to national levels, the difficulty of recruiting labour for a new project, and, similar to all new

[46] Soxna Aïssa Cissé, interview with author, 10 June 2013, Ndem, Senegal.

projects in a cash-strapped place, finding continued financial support. I argue that the project's early and ongoing success depends on its use of local knowledge, religious traditions, and philosophies to address the local needs that arise from these challenges. For Mbakke Kajoor leaders and workers, this local knowledge comes from West African Islamic scholars, including an emphasis on inclusive, not exclusive or elitist education; integrating religious and agricultural education; and using spiritual motivations to recruit participation.

The same argument was true for Bamba when he set out to form his new Murid community, and for Ndem's leaders when they established the *daara* in the 1980s. That is, they employed the history of the region, its religious traditions, and its types of knowledge to meet their era's needs. In the late 1800s, central regions of Senegal were facing rapid deterioration at the hands of the French colonial administration. The 1873 global recession had hurt global trade, particularly in Europe. Several European powers addressed their economic woes by investing in natural resource extraction in their occupied territories, particularly in Africa.[47] The French were among those powers: their policies in Senegal sacrificed sustainable farming techniques for peanut cash-cropping. Along with these harmful agricultural mandates, people in the Senegambian region experienced the social upheaval of colonialism, guerilla warfare against this occupation, and battles over territory that had little to do with European imperialism. Bamba's new *daaras* provided spaces that were ideologically separate from both monarchical and colonial powers. People of varying castes, classes, and ethnicities were attracted to his new educational philosophies, inspired by earlier West African Sufi scholars yet designed to address their needs. He was responding to the demands of his time and place, and drawing from religious traditions to do so.

Ndem faced similar challenges of an environmentally degraded region: after colonial and state control, the region was emerging from the 1970s droughts, only to face another drought in 1982–4. Senegal was also in the middle of economic restructuring during the 1980s. This was a series of changes that many nations faced in response to World Bank and International Monetary Fund policies of the time. Put in place following the 1970s global economic recession, these policies demanded that states restructure their economies in return for continued access to loans. These loans were necessary for many newly independent nations following the devastation of colonial occupation, to start their national economies.[48]

[47] William G. Hynes, *The Economics of Empire: Britain, Africa and the New Imperialism, 1870–95* (London: Longman Group Limited, 1979) 28, 89, 97–8; Kevin Narizny, *The Political Economy of Grand Strategy* (Ithaca, NY: Cornell University Press, 2007) 181.

[48] Simon Commander, 'Structural Adjustment Policies and Agricultural Growth in Africa', *Economic and Political Weekly*, 23, 39, 1988, A98.

While Senegal had continued with state control over agriculture following independence, structural adjustments lessened this control. It also, though, reduced state support and extension services for agriculturalists.[49] On top of the Sahelian droughts, this devastated rural economies, including villages such as Ndem.[50] Agriculture was no longer viable under these conditions, and young people left their rural villages to seek work and opportunities elsewhere. The resulting mass rural to urban migration across the Sahel both hurt the populations in rural areas and flooded urban areas and created unsustainable population levels. Ndem's *daara* specifically addressed these issues: to train several generations with the skills they needed to revitalize their communities. Sëriñ Babacar and Soxna Aïssa, along with Ndem's managers, drew on the region's history of artisanal production and agriculture, updating the professions with new technologies, to provide a new economic base for the *daara*. They combined religious education with professional development for adults and combined religious and secular schooling for children. Following Bamba's example, Ndem's *daara* leaders believe that economic and spiritual revitalization is intertwined.

Establishing Mbakke Kajoor's *daara*, starting in 2015, carries echoes of establishing Bamba's and Ndem's *daaras*. The region continues to struggle with severe land degradation, after over a century of drought. In addition, global environmental shifts have affected the timing of the annual rainy season, notably since 2014, pushing it one month later into the year, and thus affecting agricultural patterns. Farmers have had to adapt to this new growing season, on top of the continuing challenge of dealing with drought.[51] The 2007–11 global recession affected Senegal's businesses' trade, particularly with the European Union. Once

[49] Gilles Duruflé, 'Bilan de la Nouvelle Politique Agricole au Sénégal', *Review of African Political Economy*, 22, 63, 1995, 74; Bernard Lecomte, 'Senegal: The Young Farmers of Walo and the New Agricultural Policy', *Review of African Political Economy*, 55, 1992, 88.

[50] Laura L. Cochrane, 'Land Degradation, Faith-Based Organizations, and Sustainability in Senegal', *CAFE: Culture, Agriculture, Food, and Environment*, 35, 2, 2013, 115.

[51] See BRACED/ 'Building Resilience and Adaptation to Climate Extremes and Disasters. 2015', Senegal Floods 2015, http://www.braced.org/reality-of-resilience/i/?id=3dc7ca27-bc7d-466f-a6af-4dae3bc12abd. Accessed 14 September 2016; NOAA, 'Climate Prediction Center's Africa Hazards Outlook September 8 – September 14, 2016', http://www.cpc.ncep.noaa.gov/products/international/africa/africa_hazard.pdf; Malick Wade et al., 'On the Spatial Coherence of Rainfall over the Saloum Delta (Senegal) from Seasonal to Decadal Time Scales. Frontiers in Earth Science', 2015, http://dx.doi.org/10.3389/feart.2015.00030. Accessed 14 September 2016. This topic was also part of informal conversations during my 2015 and 2016 research trips to Senegal.

again, environmental degradation and global economic recession had local effects on the central regions of Senegal. The educational centre planned for Mbakke Kajoor seeks to address both unemployment and a changed agricultural landscape through training in professions that match the region's needs and organic agriculture that uses new technologies. Combining these educational goals with religious education, and doing so within a traditional *daara* environment, is using West Africa's religious traditions and agricultural and cultural heritage, all to address current circumstances.

At these moments in history – the late 1800s, the 1980s, and the years following the 2007–11 economic recession – people in the central regions of Senegal have dealt with the aftermath of global economic recession along with severe land degradation. Leaders of these different communities – Bamba's *daaras*, Ndem's *daara*, and the new *daara* at Mbakke Kajoor – responded with a *daara*, a spiritual community with educational philosophies designed to specifically respond to their time and place. These similarities are not coincidence, and not lost on those who have started the new Mbakke Kajoor *daara*. Soxna Aïssa explained that they are modelling their work on Bamba's and Fall's examples and Bamba's teachings.

> We have to find new ways to revalorize Senegal. We need a new model for education, according to the teachings of Sëriñ Touba and Shaykh Ibra Fall, because they taught us to work in dignity and for the love of God. All his teachings are about peace and how to awake a consciousness to the Creator.[52]

Reaching back to Islamic scholars' teachings, and using them to address contemporary challenges, is also a lesson from Bamba, who used early scholars' writings to implement his *daara*.

The model of education that Bamba set up was designed to be inclusive, receptive to scholars, labourers, those of the Wolof slave caste, the artisans, the royalty, and those freeborn. Until then, Sufi models of education in Senegal were for those who were already intellectuals, or young people who came from an intellectual family lineage.[53] In Ndem, this lesson is carried out through the artisanal centre and other activities that financially support the *daara* and its activities. People from Ndem and the surrounding fifteen villages who have often never been employed before learn agricultural or artisanal skills along with how to be in a work setting and other professional skills. However, revitalizing an entire region via spiritual and trade-based education is a long-term and ambitious strategy. The Mbakke Kajoor project has a similar goal, but is more explicit about education, with centres devoted to specific aspects of their integrated religious, trade,

52 Soxna Aïssa Cissé, interview with author, 7 June 2015, Louga, Senegal.
53 Ware, *The Walking Qur'an*, 184–6.

and agricultural educational goals. Sëriñ Babacar explained these goals simply: 'These are things that everyone needs.'[54]

The beginning of the Mbakke Kajoor project has closely adhered to the goals for the site. Emphasizing labour participation as well as financial contribution, Sëriñ Babacar encourages community involvement that corresponds with Murid and Baay Fall principles of working together for a community. Soxna Aïssa emphasized this spiritual motivation: 'With the help of God, our spiritual base, and solidarity with others bringing the money in, we are building little by little.'[55] The gradual building is necessary because of limited resources, but also their plan of building everything by hand. Through this slow work, the project's leaders hope to increase participation from not only the Murid community at large, but also the villages surrounding the new *daara*. Their strategy is to foster a sense of ownership through this involvement. In turn, they hope that the educational centres will serve the region. Their goal is economic revitalization along with renewed spiritual education, as Soxna Aïssa described it above, 'a marriage of spiritual education and practical trades'. Because they are rooted in the region's traditions of agriculture, religious education, and community, and founded on an important religious and historical site, their project has had resonance within the Murīdiyya.

[54] Sëriñ Babacar Mbow, interview with author, 12 February 2016, Mbakke Kajoor, Senegal.

[55] Soxna Aïssa Cissé, interview with author, 14 June 2015, Mbakke Kajoor, Senegal.

CHAPTER 12

Islamic Education and the 'Diaspora': Religious Schooling for Senegalese Migrants' Children

Hannah Hoechner

For my doctoral research, I spent the best part of the year 2011 on fieldwork in Kano in northern Nigeria, trying to find out how young boys experience their enrolment in Qur'ānic schools there. A major challenge was to make the children open up to me and talk. Wider norms on the appropriate behaviour for juniors encourage children to be bashful and demure in the presence of adults. Collecting data on children's opinions required me to be patient, to have as unobtrusive a presence as possible, to learn from observing, and to find research formats that allowed my research participants to talk to each other rather than to me, for example by conducting tape-recorded 'radio interviews' among each other in my absence.

The situation I encountered in Dakar, Senegal, where I studied Islamic schools receiving children from the Senegalese 'diaspora'[1] between 2014 and 2016 – including many children born and raised in the United States – could hardly have been more different. Here, the ten-year-olds scrambled to be 'selected' for an interview, talked a mile a minute, and were upset when I told them it was time to return to class as we had already overstayed the time their teacher had granted us. Here the challenge was not to make children talk, but rather to find a breathing pause in their word flow to slip in my questions. 'Five Americans are tantamount to forty Senegalese children!'[2] one of the teachers confided to me, exhausted after a day's work of trying to tame the buoyant crowd. Profound cultural differences

[1] For the purpose of this chapter, I use the term 'diaspora' broadly to refer to people with Senegalese ancestry who more or less fulfil the three overarching criteria identified by Rogers Brubaker ('The "disapora" diaspora', *Ethnic and Racial Studies*, 28, 1, 2005, 5–6), namely 'dispersion in space', an 'orientation to a "homeland"' – in this case Senegal – and a certain degree of 'boundary-maintenance' or the 'preservation of a distinctive identity vis-à-vis [the] host society'.

[2] '*Cinq américains, ça vaut quarante sénégalais!*' (The translation from French is mine.)

between children raised in a West African setting and youngsters having grown up in Western contexts had implications not only for me as a researcher, but also for the teachers dealing with them every day in class.

About a third of the students in the school described here (IQRA Bilingual Academy) are children from the Senegalese diaspora, mostly from the United States, but also from France, Italy, and Belgium. The rest of the student body is made up of Senegalese middle- and upper-class children as well as children of other nationalities whose parents work in Dakar as diplomats. The students study secular subjects, modelled on the American curriculum, as well as Arabic, Islamic studies, and the Qur'ān. Some of the diaspora children have been to Islamic schools in the countries where they were born, but for many, IQRA Bilingual Academy is the first faith-based full-time educational institution they attend.

This chapter takes the opening of schools like IQRA Bilingual Academy as a starting point to explore a force of change within Islamic educational practices that has received very little scholarly attention to date: the diaspora. The literature on Islamic schooling has widely acknowledged the importance of mobility and migration for the acquisition of religious education.[3] The role of returnees from the Arab countries as agents of change in Islamic educational practices in Africa has received due attention in the literature.[4] Yet, the literature is largely silent on the role of returnees from Western countries and on the ways in which African Muslim diasporas[5] may influence Islamic educational practices on the continent more widely. Drawing on data collected among Senegalese migrants in the US, and in Islamic schools receiving migrants' children in Senegal, this chapter seeks to step into this gap.[6] The first part of the chapter reviews the literature on

[3] C. Fortier, 'Le corps comme mémoire: Du giron maternel à la férule du maître coranique', *Journal Des Africanistes*, 68, 1–2, 1998, 197–224; Hannah Hoechner, 'Mobility as a contradictory resource: peripatetic Qur'ānic students in Kano, Nigeria', *Children's Geographies*, 13, 1, 2105, 59–72; Ousmane Kane, *Beyond Timbuktu. An Intellectual History of Muslim West Africa* (Cambridge, MA: Harvard University Press, 2016).

[4] See for example Alexander Thurston, *Salafism in Nigeria. Islam, Preaching, and Politics* (Cambridge: Cambridge University Press, 2016); Rudolph T. Ware III, *The Walking Qur'an. Islamic Education, Embodied Knowledge, and History in West Africa* (Chapel Hill: University of North Carolina Press, 2014).

[5] For a discussion of whether it is appropriate to extend the use of the term 'diaspora' to religious groups, or whether it should be reserved for ethnically defined groups, see S. Vertovec, 'Religion and Diaspora', in P. Antes; A.W. Geertz; R. Warne (eds.), *New Approaches to the Study of Religion* (Berlin and New York: Walter de Gruyer, 2004) 275–304.

[6] I conducted seven months of fieldwork in Dakar in Senegal between 2014 and 2016, and seven months of fieldwork in New York and New Jersey in the United States in

Islamic education, and makes a case for paying greater attention to migrants and 'diasporas' as agents of change. I then turn to the Senegalese case. Drawing on data collected among Senegalese migrants in New York in 2017–18,[7] I outline their demand for homeland education for their children. I argue that this diaspora demand has contributed to the emergence of a new type of school in Senegal that is both Islamic and international in outlook. The last part of the chapter portrays one such school.

Some migrants' children spend all their childhood and youth in Senegal and return to the US only for high school or college, or to start work. Others spend only their early childhood (around two to five years) in Senegal.[8] Other children leave the US when they are old enough to be accepted into a Qur'ānic boarding school, usually around age six or seven, and return to the US one or several years later after having acquired some knowledge of the Qur'ān. Another frequent practice is to send young people, especially boys, back at the beginning of adolescence for 'disciplining' or to get them out of trouble. While my research in Senegal focused on young people in the latter two categories (those enrolled in Qur'ānic boarding schools and those sent back in early adolescence), in my research in the US I also interviewed young people who had spent most of their childhood and youth in Senegal and returned to the US only for middle or high school. The next section explores how migrants and diasporas have been discussed in the literature on Islamic education.

Islamic Educational Practices, Migration and Diasporas

It has been argued that as a result of deeper-seated barriers confining scientific analysis to neatly circumscribed disciplinary terrains, scholars have paid insufficient attention to the ways in which Islam articulates with migratory processes to non-Muslim lands. Sophie Bava, for example, claims that 'Islam in a migratory context is not a field that has attracted scholars specialized in the study of Islam

---

2017 and 2018. I collected data through participant observation in different schools (including Islamic schools) in both Senegal and the US, where I attended classes, and in some cases offered lessons myself (English and Yoga). I also conducted semi-structured interviews with both headmasters, teachers and students. Finally, I collected data more widely through semi-structured interviews, group conversations and casual interactions with Senegalese migrants and their children in non-school settings in both Senegal and the US.

[7] I chose New York as a field site because many of the migrants' children I encountered in Senegal came from there.

[8] In this case, it is usually mothers who take the initiative of sending them back because they are overwhelmed by straddling childcare and work obligations.

itself.'[9] Scholars of Islam 'study the "real" Islam in its countries of origin', leaving the study of 'hybrid forms of Islam as they are reshaped through migration' to scholars from other disciplinary horizons.[10] Bava traces this divide back to the long-standing – now highly criticized – tradition within Islamic studies of distinguishing between '"learned, scriptural, orthodox Islam"' and 'local expressions of the religion, described as "vestiges of the pre-Islamic age"'.[11]

These overarching trends notwithstanding, a growing number of Islamic studies scholars explore today how Muslim migrants to the Western world seek to ensure the religious education of their children.[12] Importantly, these studies bring to light how questions of 'belonging' and 'identity' in minority situations are negotiated through Islamic schooling. Mandaville, writing about Islamic schools in Britain,[13] for example posits that 'education has emerged as a primary space in which fundamental questions about the societal inclusion and belonging of minority communities are negotiated'. Similarly, Zine notes about Islamic schools in Canada that '[i]t is within the nexus of resisting cultural assimilation and engaging cultural survival that the need for Islamic schools emerges'.[14]

While this literature offers valuable insights on how young members of the diaspora develop their religious selves, very little has been said within this body of literature about young diaspora members of African origin and their educational trajectories. What is more, the heavy focus on identity formation has to some extent obscured other dynamics. As Bava remarks insightfully, religion is not only relevant for identity formation. It 'is also objectively and/or symbolically constitutive of migratory paths themselves. In fact, religion is not only a burden or a resource (material and spiritual), or a value in which migrants in exile can take refuge. It actually generates specific trajectories.'[15]

[9] Sophie Bava, 'Migration-Religion Studies in France: Evolving Toward a Religious Anthropology of Movement', *Annual Review of Anthropology*, 2011, 497.

[10] Bava, 'Migration-Religion Studies in France', 497–8.

[11] Bava, 'Migration-Religion Studies in France', 498, quoting Sossie Andezian, *Expériences du divin dans l'Algérie contemporaine: Adeptes des saints dans la région de Tlemcen* (Paris: CNRS, 2001) 18.

[12] Yvonne Yazbeck Haddad; Farid Senzai; Jane I. Smith, *Educating the Muslims of America* (Oxford and New York: Oxford University Press, 2009); Peter G. Mandaville, *Global Political Islam* (London and New York: Routledge, 2007); Jasmin Zine, *Canadian Islamic Schools* (Toronto: University of Toronto Press, 2008).

[13] Mandaville, *Global Political Islam*, 226.

[14] Jasmin Zine, 'Safe havens or religious "ghettos"? Narratives of Islamic schooling in Canada', *Race Ethnicity and Education*, 10, 1, 2007, 71–92.

[15] Bava, 'Migration-Religion Studies in France', 501.

This is particularly true for Islamic education. Migration and mobility are long-standing themes in emic narratives about Islamic learning. Given the scarcity of scholars in the early days of Islam, in many places, acquiring religious knowledge necessitated moving away from home to live with a renowned scholar in one of the emerging centres of learning.[16] In large parts of West Africa, peripatetic traditions have survived to this day. Islamic boarding schools (both 'modern' and 'classical') are popular with many Muslim parents, who justify their school choices by arguing that a child cannot learn well within the comfort of home, and that religious maturation requires leaving behind old routines and familiar faces.[17]

In the present-day Muslim diaspora, too, acquiring religious knowledge may make it necessary to relocate. Migrants from several West African countries, including Senegal, The Gambia, Mauritania, Guinea, and Mali, are known to be sending their children 'back'[18] to their home country for the sake of religious education.[19] Of course, migrants' children travel back to the homeland not only for religious study. A growing body of literature documents how children are being sent back to their parents' homelands for 'disciplining', to protect them from what are considered to be the morally corrupting or outright physically dangerous

[16] Ousmane Kane, *Beyond Timbuktu.*

[17] See for example Hannah Hoechner, *Quranic Schools in Northern Nigeria: everyday experiences of youth, faith, and poverty* (Cambridge: Cambridge University Press, 2018); Ware, *The Walking Qur'an.*

[18] R. King; A. Christou, 'Of Counter-Diaspora and Reverse Transnationalism: Return Mobilities to and from the Ancestral Homeland', *Mobilities*, 6, 4, 2011, 451–66 write aptly that '[i]n many respects, second-generation returnees are first-generation immigrants in their homelands'. Being sent back can mean for some second-generation children going to a country they have never been to and that they know only indirectly from their parents' tales, or phone calls with relatives there.

[19] See for example Ousmane Kane, *The Homeland is the Arena* (Oxford: Oxford University Press, 2011) on Senegalese migrant families in the US; P. Kea, 'Photography and Technologies of Care: Migrants in Britain and their children in the Gambia', in J. Cole; C. Groes (eds.), *Affective Circuits. African migrations to Europe and the pursuit of social regenerations* (London: University of Chicago Press, 2016) on Gambian migrant families in the UK; É. Razy, 'De quelques "retours Soninké" aux différents âges de la vie. Circulations entre la France et le Mali', *Journal Des Anthropologues,* 2006 and É. Razy, 'La famille dispersée (France/Pays Soninké, Mali). Une configuration pluriparentale oubliée?', *L'Autre*, 11, 3, 2010 on Malian Soniké migrant families in France.

influences of Western society,[20] to prevent school failure[21] or, finally, to free up their parents' time to work.[22]

Even when Muslim diaspora children travel to the homeland for reasons other than religious education, their 'returns' may implicate Islamic schools. Religious school enrolment may provide a solution to concerns that extend well beyond purely religious matters. For example, Islamic schools may be sought out for their disciplinary function,[23] even by parents who are not particularly strictly practising Muslims. Also, as many Islamic schools provide boarding facilities, they are an attractive option for parents who send their children back for one reason or another, but don't want to entrust them to relatives for the duration of their stay (see below). The following pages introduce the Senegalese diaspora before reflecting on the ways in which it has become involved in the (Islamic) education sector in Senegal.

The Senegalese Diaspora and Demands for Homeland Education in New York

Senegal looks back on a long history of emigration. Until the mid-1970s, other African countries and France were the major destinations of Senegalese migrants. Yet, this has changed in the wake of tighter immigration controls in France and political instability and economic crisis in some of the African destination countries. New migration destinations have emerged, which include southern Europe (Italy and Spain) and the United States.[24]

[20] See C.H. Bledsoe; P. Sow, 'Back to Africa: Second chances for the children of West African immigrants', *Journal of Marriage and Family*, 73, 4, 2011, 747–62 on children sent 'back' to various parts of West Africa; see also M. Timera, 'Righteous or rebellious? Social trajectory of Sahelian youth in France', in D. Bryceson; U. Vuorela (eds.), *The Transnational Family. New European frontiers and global networks* (Oxford: Berg, 2002) 147–54.

[21] See H. Dia, 'Pratiques de scolarisation de jeunes Français au Sénégal. La construction de l'excellence par le pays des "ancêtres"', *Cahiers d'études Africaines*, 1, 221, 2016, 199–218 on children sent from France to Senegal.

[22] See A. Grysole, 'Private school investments and inequalities: Negotiating the future in transnational Dakar', *Africa*, 88, 4, 2018 on Senegalese migrants in the US and Italy.

[23] See M. Last, 'Children and the Experience of Violence: Contrasting Cultures of Punishment in Northern Nigeria', *Africa: Journal of the International African Institute*, 70, 3, 2000, 359–93.

[24] S.M. Tall, 'La migration internationale sénégalaise : des recrutements de main-d'oeuvre aux pirogues', in M.-C. Diop (ed.), *Le Sénégal des migrations. Mobilités, identités et sociétés* (Paris: Karthala, 2008) 37–67.

Reliable data on the total number of Senegalese international migrants[25] (let alone of their foreign-born children) do not exist, and estimates vary widely.[26] The World Bank puts the total number of Senegalese emigrants at around 636,200, or 4.9 per cent of the population in 2010.[27] As a corollary, we do not know the exact number of Senegalese migrants in the United States either. According to the American Community Survey, just over 21,000 Senegalese lived in the US in 2011–13.[28] Given that many Senegalese migrants are unauthorized in the US, this figure clearly underestimates the real number. Kanté,[29] for example, estimates that around 110,000 Senegalese live on the East Coast alone, and some 25,000 in New York. Kane estimates that at least two-thirds of Senegalese migrants in the US are men.[30] While the educational and socio-economic profiles of Senegalese migrants in the US are fairly diverse, including both university graduates and so-called *modou-modous* without any formal education, most work in professions for which no formal diplomas are required. According to Kane, the top three professions Senegalese are engaged in in New York are selling and driving (for men), and hair braiding (for women).[31] However, the professional profiles of Senegalese have diversified substantially over recent decades. This is particularly true for the 'second' and '1.5th' generations,[32] which are far more likely to have attended high school and college in the US than their parents.

Senegalese in 'home' and 'host' countries have maintained close and continuing relations, as evidenced for example by the high volume of remittances

[25] Commonly defined as persons who have spent at least the past year outside the country in which they were born.

[26] See for example P.D. Fall, 'Des francenabé aux modou-modou: géographie de la migration internationale des sénégalais', PhD diss., Université Cheikh Anta Diop, Dakar, 2013.

[27] World Bank, *Migration and Remittances Factbook 2011* (Washington, DC: World Bank, 2011) 217; see also Aymar Narodar Some, *Migration au Sénégal: Profil National 2009* (Geneva: International Organization for Migration, 2009) 52 seq.

[28] American Fact Finder, 'Selected Population Profile in the United States: 2011–2013 American Community Survey 3-Year Estimates', American Community Survey 2013, http://factfinder.census.gov/faces/tableservices/jsf/pages/productview.xhtml?pid=ACS_13_3YR_S0201&prodType=table.

[29] S. Kanté, 'Les Sénégalais émigrent aussi vers les États-Unis', *Population & Avenir*, 4, 689, 2008.

[30] Kane, *The Homeland Is the Arena*, 77.

[31] Kane, *The Homeland Is the Arena*, 79.

[32] The term '1.5 generation' has been coined to refer to young people who have been born in the 'homeland', but have spent their 'formative' years in the country of immigration (King; Christou, 'Of Counter-Diaspora and Reverse Transnationalism', 459).

Senegalese send home.[33] According to the World Migration and Remittances Factbook, remittances accounted for 10.3 per cent of GDP in 2014, or US$ 1.6bn in 2015.[34] The proximity between migrants and people who have stayed behind finds its expression also in the practice of sending children back to Senegal for their education. This section explores the reasons underpinning this practice among Senegalese migrants in New York. Various social and economic pressures push parents there to send children back to Senegal. In addition, young people are believed to face particular social risks in this context. Finally, parents feel unable to ensure that their children acquire the requisite religious knowledge to withstand these risks.

The costs and opportunity costs of raising children in the US provide the subtext for decisions to send children home. Most Senegalese in the US, both men and women, work full-time to earn enough to both cover the high costs of living in New York and remit money home. Babysitters must be paid for children too young to stay by themselves. Older children create significant expenses because parents need to rent apartments big enough to accommodate everyone (including separate bedrooms for boys and girls).

Family breakups also occasion children's return to Senegal. Marriages are extremely fragile in a context where both spouses work long hours outside the home. This triggers conflicts about the distribution of domestic chores, and about financial responsibility for the household budget.[35] I was told that some people marry 'for convenience' rather than love, given the high prices of rent in New York. Such marriages are unlikely to last long. To raise children as a single parent is even more challenging than raising children within a couple. Such children are particularly likely to be sent back to Senegal.

Many of the parents I interviewed were afraid of 'losing' their children. Child protection laws forbid the physical punishment of children. Many parents, convinced of the necessity of beating for a child's character formation,[36] disregard this prohibition. If the social services become aware of this, parents ultimately risk having their children taken away from them. With respect to older children/

[33] R. Grillo; B. Riccio, 'Translocal development: Italy–Senegal', *Population, Space and Place*, 10, 2004, 99–111.

[34] World Bank, *Migration and Remittances Factbook 2016* (Washington, DC: World Bank, 2016) 1–232.

[35] See Kane, *Beyond Timbuktu*, 167ff for an extensive discussion of the renegotiation of gender roles and the resulting marital conflicts among Senegalese couples in New York.

[36] See Ware, *The Walking Qur'an* on the reasoning behind physical punishment in Qur'ānic schools in Senegal.

youths, parents are afraid of losing them to gang violence, drugs and delinquency. For girls, protecting their sexuality is a major concern.

Parents, moreover, desire that their children receive a solid religious foundation. Ware has argued that Qur'ānic learning involves not only the acquisition of knowledge of the Qur'ān, usually through memorization, but that it ultimately aims at personal transformation, by way of imitating the comportment of the teacher.[37] Such an approach to Qur'ānic learning is useful to understand the context of the present study where Qur'ānic knowledge is sought after not only for its own sake, but also as a form of protection against the perceived evils of Western society I just mentioned. The difficulties involved in ensuring that children receive an adequate religious training in New York constitute another reason for sending children back to Senegal.

There are a number of full-time private Islamic schools in New York and adjacent New Jersey. Yet, they are not necessarily located in the neighbourhoods where most Senegalese live, which means that the children attending them face lengthy commutes. There is one Islamic school in Manhattan (on the Upper East Side on 96th St), yet none in Harlem, and the only Islamic school operating in the Bronx had to close in 2017 for financial reasons. What is more, private full-time Islamic schools mostly have to charge fees of $400 minimum per month to keep their doors open, which is beyond the financial reach of most migrant families, especially if they have to cater to several children simultaneously.

Whereas full-time Islamic schools are scarce, weekend Qur'ānic schools, mostly located inside mosques and catering to children from several West African countries, are widespread in Harlem and the Bronx. However, frustrations about their limited ability to produce the desired religious sensibilities abound. Teachers complain about their students' indiscipline yet feel that their hands are tied by legal provisions against the physical punishment of children. Also, the time available for religious study is limited: most teachers must carve time for teaching out of a busy work schedule. School attendance and homework take up children's time during weekdays, leaving them free to study their religion basically only on weekends. Teachers doubt their ability to instil Islamic sensibilities during such a small time window. As one teacher put it, 'society is crushing more than you built'.

As indicated in the introduction, young people are being sent back to Senegal at various ages and into a range of different arrangements that include both family homes and boarding schools. Family homes are likely to be considered preferable for very young children (and most boarding schools don't accept them), and many migrants would like their children to know their Senegalese relatives. Yet,

[37] Ware, *The Walking Qur'an.*

there are also downsides to leaving children with family members. It may open the door to 'excessive' demands for money, and it may mean having to haggle over the use made of remitted money. I also heard complaints about grandparents overly 'spoiling' their grandchildren.[38] Finally, supervision is a concern. Adults in Senegal don't usually survey a child's every movement, and often children disappear with their peers for entire afternoons. This may leave migrant parents with the feeling that their children's education is taken care of by the street, and that the close supervision of a boarding school may yield better results. Finally, for girls, extended family settings may be perceived as insufficient protection of their sexuality.[39]

Quantitative studies evaluating what percentage of all young people are sent back to their homeland at some point during their childhood and youth are few and far between. A survey carried out in France finds that 16 per cent of children of sub-Saharan African parents have spent over one year abroad before their eighteenth birthday, whereas the average among all immigrant children is 5 per cent.[40] Unfortunately, this survey does not provide country-specific statistics. A study carried out among Gambians in Girona, Spain, found that almost one-third of children had been sent back to Africa for a significant amount of time.[41] I don't have any quantitative data to evaluate what percentage of all young people are sent back from New York to Senegal, and into what kind of arrangement they are sent. Given the lack of reliable statistics on the number of Senegalese international migrants, estimating the total number of sent-back children is even greater guesswork. However, we have reason to believe that this number is quite significant, given the very high rent prices there and the (perceived) concentration of problems affecting youths (such as gang violence and drug trafficking). New Yorkers made up a significant portion of the migrants' children I encountered in the schools I visited in Senegal. The next sections explore these educational institutions in more depth.

[38] C. Coe, *The Scattered Family. Parenting, African Migrants, and Global Inequality* (Chicago and London: University of Chicago Press, 2014) 76.

[39] C. Coe, 'Child circulation and West African migrations', in C. Ni Laoire; A. White; T. Skelton (eds.), *Movement, Mobilities, and Journeys* (Singapore: Springer Science+Business, 2017) 401.

[40] A. Grysole; C. Beauchemin, 'Les allers-retours des enfants de l'immigration subsaharienne: "Les filles ou les garçons d'abord"?', *Migrations Société*, 3, 2013.

[41] Bonet i Farjas 2002, cited in Bledsoe; Sow, 'Back to Africa', 749.

The Topography of the Educational Landscape in Dakar in Senegal

Migrants' children can be found in all schools deemed to be of quality in Dakar, including in Qur'ānic schools (*daaras* and *daaras modernes*) and so-called *franco-arabe* schools (which combine instruction in religious and secular subjects), and in private secular schools (*écoles laïques*), and private Catholic schools (*écoles privées catholiques*). This section briefly introduces these different schools, discussing to what extent they meet the demands of migrants' parents before outlining some of the persistent misgivings about them.

Qur'ānic schools or *daaras*, which focus on memorization of the Qur'ān as well as on character training, often in a very deprived study environment, were for a long time the foremost educational institutions in the region. So-called *daaras modernes*, which have emerged over the last decades, resemble the classical *daaras* in their emphasis on Qur'ānic memorization, but seek to provide a somewhat more comfortable or salubrious study environment.[42] Most such schools charge fees (of the order of 30,000–60,000 FCFA per month, c. €45–90), not least to be able to afford the provision of food and hygiene facilities. Like the classical *daaras*, many *daaras modernes* accept students as boarders. In particular, the slightly more 'comfortable' *daaras modernes* in Dakar receive significant numbers of migrant children.

Next, there are so-called *franco-arabe* schools, which have been set up since the mid-twentieth century, and especially from the 1980s onwards, in an impetus to address the shortcomings of the classical Qur'ānic schools. These schools emphasize Arabic language tuition, offer lessons in several Islamic subjects, and often include secular subjects.[43] They are widespread today in Senegal, especially in urban areas. Many of them offer boarding facilities, which makes them particularly attractive for some migrant parents. In Dakar, where I conducted fieldwork in 2016, several *franco-arabe* schools received significant numbers of migrants' children.[44]

42 See for example J.É. Charlier, 'Les écoles au Sénégal: de l'enseignement officiel au daara, les modèles et leurs répliques', *Cahiers de La Recherche Sur l'education et Les Savoirs*, 3, 2004, 35–53.

43 Muslims from various ends of the religious spectrum, including Muslims from within the Sufi and 'reformist' Muslims, including so-called *arabisants*, returnees from study stays in the Arab countries, have opened *franco-arabe* schools. See Cheikh Anta Babou, 'The al-Azhar School Network: A Murid Experiment in Islamic Modernism', in Robert Launay (ed.), *Islamic education in Africa. Writing boards and blackboards* (Bloomington: Indiana University Press, 2016) 173–94; Ware, *The Walking Qur'an.*

44 Particularly popular were the school of Mariama Niasse at Patte d'Oie (which also includes a boarding section; its association with the Niassène branch of the Tijāniyya

Finally, there are numerous secular education options. Since the reputation of the public education system is overwhelmingly poor (see for example Charlier, 'Les écoles au Sénégal'), few parents enrol their children in it if they can also afford private education.[45] Yet, various private schools offer secular education modelled after the French system today (*écoles laïques*). There are also several private Catholic schools (*écoles privées catholiques*), which are reputed to provide the best-quality non-Islamic education today. In Dakar, migrants' children can be found in very much all Catholic and private secular schools with a decent reputation.[46]

While the schools described so far all receive significant numbers of migrants' children, and notably young people who have spent several years schooling outside Senegal, they don't always produce satisfactory results. As regards the *daaras* or Qur'ānic schools, migrant parents are arguably increasingly aware of the difficulties young people without any formal education are likely to face upon their return to the United States, which discourages them from schooling their children exclusively in Qur'ānic schools. This is valid also for migrants who themselves have received only a Qur'ānic education. The founder of an English–French bilingual school in Dakar,[47] which is very popular among migrants, for example, told me that some parents approached him with regrets about having enrolled their children in a *daara*:

> At some point, they realise the kid is not speaking any French, is not speaking any English anymore, he's not doing any academic work, and then they say: ok, what will my kid get from this? Will he have a *bac* [equivalent of A-levels]? Will he have a BFEM [*Brevet de Fin d'Études Moyennes*, equivalent of middle school leaving certificate]? Will he attend college? At that trend, he will not attend college. So he'll be like me. Do I want that? No.[48]

Yet, parents may opt to enrol their children in a *daara* hoping that a stint in this sobering environment might either, in the case of older children/youths, bring

---

Sufi order notwithstanding, it is a popular choice also among parents with other religious affiliations), and the schools of *Maison de la Sagesse/Darou Hiqma* (Castor and Boulevard Bourguiba), which pursue a 'reformist' agenda. *Darou Hiqma* also has a boarding school.

45 Given the very varied levels of economic success of Senegalese international migrants, admittedly some migrant parents may not be able to afford private education for their children.

46 I visited, among others, Notre Dame du Cape Vert, Practiciens, and École Seydou Nourou Tall in Pikine, Immaculée Conception and St Michel on the Plateau, and College Cardinal Hyacinthe Thiadoum in Grand Yoff.

47 See below.

48 Interview with Sidy Cissé, co-director of the Dakar Success Academy, 10 October 2016.

them back to the 'straight and narrow', or, in the case of younger children, help them memorize a significant portion of the Qur'ān in a relatively short period of time and achieve the concomitant character transformation discussed above. Migrants' children may also attend Qur'ānic school during weekends and secular school holidays.

Alas, the integration of these young people does not always work smoothly. Children who return to Senegal at an older age may lack fluency in Wolof (which is the language of communication in most *daaras*) and, with the exception of children returning from France, most speak hardly any French,[49] which makes their integration into French and *franco-arabe* schools difficult. What is more, such children have usually become accustomed to the behavioural expectations of Western school settings (where beatings for example are forbidden, and where students are encouraged to be assertive and outspoken rather than demure vis-à-vis their teachers), which can cause frustration for both children and teachers. I heard parents in the US voice concern about the judgement their US-raised children would likely be exposed to in Senegal for behaving as they did in the US – and indeed, in Senegal, I frequently heard deprecating comments about 'American' children's presumed lack of manners and respect.[50] What is more, confronted with 'problem youths' raised on the streets of American inner cities, teachers accustomed to Senegal-raised students might be out of their depth. I met several youths, for example, who had been beaten up in the classical *daaras* or *franco-arabe* schools they had been sent to for 'disciplining'. Rather than making them see 'reason', this experience confirmed them in their oppositional attitude. In some cases, Western-raised youths end up boycotting schools they dislike, so as to prove their parents 'wrong' for sending them to these schools.

Finally, there is the question of learning or maintaining one's English. Even from good private French schools, students rarely graduate with sufficient mastery of the English language to directly attend college in the US.[51] Even students who have spent their high school years in the US don't necessarily acquire enough English to do well in college admission tests like the SAT (Scholastic Ability Test), which means that they are limited to second-rate colleges.

49 While most of the migrants' children I met in New York understood Wolof, most answered back in English when spoken to. Finally, apart from children attending the New York French American Charter School (NYFACS), most children did not learn any French in the United States.

50 US-raised children, for example, often neglect the extensive greetings people in Senegal regard as an essential sign of respect.

51 Students have to take ESL (English as a Second Language) classes before enrolling in college.

A New Market Niche

In Dakar, educational entrepreneurs have acknowledged the demand for English-language schooling and responded accordingly. Starting in the 1990s and gathering pace over the last decade, numerous so-called 'bilingual' schools, which promise education in both English and French, have opened in the Senegalese capital. They cater not only to Senegalese migrants, but also to the growing international community living in Dakar and staffing the offices of the various international organisations and NGOs located there. 'Bilingual' schools are also sought after by better-off transnationally oriented Senegalese families who expect their children to acquire English in anticipation of future transnational mobility.[52] The bilingual schools I visited in Dakar all confirmed that migrants were one of their primary target groups.[53] Several headmasters in Dakar told me that they advertise their schools via personal contacts and Senegalese 'community radios' in the US. Over half of the students at Dakar Success Academy were children of Senegalese migrants to the US in 2015/16.[54] At the Senegalese American Bilingual School (SABS), migrants' children make up some 30 per cent.[55]

Finally, the most recent innovation on the education market are English–French 'bilingual' Islamic schools, which 'feeds two birds with one scone', as it were, offering both religious instruction and an English–French bilingual curriculum. At the time of my research, there was IQRA Bilingual Academy (IQRABA) at Point E, which I mentioned in the introduction to this chapter, IBAD – Islamic Bilingual Academy Dakar (offering crèche, preschool, and elementary) on the Plateau,[56] and a third school, NIA – Noor International Academy in Mermoz,[57] with a similar profile had just been opened, with fourteen students, by a former IQRABA teacher. Both headmasters I interviewed were confident that their schools would grow – or continue to grow – quickly. The trajectory of IQRABA justifies this optimism. The school had opened in 2010 with 20 students. At the time of my research some six years later, it counted already almost 300 students, and faced

[52] These schools charge fees from 60,000 FCFA (c. €90) upwards.

[53] These included SABS (Senegalese American Bilingual School, https://www.sabseducation.org/), Dakar Success Academy (http://www.dakarsuccessacademy.com/), International Bilingual School (http://www.ibsdakar.org/) and WACA (West African College of the Atlantic, http://www.waca-school.com/).

[54] Interview with Sidy Cissé, co-director of the Dakar Success Academy, 10 October 2016.

[55] Interview with Saliou Ndaw, vice director of SABS, 26 August 2016.

[56] http://www.ibadacademy.com/ The acronym IBAD means 'worship' in Arabic. Despite several emails, various phone calls and a visit, the director was unfortunately not available for interview.

[57] http://noorinternationalacademy.org/ The acronym NIA means 'intention' in Arabic.

space constraints. Since my departure from Dakar, the school has acquired a new building and further expanded.

IQRA Bilingual Academy

What is the recipe for success of IQRA Bilingual Academy? It took seriously a demand that had not been served previously. Prior to the opening of IQRABA, no Islamic school existed with an explicitly international orientation and commitment to prepare its students for college admission in the Western world[58] – despite the presence of a considerable stratum of religiously minded 'cosmopolitans' who were clearly dissatisfied with having to choose between either a *daara* or *franco-arabe* school or a secular international/'bilingual' school. The founder of IQRABA, a black American Muslim woman from Brooklyn married to a Senegalese man, explained the dilemma she faced herself as a mother with cosmopolitan aspirations for her own children as she was trying to raise them in Senegal:

> My husband and I decided not to place our children in a traditional *daara* where they may have little to no exposure to technology or the English language. Of course we really want them to know and practice their *deen*, but we also want their academic profile to propel them towards their collegiate and professional aspirations on an international scale.[59]

According to the founder of the school, not only parents had been waiting for a school of this type to open, but also Senegalese teachers who had gained teaching experience in the West:

> Even Senegalese teachers who wanted to come back have acquired an education, pedagogy, and methodology that doesn't necessarily thrive within the French system all the time … now they have more options. They can teach in the bilingual schools and have an easier time applying the knowledge and skills they learned abroad.[60]

58 The school of Mariama Niasse is very 'cosmopolitan' in the sense that it attracts students from Niassène families from across West Africa (Kane, *Beyond Timbuktu*). Yet, while its graduates are perfectly francophone, they do not learn English to the same level as their age mates at IQRABA.

59 Email exchange with Mme Nieshaakema James-Sarr, director of IQRABA, 11 February 2018.

60 Email exchange with Mme Nieshaakema James-Sarr, director of IQRABA, 11 February 2018.

And indeed, many if not most of the teachers at IQRABA were themselves Senegalese return migrants (from the US and Canada). Many others were international migrants (primarily from Anglophone parts of West Africa, and from the US, including both black and white Americans). I saw similar patterns in the other bilingual schools I visited. Several of these schools have been opened by return migrants themselves.[61] By having lived in the US or other English-speaking countries themselves, teachers had gained the necessary language skills and 'cultural competence' to teach American-raised youngsters.

IQRABA was in 2017 accredited by the Middle States Association of Colleges and Schools (MSA), which means that it can pride itself on meeting United States Department of Education standards. Its high school students prepare for the SAT and ACT (American College Testing), which are the major college admission tests in the US, and according to its founder, graduates have found admission into universities in the US and elsewhere with relative ease. IQRABA has managed to become the official school of the embassies of several Muslim countries (including Egypt, Sudan, Dubai, Saudi Arabia and Qatar), which means many embassy workers enrol their children there. Furthermore, there are children from Senegalese upper-middle and upper-class families in Dakar who can afford the 100,000–200,000 FCFA (c. €150–300) monthly school fees. Finally, a large share of the student population is made up of Senegalese migrants' children, including both young people 'returning' with their parents and young people 'sent back' on their own. According to the founder, about a quarter of its students are in Senegal without their parents. In 2016, the school opened a boarding school with eight students, which has subsequently been growing.

In addition to following American core curriculum standards, as mentioned in the introduction, IQRABA teaches Arabic, Qur'ān (recitation and memorization), and Islamic Studies, a course which covers the basics of Islamic beliefs and worship, Islamic history, and Islamic manners and morals. The school expects female students and teachers to come with their hair covered (the school uniform for girls consists of an ankle-long gown and a headscarf), and daily prayers are performed together by staff and students in the school courtyard.

While the integration of Islam into their daily school life is likely to be new, especially to students from the US, in many ways, the school seeks to establish continuity with its students' prior and likely future experiences in the US. Beating is strictly prohibited, for example.[62] The school organizes spelling bees and school sleepovers, echoing American cultural practices. The cafeteria serves

[61] The 'Dakar Success Academy' mentioned earlier, for example, was opened by the former president of the Association des Sénégalais d'Amérique, Dr Fallou Gueye, and his friend Sidy Cissé, also a returnee from the United States.

[62] Albeit, not all the school's teachers and parents think this is a wise idea.

pizza and hotdogs (alternating with typical Senegalese dishes) to meet the tastes of American-raised kids. Basketball rather than football dominates the lunch breaks.[63] Instead of offering a panoply of subjects as prescribed by the Senegalese curriculum (students typically study up to eighteen simultaneously), the secular curriculum consists 'only' of Maths, Science, History, English, French, and Physical Education, as is common in the US. (Except French, all subjects are taught in English.) A time slot is also reserved for extracurricular activities, and, besides the yoga classes I offered, students could sign up, for example, for basketball, cooking lessons, and art classes. As one can imagine, the environment of the school described here is very different from 'typical' Senegalese Islamic schools, with students – rather than copying quietly from the blackboard – interrupting their teachers repeatedly with questions about anything and everything, prompting teachers to sigh about the irreverence and impetuousness of returnee students, as indicated in the opening vignette.

While having lived in the West themselves meant that teachers could better gauge their students' likely previous experiences, the school showed little tolerance for 'Western' behaviours that were considered un-Islamic. For example, there were recurrent conflicts over hair. Many of the American-raised male youths let their hair grow into fashionable hairstyles and clashed over this with the school administration, which insisted on short hair. Listening to rap music was another contentious issue. During the weekly whole school assembly, the head *Oustaz* (Islamic teacher) emphasized on several occasions the sinful nature of smoking and drug use, and highlighted that Islam encouraged respectful behaviour towards one's elders and parents.

While its strict Islamic discipline is one of IQRABA's main selling points, it is also in a way its weakness, at least as far as middle and high school are concerned. The founder confided to me that while the elementary school was booming,

> our challenge is middle school, high school. Because IQRA is not a school … that you as a child would … naturally gravitate towards in your teenage years. We're not gonna be partying … you're not gonna have any relationships … So it's something that your parents put you here … [Once the students are enrolled at IQRA], they're trying to be here on their best behaviour … so that they can say: see, we're good, now, can we go back to the States or can we leave IQRA?[64]

[63] Arguably, other expensive private schools in Dakar also serve 'junk food' for lunch and encourage basketball rather than football, reflecting a certain 'Americanization' of Senegalese middle/upper-class eating habits on the one hand, and an attempt to distinguish oneself from Senegalese 'popular culture' on the other hand. I am grateful to Amélie Grysole for drawing my attention to this fact.

[64] Interview with Mme Nieshaakema James-Sarr, director of IQRABA, 15 August 2016.

The high fees also push parents to put their children into cheaper schools as soon as they observe an improvement in the latter's behaviour. Many youths stay no more than two or three years at IQRABA. On the upside, IQRA is very good at making even recalcitrant teenagers 'calm down', not least because their behaviour does not easily ruffle the Brooklyn-raised director.[65] As one of the students explained to me, she had understood very well that in the beginning, youths who were brought back to Senegal against their will did anything and everything to get expelled from school. She would just wait, and eventually even the most wayward youths would calm down and change their strategy, 'doing good' instead and hoping that this might eventually earn them a plane ticket back to the US.

Despite the challenges IQRABA may be facing, its quick rise to success has clearly left a trace on the education market. Two of the non-Islamic 'bilingual' schools, for example, considered adding Arabic classes to their curriculum at the time of my fieldwork, both to meet parents' demands, and to stay competitive.

Conclusion

A growing body of literature investigates today the dynamics underpinning change in Islamic educational practices on the African continent. This chapter has made a case for studying an agent of change that has received astonishingly little attention to date: the African Muslim diaspora. Drawing on data collected among Senegalese migrants in New York and in schools, including Islamic schools, receiving migrants' children in Dakar in Senegal, this chapter has illustrated how diaspora demands for homeland education have triggered transformations within the Islamic educational landscape in Senegal. Migrants, including Senegalese return migrants, have been at the forefront of these transformations, which have resulted, among other things, in the opening of a new type of school in Senegal which is both Islamic and international in orientation.

Yet, arguably, the opening of new schools is only the tip of the iceberg: other transformations within the Islamic educational landscape are less easily perceptible. We may, for example, think of the ways in which the presence of migrants' children has affected Islamic educational institutions (notably *daaras* and *franco-arabe* schools) that weren't targeting them in the first place. How does the presence of diaspora children influence the schooling experiences of other children? Does it trigger new migration aspirations? Or does it 'educate' local children, parents, and teachers about the potentially 'harmful' social and religious implications of migration to the West, for example because diaspora children may be seen

[65] Among the students were youths who had been expelled from other Islamic schools because of their unruly behaviour.

to lag behind in terms of their prior religious knowledge, their (local) language skills or their behaviour?

Finally, diaspora demands for Islamic schooling may affect the religious educational landscapes of their 'home countries' remotely. Several of the migrants I met in the US had engaged Qur'ānic teachers in Senegal who taught their children the Qur'ān via Skype/WhatsApp. This opens up a market niche for technology-savvy Islamic scholars in Senegal, while making Qur'ānic lessons easier to slot into the busy days of diaspora families.

In the current context of growing Islamophobia and increasingly aggressive secularism in Western countries, many immigrant parents in the West are hard-pressed to bring up their children as practising and self-respecting Muslims. It would not come as a surprise if Muslim homelands were to gain in importance in the future as places to educate diaspora children. This chapter has provided a first exploration of this issue, while indicating at the same time the many questions that remain open.

CHAPTER 13

What does Traditional Islamic Education Mean? Examples from Nouakchott's Contemporary Female Learning Circles[1]

Britta Frede

> Umm al Quraa is like a time capsule – it's easy to forget which century you're in sometimes, as very little resembles modern life. For those that want a glimpse of the conditions the Prophet Muḥammad and his companions lived in, you won't come closer than this. In Mauritania, I met people whose hearts were alive, vigorously beating with faith, which invigorated their limbs, allowing them to wake up early in the mornings to worship and study late into the night with torches to illuminate their books.[2]

Umm al-Qura is a village around 60km east of Nouakchott, the capital of Mauritania. This village has achieved international fame due to its *maḥḍara*, an institution for transmitting Islamic knowledge that ties in the tradition of an Islamic learning circle (*ḥalqa*). Its fame was based on the work and appeal of Shaykh Muḥammad Sālim b. ʿAddūd (ʿAbd al-Wadūd; 1929–2009), who was considered among the most learned scholars (*ʿulamāʾ*) of twentieth-century Mauritania, especially in the field of Mālikī jurisprudence (*fiqh*), Arabic language (*lugha*), grammar (*naḥw*), poetry (*shiʿr*), and the biography of the Prophet Muḥammad (*sīra*). Looking at one of the short biographical notes published after

[1] I would like to thank the members of research section 'learning' from the Africa Multiple Cluster of Excellence at the University of Bayreuth, funded by the Deutsche Forschungsgemeinschaft (DFG, German Research Foundation) under Germany's Excellence Strategy – EXC 2052/1 – 390713894 for commenting on and discussing my draft. The debate and comments helped to improve the text.

[2] Omar Shahid, 'Why I left Britain to live in an Islamic State', 2 March 2016, https://omarshahid.co.uk/2016/03/02/why-i-left-britain-to-fight-jihad-in-an-islamic-state/. Accessed 4 July 2020.

his death in April 2009,[3] we see that *maḥḍara* education in post-independent Mauritania allowed him to enter influential posts within state institutions.

Shaykh Muḥammad Sālim b. ʿAddūd was born in 1929 during French colonial rule and trained in the *maḥḍara* of his father, al-Jalīl Muḥammad ʿĀlī b. ʿAddūd (ʿAbd al-Wadūd). Coming from a well-known prestigious scholarly family, he developed himself into a famous scholar, jurist, and teacher. The first teaching position he held was during the 1950s at the Maʿhad Būtilimīt al-Islāmī, the first and only successful French *medersa*[4] in the colony of Mauritania, which had been founded in 1918 and introduced new teaching methods and a modified curriculum into the *maḥḍara* institution. However, during his later life, he was a director of an internationally frequented *maḥḍara* in Umm al-Qura. But scholarly activities were not his only occupations: he was also very much involved in contemporary politics and designing post-independence Mauritania, especially the relationship between religious institutions and the state. He held the position of the head of the Supreme Court (*maḥkamat al-ʿālīya*) between 1982 and 1988, then from 1988 to 1991 he was appointed as minister of culture and Islamic orientation (*wizārat ath-thaqāfa wa l-irshad al-islāmīya*), as well as being the head of Mauritania's Supreme Islamic Council from 1992 to 1997.

The example of Shaikh Muḥammad Sālim b. ʿAddūd illustrates that, more often than not, it was the people trained in these *maḥḍara* institutions who were later involved in forming and developing state facilities with the aim of giving the government control over Islamic institutions in the country. He was not the only person with such a profile. Others included: ʿAbdallāhi b. Būyā (b. 1935), high commissioner for Islamic affairs during the presidency of Ould Daddah (1924–2003; 1961–78) and ideological father of Mauritanian Islamic socialism; and Issilmū b. Sīdī al-Muṣṭafā (b. 1948), who was minister of culture and

[3] Islamweb, 'Wafāt al-'Allāma Muḥammad Sālim 'Addūd', *islamweb.net*: *tarīkh wa-ḥadāra*, 29 April 2009, http://articles.islamweb.net/media/index.php?page=article&lang=A&id=151027. Accessed 4 July 2020.

[4] The French term *medersa* needs to be distinguished from the Arabic term madrasa. The French *medersa* was an institution that was developed and introduced by the French colonial administration with the aim of reaching out with their *mission civilisatrice* to Muslim elite families. These schools were a kind of integrated school, combining the curriculum of colonial schools with the ones used in Islamic educational institutions, like a madrasa or a *ḥalqa*. For more about the principles of French *medersa*, see Christopher Harrison, *France and Islam in West Africa, 1860–1960* (Cambridge: Cambridge University Press, 1988) 63–7; Louis Brenner, *Controlling Knowledge. Religion, Power, and Schooling in a West African Muslim Society* (London: Hurst & Company, 2000) 41–54; Rudolph T. Ware III, *The Walking Qur'an: Islamic Education, Embodied Knowledge, and History in West Africa* (Chapel Hill: University of North Carolina Press, 2014) 163–202.

Islamic orientation (1998–2003) and the first director of the Islamic University in Nouakchott (ISERI).[5] All these personalities started their training in the *maḥḍara,* some later continuing with various kinds of Islamic educational institutions within Mauritania or in Saudi Arabia. Such examples impressively demonstrate that being trained in a *maḥḍara* by no means excluded people from joining national elite positions. Further, we learn that diplomas from state educational institutions were not the only way to start a prestigious career in the post-independence western Saharan state. These cases illustrate that in Mauritania, contrary to other former African colonies, Muslim traditional schooling remained valued during the twentieth century and continued to coexist and compete with state education.

The questions that arise are about the consequences of the continuation of *maḥḍara* education alongside state education. I will look at aspects of how these different regimes affected each other in what was, to a certain extent, a competitive interaction. In the following sections, I shed light on these issues through the lens of female adult learning in the capital Nouakchott, where more and more students enrol in state schools and universities while, at the same time, the number and visibility of *maḥḍara* institutions focusing on transmitting Islamic knowledge to adult women is steadily rising.[6] While most of the studies on Islamic education focus on children, I am especially interested in adult education given that this is a good setting to demonstrate the shifts, mutual entanglements, and transformations that happen in knowledge transmission. I argue that, to some extent, these transformations concern the curriculum itself, but to a much broader extent they also concern the techniques of learning and the performance of knowledge transmission. In the end, such technical and performative renewals might result in an epistemological change of knowledge. Launay has emphasized in his recent collected volume that the dichotomy of writing boards (*lawḥ*) and blackboards signifies symbolically the two competing knowledge regimes that are grounded in different epistemologies and that are shaped by distinguishable performances of knowledge.[7] I will present selections of my findings, based on three short field research stays between 2012 and 2014 in Nouakchott, in the field of traditional female learning among Ḥassānīyaphone as well as Pulaarophone women.

[5] Ursel Clausen, *Islam und nationale Religionspolitik: das Fallbeispiel Mauretanien* (Hamburg: 2005) 6–10, https://www.liportal.de/fileadmin/user_upload/oeffentlich/Mauretanien/Islam_und_Religionspolitik_Mauretanien.pdf. Accessed 4 July 2020.

[6] Britta Frede, 'Following in the Steps of 'Ā'isha: Hassaniyya Speaking Tijānī Women as Spiritual Guides (*muqaddamāt*) and Teaching Islamic Scholars (*limrābuṭāt*) in Mauritania', *Islamic Africa*, 5, 2, 2014, 225–73, 255.

[7] Robert Launay (ed.), *Islamic Education in Africa. Writing Boards and Blackboards* (Bloomington: Indiana University Press, 2016) 21–3.

A Brief History of Encountering: *Maḥḍara* and State Education

State schools were introduced in Mauritania in two stages, the first being in the southern part populated predominantly by Wolofophone, Pulaarophone and Soninkophone people. Here, the French followed the strategies they used in other parts of sub-Saharan Africa and tried to destroy already existing institutions of Islamic education and to replace them with colonial schools that better suited their goals.[8] French was the language of instruction and local languages were not taught at all. However, for the Saharan regions of the country, colonial schools were introduced much later and followed the Algerian model by introducing French-Arabic *medersa* schools and leaving the nomads with their *maḥḍara*.[9] Colonial tent schools for the Ḥassānīyaphone nomads were introduced only during the 1950s, ten years before independence, and rarely completely covered the primary education sector.[10] During colonial times, Muslim families were generally hesitant to send their children to colonial schools.[11] They were perceived as 'Christian' (*naṣrānī*) institutions even if the French had developed laic principles for their school curriculum. The introduction of the *medersa* did not remove their reluctance: despite the *medersa* school in Boutilimit, these institutions turned out not to attract enough students.

In post-independence Mauritania, state schools became more and more accepted, first for boys, and then eventually also for girls during the 1980s. However, Mauritania's state schools suffered from significant structural problems from the start. The quality in the primary sector was poor as the teacher to pupil

[8] Ibrahima Abou Sall, *Mauritanie du Sud. Conquêtes et administration coloniales françaises 1890–1945* (Paris: Karthala, 2007) 664–5.

[9] Harrison, *France and Islam*, 57–67; Britta Frede, *Die Erneuerung der Tiǧānīya in Mauretanien. Popularisierung religiöser Ideen in der Kolonialzeit*, ZMO Studien, 31 (Berlin: Schwarz-Verlag, 2014) 225–7; Marc Lenoble, 'Les premières écoles de campement en Mauritanie', in Edmond Bernus; Pierre Boilley; Jean Clauzel; Jean-Louis Triaud (eds.), *Nomades et commandants: Administration et sociétés nomades dans l'ancienne* A.O.F. (Paris: Karthala, 1993) 139–44.

[10] Frede, *Erneuerung der Tiǧānīya*, 456.

[11] Yahya Ould el-Bara, 'Les théologiens mauritaniens face au colonialisme française. Etude de fatwa-s de jurisprudence musulmane', in David Robinson; Jean-Louis Triaud (eds.), *Le temps des marabouts. Itinéraires et stratégies islamiques en Afrique occidentale française v. 1880–1960* (Paris: Karthala, 1997) 85–117; Yahya Ould el-Bara, 'Les réponses et les fatâwâ des érudits Bidân face à l'occupation de la Mauritanie', in Mariella Villasante Cervello; Christophe de Beauvais (eds.), *Colonisation et héritages actuels au Sahara et au Sahel*, vol. 2 (Paris: L'Harmattan, 2007) 155–92; al-Khalīl an-Naḥwī, *Bilād Šinqīṭ. al-Manāra wa r-ribāṭ* (Tunis: al-Munaẓama l-'Arabīya li-t-Tarbiya wa th-Thaqāfa wa l-'Ulūm, 1987) 346–70.

ratio rose due to population growth and an increased take-up of schooling.[12] The state had failed to produce enough teachers, so they instead started to integrate *maḥḍara* teachers into the state system to respond to the quickly rising demand for staff. Furthermore, in 1978, three years before the first state university was founded, the ISERI was created to integrate *maḥḍara* students within the state administration.[13] Zekeria Ould Ahmed Salem describes the hegemony between both educational regimes, highlighting the prominent role of *maḥḍara* education in post-independence Mauritania as follows:

> L'éducation religieuse reste ainsi au cœur de la vie familiale et éducative, ainsi que des politiques de construction nationale, d'émergence d'un sujet moral et d'élaboration collective d'une éthique publique. Alors que les madrasas au Maroc ont été reléguées dans 'une mémoire collective néanmoins valorisée', en Mauritanie elles vont être au centre de la séquence postcoloniale de la formation de l'État.[14]
>
> [Religious education thus remains at the heart of family and educational life, as well as of policies for national construction, the development of moral individuals and the collective development of a public ethic. While the madrasas in Morocco have been relegated to 'a collective memory which is nonetheless valued', in Mauritania they will be at the centre of the postcolonial sequence of state formation.]

The administrative rules that the Mauritanian government introduced to integrate students from the *maḥḍara* institutions into state positions were remarkable and might be one of the main reasons why *maḥḍara* education was not automatically marginalized, replaced by reformed institutions, or sought re-traditionalization as in numerous other Muslim communities throughout the later twentieth century. There is no doubt that such a prominent role for traditional education is special in the contemporary world, however, we need to critically question what effects this has had on the tradition itself. Does the traditional knowledge regime remain what it was or is it, nevertheless, being transformed along a reforming path shaped by state schools because of the coexistence of diverse knowledge conceptions and the competition between such institutions producing knowledge?

12 Michael Hirth, *Traditionelle Bildung und Erziehung in Mauretanien. Zum entwicklungspolitischen Potential der maurischen mahadra* (Frankfurt: Peter Lang, 1991) 60–70.

13 Zekeria Ould Ahmed Salem, *Prêcher dans le désert. Islam politique et changement social en Mauritanie* (Paris: Karthala, 2013) 73.

14 Ould Ahmed Salem, *Prêcher dans le désert*, 74.

A Brief Remark about the Term 'Traditional'

While Launay criticizes the usage of the term 'traditional' in this context as describing static and non-dynamic patterns, preferring to replace it with the term 'classical', I would like to argue against this and keep the term traditional.[15] It is true that we do find various academic publications in which the term was used exactly in the way Launay criticizes: a term that describes static practice combined with the negative view of belonging to a primitive African-ness that was not capable of understanding the complex dimensions of the more civilized practice in the Muslim Mediterranean. However, I do not understand why we should get rid of a term because it was used by various authors in an approach of normative presumptions. Instead, I would like to emphasize the multilayered reflection done by other authors calling for a more conscious use of the term. If understood in this way, the term traditional turns out in the end to be quite a useful descriptive term. As I will illustrate, the understanding of a practice or institution as traditional is not as an unchanged entity but rather one that undergoes transformations while claiming continuity. The classification as traditional in this sense, despite all its claims for unchanged continuities, is not resisting change but is formed by dynamic interactions of transmitted values, ideas, and ways of doing something from the past and understanding of achieving, selecting, and praising values, ideas, and practice in the present. Understood that way, the term traditional describes a multilayered phenomenon, the pretension of stable continuities while being constantly within a process of dynamic transformation. The term classical in contrast, at least to my understanding, refers to a specific historical period in which certain practices and a compendium of texts have been established, but does not hint at the double face value contained in the term traditional as a kind of transformative doing while claiming continuous repetition.

Further, the reference to a traditional institution goes along with labelling an institution or a practice as authentic. This is the point where the notion of a static concept becomes most prominent since traditional practice is often understood as connecting to a specific historical moment that becomes preserved and carries on unchanged into the present. However, such a claim to be practising (an unchanged) authentic tradition might not hold true when examined historically. A traditional institution or practice that is labelled as authentic is always somehow invented because adaption to contemporary needs and demands brings in change.[16] This is true to the time when a tradition has been founded as well as to its transmission from one generation of tradition-keeper to the next. Such a process of transmission

[15] Launay, *Islamic Education*, 3.

[16] Eric Hobsbawm; Terence Ranger (eds), *The Invention of Tradition* (New York: Cambridge University Press, 1983).

is best understood as mediation, in which a specific moment in a historical and/or mythical past is mediated into different social realities of the present. Kazmi distinguishes, in this sense, between a normative and an ontological understanding of the term tradition.[17] While the normative understanding, inspired by thinkers of the enlightenment period, highlights the dichotomy of tradition versus modernity, the ontological understanding inspired by Heidegger and Gadamer allows us to highlight the transformative character of tradition by emphasizing the multiple clusters of conversation between the past, the present, and the future that come along with the preservation of tradition.[18] In this sense, a tradition is in an ongoing process of transformation.

The close relation between tradition and authenticity also becomes obvious when looking at the epigraph at the beginning of this chapter. The author claims that if you want to get a glimpse of the realities in which the Prophet once lived and taught, go to Mauritania, and there you will be closest to the authentic Muslim community. Obviously, for this author, the *maḥḍara* as a traditional institution works especially well as it successfully mediates the reality of the Prophet into the present. We need to keep in mind that the *maḥḍara* has been developing in the Western Sahara into the form as we know it today since the seventeenth century. Therefore, it is a specific Western Saharan tradition that claims its roots in the early Islamic period. It further predates colonial and post-independence educational institutions in the country. This reference to an earlier origin than the state schools is reflected by the Arabic term *taʿlīm al-ʿaṣlī* (original teaching) that is used in national political debates to describe the teaching in *maḥḍara* institutions.[19]

A claim of authenticity for the traditional education is very much welcomed by Mauritanian scholars as they have been propagating such an image for a long time throughout the Islamic world.[20] Being a highly mobile scholarly elite,

[17] Yedullah Kazmi, 'Islamic Education: Traditional Education or Education of Tradition?', *Islamic Studies*, 42, 2, 2003, 259–88, 261, 269.

[18] Kazmi, *Islamic Education*, 279.

[19] The Arabic term *taqlīdī*, which corresponds closely to the English term traditional, also embeds an ambiguous controversy among Muslim scholars, especially since scholars from the eighteenth-century *Ahl-i Ḥadīth* movement attacked the term *taqlīd* understood as following a certain Sunni school of law (*madhhab*) as an unallowed innovation (*bidʿa*). The term is rarely used by Mauritanian Muslim scholars when describing the *maḥḍara*. Nevertheless, an-Naḥwī (*Bilād Šinqīṭ*, e.g. 445), for example, categorizes the *maḥḍara* education explicitly as *tarbiya taqlīdīya* (traditional education). Further, in international political contexts when using French we frequently read the term *éducation traditionelle* (traditional education) referring to *maḥḍara* education in policy papers.

[20] See for example, Chouki El Hamel, *La vie intellectuelle islamique dans le Sahel ouest-africain, XVIe–XIXe siècles: une étude sociale de l'enseignement islamique*

Mauritanian scholars have frequently explained their home education to their host communities in diverse texts, proving that they are well-trained Muslim scholars and, in more recent times, even successfully advertising a kind of study 'tourism' for Western, North African, and Gulf Muslims to come and attend Mauritanian *maḥḍara* institutions. In this sense, the term traditional suits very well, especially if read in a more Weberian sense.[21] Weber defines traditional rule as rooted in a divine sphere. The same is true for Islamic traditional education as it starts with the divine word of the holy book, the Qur'ān, that was mediated to mankind through the Prophet and signs the beginning of all knowledge. As Ware points out, the Qur'ān in traditional education is not studied for the meaning at first hand, but to incorporate the divine text as a beginning and requirement for studying the text and its meaning.[22] Such incorporation best comes about by connecting back to the original moment when God transmitted this knowledge to humankind: the mediation of the Qur'ān by the Prophet.

Therefore, the recreation of the era of the Prophet's time plays prominently into the knowledge transmission process. Seesemann has interpreted this cross-temporal connectivity as being firmly embedded within the teaching of the Mālikī tradition that 'should not be taken simply to refer to a school of jurisprudence but to describe a specific approach to reenacting the *Sunna*, the example of the Prophet'.[23] In this sense as well, *maḥḍara* education is traditional since it refers to the divine root of knowledge. Despite the changes of teaching methodologies and performance of knowledge transmission and authority within the institutions, the texts taught within Mauritanian traditional institutions have not yet been replaced by reformed textbooks. Most of the *maḥḍara* institutions still teach the curriculum as former generations did: a locally produced didactic literature that has been derived from ninth- and tenth-century texts, written mainly by Andalusian and North African authors.[24] Even in this sense, the *maḥḍara* institutions are traditional and maybe classical at the same time.

---

en Mauritanie et au nord du Mali, XVIe-XIXe siècles (trans. 'Fatḥ al-šakūr' by al-Bartīlī al-Walātī (mort en 1805) (Paris: L'Harmattan, 2002); or Aḥmad b. al-Amīn al-Shinqiṭī, *al-Wasīṭ fī tarājim 'udabā' Shinqīṭ: kalām 'alā tilka l-bilād taḥdīdan wa taḥṭīṭan wa 'ādātuhum wa akhlāquhum wa mā ta'laqu bi-dhālika* (Nouakchott: Mu'assasat Munīr, 1989).

21 Max Weber, *Wirtschaft und Gesellschaft: Grundriss der verstehenden Soziologie* (Frankfurt a.M, Zweitausendeins, 2005), part 1, chap. 3.

22 Ware, *Walking Qur'an.*

23 Rüdiger Seesemann, 'Embodied Knowledge and The Walking Qur'an: Lessons for the Study of Islam and Africa (Review)', *Journal of Africana Religions*, 3, 2, 2015, 201–9, 203.

24 Mohamed Lahbib Nouhi; C.C. Stewart, 'The Maḥaẓra Educational System', in

Maḥḍara Education and State Education in Mauritania: the Most Significant Features

Most people born in Mauritania after 1970 went to state schools at least for primary education. It is hard to believe that such experiences of different knowledge regimes would not affect traditional education per se. The teacher's role is more as a mediator of divine knowledge to the student. Islamic knowledge is transmitted and mediated by a person but not taught as an abstract object. Therefore, we need to consider the student's role as well. The moment students are exposed to state education with its own knowledge regime, the teacher as mediator must respond to these diverse experiences of his audience. Even if in Mauritania, traditional education did not become devalued to the same extent as in other Muslim societies, state education is nevertheless widely spread. As both educational regimes propagate a distinctive approach to knowledge, it is only natural that we will find a mutual transformation that might produce hybrid knowledge conceptions.

What is it that differentiates *maḥḍara* education from state education? I will try to briefly sketch in the following paragraph the main differences in the methodology of learning and its performance. While the writing board stands emblematically for traditional education, the blackboard is the significant tool for state education. However, today some *maḥḍara* institutions will use the blackboard as well, and the writing boards disappear from use once a student has successfully embodied the Qur'ānic text. The difference of the performance and the means of discipline that are always an aspect of educational formation can be clearly seen in a documentary of 1970.[25] In it we visit a nomadic camp and the film describes all kinds of life-cycle rituals as well as the school. The camp of this nomadic group has a Qur'ānic school and a state school in their tents. We can see that even in early post-independence Mauritania, state education reached the countryside as well, at least for primary education.

Qur'ān lessons in this documentary are performed mainly by naked kids.[26] They gather closely in a half circle before the teacher where everybody busily recites with a loud voice his own Qur'ānic verse. Everyone follows his own rhythm and speed. The teacher holds up the stick as a symbol of corporal discipline and the pain of incorporating the divine text. He shows nearly no emotions but punishes from time to time by tearing the ear of a student or gently using the

---

Charles C. Stewart (ed.), *Arabic Literature of Africa, Vol. 5: The Writings of Mauritania and the Western Sahara*, 1 (Leiden: Brill, 2016) 18–50.

25 Jean-Luc Magneron, 'Les fils des nuages', Office de Radiodiffusion télévision française, 25 November 1970.

26 During the 1970s, it was still a local custom not to dress children before their milk teeth were replaced – and it is mainly at this early age that children study the Qur'ān.

stick if someone does not sit properly or makes some mistakes in their recitation. It is a special gift to be able to listen to so many students at the same time, picking up on any and all mistakes, then offering correction until every student in his own speed of learning has succeeded with one part after the other of the Qur'ān.

After this scene, the documentary switches to the state school. It starts by gathering all kids for lessons in front of the tent. Every pupil is dressed in proper clothes and lines up for entering the class by holding the other's shoulder. They go into the tent and sit down on the ground in lines. Each student holds a small blackboard in his hand, the teacher a slightly bigger one. They do some maths. The results of the exercises need to be noted down on each student's blackboard and everybody, including the teacher, holds up their blackboard with the result inscribed. Every student is quiet, only speaking up if the teacher invites one or more students to do so. Otherwise, it is only the teacher talking and asking questions. After the accounting exercises, a poem concerning maths is recited. A couple of students present a bodily performance in front of the class. With this the scenes of children's schooling ends.

The very brief descriptions of both educational regimes already give some idea of the differences in performance of transmission and approaches toward knowledge. The idea of discipline obviously shifts from corporal discipline to a new order of human interactional conduct and spatial organization. The individual aspect of Qur'ānic teaching that allows each student to progress at their own speed and to succeed in their own capabilities alongside their own cognitive abilities differs substantially from the cohort-focused transmission of knowledge in state schools, where all students go through the same training at a similar speed, remaining quiet while the teacher or another student speaks. The order of sitting is completely different, as students sit in rows, everybody has his own place, and the teacher stands in front. Therefore, the performance of authority differs as well. While the teacher of the Qur'ān school was hiding gestures of emotion, the teacher in the math class articulates the poem performance together with the kids.

Women and the *Maḥḍara*

Unlike children's education, the courses for adult women offered in *maḥḍara* institutions do not strictly follow a certain curriculum compared to the ones that train pupils to prepare them for adult life. In these institutions, students will be involved full time, and the aim is to prepare them for their future tasks either as *imām*, *ʿālim*, *faqīh* or preacher and the like; or parents might choose an integrative institution that combines knowledge disciplines common in state schools that will prepare them for the general wage labour market as well. Most of these full-time *maḥḍara* education settings will be dominated by boys, especially from the intermediate level on. Girls who study to the level of a fully-fleshed *ʿālima* are a tiny minority and might study more in private homes than by following *maḥḍara* sessions. However, the *maḥḍara* was never limited to boys only.[27] In general, any age, gender, or social group is invited to join the sessions. This explains why *maḥḍara* institutions differ tremendously in the level of the courses they offer, especially for their adult public.

Even though *maḥḍara* education is generally open to anybody, one must consider the social and gender-specific obstacles that hinder certain people from following the *maḥḍara* education for a long period. Such obstacles arise for women, as I outlined earlier, especially due to their obligations for child-bearing and household tasks in combination with their dependence on the goodwill of their male family members.[28] Women, therefore, continue to face serious obstacles in developing into Islamic scholars. Nevertheless, women scholars have been found in Mauritania since the later eighteenth century, the overwhelming majority, just like their male counterparts, having grown up in scholarly families.[29] This does not seem to have changed in traditional Islamic education in the twenty-first century.

The knowledge that is transmitted in these sessions for women concerns the same texts that men study in various Islamic disciplines such as the Qur'ān, *sīra*, *tajwīd* (elocutions concerning the recitation of the Qur'ān), *fiqh*, *ḥadīth* (accounts of speech and action of the Prophet Muḥammad) and *tafsīr* (explanation of the Qur'ān). However, most of the texts taught in the courses are at the introductory level. Qur'ānic recitation can form an important part of the curriculum. While the complete memorizing of the divine text might not be the first aim, the proper utterance of the Qur'ānic word is trained since the ability to recite is considered to be something valuable that deepens your spirituality and will bring benefit to you and your listeners. Interestingly the discipline of *sīra*, the history of the life of the Prophet and his companions, was never formalized as a proper discipline in the Middle Eastern madrasa institutes, but is in the *maḥḍara* institutions of Mauritania. It holds an especially prominent place in the curriculum in the women's sessions that I studied. Furthermore, numerous female scholars stated to me that *sīra* is a field of knowledge in which Mauritanian women are often well versed and are prominently present in the field of teaching for children, men, and women alike.

The women I interviewed between 2012 and 2014 were from different ethnic backgrounds, ages, and educational backgrounds. Their female *maḥḍara* institutions differed in size, level of teaching, and the social background of their

[27] an-Naḥwī, *Bilād Šinqīṭ*, 288–90.

[28] Frede, 'Following in the Steps of 'Ā'isha', 239.

[29] Britta Frede, 'Arabic Manuscripts of the Western Sahara: Trying to Frame an African Literary Tradition', *Journal of Islamic Manuscripts*, 8, 1, 2017, 57–84, 76–8.

students. When I started looking for them, I asked around among educated pious families I knew from previous research in Mauritania and went on to mosques in different town districts asking the local *imām* if he knew of women teaching adult women in his neighbourhood. It took a while, but I was able to find several women, meeting some of them only once while others several times. I conducted interviews about the biographical background of these women and I asked questions about teaching methods, their understanding of knowledge, etc. For most of the women, I participated at least once in their lessons (*dars*) in order to get a proper idea about what their teaching looked like and the social composition of their audience.

Any Kind of Learning is a *Maḥḍara:* from Khadja Dia to Mariyam as-Sālma Mint Limrābuṭ aṭ-Ṭulba

As I already mentioned, for most of the people I talked to, any kind of traditional learning in Mauritania is considered as *maḥḍara*. Therefore, what is offered under this label differs tremendously and one needs to decide how to choose an appropriate institution for studying Islamic knowledge. In Mauritania, when I asked many scholars how to find a good teacher they emphasized that, if you want to study *ʿilm*, it doesn't matter which doctrinal orientation the teacher is following, but you should choose the one who is strongest in his discipline. As for the women's education courses offered in the *maḥḍara*, they generally remain at an introductory level. Therefore, the capacity of the teacher in a certain discipline might not be the first reason for choosing that teacher. Teachers, even in the urban context of Nouakchott, are often chosen from the community one belongs to.

Neighbourhoods in Nouakchott tend to be homogenous.[30] Families from certain lineages or ethnic groups who originate from the same region often settle close by. Furthermore, families that originate from the same village and belong to the same extended family often stay in contact even if living far from each other. A teacher is often chosen through these contacts, be it either neighbourhood or family alliances. Family alliances seem to be especially important among women coming from families with a scholarly background. In social enivronments where there are a significant number of female teachers present in a town, there is a choice, and we find quite high mobility among these urban women, who also develop a strong relationship with their teacher and their learning circle. In social environments that do not produce a significant number of female teachers, the choice among these women remains small and they will normally go to the teacher in their neighbourhood. I will now present two examples that emphasize these

[30] Amselle Choplin, *Nouakchott: Au carrefour de la Mauritanie et du monde* (Paris: Khartala, 2009) 140–3.

different choice modes. The first female learning circle is guided by Khadja Dia, a Pulaarophone teacher with deep Arabic training who teaches in a poor neighbourhood on the outskirts of Nouakchott. The second example is at the opposite social range of possible learning circles, that is Mariyam as-Sālma's institution that teaches women from her home region who already have a deep elementary training in Islamic education from a young age.

Khadja Dia (b. 1965) – Dia's family originates from Bogué and she is from a well-known Pulaar scholarly family. Her grandfather was the seventh *almami* of Bogué and specialized in prophetic medicine (*ṭibb an-nabawī*). Her father moved to Tidjikja to the Ḥassānīyaphone scholar Muḥammad Maḥmūd Ould Ṣāliḥī and studied the Qur'ān with him. Then, he continued studying in Moudjéria, where she was born. She studied along with her father, but never received a licence (*ijāzā*) in any discipline. She speaks Ḥassānīya fluently and reads Arabic. She even studied in the state school for a year and has learned some French. However, her father was a well-respected scholar who studied with several Ḥassānīyaphone scholars in the Tagant region, where she profited from the scholarly environment. Still, direct access to the text was not permitted to her, and she has said that this was only possible for men. Nevertheless, she started teaching at the age of twenty (1985) when her first child was born. She moved to Nouakchott around 1997. Her learning circle has around fifteen students and during holidays the group can even rise up to twenty-five. The teaching is free for the women of her neighbourhood. It is a very poor neighbourhood, however those that can give whatever they can afford.[31]

The teaching practice follows the traditional path. Students come to her private house twice a week after Maghreb prayers. They gather in a circle in the courtyard and read some elementary books. Khadja does not sit on a special carpet or at any other particular place like we often see in some of the learning sessions, but she sits within the circle. Khadja states that most of her students had never received any Islamic education before. She mentions that some of them did not even know how to pray when they first started coming. She teaches them some verses from the Qur'ān and then starts with al-Akhḍarī talking about the principles of *fiqh* concerning ritual purity. She reads the text in Arabic from a textbook and then explains it in Pulaar. At the end of the session, some students will read a few verses that were read during the previous session. Some will read in Arabic and then explain in Pulaar, others will only describe the text in Pulaar. Khadja does not systematically teach them how to write and to read. She uses a textbook to present the text they will study; a wooden board (*lawḥ*) is not used within the sessions. Despite the existence of a textbook, the knowledge is transmitted and achieved

[31] Khadja Dia, interview with author, Nouakchott, March 2012.

orally. Reading and writing skills are not part of the knowledge transmission. The focus is on enabling these women to acquire the elementary knowledge necessary for performing their ritual obligations, not to train them systematically in the disciplines of Islamic education.

Mariyam as-Sālma bt. aṭ-Ṭulba (b. 1955) – The *maḥḍara* of Mariyam as-Sālma was founded 1975, when she was only twenty years old and still living in Baraina, a village in south-western Mauritania (Trarza, Gible). Baraina is a village of Idaw ʻAlī, a lineage famous for their engagement in Islamic knowledge and their activities in spreading the Sufi movement Tijānīya in Mauritania.[32] Mariyam as-Sālma is the daughter of the Hāfiẓī *khalīfa* Limrābuṭ aṭ-Ṭulba (d. 1989) who represented the Ḥāfiẓiyya branch of the Tijānīya in Mauritania from 1957 to 1989.[33] She is therefore of the classical Sufi *ʿulamāʾ* milieu. She completed her education under local well-known Islamic scholars: Arabic grammar (*naḥw*) with Bābā Ould Fettan and Aḥmaddū Ould Limrābuṭ; and Islamic jurisprudence (*fiqh*) and the life of the Prophet and his companions (*sīra*) with Bāh Ould ʻAbdallāh, who is considered to be one of the best contemporary scholars of the region and who runs a *maḥḍara* with an international reputation in Noubaghia, another Tijānī-dominated village of the Idaw ʻAlī. She holds a licence (*ijāza*), which formally allows her to teach.[34]

In 1990, Mariyam as-Sālma moved to Nouakchott because she wanted her daughters to get their higher state education in the capital. Mariyam as-Sālma has even written on different topics, which can be bought as small booklets in the market. Her *maḥḍara* is situated in a specific building close to her private house, lessons are given daily during the morning (around 8.00 a.m. to 12.30 p.m.) and in the evening hours (around 5.00 p.m. to 7.00 p.m.). Her school is called *Maḥḍarat al-ummahāt al-muʾminīn li-taʿlīm nisāʾ wa abnāʾ al-muslimīn al-muhimm min ʿulūm ad-dīn.*[35] In Nouakchott she teaches women from the age of twenty-five onwards. Some of them live close by the school, others travel daily from districts further away. They mostly originate from Trarza and Tijānī families. She has more than thirty female students who come regularly to her lessons. She teaches grammar (*naḥw*), the life of the Prophet and his companions (*sīra*) and Islamic jurisprudence (*fiqh*). The school year in Nouakchott lasts from October to June, just like in the state schools. During the summer break, she returns home to

[32] Frede, *Erneuerung der Tiğānīya*, 80, 84–90, 461–81.

[33] Frede, *Erneuerung der Tiğānīya*, 378.

[34] Mariyam as-Sālma Mint Limrābuṭ aṭ-Ṭulba, interview with author, Nouakchott, Feb. 2012. For more about the regional particularities of *maḥḍara* education in Trarza, see Corinne Fortier, 'Une pédagogie coranique: Modes de transmission des savoirs islamiques (Mauritanie)', *Cahiers d'Etudes Africaines*, 169–170, 1–2, 2003, 235–60.

[35] English translation: *Maḥḍara* of the mothers of believer for the teaching of women and sons of Muslims the important things of the religious disciplines.

her village Baraina, where she teaches people in the village. While in Nouakchott, she doesn't have male students, whereas in Baraina she frequently does.

The morning lessons in her *maḥḍara* in Nouakchott start with training in reciting the Qur'ān. This is taught by her best students. Mariyam as-Sālma only personally assists the lessons from 11.00 a.m. onwards. The lessons always start with a recitation of a Qur'ānic verse, which was discussed the day before. She then continues reading the next verses, explaining their meaning. After finishing the Qur'ānic reading, she will start with a lesson in one of her specialized disciplines. Her best students are learning the Qur'ān by heart and are even memorizing and reading the poetry that is used as the base of the different subjects of study. Even here, the wooden board is not used for the transmission of knowledge. Some women have textbooks, others only learn by listening. Mariyam as-Sālma reads verses of mostly locally written didactic poetry (*naẓm*) and then continues to explain the content. While the poetry is written in standard Arabic (*fuṣḥā*), the explanations are given in the local dialect of Ḥassānīya. Classical Arabic words and expressions used in the recited text will be explained first before she turns to the overall meaning of the complete verse. Her method of teaching can thus be seen as a traditional method practised for generations in the Mauritanian *maḥḍara* system. New technologies of teaching are not implemented. In a corner of the classroom, there is a blackboard but Mariyam as-Sālma does not use it for her lessons. Only her students teaching the Qur'ān and recitation sometimes use it to explain the rules of pronunciation. The students participate in Mariyam as-Sālma's lessons to different degrees. Some use a notebook to write something down, some have small booklets with the printed poetry, but most sit in the circle, listen, and ask questions from time to time or add remarks on what Mariyam as-Sālma has said. From the thirty to forty students who attend the lesson, maybe three to five can be seen as being extraordinarily engaged, trying to reach a certain level so that in future they might be able to take over some teaching themselves.

The strict combination of reading the Qur'ān at the beginning of each lesson and completing the whole text during one year of schooling emphasizes the importance of the book on which Islamic knowledge is based. Sometimes the lesson is followed by a *madḥ* session (praising of the Prophet). Not everybody stays and participation is voluntary and based on individual capabilities. The same goes for the funding of the *maḥḍara* in which women circulate a box during the lesson and everyone gives what she can. Most of the female students are housewives and family duties come first. However, the number of regular attenders seems to be quite high, at least for the lessons of Mariyam as-Sālma, the room filling up with students quickly. They know each other well since most of their families originate from Trarza and the Tijānī milieu. Even though the *maḥḍara* is principally open to everybody, the participating students are from common *bīḍān*, *zwāyā*, and *tijānī* backgrounds of south-western Mauritania sharing a common socialization.

Competing with Contemporary Means of Learning: Mariyam Mint Maḥanḍ

While the first two examples demonstrate the variety of knowledge levels captured by the term *maḥḍara*, the third example illustrates how the diverse educational experiences of students and teachers alike initiate modifications of the learning procedure. I will talk about a mother and her daughter who direct the *Maḥḍarat at-tarbawiya li-ta'līm al-mar'a bi-l-manāhij al-'aṣrīya*[36] located in Dar Na'im. The *maḥḍara* of 'Ā'ishatu bt. Mukhtār b. Ḥāmidun is a state-registered school but categorized as a Qur'ānic school. In the school they offer Qur'ānic teaching to children and women during the mornings and afternoons. Twice a week at 5.30 p.m. they teach courses in *tajwīd* and *fiqh* (jurisprudence) for women only. These courses are offered late in the afternoon to give employed women the opportunity to study.[37] The school was founded by 'Ā'ishatu bt. Mukhtār b. Ḥāmidun in 1983 in Nouhadibou.[38] When 'Ā'ishatu started her teaching activities, she first offered courses in her home. Only later, women started to feel uncomfortable entering houses owned by a man not belonging to their own family and, therefore, they moved the school out of the private house.[39] 'Ā'ishatu taught at the school until 2010. Since then, her youngest daughter Mariyam bt. Maḥanḍ (b. 1976) has replaced her.

'Ā'ishatu was born in Atar into a family of Islamic scholars. Her father was Mukhtār b. Ḥāmidun (1897–1993).[40] Her mother was Mariyam bt. Aḥmad al-Bashīr, who grew up in a famous scholarly family from Chinguetti. 'Ā'ishatu's father and her brother Muḥammadan Mukhtār b. Ḥāmidun (d. 1992) taught her. She was a curious young girl, so she even studied in several *maḥḍara* institutions in the region of Trarza and Tichit. She had a number of female private teachers studying the Qur'ān, *Qurrat al-abṣār*,[41] and *al-Akhḍarī* (comprehensive work for Mālikī jurisprudence). The first *maḥḍara* she studied in was the *maḥḍara*

[36] English translation: Educational *maḥḍara* for teaching women with contemporary methods.

[37] Mariyam bt. Maḥanḍ, interview with author, Nouakchott, February 2012.

[38] *Sīra dhātīya*, a single-page text, handed over to me by Mariyam bt. Maḥanḍ during my first visit to the school. It is divided into three parts: her studies; her writings; her teaching.

[39] Mariyam bt.. Maḥanḍ, interview with author, Nouakchott, February 2012.

[40] An Islamic scholar and historian who authored the Encyclopedia *Mausū'a ḥayāt Mūrītāniyā* which even today is only edited and published in parts. He moved to Medina (Saudi Arabia) in 1982, where he stayed until his death. For more about his work and life, see Ulrich Rebstock, *Maurische Literaturgeschichte*, 2, 822–3, entry 2486 (Würzburg: Ergon Verlag, 2001); Stewart, *Arabic Literature*, 522–7, entry 494.

[41] A poem concerning *sīra* (life of the Prophet and his companions) composed by Abd al-'Azīz b. 'Abd al-Wāḥid al-Lamṭ al-Maknāsī al-Maimūnī (1475–mid-sixteenth century).

of the Ahl Maḥanḍ b. Bābah b. Aʿbaid, where she spent a year studying the *Mukhtaṣar al-Khalīl*, another comprehensive outline of Mālikī jurisprudence. Further, she studied in Boutilimit in the *maḥḍara* of Shaykh Muḥammad ʿAlī b. ʿAbd al-Wadūd (known as ʿAddūd; d. 1982) and at the *maḥḍara* of the famous Mauritanian scholarly family Ahl al-Aufā who are specialized in *ṭibb* (healing). Moreover, she studied in Tichit at the *maḥḍara* of the Ahl Muḥammad b. Aḥmad aṣ-Ṣaghīr specializing in *tajwīd*. During her studies in Boutilimit and Tichit she lived with the family of her maternal aunt, only going to the *maḥḍara* for lessons. Later she studied with her paternal nephews in the *maḥḍara* of the Ahl Maḥanḍ Bābah in Maʿta Moulana (Trarza), further specializing in *fiqh* and *tajwīd*. During her studies at these diverse *maḥḍara* institutions she achieved several licences (*ijāza*), some written, some oral.[42] Written and oral licences are common practice among traditional Islamic scholars in Mauritania. They attest to authoritative transmission of a certain Islamic knowledge and legitimate teaching activities. These licences were not always written on papers. Among well-known scholars, oral licences were enough, because trust was considered as one of the most important principles of teacher–student relations. Written licences would only become important if somebody intended to study outside the scholarly networks of his teachers. Nevertheless, for women it was not taken for granted that written licences would be handed over to them. Some scholars hesitated to give girls or women written licences.[43]

ʿĀʾishatu married at the early age of eleven and is the mother of eight children. Despite her family duties, she did not stop studying the traditional curriculum of the local *maḥḍara* institutions. Her husband moved a lot in the country because he worked for the government, but he always settled close to a well-known *maḥḍara* so that she could continue her studies. She founded her school while living with him in Nouhadibou, although later they had to move to Rosso. During the 1980s they stayed in Mecca and Medina (Saudi Arabia) for several months, hoping to be able to finally settle there after her father had retired to Medina in 1982. She had been collecting her own books in different disciplines of Islamic knowledge since she was young. She wrote several texts on her own in the disciplines of *tajwīd*, *sīra*, the benefits of the Qur'ān and devotional literature, such as the explanations of the names of God. Her texts are not published, because she does not have the means to finance the printing. During her several months in Saudi Arabia, she was continuing to teach among the Ḥassānīyaphone women living there and to study.[44] After her return from Medina, she finally settled in Nouakchott, further continuing her teaching activities. Since then, her school has only moved between

[42] ʿĀʾishatu bt. Ḥāmidun, interview with author, Nouakchott, November 2012.
[43] Umm Kalthūm bt. Anbūja, interview with author, Nouakchott, March 2012.
[44] ʿĀʾishatu bt. Ḥāmidun, interview with author, Nouakchott, November 2012.

different quarters of the town in the districts of Dar Na'im and Toujounine. The students live in different quarters of the town and the majority come from districts like Tevragh Zeina, Arafat, and Dar Na'im.[45] ʿĀʾishatu has been affiliated to a Sufi community of the Qādirīya, but recently changed her affiliation to the Tijānīya after the death of her Qādirī shaykh in 2009.[46]

Her daughter Mariyam bt. Maḥanḍ has since 2010 slowly taken over the teaching activities of ʿĀʾishatu in the disciplines of Islamic jurisprudence (*fiqh*) and recitation (*tajwīd*), and her brother is responsible for the teaching of the Qur'ān and Arabic. Mariyam's own field of specialization is classical Arabic poetry. Beside her teaching activities in the school, she gives private lessons in her field of specialization. Her private students are mostly men. Mariyam went to a state school and, at the same time, she studied the classical Islamic curriculum at home. Since her mother retired from teaching, Mariyam longs to reform her mother's school from within, particularly the didactic teaching methods. She writes important things on the blackboard in front of the room, where she is either sitting on a chair or is standing in front of the students. The students are sitting on the ground but they do not sit in a circle like in the former study circle. Instead, they sit in rows similar to state schools. The texts she teaches are typed in advance on her computer and then copied for the students, so that they can recite and memorize them at home if they want, when preparing next week's lesson. At the beginning of the lesson, the students start reciting the text that Mariyam gave them the week before. Most of the students will read them from their papers and then Mariyam explains the meaning of the text. The texts themselves are the same texts as those taught by her mother, most of them being didactic poetry composed by local scholars since the seventeenth century for teaching *fiqh* and *tajwīd*. In the near future, Mariyam intends to add courses in French and English. She considers foreign languages to be important in our global world. Payments for the *maḥḍara* courses follow a regular fee system, therefore a course in Islamic jurisprudence (*fiqh*) in 2012, for example, would be 3,000 UM (around US$14) per month.[47]

The fact that Mariyam has taken over her mother's school is quite special. Numerous schools disappear when their directing Islamic scholar retires. This might be due to the fact that the *maḥḍara* in general is a semi-institutionalized setting. It is a learning circle very much bound to the personality of the scholar who teaches. If the scholar stops teaching activities, the *maḥḍara* stops as well. Only a few schools have developed into institutions lasting for several generations and are mostly in the footsteps of one family.[48] These institutions are normally in

[45] Mariyam bt. Maḥanḍ, interview with author, Nouakchott, February 2012.
[46] ʿĀʾishatu bt. Ḥāmidun, interview with author, Nouakchott, November 2012.
[47] Mariyam bt. Maḥanḍ, interview with author, Nouakchott, February 2012.
[48] Some of these outstanding *maḥḍara* institutions were founded during the nineteenth

the hands of male scholars. However, Mariyam's attempt to reform the school from within hints at a general trend in Mauritania's traditional education. Reasons for the reform trend are found in the competition between the traditional schools and the private faith-based schools and state schools. Her intention to introduce English and French courses indicates the international demand for Mauritania's traditional Islamic education. Converts or reverts, depending on how you describe those who recently embraced Islam, the increasing number of Muslims from North America and Europe, West Africa, Pakistan, and the Arab world, come to study for a couple of weeks and up to a couple of years in several *maḥḍara* institutions in and outside Nouakchott.

Conclusion

The Mauritanian *maḥḍara* is a traditional institution well embedded within the national identity as part of the cultural heritage that makes Mauritania part of Islamic history. It also proves the authenticity of Islam as practised and lived in the country. Such evidence has been presented to the non-Mauritanian world in several historical moments and documents. This has lasted until today since the *maḥḍara* still attracts lots of attention among all kinds of knowledge seekers within the contemporary Islamicate world from nearly any geographical background. The *maḥḍara* in Mauritania is not only widespread among the Ḥassānīyaphone population, because this educational institution is part of all ethnic groups, be they Pulaarophone, Wolofophone, or Soninkophone. This means it is a real national cultural heritage shared perhaps not by all social groups, but within the traditions of parts of the elite of all ethno-linguistic identities. In post-independence Mauritania, it has become part of a traditional, national cultural heritage. The *maḥḍara* have managed to remain a vivid and important institution beyond the direct control of the government. There has been no state-guided reform that reshaped the curriculum or pedagogical methods within the institution. It remains, until today, based on private initiative and without quality control from state organizations. Consequently, the institution has many different forms and elements concerning the level of education, the level of the student or the teacher, the frequency of lessons, the audience studies are directed at (their age, social status, gender, etc.), the way in which the teacher is financed, and even the site where the lessons are taking place.

---

century and have been mentioned in this chapter, for example *maḥḍara* of the Ahl Maḥanḍ b. Bābah b. Aʿbaid, Ahl al-Aufā, Ahl Muḥammad b. Aḥmad aṣ-Ṣaghīr. More information about the scholarly works of the founding fathers and their sons can be found in Rebstock, *Maurische Literaturgeschichte* and in Stewart, *Arabic Literature*.

Nevertheless, even if the *maḥḍara* is still an institution founded by private initiative without any or only little governmental control, it is recognized as a possible primary and secondary education within the national educational system. This has led to transformations through its competitive encountering with state schools and their pedagogy, curriculum, and conception of knowledge. This is not only true for the *maḥḍara* targeting children and young adults, but also for adult education, as this chapter has illustrated. Because the teacher of the study circle needs to transmit Islamic knowledge to her audience, she needs to adapt to the modes of knowledge transmission and the performance of authority her students understand. In this way, the Mauritanian *maḥḍara* constitutes a traditional institution, although I want to emphasize once more that the term traditional in this context is not understood as opposing 'modern'. The term is established in its ontological interpretation. It contains an important aspect of temporality, in the sense of transmitting ideas and practice from the past to the present. Further, it describes the tension between a pretense of continuity and a transformative doing that is inherent in the process of mediating by the necessity of responding to the needs of the student. The mutual entanglement of a transmitting scholar and an achieving student in producing *maḥḍara* education is an aspect of the transformative process that demands further exploration.

Interviews

ʿĀʾishatu bt. Ḥāmidun, Nouakchott, November 2012
Khadja Dia, Nouakchott, March 2012
Mariyam bt. Maḥanḍ, Nouakchott, February 2012
Mariyam as-Sālma Mint Limrābuṭ aṭ-Ṭulba, Nouakchott, February 2012
Umm Kalthūm bt. Anbūja, Nouakchott, March 2012

PART IV

'AJAMĪ, KNOWLEDGE TRANSMISSION, AND SPIRITUALITY

Introduction

Jeremy Dell

In the ever-growing field of research concerned with the ways the Arabic script has been adapted to the phonetic needs of other languages – or what African Studies scholars have come to call '*'Ajamī*' – the nineteenth century looms large. It is striking how often this period provides the backdrop for the expansion of this particular orthographic practice as a tool of Islamic education. In locations as varied as southern Somalia, Senegambia, and the Kenya coast (the settings of the following three chapters), the fusion of Sufi identity, poetic expression, and *'Ajamī* (lit. 'non-Arab') is paramount. Why?

Together, the chapters in this section begin to provide an answer. In 'Bringing *'Ilm* to the Common People: Sufi Vernacular Poetry and Islamic Education in Brava, c. 1890–1950', Lidwien Kapteijns and Alessandra Vianello describe the emergence of new forms of religious instruction in the port city of Brava on Somalia's southern Benadir coast. Led by the legendary scholar Shaykh 'Uways (1847–1909), Brava's poets used Chimiini, or the 'language of the town', to write didactic verse aimed at educating Brava's entire population in Islamic precepts, regardless of social background. Drawing on not only the broader Islamic scholarly tradition, but also on the more specific networks of the western Indian Ocean that linked Brava to southern Arabia and the Swahili coast, these scholars composed *s̱teenzi*: didactic poems about foundational Islamic concepts (*tawba, taqwa, tawakkul*, etc.) that were deliberately easy to memorize and often recited in public. Such gatherings came to be associated with the Qādiriyya community in Brava, but they were not exclusive to any particular *ṭarīqa*, as shown by the scholar-poet Mallim Nuri's Ahmadiyya affiliation. The most unique *s̱teenzi* author, however, was the female scholar Mana Sitti Habib Jamaladdin, or Dada Masiti (c. 1820–1919), whose life as a celibate female saint drew comparisons to the eighth-century mystic Rābi'a al-'Adawiyya and whose poetry most vividly evoked Brava's local character. She perhaps best exemplifies the intense (and intensely local) religious expression that Kapteijns and Vianello conclude lay at the heart of a new movement for Islamic education of the common people at a time of intensifying European presence in East Africa.

The intensity of Sufi adherence and local poetic production in non-Arabic languages is also captured in Khadim Ndiaye's study 'A Senegalese Sufi Saint and *'Ajamī* Poet: Sëriñ Moor Kayre (1874–1951)'. A member of the first generation of Murid poets to write in Wolof using the Arabic script, or '*Wolofal*' (lit. 'to make Wolof'), Kayre came from a family of Tijanis with roots in the Senegal River Valley region of Fuuta Tooro. He joined the nascent Murid community in his teens, having met its founder Amadu Bamba before the latter's arrest and imprisonment at the hands of the French in 1895, and was later among the few disciples who followed Bamba to Mauritania during his second period of exile in 1907. He remained with Bamba after his return to Senegal, eventually founding a village near the home of Bamba's son and the first caliph of the Murīdiyya, Mamadu Mustafaa Mbàkke. Using recently obtained manuscripts from Kayre's descendants, Ndiaye provides a uniquely detailed window onto Kayre's poetry, offering a counterpoint to the perhaps better-known case of Sëriñ Muusaa Ka (1883–1967), another Murid poet who was Kayre's contemporary and friendly rival. The principal message of Kayre's poetry is one of piety, devotion to one's shaykh, and the sanctity of work, all expressed in intricately metered Wolof verse. While largely universal in approach, he also localizes his work through his use of place names specific to Senegal.

Abdulkadir Hashim's 'Praise and Prestige: the Significance of Elegiac Poetry among Muslim Intellectuals in the Late Twentieth Century Kenya Coast' discusses literary works written in Swahili using the Arabic script. Like Kapteijns and Vianello, Hashim argues that Swahili poetry facilitated a wider distribution of Islamic knowledge beyond the circles of elites often recognized as religious authorities on the Swahili coast. He focuses in particular on elegies as a way of marking the passing of prominent scholars. With reference to Mauss's canonical notion of gift exchange, he argues that elegiac poetry establishes obligations between students and their teachers. The 'Alawiyya scholars based in Lamu are presented as especially prominent promoters of Swahili poetry, though Hashim is careful to note that the composition of such elegies was not restricted to 'Alawi communities. Despite taking his exploration of elegies from the Kenya coast up to the late twentieth century, Hashim traces the oldest surviving examples of written Swahili poetry to the early eighteenth century, with the nineteenth century presented as an especially fertile period in the history of Swahili composition, as evidenced by the careers of scholars like Mwenye Manṣab (1828–1922). Manṣab's student Shaykh Muḥammad ʿAli al-Maʿāwī (d. 1960) taught many of the twentieth century's most prominent Swahili poets in turn. Hashim ends his contribution with a brief consideration of the emergence of 'reformist' scholars on the Kenya coast in the late twentieth century. Often graduates of Islamic universities outside of East Africa, they exist outside of the region's tradition of master–disciple relations, providing what Hashim calls a 'counter-position' to the ʻAlawiyya and at times even composing their poetry in Latin, rather than Arabic, script.

Though a diachronic account of the emergence of *ʻAjamī* across Africa still remains to be written, it is striking how often its expansion can be traced to the late nineteenth century. Whether it was through *s̱teenzi* in Brava, *xasida* in Senegal, or elegies on the Kenyan coast, ʻ*ʻAjamī*ʼ was seen as a powerful tool in the late nineteenth century for expressing foundational Islamic concepts and strengthening the bonds of Sufi identity, suggesting a more general trend beyond the specificities of particular localities. Building on this point, it bears mentioning that this widespread phenomenon was in no way unique to African settings. To cite just one example, Khwaja Ghulam Farid (1845–1901 CE), the most celebrated Sufi poet of the Siraiki language of Pakistan, was active during this same period.[1] Future research in *ʻAjamī* should seek to demonstrate how such parallels are not just the result of individual acts of improvisation, but are embedded in larger social and political contexts that make such creativity possible in the first place.

It is also important to note that while *ʻAjamī* grew in prominence, it did not grow at the expense of Arabic. That *ʻAjamī* texts reached audiences not literate in Arabic is amply illustrated in the following chapters, but these dynamics were rarely so straightforward. For one, *ʻAjamī* was used in all kinds of writing, not only poetry. Correspondence, interlinear glosses and talismanic texts have all been composed in African languages using the Arabic script. One Senegalese scholar, upon finishing a complete commentary on the Qur'ān in Wolof, even stipulated that it should only be read by those who were already literate in Arabic.[2] *ʻAjamī* and Arabic, in short, never had a zero-sum relationship. Both were at play in the sophisticated transmission of Islamic knowledge.

[1] See Jamal J. Elias, ʻSufi Poetry and the Indus Valley: Khwāja Ghulām Farīdʼ, in John Renard (ed.), *Tales of God's Friends: Islamic Hagiography in Translation* (Berkeley: University of California Press, 2009).

[2] See Jeremy Dell, ʻUnbraiding the Qur'an: Wolofal and the *Tafsīr* Tradition of Senegambiaʼ, *Islamic Africa*, 9, 2018, 55–76.

CHAPTER 14

Bringing *'Ilm* to the Common People: Sufi Vernacular Poetry and Islamic Education in Brava, c. 1890–1959

Lidwien Kapteijns and Alessandra Vianello

In the small Indian Ocean port city of Brava, on the southern Benadir coast of Somalia, religious life at the turn of the twentieth century was characterized by the emergence of a new mode of religious instruction, namely Sufi religious poetry composed by Brava's *'ulamā'* in the language of the town (Chimiini or Chimbalazi),[1] a Bantu language related to Swahili with a substantial proportion of Arabic and Somali vocabulary. This kind of emphasis on religious instruction of the common people in their own vernaculars was a regional phenomenon in the period under study[2] and coincided with the establishment (or intensification) of European rule in East Africa.

The Bravanese *'ulamā'* who composed these teaching poems were an integral part of the regional network of religious scholars that connected Brava with Zanzibar, the Swahili coast, the Hadramawt, and the Hijaz (Mecca and Medina). They drew on their wide knowledge of Islamic scholarship and devotional texts in Arabic to fashion concise, vivid, accessible, and easy-to-memorize nuggets of religious instruction in the vernacular for the population of the town of Brava. Drawing from the recently published source publication of Brava's Sufi religious

[1] The vernacular of Brava is commonly called Chimiini by its speakers and we follow that use in this essay. Chi- is a prefix denoting 'language', as in Ki-Swahili, and Miini, or Mwiini, is the name the inhabitants give to their town (which they never call Brava). However, our poets consistently call the language they use 'Chimbalazi', which refers to a more formal and literary form of the language, which has a parallel in the 'Kingozi' language of Swahili poetry (Lyndon Harries, *Swahili Poetry* (Oxford: Clarendon Press, 1962) 14). We have transliterated Bravanese personal names as they are pronounced in Chimiini, and, therefore without Arabic diacritics.

[2] This is the subject of Anne K. Bang, *Sufis and Scholars of the Sea. Family Networks in East Africa, 1860–1925* (London: Routledge, 2014).

poetry in Chimiini,[3] this paper's main focus is on the poems of three Bravanese *'ulamā'*: the female scholar-poet Mana Sitti Habib Jamaladdin or Dada Masiti (c. 1820–1919); the learned and prolific Shaykh Qasim b. Muhyidin al Wa'ili (1882–1922), both affiliated with the Qādiriyya; and Ahmed Nur b. Haji Abdulqadir bin Abdio Hasan, better known as Mallim Nuri (1881–1959), who was affiliated with the Aḥmadiyya.[4] The latter adopted the practice of versified religious instruction in Chimiini later than Shaykh Qasim and Dada Masiti, producing his vast opus in the period between the end of World War I and his death in 1959.

These *s̱teenzi* (as these poems are called in Chimiini) offer insight into how the *'ulamā'* engaged in a particular form of knowledge production and transmission that was meant to influence and transform local religious practice. Apart from the intellectual and didactic dimension of the *'ulamā*'s writings, the *s̱teenzi* also convey something about the lived religious experience of the people of Brava in this time-period, and about how they leveraged orality and writing in all aspects of creating, learning, using, and transmitting this corpus of Islamic learning and devotion.

After a brief description of Brava and its regional context at the turn of the twentieth century, this chapter will first introduce the three poets; then present the *s̱teenzi* as a genre and describe the combination of oral and written techniques their authors and audience used to compose, recite, and transmit them; and, finally, present an analysis of the *s̱teenzi*'s themes.

Early Twentieth-Century Brava in a Regional Context

In the last decade of the nineteenth century, when the *s̱teenzi* emerged, Brava went from having been a peripheral part of the wide-flung dominions of the sultan of Zanzibar (from 1837 onwards) to becoming, in 1893, an early toehold for what was to become the full-fledged Italian colony of Somalia Italiana. In this period, the town of Brava had approximately 5,000 inhabitants, of which the most important groups were the Somali Tunni of the town, who usually had Chimiini as their

[3] Alessandra Vianello; Lidwien Kapteijns; Mohamed M. Kassim (eds.), *'Stringing Coral Beads': The Religious Poetry of Brava (c. 1890–1975): A Source Publication of Chimiini Texts and English Translations* (Leiden: Brill, 2018). It consists of fifty-six poems by six *'ulamā'*-poets. Vianello transcribed the poems from audiocassettes or obtained them in the form of manuscripts (in Arabic or *'Ajamī* script), either 'home-made' or produced on commission by Bravanese copyists. Below we occasionally refer to a manuscript (M) or oral (O) source text. The full list of these is included in the book. Brill allowed us to draw on this book.

[4] For more information, see Sean O'Fahey, *Enigmatic Saint: Ahmad ibn Idris and the Idrisi tradition* (Evanston, IL: Northwestern University Press, 1990). The Aḥmadiyya was also called Idrīsiyya or Āl Aḥmad in Brava.

second language; two groups that traced their (patrilineal) origins to different parts of southern Arabia (the Hatimi and the Bida); several families of Ashrāf who had settled in Brava in the more distant past; more recent immigrants from Arabia; and about 400 slaves, brought from the south and west.[5] That the local Bantu vernacular of Chimiini, shared by all town dwellers, was (and is) unique to Brava and the Bravanese testifies to the town's long history as an autonomous urban community and city-state. For the people of Brava it was, and continues to be, a key feature of their common identity. Given that Chimiini, as a minority language, never received support from any government (colonial or Somali),[6] it was the tenacity with which the Bravanese themselves held on to their language that allowed it to survive. The religious didactic poetry under study here is an expression of such a cultural investment in the language and communal identity of Brava.

Today, as a result of more than twenty-five years of civil war in Somalia, the Chimiini-speaking community has been dispersed all over the world, to diaspora locations extending from Arabia and Europe to the USA, Canada, and Kenya. Since the younger generations no longer use Chimiini as their first language, this unique language, which is believed to have emerged in c. 1100 CE, has been seriously declining.[7]

In Brava, as in other East African coastal towns, the partly overlapping social categories of mercantile class and *'ulamā'* were the backbone of the town's social elite. Historically, Brava was known for two characteristics. It was an important import-export market and a centre of religious learning. *'Ulamā'* of Bravanese origin were famous and held important judgeships all over East Africa.[8] Those

[5] The Ashrāf claimed descent from Prophet Muḥammad through his grandsons Ḥasan and Ḥusayn. Of the three poets studied here, Shaykh Qasim belonged to the Bida; Dada Masiti to the Ashrāf, and Mallim Nuri to Brava's Tunni.

[6] The strong emphasis on Somali as the official language in the early 1970s, also the period during which over 2,000 Somalis affected by drought were resettled in Brava, put further pressure on Chimiini.

[7] The number of Chimiini speakers before the major dispersion of the community in the early 1990s has been estimated at 10,000 to 15,000 (Bana Banafunzi; A. Vianello, 'Chimi:ini in Arabic Script: Examples from Brava Poetry', in Meikal Mumin; Kees Versteegh (eds.), *The Arabic Script in Africa* (Leiden: Brill, 2014) 293–311, 294–5. For the estimated date of the emergence of Chimiini, see Derek Nurse; Thomas Spear, *The Swahili: Reconstructing the History and Language of an African Society, 800–1500* (Philadelphia: University of Pennsylvania Press, 1985) 59; and Derek Nurse; Thomas J. Hinnebusch, *Swahili and Sabaki: A Linguistic History* (Berkeley: University of California Press, 1993) 487.

[8] Examples are Muḥyī al-Dīn b. Shaykh al-Qaḥṭānī and 'Abd al-'Azīz b. 'Abd al-Ghanī al-Amawī. See Alessandra Vianello; Mohamed M. Kassim (eds.), *Servants of the*

resident in Brava taught their advanced students in mosque- and home-based settings, while all Bravanese children (boys and girls) attended Qur'ān schools, which were often taught by women.

Some *'ulamā'* of Brava travelled widely to expand their knowledge, as was the case with the renowned Shaykh Uways (1847–1909), also the teacher and mentor of Shaykh Qasim, under study here. Shaykh Uways was born and educated in Brava, studied in Baghdad and Mecca and, after his return to East Africa,[9] actively spread the teachings of the Qādiriyya brotherhood among the common people of the hinterland. Shaykh Uways was one of the most influential advocates of instructing people of all, even lowly backgrounds, in their own vernaculars. His return to East Africa in 1882 therefore represents an important milestone in the history of Islamic education there. Shaykh Qasim explicitly attributes his decision to compose didactic religious poetry in Chimiini to the inspiration of Shaykh Uways.[10]

The coastal networks of *'ulamā'* of the period between c. 1880 and the beginning of World War II have been the subject of the two recent monographs by Anne Bang, *Islamic Sufi Networks in the Western Indian Ocean*[11] and *Sufis and Scholars of the Sea*.[12] Particularly in the latter, Bang documents an important intellectual and social innovation, namely a new region-wide emphasis on teaching ordinary people in the vernacular. This new phenomenon was not, she argues, the result of a Sufi or Neo-Sufi revival, as Sufism had not been in decline.[13] What is new, Bang

Sharia: the Civil Register of the Qadis' Court of Brava, 1893–1900 (Leiden: Brill, 2006), 2 vols., 51, and Bang, *Sufis and Scholars*, 94.

9 Scott Reese, *Renewers of the Age: Holy Men and Social Discourse in Colonial Benaadir* (Leiden: Brill, 2008) 113.

10 Shaykh Qasim, 'Chidirke ya Rasuul A<u>ll</u>ah' ('Rescue us, O Prophet of God'), stanzas 6–7.

11 Anne K. Bang, *Islamic Sufi Networks in the Western Indian Ocean* (Leiden: Brill, 2014).

12 Anne K. Bang, *Sufis and Scholars of the Sea* shows that these networks spanned Zanzibar, the East African coast as far south as Mozambique and South Africa (Cape Town), the Hijaz (Mecca and Medina), the Hadramawt, the Comoros, and Madagascar.

13 For a recent reevaluation of the concept, see John O. Voll, 'Neo-Sufism: Reconsidered Again', *Canadian Journal of African Studies*, 42, 2/3, 2008, 314–31. The Bravanese poems under study here do not give evidence of a new stage of intensified organization and centralization of the Sufi brotherhoods, a phenomenon associated with Neo-Sufism in scholarship of the past. Moreover, while the Bravanese *'ulamā'*'s insistence that every Muslim's beliefs and devotional practice must be in conformity with the authoritative religious scholarly texts is central to these poems, it is unclear to what extent this philosophical emphasis, rather than its tangible expression in vernacular poetry for the common people, was new. Teaching in the vernacular,

argues, especially on the East African coast, was the renewed emphasis on teaching Islam to the common people. While in southern Arabia, where this impulse was of longer standing, the issue of teaching in any language other than Arabic had not arisen, in East Africa this new form of religious instruction developed in tandem with teaching in the vernacular. The emergence of the Sufi teaching poems in Chimiini must be understood in this context of enormous and multifaceted religious activity and change in the wider region.

The Poet-Scholars of Brava

The backgrounds and expertise of the three poet-scholars under study here are quite different. Shaykh Qasim, more than any other Brava *'ālim*, fits the portrait Bang sketched of the Sufi scholars of East Africa, as he was fully integrated in the networks of religious education and scholarship, and the webs of family and friendship of his time and region. The *manāqib* devoted to him[14] note that he travelled to the holy cities at least twice, both times in the company of family members and other students and shaykhs of the Benadir, and with the objectives of both performing the pilgrimage and studying at the feet of particular Shāfi'ī scholars such as Sayyid 'Umar b. Abūbakr b. Muḥammad Shaṭṭā, with whom he studied grammar (Ibn Mālik's Alfiyya'). While in Mecca, another important Sufi scholar of the network analysed by Bang arrived in that town, Shaykh 'Abd al-'Azīz al-Amawī from Zanzibar. It was in the company of the latter (among others) that Shaykh Qasim then travelled to the Hadramawt to study *ḥadīth* and *fiqh* with Sayyid 'Alī al-Ḥibshī, visiting also the 'Alawi shaykhs of 'Inat. Shaykh Qasim also followed Shaykh 'Abd al-'Azīz al-Amawī to Zanzibar, where he studied prosody and esoteric knowledge with him, eventually writing a praise poem (*qaṣīda*) in Arabic for this teacher.

However, Shaykh Qasim, who belonged to the Bida of Brava, began his education much closer to home. According to the *manāqib*, he went to serve and study under Shaykh Uways in Brava, his birthplace, at the young age of seven. Later he studied for several years in relatively nearby Mogadishu with Shaykh Sufi ('Abd al-Raḥmān b. 'Abdallah al-Shāshī), under whose guidance he studied grammar, morphology, rhetoric, *ḥadīth* and *fiqh* (jurisprudence), and who also gave him a

---

which Levtzion initially presented as an important aspect of 'Neo-Sufism' in the eighteenth- and nineteenth-century Islamic world (Voll, 328), is indeed central to the late-nineteenth- and twentieth-century corpus of Bravanese didactic Sufi poetry presented here.

14 Shaykh Abūbakr Nūrshe Muḥyīdīn', 'Manāqib'. Mohamed Kassim, co-editor of the source publication, provided a summary translation. See also Reese, *Renewers*, 95, n. 94.

relative in marriage. He had many dream visions of Prophet Muḥammad, and was associated with a number of miracles. In one of these, he successfully called upon Shaykh 'Abdulqādir al-Jīlānī to save the leaking ship on which he was travelling back to Brava from Zanzibar. In another, which took place during a drought, he successfully prayed for rain at the tomb of Shaykh Nur Chande, a Bravanese Sufi saint of the seventeenth century.[15]

As a result of this peripatetic learning, Shaykh Qasim was, in terms of formal education, among the most learned Bravanese *'ulamā'*, known for his superior knowledge of Arabic and his beautiful handwriting. By the time of his death in 1922, he had authored an impressive body of scholarly and devotional works in Arabic prose and poetry. These included the earliest *manāqib* of Shaykh Uways titled *Ins al-Anīs* (c. 1917), praise poetry for the Prophet and Shaykh 'Abdulqādir al-Jīlānī, as well as a compilation of religious poetry by famous contemporaries. The latter included Arabic praise poems for Prophet Muḥammad and Shaykh 'Abdulqādir composed by two of his teachers (Shaykh Uways and Shaykh Sufi), to which Shaykh Qasim, following the well-established genre of *takhmīs*, added his own poetic lines.[16] Shaykh Qasim's erudition is also evident in his didactic poetry in Chimiini, about which more below.

A very different portrait emerges from the sources we have for the greatest female poet in Chimiini, Mana Sitti Habib Jamaladdin, whom the Bravanese fondly remember as Dada Masiti ('Grandmother Masiti'). Perhaps because she was a woman, she did not become the subject of written *manāqib* devoted to her life and achievements, so we do not have the detailed information about her religious instruction, scholarly contacts, and travel so often contained in such a source. However, she is vividly remembered in oral sources.[17] From them we know

[15] Reese, *Renewers*, 6, 41.

[16] Reese, *Renewers*, 158, and n. 53; Scott Reese, 'The Best of Guides: Sufi Poetry and Alternate Discourses of Reform in Early Twentieth Century Somalia', *Journal of African Cultural Studies*, 14, 1, 2001, 49–68, 56–8; Alessandro Gori, *Studi sulla letteratura agiografica islamica somala in lingua araba* (Florence: Dipartimento di Linguistica, Università di Firenze, 2003) 16–17; Enrico Cerulli, 'Note sul movimento musulmano nella Somalia'. In *Somalia: Scritti Vari ed Inediti, Vol. I* (Rome: Istituto Poligrafico dello Stato, 1957) 177–210, 188, 196. The *'Majmū'at qaṣā'id fī madḥ Sayyid al-anbiyā' wa al-tawassul bi-tāj al-awliyā' Sayyid 'Abd al-Qādir al-Jīlānī'* consists of two poems by Shaykh Uways, two by Shaykh Sufi, and four by Shaykh 'Abd al-Raḥmān al-Zaylā'ī.

[17] These oral sources consist of information collected by Vianello in decades of connections with the Bravanese community. This section is based on Alessandra Vianello, 'Dada Masiti', in Emmanuel K. Akyeampong; Henry Louis Gates (eds.), *Dictionary of African Biography* (New York: Oxford University Press, 2012), vol. 2, 150–1.

that she belonged to the Ashrāf on the sides of both her father and mother. Dada Masiti's experiences as a young woman strongly influenced her spiritual development. The most common version of these events holds that she was kidnapped as a child of six and sold into slavery in Zanzibar. However, another version, supported by relatives who are still alive, holds that she staged a kidnapping to elope with a suitor of whom her family disapproved. The couple escaped to Pate, where Dada Masiti, after the marriage deteriorated, lived in circumstances described as virtual slavery, until, after ten years, Shaykh Omar Qullatayn of Zanzibar, a relative on her mother's side, helped her return to Brava. In her poetry, Dada Masiti refers only indirectly to these events, but repeatedly expresses her deep remorse about having given in to worldly temptations, always asking God to forgive her. Her poems also often make fond and special mention of Shaykh Omar Qullatayn in her invocations of God's blessings.

Although Dada Masiti's poetry reveals that she had a more than basic knowledge of Arabic, it was all in Chimiini and, while it shows great familiarity with the Qur'ān and *ḥadīth*, on which it often draws directly, it makes no reference to written religious scholarship. When speaking of her progress on the Sufi path, Dada Masiti refers rather generally to 'advice and warnings', which might suggest that she received her instruction orally. She belonged to the Qādiriyya and had close personal bonds with two *khalīfas* of this *ṭarīqa*: Omar Qullatayn in Zanzibar and Sharif Alawi b. Habib Makka in Brava. When she was young, she is said to have had a mentor called Shaykh 'Ma Janaale', probably Shaykh Muḥammad Jenay al-Baḥlūl, who was an adherent of the Qādiriyya and a teacher of Shaykh Uways.[18]

Even in her lifetime, Dada Masiti became a paragon of piety and wisdom, and was admired as a powerful and inspiring poet. The Bravanese *'ulamā'* who were her contemporaries held her in great esteem and two of them expressed this in their poetry. She was still alive when Shaykh Qasim composed a poem for her that opened with 'Daada Maasiṯi nsoomela du'a' ('Dada Masiti, pray for me'), in which he called her 'a treasure to be jealously preserved', and impressed on listeners that love for her was 'the foundation of all true faith'.[19] Some of this admiration may have been related to the fact that she was a descendant of the Prophet. However, after her death, Mallim Nuri praised not only her piety, noble lineage, and the spiritual rewards of the annual *ziyāra* to her grave, but also, explicitly, her poetic skill: 'Masiti, a woman who had a fine mind,/ eloquence, and great discernment,/ who could compose a full *shṯeenzi* in faultless poetic

[18] Vianello, interview with Mohammed Gaduud, Mogadishu, 1982; Reese, *Renewers*, 112.

[19] 'Dada Masiti, pray for me', 3.

meter.'[20] Another Bravanese *'ālim*, Shaykh Nureni, who died in 1909, engaged Dada Masiti's poetic services directly; when he felt his death drawing near, he asked her to compose a poem that would guide his followers toward accepting his death, when it came, as the inevitable and even joyful transition from this world to the afterlife. 'After life comes death: when the Shaykh dies no one should weep' (the opening of 'Ba'di ya hayy ni mawti̱') is one of Dada Masiti's finest and most moving poems.

Dada Masiti did not remarry and had no children. When she died, she was buried on the site of her small house. Given the gender ideology of the period, one may wonder whether Dada Masiti could have reached the heights of wisdom and piety in the eyes of her contemporaries if she had been a wife and mother. This is not a question we can answer with any certainty, but it is worth mentioning that there are striking similarities between the details of the life of the mystic Rābi'a (described, for example, in Smith's *Rābi'a the Mystic*) and those associated in Bravanese memory with that of Dada Masiti. Like Rābi'a, Dada Masiti was a celibate saint, who matched or exceeded her male contemporaries in piety and understanding. The two female mystics were even believed to have had the early life-experience of kidnapping and enslavement in common.[21]

Mallim Nuri, the third poet under study here, was born into the most prominent and influential family of the Somali Tunni Dafaradhi group. His father and brother, as well as the father and brother of his mother, had held leading positions among the Tunni from before the establishment of Italian colonial rule. Tradition has it that Shaykh Nureni Mohamed Sabir, the foremost jurist and *'ālim* of the time, saw him playing with other children on the beach of Brava and invited him to become his student. Under Shaykh Nureni's guidance, Mallim Nuri acquired great proficiency in *fiqh* and became affiliated with the Aḥmadiyya Sufi order.[22] Unlike his teacher Shaykh Nureni, who used only Arabic, Mallim Nuri authored texts in both Arabic and Chimiini. His religious poetry in Chimiini put special emphasis on, as Reese put it, 'adherence to the *sharī'a* as an indispensable element of spiritual

[20] 'Sẖteenzi cha Masadaati̱' ('The poem of the Ashrāf'), 41. Here *mizaani* (weight or measure) can refer to either the perfect metrics of Dada Masiti's poems or the 'just measure' of their content. Dada Masiti was the most accomplished Bravanese poet using the Swahili *utenzi* metre, that is to say stanzas of four hemistiches, of which three rhyme with each other, while the fourth is the same throughout the poem. She also composed mono-rhyme poems in the literary tradition of Arabia.

[21] Margaret Smith, *Rābi'a the Mystic and her Fellow Saints in Islam* (Cambridge: Cambridge University Press, 1984; first edition 1928) 6, 19.

[22] After the death of Shaykh Nureni in 1909, he composed a poem in honour of his teacher (in Chimiini) and also wrote his *manāqib* or hagiography (in Arabic). See Reese, *Renewers*, 30.

development'.[23] The poem Bravanese consider his masterpiece is the 284 line long 'Zubadi' ('The Cream'), his Chimiini version of part of the Arabic poem 'Matn al-zubad fī' l-fiqh', composed by the fifteenth-century *'ālim* Aḥmad b. Raslān al-Ramlī. Based on an original Arabic text of one thousand lines, Mallim Nuri's 'The Cream' gives detailed instruction in the principles of *fiqh* relating to ritual purity, and proper forms of prayers, fasting, and so forth, according to Shāfi'ī jurisprudence.

The Composition, Recitation and Transmission of the *Sṯeenzi*

The *sṯeenzi* of Brava are didactic devotional poems meant for recitation, each poem chanted in a particular melody and rhythm, often in formal and informal group-settings.[24] In structure, they consist of strings of stanzas that are both grammatically and thematically self-contained, can follow each other in unlimited numbers, and are relatively easy to memorize.[25] The oldest *sṯeenzi* now extant date to c. 1900, when, as mentioned above, the charismatic Shaykh Uways (1847–1909) began to use poetry in the East African vernaculars (including Somali and Chimiini) to teach Islam to the common people of town and countryside who did not know Arabic and may not have been literate. From the beginning the objective of these didactic poems was therefore that they would be memorized and recited orally.

Whether the poet-scholars of Brava composed their *sṯeenzi* orally or in writing cannot be known with certainty. However, it is quite possible that most *sṯeenzi* were composed in writing. This is practically certain for those poems that are Chimiini versions of Arabic texts, such as Mallim Nuri's 'The Cream', as well as for those that were composed in adherence to a particular formal structure, such as Shaykh Qasim's 'Chidirke ya Rasuul Aḻḻaah' ('Rescue us, O Prophet of God'), in which the initial letters of each line formed an acrostic. Many Bravanese believe today that even an exceptionally talented poet like Dada Masiti composed her poems in writing. The great-grandson of the shaykh for whom Dada Masiti wrote 'After life comes death', related that the shaykh, already bed-ridden when Dada Masiti sent him the poem, had it read out to him aloud from a piece of paper.[26] Moreover, when Shaykh Qasim composed the urgent plea 'Rescue us, O Prophet of God', in response to the establishment of an Italian mission school in Brava in

[23] Reese, *Renewers*, 21.

[24] The below is based on Banafunzi and Vianello, 'Chimi:ini in Arabic Script'.

[25] There are four basic forms of *sṯeenzi*. Two of them consist of stanzas (four hemistiches in two lines) and two consist of lines (each line formed by two hemistiches).

[26] Mohamed Kassim, interview with Sayyidi b. Shaykh Nureni b. Banafunzi, the son of Shaykh Nureni's daughter (unpublished, Mombasa, September 1993).

1908, the poem's text, as Mohamed Kassim reported, 'was quickly distributed, in writing, to all the households in Brava and people were asked to recite it every evening before the evening prayers'.[27]

In Bravanese memory, two poems were unquestionably composed orally. One is the short, four-stanza poem of advice titled 'Ndruuza kasaani sowṯiya' ('O brothers, listen to my voice') Shaykh Qasim recited during a teaching session with his students just before his death.[28] The other poem, also one of last advice before death, is the eight-stanza poem 'Iyi ni bishaara' ('These are glad tidings') by Shaykh Mohamed Sufi (d. 1968).[29] In Somalia as a whole, the ability to compose, transmit, and memorize poetry without resorting to writing was certainly quite common in this period. However, it is evident that among the highly educated *'ulamā'* of Brava the oral and written medium coexisted; they purposefully used both.

As has been explained by Banafunzi and Vianello in their 'Chimi:ini in Arabic Script', the *'ulamā'*-poets used a modified Arabic script (*'Ajamī*) to write Chimiini.[30] This script appears to have been pioneered by Shaykh Uways, who, as mentioned above, made short compositions in different Somali dialects and languages (including Chimiini). However, his example, while widely followed, did not lead to a unified or standardized way of writing Chimiini in Arabic script.[31] Knowledge of Arabic had always been a central feature of religious education in Brava and most townsmen, as well as many female members of middle-class and elite families, were literate in Arabic. This literacy often went beyond what they learned as young children in Qur'ān school, as men went on to study in the semi-formal setting of the shaykh's house or mosque circle and women were often tutored in private settings.

During the overlordship of Zanzibar (1837–93/1905), Arabic had been the official language on the Benadir coast. This continued to be the case during the first decades of Italian colonial rule (roughly until World War I), when Arabic was used in the qāḍī's courts, as well as in official announcements and proclamations to the population. Moreover, the *ṭarīqa*s with which the Bravanese *'ulamā'*

[27] Mohamed Kassim, 'Colonial resistance and the local transmission of Islamic knowledge in the Benadir Coast in the late 19th and early 20th centuries', PhD diss., History, York University, 2006, 231.

[28] Abū Bakr b. Nūrshe, 'Manāqib Shams al-Dīn', manuscript, 38.

[29] Shaykh Mohamed Sufi's work is discussed in the source publication Vianello et al., '*Stringing Coral Beads*'.

[30] The below is based on Banafunzi and Vianello, 'Chimi:ini in Arabic Script', 297–300.

[31] Banafunzi and Vianello, 'Chimi:ini in Arabic Script', 298; Cerulli, 'Note sul movimento', 188.

were especially affiliated, the Qādiriyya and the Aḥmadiyya, put special emphasis on education, the former emphasizing language-related fields of scholarship and the latter Islamic law and jurisprudence.[32] That the *'ulamā'*-poets of Brava were therefore highly literate and composed in *writing* poems intended for *oral* recitation and memorization is therefore very likely.

A combination of oral and written media characterized how the men and women for whom the *s̱teenzi* were composed learned, recited, read, transmitted and preserved them. The authors of *s̱teenzi* repeatedly state that they intended their poems to be a guide for 'women, men, free-born and slaves', an intended audience that had various levels of literacy, with women of non-elite households, as well as slaves or former slaves, often illiterate. Moreover, much of this audience was also not directly accessible to the *'ulamā'*-poets, for women were confined to their homes and did not, for example, attend mosques. A shaykh's disciples would therefore have been the first to hear a new composition and would have committed the texts to writing, by ear or by copying the shaykh's text. They would also have memorized the melody specific to the poem.

A major venue in which the *'ulamā'*-poets and their disciples recited the *s̱teenzi* were the large public gatherings for ritual *dhikr* chanting, promoted in particular by Shaykh Uways and later taken up by the Qādiriyya in Brava. Men of all age groups and social classes attended these gatherings. The audience would first participate by repeating lines as a group and then gradually learn melody and text by heart. (Until very recently this was also how Qur'ānic schoolteachers taught the *s̱teenzi* to young children.)[33] Women learned from close male relatives who had attended such gatherings or were affiliated with the shaykh and his *ṭarīqa*. In Brava, fathers, husbands, brothers, and so forth, are said to have taught their close female relatives habitually.[34] In elite households, where women were literate in Arabic, manuscripts might have also circulated, but even then the melody would have to be transmitted orally. The written and oral mediums were therefore not mutually exclusive but used simultaneously.

However, women especially embraced the *s̱teenzi* and made them their own, regularly chanting and reciting them as part of their everyday lives. This they did both informally, while sewing in their homes or in the small Qur'ān schools for girls that in Brava were commonly taught by women and, more formally, when they gathered in private homes to congratulate newly-weds or visit a widow during her *'idda* (mourning period). They also used them as reference

[32] Banafunzi and Vianello, 'Chimi:ini in Arabic Script', 296–7.

[33] In source O.11, a recorded cassette, the male teacher chants a small part of the poem (a stanza or set of lines) at a time, and each time the boys of his class repeat the refrain (the first stanza) after him as a group.

[34] Kassim, 'Colonial resistance', 251.

when questions about belief or practice arose. Women also specialized in the oral rather than written medium. Scholars who have written about the Swahili *utendi* genre have commented on the vast amount of poetry Muslim women of the coast were able to memorize.[35] This is also true for Brava. For example, one elderly Bravanese woman, recorded in the mid-1990s, was able to recite from memory, without recourse to any written document, a number of very long *s̠teenzi*, including Shaykh Qasim's 'Rescue us, O Prophet of God' (fifty-five stanzas) and his 'Ya Sheekhi Abdul̠qaadiri' ('O Shaykh Abdulqadir'), which has fifty-nine stanzas. A comparison with the available written texts revealed how perfectly she remembered the poems. Meanwhile, men often relied on the written texts. Because Chimiini in Arabic script is not easy to read even for an experienced reader of Arabic, their reading-based recitations are often less fluent than those done from memory.[36]

New *s̠teenzi* production continued in the period between the two world wars, but the oldest ones remained important to people and it was in this period that individual Bravanese commissioned written copies of these from the best copyists in Brava.[37] These copyists used the *'Ajamī* script devised for Chimiini to reproduce the sounds of this language as faithfully as possible.[38] However, the number of manuscripts that were produced using only the Arabic alphabet to transliterate Chimiini is much higher. These were usually written by men for the use of their female relatives (and upon the latter's request) as simple aids to memory during oral recitations in domestic surroundings. Again, oral and written transmission and preservation coincided and overlapped, because Bravanese women, as the *s̠teenzi*'s true custodians, kept the poems alive through memorization and oral transmission but also jealously preserved written transcriptions.

The introduction of tape-recorders in Brava in the mid- to late 1970s[39] triggered a real revolution in the diffusion of the *s̠teenzi*, as the number of oral recordings grew exponentially. Those who made such recordings included individual *'ulamā'*, men in private gatherings, women (who did so only for circulation among other women or close relatives), and even singers of Chimiini love songs, who

35 See, for example, J.W.T, Allen, *Tendi: Six Examples of a Swahili Classical Verse Form with Translations and Notes* (London: Heinemann, 1971) 9.

36 This is evident in sources O.1 and O.11.

37 Among the sources gathered by Vianello are photocopies of two manuscripts (M.1 and M.2) in the same hand, said to be the work of the copyist Shego Bakari, and probably dating from the mid-1930s.

38 The name '*'Ajamī*' refers to a script that uses the Arabic alphabet plus extra letters.

39 This was made possible by the improved economic conditions of many Bravanese households, after their young men had gone to work in the Gulf States and Saudi Arabia.

recorded *s̱teenzi* on cassettes that were then offered for sale.[40] The last twenty-five years have witnessed further developments in the preservation and dissemination of the *s̱teenzi*.[41] In the wake of the civil war, some Chimiini-speakers in exile throughout the world have gained a new, heightened appreciation of the *s̱teenzi* as a significant aspect of their surviving cultural heritage. They have used computers to create and disseminate computer-generated texts of *s̱teenzi* and have created internet sites that include recordings of *s̱teenzi* recitations.[42]

The Themes and Subject Matter of the *S̱teenzi*

As learned, Sufi, didactic and devotional poems, the *s̱teenzi* have many commonalities.

The *S̱teenzi* are Didactic in Nature

The *s̱teenzi* are didactic, composed to guide and teach *'ilm* to all Chimiini speakers without distinction of socio-economic status and gender. Although the Bravanese *'ulamā'* were well versed in the range of scholarly fields constituting the *'ulūm al-dīn*, in the poems they refer to *'ilm* without further specification. It is evident from the corpus of *s̱teenzi* as a whole that they were meant to educate their audience broadly in areas ranging from early Islamic history to those aspects of theology and *fiqh* that would guide them towards correct beliefs, the correct performance of acts of worship, and the observance of properly Islamic moral values and social conduct.

The poets contrasted *ilmu na ujahli* (knowledge and ignorance), that is to say, they wanted to remedy the problem of ignorance (*jahl*) with the religious knowledge of *'ilm*. In the context of Brava, which had been a Muslim town for centuries, *jahl* did not refer to the ignorance of people who were not yet Muslim but to Muslims who needed to correct and perfect their beliefs and behaviour. The *'ulamā'* insisted that *'ilm* was closely connected to worship and that actively pursuing and seeking it was a duty for everyone irrespective of social status. Shaykh Qasim especially emphasized this in several poems:

> It is the duty of everyone, woman, man,
> freeborn and slave, to learn these pillars of the faith.

[40] The sources gathered by Vianello include examples of all these types of oral recitations.

[41] The following is based on Banafunzi and Vianello, 'Chimi:ni in Arabic Script', 300.

[42] See for example, http://www.albarawi.com/stenzii.htm, accessed 19 June 2017, which includes a male voice recording of Mallim Nuri's 'Shṯeenzi cha mi'raaj' ('The poem of the *mi'rāj*'). An example of such a computer-generated text in *'Ajamī* is source M.3.

> The ignorant should learn and ask – it is a religious duty.
> Do not be lax and do not tire [of seeking knowledge].
> Whoever is ignorant should seek [knowledge] and whoever fails to find it
> should go and look for a teacher, even as far as Aden.
> Worship is closely linked to knowledge, and for every act
> you perform you should learn its *'ilm*.[43]

The poet strongly condemns (in fact, goes as far as to insult!) those who do not seek knowledge: 'Whoever does not know these [pillars of Islam] is [like] the worst of savages./ Everyone must learn them – you should note this.'[44]

Mallim Nuri too put special emphasis on proper worship based on *'ilm*:

> O human soul, be firm in your faith,
> do not quickly mumble your prayers,
> either the obligatory or the voluntary ones,
> [since] worship is your real capital.
> Let the prayers be complete.
> Let the fasting be faultless.
> Beware of any action that would nullify it.
> Only the ignorant does not consider this.[45]

The central themes of the *s̱teenzi* bear witness to the wide-ranging nature of their didactic message. The *'ulamā'* continuously cautioned their audience to forswear all aspects of behaviour that were incompatible with the teachings of the Qur'ān and *ḥadīth*. To their minds, central to such ignorant, un-Islamic behaviour was the mindless pursuit of worldly pleasures and the importance given to wealth and power. Instead, listeners should be aware that the world is only a temporary abode; that death comes unexpectedly, and that wealth and riches are useless in the afterlife. As Dada Masiti puts it:

> The world is deceitful.
> Do not let its pleasures tempt you ....[46]
> How many/ mighty as princes, I saw
> [congregate] and then disperse and depart,
> [though] many were full of vitality and wealthy.
> They left their wealth behind
> and their aspirations are no more.

[43] Shaykh Qasim, 'L̲a Ilaaha' ('There is no god but God'), 26, 27, 29, 55.
[44] Shaykh Qasim, 'L̲a Ilaaha', 54.
[45] Mallim Nuri, 'The poem of the Ashrāf', 20–1.
[46] Dada Masiti, 'O Exalted Lord', 19.

What they left behind is no longer theirs,
for it will be inherited by the living.
If you look at the living
[and] at those who are bereft of speech and voice,
[you will realize that] after life comes death.
This is a certainty I never forget.[47]

A second recurring theme of the *sṯeenzi* is the crucial importance of sincere intention, of a faith based on inner conviction, and the condemnation of a mechanical approach to worship or simply following habit. Shaykh Qasim presents sincere intention as the first principle of the Qādiriyya.

My friends, follow the directives
of the Qādiriyya brotherhood:
to start fearing God
with a clean heart and pure intention.[48]

Combining Islamic practices with local customs that were not strictly Islamic was part of the *jahl* the poems' *'ilm* was meant to remedy. This receives particular emphasis in the poems by Mallim Nuri, the shaykh who emphasized practical matters of *fiqh*, in line, it appears, with the teachings of the Aḥmadiyya.[49] He condemned the observance of 'old customs and traditions' just because people might talk or judge if one broke with such custom, and singled out for criticism customs associated with funerals, such as spending extravagant amounts of money, exaggerating praise for the dead, and so forth:

Follow the Sharī'ah and do not observe custom
when you commemorate the dead in their graves.[50]
Instead of following old customs and traditions
because of your fear of shame and criticism,
you should look quickly for the way
to enter through the Lord's door. [51]

[47] Dada Masiti, 'O Exalted Lord', 12–14.
[48] 'O Shaykh 'Abdulqādir', 35. See also 'There is no god but God', 33: 'You should have virtuous intentions and a pure heart/ Fear the punishment of Hell and strive to be placed in Paradise.'
[49] From the perspective of the corpus of *sṯeenzi*, the Aḥmadiyya placed much educational emphasis on *fiqh* and thus on the practical aspects of everyday worship, whereas the Qādiriyya emphasized theology and aspects of belief.
[50] Mallim Nuri, 'Shṯeenzi cha sabri' ('The poem of forbearance'), 22.
[51] *Shṯeenzi cha Hasani na Huseeni* ('The poem of Ḥasan and Ḥusayn'), stanza 16. See also, this same poem, *passim*, and 'The poem of forbearance', 16–17.

The *S̱teenzi* are Sufi in Nature

In addition to conveying the central religious values noted above, the *s̱teenzi* are also explicitly Sufi and present the Sufi path as a certain way to gain access to Paradise. The *s̱teenzi* show that the poets embraced the mystical tenets of Sufism and guided their audience toward Sufi knowledge, beliefs, practice, and principles of behaviour. For both the poets and their audience the *s̱teenzi* constituted Sufi devotional acts of worship and religious instruction. The Sufi themes of the *s̱teenzi* are as follows:

1) Acknowledging the Qur'ān and *ḥadīth* (*Sunna*) as the basis for all worship and behaviour, Mallim Nuri articulated this explicitly when he said: 'The principles of *'ilm* are found in the Qur'ān/ [and] in the *ḥadīth* of the Prophet, the offspring of 'Adnān.'[52]

2) Belief in the centrality of the Prophet in God's design for His creation (*al-Nūr al-Muḥammadī* or Muḥammadan Light) and the Prophet's crucial role as intercessor for mankind. Shaykh Qasim presented the Prophet as the cure for and protector against all ills, and Dada Masiti said about Prophet Muḥammad:

> His equal has never been created,
> he is our Master, the most richly endowed with virtues.
> His radiant and dazzling Light
> has existed since the beginning of time.[53]

3) Knowledge of the life of the Prophet, his lineage, wives, and children; of the events of his ascent to Prophethood and leader of the first Muslim community; and of the miracles he performed during his life. Some of the Prophet's miracles, for example, are narrated in Shaykh Qasim's 'Meezi wa keendra' ('In the ninth month') and in his Chimiini translation of al-Būsīrī's Hamziyya, which mentions some of the 'astonishing signs' that manifested themselves in the world on the day the Prophet was born: the spontaneous collapse of the palace of Khosrow, ruler of the Persians; the drying up of Persian wells; and the extinction of the fires in the Zoroastrian temples.[54]

4) Appealing to the Prophet to intercede for his community. For authors and audience, the *s̱teenzi* were expressions of devotion to the Prophet, which took the form of praising him and asking him to advocate for them with God.[55] Shaykh

[52] Mallim Nuri, 'Shṯeenzi cha A'isha' ('The poem of A'isha'), 2.

[53] Dada Masiti, 'O Compassionate Lord', 17. See also Shaykh Qasim, 'Rescue us, O Prophet of God'.

[54] Shaykh Qasim, 'Hamziyya', 15–17.

[55] Poems usually open with praise for God and His Prophet, and even Shaykh Qasim's 'Chidirke ya Rasuul Allaah' ('Rescue us, O Prophet of God'), which is dedicated to the Prophet, includes a prayer addressed directly to God (2:31).

Qasim praises and invokes him as the ultimate intercessor, the healer of all physical and spiritual ills, the greatest protector, unequalled in rank by any other prophet, and the one whose Light was eternal and emanated immediately from God.[56] In his 'Rescue us, O Prophet of God', he prays:

> Rescue us, O Prophet of God.
> Support us, O Messenger of God.
> Heal us, O God's Beloved.
> O Prophet, we are under your protection.[57]

Dada Masiti echoes these sentiments in her 'O Compassionate Lord':

> I am under the protection of the Prophet.
> His pleas for me are accepted [by God],
> [and] his intercession does not fail
> in the Hereafter and in this world.[58]

Mallim Nuri begins his poem 'Mt̠awasuleeni Mus̠tafa' ('Seek the intercession of the Chosen One') with the lines:

> Seek the intercession of the Chosen One,
> the most honorable Muḥammad.
> [Invoking] his name has healing powers
> both during [your] life and after death.[59]

Praise and blessings invoked upon the Prophet's beloved and morally pure daughter Fatima also feature prominently in the *s̠teenzi*, several of which are devoted completely to her.[60] In 'O Exalted Lord', Dada Masiti prays:

> O Lady [Fatima], be the guarantor of my salvation,
> hold me tight like something entrusted to you.
> You are the healer of souls on the day of the fierce heat and the questioning.[61]

Mallim Nuri expressed the idea of Fatima as an intercessor as follows:

[56] See Shaykh Qasim, 'Hamziyya', 1–2, and 'Rescue us, O Prophet of God', 11, 16, 17.

[57] Shaykh Qasim, 'Rescue us, O Prophet of God', 54.

[58] Dada Masiti, 'O Compassionate Lord', 16.

[59] Mallim Nuri, 'Seek the intercession of the Chosen One', 1.

[60] See Mallim Nuri, 'Chidirke Maana Faatima' ('Come to our help, O Lady Fatima'); 'Sht̠eenzi cha Faatima' ('The poem of Fatima'); and Dada Masiti, 'Sayiidi yiitu Siteeni' ('O Our Lady').

[61] Dada Masiti, 'O Exalted Lord', 37.

Help us, O Zahra‘, on the day of reckoning
and in all hardships that await us tomorrow in the Hereafter.[62]
O God, for the sake of Lady Fatima,
take away our afflictions and grant us a good end to our lives.[63]

He also praised Fatima as a perfect Muslim, as a loyal and obedient wife to her husband, and as a woman whom God had spared from menstruation and other burdens of womanhood.[64] In addition to Fatima, the Prophet's mother, wives, and other close relatives were also a significant focus of devotion and prayers for help and intercession, as is, for example, immediately evident from the titles of the *steenzis* by Mallim Nuri.

5) Performing the *ḥajj* and visiting the Prophet's tomb. The pilgrimage to Mecca features in many of the *steenzi*, including in the 'Alfeeni msalileeni' ('Ask God to bless him two thousand times') by Shaykh Uways. Shaykh Qasim completely devoted his 'In the ninth month' to it, giving his audience a detailed description of what to expect and what to do. He also reassured his listeners that Shaykh 'Abdulqādir's miraculous powers would keep them safe at sea:

Those who are at sea
he saves from danger
and averts [all] evils from them,
so that they reach port safely.[65]

Dada Masiti included prayers for the safety of the pilgrims in her 'Sayyidi yiitu Siteeni' ('O Our Lady'), in which she invoked Fatima, the Prophet's daughter, on their behalf:

Pray for the pilgrims
to be successful. May God
grant them [favourable] winds and seas,
and [put] joy into their hearts.
May He grant them a safe pilgrimage
and eternal happiness.[66]

Mallim Nuri devoted two whole poems to pilgrims and the pilgrimage: 'Shteenzi cha hija' ('The poem of the pilgrimage') and 'Shteenzi cha mahaaji' ('The poem of the pilgrims'). Both start with a prayer to God to ensure the pilgrims' safety:

62 Mallim Nuri, 'The poem of Fatima', 18.
63 'Shteenzi cha udh'hiya' ('The poem of ritual sacrifice'), 1.
64 Mallim Nuri, 'The poem of Fatima', 38–9; 'The poem of ritual sacrifice', 2–3.
65 Shaykh Qasim, 'O Shaykh 'Abdulqādir', 24.
66 Dada Masiti, 'O Our Lady', 10–11.

O God, for the sake of the noble Prophet,
ease the journey of the pilgrimage.
O God, for the sake of your Messengers,
make the pilgrimage easy this year.[67]

O God, protect all pilgrims,
particularly those who visit the Prophet, our Light.
For the sake of the Prophet and the angels,
protect pilgrims every year.
For the sake of the Prophet, the father of al-Batūl
allow them [to perform] a pilgrimage that is acceptable to you.
O God, make their journey safe and joyful
and allow them to visit Muḥammad every year.[68]

6) Honouring the *ṭarīqas* founders and *awliyā'*. Sufi saints play a central role in the *steenzi* and the poets guide their audience towards recognizing the special gifts God bestowed upon these holy men (*barakah* and *karāmāt*) and appealing to them for intercession with God.[69] In the praise poems Shaykh Qasim and Dada Masiti composed for the founder of their *ṭarīqa*, they assured their audience that the shaykh was ready to ease the path of all those who called upon him and that his powerful intercession would help them in this life and after death. Shaykh Qasim's poem 'O Shaykh 'Abdulqādir' praises the Shaykh, narrates parts of his life and his miracles, and affirms his power, and guarantees the Shaykh's readiness to protect and intercede for his followers:

Even when a disciple is far away,
[the Shaykh] can hear his voice.
He does not forget you when you need help to succeed,
al-Jīlānī, the greatest Shaykh.

If you, his disciple, invoke him
[saying] 'Shaylillah, Shaylillah,'
he immediately comes to you,
bringing you joy and bestowing his favor.

Whoever makes a vow
to Shaykh 'Abdulqādir
receives a clear response
that brings blessings and joys.

[67] Mallim Nuri, 'The poem of the pilgrimage', 1–2.
[68] Mallim Nuri, 'The poem of the pilgrims', 1–4.
[69] See, for example, Shaykh Qasim, 'There is no god but God', 37–8, cited below.

You are a Shaykh who possesses *baraka*,
you are undoubtedly a *walī*,
you are the lord
of all the flawless *awliyā'*.[70]

In her 'Mawl̲aana Muhyidiini' ('O our lord Muḥyī al-Dīn'), Dada Masiti paid this tribute to her shaykh:

Our Shaykh has miraculous powers:
a disciple of his has no worries,
a disciple of his is in a happy state,
and has no reason to be troubled.

To the disciples of Jīlānī
God has granted future bliss:
[they will enter] Paradise without [being submitted to] any reckoning,
[because] their Shaykh vouches for them.[71]

7) Acknowledging the teachings of all *ṭarīqas* and the equal legitimacy and worth of all *awliyā'*. There are no immediately discernable differences between the teachings of the Qādiriyya and Aḥmadiyya in the texts of the poems. The *'ulamā'* of both *ṭarīqas* share the same beliefs and stress the same points in their teachings, with this specification: the Qādirī Shaykh Qasim went into considerable detail about theological points (as in his poems 'Nakaanza khṯuunga marjaani' ['I start stringing coral beads'], his Chimiini translation of the 'Aqīdat al-'Awāmm', and 'There is no god but God'), while the Aḥmadī scholar Mallim Nuri saved such detail for practical rules of the *Sharī'a* and *fiqh* (as in his 'The Cream').

While the different *ṭarīqas* may have been competing for followers and differed somewhat in devotional practice (as to what *dhikr* and *wird* texts to read and recite), no such competition finds expression in the *s̲teenzi*. In fact, the *'ulamā'* of Brava actively discouraged making distinctions between *ṭarīqas*, *ṭarīqa* shaykhs, or *awliyā'*. Thus Shaykh Qasim asserted:

And all *awliyā'* are righteous and truthful:
you should not make any distinction between them or belittle them.
Whoever belittles them will be damned
and will be punished in the deepest chasms of Hell.[72]

[70] Shaykh Qasim, 'O Shaykh 'Abdulqādir', 21–5, which also praises Shaykh Uways, Shaykh Sufi and the founders of other *ṭarīqas*.
[71] Dada Masiti, 'O our lord Muḥyī al-Dīn', 23, 36.
[72] Shaykh Qasim, 'There is no god but God', 37–8.

Similarly, in her poem 'Sayyid Jamaladiini' ('Sayyid Jamāl al-Dīn'), Dada Masiti prays in one breath for the intercession of the shaykhs of different *ṭarīqas*, namely 'Abdulqādir al-Jīlānī and Aḥmad b. Idrīs, the founders of the Qādiriyya and the Aḥmadiyya, and the two main local representatives of these two *ṭarīqas*, Sharif Alawi and Shaykh Nureni.[73]

The Aḥmadiyya-affiliated Mallim Nuri mirrored this validation of all *ṭarīqas*:

> You should regard [all] the Sufi orders as valid,
> all brotherhoods as sanctioned.
> God examines our intention.
> My heart loves them all.[74]

In spite of this inclusive attitude, however, the poets under study also praised their own *ṭarīqas*, the Qādiriyya and its founder Shaykh 'Abdulqādir al-Jīlānī in the case of Shaykh Qasim and Dada Masiti, and the Aḥmadiyya in the case of Mallim Nuri. Shaykh Qasim opened his poem for al-Jīlānī with the following lines:

> O Shaykh 'Abdulqādir,
> your miraculous powers are evident.
> Whoever rejects you is an unbeliever
> who lacks true faith.[75]

Dada Masiti praised Shaykh 'Abdulqādir with the words:

> O our lord Muḥyī al-Dīn,
> your *ṭarīqa* is the true one.
> Whoever does not follow it is reprehensible.
> He has no light in his heart.[76]

Mallim Nuri paid special tribute to his own spiritual guide, Shaykh Aḥmad ibn Idrīs of the Aḥmadiyya:

> But my greatest love
> is for my Shaykh, the Sun of the West,
> Ibn Idrīs, my succor,
> who is the guide of my soul.[77]

8) Performing *ziyāras* or visitations to the graves of the Prophet's close relatives (the Ahl al-Bayt) and all the *awliyā'*, especially on the anniversary of their

[73] Dada Masiti, 'Sayyid Jamāl al-Dīn', 6–9.
[74] Mallim Nuri, 'The poem of forbearance', 31.
[75] Shaykh Qasim, 'O Shaykh 'Abdulqādir', 1.
[76] Dada Masiti, 'O our lord Muḥyī al-Dīn', 1.
[77] Mallim Nuri, 'Seek the intercession of the Chosen One', 32.

death. For example, in his 'Mooja chiloongole' ('May God guide us'), Mallim Nuri gave the following general guidance: 'It is *Sunna* for men to visit the graveyards, as it is more meritorious to go and remember the Day of Judgment.'[78] He also reminded his audience of the precise dates for *ziyāras*, both to the Ahl al-Bayt and, locally, to Dada Masiti.

9) Acknowledging the special status of the Ashrāf, who must be loved as descendants of Muḥammad. This love (enjoined by the Qur'ān, in Sufi views) was also seen as a reward due to the Prophet, to repay him all he did for humankind. In Mallim Nuri's words:

> O human soul, always love
> the descendants of the Father of Qāsim;
> to love them is a duty
> dictated by God, The Ruler.
> The Prophet led his followers onto the right path.
> His reward is that we love him,
> cherish all his relatives,
> and especially his descendants.[79]

10) Pursuing specific steps on the Sufi path. Historically, Sufi shaykhs have often had two kinds of followers: a small group of full-time disciples who, under the shaykh's guidance, hoped to reach the highest level of Sufi knowledge, and a much larger number of followers, who benefited from the shaykh's teachings and exhortations 'in a less structured form' (as Shoshan put it in another context).[80] The audience of the *s̠teenzi* consisted of the latter category of people. Although the poets use many terms associated with the Sufi way, they do not refer to the highest levels of Sufi *ma'rifa* or use a lyrical discourse of love for God replete with the metaphors of earthly passion that are so common in the Sufi poetry of Arabia, Turkey, and Persia. It is possible to discern in the *s̠teenzi* terms that coincide with the names of some of the spiritual stages of the Sufi journey.[81] However, such terms might also simply refer to central Islamic values. They include:

[78] Mallim Nuri, 'May God guide us', 54.

[79] Mallim Nuri, 'The poem of the Ashrāf', 2–3.

[80] Boaz Shoshan, *Popular Culture in Medieval Cairo* (Cambridge: Cambridge University Press, 1991) 11–12.

[81] For example, in her book about Rābi'ah, Smith (*Rābi'a the Mystic*, 51) lists the following stages on the Sufi path: *tawba*, *ṣabr*, *shukr* (gratitude), *rajā'* (hope), *khawf*, *faqr* (voluntary poverty), *zuhd* (abstention, asceticism), *tawḥīd* (abnegation of personal will in the Will of God), *tawakkul* (complete dependence upon God), and finally *maḥabba* (love), which includes *shawq* (passionate longing), *uns* (intimacy with God) and *riḍā'* (satisfaction).

Tawba (repentance), the acknowledgement and repenting of sins that might be brought about by the advice and warnings from a shaykh, about which Dada Masiti said: 'My soul turned to God in repentance./ It gave heed to admonitions and stern warnings',[82] as well as 'I feel remorse for [my] sins/ as now my life nears its end,/ [for] much of my time/ has been spent in trivial pleasures.'[83]

Ṣabr, patience and forbearance in the face of the challenges of life, one of the most emphasized values in the *s̱teenzi*, to which Dada Masiti referred when she said: 'Early on I obtained [the virtue of] fortitude/ through the virtuous Prophet's prayers of intercession.'[84]

Rajā', hope that God will pardon one's sins and accept the repentant in Paradise.[85]

Khawf and *taqwah*, holy fear of God and obedience to God, about which Shaykh Qasim said: 'To be God-fearing is a treasure/ more precious than pearls./ My friends, stop being negligent/ [and] you will attain glory in the afterlife.'[86]

Zuhd, abstention from the pleasures of this world, which is implicit in the poets' views that the world and its pleasures are impermanent and should not be sought or given importance.

Tawakkul, complete trust and dependence on God in everything one may do or experience, to which Dada Masiti referred when she said: 'I am sitting down trusting (with *tawakkul*) in You/ waiting for Your order/ to leave the abode of delusion/ [and] go to the abode of the grave.'[87]

11) Acquiring *'ilm* from Sufi shaykhs. The preferred way of acquiring such knowledge, the *s̱teenzi* suggest, was at the feet of a shaykh. Dada Masiti gave this advice:

> We can benefit by sitting with the Shaykh
> as it is a means of achieving greatness.
> Next to him one acquires faith,
> a treasure worth preserving.
>
> Next to him one acquires religious knowledge,
> which is beneficial for all to use.

[82] Dada Masiti, 'O Exalted Lord', 24. See also Dada Masiti, 'O Exalted Lord', 18 and Shaykh Qasim, 'I start stringing coral beads', 62.

[83] Dada Masiti, 'O Exalted Lord', 16.

[84] Dada Masiti, 'O Exalted Lord', 43; Mallim Nuri's 'Ahl̲u al-sabri' ('Those who were steadfast in adversity') is completely dedicated to this virtue.

[85] Dada Masiti, 'O our lord Muḥyī al-Dīn', 13–14.

[86] Shaykh Qasim, 'O Shaykh 'Abdulqādir', 36.

[87] Dada Masiti, 'O Exalted Lord', 33.

Next to him one acquires wisdom,
a precious thing worth looking for.[88]

However, those who seek knowledge should not follow a shaykh's teaching mindlessly. Shaykh Qasim cautions his audience: 'And if you see any mistakes, correct them/ all men err, no matter who they are.'[89] This was echoed and further elaborated by Dada Masiti:

The words the Shaykh uttered
should be carefully sifted:
Write down the meaningful ones
and leave out those which are worthless.

Leave out the worthless ones;
many should be discarded.
Where there are mistakes and errors
I do not object to their rejection.[90]

Because the poets regarded *'ilm* as light and ignorance as darkness, a good teacher was like a lamp.[91] In 'After life comes death', Dada Masiti evokes the sadness that will weigh on Brava after Shaykh Nureni's death: '[Now] the mosque is dark/ even when a lamp is lit/ for he was the lamp/ the bright light we all watched.'[92]

The *S̱teenzi* are Local in Nature

As mentioned above, a central feature of the *s̱teenzi* is that they represented a new genre of religious poetry specially produced to transmit general Islamic knowledge to a local audience in the local language of their town. This means that the *'ulamā'*'s whole oeuvre in Chimiini was composed for a small urban community of c. 5,000 people. The very existence of this poetry therefore speaks to the value the *'ulamā'* attached to their community, a sense of community that their Chimiini poems both expressed and deepened. For this Chimiini-speaking community, this new form of knowledge production was revolutionary. It is true that, when religious instruction in Chimiini was introduced, Islam was already at the heart of the town's identity and that its population was already known for the

88 Dada Masiti, 'After life comes death', 29–32.

89 Shaykh Qasim, 'I start stringing coral beads', 60.

90 Dada Masiti, 'After life comes death', 43–6.

91 Mallim Nuri noted in 'Udh'hiya' ('The poem of ritual sacrifice'), 24: 'Knowledge (*'ilm*) is light, ignorance is darkness'. See also Dada Masiti, 'Sayyid Jamaladiini' ('Sayyid Jamāl al-Dīn'), 30: 'O Lord, remove from us the darkness of ignorance,/ direct our minds to words of advice and divine warnings'.

92 Dada Masiti, 'After life comes death', 101–2.

importance it attached to Islamic education and devotion. However, direct access to the central, authoritative religious texts was restricted to a small number of almost exclusively male *'ulamā'*. With the introduction of the *s̱teenzi*, explicitly composed for an audience of 'men and women, freeborn people and slaves',[93] common people gained new and more direct access to the formal teachings of Islam. This is how Shaykh Qasim, in reality an accomplished Arabist, explained why he was dispensing religious instruction in vernacular verse:

> This is an abridgement of the 'Aqīda[94]
> for those who are ignorant and do not know their [religious] obligations
> It is easy to learn these verses,
> and you should understand their explanation in Chimbalazi.
>
> And my words are in Chimbalazi
> because I [i.e. we, the people of our town] do not know Arabic.
> O friends, study them thoroughly
> [so that] you will know them line by line.
>
> For I am just an ignorant man,
> but I wanted our people
> to learn the attributes of God
> and the prophets, at least in our language.[95]

The poet attributed his decision to write in the vernacular to the influence of Shaykh Uways:

> My words in the Chimbalazi language
> are one of your [the Prophet's] miracles.
> It was my light, the Shaykh, who inspired [me].
> O Prophet, we are under your protection.
>
> Haji Uways, our Shaykh,
> the Shaykh of our *sharīfs*,
> who saw you, our Prophet.
> O Prophet, we are under your protection.[96]

[93] Shaykh Qasim, 'There is no god but God', 26.
[94] The ''Aqīdat al-'Awāmm' ('Creed of the Muslim Laymen'), by Aḥmad b. Muḥammad al-Marzūqī (a nineteenth-century Mālikī scholar), which Shaykh Qasim translated into Chimiini in his 'I start stringing coral beads'.
[95] Shaykh Qasim, 'I start stringing coral beads', 51, 59, 61.
[96] Shaykh Qasim, 'Rescue us, O Prophet of God', 6–7.

Mallim Nuri too was explicit about the didactic value of using Chimiini (Chimbalazi) instead of Arabic:

> Beg God for worldly and religious [gains]
> in Chimbalazi, a language that provides you with the ability to discern.
> It is not necessary to know the Arabic language,
> but only to follow the Prophet in proper behavior.[97]

For Bravanese with no or limited Arabic, being able to recite core texts they had been reciting in Arabic in their own, distinctive town language allowed for a new, more personal and intimate connection to such texts.[98]

This intimate setting of Bravanese *'ulamā'* instructing the people of Brava in their own language also reveals itself in how the poets address their audience. The term they use most often is that of *ndruuza*, or 'my kinsfolk'. This in fact reflected actual relationships in Brava, where most members of the community were connected to each other in a complex network of multiple crisscrossing relations of descent and marriage.[99] Another term the poets often use, that of *akhuaani* or *ikhwaani* ('brothers'), emphasized the community's connectedness to the Islamic *Umma*.[100] However, the *s̠teenzi* also reflect a new emphasis on the relationship of equality between poet and audience, between scholar and common people. As we saw above, the learned Arabist Shaykh Qasim takes his identification with his audience so far that he explains his decision to compose in Chimiini with the statement 'because I do not know Arabic'.

The local nature of the poems further expresses itself in how the *s̠teenzi* refer to the activities in which local people regularly engaged. Brava was an Indian Ocean port town and thus served as the terminus of caravan routes to and from the interior. Many of its inhabitants were involved in commerce and thus often travelled by land and sea to other towns of the Benadir and Swahili coasts, or inland to Bardera.[101] The *s̠teenzi* reflect this in that they often include prayers for the safety of travellers, including, as mentioned above, pilgrims to the holy places.[102]

97 Mallim Nuri, 'The poem of the pilgrims', 31–2.

98 For example, Shaykh Qasim's 'Ya nabiyi salaam aleika' ('O Prophet, peace be upon you') is a translation of the Arabic panegyric that was a regular part of *mawlid* celebrations: al-Barzanjī's 'Yā nabī'.

99 See Shaykh Qasim, 'I start stringing coral beads', 59; 'O Shaykh 'Abdulqādir', 35, 36; 'In the ninth month', 7; 'There is no god but God', 6.

100 Both Shaykh Qasim (in 'There is no god but God', 22) and Dada Masiti (in 'After life comes death', 107–8, and 'Sayyid Jamāl al-Dīn', 19, 23) use *akhuaani* ('brothers') with this meaning.

101 Vianello and Kassim, *Servants of the Sharia*, 31–2.

102 Dada Masiti, 'Sayyid Jamāl al-Dīn', 13; 'O Compassionate Lord', 6–7.

In his 'O Shaykh 'Abdulqādir', Shaykh Qasim reassured his listeners that Shaykh 'Abdulqādir's miraculous powers would keep them safe at sea:

> Those who are at sea
> he saves from danger
> and averts [all] evils from them,
> so that they reach port safely.[103]

Brava was also dependent on animal husbandry and farming. After the Webi Gofka canal that had channelled water to Brava's immediate agricultural hinterland from the Webi Shabelle had been obstructed during regional warfare in the 1870s, the fields of the Bravanese depended exclusively on seasonal rainfall. Drought ruined the crops, harmed cattle, and thus brought famine, while rains meant prosperity. Prayers for rains feature in many of the poems:

> O Lord, grant [us] beneficial winds/ that bring rain and plenty.[104]

> Bring us abundant rains – we beg You/ so that people and cattle may rejoice, O Beneficent God.[105]

> O Lord, bring rain to us./ O Lord, save us from hunger,/ from famines and great calamities./ Grant us your never-ending mercy.[106]

> Free us from affliction, distress and calamity/ and from every evil and famine./ Pray for rain [on our behalf]./ O Prophet, we are under your protection.[107]

Rain was so important in Brava that the poets also use it metaphorically. Thus Shaykh Qasim compares Shaykh 'Abdulqādir al-Jīlānī to nourishing and indispensable rain: 'al-Kīlānī averts all calamities/ when his follower invokes him./ He is our succor, our rain/ who will intercede for us in the Hereafter.'[108] Rain as theme and metaphor also features in both secular and religious Somali poetry, but is absent from Swahili poetry, perhaps because the area south of Somalia enjoyed more regular rainfall.[109]

[103] Shaykh Qasim, 'O Shaykh 'Abdulqādir', 24.
[104] Dada Masiti, 'O Compassionate Lord', 8.
[105] Shaykh Qasim, 'There is no god but God', 61.
[106] Shaykh Qasim, 'O Shaykh 'Abdulqādir', 54.
[107] Shaykh Qasim, 'Rescue Us, O Prophet of God', 20.
[108] Kīlānī is Jīlānī. Shaykh Qasim, 'O Shaykh 'Abdulqādir', 51.
[109] For an example of this in Somali Sufi poetry, see Abdisalam Yassin Mohamed, 'Sufi Poetry in Somali: its Themes and Imagery', PhD diss., University of London, 1977, 224–6.

Occasionally the *s̱teenzi* provide a brief window on specific local events. As mentioned above, Dada Masiti's 'After life comes death' marked the death of the deeply beloved local Islamic judge and scholar Shaykh Nureni in 1909. Another example is Shaykh Qasim's 'Rescue us, O Prophet of God', which was triggered by his concern about the establishment of Catholic mission schools in Brava in 1908 and was instrumental in preventing their success. In her 'Sharrul̲ bilaadi' ('The evil that plagues the country') Dada Masiti cried out against the danger Italian town planning represented for her small house, which, in the end, was spared (1912). Finally, in 1941, when the fighting of World War II had also reached Brava, Mallim Nuri called upon Fatima to protect the people of Brava against the evils of that time. His 'Chidirke Maana Faat̲ima' ('Rescue us, O Lady Fatima') railed against foreign aggression in the form of British troops that drove the Italians from Brava (and eventually Somalia as a whole.) It includes the lines:

> O Zahra, mother of Ḥusayn, come to our help,
> implore God to save us from the foreigners.
> O Prophet, O Messenger of God, come to our help!
> May God turn their gunpowder into water.
> O God, we have no recourse against [their] explosives:
> Save us, O Sublime, You who have created us.
> O God, keep them [the foreigners] in their own country,
> let their fire burn *them* [and not us].[110]

Included in the religious guidance offered by the *'ulamā'* in the *s̱teenzi* was advice on how to keep local community and family life harmonious. Thus Shaykh Qasim preached good relations among relatives and neighbours: 'Maintain close ties with your relatives, do not become estranged [or] slander each other/ Be mindful of the rights of your relatives and neighbors/ Forgive each other in all circumstances/ whoever forgives his fellow men will dwell in Paradise.'[111] He also cautioned: 'And we must respect and take care of our parents, O brothers. Those who trouble them will be put in Hell – you should fear this.'[112] Mallim Nuri complained that such respect was declining: 'Proof of this [the work of the Devil] is that compassion no longer exists:/ Children do no longer give their mothers the respect they deserve.'[113]

The *'ulamā'* considered good relations between husband and wife of special significance. Thus Shaykh Qasim told married couples: 'You should live together in harmony, not become estranged./ If wife and husband love each other, they find

[110] Mallim Nuri, 'Come to our help, O Lady Fatima', 19, 33–5.
[111] Shaykh Qasim, 'There is no god but God', 35–6.
[112] Shaykh Qasim, 'There is no god but God', 32.
[113] Mallim Nuri, 'Come to our help, O Lady Fatima', 16.

contentedness.'[114] Mallim Nuri presented Ḥawwā' (Eve) as a role model to make the same point:

> It is commendable for husband and wife to help each other
> in [matters of] the world and of religion.
> Ḥawwā' was the first to do so. She helped Adam,
> and through her deeds she served and honored him.
> For a wife, helping her husband is a source of pride;
> this is the ideal conduct, and Ḥawwā', that shining moon, was the
> first to display it.[115]

Dada Masiti addressed herself especially to women: 'Paradise is easily accessible to women, if they choose to be gentle./ You should strive to be agreeable/ and obey your husbands.'[116]

However, the *'ulamā'* did not just exhort others to preserve social harmony in Brava. They themselves maintained close and friendly relations with each other, irrespective of descent, social status, socio-economic background, age, gender, or *ṭarīqa* affiliation. The *s̱teenzi* show that they befriended and visited each other, prayed for the health of those who were ill, praised each other in their poems, asked for each other's blessings, and even made the pilgrimage together.[117]

The personal and vividly visual nature of Dada Masiti's poetry mentioned above best exemplifies the intimate local atmosphere of the *s̱teenzi*. It is in her poems that one finds reference to women's domestic habits such as burning sweet-scented incense to make a room smell good; keeping money for alms at hand near the bed of someone who was ill or a woman in labour, or preparing the body for burial after death.[118] Indeed, the poetry of Dada Masiti stands out among all other *s̱teenzi* in its ability to evoke local places, people, and events in ways that are so vivid and visual that they are almost film-like. In 'After life comes death',

[114] Shaykh Qasim, 'There is no god but God', 50.

[115] 'Mooja ondrola dhibu' ('O God, remove troubles'), also called 'Shṯeenzi cha nuuru za Mtume' ('The poem of the Prophet's light'), 17–18, 23.

[116] Dada Masiti, 'O Our Lady', 21. Other poems portray men and women as each other's helpmates, e.g. Mallim Nuri in 'Mooja ondrola dhibu' ('O God, remove troubles'), 17: 'It is commendable for husband and wife to help each other in [matters of] the world and of religion.'

[117] Examples from the turn of the twentieth century are the friendship between Shaykh Uways and Shaykh Nureni, that of Shaykh Qasim and Shaykh Nureni with Dada Masiti, and the warm feelings that inspired Shaykh Qasim's prayers for the Bravanese Ashrāf Omar Qullaten and Alawi b. Habib Makka in his 'Rescue us, O Prophet of God'.

[118] See for the former two customs, Dada Masiti, 'O Our Lady', 17; and for the latter, 'Sayyid Jamāl al-Dīn', 17–22.

she evokes the funeral procession for the departed and beloved Shaykh Nureni, portraying not only people's emotions but also Brava's 'sacred geography': as the men wound their way out of Brava to the grave site, the women watched from the roofs of their houses, from where angels were showering blessings on all.

The *S̱teenzi* Express the Unique Characteristics of their Authors

Although the *s̱teenzi* have in common that they are Sufi, didactic, devotional poems that represented the *'ilm* of the wider *umma* to all members, high and low, male and female, of a specific local community, each of the poet-scholars discussed here (as well as the others who feature in the recent source publication) leaves a personal stamp on his or her poems, a unique educational emphasis and approach, a special style, tone, technical virtuosity, and so forth. A full study lies beyond the scope of this chapter, but the striking difference in approach in the *s̱teenzi* of Shaykh Qasim and Dada Masiti, even though they share the common features of the *s̱teenzi* outlined above, exemplifies the idiosyncrasies of each poet. Shaykh Qasim's enormous erudition and his unique educational emphasis on complex matters of theology, already mentioned above, deserve further illustration.

Shaykh Qasim's poems convey more complex aspects of theology and refer by name to more Sufi saints, shaykhs, scholars, and poets than those of any other of the *s̱teenzi* poets. Apart from his prose and poetry texts in Arabic, his Chimiini oeuvre includes translations of classical religious texts. His 'Jisi gani khpaandra mitume' ('How could the [other] prophets …') is a translation of the Hamziyya, a eulogy of the Prophet composed in Arabic by the thirteenth-century poet of Mamlūk Egypt Abū 'Abd Allāh Muḥammad b. Sa'īd al-Būṣīrī, which gained immense popularity in East Africa.[119]

Shaykh Qasim translated approximately the first one hundred lines of the Hamziyya, i.e. the part devoted to the Prophet's life from his birth to his flight to Medina. From a formal point of view, he did not attempt to adhere to the original, for he divided his poem into stanzas formed by four rhyming hemistichs. While two of these hemistichs translate the Arabic text, the other two interpret and expand the concepts and metaphors alien to his local audience, or contain Shaykh Qasim's own comments and asides.[120] The great accomplishment of Shaykh Qasim is that, when recited, his Chimiini verses achieve a faithful reproduction of the rhythm of the Arabic poem, despite the difference in prosodic rules and hemistich length. However, the translation is couched in highly sophisticated but often

[119] The original title was 'Qaṣīdat Umm al-Qurā fī Madḥ Khayr al-Warā'. The poem is popularly known as the Hamziyya because all its lines rhyme in *hamzah*.

[120] The addition of these two hemistichs to each stanza makes the Chimiini text twice as long as the original. Different oral and written versions give between 98 and 108 stanzas.

obscure language, mirroring the linguistic complexities of the Arabic original. Most Chimiini speakers who recited it therefore did so for devotional purposes, without necessarily understanding every word.[121]

Other poems that attest to Shaykh Qasim's great erudition are his 'I start stringing coral beads', the Chimiini translation of the above-mentioned 'Aqīdat al-'Awāmm'; his 'La ilāha' ('There is no god but God'), which is based on the Umm al-Barāhīn ('The Mother of Proofs ...') by Shaykh Muḥammad b. Yūsuf al-Ḥasan al-Sanūsī (d. 1489), and which in sixty-six stanzas goes into great detail about God's attributes – both the attributes He necessarily has and those that can of necessity *not* be attributed to Him; his 'Ya nabiyi salaam aleika' ('O Prophet, peace be upon you'), a translation of the poetic part of the mawlid of al-Barzanjī, and his 'Salaatun salaamun 'alā al-Mustafa' ('Peace and blessings upon the Chosen One'), which provides versified advice about marriage by drawing directly on a rarely cited *ḥadīth*. Finally, in his 'Rescue us, O Prophet of God', a cry for help directed at the Prophet, Shaykh Qasim refers by name to about twenty scholars of different time-periods, including the founders of four *ṭarīqas*, authors of famous praise poems for the Prophet, Hadramawt scholars of the past, and shaykhs who were his (near-)contemporaries – a fascinating window on his intellectual and social network.

While Shaykh Qasim occasionally also expressed great emotion, as when describing his eagerness to visit the Prophet's tomb and his reference to the tears he shed at leaving Medina,[122] there is no doubt that Shaykh Qasim engaged his local audience by presenting them with instruction in texts of great difficulty and intellectual complexity.

As was already touched on above, Dada Masiti left a different stamp on her poems. While she never flaunted her formal religious knowledge, her poems show, as was mentioned above, her knowledge of Arabic and her familiarity with the Qur'ān and *ḥadīth*. For example, the Qur'ānic verse 'Take necessary provisions with you for the journey, and piety is the best provision of all'[123] is echoed in her lines: 'Provisions lie ahead/ for the pious who have done good [in this world]/Their souls are chosen [to dwell]/ in the highest level of Heaven that has been reserved for them.'[124] Another poem contains insightful meditations about the deeper meaning of 'al-Raḥmān' and 'al-Raḥīm' as attributes of God.[125]

[121] In the source publication we present only the first fifty stanzas, with special acknowledgement of our fellow-editor Mohamed Kassim.

[122] 'Meezi wa keendra' ('In the ninth month'), especially 7–8 and 15.

[123] The Qur'ān 2:97.

[124] 'O Exalted Lord', 11. Her knowledge of Arabic is evident from, for example, 'The evil that plagues the country' and 'Sayyid Jamāl al-Dīn'.

[125] 'Sayyid Jamāl al-Dīn', 2–3.

Dada Masiti's poems are unique in the extant corpus of *s̱teenzi* in two ways. First, as we saw above, her poetry had an almost filmic visual quality that brought to life concrete aspects of the everyday in Brava so familiar to her audience. Second, her poems occasionally make reference to personal emotions. Dada Masiti does not only speak about her past as a source of deep and painful remorse but also laments the indignities and physical challenges that come with old age. Gone the confidence, boldness, and arrogance of youth; gone health and strength. Now her breathing has become laboured, her joints are faltering, and her veins have 'dried up like the grass in the season without rain'.[126] In a less explicitly intellectual way, she reached her audience, men and women – but especially women – with her seemingly effortless, intimate, personal, and visual poetry.

Mallim Nuri too left a unique stamp on the *s̱teenzi*. The Bravanese addressed him as 'Maalimu' (Teacher) rather than as shaykh and he was indeed the teacher par excellence among all the *s̱teenzi* poets. First of all, with twenty-four *s̱teenzi* to his name, Mallim Nuri was the most productive poet in Chimiini.[127] Second, his poetic production bears testimony to his aim of including as many nuggets of religious instruction as possible in any one poem. It is true that no *s̱teenzi* are monothematic; all weave together prayers and supplications, praise of the Prophet and the *awliyā'*, Islamic history and legends, aspects of theology, rules of *fiqh*, social commentary and advice, and so forth. However, this feature is especially evident in Mallim Nuri's *s̱teenzi*. At times he crammed so many topics into a poem that the sudden transitions from specific event to general advice or historical epoch affected the poem's cohesion and flow. For example, his poem 'Sht̲eenzi cha Haawa na Aadamu' ('The poem of Eve and Adam') deals with as many as sixteen unrelated different topics! While a modern audience might see this as a shortcoming, the people for whom he composed his poetry greatly appreciated this.

Ease of learning was also a central objective in the form Mallim Nuri chose for his poems. Thus he couched his poems in the Chimiini of everyday speech that was accessible to all.[128] Moreover, in contrast to Shaykh Qasim, whose linguistic brilliance at times made a poem's meaning opaque, Mallim Nuri never used obscure language, even when translating Arabic *fiqh* into Chimiini verse (as in 'The Cream'). Of course, the rules of *fiqh* may have lent themselves to clarity of expression more than Shaykh Qasim's dense theological subject of God's attributes (as in 'I begin to string coral beads'), but Mallim Nuri aimed for ease

[126] 'O Exalted Lord', 29.

[127] This is the number that was included in the source publication mentioned above. There are other poems for which we do not have complete texts or for which his authorship is not certain.

[128] This in spite of the fact that Mallim Nuri himself refers to the language of his poetry as Chimbal̲azi, the literary form of Chimiini ('The Cream', 4).

of understanding and memorization even in the metre and rhyme he chose for his poems. In twenty-one out of his twenty-four poems, the rhyme is restricted to two hemistichs only (pattern a-a, b-b, c-c, etc.). In these ways Mallim Nuri too left the stamp of his personality on the *s̱teenzi*.

Conclusion

As a body of Islamic knowledge production that emerged around the turn of the twentieth century, the Chimiini *s̱teenzi* are religious, Sufi, instructional and devotional texts created to connect a specific local community on Somalia's Benadir coast to the religious knowledge of the wider Islamic *Umma*. Their major features, themes and objectives allow us to place the Chimiini *s̱teenzi* within the developments of East African Islam in this period, especially with regard to the new emphasis on expanding religious knowledge beyond the educated (coastal) elite to men and women of all social backgrounds, and on producing such knowledge in the local vernaculars.

The *s̱teenzi* purposefully guided local believers towards Islamic beliefs and acts of worship that were based on *'ilm* and thus in line with what their authors considered authoritative religious texts. This allows us insight into the intellectual framework and religious knowledge of the poets, each with his or her own specialty, emphasis, and personal touch. The impressive list of scholars and texts mentioned in the poems gives a glimpse of the *'ulamā'*'s formal Islamic knowledge, but the poems themselves, with their general Islamic and specific Sufi religious and social guidance, bear the fullest testimony to their authors' knowledge and insights. This corpus of poems shows them as well-integrated into the networks of Islamic learning in the western Indian Ocean, that is to say, the Hijaz; southern Arabia, especially the Hadramawt; the Swahili coast; and the Somali Benadir coast, with, to an increasing extent that is as yet not fully understood, inroads into the East African interior.

However, the poems also bring into view the uniquely *local* dimension of Islam in Brava. That they used the linguistic medium of the vernacular unique to Brava is an important aspect of this, for this language was, and is, central to the communal identity of this old, historical town. The *s̱teenzi* engaged the local to transmit the universally Islamic in other ways as well, namely through references to local or locally known people, places, customs, events, livelihoods, and the physical and social environment. In this way they offer insights into how a small East African port city at this moment in time learned and lived Islam.

The *s̱teenzi* show that the medium the people of Brava chose to create and preserve this living and enduring popular heritage was one in which orality and writing did not form an oppositional binary but coincided, overlapped, and reinforced each other; this combination helped to make the *s̱teenzi* a powerful, embodied intellectual and social experience, and a unique and resilient component of Brava's Islamic heritage and communal identity.

Finally, we would like to modify Mohamed Kassim's argument that anti-colonial resistance was central to the *st̠eenzi* of Brava (and the Islamic knowledge production of the Benadir in this period more generally).[129] As mentioned above, some poems (such as Dada Masiti's 'The evil that plagues the country' and Mallim Nuri's 'Rescue us, O Lady Fatima') decried specific aspects of colonial rule and aggression. Nevertheless, the 'resistance' of the *st̠eenzi* does not lie primarily in the occasional explicit expression of resistance to an aspect of colonial rule. Rather, this resistance lies in their very existence as an intensely local form of religious knowledge production intended to strengthen the Islamic values that lie at the heart of Brava's traditional, deeply religious, communal identity.

[129] Kassim, 'Colonial resistance'.

CHAPTER 15

A Senegalese Sufi Saint and *'Ajamī* Poet: Sëriñ Moor Kayre (1874–1951)

Khadim Ndiaye

The numerous manuscripts in *'Ajamī* discovered in Africa are in striking contrast with the myth of Africa being devoid of writing and significant literature, as conveyed by colonial hegemonic discourses. Alongside the 'Colonial Library'[1] or the writings produced by Europeans about Africa during the colonial period and by African intellectuals in French, English, and Portuguese, other libraries have thrived, among which is the Islamic library produced by 'Non-Europhone Intellectuals'.[2] These intellectuals wrote both in Arabic and in their native African languages (Fulani, Hausa, Swahili, Yoruba, Somali, Amharic, Kanuri, and so on) by using the Arabic script. This form of writing, called *'Ajamī*, enabled these 'Muslims beyond the Arab world'[3] to produce a body of works of high intellectual quality and value, dealing with a variety of subjects touching their lives.

The official language in Senegal is French, which is a relic of the country's colonial past. It is the language of instruction despite being inaccessible to a majority of Senegalese.[4] Alongside it, local languages are elective subjects for college students, are used as a medium of communication, and for other purposes in non-formal educational settings. *'Ajamī* writing is nevertheless widely used in Senegal in its Wolof form known as Wolofal, especially among followers of the Murīdiyya Sufi order,[5] founded by Shaykh Amadu Bamba (1853–1927). The most

[1] V.Y. Mudimbe, *The Invention of Africa: Gnosis, Philosophy, and the Order of Knowledge* (Bloomington and Indianapolis: Indiana University Press; London: James Currey, 1988).

[2] Ousmane Kane, *Non-Europhone Intellectuals* (Dakar: CODESRIA, 2012).

[3] Fallou Ngom, *Muslims beyond the Arab World: The Odyssey of Ajami and the Muridiyya* (Oxford: Oxford University Press, 2016).

[4] Mamadou Cisse, 'Langue, Etat et société au Sénégal', *Sudlangues*, 5, 2005, 99–133.

[5] There are several studies of this Sufi order. See in particular Cheikh Anta Mbacké Babou, *Fighting the Greater Jihad: Amadu Bamba and the Founding of the Murîdiyya of Senegal, 1853–1913* (Athens: Ohio University Press, 2007); John Glover,

prolific *'Ajamī* poets of this brotherhood are Sëriñ Moor Kayre (1874–1951), Sëriñ Sàmba Jaara Mbay (1870–1971), Sëriñ Muusaa Ka (1883–1967), and Sëriñ Mbay Jaxate (1875–1954). This group of *'Ajamī* poets were dubbed by some authors the 'Pléiade mouride',[6] in reference to the group of sixteenth-century French Renaissance poets.

This chapter examines the poetic work of a leading Mouride scholar, Sëriñ Moor Kayre, whose work caught my attention. With the exception of his close followers and specialists of Wolof *'Ajamī*, his work is unknown to the general public.

The study of his manuscripts is premised on the alarm sounded by Senegalese historian Cheikh Anta Diop in *Nations nègres et culture*[7] regarding the urgency of preserving Africa's rich intellectual leagacy, especially its written literary sources. Diop emphasized particularly the national prominence of these four great scholars and Wolofal poets. In his view, the poetic legacy of Sëriñ Moor Kayre and his peers 'should be carefully guarded before it disappears'.[8]

This chapter is part of a larger research project on the life and intellectual legacy of Sëriñ Moor Kayre, a prominent Murid poet and disciple. It draws from an unpublished biography, collections of poems, and other excerpts from the author's extensive poetic work. His poetry is inseparable from his discipleship to his master Bamba. In what follows, I will address his family background, life story, achievements, and companionship with Bamba as they appear in his poetry, and then offer a thematic analysis of selected verses of his poetic works.

Sëriñ Moor Kayre's Life and Work

Overview of Sëriñ Moor Kayre's Life

Sëriñ Moor Kayre was born in 1874 in Kayre Alleu, a village five kilometres from Khombole, bordering Baol and Cayor.[9] Son of Useynu Kayre and Soxna Anta

Sufism and Jihad in Modern Senegal: The Murîd Order (Rochester, NY: University of Rochester Press, 2007); Cheikh Guèye, *Touba : la capitale des mourides* (Paris: Karthala, 2002). See also David Robinson, *Paths of Accommodation: Muslim Societies and French Colonial Authorities in Senegal and Mauritania, 1880–1920* (Athens: Ohio University Press, 2000).

6 Samba Mbuup, 'Littérature nationale et conscience historique. Essai sur la perspective nationaliste dans la littérature d'expression wolof de 1850 à nos jours', PhD diss., Université de Paris III, 1977.

7 Cheikh Anta Diop, *Nations nègres et culture* (Paris: Présence Africaine, 1979).

8 Diop, *Nations nègres*, 530.

9 Baol and Cayor are regions of Senegal. Here, the names of the localities are written in their usual form. The names of people are Wolofized.

Jénn, Kayre came from a renowned literate Muslim family. In his biography,[10] he says the following about his family:

> Koo gis cosaanam di Kajoor ak Mbaakol
> Am na ci waa Njaxate maam mbaatew Syll
>
> Ngir ñooy cosaani doomi soxna ya fi woon
> Delluy cosaani nit ñi yiw yi fi njëkkon[11]
>
> [Anyone from Cayor and Mbakol
> Has ancestry in the Njaxate or Syll[12] families
>
> They had given birth to renowned scholars
> And to the first great virtuous people who lived there]

Regarding his ancestry he further added:

> Man Kayre nak sama ñetteelub maam ci baay
> Ndéy jaa juddoo Njaxate, wax lii du lu aay
>
> [As for me, Kayre, my great-great paternal grandfather
> Came from the Jaxate family, without any doubt]

Sëriñ Moor Kayre's family is divided into two branches, one coming from Fouta[13] and the other from Cayor:

> Sunuy coosaan bu leen ko feetale Bawal
> Fuutaak Kaajoor ñooy maami gîr yi ñu lawal
>
> [Do not tell that we originated from Bawol
> Our ancestors came from Fouta and Cayor]

According to his only living son, Sëriñ Abdu Kayre,[14] the name Kayre derives from Hayre, which is the name of a locality in Fouta, Hayre Lao,[15] his paternal ancestors' village. His mother came from Cayor. Therefore Kayre is not his

[10] This document was in the possession of Sëriñ Xaadim Kayre, Sëriñ Moor Kayre's grandson.

[11] In this chapter, each verse of poetry is followed by its translation.

[12] These last names are also spelled Diakhaté and Syll or Sylla.

[13] Fouta-Toro is a region of northern Senegal bordering the left bank of the Senegal River.

[14] His full name is Sëriñ Abdu Rahmân Kayre. I interviewed him in my documentary film about his father.

[15] Also spelled in this form: Aéré Lao or Haere Lao. The paternal lineage of Amadu Bamba originated in the village of Abdallah in the province of Lao in Fouta-Toro. See Babou, *Fighting the Greater Jihad*, 34.

family name. Moor Kayre's real family name is Baro,[16] a common family name in Senegal. His father, a Tijāniyya affiliate, taught him the Qur'ān and religious sciences. After his studies, he earned his living as a tailor. He was an accomplished, erudite and pious Muslim who was fascinated by Prophet Muḥammad's life story. He demonstrated his eagerness to go to Mecca and Medina. His fascination for the Prophet of Islam finally led him to Shaykh Amadu Bamba, as he puts it:

Ba ma jogé cëg njëkk Màkka laa nàmmoon
Ak Màddina ak Saam ndeke boobu Mbàkke laa jëmoon

Leerug Bàmba ji moo ma ñoddi may dox di tem-temi ba Yàllaa ma ko won

Ma nga ma booleeg moom ci ay nelaw won ma melow yonent ba dootu ma selaw

[When I entered the Path, I was captivated by Mecca
Medina and Shâm when in reality I was heading for Mbacké

Allah constantly directed Bamba's hypnotizing light to me

He showed it to me in a dream. He has the characteristics of the Prophet, which delighted me]

Attracted by the prophetic light, Kayre finally joined Bamba who, in turn, commanded him to praise the Prophet of Islam in his poems:

Bàmba ma may man Kayre may wone xarbaax i Yonent

[Bamba has endorsed my verses extolling the prowess of the Prophet]

He met Shaykh Amadu Bamba in 1890 in his new homestead of Touba, where Bamba settled with his family in 1888.[17] He stayed in Touba after pledging his allegiance. Later he followed him to Mbacké-Bari (Djolof), where he lived until 1895, when his master was arrested. Bamba sent him and other followers to stay with his brother Maam Cerno Mbàkke prior to his deportation to Gabon (1895–1902).

During Bamba's second exile in Sarsara, Mauritania (1902–7),[18] he decided to join him. He was among the fortunate disciples who received the famous qasîda '*Ina-l la zîna ilâ Sarsâra*' ('Those who went to Sarsara ...') from the shaykh, where he wrote that: 'those who came to Sarsâra with the intention to pay me a visit are absolved of their sins'. He stayed in Sarsara with the shaykh before they

[16] According to his son, Abdu Kayre. Also written Barro.
[17] Guèye, *Touba*, 75.
[18] Sarsara is located 27 kilometres from Boutilimit, a town in Mauritania.

travelled back to Thiéyène (Djolof) in 1907. Once in Thiéyène, he was allowed by the shaykh to visit his family. Later on, Sëriñ Moor Kayre went on touring the country, visiting many places like Ndiégam, a Seereer[19] locality and the home of his disciple Gàjji Fay. He penned this stanza about the village:

Njégam la jaaye mbaamum deex
Sa réew Seereer ya la xame Seex
Ba sàlli ngëneel dootu fa jeex
Budul woon Seex ma sàmmaani

[It was in Ndiégam that I sold a racy donkey
I became a Shaykh in Seereer country
This village was the land of plenty
Had it not been the Shaykh, I would have been a shepherd]

Following his master's death, he renewed his allegiance to his son and first successor, Mamadu Mustafaa Mbàkke, who sent him to Taïf.[20] He founded the village of Ndony near the vicinity of Taïf. Later on, he settled in the eponymous village of Kayre that he had created, where he died before noon on Sunday, 17 June 1951 (12 Ramadan). His family and disciples commemorate his death each year in Touba. His son Mame Thierno Kayre took over from him and perpetuated the family legacy from 1951 until his death in 1998. Sëriñ Abdu Kayre took over from him from 1998.

There are no photographs of Sëriñ Moor Kayre. However, according to the description given by Abdu Kayre, he was a sturdy light-skinned man, always smiling and affectionately nicknamed 'Baay Maaka' (Father-Maaka) since he loved wearing conical straw hats that are also highly coveted by Fulani herders of the Sahel. His kindness was legendary, as reported by his disciple Mustafaa Sëy.[21] One day a beggar entered his home begging for clothes to wear so Moor Kayre borrowed a loincloth from his wife, Xari Gumba, wore it, and took off his clothes which he gave to the beggar.

Sëriñ Moor Kayre had a great many followers, who each shone according to the extent of their piety. Beside Gàjji Fay, these included Sëriñ Moor Marem Njaay and Sëriñ Moor Koddu Njaay. The latter was a gifted medium. Others of his followers who are still alive are Sëriñ Umar Njaay and Sëriñ Mustafaa Sëy.

Moor Kayre was one of the first *'Ajamī* poets to sing the praises of his master Bamba. He also maintained excellent friendship bonds with his fellow poets in their years of discipleship. These bonds of mutual respect fostered the recognition

[19] The Seereer people are the third-largest ethnic group in Senegal.
[20] Located east of the department of Mbacké, in the region of Diourbel.
[21] Interviewed in the documentary film.

of their followers when they were promoted to the rank of shaykh. Sëriñ Moor Kayre was second after Sëriñ Sàmba Jaara Mbay to write *'Ajamī* poems praising their master's exceptional human qualities and virtues. Moreover, Sëriñ Sàmba Jaara Mbay recalled their relationship and respective roles as pioneers of Murid *'Ajamī* poetry:

> Yow Taala yal na nga gudduw fan
> siggil nga ma man mi njëkk woy
> Seex ba tay woykat yi yépp a ngi woy
>
> [I wish you Taala a very long life[22]
> You honoured me as the first to sing the Shaykh's praises
> And now all the singers are imitating me]

Sëriñ Moor Kayre profusely returned the favour to Sëriñ Sàmba Jaara Mbay and conceded his rank as the second most prolific poet singing his Shaykh's praises:

> Ka njëkk a woy Bàmba maa ca topp ñuy
> Woyandoo, ñu woye fa gànnaari woy
> Jurbel ba ñépp a ñu roy
>
> [I was the second poet to sing the merits of Bamba
> And together we kept singing
> We sang in Mauritania and Diourbel until everyone started imitating us.]

The great talent of these two pioneers of Murid Wolofal was acknowledged and endorsed as Sëriñ Moor Kayre puts it in the following verse:

> Ñun ñaar la Bàmba ni seen woy day
> Hikam, du Wolof, Maak Sàmba Jaara la wax lii
> Loolu sax dafa doy
>
> [Bamba said your poetry is a source of wisdom,
> It is not Wolof he said to Sàmba Jaara and I
> His words are heart-warming]

The youngest of the group and a virtuoso, Sëriñ Muusaa Ka, for his part said he was indebted to the two 'giants' of Wolof *'Ajamī* poetry:

> Maam Sàmba Jaara ak Jaxateek Moor Kayre
> Ñépp a nga dengoo, Njàmme jël seen bayre

[22] A nickname of Sëriñ Moor Kayre, which he uses to name him in his poetry.

[The pioneers Sàmba Jaara and Moor Kayre
Wrote verses and Njàmme[23] inherited their charisma]

His admiration was echoed in other verses, without mentioning Sëriñ Sàmba Jaara Mbay:

Dexug Kayre man laa naane ak Baabakar sadiix
Nde ñoo xuus ci géejug Bàmba bay xelli ndox mu neex

[I drank at Kayre's river with Baabakar, The Truthful
They dived into Bàmba's ocean until they became his flowing streams.]

Sëriñ Moor Kayre continued corresponding with Sëriñ Muusaa Ka because the latter praised the virtues of Sëriñ Mamadu Mustafaa Mbàkke, first caliph of the Murīdiyya and successor of the great 'mystical pole' ('*Ku wuutu xawsu*').[24] Sëriñ Muusaa Ka later extolled his fellow disciple's qualities and prayed to the Lord to save his soul. He also mentioned to Sëriñ Muusaa Ka that, with a new caliph, their poetry had been taken to a new level and his presence warranted the end of their mourning for their master. The stanza used here is called *muqtadib:*

Ñjàmme góor nga jaajëfe waay
Kayre kañ la faf di la woy
Yaw ki woy mbërëm mi fi man
Yaw siraat ja yalna nga wéy

Ñjàmme nag ma *wax* la lu tuut
Mustafaaay kuloor sunu woy
Ngir ku wuutu xawsu du maas
woykatam du jooy du ne 'woy'!

[Thank you Njàmme, you are a gentleman
I honour you and praise your merits
You who magnified the achievements of my hero
I pray you to cross the bridge Sirât[25] without fear

Let me tell you something dear Njàmme
It is Mustafaa who embellishes our poems
As a successor of the Pole, he is eminent
His thurifer never sheds tears of sorrow]

[23] Njàmme is one of the nicknames used by Sëriñ Muusaa Ka in his poetry.
[24] *Xawsu* is derived from *Ghawth*. In Sufism, *Al-Ghawth al-A'zam* is the Supreme Helper.
[25] According to the Islamic tradition, *Sirât* is the bridge, thinner than a hair, stretched over hell, which all human beings must traverse to reach paradise.

If Sëriñ Moor Kayre and his poems were loved by everyone, Sëriñ Muusaa Ka later became the public's favourite, the poet whose lyricism moved everyone. In the view of Baay Maaka, his fellow disciple is an admirable poet who has eclipsed them all. Sëriñ Moor Kayre beautifully recounts his positive view of the poetic talent of Sëriñ Muusaa Ka in this poem:[26]

Man Taala mii du ma iñaan ku riisaa
Daa koy sibooru ndax mu may ma wiisaa

[I Kayre never envy an eminent poet
I'd rather flatter him so that I can gain his recognition]

The following anecdote from Sëriñ Abdu Kayre sheds light on the close relationship between the two poets and the admiration of Sëriñ Moor for Sëriñ Muusaa Ka. One day, Sëriñ Muusaa Ka was visiting Sëriñ Moor Kayre's house. He scribbled a few words on a piece of paper as soon as he arrived and told the young disciple accompanying him to take the note to Sëriñ Moor Kayre. He read the words in the note '*Sëriñ Moor, tay jii de dinaa la jommal*' (Sëriñ Moor, I have come to amaze you) and Sëriñ Moor responded '*Manoo maa jommal, da nga may jàmmal*' (You cannot amaze me, on the contrary you are going to appease me).

Sëriñ Moor Kayre was also very close to Sëriñ Mbay Jaxate, the moralist-poet whose aphorisms are well grounded in Wolof culture. Sëriñ Abdu Kayre added that one day, Sëriñ Mbay Jaxate told Sëriñ Moor Kayre that he had lost his inspiration after Bamba's death, so Sëriñ Moor Kayre encouraged him to start singing the virtues of the first caliph, Sëriñ Mamadu Mustafaa Mbàkke. Sëriñ Mbay Jaxate followed his advice and soon after rediscovered his eloquence by writing poems on the qualities and virtues of Amadu Bamba's eldest son. Sëriñ Moor Kayre encouraged Sëriñ Mbay Jaxate to pursue his important mission to write poems. He wrote 'he was the captain whose success rests on steering his ship'. If Moor Kayre was the *bashîr*, the announcer of good news, Sëriñ Mbay Jaxate was the *nazîr*, the warner whose verses invite followers to moral rectitude:

Seex Baabakar jaxatil gaalug ndigal gi nga war
Soo joowatul jaxatoo teertil te doo bari ndam

Capteen bu muy bàyyi baarub gaal gi kon di na toj
Buy fiiru doc ne rajax! Góor jooy fa jooyi ndayam

Seen gaal gi may joowlu mooy seen itte jogatul
Laabiire leen say waxay may itte kuy bëga dem

[26] Several verses of this poem are presented in the last part of this study.

Man maay 'bashî'r ngay 'nazîr' te *bégle* naa jariñul
yaw nag xuppeel ndax ku làmboo itte jàjju wedam

Kuy nit te xelu bu seetloo say bayit bewetul
Day bàyyi lépp ludiy caaxaan te sàmmi jëfam

[Shaykh Baabakar please steer the ship which is on a mission
If you no longer hold the rudder, get out of the ship, you will no longer be successful

A captain who fails to control his ship will cause a shipwreck
He leaves it at the mercy of rocks and makes his passengers suffer and cry

The ship that does not fail is the salvation of the disciples
Talk to them because your words are useful to Murids

You are the *Nazîr* and I am the *Bashîr* who wants to be helpful for you
Spread the word because someone who is ambitious must be motivated

Any reasonable man who understands your writing
Will likely abhor foolishness and control his actions]

Like other followers, Moor Kayre was saddened by Bamba's death in 1927, and his sorrow lingered. His lamentations can be heard in his elegy to his master:

Sama seex bee ma daa bégal di ma berndeel
Di ma yaatal ba xey ma nax ñibbi Tuubaa

Bu ma jooyee damaa gisul ka ma miinoon
Su ma doon ndaw danaa yërëmlu ji Tuubaa

[My Shaykh who used to welcome and entertain me with grand pomp
Has suddenly returned to Tuubaa

I cry because my good friend is gone forever
if I was young, I would go to lament in Tuubaa]

Overview of Sëriñ Moor Kayre's Work

Seriñ Moor Kayre wrote about seventy manuscripts, a compendium of six thousand verses. Before translating some verses from selected themes, it might be instructive to make a few comments on the poet's work.

Literary Genres and Themes

The texts of Sëriñ Moor Kayre are classified as Islamic inspired poetry. The main themes explored in his poetry revolve around the work of his spiritual master, the Sufi saint Shaykh Amadu Bamba. Bamba and his writings are the main source of inspiration for all Murid-driven *'Ajamī* poetry and scholarship. The poetry of Wolof scholars is epic, didactic, historical, elegiac, philosophical, and mystical. Sëriñ Moor Kayre's poems, written at different stages of his life, deal with hagiography, theology, praise songs, social criticism, moral and religious education, and so on. The Senegalese historian Cheikh Anta Diop is one of the first to point to the array of topics covered by Wolof *'Ajamī* poets and authors. In his view:

> this poetry also deals with satirical verses (Alioune Thioune), polemics in the form of epistles (Mor Talla Fall). It abounds with versification of physiological and moral topics (Sëriñ Mbay Jaxate), casting picturesque description of the lifestyle in royal courts. In addition to the clerics' attitude of subordination, the portrayal of customs, and relationships therefrom, in the early days of Muridiyya.[27]

The Wolofal poems of Sëriñ Moor Kayre follow the rules of Arabic poetry as reflected in his manuscripts, but in some cases, the metric rules used are mentioned. If the rules are driven by Arabic prosody, a blend of local colouring is added. The national consciousness equation[28] pervades the poetry of Wolof *'Ajamī* scholars. According to Diop, 'given the way of life, one can feel, even through religious expression, the ever-diversified Negro pulse generating art'.[29] Sëriñ Moor Kayre, like other poets, can relate to the issues his generation faced, giving it context by using his mother tongue. The terminology they used might come from various sources. In addition to using Arabic, Wolof *'Ajamī* poets borrowed foreign words and used loan words that they blended with their own Wolof linguistic reality. These loan words are Wolofized. Sëriñ Moor Kayre used many foreign words and expressions in his poetry, French in particular. Here's an example:

> Man Taala mii du ma iñaan ku riisaa
> Daa koy sibooru ndax mu may ma wiisaa
>
> [I Taala never envy an eminent poet
> I'd rather flatter him so that I can gain recognition]

The term '*riisaa*' comes from the French '*riche*' (rich), the word '*wiisaa*' from 'visa'.

Sëriñ Moor Kayre used several metric forms in his poetry such as *rajaz*, *mutadārik*, *mutaqārib*, *munsarih*, *muqtadib*, etc. But his poems did not always

[27] Diop, *Nations nègres*, 531.

[28] Ngom, *Muslims Beyond the Arab World*, 26 and following.

[29] Diop, *Nations nègres*.

stick to the Arabic metric standards. Instead they copied their master, Shaykh Amadu Bamba, who in many instances used his own metric like the *tashmīd* in his poem *Jazbul Qulūb*, meaning attraction of hearts.[30] In doing so, Moor Kayre and his peers invented their own standards to follow whenever they needed to.

His Audience

The poetry of Shaykh Moor Kayre and his fellow Murid poets and disciples catered for public gatherings during Murid religious events; his primary audience was the Murid disciple of Wolof background. In Shaykh Amadu Bamba's educational programme, no one should be left behind.[31] Those who could not learn his teachings in Arabic should be able to access them in their mother tongue. In furtherance of this aim, he had personally tasked some of his disciples and gifted *'Ajamī* poets to instruct these disciples through *'Ajamī* poetry in Wolof. Thus, in his poem '*Xarnu Bi*' ('The Century'), the poet Sëriñ Muusaa Ka said his master Amadu Bamba made him his interpreter '*Tay jii ma wax bani tareet Ngir yaa ma def antarpareet*', which means 'I will talk to be astounded because you made me your interpreter'. In the writings of Sëriñ Moor Kayre, the expression '*Mooma soññi loo*' that translates literally as 'the Master tasked me to talk to the disciples' appears quite often in his poetry. Defining their target audience, these poets acted as soldiers whose only mission was to prepare their fellow disciples on how to claim ownership of their master's teachings.

Dissemination and Translation Issues

The Wolofal texts and the other Islamic manuscripts of Kayre are jealously guarded by the author's relatives or disciples, who view them as a valuable legacy that must be treasured by the family and kept away from the public. These revered manuscripts are hidden in private libraries and collections. It is a challenge to convince wary self-proclaimed curators of the utility of sharing them with researchers and the public in general. It was fortunate that Seriñ Moor Kayre's grandson was aware of the importance of recording his grandfather's manuscripts and making them available to researchers and academic institutions.

Another challenge to people doing fieldwork is the 'double translation' dilemma. This is an expression used by the Senegalese linguist Pathé Diagne[32]

[30] Mamadou Lo, 'Un aspect de la poésie wolofal mouride : traduction et analyse de quelques titres de Sëriñ Mbay Jaxate', Master's thesis, Université Cheikh Anta Diop de Dakar, 1993.

[31] Fallou Ngom, 'Amadu Bamba's Pedagogy and the Development of 'Ajamī Literature', *African Studies Review*, 52, 1, 2009, 99–123, 109.

[32] Pathé Diagne, 'Table ronde sur 'l'éducation en Afrique', *Présence Africaine*, Nouvelle série 64, 4e trimestre 1967, 59–96.

to illustrate the fact that a minimum proficiency in Arabic, some knowledge of the poets' social and religious background, and a mastery of the *'Ajamī* writing system with its particular forms and signs, are required for someone to be able to transcribe Wolof *'Ajamī* texts into Latin characters before translating them into another language. These necessary skills are often lacking in students and other researchers trained only in European languages such as French or English. Another challenge is recognising in the poet's manuscripts the words borrowed from the writings of Shaykh Amadu Bamba or verses quoted from the Qur'ān. In short, it is a prerequisite for researchers to be versed in Islamic sciences and to be familiar with the writings of the shaykh, in order to grasp and translate the true meaning of some of these poems. The accurate and complete translation of Sëriñ Moor Kayre's *'Ajamī* poetry will contribute to disseminating the work of this gifted yet unknown intellectual, whose legacy is part of the cultural heritage of Africa.

In addition, one must salute the steps taken by the late Sëriñ Abdu Lahad Mbàkke (1914–89), son of Shaykh Amadu Bamba and third caliph of the Murīdiyya, to record on audio tapes the writings of the four most famous Wolof *'Ajamī* poets. Sëriñ Abdu Lahad Mbàkke found one of the greatest voices of the Murīdiyya order to chant all their repertoire. As a result, many of Sëriñ Moor Kayre's poems are well preserved today. Audio files of his chanted *'Ajamī* poems are now available online for listening or free download.

As a contribution to the dissemination of Sëriñ Moor Kayre's work and success story, we initiated in 2014 a documentary film project titled *Baay Maaka*, which recounts his life story and achievements. It took several weeks for the production team and shooting crew to finish the project. They travelled hundreds of miles, meeting with the poet's relatives who are living in different towns and villages, securing the approval and involvement of specialists in *'Ajamī* poetry, for a fifty-minute documentary. They visited the poet's birthplace and his home in Touba. Many of his poems are chanted and commented upon in the film and the topics of his poetry discussed. His only surviving son also features in the documentary, some of his grandchildren, and a few surviving disciples. The film aired on Senegalese national television on 6 December 2014.

Verse Translation

Moor Kayre's poetry tackles an array of topics that can also be found in the works of other Wolofal poets. We have selected verses from Sëriñ Moor Kayre's work to highlight some of these topics.[33]

[33] All the texts presented here come from his grandson Sëriñ Xaadim Kayre. Some

His Relationship with the Shaykh Amadu Bamba

Sëriñ Moor Kayre wrote many verses dedicated to his master Shaykh Amadu Bamba. In his view, the shaykh's persona is unique:

> Alhamdou lilaahi nu sant sunu Boroom
> Bi ma xamal Bàmba mi mësla am moroom
>
> [In the name of God, Praise be the Lord
> Who guided me toward Bamba who has no equal]

His master is the great saint whose achievements earned him the title of Servant of the Prophet of Islam. His holy city of Touba is the blessed land where all Murid disciples want to be buried:

> Nimu nekkee jëfal Nabii ci Wolof yii
> Ba tuddoo Xaadimu Rasuuli fa Tuubaa
>
> Dadi Xaadim di gën ji xutbu di waasil
> Ta di xawsu ku wax na feete na Tuubaa
>
> Gile Tuubaa ku Yàlla def nib xaritam
> La ñu koy rob mu dékki dem gële Tuubaa
>
> Ku fi gëm lii na ñaan ñu rob *ko* ci sii suuf
> Bu fi dékke ëlëk ñu *yobbuko* Tuubaa
>
> [He served the Prophet so well among the Wolofs
> That he earned the title of Xaadimu Rasuul in Tuubaa
>
> He is the Servant, the Intercessor, the greatest Pole
> Of those who pick Tuubaa as residence
>
> When the one befriended by God is buried in Tuubaa
> He resurrects and goes to the Heavenly Tuubaa
>
> If you believe it pray to be buried there
> After resurrection, he will be moved to Tuubaa in Heaven]

For our poet, only the shaykh can bring joy to the disciples. For this reason, extolling his qualities is a way of gratifying him. He credited his ability to write poetry in Wolof and Arabic to his shaykh.

> Wedamloo nga ña daa reetaan sa murid
> Ba ñu xam ni sa waay du torox ci mujjam
> ku fi am li nu am da na doon sa géwal

---

poems are listed in the Fallou Ngom Collection, which is part of the Endangered Archives Programme 334.

Woy war na géwal ci ku sotti mayam
Seex yaa nu xamal ba nu mel ni Arab
Bay woy ci arab ak a woy ci ajam

[You stunned those who laughed at your disciple
They now know your follower will never lose
Anyone who has such master will become his bard
The generous is always praised by the bard
O Shaykh! we are as eloquent as Arab poets
We can now write poems in Arabic and Ajam]

For Sëriñ Moor Kayre, the shaykh is the true heart surgeon, the perfect physician of ailing souls. His master has the capacity to turn the heart's evil inclinations into good ones:

Sëriñ bee gis ku daa ñeetaan
Mu def ko ni waa ju daa reetaan
Te moo fiy fal ku dee faa daan
Bamuy niru waa ju daa daane

[When the Shaykh encountered a distressed person
He made him very euphoric
When he crossed paths with a loser
He made him a perpetual winner]

Here Sëriñ Moor Kayre recounts his sincere allegiance to the Shaykh:

Ku xawsu bindug baaxam bu leen seetatig bonam
Ku seet ag bonam kat xawsu lay weddi ay waxam

Te man Kayre Bàmbaa bind saag jub ci aw këyit
Taxit sant naa man mii ku may bañ du jëm kanam

Sëriñ bee ma *noon* deel sant yow aw nga yoonu jub
Bul jàqati ba ngay jooy xanaa doyna ag ngërëm

Mu dellooti cib yoor-yoor beneen lal ma woo ma ñëw
Mu jox maw këyit wow bégle laa fekk ciy mbindam

Mbindam maa ma wax saag jub teyit moo ma soññi loo
Ku yëg lii bu may gotteeti mooy feeñalug dëngëm

[When the elect of God praise somebody's goodness
Do not conjecture, otherwise you contradict him

As for me, Bamba endorsed my righteousness on paper
Therefore, I am grateful and my enemy will be lagging behind

He summoned me one afternoon
And gave me a written note that made me happy

The Master enjoined me to be grateful for I was on the right path
He told me not to worry, I was so elated

This note attests to the sincerity of my mission as a preacher
Be advised I am tasked to correct what is wrong]

Verses Extolling the Prophet

A great deal of Sëriñ Moor Kayre poems is dedicated to the Prophet of Islam, his family, and his companions as demonstrated in the following verses:

Bismi Laahi Kayre woy ki fiy gën ji Adnaanaa
Ki tax Yàlla sos nit ñeek jinneey gën ji Adnaanaaa

Ki tax Yàlla sos mbooleem malaakaam ya ak 'Arash'
te sos ngir jëmmam 'Kursiyyu' mooy gën ji Adnaanaa

Ki tax 'asamaaw' yeek suuf yi deydeele laa di woy
Muhammadu Abdu Laahi mooy gën ji adnaanaa

[In the name of God, I Kayre am praising the best of 'Adnān lineage
God created human beings and Jinns out of the best of 'Adnān's family

For his sake God created the angels and the Throne
Everything else was created for His Majesty, the best of the 'Adnāns

My verses are praising the one for whom the heavens and earth were created
His name is Muhammad 'Abdu Lâhi the best of the 'Adnāns]

On *Tawḥīd* (Oneness of God)

This text on Tawḥīd shows that Sëriñ Moor Kayre was also versed in theology. Here he uses the equine metaphor to teach the disciples about faith, patience, solitude, piety, and hard work:

Bu Tawhiid defoon aw naaru-góor
Gëm di wuddam baa
Ragal Yàlla dim ñàddam
Nangoo muñ di gettam baa

Ndigël moo di ay buumam
Ya koy yeew ba doo tu dem
Nangoo wéet di ab jéngam
bu saay-saay yorul doom baa

[If Tawḥīd is a thoroughbred
Then faith is its stable
Piety its fence
And patience its enclosure

Injunction is its rope
Which bridles and controls it
Solitude is its chains
That a fool does not possess]

Exhortation of the Disciples

Inspired by the Shaykh's teachings, Sëriñ Moor Kayre devoted a great deal of verses urging his fellow disciples to remain steadfast in the path of righteousness. As he already hinted, the Shaykh tasked him to embolden ('*Mooma soññi loo*') his fellow disciples' faith:

Bisim Laay Kayre santaane
Jubal yoon ak di distaane

Muriid kaay leen nu waxtaane
Lunuy tax a muslu saytaane

Di leen xool yoon te wàttuy pax
Te wàttum ndog mu melniy sox

Xalam leen dee nde kon ngeen sax
Ci jàkk ak dox di diistaane

Bu ngeen sóoboo bu leen moy yoon
Di wut ku fi xam mu ànd ak yéen

Bu leen koy fàtte yobbalu leen
Ku yobbalu moom du ñeetaane

[And here is Kayre the messenger
Who blazes the trail and proclaims

Fellow Murids, gather around me
Let's talk about how to ward off Satan

Beware on the path and avoid any pitfalls
Shun obstacles that can cause gunshot injury

Practice meditation that brings you closer
To God and makes you truth-seekers

Once you begin your journey, remain steadfast
Seeking good masters who can guide you

Take a viaticum, do not forget it so
you will never be disillusioned]

In the following verses, Sëriñ Moor Kayre reminds the disciples of the criteria for selecting a trustworthy master and how to avoid the impostor who can fool them in God's path. Sëriñ Moor Kayre uses *mutaqārib* metric form in this poem:

Muriid, deel takook seex bu mat tey bu xam
Bu lay laayebiir tey buy sellal jëfam

Bu xam péey ba xawsook rijaal yay dajee
Bu ràññee sariiha ak haqiiqaak jëmam

Te xam kay Boroom péey ba xam yonenam
Bileb seex dawal leen ko màggal mbiram

Ku dul bii sëriñ daw ko yow miy Muriid
Nde kuy réer di réeral Mariid mooy turam

Muriid, ak Mariid, ak Muraad bokkewul
Muraad moo di seex bub jubam def alam

Muriid mooy ku gëm Yàlla jox koy mbiram
Mariid mooy ku seytaane wommat xolam

Na ngay muslu saytaane yow kiy murid
Te wut seex bu lay tàggaleek ay ndogam

Melow seex bi may wax du kuy seex di moom
Du foo dem ñu am nattangoom, noo ko am

[Murid, seek after a true and learned Shaykh
The one who is prodigal and sincere

The one who knows the place of the elect of God
The one who is apt to discern *Sharī'a*, *ḥaqīqa* and his own self

And knows the Lord and His messenger
Serve this kind of Shaykh and exalt his deeds

O Murid, shun any Shaykh who lacks these qualities
Marîd is an impostor who misleads people

The Murid, Marîd and Murâd are very different in nature
Murâd is a Shaykh whose sincerity is evident

Murid is the one who believes only in God and entrusts Him with his business

Marîd is the one whose heart is controlled by Satan

O Murid do your best to avoid Satan's tricks
Find a Shaykh who pulls you out of his evil plots

The Shaykh I evoke has no equal
This Shaykh is unique and he is our Shaykh]

On Meditation and the Use of Reason

Sërin Moor Kayre wrote many poems emphasizing the importance of reason and meditation for disciples seeking God:

Saadix dafay nangoo xalam
Dëkkal lu baax ci am xelam

Tey rafetal yeeney xolam
Bu dee sikkar xolam xalam

Baatiin xalam nga koy xamee
Yàlla xalam nga koy gëmee

Ku xalamul bu *gëlemee*
Moo silmaxaal bëti xolam

Kuy seetlu door a wax du juum
Du dox di reccu ak di miim

Ab seetlukat du sànku moom
Dof mooy ku jiitalul xelam

[The sincere disciple must meditate
He vivifies good things in his heart

His intentions are sincere
He purifies his heart during meditation

Secret knowledge is transcended through meditation
Meditation boosts your faith in God

If you don't think twice in anger
You closed the eyes of your heart

If you think twice before you talk
You never have regrets or are in denial

A wise man is never lost
A fool does not use his mind]

Verses Addressed to His Peer Sëriñ Muusaa Ka

His good relationship with his peer Sëriñ Muusaa Ka was mentioned above. Here are other verses in which he emphasizes, without reservation, his gifts in the art of poetry. His verses dedicated to Sëriñ Muusaa Ka are among the finest ever written in the Wolof language:

Kayree ngi naa Muusaa fi sut ci yii saa
Ku ko rawoon lu jiitu dabtil Muusaa

Man sippinaa yaa saf sebul te noosaa
Say woy a siiw xaayaki reewi Muusaa

Njëk njëkk saa woy wee safoon suuf soosaa
Yaw nak sa woy jël na dombook waa roosaa

Man taala mii du ma iñaan ku riisaa
Daa koy sibooru ndax mu may ma wiisaa

Lii kat misaal la bul ma fàtte Muusaa
Yaw deema ñaanal tey jileek soosee saa

Ku sax ci ñaan kookee du koy taxoo saa
Jombul bu faatoo sax dëkkak Idriisaa

Yal na nu Yàlla may nu bokku keesaa
Fa kër ya naa Aljanna bokku miisaa

May nug téxey ëlëk fégal nu 'buusaa'
Yal na nu Yàlla ubbi maak mii Muusaa

Amiina yaa Rabbi ku ñaan mooy *'luusaa'*
Kudul yaxantu sax du def ku riisaa

Yaxantu naa ci tagg Bàmba ay saa
Taggam wi def ma may nirook 'ru'uusaa'

Taggam wi feesal na samay 'ko'oosaa'
ba maa ngi mandal tay samay 'juluusaa'

Tonoy woyam wee fi saxal ab soosaa
Saxal kafeek mburook fegalmay tiisaa

Taggam wi mooma may muriid yu woosaa
Ngir bëgg a am ngërëm lu mbóot ma diisaa

Tagg Sëriñ bi mooma def 'mahruusaa'
Man defe naa sax mooma def 'ra'iisaa'

Man tagg naa Sëriñ bi ay '*taxmiisaa*'
Mu wan ma xayrun naasi kay 'naamuusaa'

Laayay fa xadiis[34] mooma tax di xuusaa
Ci yile xeewal ndax ku santaay 'luusaa'

[Kayre is confirming that Muusaa is the best of all
He surpassed his colleagues who now follow his footsteps

You are seductive while I have lost my verve
Your verses are celebrated from Kayes[35] to the land of Moses

Once my poems were very captivating in this land
Now people of Rosso[36] are pleased with your verses

I, Taala, never envy an eminent poet
On thc contrary, I follow him in order to learn from him

O Muusaa! Do not walk away from me
Please pray for me all the time

Prayers do not prevent death
But can make us the neighbour of the Prophet 'Idrīs

May God welcome both of us
In the afterlife abodes of Paradise

May God welcome Muusaa and I
And reward us with redemption and bliss

Amen! God accepts all prayers addressed to Him
Without skills you cannot reap any profits from your trade

My business is to praise the qualities of Bamba
Now I feel like a leader just praising him

The way I praise him filled my purse
Of which I lavishly address my assemblies

Thanks to this praise the victuals were abundant
Bread and coffee plentiful and my affliction dissipated

[34] Here Sëriñ Moor Kayre refers to the Qur'ānic verse '*Wa 'mmā Bini'mati Rabbika Fañaddith*' ('And of your Lord's Blessings, proclaim it', The Qur'ān, 93:11).
[35] A region of Mali.
[36] City of northern Senegal, on the border with Mauritania.

By his praise, the disciples came closer to me
To enjoy listening to my high-value texts

The praises I addressed him are my shield
He made me a very rich man

I produced verses to praise the Shaykh
Who showed me the Prophet who possesses the virtuous qualities

Proclaiming the Lord's blessings is my motivation
To seek favours granted only to the grateful]

Poem about the Bawol Region

According to Sëriñ Moor Kayre, Bawol is the best region of the country since it is the shaykh's birthplace and it is where he founded the city of Touba. Kayre argues that cities surpass one another by the intrinsic human quality of their inhabitants rather than by the beauty of their landscape:

Kuy xas Bawal te dib Ajoor na jug Bawal
Ñibbi Kajoor nde kon mu xëy ñee waa Bawal

Bawal bonoon na wànde tey moo gën feneen
Fudul Bawal ngir ñi ko dëkkee gën ñeneen

Réew gënewul moroom ma joor gu tàlli ngir
Woy-dëkke ñay gënënte góor yu làkki ngir

Bu joor gu tàlli doon waral gënug barab
Makaag Medinaa kon du gën dëkki Arab

Ngir doc yu gudd a leen wër'ak tund'aki xur
Wànde worom ma gën ña baax ak na soxar
Lii tax bawal mujj di peeyub Yàllaam
Bamuy kërug Seex Bàmba xutbub lislaam

Réewum Bawal bamu amee Tuubaa la gën
Ku weddi lii deful Sëriñ bi ni bàkkan

Tuubaa di gën ji dëkkuwaay ñi ko dëkke
Di ngën ji woy-dekke fi lay ñëmbët tegee

Koo xam ni boo fa dëkkulit ñaan faa dëkke
Boo dundatul feexal sa ruu difa dogee

Bii làmbi lislaam sàjjiwul fudul Bawal
Fi Mbàkke yeen Kajoor nangeen wutsi Bawal

[Let him leave Bawol this Cayorian who hates it
He will surely envy the inhabitants of Bawol when he returns to Cayor

Once Bawol was a bad town, but it is today the best
And because its residents are the best

Cities are not ranked by the beauty of their landscape
They are distinguished by the character of their residents

If appearance were the single defining criterion
Then Mecca and Medina would not shine in Arabia

They are surrounded by mountains, dunes and caves
The only difference is that the Prophet resided there
Thus Bawol also became a City of God
Since the Pole Shaykh Bamba lived there

Bawol has been excelling since it gave birth to Tuubaa
Whoever undermines this fact does not praise the Shaykh

Tuubaa is the city of choice to its residents
It shines by the human quality of its inhabitants

If not yet done, try to live there
And make sure you will be buried there

This light of Islam shines only in the Bawol
O you Cayorians! Come to Bawol via Mbàkke]

Verses Devoted to Friendship

Sëriñ Moor Kayre has also written many verses dedicated to friendship:

Kuy seet teraanga du tàggook gis teraanga yu mat
Kuy seeti bon-bon du tàggook gis lu muy nemmiku

Bul seeti bon-bon ba réerook sab xarit dana tax
Ngay noonu fekk ludul bég loola moom nammu ko

Bul dégg cib soppe ay wax *deel* janook la mu def
Ngay doora yuqet ku am xel dégg yàqalu ko

Ngir ab rambaaj dana *sos* aw fenn mu mel ni lu am
Fum toll, waaye borom xel ab rambaaj jëlu ko

Yow Kayre bul geesu kuy ñaawal sa jikko maneel
Bu ñaar manee kenn wii léeb kuy wolof solo ko

[Whoever seeks good will find good
Anyone seeking evil will find it on their path

Do not push your friend's loyalty to the limit
You may ruin your friendship

A reasonable person is always a good listener
Do not listen to rumours and hearsay about your friends

The perfidious makes up untrue stories
However he cannot manipulate the wise man

O Kayre! Pay no mind to foolish talks
In friendship, the regulator is the wise one, as the Wolofs say]

Verses Devoted to the Sanctity of Work

The sanctity of work is celebrated in the Murīdiyya as attested by Murid scholars. The expression '*dafa wàcc liggéey*', literally meaning 'he stopped working', is used in Murid parlance to convey the idea that that person has passed away. The sanctification of work stemming from the new breath infused by Amadu Bamba was propagated in the masses by Murid poets. These following verses of Sëriñ Moor Kayre perfectly illustrate this philosophy:

Kuy sàkku ag àgg'ak ngërëm liggéeyi
Liggéey du wor saadix, di leen liggéeyi

Liggéey du rusloo kenn kuy sellal ndigël
Da koy kaweel mu yor melow ka koy digël

Ku masa gën maasam liggéey la ko gëne
Ku weddi lii ndaw la lu dul am lu gëne

Kon lu fi waay am ci liggéey la ko ame
Lii mooy ndigël lol ku ko def daa di ame

[Get to work if you seek success and blessings
Work warrants protection and dignifies the sincere disciple

Working causes no affliction to one who follows order
He is highly regarded just like his master

Hard work is the only criterion of success
Anyone who undermines this truth is bound to failure

Wealth is generated by hard work
This is the golden rule of the successful]

Conclusion

In this paper we have attempted to present the life story and intellectual legacy of a pioneer of Wolof *'Ajamī*, Sëriñ Moor Kayre, who is the least studied figure of the 'Pléiade Mouride'. Contrary to the widely held claim that Africa has no intellectual legacy, this chapter has tried to underscore the rich *'Ajamī* literary tradition that flourished within the Murid community during colonial times by positing the poetry of Sëriñ Moor Kayre. In addition to his Islamic content, his poetry reveals a strong nationalist consciousness. The subjects tackled are varied and the writings of Amadu Bamba constitute the main source of inspiration.

However, our study does not claim to be exhaustive. We have not yet had possession of his complete works. Since some of his poems are lost,[37] it will be difficult or even impossible to publish his complete works. Most of the poems are untitled and establishing a chronology is also a challenge since most of them are not dated. Regarding the inventory and conservation of the manuscripts, attempts have been made to digitize and transcribe the poems made available by members of the poet's family. To this end, as part of the project called EAP 334,[38] Dr Fallou Ngom's team's efforts at Boston University are critically acclaimed. His team is working in collaboration with the Digital Preservation of Senegal's Wolof *'Ajamī* manuscripts. This project aims to safeguard the Senegalese Wolof poets' writings, including Sëriñ Moor Kayre's. Dozens of the poems he authored have already been digitized and preserved.

We have personally collected dozens of manuscripts thanks to our regular contacts with one of Sëriñ Moor Kayre's grandsons, Sëriñ Xaadim Kayre, in order to record and transcribe the writings of the poet. So far we have transcribed one thousand or so verses into Latin characters. Our objective is to facilitate the dissemination of his poetic work. This project will help form the basis of a future anthology of Wolofal poetry following collection of sufficient texts. It should be noted that a small circle of Sëriñ Moor Kayre's disciples in Senegal is working relentlessly to create a collection of his writings. All these endeavours will undoubtedly contribute to saving a large portion of Sëriñ Moor Kayre's work from oblivion.

It is important for Sëriñ Moor Kayre's manuscripts and other writers of Wolofal poems to be exhumed because, not only will it prevent their disappearance, but a whole section of Africa's prestigious intellectual past will be saved. This work will make it possible to highlight the profound significance of these texts for the African masses who need to reconnect with these writers and their histories.

[37] All this information has been provided by his grandson, Sëriñ Xaadim Kayre.

[38] EAP (Endangered Archives Programme). Refer to Maja Kominko (ed.), *From Dust to Digital: Ten Years of the Endangered Archives Programme* (Cambridge: Open Book Publishers, 2015) 722.

CHAPTER 16

Praise and Prestige: The Significance of Elegiac Poetry Among Muslim Intellectuals on the Late Twentieth-Century Kenya Coast[1]

Abdulkadir Hashim

Introduction

Swahili poetry was used for various functions which included, *inter alia*, social functions, political activities and inculcating and disseminating Sufi tradition. During the funeral ceremonies of prominent intellectuals, elegiac poetry was recited by their peers paying tribute to their departed fellows. A salient feature of the poetic heritage on the Kenya coast is Muslim women's contribution in composing poems. This chapter explores these poetical trajectories and highlights patterns of poetical heritage on the late twentieth-century Kenya coast.

The main argument of this chapter is premised on the fact that poetic culture, particularly elegiac poems, is considered to be a cultural asset among *'ulamā'* on the Kenya coast. It was transmitted through an intellectual chain that passed from one generation to the next, which ensured continuity of their cultural heritage over time. Elegiac poems composed by learners reflected adoration of their mentors who represented the apex of literary heritage along the Kenya coast. The mentor–learner connection served as a breeding forum to mentor as well as 'manufacture' future poets. This chapter shows examples of intellectually linked scholars-cum-poets and illustrates some of their poetical works.

'Ulamā' on the Kenya coast, particularly the traditionalist 'Alawiyya scholars, revered poetic culture that seemed to be part and parcel of their daily intellectual life. This chapter focuses on the poetical works of 'Alawiyya scholars and their students, who established a scholarly network that formed a constellation of reputed poets linked by an intellectual chain on the Kenya coast giving examples

[1] I thank Professor Saad S. Yahya for his useful comments on improving the text of this chapter.

of various poems composed by the 'Alawiyya *'ulamā'*. These *'ulamā'*-cum-poets were born and bred locally albeit their masterly poetical skills in composing artistic poems of high degree were recognised and admired by their peers along the Kenya coast and beyond. The chapter will highlight the traditionalist 'Alawiyya poets, who enjoyed considerable prestige in the poetic culture on the Kenya coast. The chapter will illustrate examples of elegiac poems composed by two renowned 'Alawiyya *'ulamā'*, Sayyid Ali Badawī and Ustāḍ Muḥammad b. Sa'īd al-Biḍ, who are arguably among the most profound writers of poems and prose along the Kenya coast. In addition to the 'Alawiyya *'ulamā'*, the chapter will also demonstrate the dwindling role of the reformist Salafī *'ulamā'* in the poetical culture on the Kenya coast. Despite having the advantage of studying in Arab-speaking countries, the reformist Salafī *'ulamā'* isolated themselves from the poetical world upon their return to their home towns and focused on teaching and proselytizing their belief.

Significance and Use of Poetry on the Kenya Coast

Poetry is a remarkable heritage of the Swahili littoral that reflects its cultural and intellectual history. The tradition of writing poetry along the Kenyan coast, and in particular praise poetry, continued over centuries. Since the mid-fourteenth century, poetry has played a significant role in shaping Islamic intellectual tradition on the Kenyan coast. When the globetrotter Muḥammad b. 'AbdAllāh ibn Battuta (d. 1377) visited Mogadishu, Mombasa and Kilwa in 1332, he met local poets who composed Swahili poems using the Arabic script.[2]

The earliest known Swahili poet is Fumo Lingo, whose works date between the fourteenth and seventeenth centuries.[3] The earliest written poetry on the Kenya coast was composed by Syd. Aydarūs b. 'Uthmān b. 'Alī b. Sh. Abū Bakr b. Sālīm (d. 1750) of Lamu, who translated the well-known *Qasīda Umm al-qurā* by Sharaf al-Dīn Muḥammad b. Sa'īd al-Būṣīri (1213–95) into Swahili using the Arabic script in 1652. The poem was later known as *Utendiwa Hamziyya* or *Maulidiya Hamziyya* (481 vss.).[4]

Another Swahili poem entitled *Al-Inkishafi* ('The Soul's Awakening') by Syd. 'AbdAllāh b. 'Alīb. Nāṣir b. Aḥmad b. 'AbdAllāh b. 'Alī b. Sh. Abū Bakr b. Sālīm

[2] M.A. Ibn Baṭṭūṭah, *Tuḥfat al-nadhar fī Gharā'ib al-amsār wa al-asfār* (Cairo: Matbaal-Istiqama, 1967).

[3] J.W.T. Allen, *Tendi: Six Examples of a Swahili Classical Verse Form with Translations and Notes* (London: Heinemann, 1971).

[4] Kineenewa Mutiso, 'Archetypal Motifs in Swahili Islamic Poetry: Kasidaya Burudai, PhD diss., Department of Linguistics and African Languages, University of Nairobi, 56.

(1720–1820) of Lamu is considered to be one of the finest literary works in which the author pleaded with his heart not to fall victim to *ghurūr* (self-deception) but to prepare for death's journey and realization of the afterlife.[5]

In 1835, Syd. ʿUmar b. Amīn b. Nāṣir al-Ahdal (1798–1870), who was a *qāḍī* of Siu on the Kenya coast, composed an epic entitled *Utendiwa Ayubu* and a poem whose title is given in the last verse: *Durar al-Mandhuma* ('String of Pearls'). The poem was originally written using Arabic script, and was transcribed into Roman script over time. Composition of the poem follows the Arabic alphabet framework (60 vss.):

Andika mwandishi khati utuze
Isumu ya mola utanguize
Utie nukuta na irabuze
Wasikulahini wenye kusoma

Baada ya ina kulibutadi
Bijahi Rasuli tutahimidi
Bushira ya pepo nasi tufidi
Mola atujazi majaza mema

[Write ye, scribe and keep steady your writing
Preface it with the name of God
And put the dots and vowels in place
That the readers may not find fault with it.

After starting with the Name
With honour let us praise the Prophet
That we may earn the happiness of Paradise
And God bestow upon us His blessings][6]

Most of the Swahili literary works were written in a modified form of the Arabic script long before the advent of Roman script. Swahili people modified the Arabic script to suit the phonetic needs of their language. Hence, a great deal of Swahili literary and historical works were written in the Arabic script and preserved for posterity.[7] The presence of Arabic script many centuries before the advent of European colonialism was a primary driver behind the development of

[5] M.H. Abdulaziz, 'The Influence of the Qasida on the Development of Swahili Rhymed and Metred Verse', in S. Sperl; C. Shackle (eds.), *Qasida Poetry in Islamic Asia and Africa: Classical Traditions & Modern Meanings* (Leiden: E.J. Brill, 1996), 1–2, II, 421.

[6] L. Harries, *Swahili Poetry* (Oxford: Clarendon Press, 1962) 118.

[7] M.H. Abdulaziz, *Muyaka: 19th Century Swahili Popular Poetry* (Nairobi: Kenya Literature Bureau, 1994) 11.

Swahili literary works.[8] Writing Swahili in Arabic script was not confined to the learned classes on the Kenya coast but was also used as a means of communication and expression between people at official as well as domestic levels. The advent of European missionaries diminished the use of the Arabic script and replaced it with Roman script.[9] In the mid-twentieth century, a number of researchers were offered grants to study Swahili literary works and collect manuscripts with the objective of preserving them. However, the researchers' efforts did not do much to resolve the dilemma of Swahili written in the Arabic script.[10]

Muslim women contributed to the intellectual history of the East African coast. Most of the women intellectuals wrote poems and others taught the Qur'ān in their homes. Not only were women poets, they were also custodians of poems. They were prominent in preserving poetry and the majority of the best manuscripts were held by women in their houses.[11] The earliest reported poem by a Muslim woman, entitled *Siri al-Asrari* ('The Secret of the Secrets'), was composed in 1663 by Mwana Mwarabu bt. Shekhe Mwana Lemba (563 vss.)[12]. In 1807, a female scribe calling herself the daughter of Sa'īd Amini b. Sa'īd b. Uthmān from the Mahdalī clan composed *Mwana Fatuma* ('The Epic of Princess Fatuma') praising Fatima, Prophet Muḥammad's daughter (446 vss.). In 1858, Mwanakupona bt. Msham (1810–60), the widow of Sh. Mataka b. Mbārak (1779–1856), composed *Utendi wa Mwanakupona* ('Mwanakupona's Poem') (102 vss.), one of the most popular poems in Swahili literature written by a woman. Mwanakupona wrote the poem for her daughter Mwana Hashima bt. Shaykh (1841–1933).[13]

Swahili poetry was used as channels of expression that covered a wide range of social fucntions as well as political activities. In 1871, Swahili poetry was used on the Kenya coast as a tool to send 'secret' messages orally to Mbāruk b. Rāshid al-Mazrū'ī, the last of the Mazrū'ī rulers, who campaigned for the re-establishment

[8] M.H. Abdulaziz, 'The impact of Islam on the development of Swahili culture', in Mohamed Bakari; Saad S. Yahya (eds.), *Islam in Kenya Proceedings of the National Seminar on Contemporary Islam in Kenya* (Nairobi: Mewa Publications, 1995) 154.

[9] For instance, one report reads 'In order to meet the advance of Islam in East Africa, the German missionaries are supplanting the Arabic Alphabet in the vernaculars by Latin, and we are told that this will prove a blow to Islam.' Samuel Zwemer, *The Moslem World*, II, 2, 1991, 218.

[10] For instance, J.W.T. Allen remarked 'it is also generally held that Arabic script is a poor vehicle for writing the Swahili language. Without some adaptation it certainly is; but we must remember that the Roman alphabet needed some adaptation to make it suitable for Swahili.' J.W.T. Allen, 'Arabic Script for Students of Swahili', *Tanganyika Notes and Records*, Supplement, November 1945, 7–78.

[11] Allen, *Tendi*, 9.

[12] Mutiso, 'Archetypal Motifs', 57.

[13] Allen, *Tendi*, 55.

of the Mazrūʿī rule and revolted against El-Būsaʿīdī rule in Mombasa. The carriers of the message, who were singing the song on the way to Mbāruk's realm, were not aware of the messages composed in parables. Mbāruk grasped the message about the impending attack and moved his forces out of harm's way. The poem was composed by Mbāruk's friend Suʿūd b. Saʿīd al-Māʿamirī and reads:

Jamii watejeme vaapagaro
Wangojee wajeni wadungumaro
Mganga situje wajapo wangaro

[The throngs of wizard's followers have donned their beaded cords
So wait ye now the coming of these strange-garbed demon hordes
O wizard, be prepared for those who leap high on the swords!][14]

Swahili poetry was also used as a way of expressing the importance of musical instruments in religious gatherings. The following is a poem composed by Ustādh Muḥammad Sharīff Saʿīd al-Biḍ (d. 2013) that talks of keeping alive performers as well as listeners at the festivals and relieving and healing their sorrow. The poem is charged with lyrical connotations which demonstrate the poet's adoration of music and its instruments. Ustādh Muḥammad, a bold and vocal poet-scholar, was responding to his rivals who opposed the use of musical instruments in religious functions (10 vss.):

الناي و الطار و المرواس تحيينا   وتذهب الشجو عنا ثم تشفينا
إن الغناء غنى بل في السماع منى   يا ليت عاذلنا يصغي فيدرينا
لآل داود مزمار صفا وزهى   وسر مزماره باق بأهلينا

[The flute, tambourine and Almarwas keep us alive
They relieve us from sorrow and then heal us
Singing is wealth and its hearing is a desire
We wish those blaming us listen and inform us
The people of Daud had flutes that flourished with purity
And the secret of his flute remains with our people][15]

Elegiac Poetry on the Kenya Coast

Composition of elegiac poems on the Kenya coast has for long been considered a laudable pursuit among the *'ulamā'*. Hardly a scholar's death would pass without his peers or students composing elegiac poems to lament his departure. Elegiac

[14] M.A. Hinawy, *Al-Akida and Fort Jesus, Mombasa* (Mombasa: Muscat Bait Alghasham for Publishing & Translating, 2015) 41.

[15] I thank Hassan Nandwa for reviewing all poems written in Arabic and Swahili, which I translated.

poems composed by learners reflected their adoration of their mentors, who represented the apex of literary heritage on the Kenyan coast. During the funeral of notable intellectuals elegiac poems were also recited by their peers paying tribute to their fellows.

The poetical tradition in composing elegiac poetry was highly revered on the Kenya coast, particularly in the Lamu archipelago. In addition to mastering their respective religious disciplines, a considerable number of the *'ulamā'* in Lamu were poets in their own right. *'Ulamā'*'s command in composing elegiac poems has long been evident, as in the case of Bwana Yasini, a qāḍī of Rasini in Lamu, lamenting the death of his young son, Akheri, who became sick in Zanzibar and died there:

> Ai kilioshadidi kwangu kimezokithiri
> Mwanangu kufa baidi tusandikane nadhari
> Liwcle halibudi illa nilenye kujiri
> Ayuha al maghruri ina khada duniya
>
> [O, this bitter weeping of mine that never ceases
> My little son to die so far away without the last farewell
> What is decreed to occur must happen
> O you deceived one. What treachery has this world?][16]

Composition and Recitation of Elegiac Poems

Swahili poetry developed out of Arabic antecedents which comprise over 90 per cent of all traditional poetic expression, both written and oral.[17] Elegiac poetry, similarly to other poems, reflects a close connection with classical Arabic literary works. Hence, a substantial part of Swahili poetry is influenced by the Islamic tradition and conveys Islamic concepts and images from Muslim teachings.[18] Most of the poems composed on the Kenya coast owe their origin to traditional Arabic literary forms while retaining the distinctiveness of the Swahili prosodic system.[19] Almost all the written elegiac poetry of the late twentieth-century Kenya coast has been preserved by either the composer's family or their students. It was a normal practice for students to ask their mentors for copies of the poems and in some cases even transcribe them in the absence of copying facilities. Besides being recited in public gatherings praising Prophet Muḥammad, particularly during the

[16] Abdulaziz, 'The Influence of Qasida', 426.

[17] Abdulaziz, 'The Influence of Qasida', 411.

[18] F. Topan, 'Projecting Islam: Narrative in Swahili Poetry', *Journal of African Cultural Studies*, 14, 1, 2001, 115.

[19] Abdulaziz, *Muyaka*, 11.

mawlid festivals (celebration of Prophet Muḥammad's birth), the recitation of elegiac poems was also done during mourning periods and commemorations in honour of the deceased.

The public recitations symbolized the recognition of the deceased in the eyes of the mourners and were designed to be heard and remembered by all members of the community.[20] They were important exercises in disseminating poems to wider society. It was through praising a departed scholar by the recitation of elegiac poems that his prestige was appreciated by society. In addition, elegiac poems were also used to disseminate Sufi teachings based on the 'Alawiyya *ṭarīqa*. Through composition and recitation of poems, Sufi traditions were transmitted to the performers as well as the listeners. Sufi teachings inculcated in the *murīds* (followers) great respect for their teachers. Quoting Sh. Abdalla Saleh Farsy, Pouwels noted how Sh. ʿAbd Allāh Bākathīr respected his mentor Syd. Aḥmad b. Sumayṭ to such an extent that 'he would not sleep in the same room as Syd Aḥmad, nor even in the same house nor at the same location. Sh. ʿAbdAllāh acted in Syd. Aḥmad's presence the way a child acts in his father's presence.'[21] However, after the death of a scholar, his students would take the liberty of composing elegiac poems praising their departed saint without any reservation.

Elegiac Poetry as a Gift of Exchange

Elegiac poetry on the Kenya coast subscribes to Mauss's formulation of ritual exchange which presumes three obligations – giving, receiving and repaying – which establishes a bond of clientage between the poet and the patron.[22] Hence, poetry is regarded as a gift of exchange that demands to be paid back, and failure to return the gift means a loss of dignity.[23] It follows, therefore, that when students compose elegiac poetry to lament the death of their master, the burden of repaying shifts to the second generation of students, who would be expected to 'pay back' what their teachers did for their masters. The responsibility to pay back continues downwards and in some cases passes horizontally to include students' peers and friends.

[20] S. Sperl; C. Shackle (eds.), *Qasida Poetry in Islamic Asia and Africa: Eulogy's Bounty, Meaning's Abundance. An Anthology*, Vol. II (Leiden: E.J. Brill, 1996) 36.

[21] R.L. Pouwels, *Horn and Crescent: Cultural Change and Traditional Islam on the Kenyan Coast* (Cambridge: Cambridge University Press, 1987) 155.

[22] S.P. Stetkevych, 'Abbasid Panegyric and the Poets of Political Allegiance: Two Poems of Al-Mutanabbi on Kafur', in S. Sperl; C. Shackle (eds.), *Qasida Poetry in Islamic Asia and Africa: Eulogy's Bounty, Meaning's Abundance. An Anthology* (Leiden: E.J. Brill, 1996) 38.

[23] Stetkevych, 'Abbasid Panegyric'.

Elegiac Poetry and Power

Poetry as part of everyday life is linked to discourses of power and politics.[24] Since its inception, poetry has been speaking of power and self-praise.[25] Elegiac poems on the Kenya coast are no exception to the connection between poetry, power and self-praise. The association between poetry and power is clear in elegiac poems that praise the departed from the learned class, which in turn attributes special status in society to the person praised. The power of an elegiac poem propels it and guarantees its dissemination beyond the geographical and chronological limits of the praised's dominion. In addition to its societal function, elegiac poetry was used to establish the authority of the poets and their patrons. As demonstrated below, elegiac poems were used to outlast the power of the ones being praised and to eternalize their memory to the extent of even outliving the power of time.[26]

Transmission of Elegiac Poetry Through an Intellectual Chain

'Ulamā' on the Kenya coast regarded poetry to be their cultural asset and passed it from one generation to the other to ensure continuity of their poetical heritage. Poetry was transmitted through an intellectual chain linked to the teacher–student connection. The chain continued unbroken from the patron to the poet and their students. The teacher–student link cemented relationships that established a network, within which prospective poets were mentored and 'manufactured' to be future poets. Poetry forums served as spaces for interaction and mentorship between teachers and students. Through teaching and learning of poetry, the oral tradition of transmitting Islamic knowledge 'helped to establish the authority of teachers who were to follow and it served as the criterion to distinguish one student from another as far as his closeness to the master'.[27]

It has been argued elsewhere that Islamic knowledge along the East African coast was stratified socially and handed down within families from generation to generation. However, this chapter argues that the poetical heritage of the Kenya coast transcended clan boundaries and reflected a diversity of learners from different family backgrounds that did not necessarily belong to the 'Alawiyya clan.[28]

24 K. Kresse, 'Enduring Relevance: Samples of Oral Poetry on the Swahili Coast', *Wasafiri*, 2, 2011, 109.

25 J.C. Burgel, 'Qasida as Discourse on Power and its Islamization: Some Reflections', in S. Sperl; C. Shackle (eds.), *Qasida Poetry in Islamic Asia and Africa: Eulogy's Bounty, Meaning's Abundance. An Anthology* (Leiden: E.J. Brill, 1996) 451.

26 Burgel, 'Qasida as Discourse on Power'.

27 S.H. Nasr, 'Oral Transmission and the Book in Islamic Education: The Spoken and the Written Word', *Journal of Islamic Studies*, 3, 1, 1992, 1.

28 For instance, see A. Bang, *Sufis and Scholars of the Sea: Family Networks in East*

The Traditionalist *'Ulamā'*

The *'ulamā'* along the Kenya coast showed a wide range of interests from poetry to jurisprudence, and composed poems in Arabic as well as writing Swahili poems using the Arabic script. The majority of the *'ulamā'* who composed poems subscribed to the traditionalist 'Alawiyya *ṭarīqa.* A striking feature of these *'ulamā'*-cum-poets is that they were products of the local intellectual tradition. Almost all *'ulamā'* mentioned below studied under local teachers without recourse to the outside world. Those who were lucky enough would travel to Yemen to visit their ancestors' homeland for a few months. Strikingly, despite their mastery of the written script, most of the *'ulamā'* on the Kenya coast would hardly speak Arabic. This disparity was partly due to lack of exposure to an Arabic-speaking environment.

Ḥabīb Ṣāleḥ b. ʿAlwī Jamal al-Layl (d. 1935)

The 'Alawiyya *ṭarīqa* rose to prominence on the Kenya coast through Ḥabīb Ṣāleḥ b.ʿAlwī Jamal al-Layl. He was given a portion of land by Syd. Abū Bakr b. ʿAbdal-Raḥmān (Mwenye Manṣab) (d. 1922) and established *Riyāḍa* mosque-college in 1889. The *Riyāḍa* mosque-college provided Islamic knowledge to the underprivileged and lower social strata drawn from ex-slaves and local people of Haḍramī and Comorian origin.[29] Ḥabīb Ṣāleḥ was also responsible for establishing the celebration of *mawlid nabawī* in 1890. Ḥabīb Ṣāleḥ is considered to be the founding father of the traditioinalist'Alawiyya *ṭarīqa* in Lamu.

Ḥabīb Ṣāleḥ first came to Lamu to visit his uncle Mwenye Sayyid Ali from the Comoro Islands. At the age of eighteen, Ḥabīb Ṣāleḥ experienced pain in his leg. His father Sayyid ʿAlwī sent him to his uncle in Lamu for treatment. Ḥabīb Ṣāleḥ later returned to Comoro, where he married. In 1870, he took permission from his father to travel and settled in Lamu.[30]

A number of Ḥabīb Ṣāleḥ's students and Murids composed elegiac poems. The culture of composing stretched downwards to include generations of students. Not only would the immediate students of a patron adore their master and compose elegies for him, but we also find students composing poems to lament for their teacher's patron. The following is a poem written by Sh. ʿAbdAllāh b.

Africa, 1860–1925 (London: RoutledgeCurzon, 2003) 124; R. Loimeier, *Between Social Skills and Marketable Skills: The Politics of Islamic Education in 20th Century Zanzibar* (Leiden: Brill, 2009) 68.

[29] K. Kresse, 'Cosmopolitanism Contested: Anthropology and History in the Eastern Indian Ocean', in Roman Loimeier; Rüdiger Seesemann (eds.), *The Global Worlds of the Swahili* (Berlin: LIT Verlag, 2006) 218.

[30] Ṣāliḥ Muhammad 'Alī Badawī, *Al-Riyāḍ bayna maḍīhī wa ḥāḍiriḥi* (Lamu: Ṣāliḥ al-Badawī, 1989) 18.

Muḥammad al-Husnī (Barʿede) (a student of Ḥabīb Ṣāleḥ's students) lamenting the death of Ḥabīb Ṣāleḥ (40 vss.):

مُقْلَـةُ الْقُطْـرِ بِالأَسَى عَمْيَـاءُ　　كُـلُّ رُزْءٍ مِنْ بَعْـدِ هَـذَا هَبَـاءُ
غَابَ نَجْمٌ بَلْ غَابَ نُـوْرُ وَشَمْسٌ　　كَانَ مِنْهَـا الضِّيَـاءُ وَالإِهْـتِـدَاءُ
غَابَ بَـدْرٌ بَلْ قَدْ تَهَـدَمَ رَكْـنٌ　　كَانَ مِـنْـهُ السَّنَـاءُ والإِلْتَجَـاءُ
وَطَبِيْـبٌ لِكُـلِّ رُوْحٍ وَنَفْسٍ　　إِنْ عَـرَّتْـهَـا الأَمْـرَاضُ وَالأَدْوَاءُ

[My eyeball turned blind due to sorrow
All loss after this is dust
A star has disappeared, actually rather light and sun have disappeared
From them is brightness and guidance
A crescent has disappeared, actually rather a pillar has been destroyed
From them brilliance and asylum
And the doctor of every spirit and soul
If they are infected by diseases and illness]

Due to the exposure they acquired in their homeland and other centres of Islamic learning in the Muslim world, the ʿAlawiyya *'ulamā'* came to the Kenya coast having studied in the written Islamic tradition and were therefore responsible for bringing that written tradition with them.[31] As a result, the ʿAlawiyya *'ulamā'* enjoyed considerable prestige both in their original and adopted homelands.[32] The ʿAlawiyya *'ulamā'* had the privilege of being bilinguals who mastered Arabic linguistic and literary sciences and were able to manipulate Swahili so as to steer it closer to the Arabic especially in poetic form and diction.[33] Compared to other brotherhoods which focused on esoteric devotion, the ʿAlawiyya *ṭarīqa* emphasized ritual and erudition in the sciences as important elements in their religious commitments.[34] All these attributes together contributed towards the prominence of the ʿAlawiyya *ṭarīqa* in the development of Islamic literary tradition and poetical heritage along the East African coast.

Sh. Muḥammad b. ʿAli al-Maʿāwī (d. 1960)[35]

Scholar-poet Sh. Muḥammad b. ʿAlī al-Maʿāwī was born in Lamu and is considered to be the doyen of poetry in Lamu. Though not linked to the ʿAlawiyya lineage, Sh. Muḥammad was closely attached to his ʿAlawiyya teachers and the ʿAlawiyya *ṭarīqa*. He established a scholarly network that formed a constellation

[31] Pouwels, *Horn and Crescent*, 130.
[32] Bang, *Sufis and Scholars of the Sea*, 10.
[33] Abdulaziz, 'The Influence of Qasida', 412.
[34] Pouwels, *Horn and Crescent*, 197.
[35] Interview with Sh. ʿAlī al-Maʿāwī (d. 2016), Mombasa, 15 December 2007.

of reputed poets along the Kenya coast including Sh. Muḥammad b. Qāsim al-Mazruʿī (d. 1982) and Syd. ʿAlī Aḥmad Badawī (d. 1987). The latter produced a number of scholar-poets who include Syd. Muḥammad Ṭālib Rudaynī (d. 1981), Ustādh Muḥammad Sharīff Saʿīd al-Biḍ (d. 2013), Sh. Muḥammad al-Wāilī (d. 2014), Sh. Muḥammad ʿUmar Dumila and Aḥmad Sh. Nabahanī (d. 2017).

Sh. Muḥammad was a scholar with a deep love of the Arabic language. His masterly skills in composing Arabic poetry can be seen in the following poem that indicates in the last verse the dates of birth, death and life (in Hijri) of Syd. ʿAlī b. Muḥammad b. Ḥusayn al-Ḥibshi (1843–1915). The dates are computed by adding together the values of each of the underlined Arabic words, which adds up to the respective date:

في مدة العمر للحبشي ومولده   ثم الوفاة بشارات باعلان
إن شئت تحفظها تحظى ببركته   فاكها ضمن بيت ماله شان
نهج أغر لميلاد ومدته   سيد وعام الوفا أرخ بغفران
1259   74   1333

[The life of al-Ḥibshi and his birth
Then his death is good tidings to be announced
If you wish to memorize them you will receive his *baraka*
These are the dates in a verse that has no significance
An illustrious path for a birth and its duration
Master and the year of death date it with forgiveness]

The above poem demonstrates Sh. Muḥammad's mastery of Arabic prose and his skill in accurately placing in a meticulous manner the dates of birth, death and life of Syd. ʿAlī al-Ḥibshi. In addition to his mastery of the Arabic language, Sh. Muḥammad was also deeply versed in other Islamic disciplines including *tafsīr* (exegesis), *ḥadīth* (Sayings of Prophet Muḥammad), *fiqh* (jurisprudence) as well as *taswwuf* (mysticism).

Sh. Muḥammad wrote a number of Arabic poems on various matters which included praise for Prophet Muḥammad. His famous poem is read during the *mawlid* annual celebration on the Kenya coast (19 vss.):

ياربنا بالمصطفى تتوسل   وبقطبنا الحبشي علي الاكمل
يا من بذكرك كل صعب يسهل   وببركة اسمك كل قصد يحصل
يا مفردا في عصره ومجددا   للدين نلت به مقاما يفضل

[O our Lord we seek intercession through the Anointed
And our Pole al-Ḥibshi ʿAlī the perfect
O with your remembrance all hardship becomes ease
And with your name's blessings every wish is accomplished
O you the only one in your time and the reviver
Of the religion you achieved a rank that is preferred]

Sh. Muḥammad adored Ḥabīb Ṣāleḥ and wrote a number of poems praising him. Sh. Muḥammad composed an elegiac poem lamenting the death of his teacher Ḥabīb Ṣāleḥ (8vss.):

عظمت فعين الدهر أمست باكيه   لافول شمس ضيائها المتلاليه
عظمت رزيئتنا بفقد أنيسا   وطبيب أنفسنا إذهي شاكيه
قطب العلم الذي هو مفرد   في عصره رفع الاله مبانيه

[Great sorrow the eyes of time turn crying
for the disappearance the Sun its light shining
Our loss is great for missing a friend
and a doctor of our souls, start complaining
The Pole of the people the only one
in his time Allah has elevated his status]

Among Sh. Muḥammad's intellectual works is a booklet on the science of prosody (*ʿilm al ʿarūḍ*) entitled سلم النهوض إلى ارتقاء درج العروض Sh. Muḥammad b. ʿAlī al-Maʿāwī has left a number of poems which are being compiled into an anthology.

Syd. ʿAlī Aḥmad Badawī (1907–87)[36]

Syd. ʿAlī was born in Lamu. He was briefly taught by his great grandfather Syd. ʿAlīb. Syd. ʿAbdAllāh (brother of Syd. ʿAlwī b. ʿAbdAllāh, the father of Ḥabīb Ṣāleḥ). Syd. ʿAlī was also taught by his paternal grandfather Ḥabīb Ṣāleḥ and father Syd. Aḥmad Badawī. While in Zanzibar, Syd. ʿAlī was briefly taught by his maternal grandfather ʿAbdAllāh Bākathīr (1860–1925) and then his uncle Abū Bakr b. ʿAbd Allāh Bākathīr. Syd. ʿAlī also studied under Sh. Muḥammad b. Ali al-Maʿāwī, who was considered to be his *Shaykh Fat-hi-hi* (main teacher). Sh. Muḥammad taught Syd. ʿAlī Arabic linguistics and literary sciences. The teacher–student connection between Sh. Muḥammad b. Ali al-Maʿāwī and Syd. ʿAlī Aḥmad Badawī is arguably the start of the poetical intellectual chain along the Kenya coast.

A humble scholar, well known for his uncontroversial stances, Syd. ʿAlī was privileged with a prodigious memory and 'got down to the serious business of teaching and spent the rest of his time preparing manuscripts and enlarging his personal poetry anthology'.[37] Syd. ʿAlī did not only continue the legacy of his

36 ʿAbd Allāh Ṣāleh Farsī. A.S. *Baaadhiya Wanavyuoniwa Kishafiwa Mashirkiya Afrika*, 1972, 42, Ḥārīth Ṣāleḥ. (2004). *Chaguo la Wanavyuoni* (Mombasa: Bajaber Printing Press, Ramadhan 1425), 52, خ باحسن), الرياض بين ماضيه وحاضره, الطبعة الاولى ه1410–1989 p.40 Interviews: with Sh. Bahsan, Malindi, 20 August 2006; Syd. Muhsin Syd. Ali, Lamu, 22 December 2007.

37 M. Bakari, 'The New 'Ulama in Kenya', in Mohamed Bakari; Saad S. Yahya (eds.),

teacher Sh. Muḥammad b. ʿAlī al-Maʿāwī in composing poems but rather surpassed his mentor by composing poetical works of a technical nature on Islamic knowledge that included Arabic syntax (*naḥw*), inheritance (*mirāth*), prayer times (*awqāt al al Salāh*) and the direction of the *Qibla* (*ittijāh al-Qiblah*).

Syd. ʿAlī was so attached to Lamu that he would rarely travel outside the island. In one of his poems, Syd. ʿAlī expresses his affection for Lamu:

رأيت الناس قد لاموا　　محبا لم يزر لامو
أرى قلبي يحن إلى لام　　و وإن عذل لجّ في العاذلون وإن لاموا

[I saw people blaming
A lover who has not visited Lamu
I see my heart attached to Lamu
Even the critics reproach and blame]

Syd. ʿAlī is arguably the most prominent writer of poetry along the Kenya coast. His poetry covers a variety of Islamic disciplines. He composed a number of elegiac poems lamenting the deaths of his wife, parents, grandparents, peers, teachers as well as his students. The following are samples of Syd. ʿAlī's elegiac poetry:

1) An elegy lamenting the death of Syd. Abdulrahman b. ʿUbayd Allāh Al-Saggaf (1863–1956) the *Muftī al-diyār al-Ḥaḍramiyya* (Mufti of Ḥaḍramawt) (50 vss.). It opens:

بأي قول أفي الحق الذي وجبا　　من الرثاء وبحر العلم قد نضبا
وأي نور بيان أستضيئ به و　　الشرق أظلم مذ نجم العلا غربا
وأي ركن اصطبار نستكن به　　وركننا انهدم والاسلام قد نكبا

[With which statement can I fulfil the incumbent right
To elegy, yet the ocean of knowledge has drained
And with which light of explaining, will I illuminate
Yet the East has darkened since the star of eminence has set
And which pillar of patience we lean on
Yet our pillar has been demolished and Islam is bereaved]

2) An elegy for Syd. Abū Bakr b. ʿAbd al-Raḥmān b. Sh. Abū Bakr b. Sālīm (Mwenye Manṣab), mentor of Syd. ʿAlī's grandfather Ḥabīb Ṣāleḥ (24 vss.). It reads:

يا جيرة بالحما الارجب　　عطفا على الهائم المحتار
عطفا على رق القلب الصّب　　قد حرّكه ساجع الاسحار
مستّني حسن بدى أعجب　　في وصفه حارت الافكار

Islam in Kenya: Proceedings of the National Seminar on Contemporary Islam in Kenya (Nairobi: Mewa Publications, 1995) 180.

[Ooh Neighbours on the pillar of refuge
Be kind on the strayed and the confused
Be kind on the adoring softened heart
It has been moved by the early morning composer
I have been touched by beauty that appeared strange
In its description, minds are confused]

3) An elegy on the commemoration of fifty years since the death of Syd. ʿAlī's grandfather Ḥabīb Ṣāleḥ (50 vss.). It opens:

ذكرى تبشرنا بنيل كل رجا　　كما تكون لنا من همنا فرجا
ذكرى تصف قلوبا بالجفا انكدرت　　واليسر تدني وتقصى العسر والحرجا
ذكرى تجدد بالوفاء ويشملنا　　منها الهنا والعنا تزيل والعوجا

[Remembrance gives us glad tidings to achieve all hopes
As well as being our comfort from our sorrow
Remembrance cleans hearts that have been spoiled by cruelty
And brings near the ease and moves away the difficulty and discomfort
Remembrance that renews faithfulness and covers us
From its happiness and removes hardship and deviation]

4) An elegy for Syd. ʿAlī's maternal grandfather Sh. ʿAbd Allāh Bākathīr (1860–1925), who died in Zanzibar (9 vss.). It opens:

لم نلق فى هذا الز مان وأهله　　وحوا دث فيه لروحك منعشا
إلا موا جهةالحبا ئب من لهم　　قصدعلى السننالسنية عر شا
من أهل بيت المصطفى سفن النجا　　ه ومن على آثار هم حزما مشى

[We have not got in this era with its people
And its events to your soul a refresher
Except facing the beloved ones whom
Desire to follow the footpath
From the house of the Anointed, ships of salvation
And the one in their footsteps with determination he followed]

5) An elegy on the death of Syd. ʿAlī's colleague Sh. Abddalla Husni Barʿede (86 vss.):

لِلْمَوْتِ فَتْكٌ لاَيُرَدُّ ذَرِيْعُ　　كُلٌّ وَإِنْ يَسْلَمْ لَدَيْهِ صَرِيْعُ
هَذَا الَّذِي نَبْكِيْ عَلَيْهِ فَفَقْدُهُ　　للدين نقص لا يقاس شنيع
هَذَا الَّذِي تَبْكِيْ عَلَيْهِ مَعَابِدٌ　　وَمَجَامِعٌ وَمَجَاهِلٌ وَصُقُوعُ
لَمْ تَبْكِهِ(كِيْنْيَا)فَحَسْب فَكُلُّ إِقْـ　　ـلِيْمِ بِأَفْرِيْقَا بِهِ مَفْجُوْعُ

[Death has devastation that cannot be reversed approaching
Everybody even if he is safe, he has to be wrestled down
This one that we are bewailing, by his loss

The religion has diminished with immeasurable ugliness
This one that places of worship are bewailing
As well as meeting places, unexplored and frost lands
It's not only (Kenya) that is weeping but all
Places in Africa are bereaved]

6) An elegy on the death of Syd. ʿAlī's student Syd. Muḥammad Twalib Rudaini (d. 1981) (48 vss.):

سلاح المنايا لايفل له حد   وجيش الرّزايا لموقفه حد
فكم شنّ فينا غارة تلو غارة   من العقد المحتوم ما إن له رد
وأفنى كبيرنا وأبلى صغيرنا   وذا الحكم فيه يستوي الشيب والمرد

[The weapon of death its edge cannot stop being sharp
And the army of calamity has no limit
How many raids did it launch in our midst one after another?
From the ultimate contract which cannot be returned
It has exhausted our elder persons and worn out our young ones
And before the Owner of its Judgment, an older man is equivalent
to a young man]

Syd. ʿAlī's death was mourned by various poets who include Syd. ʿAbd al-Qāḍīr Junayd in the following elegiac poem (46 vss.):

دعني انوح فلا ملام واندب   اذ غاب من افق المعالي كوكب
دعني انوح فلا ملام فقد سطا   سيف المنون على المفارق يضرب
سلب المنون من السراة زعيمهم   فغدت محاجرهم بدمع تسكب

[Leave me alone to mourn without blame
A star has vanished from the horizons of excellence
Leave me alone to mourn the sword of
death has attacked and killed the departed
Death has robbed the elites of their leader
Leaving their eyeholes pouring tears]

Syd. ʿAli wrote a number of manuscripts which have been partly published. His intellectual works written in Arabic, both prose and poetry, include:

نزهة النظر (نظم نخبة الفكر مصطلح الأثر للحافظ ابن حجر)
الطريقة السهلة لمعرفة الأوقات والقبلة
الأرجوزة الوجيزة المسماة ببلة الأوام في أحكام ذوي الأرحام – دار البحث للطباعة والنشر بعدن
خير الندا نظم قطر الندى
طرفة الأصحاب نظم متن تحفة الأحباب في استخراج الأوقات والقبلة بالحساب للعلامة المتبحر المرحوم الشيخ الأمين بن علي بن عبدالله المزروعي

مختصرربع المجيب (نظم)
طريقة الخلان في فن البيان (نظم تحفة الاخوان)
المدمع الهاطل علي داعي السواحل
جدول ميل الشمس المسمى بالميل الأول على ترتيب أيام الشهور الميلادية
جنى ثمر نزهة النظر منظومة نخبة الفكر للحافظ ابن حجر

Syd. ʿAli taught a generation of poets who include: Syd. Muḥammad Ṭālib Rudaynī (d. 1981), Ustādh Muḥammad b. Saʿīd al-Biḍ (d. 2013), Sh. Muḥammad al-Waili (d. 2014), Aḥmad Sh. Nabahanī (d. 2017), Sh. Muḥammad Omar Dumila and Sh. Maḥmud Aḥmad ʿAbd al-Qādīr (Mau).

Syd. Muḥammad Ṭālib Rudaynī (1927–81)[38]

Syd. Muḥammad Ṭālib was born in Witu. He started his learning in Witu and then his uncle Sayyid Muḥammad ʿAbd Allāh Rudainī took him to Madrasa al-Najah in Lamu. Among the teachers of Sayyid Muḥammad Ṭālib in Lamu were his uncle Sayyid Muḥammad ʿAbd Allāh Rudainī, Sayyid Ali Badawī, Sayyid Muḥammad ʿAdnān, Shaykh Muḥammad b. Ali al-Maʿāwī and Shariff Saʿīd al-Biḍ. The poetical intellectual chain is noted in Syd. Muḥammad Ṭālib's case in which it extends downwards from his teachers Sh. Muḥammad b. 'Ali al-Maʿāwī and Sayyid 'Ali Badawī.

Syd. Muḥammad Ṭālib composed poems in Arabic for various occasions which include elegies and praises for his teachers and peers. He composed an elegiac poem lamenting the death of King Fayṣal b. ʿAbd al-ʿAzīz of Saudi Arabia. He also composed several poems lamenting the death and commemoration of his teacher and close colleague Shariff Saʿīd al-Biḍ. Two of the poems are recited during the *Ziyāra* (commemoration) of Shariff Saʿīd al-Biḍ. The following is an elegiac poem composed by Syd. Muḥammad on the seventh anniversary of the death of his teacher Shariff Saʿīd al-Biḍ (27 vss.):

لذكرى سعيد القوم ينشرح الصدر ويـنفك قيد الحزن حيث أتى اليسر
لذكرى طبيب الروح و الجسم لذة يذوق صفاها من له الفهم و القدر
لذكرى إمام أمة ذي شهامة تشرّفت الآحاد و الشفع و الوتر

[For the remembrance of the good people the chest is delighted
And the chains of sorrow are untied whenever ease comes
Verily, remembering the doctor of the soul and body is delicious]

38 Interviews with: Sh. Aḥmad Nabahanī, Mombasa, 17 December 2007; Abu-Bakr Salim Muḥammad al-Kindy (Sheikuna), Malindi, 7 January 2008; Bibi Khadija Binti Shariff Salim al-Ahdali (wife of Muḥammad Ṭalib), Malindi, 7 January 2008; Hon. Abu-Bakr Din, Malindi, 7 January 2008; email by Sayyid Aḥmad Muḥammad Ṭalib Rudainī dated 30 April 2008.

[He tastes its purity whoever has understanding and ability
For the remembrance of the *Imām* of the *Umma* a man of nobility
Honoured by the singles, evens and odds]

Ustādh Muḥammad b. Saʿīd al-Biḍ (d. 2013)

Ustādh Muḥammad was born in Lamu and is a product of the local intellectual tradition and an example of an ʻAlawiyya scholar born and bred locally. He studied under ʻAlawiyya scholars, particularly Sayyid Ali Badawī, whose tutelage demonstrates continuity of the poetical intellectual chain along the Kenya coast. A highly intelligent and articulate intellectual, Ustādh Muḥammad is considered to be one of the most widely read scholars on the Kenya coast.[39] Due to his distinguished scholarship and passion for academic excellence, he earned the title of ʻUstādh' (equivalent to professor) among his peers and students. He was among the few scholars who preferred to be financially independent and avoided being on the payroll of any organization. Keeping a distance from donor funding earned him peace of mind and a reputation of independence in his academic zeal. He used his intellectual standing in society to mobilize funds from local sympathizers for the establishment and maintenance of ʻAlawiyya institutions in the Eastern African region.

A vocal and aggressive scholar, Ustādh Muḥammad was among the key actors in sustaining and reviving the ʻAlawiyya intellectual tradition in East Africa. He managed to get the best of both worlds: knowledge from his maternal uncle Syd. ʿAlī Aḥmad Badawī and travelling from his father Sharīff Saʿīd. However, Ustādh Muḥammad differed from his predecessors in his *daʿwa* approach in that he was at the forefront of public criticism of his opponents. He took advantage of public gatherings particularly during *mawlid* celebrations to defend the ʻAlawiyya *ṭarīqa* and dispel his rivals' allegations against the *ṭarīqa*.

He was in the forefront of advocating the Sufi tradition of the Banīʿ Alawī clan of the ʻAlawiyya *ṭarīqa*. In the following poem, Ustāḍ Muḥammad describes Banīʿ Alawī's *ṭarīqa* and its commitment to *Taṣawwuf* and knowledge. The poem explains the mystical approach methods as prescribed by the Banīʿ Alawī. It is centred around Sufi devotions, which refer to the *ḥaqīqah* (the Reality) often indicating the ʻDivine Light' radiating from God which is understood as eternal spiritual essence.[40] It opens thus (14 vss.):

طريقة آل باعلوي   تسوق النفس للعلوي
طريقتهم عبادات   ومنهل علمهم يروي
لمنهج الحقيقة و   التصوف كلهم يحوي
وأحياء علوم   الدين مطمعهم بلا غرو

[39] Bakari, ʻThe New ʻUlama in Kenya', 187.
[40] Bang, *Sufis and Scholars of the Sea*, 18.

[The paths of the people of Ba'alawi
Steers the soul to eminence
Their path is rituals
the spring of their knowledge is reported
The path of truth and
Sufism all of them carry
And revival religious sciences
their ambition without doubt]

Ustādh Muḥammad composed a considerable amount of poetry in Arabic and Swahili using the Arabic script and compiled an anthology, of around 530 pages, which includes his poems and those of local and foreign poets. Ustāḍ Muḥammad followed in the footsteps of his teacher Sayyid Ali Badawī in writing poems and prose.[41]

The following is some of Ustādh Muḥammad's elegiac poetry:

1) An elegy for his mentor Syd. 'Umar b. Sumayt (1886–1973) (24 vss.):

أيا قطب هذا العصر تنقل ناعما　　وتترك هذا الدهر خلوا مبددا
حبيبي شجاع الدين وابن شهابه　　أترحل عنا بعد أن كنت مرصدا
ويا سيدي ياعمر القطب كنت　　غوثنا الفرد يا من عشت نورا مؤيدا

[Ooh the pole of this age you depart blessed
And you leave this world empty dispersed?
My beloved brave of the religion and son of its star
You depart us after you have been our telescope?
Ooh my dear Oh the pole the age you were our only relief
Our only relief Ooh you have lived as a supported light]

2) An elegy for his teacher Sayyid Muḥammad 'Adnān Al-Ahdal (1896–1963) (26 vss.):

سهام الرزء قد رمت بقلبي　　وآلمني الآسى فازداد كربي
مصاب أدهش الاقطار طراّ　　وألهب ناره في كل جنب
يعزّ على صبر أو سلو　　أأسلو والطبيب نأى بطبّ

[The arrows of loss have been thrown at my heart
And grief has caused me pain and added my agony
A disaster has puzzled all the territories
And its fire blazed all the sides
It holds dear for patience or comfort
How do I be in comfort yet the doctor has gone is far with medicine?]

[41] The compilation is in a handwritten manuscript preserved by Ustāḍ Muḥammad's family.

3) An elegy for his colleague Syd. Muḥammad Ṭālib Rudaynī (31 vss.):

لطعن القلب بالرمح الرديني   أراه أخف من رزء الرديني
وحسبك لو دريت ما دهانا   فتسعدنا دما عن دمع عين
وذاك لما طمى ما هدّ ركنا   ركينا عين مجد أي عين

[The stabbing with Rudaynī's spear
I see it lighter than Rudaynī's loss
Sufficient for you if you knew what has stormed us
So that you lend us blood instead of tears of an eye
That is when it overflew what destroyed a pillar
A cornerstone a fountain of glory what a fountain!]

Ustādh Muḥammad was mourned by several local poets as well as his peers from abroad. The following is an elegiac poem composed by Syd. Abū Bakr Al-ʿAdanī lamenting the death of Ustāḍ Muḥammad (26 vss.):[42]

رحل المجاهد بالمحيط الاطلسي   من بعد عمر حفا بالانفس
رحل الشريف الحر عنا قائلا   من لي بحامل غايتي وتجانسي
ذاك الامام محمد البيض الذي   شحن الافارق بالسلوك الاقدس

[The Mujāhid of Atlantic Ocean departed
After a friendly age with souls
The independent Sharīf departed us saying
Who will take charge of my objective and likeness?
That is the *Imām* Muḥammad Al-Biḍ who
Loaded Africans with most glorious behaviour]

Ustādh Muḥammad had an annual routine of visits holding *darsas* particularly in the month of Ramadan and during *Mawlid* celebrations in the month of Rabī al-Awwal across the East African region. His travels outside the area included Yemen, Saudi Arabia, United Arab Emirates and the United Kingdom.

Despite his busy teaching and travelling schedule, Ustādh Muḥammad found time to compose poems in various disciplines and wrote a number of books in Arabic and Swahili using the Arabic script. Some of his intellectual writings have been published while a substantial part is in a manuscript form.

Sh. Muḥammad b. Sh. Abū Bakr al-Wāilī (1936–2014)

Sh. Muḥammad was born and bred in Lamu. Though not of ʿ*Alawī* descent, most of Sh. Muḥammad's teachers and mentors were from the ʻAlawiyya scholars. His main teachers were Syd. ʿAli b. Aḥmad Badawī and Sh. Muḥammad ʿAli

[42] Syd. Abū Bakr Al-ʿAdanī is a poet from Hadramawt in Yemen who had close connections with Ustāḍ Muḥammad b. Saʿīd al-Biḍ.

al-Maʿāwī, from whom he learnt a great deal of poetry. This teacher–student connection further demonstrates the continuity of the poetical intellectual chain. Sh. Muḥammad al-Wāilī is famous in Lamu for Swahili poems which he composed using the Latin script. He also published a timetable for prayer and fasting for three towns – Lamu, Malindi and Mombasa – that he prepared when he was the qāḍī of Malindi.

The following is an example of an Arabic elegiac poem composed by Sh. Muḥammad al-Wāilī lamenting the death of his teacher Sharīff Said Al-Biḍh (20 vss.):

رزء به أكبادنا تتقطع   دوما في الاحشاء نار تدلع
سمت عيوني بالدوموع كآبة   وفؤادي المكلوم ذا يتوجع
مذ غبت عنا حل في افريقيا   وطأ البلا لم يبق منها موضع

[A loss that tears our livers apart
always erupts fire in our intestines
My eyes bear tears out of sorrow
and my wounded heart is in pain
Since you departed us Africa
was afflicted by a disaster not sparing any place]

In the same way as his teachers, Sh. Muḥammad al-Wāilī expresses his sorrow and surge of emotion on the death of his patron that tore apart his liver.

Sh. Muḥammad ʿUmar Dumila

Sh. Muḥammad was taught by Syd. ʿAli b. Aḥmad Badawī, which demonstrates continuity of the poetical intellectual chain stretching downwards to include a new generation of poets. Sh. Muḥammad was a colleague and close friend of Syd. Muḥammad Ṭālib Rudaynī. The latter held *darsas* on the commentary of the Qur'ān for almost thirty years and by his death had reached the last chapter of the Qur'ān. Sh. Muḥammad ʿUmar Dumila continued the *darsas* and completed the commentary of the Qur'ān.

Sh. Muḥammad composed several poems in Arabic. The following are some of them:

1) An elegy on the death of his teacher Syd. ʿAli b. Aḥmad Badawī (37 vss.):

خطب أجل من الدهور وقوع   وأحرّ من بين العيون دموع
خطبألم على السماء فأظلمت   أرجائها وانسد عنا نجوع
خطب ألم بشمسنا فتكسفت   وعرى على باقي النجوم رجوع

[A disaster bigger than what happened in ages
and hotter than tears within the eyes
A disaster that befell the skies and darkened
its edges and obstructed its horizons

A disaster that befell our Sun causing its eclipse
and other stars were deprived of re-emerging]

2) An elegy on the death of his colleague Syd. Muḥammad Ṭālib Rudaynī (25 vss.):

بحر الاسى قلب الكئيب يذوب   وتجري دموع في الفؤاد سروب
لنبك ابن عبدالله وهو محمّد   أخا العلم والارشاد وهو أديب
بأخلاقه قد فاق كل قرينه   ومنيحي أخلاق النبي غريب

[Ocean of sorrow leaving the heart of the depressed melting
And tears run leaking from the heart
We cry Muḥammad the son of Abdallah
Brother of knowledge and guidance and a poet
His attributes surpassed all his fellows
And whoever revives the Prophet's character is a stranger]

The Reformist *'Ulamā'*

The traditionalist 'Alawiyya *ṭarīqa* dominated Muslim discourses on the East African coast from the early twentieth century until the 1980s, when a new generation of reformers developed. Towards the end of the twentieth century, the Kenya coast witnessed the emergence of a new wave of reforms from young graduates coming from foreign Islamic universities, particularly from Saudi Arabia. These young and modern *'ulamā'* came with a Salafī orientation that was different from their home-grown tradition. Most of them were from underprivileged communities that could not get easy access to either formal secular education or informal religious education. With the outbreak of civil war in Somalia in the early nineties, an influx of Somali scholars sought refuge in Kenya. With all these reinforcements from within and abroad, the reformist *'ulamā'* gained momentum on the Kenya coast. Their movement was seen as a powerful counter-position to the locally dominant 'Alawiyya *ṭarīqa*, increasing the internal pluralism of scholarly positions as well as sectarian competition.[43] The emergence of a new wave of reformist religious ideas was perceived as a threat to the existence and continuity of the traditionalist 'Alawiyya *ṭarīqa*.

The reformist *'ulamā'* adopted more radical positions which opposed the established practices of the traditionalist 'Alawiyya *ṭarīqa*, which were considered as un-Islamic innovations (*bida'*). The traditionalists' *'ulamā'* were challenged by

[43] K. Kresse, *Philosophising in Mombasa: Knowledge, Islam and Intellectual Practice on the Swahili Coast* (Edinburgh: Edinburgh University Press, 2007) 184.

the reformists, who saw the 'Alawiyya *ṭarīqa* and Sufi traditions being incapable of providing answers for contemporary challenges.[44]

Furthermore, the reformists were no longer attracted by charismatic teaching personalities but preferred to be identified by their institutional affiliation.[45] This resulted in a disconnect in the teacher–student bond that was a hallmark of the traditional system of Islamic learning on the Kenya coast. A striking feature of the reformist *'ulamā'* is that they seem to have lost touch with their poetical heritage. Despite having the advantage of learning at various universities in the Arab and Muslim world, the new reformist *'ulamā'* hardly composed any elegiac poetry.

Sh. Mahmoud Ahmed Abdulkadir (Mahmoud MAU) (b. 1952)

Sh. Mahmoud, born in Lamu, represents the reformists' movement. He was taught by traditionalist 'Alawiyya scholars including the scholar-poet Syd. ʿAli b. Aḥmad Badawī. Sh. Mahmoud followed in the footsteps of the pioneer reformist in Lamu, Sh. Fayṣal b. ʿAlī al-Lāmi (d. 1918). Sh. Fayṣal differed with 'Alawiyya scholars but did not engage in debates. In order to avoid controversies, Sh. Fayṣal left Lamu and settled in the nearby village of Shela. He taught a generation of scholars who include Sh. Muḥammad Al-Maʿāwī and Syd. ʿAlī Aḥmad Badawī.

Sh. Mahmoud has composed a number of Swahili poems on topical issues, mostly written using the Latin script. The following is an example of his poetry, entiled *Wasiya wa Mabanati* ('Advice to Girls'), composed in 1974, regarding the temptations, challenges and sufferings that face young girls on the Kenya coast. It reads:

Sikiza mwanagu   Nikupe wasiya
Mimi ulimwengu   Ninauweleya
Mingi miaka yangu   Katika duniya
Nawe haya yangu   Hela zingatiya

[Listen my child   to the advice I shall give you
I understand   the ways of the world
I have spent many years   on this earth
And what I tell you now   you should bear in mind][46]

The following are titles of Sh. Mahmoud's poems in epic form (*tendi*) composed in Swahili using the Latin script: *Wasiya wa mabanati* (1974), *Kimondo* (1, 2, 3) (1975), *UKIMWI Nzimwi* (1990), *Hakiza watoto* (2000), *Uzunduzi* (2001), *Mwangaza* (2003), *Mukhadarati* (2004), *Ramani ya maisha (mume)*

[44] Loimeier, *Between Social Skills and Marketable Skills*, 109.

[45] Loimeier, *Between Social Skills and Marketable Skills*, 124.

[46] Kresse, 'Enduring Relevance', 49.

(2006), *Ramani ya maisha (mke)* (2006), and *Kikuba* (2010). Sh. Mahmoud also composed short poems which include: *Tunda* (1976), *Kipande cha ini* (1989), *Msichana wa kiislamu* (1990), *Kitabu* (2000), *Jahazi* (2002), *Swahili* (2003), *Mlango t'aushindika* (2005), *Ufisadi* (2006), *Asochake!* (2006), *Tahadharina UKIMWI!* (2006), *Mama musimlaumu* (2006), *Bandari* (2009), *Yatima* (2009), *Tupijeni makamama* (2010), *Tulindeni Swahili* (2010), and *Bandari inamawimbi* (2010).

Conclusion

Poetry has significantly contributed to the literary tradition of Swahili culture. The above elegiac poems exhibit patterns of Arabic literary influences which over time were adopted and adapted in Swahili poetry. The transmission of elegiac poems on the Kenya coast established a network of *'ulamā'* and poets who were closely attached in their lives as well as after the departure of their peers. The poetic network extended across the Indian Ocean, establishing an interface between local poetic expression and the wider world, reaching as far as Arabia.

The elegiac poems cited above exhibit poetic power and its close connection with establishing religious rituals. Elegiac poems were also used as instruments of acquiring authority and power, particularly in recitation and performance of the poems in public settings. Recitation in public settings was not only meant for the deceased scholar but also symbolized recognition of the *ṭarīqa* subscribed to by the departed patrons.

In addition to their literary value, elegiac poems were used as vehicles for inculcating mystical values and Sufi messages, particularly those prescribed by the 'Alawiyya *ṭarīqa*. Poetry also contributed to the dissemination of both the esoteric and exoteric teachings of the 'Alawiyya *ṭarīqa* on the Kenya coast and beyond. *'Ulamā'*, mainly subscribing to the 'Alawiyya *ṭarīqa*, presented in this chapter were products of the local intellectual tradition. They demonstrated an intellectual standing that was admired by their peers in the region and beyond. In addition to mastering their respective religious disciplines, a considerable number of the *'ulamā'* were outstanding poets who demonstrated their mastery of poetical skills.

Elegiac poetry was also used as a channel of social expression for poets to express their appreciation and sorrow for their deceased patrons and peers. Poetry on the Kenya coast in its various expressions needs to be studied further in order to reveal its living spirit and its enduring relevance to the Swahili people and their culture.

CONCLUSION

The Study of Islamic Scholarship and the Social Sciences in Africa: Bridging Knowledge Divides, Reframing Narratives

Ebrima Sall

This book showcases cutting-edge research in the study of Islam and Islamic scholarship in Africa. In many ways, it also shows how the study of Islamic scholarship in Africa has led to a formidable extension of the frontiers of the study of Africa, and of African scholarship.

I would like to begin with a personal experience. In the mid-1990s, while I was programme officer at CODESRIA, Ousmane Kane, who was then head of the Department of Political Science of Gaston Berger University, in Saint-Louis, Senegal, invited me to teach a course on 'Contemporary political problems' in his department. For five years, during the second semester, I used some of my leave days to go every week on an overnight trip to Saint-Louis, which is 260 km to the north of Dakar, to teach the course. Instead of using the accommodation provided by the University, I used to spend the night in Ousmane's house. Through our conversations, I came to realize how segmented the African intellectual community was.

One evening, I was looking at Ousmane Kane's *Handlist of Manuscripts in the Libraries of Shaykh Mor Mbaye Cissé, al-Hâjj Malick Sy & Shaykh Ibrahima Niasse*,[1] and listening to Ousmane explain with passion, but also with great anxiety, how tens of thousands of precious manuscripts lying in private libraries all across West Africa, particularly in great centres of learning like Timbuktu in Mali, and Pir, Koki, Touba, Tivaouane and Medina Baye in Senegal, could be lost through serious deterioration if something was not urgently done to preserve them. It then dawned on me that even with all the research and publishing that CODESRIA was doing as the leading pan-African social science research council, we actually

[1] Ousmane Kane, *Handlist of Manuscripts in the Libraries of Shaykh Mor Mbaye Cissé, al-Hâjj Malick Sy & Shaykh Ibrahima Niasse* (London: Al-Furqan, 1997).

knew very little about what the thousands of manuscripts that Ousmane was talking and writing about were discussing, in part because most of the manuscripts were written in Arabic or were using the Arabic script (*'Ajamī*). It was clear that there were other important intellectual debates that had been going on in Africa that neither CODESRIA, nor most of the African universities and research centres modelled on those of the West, were engaging with. Very few were the African scholars who had read the Timbuktu manuscripts, for instance, and were familiar with the debates captured in the huge number of manuscripts to be preserved. So, I concurred with Ousmane, but also asked: apart from preserving the manuscripts, how about developing research projects whose aim would be to bring out what is in the manuscripts, engage with the debates in them, connect the debates in them with our debates, and connect the different sub-groups of what should be one large and diverse African intellectual community?

From our conversation came the idea of writing a concept note for a CODESRIA 'green book' (which was the name given to the state-of-the-art reviews that CODESRIA used to commission prior to the launching of each one of its Multinational Working Groups). This green book would serve as a foundation for launching research networks and working groups on the debates among the Islamic and other scholars who were not really seen to be part of the mainstream African scholarly community. Ousmane then drafted and submitted to CODESRIA a concept note for a green book on 'Non-Europhone intellectuals'. CODESRIA approved the concept note and sponsored the research leading to the writing of the green book.

It should be noted that Cheikh Anta Diop and other founding members of CODESRIA were aware of the existence of the huge body of knowledge produced by Islamic scholars. Ousmane Kane's *Non-Europhone Intellectuals*, published in 2003, was the first major CODESRIA publication on the study of Islamic scholarship, which is an important strand of African scholarship. The French edition of Ousmane's green book was published several years before the conference in Cape Town was held that led to the publication of *The Meanings of Timbuktu*, edited by Shamil Jeppie and Souleymane Bachir Diagne. CODESRIA was already keenly interested in 'endogenous knowledge' and had set up a multinational working group on the subject, led by Paulin Hountondji, and the group came up with a book with the same title that sparked off a lively debate on endogenous knowledge in the *CODESRIA Bulletin*. However, that debate did not touch on the study of Islamic scholarship.

Indeed, one consequence of the introduction of the social sciences and humanities in tropical Africa in the wake of the European Enlightenment was the sidelining of the endogenous and other 'non-Europhone' knowledges and institutions of higher learning that existed in the region. Islamic scholars from the region, whose works were read along with the classics of Arabic and Islamic studies, suddenly became downgraded to the status of 'pre-modern', exotic, non-scientific intellectuals, whose huge production (that includes oral texts, *'Ajamī* works, and Arabic texts dealing with philosophical, social, medical, spiritual, ecological, economic and other issues) could, at best, be objects of study by 'Europhone' scholars. Philosophies, languages, and religions were also reclassified along similar lines. Beyond the reclassification, Boaventura de Sousa Santos, Walter Mignolo, Sabelo Gatsheni-Ndlovu and other decolonial thinkers have argued that these processes of epistemological and linguistic annihilation should be called 'epistemicide' and 'linguicide'.[2] They have, in effect, led to a narrowing down of the field of African studies as institutionalised in the 'modern' universities of the West, or those modelled on them, and of the scope of the social sciences and humanities. Much more devastating have been the effects on the languages, cultures and endogenous knowledges of the communities and societies that were subjected to the processes. The understanding of what accounts for the resilience and, in some instances, real dynamism of African societies over the centuries was therefore limited to what 'received social science'[3] could capture. The chapters of this book therefore bring fresh insights into social sciences and humanities debates. Extending the frontiers of the study of Islamic scholarship in Africa and bridging the 'europhone'/'non-europhone' knowledge divides could significantly advance decolonial thinking, and significantly extend the frontiers.

In what follows, I first situate the questions posed and ambitions set for the conference and workshop hosted by Harvard University in the broader context of knowledge divides and how the latter play out in the study of Africa. These meetings were held respectively in February and October 2017, and it is the papers presented there that were later developed into the chapters published in this book. I then present one African response to the knowledge divides, that of the Council for the Development of Social Science Research in Africa (CODESRIA), and discuss the various ways in which African scholars working with CODESRIA have been contributing to the transformation of the global epistemological order; the same order under which Islamic scholarship and endogenous and indigenous knowledges have also been sidelined, if not simply suppressed. I also show the

[2] Boaventura de Souza Santos, *Epistemologies of the South. Justice Against Epistemicide* (Boulder, CO: Paradigm Publishers, 2014); Walter D. Mignolo, *The Darker Side of The Renaissance: Literacy, Territoriality and Colonization* (Ann Arbor: University of Michigan Press, 1995); Walter D. Mignolo, *The Darker Side of Western Modernity: Global Futures, Decolonial Options* (Durham, NC and London: Duke University Press, 2011); Sabelo Gatsheni-Ndlovu, *Coloniality of Power in Post-Colonial Africa: Myths of Decolonization* (Dakar: CODESRIA, 2013).

[3] Claude Ake, 'The Social Sciences in Africa: Trends, Tasks and Challenges. A Lecture Given on the Tenth Anniversary of CODESRIA' (Dakar: CODESRIA, 1986).

various ways in which the studies offered in this collection contribute to the epistemic struggle in which CODESRIA and like-minded social sciences consortiums in Asia and Latin America are engaged. In the third and last section of this chapter, I highlight some of the key issues raised by the chapters of this book that seem to me to be items of a new research agenda that could greatly increase the contributions to decolonial thinking coming from the study of Islamic scholarship in Africa and African studies.

***

As noted in the introduction to this book,[4] CODESRIA was set up in 1973 with the aim of promoting social science research in Africa. It quickly became a platform for African intellectuals seeking to transcend all knowledge divides and transform what has been called the 'colonial library'[5] and the larger, and more complex imperial library whose metamorphosis is an ongoing process. CODESRIA has been promoting independent and bold thinking on the problems of the contemporary world from within Africa. This was an attempt, as Amilcar Cabral would say, to look at the world 'with our own eyes', and from where we are,[6] and boost knowledge production with such a perspective, from within Africa.

Knowledge Divides

The intellectual communities engaged in the study of Africa, both within and outside of the continent, have been segmented for far too long. In the Western academies, the logic of 'area studies' and the specializations that one finds in the humanities and social science disciplines have contributed to the fragmentation of both African studies and Islamic studies.[7] Within the African continent

[4] See Ousmane Kane, 'Where Have We Been and Where Are We Going?', the introduction to this volume.

[5] V.Y. Mudimbe, *The Invention of Africa: Gnosis, Philosophy, and the Order of Knowledge* (Bloomington and Indianapolis: Indiana University Press; London: James Currey, 1988); Valentin Y. Mudimbe, *The Idea of Africa* (Bloomington: Indiana University Press; London: James Currey, 1994).

[6] Amilcar Cabral used to say that 'we should think with our own heads, in the context of our realities'; Walter Mignolo has argued that our identity is not determined solely by our capacity to think, but also where we think and act from. Therefore, we should go beyond Descartes' famous phrase: 'I think, therefore I am' and instead say: 'I am from where I think and do'.

[7] In his introduction to this book, Ousmane Kane gives a good illustration of this by explaining how, even at Harvard, it turned out to be difficult to situate 'Islam in

itself, 'Europhone' and 'non-Europhone' intellectuals often work in silos, with the former claiming 'scientific' legitimacy for themselves and for the knowledges they produce in universities and research centres modelled on those of the West and denying such legitimacy to any other category of intellectual or knowledge.[8] The Non-Europhone scholars also tend to read and engage one another much more than they would engage the Europhone scholars in serious scholarly or public debates.

The divides separating the Europhone epistemic communities (that are far from being homogenous) from the Non-Europhone epistemic communities (that are equally heterogenous) are just a few of the many 'knowledge divides' that exist at the global level, as well as within the various regions and countries of the world. The 2010 International Social Science Council and UNESCO *World Social Science Report* on 'Knowledge Divides' shows the extent to which what could otherwise have been a global intellectual community is highly segmented and traversed by asymmetries of power that are as formidable as those that characterize what is often called the 'global community'.[9] What Paul Tiyambe Zeleza calls the 'global epistemological order'[10] is 'Western-centric' and does not only mirror the global socio-political and economic order: it also supports as much as it is a product of the latter. 'Epistemicide', i.e. the annihilation of other ways of knowing, has been part of the imperial project. Eurocentric epistemologies were presented as the only 'scientific', i.e. 'legitimate', epistemologies. European languages became the dominant languages of scholarship. Bridging the knowledge divides should be the logical consequence of the recognition of the plurality of knowledge; it therefore would be part of the processes that could lead to the transformation of both the global epistemological order and the

---

Africa', a field of study that concerns many departments and faculties but does not fit very neatly into the current institutional map of the university. The place of 'Africa in the disciplines' is also well documented, see Robert H. Bates; V.Y. Mudimbe; Jean F. Obarr (eds.), *Africa and the Disciplines. The Contributions of Research in Africa to the Social Sciences and Humanities* (Chicago, IL: University of Chicago Press, 1993).

8 Ousmane Kane, *Intellectuels non Europhones* (Dakar: CODESRIA, 2003), translated in English as *Non Europhone Intellectuals* (Dakar: CODESRIA, 2012); Mudimbe, *The Invention of Africa*; Mudimbe, *The Idea of Africa*.

9 *World Social Science Report 2010* (Paris: International Social Science Council and UNESCO, 2010).

10 Paul Tiyambe Zeleza (ed.), *The Study of Africa, Volume II: Global and Transnational Engagements* (Dakar: CODESRIA, 2006).

global socio-political order to make them more equitable and just.[11] *Epistemic justice*[12] is a precondition for global justice.

Within the African continent, the fragmentation of the intellectual communities along disciplinary lines is aggravated by language divides, divides between 'orthodox' and vernacular forms of expression, generational and gender divides, the marketization of higher education and the social sciences and humanities that has led to not only narrow institutional and area specializations, but also a reclassification of the disciplines and fields of study that is more or less based on their perceived market value. Therefore, the big divide between Europhone and non-Europhone intellectuals and knowledges is made much more complex by the separation but also the overlapping of 'areas', fields and spheres. 'We live in a world of structural heterogeneity.'[13] The asymmetries exist not only between what Beigel, Ouedraogo and Connell rightly call 'imperial' [rather than 'Western'] social science, but also within the countries of the Global South itself. 'Imperial' social science feeds on data, concepts, indigenous knowledges, and the intellectual labour of communities and societies not only of the Global North, but also of the Global South, including those of the indigenous peoples. Imperial social science has a formidable capacity to absorb, assimilate, digest, repackage, rebrand and re-export knowledge products (theories, concepts, paradigms, publications) whose constitutive elements are drawn from the whole world. In the process, it exerts enormous influence on social sciences and humanities, and on the knowledge systems of the world.

The relationships between the disciplines, intellectual communities and knowledges are, therefore, far from being equal or always harmonious. The rise to hegemonic positions of particular kinds of institutions, such as the modern university, the dominant Euro-American languages, epistemologies, and knowledges in and of the West led to the downgrading of the value of many other institutions,

[11] The theme of the 2009 ISSC General Assembly held in Oslo was 'One Planet, Worlds Apart'. The 'knowledge divides' discussed in the *World Social Science Report 2010* are an aspect of the fragmentation and asymmetry that characterize our planet. Held in Durban, in post-apartheid South Africa – one of the world's most unequal societies – the theme of the 2015 Assembly focused on the need for transformation of both the world of knowledge production and the rest of the world: 'Transforming Global Relations for a Just World'.

[12] Santos, *Epistemologies of the South*; Mignolo, *The Darker Side of The Renaissance*; Mignolo, *The Darker Side of Western Modernity*; Gatsheni-Ndlovu, *Coloniality of Power in Post-Colonial Africa*.

[13] Fernanda Beigel; Jean-Bernard Ouedraogo; Raewyn Connell, 'Building Knowledge from Fractured Epistemologies'; *METHOD(E)S: African Review of Social Science Methodology*, Special Issue on Epistemological Fractures in a Globalized World: Normalizations, Debates and Alternatives in the Social Sciences, 1–2, 2017, 62–78.

cultures and languages, epistemologies and modes of learning and knowledges that existed, both in the West and elsewhere. The results were the 'epistemicide' referred to above and the marginalization – and, in some cases, the death – of local knowledges and languages that in Africa were overrun by those of the former colonial powers, particularly English, French and Portuguese. Paradoxically, for the societies of the South, particularly the indigenous peoples of the Americas, and the Africans, the encounter with the West in the aftermath of the European Renaissance and Enlightenment whose 'darker sides'[14] have now been exposed, were major turning points in these processes.[15] This was when coloniality took shape, and coloniality was, and still is, an all-round, pervasive rapport that has become the DNA of imperial domination of societies around the world.

> 'Western modernity' has been an enormous contribution to the many histories of cultures and civilizations, but it shouldn't be taken as the point of arrival of human existence on the planet ... It was during the Renaissance that the invention of the Middle Ages and the invention of America appropriated the idea of history and colonized time and space and located Europe as the point of reference of global history .... Western civilization is the most recent, which doesn't mean that it is the best. However, the idea that European modernity was the point of arrival of humanity and the model for the entire planet came to be taken for granted.[16]

The 'subjugation of indigenous understandings of the world [was] part of the colonial process'.[17] One major outcome of these processes was the transformation of economies and political systems, bodies, race, gender and inter-generational

[14] Mignolo, *The Darker Side of the Renaissance.*

[15] Mignolo, *The Darker Side of the Renaissance*; Mignolo, *The Darker Side of Western Modernity*; Enrique Dussel, *The Invention of the Americas: Eclipse of 'the Other' and the Myth of Modernity* (New York: Continuum, 1995); Anibal Quijano, 'Coloniality and Modernity/Rationality', *Cultural Studies*, 21, 2–3, 2007, 168–78; C.B. Rougier; P. Colin; Ramon Grosfoguel, *Penser l'envers obscur de la modernité : une anthologie de la pensée décoloniale latino-américaine* (Limoges: Presses Universitaires de Limoges, 2014); Samir Amin, *Eurocentrism: Modernity, Religion, and Democracy A Critique of Eurocentrism and Culturalism* (New York: Monthly Review Press, 2009, 2nd edition); Santos, *Epistemologies of the South*; Gatsheni-Ndlovu, *Coloniality of Power in Post-Colonial Africa.*

[16] Mignolo, *The Darker Side of Western Modernity.*

[17] C. Cuneen; S. Rowe; J. Tauri, 'Fracturing the Colonial Paradigm: Indigenous Epistemologies and Methodologies', in Fernanda Beigel, Jean-Bernard Ouedraogo; Raewyn Connell (eds.), special issue on 'Epistemological Fractures in a Globalized World: Normalizations, Debates and Alternatives in the Social Sciences', *METHOD(E)S: African Review of Social Science Methodology*, 2, 1–2, 2017, 62–78.

relations, languages, cultures, religions, ways of knowing, and whole regions of the world, all of which bear the marks of coloniality.

As we know, Islam and African religions became major targets of the 'civilizing missions', in the same ways as the Africans, the Asians, and the indigenous peoples of the Americas were targeted for suppression and exploitation. These were violent processes. History itself was 'colonized', as the West claimed to be the exclusive centre, source of 'progress', and driver of human history, or rather, world history. The dominant narratives about human history and about the world were reframed accordingly, and the social and human sciences played key roles in the (re)framing of existing narratives. 'Orientalism' (Said), the 'invention of Africa',[18] and the 'invention of the Americas'[19] are good illustrations of the seminal works of great intellectuals from the South showing how the 'West' constructed entire regions of the world. More recent works have shown that the critique of the Western-centric construction of the Orient, Africa, and the Americas was itself largely framed in Eurocentric terms, using the very 'colonial' and imperial libraries they set out to critique, and in the process ignoring the Muslim, indigenous, and numerous other libraries and knowledge systems, many of which are much older than the colonial library.[20]

Similar critical analysis has also been made of the whole development discourse.[21] The economics and politics, and the cultural, ideological and spiritual bases of the division of the world into a centre (the West) and a periphery have been very well documented in a countless number of publications. Development, like modernity, was also largely seen as a vertical historical evolution of communities and societies from whatever levels of 'backwardness', 'underdevelopment' or 'primitiveness' they were in towards where the 'developed' world (i.e. the West) is today in terms of ways of life, family structures, economic and political systems. Lee Kuan Yew, the former president of Singapore, titled his book on the transformation of his country *From Third World to First.*[22] The geography of the

[18] Mudimbe, *The Invention of Africa.*

[19] Dussel, *The Invention of the Americas.*

[20] Kane, *Non-Europhone Intellectuals*, 2012; Ousmane Oumar Kane, *Beyond Timbuktu. An Intellectual History of Muslim West Africa* (Cambridge, MA: Harvard University Press, 2016); Mignolo, *The Darker Side of the Renaissance*; Santos, *Epistemologies of the South.*

[21] Arturo Escobar, *Encountering Development: The Making and Unmaking of the Third World* (Oxford: Princeton University Press, 1995); Ake, 'The Social Sciences in Africa'; Partha Chatterjee, *Nationalist Thought and the Colonial World: A Derivative Discourse?* (London: Zed Books, 1993); Partha Chatterjee, *Our Modernity* (Rotterdam/Dakar: SEPHIS and CODESRIA, 1997).

[22] Lee Kuan Yew, *From Third World To First: The Singapore Story: 1965–2000* (New York: HarperCollins Publishers, 2000).

world was a geography of development, read in ways that mirrored the hierarchy that characterizes the global order, at the top of which is the West. To this day, despite the emergence of new 'markets', 'poles', 'centres', and 'powers' (such as the BRICS countries – Brazil, Russia, India, China and South Africa) in other regions of the world, differences in levels of development and in the volume of knowledge production, just like differences in the ranking of universities, think tanks, and journals, etc., all tend to follow the North/South, West/Rest of the World divide, broadly defined.

Furthermore, some scholars from the Global South see the decentring of theory as an important aspect of the transformation of the global epistemological order that is too Western-centric and dominated. Oludamini Ogunnaike for example (chapter 6) refutes the notion that philosophy, 'as an independent discipline, more or less died out in the Maghreb, sub-Saharan Africa, and the Arab heartlands by the thirteenth century'.[23] His analysis of the philosophical works of Shaykh Dan Tafa argues persuasively that *falsafa* was alive and well in the nineteenth-century Sokoto Caliphate. Overall, Ogunnaike's work critically engages thinkers and ideas from non-Europhone African traditions just as one would more familiar Western intellectuals and theorists such as Kant, Marx, or Merleau-Ponty. This trend marks an important turn in African studies and the study of Islam in Africa, in which contemporary scholars in the West are increasingly able to productively engage with their counterparts in non-Europhone African traditions much as contemporary scholars continue to critically engage with ancient Greek, Roman and Early Christian philosophers and ideas. This is further illustrated in his *Deep Knowledge* in which Ogunnaike uses Ibn 'Arabi, a thirteenth-century Sufi and one of the most influential figures in the Islamic intellectual tradition, as a source of theory, much as one would use the work of Foucault or Bourdieu to analyse socio-political or religious phenomena.[24]

Along similar lines, in *Theory from the South*, the Comaroffs argue that history is no longer made solely from the West. If anything, they further argue, the works of Cheikh Anta Diop, for instance, who has tried to show that Egypt was the cradle of civilization that influenced many other civilizations, such as ancient Greece, which nullifies the claims to anteriority attributed to Western civilization, have shown how history is decentred. That being the case, the decentring of theory has become a necessity.[25] In truth, history was never solely made from the West,

[23] Ogunnaike, chapter 6 of this volume.

[24] Oludamini Ogunnaike, *Deep Knowledge: Ways of Knowing in Sufism and Ifa, Two West African Intellectual Traditions* (Philadelphia: Penn State University Press, 2020).

[25] Jean Comaroff; John Comaroff, *Theory from the South: Or How Euro-America is Evolving Towards Africa* (New York: Routledge, 2012); Achille Mbembe, 'Africa in

and the decentring of theory is what the pan-African movement, and the whole history of CODESRIA, has been about. Among the most significant milestones in the decentring of theory are the building of strong universities and research councils such as CLACSO (the Latin American Council of Social Sciences) and FLACSO (the Latin American Faculty of Social Sciences) in Central and South America, and CODESRIA and the Association of African Universities in Africa, and the consequent boost in knowledge production in the South. Indeed, in the words of one of its founders, CODESRIA was set up in 1973 as a platform for 'independent and audacious thinking on the challenges facing the contemporary world'.[26]

The chapters in this book give a good sense of how important and debilitating the knowledge divides have been. They also highlight the many emancipatory counter-processes and counter-narratives that the Islamic scholarship in Africa has engendered.

Bridging Knowledge Divides, Reframing Narratives

Indeed, the chapters in this book challenge many dominant narratives about Africa as well as the simplistic binary divides between civilizations of orality and civilizations that value the written word, 'tradition' and modernity, the 'formal' and the 'informal' sectors, and so forth. They also challenge the dominant narratives about Islam in tropical Africa that was often portrayed as being peripheral, its scholars being marginal in the world of knowledge production; and about Afro-Arab relations (that are often portrayed as being primarily conflictual). In sharp contrast to all those narratives, the contributors to this book present completely different pictures. For example, Ousmane Kane's work shows that cosmopolitanism was, and is still, common in Muslim societies of Africa, including within families,[27] and Zachary Wright[28] and Dahlia Gubara[29] document extensive networks and movements of scholars in the Muslim World, and show that scholars from sub-Saharan Africa participated in such networks as equal partners. Depicting Africa as the 'continent of orality' is just one of the very problematic dominant narratives. Orality in Africa did not mean the absence of other kinds of texts, including

---

Theory', paper for CODESRIA – Point Sud conference on 'Afrika N'Ko: Africa in the World – Debating the Colonial Library' (Dakar, 28–31 January 2013).

[26] Samir Amin, 'Notes on the Creation of CODESRIA', paper presented at the celebration of CODESRIA Day at the CODESRIA headquarters in Dakar (Dakar, 1 February 2016).

[27] Kane, *Beyond Timbuktu*.

[28] Wright, chapter 1 of this volume.

[29] Gubara, chapter 2 of this volume.

written texts. Indeed, the African continent has also for a long time been 'a continent of writing', as can be seen with the Egyptian hieroglyphs, the Amharic texts, Arabic and *'Ajamī*. Written texts are vocalized and audio recordings of oral translations and commentaries of sacred texts such as the Qur'ān are widely circulated. Cheikh Ibrahim Niasse's Arabic translations and commentaries of the Qur'ān (a written text) have been transcribed and there have been serious attempts to transcribe the Wolof version, translated into English and French, and publish it. Similar work has been done on 'Alī Ḥarāzim Barrada's *Jawāhir al Ma'ānī wa bulūgh al-amānī fi fayḍ Aḥmad al-Tijānī*.[30]

The classification of Africa as the 'continent of orality' was part of the colonial project: that of subjugating the continent and its people. However, 'orality' does not necessarily signify inferiority in terms of cultures, and knowledge production and classification. James Scott has even argued that if American farmers have almanacs showing crops and seasons, the hunter-gatherers of the world have always had full 'libraries' of almanacs concerning a broad range of crops, animals, fishes, etc.[31] Orality is the hallmark of most indigenous knowledges.[32] The oral text is therefore far from being an inferior text.[33] The Ibadan School of history is known for being one of the first in Africa to say that oral sources ought to be recognized as legitimate sources of history. The eight-volume *General History of Africa* (*GHA*) published by UNESCO made extensive use of oral sources.[34] Scholars such as

30 See Cisse Kane (trans.), *Jawâhirul-ma'ânî - Les joyaux des sens et l'accès aux aspirations, en l'effluve spirituel du maître, Abul 'Abbâs At-Tijânî* (Dakar: L'Harmattan, 2018).

31 James C. Scott, *Against the Grain: A Deep History of the Earliest States* (New Haven, CT: Yale University Press, 2017).

32 Paulin Hountondji (ed.), *Endogenous Knowledge: Research Trails* (Dakar: CODESRIA, 1997); Chris Cuneen et al., 'Epistemological Fractures in a Globalized World'.

33 Souleymane Bachir Diagne, *The Ink of The Scholars: Reflections on Philosophy in Africa* (Dakar: CODESRIA, 2016).

34 See: https://en.unesco.org/general-history-africa and https://boydellandbrewer.com/catalogsearch/result/?q=UNESCO, both accessed 6 July 2020. In his 2008–9 Inaugural Lecture at Gaston Berger University of Saint-Louis, Senegal, Djibril Tamsir Niane, editor of Volume IV of *The General History of Africa* (*GHA*), argued that orality has now been rehabilitated: '*aujourd'hui, en Afrique, la tradition orale a été réhabilitée. On sait qu'elle a apporté une contribution de qualité à la rédaction de l'Histoire Générale de l'Afrique réalisée sous l'égide de l'UNESCO: Histoire monumentale en huit volumes. Sans elle, des pans entiers de notre passé seraient relégués dans les siècles obscurs. Elle a été réhabilitée, la tradition orale et des campagnes de collecte ont été organisées à travers tout le Continent. ... Aujourd'hui, nous disposons de bandothèques, de bibliothèques sonores, dans les instituts de recherche,*

Akiwowo[35] and Adesina,[36] who are engaged in the study of Yoruba languages and religions, have demonstrated how 'taking our locales seriously' could enrich disciplines like sociology, linguistics, and history. The same thing could be said about the study of African religions.[37] Orality has also been evolving and taking new forms, particularly with the ITCs revolution, as de Diego González shows.[38] Furthermore, Islamic scholarship has shown how written texts are read out loudly to students and large groups of people in the course of Qur'ān *tafsīr*, etc.

This book is therefore also about rethinking education, generally, and Islamic education, more specifically – from the *daara* (Madrasa, 'traditional' Qur'ānic school) to the modern Islamic university; teacher/marabout-student/disciple relations (Is the student necessarily a disciple? Not in the modern schools!) and how that is related to the big issues – spirituality, Islam, global challenges, peace, violence, international migrations, diasporas (and their children), and population displacements. These issues are addressed in part III of the volume, which examines the transformation of Islamic education.[39] This culminated with the rise of Islamic institutions of higher education. Kane shows how the evolution of Islamic universities of West Africa and that of the modern university modelled on those of the West have tended to make the two more and more similar to one another.[40]

The bridging of the 'knowledge divides' is, as a matter of fact, as formidable a task as that of the transformation of the world to make it more inclusive and just. The struggles to transform the dominant epistemological order – and the world – are as old as the order itself. The critique of orientalism, and of the colonial library, the critique of the coloniality of power, of modernization theory, and of the dominant theories of development and globalization have led to major

dans les Universités d'Afrique, d'Europe et d'Amérique. Oui on peut écouter les voix de nos doctes griots et nos doctes doyens illétrés.'

[35] Akinsola A. Akiwowo, 'Contributions to the Sociology of Knowledge from an African Oral Poetry', *International Sociology*, 1, 4, 1986, 343–58; Akinsola A. Akiwowo, 'Indigenous Sociologies: Extending the Scope of the Argument', *International Sociology*, 14, 2, 1999, 115–38. On orality, also see Mamousse Diagne's *Critique de la raison orale* (Paris: Karthala, 2005).

[36] Olujimi O. Adesina, 'Sociology and Yorùbá Studies: Epistemic Intervention or Doing Sociology in the "Vernacular"?', *African Sociological Review*, 6, 1, 2002, 91–114.

[37] Oludamini Ogunnaike, 'From Theory to Theoria and Back Again: Decolonizing Theories of African Philosophy and Religion', paper delivered at the Meeting of the American Academy of Religion, Boston, 18–21 November 2017.

[38] De Diego González, chapter 8 of this volume.

[39] See Bolton (chapter 10), Cochrane (chapter (11), Hoechner (chapter 12), Frede (chapter 13) in this volume.

[40] Kane, *Beyond Timbuktu*, chapter 7.

shifts in the paradigms of development and social change. In the study of Islamic scholarship in Africa, more specifically, these days, a number of intellectuals on both sides are making efforts to transcend the boundaries and bridge the divides separating these epistemic communities. A growing number of non-Europhone intellectuals, who studied in the Arab world or studied in other parts of Africa but using the Arabic language, pursue postgraduate studies in 'modern' institutions in Europe and the Americas and in Africa.[41] Similarly, Arab and Islamic studies departments have been mushrooming in universities in, or modelled on, those in the West, broadly defined.[42]

We also have in this book a good illustration of the incredible dynamism and renewal going on in Islam and in our societies more generally, the blurring of certain boundaries, the closing-up of space and time differences. The book also reveals the great dynamism of the Muslim societies and of religious confraternities within these societies that, in many Eurocentric scholarly productions, are seen as 'obscurantist', with no chances of catching up with our high-tech-driven world. Yet, as has been shown in this book, Muslim Sufi orders, such as the Tijāniyya, have not only integrated the ITCs and social media into their systems, but also domesticated these technologies.[43] In the process, they (the Sufi orders) too have evolved and had some of their very fundamental constitutive elements, such as the relations between the shaykh and his disciple, redefined to take on new forms and meanings. In that regard, the Sufi orders are very 'modern' in the dual sense of having the capacity to find adequate and appropriate responses to the challenges of the contemporary world,[44] and of being simply 'up-to-date' and moving at par with the progress of science and technology. Contemporary challenges such as climate change and international migrations are also being addressed, not only in cities like Dakar, but also in rural settings such as Mbacke Kajoor in Senegal.[45]

One of the major contributions of this book, therefore, is the way it interrogates the coloniality of knowledge, as well as the coloniality of power and the coloniality of bodies – for instance by revisiting issues of race.[46] Zachary Wright and Chanfi Ahmed forcefully argue that scholars from West Africa were very influential in Cairo, Fez, Marrakesh, Mecca and Medina where they taught luminaries. In

[41] Mamadou Yuri Sall's recently published book, *La mesure de l'Arabophonie au Sénégal* (Dakar: Presses universitaires de Dakar, 2018).

[42] Kane, *Beyond Timbuktu*.

[43] See de Diego González, chapter 8 in this volume.

[44] Ali El-Kenz, *Algeria: The Challenge of Modernity* (Dakar: CODESRIA, 1991).

[45] Cochrane, chapter 11 of this volume.

[46] See, for example, Gubara, chapter 2 of this volume, and same author, 'Revisiting Race and Slavery through 'Abd al-Rahman al-Jabarti's *"Ajā'ib al-āthār"*', *Comparative Studies of South Asia, Africa and the Middle East*, 38, 2, 2018, 230–45.

the process they deconstruct the notion that racial prejudice could prevent Black African scholars from reaching the very top of the scholarly establishment. Along the same lines, Dahlia Gubara shows the notion of 'the African' or 'blackness' was simply unknown among the Muslim scholars in Al-Azhar prior to the twentieth century.[47] The book is therefore also a major contribution to decolonial thinking.

Much of the discussion in Africa over the past two decades or so has been about the challenges facing the humanities and social sciences. Taking the crises and challenges as the starting points of our stories in some ways influences the stories we tell. The papers published in this book are a clear demonstration of the dynamism of the humanities and social sciences in Africa. Connecting the debates in the different fields of study and disciplines has been an important contributory factor to the dynamism of the humanities and social sciences. One institution that worked hard to connect the study of Islamic scholarship with the study of Africa and the world is CODESRIA.

Connecting Endogenous Knowledges, the Study of Islamic Scholarship, and the Social Sciences

Quite early in its history, CODESRIA took a keen interest in reclaiming the broader and deeper intellectual history of Africa in which Islamic and Arabophone scholars played major roles, and in connecting the different kinds of intellectuals and knowledges of the continent. Africa, it should be remembered, is where some of the first institutions of higher learning of the world (that include the Qarawiyyine in Fez and the Al-Azhar in Cairo) were established. Others, like Timbuktu and Pir (in present-day Senegal) came later. Most of these institutions of higher learning that Africa had were based in Muslim societies and run by Islamic scholars. As several chapters of this book show, over the years, many other centres of learning emerged in North, West and East Africa, some of which became very famous. Reclaiming that history and working towards the re-membering ('re-piecing together') of the diverse community and the huge but highly fragmented body of knowledge was something that Cheikh Anta Diop, for instance, strongly argued for.[48] The initiatives aimed at bridging the divides between the different kinds of knowledge production sites, intellectuals and knowledges included major continental research networks on endogenous knowledges as well as what was called an 'Arabophone Initiative' that looked at the place and roles that Islam and the

[47] Gubara, 'Revisiting Race and Slavery'.

[48] Cheikh Anta Diop, *The African Origin of Civilization: Myth or Reality* (New York: Lawrence Hill & Co., 1974). It should be noted that Cheikh Anta Diop was for a few years a member of the Executive Committee of CODESRIA.

Arab language and culture have had historically and are currently having in many parts of the continent. I return to this point later.

The CODESRIA story, it should be noted, is a chapter of the larger, older and more complex story of the epistemic self-affirmation of Africa, itself being at once a precursor, companion process, and postscript to the process leading to emancipation and higher levels of self-realization that the peoples of Africa and African descent are engaged in. It is, in many ways, a continuation of the story of what decolonial scholars call 'epistemic disobedience' in Africa.

Furthermore, this is a story about reclaiming African agency in scholarship and knowledge production, and about enabling African agency through research: building a community of scholars, and, to a certain extent, an epistemic community across all the divides of a linguistic, disciplinary or gender nature. Transcending all the divides, such as those between intellectuals and knowledges (Europhones/ other intellectuals and knowledges), sub-Saharan/North African, languages, genders, generations, disciplines, regions, and so forth, was seen as a condition for the advancement of African scholarship and the increase of the volume of knowledge produced from within the continent as well as the 'relevance' of the knowledge produced to the policy agendas and to the broader continental emancipation and transformation projects.

Beyond Africa, the idea behind the creation of CODESRIA, as we now know it, in 1973 (there is a longer history) was to build a strong pan-African institution that would be 'one of the engines that are needed to promote independent and audacious African reflections on the challenges of the contemporary world'.[49] The starting point, of course, was to contest the dominant narratives about Africa, which made the transformation of the colonial library a necessity. This was done not only by confronting the dominant historical paradigms, but also the paradigms of development. CODESRIA has therefore been engaged in the struggle to decolonize the humanities and social sciences since its creation. The promotion of endogenous knowledge production called for the transformation of what Valentin Mudimbe called the 'colonial library' that had led to a major 'epistemicide' and the sidelining of what was left of the libraries and knowledge systems that preceded or co-existed with it. As noted above, the struggle to decolonize the humanities and social sciences is part of a bigger struggle for the transformation of the global epistemological order that mirrors the dominant socio-political order.

CODESRIA has therefore been engaged in the promotion of the humanities in Africa, like CLACSO and other institutions of the Global South have also been doing. Cheikh Anta Diop, Amilcar Cabral, Joseph Ki-Zerbo and others have argued that Africans ought to be the co-authors of the global narratives, by

[49] S. Amin, 'Notes on the creation of CODESRIA'.

looking at the world from where we are, and at each given moment. The starting point for being co-authors of the narratives about our world, is to be the authors or, at the very least, the co-authors of the narratives about Africa. Mamousse Diagne, a Senegalese philosopher, further argued that Africans ought to be the authors or co-authors of the 'African novel' that 'we then proudly donate to the truly global or universal library that the peoples of the world are building'.[50] This is also an issue for the Global South as a whole, which is why CODESRIA, CLACSO, IDEAs (International Development Economics Associates based in India), and other councils and networks have been deploying efforts to build South–South knowledge networks.

CODESRIA has been intervening at various levels. To begin with, how does one set a research agenda that seeks to produce knowledge about Africa and about the world 'from where we are', and determine priorities for research not according to the available sources of funding for research but on what the research and policy communities consider to be critical issues for Africa? At the time of the creation of CODESRIA, much of the research done on the continent was demand driven: funding agencies, international organizations and embassies providing funding for research on the issues that *they* were concerned about, were really the ones setting the agenda for research. This left very little room for the basic research and the exploration of issues that could lead to significant contributions to theory, and even less room for critical reflections on development and development cooperation. Where the initiatives were taken by well-meaning European and American scholars based at universities in North America or Europe, the agenda was again determined almost unilaterally by the latter, and a division of labour established, with the African scholars serving mainly as data collectors and informants. To overcome such challenges, CODESRIA decided to prioritize basic research, and priorities were discussed during the triennial general assembly. It later began developing strategic plans in which thematic priorities were set.

The second major challenge was to grow the numbers of African scholars and nurture new generations of scholars who could meaningfully engage in critical conversations about African and global issues with African policy makers, international organizations and our colleagues of the North. Indeed, with the universities being not just modelled on those of the West, but also for a time literally affiliates of universities in Europe and North America, the curricula were Eurocentric, and the capacity to engage in critical discussions was limited. Decolonizing the social sciences therefore called for the enhancement of African research capacity, through a series of initiatives such as summer institutes, methodology workshops, small grants for thesis writing, social science campuses, scholarly writing

[50] He made the point at both the African Humanities Conference in Bamako, June 2017, and at the UNESCO World Humanities Conference held in Liège in August 2017.

workshops, South–South summer institutes, launching a textbook series, etc. The cohorts of young scholars who participated in these initiatives built strong bonds among themselves, which was an important part of the scholarly community-building process.

The third level and type of intervention was in publishing. The politics of journal publishing are complex. The majority of those rated as the best international journals are published in the West. For African scholars, being published in such journals, including those that specialize in African issues, is quite a challenge. The best international journals themselves are not affordable for most African scholars and African university libraries, which means that even when they get their works published in those journals, their colleagues and students on the continent might find it difficult to have access to the journals, even with the adoption of open access policies. Equally important is the fact that the editorial policies and lines of the journals are determined by the requirements of the academic environments in which they are published. Therefore, what might be considered important issues for debate in Africa might not be seen the same way by the editors of journals published in the North. Providing publishing outlets for African scholars was therefore seen to be an important part of the CODESRIA project. Having peer-reviewed journals published in Africa and in other regions of the South increased the possibilities for scholars of these regions to read and engage with one another's work, while helping to project scholarly voices from the South at the global level, thus increasing the visibility of southern scholarship. Most of CODESRIA's journals are bilingual (English and French), and one of them is a review of books whose aim is to showcase books published from Africa or about Africa and, especially, give a chance to African scholars to express their views about the quality of the publications about Africa. One of the CODESRIA journals, *Afro-Arab Selections in the Social Sciences*, was published out of Cairo, in collaboration with the Afro-Arab Research Centre, with a view to connecting the social science debates in the European languages with those in Arabic. Important articles were translated from English and French into Arabic and published in the journal.

The fourth was in creating frameworks and instruments for determining quality, setting standards, and measuring production. The most ambitious of those initiatives so far is the attempt to build an African Citation Index (ACI). It is a well-established fact that using bibliometric studies and other conventional means for measuring scientific outputs, Africa produces only a small fraction of the articles, books and other research outputs of the world. However, it is also recognized that the citation indexes used by big, northern-based institutions such as Thompson Reuters and Web of Science do not capture the vast array of publications in languages other than English, and all those that do not meet certain criteria. The knowledges produced on the African continent are therefore not fully accounted for, and much of them remain invisible. This is the problem that ACI is meant to address. The project was first discussed in 2006, but it was only in 2015 that it really took off, with the technical assistance of the Indian Citation Index – largely as a mark of South–South solidarity.

Therefore, CODESRIA did many things to promote knowledge production in Africa and it has begun to work more systematically towards bridging the two divides that were for a long time overlooked, even in the CODESRIA community: the divide between Europhone and non-Europhone scholars and knowledges, and the divide between those who work in the European languages and the Arabophones. As mentioned in the introduction to this volume, the first major publication related to that is Kane's book titled *Non-Europhone Intellectuals*, first published in French in 2003, and then translated in English, Arabic and Spanish, followed five years later by *The Meanings of Timbuktu* edited by Shamil Jeppie and Souleymane Bachir Diagne. In 2012, an Arabophone Initiative was launched, with a view to encouraging the use of the Arabic language as a language of research within CODESRIA circles, but also to research and publish on the presence and dynamics of Arab and Islamic cultures on the rest of the African continent, the relationship between these and other cultures, and so forth and so on.

Conclusion: Towards a New Research Agenda – Issues Needing Further Exploration

The study of Islamic scholarship in Africa has, so far, largely focused on the past. This book shows how Islamic scholarship is also focusing on contemporary development, political and cultural issues, as much as it is focusing on spiritual issues. Indeed, for Muslim intellectuals, one of the major challenges of the day is that of contributing, based on Islamic philosophy and values, to the search for solutions to the major contemporary problems of the world: the challenges of globalization; environmental degradation and poverty; insecurity, terrorism and violence; climate change and the need for sustainable ecological civilizations; inequality and exclusion, etc. All these issues ought to be addressed by Muslims not so much in a defensive way, but also proactively. The chapters of this book have looked at development projects, historical experiences, the creative uses of the internet, the divides and hierarchies of knowledge and power, and many other issues confronting the world today. These are also issues that the social sciences and humanities are addressing. They are the very same issues that are at the heart of decolonial thinking.

The book also highlights important paradigm shifts that raise fundamental questions, including at the level of doctrines: disciple–master relations among the Sufi and the respective roles of the master and that of the disciple;[51] the importance

[51] See de Diego González, chapter 8 in this volume.

of physical contacts between the two in the age of the internet; initiation rites; the role of technology – ICTs – in the evolution of practices and relationships; and the very major issue of an Islamic space of meaning, in a context of multiplicity of spaces ...

Ultimately, one would also like to know where the study of Islam is thriving today and what explains the successes. How is the public sphere being reconfigured and what roles are Islamic scholars, Islamic NGOs, and Islamic civil society playing? What is the nature of the women's movement in Muslim societies?

The political economy of the study of Islam should also be looked at: who is funding the study of Islamic scholarship in Africa? How are funding regimes affecting the study of Islam? Few research funding systems allow research freedom. Therefore, the heavy dependence on foreign funding for research poses serious challenges for the study of Islamic scholarship and for African studies. That was, and still is, a major challenge that CODESRIA is also facing. Sustaining programmes and institutions is a major challenge – institutions and scholarly journals have extremely short life expectancies in Africa. What is the situation with the study of Islamic scholarship?

The modern university, it should be remembered, is at once a very conservative institution, and one where revolutions – cultural, scientific and political – are sometimes born. Islamic universities have undergone profound transformations with the advent of ICTs and social media. How are they responding to phenomena such as the massive open online courses (MOOCs)?

The CODESRIA story, interesting as it is, also raises questions: beyond decolonizing the social sciences and humanities, what do we want African humanities to be like (Binam-Bikoi[52] asked the question), and how do we build them up? We should be interested not only in what must change (what 'must fall') but also what 'must rise'.[53] How successful has CODESRIA been in straddling the various spheres and epistemic communities, and in building an African intellectual community, while still being 'in tune' and recognizable in dominant global scholarly and thinking frameworks to the point of being ranked sub-Saharan Africa's 'top think tank' in the 2016 'Global, GoTo, Think Tanks Report' of the University of Pennsylvania?

These, and many other issues, will, hopefully, be the subjects of more conferences and workshops on Islam and Islamic scholarship in Africa, and of many other great books to come.

[52] Charles Binam-Bikoi, oral communication, UNESCO Africa Regional Conference on Humanities, Bamako, 28 June–1 July 2017.

[53] F.B. Nyamnjoh, *#RhodesMustFall: Nibbling at Resilient Colonialism in South Africa* (Mankon Bamenda: Langaa Research Publishing, 2016).

Glossary

'Ālim	male scholar [Arabic]
'Ālima	female Muslim scholar [Arabic]
'Ārif billāh	an aspirant who has achieved gnosis [Arabic]
'Aqīda	theology [Arabic]
'Aqlī	'rational' (sciences) [Arabic]
Adab	good manners [Arabic]
Aga Khan Development Network	a network of private, non-denominational development agencies founded in 1967 by Shah Karim Al Hussaini, Aga Khan IV, the 49th Hereditary *Imām* of the Shia Ismaili Muslims, which work primarily in the poorest parts of Asia and Africa
Aga Khan Foundation	see Aga Khan Development Network
Aḥbāsh	Ethiopians (sing. Ḥabashī) [Arabic]
'Ajamī	language(s) of Muslim people written in the Arabic script. A tradition that became widely practised after the establishment of Islam and contains a great deal of knowledge [Arabic]
Akbarī	Ibn 'Arabī-derived [Arabic]
Al-Azhar	one of the greatest institutions of higher learning in the Islamic world. Founded in 972 CE and located in Cairo, Egypt, it has attracted students and scholars from all over the Islamic world
Al-Furqan Foundation	a charitable foundation established in the 1990s by Shaykh Ahmad Zaki Yamani for the purpose of preserving the Islamic written heritage
Al-Mukhtaṣar	a leading treatise on Mālikī jurisprudence written by Khalīl Ibn Ishāq al-Jundī
Amīr al-Ḥajj	government official in charge of the supervision of the pilgrimage [Arabic]

Amr bil-ma'rūf wa nahy 'an al-munkar	commanding right and forbidding wrong [Arabic]
Ansaroudine	in this book: International association of disciples of Senegalese Sufi Shaykh Ibrahim Niasse (1900–75)
Arabisant	a student or graduate of an Arabo-Islamic School [French]
Arabophone	a member of the intellectual tradition carried out in the Arabic language. To be contrasted with 'Europhone', although the two are not always mutually exclusive
Baay Fall	sub-group of the Murid Sufi order identified by their colourful ragged clothes, and their hair in dreadlocks [Wolof]
Baqāyā al-Ḥajj	majority of black Africans in Mecca (lit. the remains of the *Ḥajj*) [Arabic]
Bāṭin	inner, hidden, or esoteric dimension of a text or other aspects of Islam [Arabic]
Bid'a	blameworthy innovation [Arabic]
Bilād al-Sudān	Land of the Blacks, refers to sub-Saharan Africa [Arabic]
Borno	currently the name of a state in north-eastern Nigeria, but was an important part of the Kanem-Borno Empire, which was one of the first West African states to embrace Islam
Ceerno	a master, teacher, or guide, especially in a religious context [Pulaar]
Chimbalazi	see Chimiini
Chimiini	language of the town of Brava. A Bantu language related to Swahili with a substantial proportion of Arabic and Somali vocabulary. Also called Chimbalazi
Daara	Qur'ānic schools or large agricultural communities led by a Murid shaykh [Wolof]
Daara tarbiya	*Daara* with the goal of inclusive education of the soul, even for those who were not literate or of a clerical lineage, created by Amadu Bamba (1853–1927) [Wolof]
Dā'ira	Sufi association [Arabic]
***Dā'iya* (sing. *dā'ī*)**	Muslim missionaries [Arabic]

Dars	lesson [Arabic]
Da'wa	Islamic missionary activity [Arabic]
Dhākir	a person who performs the remembrance of God [Arabic]
Dhikr	ritual of remembrance of the name of God, performed daily by the Sufis and other Muslims [Arabic]
Dhul-Ḥijja	the month of the Muslim calendar when the greater pilgrimage to Mecca is performed [Arabic]
Du'ā	prayer of supplication which is separate from the mandatory five daily prayers or *ṣalāt* [Arabic]
Europhone	a term coined by Kwame Anthony Appiah to refer to African intellectuals writing in European languages
Faḍl	merit [Arabic]
Falsafa	philosophy [Arabic]
Fanā	extinction of the aspirant in the divine essence. Also called *waṣl* or *wuṣūl* [Arabic]
Faqīh	jurist [Arabic]
Fatwā	a legal case, opinion, or ruling [Arabic]
Fayḍa	outpouring or deluge referring to what is commonly called 'the divine flood' predicted by Aḥmad al-Tijānī and actualized by Shaykh Ibrahim Niasse (d. 1975), which greatly enhanced spiritual enlightenment and membership in the Tijāniyya Sufi brotherhood. [Arabic]
Fiqh	Islamic jurisprudence regulating acts of worship and social transactions, such as marriage, divorce, child custody, etc. [Arabic]
Franco-arabe (schools)	a hybrid primary or secondary school that blends modern academic training and disciplines with traditional Islamic education and includes language instruction in French and Arabic [French]
Fulani	ethnic group stretching across the Sahel that has produced a large number of prominent Muslim scholars since the twelfth century CE. Other names for this group include Peul and Fulbe or Fellata
Gamou	initially a pre-Islamic harvest festival in Senegambia. At the beginning of the twentieth century, a Sufi festival commemorating the birth of the Prophet Muḥammad [Wolof]

Gao	a city in present-day Mali that was previously an important hub of trans-Saharan trade dating back to the ninth century CE. It also became part of the Mali Empire and served as the capital of the Songhay Empire until its collapse after the Arma invasion in 1591
Ghana	a fabled West African state (c. 350–1236 CE) that covered parts of present-day Mali and Mauritania and derived much of its power from the lucrative gold and salt trade around and within the Sahara. Not to be confused with the contemporary state of Ghana, which is located in a different part of West Africa
Ḥadīth	sayings of the Prophet Muḥammad or accounts and traditions about his life whose study forms one of the most important bases for Islamic sciences and law [Arabic]
Hadiya	offerings to Sufi shaykhs or descendants of the Prophet Muḥammad [Arabic]
Ḥaḍra	spiritual presence of the Prophet or a Sufi master or collective meeting for reciting Sufi litanies [Arabic]
***Ḥāfiẓ* (m)/*Ḥāfiẓa* (f)**	a person who has memorized the Qur'ān. The term literally means 'guardian' in English [Arabic]
Ḥajj	greater pilgrimage to Mecca [Arabic]
Ḥāj	title given to a person who performed the Ḥajj [Arabic]
Halāk	eternal damnation [Arabic]
Ḥaqīqa	a truth or fact, especially divine reality [Arabic]
Ḥaqīqa muḥammadiyya	Muḥammadan reality [Arabic]
Ḥaram	sanctuary [Arabic]
Ḥarām	forbidden in Islam [Arabic]
Hassaniyaphone	speakers of the Arabic dialect of Hassāniyya in the Western Sahara
Hausa	a very large ethnic group found across many contemporary West and Central African countries such as Nigeria, Cameroon, Niger, and Chad
Ḥifẓ	memorization of the Qur'ān and a central aspect of Islamic education [Arabic]
Ḥijāb	veil [Arabic]

Hijra flight or emigration usually referring to the Prophet Muḥammad's flight from Mecca to Medina, or later migrations by other Muslims based on the original *hijra*. It is also used as the starting point for dating in the Islamic calendar, corresponding to 622 CE [Arabic]

Ibn Battuta the famous Moroccan traveller who visited numerous places in the world, including the ancient Mali Empire in 1353 CE, and wrote about his travels and experiences in his book called *al-Riḥla* or 'The Journey' (1304–69 CE)

Ibn Ḥawqal Arab geographer who wrote the first comprehensive account of the Saharan trade routes in his work *Sūrat al-Arḍ* ('Picture of the World', c. 988 CE)

Ijāza a licence or certificate that allows a person to teach a text, transmit knowledge, or instruct others in certain ritual practices [Arabic]

Ijtihād independent juridical reasoning or the process of deriving legal rulings and opinions from the Qur'ān and the *Sunna* [Arabic]

'Ilm knowledge [Arabic]

'Ilm al-Ḥadīth the science of *ḥadīths* or traditional accounts of the life and sayings of the Prophet Muḥammad [Arabic]

Īmān faith [Arabic]

Islamiyya School a hybrid primary or secondary school that blends modern academic training and disciplines with traditional Islamic education and often includes language instruction in English and Arabic

Jakhanke also called the Wangara in Senegambia: they are one of the first clerical groups in West Africa that spread Islam in the region. Involved in trade, subsistence agriculture, and clericalism, they spread and assimilated into many of the major societies and groups of West Africa, bringing the practice of Islam with them

Jihādi Islam the philosophy of radical Muslim groups who perform acts of violence, some of which target civilian populations

Kaaba	a building at the centre of Islam's most important mosque, the Great Mosque in the city of Mecca, Saudi Arabia. It is the most sacred site in Islam (also spelled Ka'ba) [Arabic]
Ka'ba	see Kaaba [Arabic]
Kalām	dogmatic philosophy [Arabic]
Kanem-Borno	a medieval empire in what is called the Central Bilād al-Sūdān and which comprised territory in present-day Nigeria, Niger, Chad, and Libya. Most likely originating in the seventh century CE, its Sayfawa dynasty embraced Islam in the eleventh century, and the empire lasted until the era of colonization at the end of the nineteenth century
Kano	one of the most populous cities in Northern Nigeria, and historically a very important town in Saharan trade and Islamic scholarship. The Kano Chronicle contains a great deal of information about the spread of Islam into this city and Hausaland in Northern Nigeria in general
Khalif général	a title created by the French for the Sufi leaders whom they deemed most prominent [French]
Khalīfa	a successor who inherits spiritual and sometimes political authority from the founder of a Sufi order but also from the Prophet Muḥammad himself (sometimes called 'caliph' in English) [Arabic]
Khalwa	ritual seclusion [Arabic]
Khidma	performing unpaid work for, or giving one's wealth to, a shaykh or the community; a pillar of Sufi doctrine [Arabic]
Khilāfa	political authority [Arabic]
Kufr	unbelief [Arabic]
Kunta	a clan of Muslim scholars from the larger Zawaya group, they were the most influential group of clerics in the Bilād al-Sūdān in the eighteenth and nineteenth centuries [Arabic]
Lawḥ	wooden writing board used in Qur'ānic schools [Arabic]

Laylat al-qadar	the Night of Destiny; one night in the month of Ramadan when the reward for acts of worship is higher than a lifetime of worship [Arabic]
Leylat al-isrā wal mi'rāj	nocturnal ascension of the Prophet Muḥammad to God [Arabic]
Madḥ	devotional poetry usually about the Prophet Muḥammad [Arabic]
Madhhab*, pl. *Madhāhib	a school of Islamic jurisprudence. There are four recognized *Sunna madhhabs* (Mālikī, Ḥanafī, Ḥanbalī, and Shāfi'ī), two Shi'ī *madhhabs* (Ja'farī and Zaidī), as well as the Ibāḍī and Ẓahirī *madhhabs* [Arabic]
Madrasa, pl. *madāris*	literally a 'school', which could refer to lower-level educational institutions or even to higher-level colleges such as Qayrawān in Tunisia [Arabic]
Maendeleo	development/progress [Swahili]
Magal	Murid festival commemorating the return from exile of Amadu Bamba, the founder of the Murid order [Wolof]
Maḥabba	Love, especially idealized love developed by the disciple for the Prophet Muḥammad or a master among Sufis [Arabic]
Maḥḍara	a traditional institution for transmitting Islamic knowledge in the Western Sahara [Arabic]
Mahdi	eschatological figure in Islamic millenarianism believed to appear at the end of time [Arabic]
Maḥmal	a decorated palanquin, perched on a camel and serving in the past to transport people, especially to Mecca [Arabic]
Malam	a master, teacher, or guide especially in a religious context [Hausa]
Mālikī madhhab	one of the four Islamic Sunni schools of law that regulate acts of worship and social transactions. It was founded by *Imām* Mālik b. Anas (711–795) [Arabic]
Mansa Musa	the legendarily wealthy king of the Mali Empire who went on *Ḥajj* in 1324 CE with an enormous entourage and brought back books, scholars, and architects which greatly strengthened the Islamic intellectual tradition in Mali and the region in general (1280–1337 CE)

Marabout	Sufi shaykh or Muslim cleric [French]
Ma'rifa	gnosis or mystical knowledge of God [Arabic]
Mbakke Bawol	village in Central Senegal, where Amadu Bamba (1853–1927), the founder of the Murīdiyya Sufi order, was born
Mbakke Kajoor	village in Central Senegal and historical site for the Murīdiyya Sufi order founded by Amadu Bamba (1853–1927)
Médersa	French hybrid schools established in Algeria, Mali and Mauritania during French colonial rule that combine Islamic and Western forms of modern education and often include language instruction in English French and Arabic
Medina Baye	the city founded by Shaykh Ibrahim Niasse (1900–75) in Senegal and the religious centre of the Niasse branch of the Tijāniyya brotherhood (Fayḍa) (also called Medina Kaolack)
Modou modou	non-Western-educated Senegalese of rural origin, often with some experience in international migration [Wolof]
Mufti	Islamic jurisconsult [Arabic]
Muḥammadan Reality	*Al-Ḥaqīqa al-Muḥammadiyya* in Arabic and an important concept in Sufism, particularly in the Akbarian tradition of Ibn 'Arabī. It refers to the nature and existence of the Prophet Muḥammad before the creation of any other being through which all things were brought into being [Arabic]
Mujtahid	an individual who is qualified to exercise *ijtihād* in the evaluation of Islamic law. *Mujtahids* must have an extensive knowledge of Arabic, the Qur'ān, the *Sunna*, and legal theory [Arabic]
Muqaddam	a deputy or intermediary authority figure who is authorized to initiate others into the secrets and practices of a Sufi Brotherhood [Arabic]
Murabbī	spiritual master [Arabic]
Murīd	a spiritual disciple, particularly in a Sufi brotherhood. More specifically in this book refers to members of the Murīdiyya, a Sufi brotherhood founded by Shaykh Amadou Bamba [Arabic]

Murīdiyya	Sufi order founded by Senegalese Sufi shaykh Amadu Bamba (d. 1927)
Murshid	guide or teacher (Sufi) [Arabic]
Muwallidūn	descendants of black slaves in Saudi Arabia [Arabic]
Naḥw	grammar [Arabic]
Ndigal	a religious authority's directive supposed to have priority over even state laws and policies [Wolof]
Pulaarophone	speakers of Pulaar language [French]
Qāḍī	a judge who interprets and implements Islamic law [Arabic]
Qādiriyya	one of the earliest and most prominent Sufi brotherhoods found in West and North Africa named after Shaykh 'Abd al-Qādir Jīlānī (d. 1166) in Baghdad. Prominent members of this brotherhood are 'Abd al-Karīm al-Maghīlī, Sidi Mukhtār al-Kuntī, and 'Uthmān Dan Fodio
Qarawiyyīn	based in the city of Fez in Morocco, it is the oldest existing and continually operating higher educational institution in the world
Qaṣā'id*, sing. *qaṣīda	poem [Arabic]
Qawā'id	legal maxims [Arabic]
Qayrawan	an ancient city in modern-day Tunisia and the name of the oldest college in the world, founded in 859 CE. The scholars responsible for establishing the *Mālikī madhhab* studied here
Ramadan	fasting month for Muslims
Riḥla	travel in the search for knowledge [Arabic]
Riwāq*, pl. *Arwiqa	hostels at important mosques and institutions of higher learning. Some were established at al-Azhar in Cairo for students coming from the central Bilād al-Sūdān dating as far back as 1258 and still exist today [Arabic]
Ṣafā and Marwa	two small hills now located in the Great Mosque of Mecca. Muslims perform a hurried walk back and forth between them seven times, during the ritual pilgrimages of *Ḥajj* and *ʿUmra*
Salaf	the venerable forefathers [Arabic]

Salafī	a person who follows the ideology of Salafism [Arabic]
Salafism	a conservative reform movement in Islam which emphasizes imitation of the Prophet Muḥammad and his earliest followers, the Salaf. It is often divided into three categories or factions: quietists who are uninterested in modern politics, activists who are intensely concerned with politics, and a smaller group of jihadists involved in political violence
Ṣalāt al-fātiḥ	a prayer on the Prophet Muḥammad, recited especially by Tijānis [Arabic]
Sanad	Support or the chain of transmitters of *ijāza* who initiate others into a Sufi order and its practices [Arabic]
Sankoré Mosque	an important Islamic institution of higher learning in Timbuktu founded in the fourteenth century that is used as the paradigm for knowledge production and transmission in this book. At its height, it was one of the most prominent intellectual centres in the entire Muslim world
Sayfawa	dynasty that ruled Kanem Borno from the eleventh to the nineteenth century
Serin	a master, teacher, or guide especially in a religious context [Wolof]
Shanāqiṭa	natives of Shinqīṭ. Refers more broadly to Mauritanians
Shaqā	damnation [Arabic]
Sharī'a	Islamic law derived from the Qur'ān and *Sunna* [Arabic]
Sharīf	a descendant of the Prophet Muḥammad who is often afforded a great deal of respect as a result [Arabic]
Shaykh	a spiritual master or guide, specifically in the context of Sufism [Arabic]
Shaykh murabbī	see *murabbī* [Arabic]
Shaykh wāṣil	one who can help link wayfarers to God through a verified mystical chain (also called *shaykh murabbī*) [Arabic]
Shinqīṭ	an important intellectual and commercial hub found in present-day Central Mauritania

Shirk	association of Allah's power and nature with something else. Sometimes also used to refer to polytheism or idolatry [Arabic]
Shiʿr	poetry [Arabic]
Sikkar	a Sufi tradition of singing *dhikr*, the remembrance of God's names [Wolof]
Silsila*, pl. *salāsil	the chain of transmitters of *ijāza* that initiates others into a Sufi order and its practices [Arabic]
Sīra	biography of the Prophet Muḥammad [Arabic]
Sirr*, pl. *asrār	secret knowledge believed to be possessed by a category of religious cleric and conferring extraordinary powers [Arabic]
Sokoto	a major city in north-western Nigeria that was the capital of the Sokoto Caliphate established by ʿUthmān Dan Fodio and still an important religious centre today
Songhay	the last of the prominent medieval West African empires. Ruled first by the Sonni dynasty from the capital Gao, later replaced by the Askiya dynasty until the Moroccan invasion in 1591 CE which effectively ended the empire
Soninke	an ethnic group that founded and led the Empire of Ghana as well as the kingdom of Takrūr. They later scattered all over the Bilād al-Sudān, and became an important sub-group that helped to spread Islam in the region
Soninkophone	speakers of the Soninke language
Sṯeenẕi	Sufi devotional poems in Chimiini, vernacular language of Brava
Sūdānī	adjective referring to the land of the black people or to black people themselves. Not to be confused with present-day Sudan, whose name also comes from the Arabic word for 'black' [Arabic]

Sufism	a term referring to the esoteric, mystical, and inner aspects of Islam through which practitioners strive to achieve union with God. Organized into various brotherhoods or *ṭarīqas*, Sufi Islam became the normative form of Islam in the Bilād al-Sūdān and is still of paramount importance in the region. Prominent brotherhoods include the Qādiriyya, the Tijāniyya, and the Murīdiyya
Sunna	the transmitted sayings, actions, teachings, and lived examples from the life of the Prophet Muḥammad and his companions that form an important basis for Islamic law and practice [Arabic]
Tafsīr	Qur'ānic exegesis or commentary [Arabic]
Tafsīr al-Jalalayn	literally 'The Exegesis of the Two Jalals', it is a widely known and studied commentary on the Qur'ān written by Jalāl al-Dīn al-Suyūtī and Jalāl al-Dīn al-Maḥallī
Taḥqīq	verification [Arabic]
Tajalliyāt	signs or divine self-disclosures [Arabic]
Tajwīd	art of the psalmody of the Holy Koran [Arabic]
Takfīr	declaring self-identified Muslims as unbelievers [Arabic]
Takkārā	name of West Africans living in the Muslim Holy Lands (also called Takārira, Takārina, or Takarna, sing. Takrūrī)
Takrūr	one of the first Islamized medieval West African states. It controlled a number of important trade routes, and because of its high profile in Egypt and the Hijaz, West African Muslims were often referred to as people of Takrūr
Ṭalāq	unilateral repudiation of a woman by a husband [Arabic]
Talibe	pupil of a Qu'rānic school or disciple of a Sufi shaykh, or follower of a Sufi order [Wolof]
Ta'līm	instruction [Arabic]
Taqlīd	blind imitation [Arabic]
Tarbiya	education; among Sufi communities, usually refers to initiation into the secrets of the Sufi path [Arabic]

Ṭarīqa	a path or way, usually used to refer to a Sufi brotherhood [Arabic]
Tarqiya	spiritual uplift [Arabic]
Taṣawwuf	refers to Sufism, the study of Sufism, or works on the practice and theology of Sufism [Arabic]
Tawba	repentance [Arabic]
Tawḥīd	term referring to the 'oneness' of God that is a fundamental aspect of Islamic philosophy and theology [Arabic]
Ta'wīl	hermeneutics [Arabic]
Tijāniyya	the most popular Sufi brotherhood in West Africa established by Shaykh Aḥmad al-Tijāni who founded the order after receiving the authority to do so from the Prophet Muḥammad in a revelation. It is centred around Fez, Morocco, but Medina Baye in Senegal is also an important centre
Timbuktu	one of the most fabled intellectual and commercial centres in West Africa. It is home to many important scholars such as Ahmad Baba and Sidi Mukhtār al-Kuntī and celebrated institutions such as the Sankoré Mosque, Sidi Yahya Mosque, and the Jingerer Ber Mosque
'ulamā'*, sing. *'ālim	scholars
'Umra	lesser pilgrimage to Mecca that can be performed at any time of the year [Arabic]
'Uzla	isolation for spiritual retreat [Arabic]
Wahhābī	term used by opponents to designate followers of a religious community founded by Muḥammad b. Abd al-Wahhāb and reputed to be very intolerant. Self-designate as *muwaḥḥidūn* or *ahl al-tawḥīd* (believers in the unity of God) [Arabic]
Wahhabism	name given by detractors to the official Islamic doctrine of Saudi Arabia based on the teachings of Muḥammad b. 'Abd al-Wahhāb and reputed for its dogmatism and intolerance
Walata	an important intellectual and commercial town in present-day south-eastern Mauritania
Walī*, pl. *awliyā	pious Muslim, or a Sufi saint among Sufi communities [Arabic]

Waẓīfa	collective ritual prayer performed by members of the Sufi order of the Tijāniyya [Arabic]
Wird	litany of prayers recited daily for spiritual uplift by members of Sufi orders [Arabic]
Wolof	a dominant ethnic group in the Senegambia and also the language spoken by this group. They are one of the ethnic groups most involved in the teaching and spreading of Islam in the area
Wolofal	*'Ajamī* used in Senegal in its Wolof form [Wolof]
Wolofophone	native speaker of Wolof language
Wuld	version of 'son' derived from *walad*; a common part of male names [Hassaniyya Arabic]
Yaqaẓatan lā manāman	vision in a waking state (often vision of the Prophet Muḥammad) [Arabic]
Ẓāhir	the apparent, manifest, or outward 'exoteric' dimension of a text or other aspects of Islam [Arabic]
Zaman al-ṭafra	expression that Saudis use to describe the period which followed the unprecedented increase in oil prices at the beginning of the 1970s and the unprecedented wealth that Saudi Arabia (state and population) acquired
Zamzam	holy water derived from a well located within the Masjid al-Ḥaram in Mecca, Saudi Arabia, 20 m (66 ft) east of the Kaaba, the holiest place. Also spelt *zemzem* [Arabic]
Zawāyā	clerical class that specialized in the production, reproduction, and dissemination of Islamic knowledge and was also largely responsible for the introduction and establishment of Sufism in the western Bilād al-Sūdān
Zāwiya	a Sufi lodge or meeting place [Arabic]
Zemzem	see *Zamzam*
Ziyāra	pious visit to a saint, pilgrimage to a saintly city

Bibliography

ʿAbd al-Raḥmān al-Jantūrī. *Nawāzil*, Badriane Library MS, 166.

Abdulaziz, M.H. *Muyaka: 19th Century Swahili Popular Poetry* (Nairobi: Kenya Literature Bureau, 1994).

Abdulaziz, M.H. 'The impact of Islam on the development of Swahili culture', in Mohamed Bakari; Saad S. Yahya (eds.) *Islam in Kenya Proceedings of the National Seminar on contemporary Islam in Kenya* (Nairobi: Mewa Publications, 1995).

Abdulaziz, M.H. 'The Influence of the Qasida on the Development of Swahili Rhymed and Metred Verse', in S. Sperl; C. Shackle (eds.) *Qasida Poetry in Islamic Asia and Africa: Classical Traditions & Modern Meanings* (Leiden: E.J. Brill, 1996) Vols. 1–2.

Abdullah, Abdul-Samad. 'Arabic Poetry in West Africa: An Assessment of the Panegyric and Elegy Genres in Arabic Poetry of the 19th and 20th Centuries in Senegal and Nigeria', *Journal of Arabic Literature*, 35 3, 2004, 368–90.

Abiodin, Abdul Ganiy Muhammad Raji. 'Shaykh Ibrahim Niass: His Revival of the Tijaniyya Sufi order and response to colonialism', PhD diss., International Islamic University Malaysia, 2016.

Abun-Nasr, Jamil. *The Tijaniyya: A Sufi Order in the Modern World* (London and New York: Oxford University Press, 1965).

Adams, Adrian; Jaabe So. *A Claim to Land by the River: A Household in Senegal 1720–1994* (Oxford: Oxford University Press, 1996).

Adesina, J.O. 'Sociology and Yorùbá Studies: epistemic intervention or doing sociology in the "vernacular"?', *African Sociological Review*, 6, 1, 2002, 91–114.

Adesina, O.O. 'Sociology, Endogeneity and the Challenge of Transformation', in *African Sociological Review*, 10, 2, 2006, 133–50.

Aga Khan Development Network. 'Education (Tanzania)', 2016, http://www.akdn.org/where-we-work/eastern-africa/tanzania/education.

Aga Khan Foundation (AKF). *The Madrasa Pre-School Curriculum* (Kampala: Madrasa Resource Centre, 2009).

Akasoy, A. 'What is Philosophical Sufism?', in P. Adamson (ed.) *In the Age of Averroes* (London: Warburg Institute, 2011) 229–49.

Ake, C. 'The Social Sciences in Africa: Trends, Tasks & Challenges. A Lecture Given on the Tenth Anniversary of CODESRIA' (Dakar: CODESRIA, 1986).

Akiwowo, A. 'Contributions to the Sociology of Knowledge from an African Oral Poetry', *International Sociology*, 1, 4, 1986, 343–58.

Akiwowo, A. 'Indigenous Sociologies: extending the scope of the argument', *International Sociology*, 14, 2, 1999, 115–38.

Al-Arawani, Mahmud Hamu. *Al-kashf 'an al-makhṭūāt al-'arabiyya wa al-maktūbāt bil-ḥarf al-'arabi fi minṭaqat al-sāḥil al-Ifrīqī*, Timbutku, undated and unpublished manuscript.

Al-Ayashi, Aḥmad Sukayrij. *Kashf al-ḥijāb* (Ed. Rāḍī Kanūn, Rabat: Dār al-Amān, 2012).

Al-Balbālī, M.; A. Al-Balbālī. *Al-Ghuniyat al-muqtaṣid al-sā'il fī-mā waqa'a fī Tuwāt min al-qaḍāyā wa-l-masā'il* (Lemtarfa, MS khizāna Lemtarfa collection): f. 635.

Al-Barāwī, Shaykh Abūbakr Nurshe Muḥyīdīn. *Manāqib Shams al-Dīn wa ibn Muḥyīdīn al-Walī al-Kāmil wa Quṭb al-Fāḍil al-Shaykh Qāsim b. Muḥyīdīn al-Barāwī al-Qādirī* (Brava unpublished manuscript, n.d).

Al-Bārikī, Muḥammad al-Māmī al-Bukhārī. *Kitāb al-Shaykh, al-Bādiya wa nuṣūṣ ukhrā* (Rabat: Centre d'études sahariennes, 2014).

Al-Barrāda, 'Alī Harāzim. *Jawāhir al-ma'ānī wa-bulūgh al-amānī fī fayḍ Saydī Abī l-'Abbās al-Tijānī* (Beirut: Dār al-Fikr, 2001).

Al-Barwani, Ali Muhsin. *Conflicts and Harmony in Zanzibar: Memoirs* (Dubai: n.p. 1997).

Al-Jabartī, 'Abd al-Raḥmān. *'Ajā'ib al-āthār fi'l-tarājim wa'l-akhbār,* 4 vols. (Cairo: Bulaq, 1880).

Al-Jabartī, 'Abd al-Raḥmān; Thomas Philipp; Moshe Perlmann (eds. and trans.) *'Abd al-Raḥmān al-Jabartī's History of Egypt* (Stuttgart: Franz Steiner Verlag, 1994).

Al-Jāmī, Muḥammad. *Amān Aḍwā' 'alā ṭarīq ad-da'wa ilā al-islām* Riyadh, al-Ri'āsa al-'āmma li idārāt al-buḥūth al-'ilmiyya wa al-iftā' wa ad-da'wa wa al-irshād 1404/1984.

Al-Kashnāwī al-Ash'arī al-Mālikī, Muḥammad b. Muḥammad al-Ghallānī. *Al -Durr al-manẓūm wa khulāṣat al-sirr al-maktūm fī'l-siḥr wa'l-ṭalāsim wa'l-nujūm* (Cairo: Muṣṭafa al-Bābī al-Ḥalabī, 1381/1961).

Al-Kattāni, Muḥammad b. Ja'far b. Idrīs. *Salwat al-anfās wa muḥādathat al-akyās* (Rabat: Dār al-amān, 2014) I, 180.

Al-Lamāṭī, Aḥmad b. al-Mubārak. *Pure Gold from the Words of Sayyidī 'Abd al-Aziz*, translated by John O'Kane and Bernd Radtke with notes and an outline (Leiden: Brill, 2007).

Al-Nabulusī, *ʿAbd al-Ghānī. al-Ḥadīqa al-nadiyya sharḥ al-Ṭarīqa al-Muḥammadiyya wa l-sayra al-Aḥmadiyya* (Beirut: Dār al-Kutub al-ʿIlmiyya, 2011).

Al-Naḥwī, al-Khalīl. *Bilād Šinqīṭ. al-Manāra wa l-ribāṭ* (Tunis: al-Munaẓama l-ʻArabīya li-l-Tarbiya wa l-Thaqāfa wa l-ʻUlūm, 1987).

Al-Naqar, ʿUmar. *The Pilgrimage Tradition in West Africa: An Historical Study with Special Reference to the Nineteenth Century* (Khartoum: Khartoum University Press, 1972).

Al-Qādirī, Muḥammad b. al-Ṭayyib. *Mawsūʿat aʿlām al-maghrib maʿhu Tadhkirat al-muḥsinīn bi-wifayāt al-aʿyān wa ḥawādith al-sinīn li ʿAbd al-Kabīr al-Fāsī wa al-Aʿlām bi-man ghabar min ahl al-qarn al-ḥādī ʿashar* (ed. Muḥammad Ḥajjī and Aḥmad al-Tawfīq (Rabat: Dār al-Gharb al-Islāmī, 2008), IV: 1593–7).

Al-Qādirī, Muḥammad b. al-Ṭayyib. *Mawsūʿat aʿlām al-maghrib maʿhu Tadhkirat al-muḥsinīn bi-wifayāt al-aʿyān wa ḥawādith al-sinīn li ʿAbd al-Kabīr al-Fāsī wa al-Aʿlām bi-man ghabar min ahl al-qarn al-ḥādī ʿashar* (ed. Muḥammad Ḥajjī and Aḥmad al-Tawfīq (Rabat: Dār al-Gharb al-Islāmī, 2008), X: 3706–7.

Al-Sāʼiḥ Muḥammad, al-ʻArabī b. *Bughyat al-Mustafīd li Sharḥ Munyāt al-Murīd* (Rabat: al-Maʼārif al-Jadida, 2017).

Al-Ṣabbān, Muḥammad Surūr. *Adab al-ḥijāz: ṣafḥatun fikriyya min adab al-nāshiʾa al-ḥijāziyya shiʿran wa nathran* (Jedda: Dār al-Iṣfahānī, 3rd edition, 1383/1963).

Al-Shinqiṭī, Sīdī Aḥmad Al-Amīn. *Al-Wasīṭ fī tarājim ʼudabāʼ Šinqīṭ: kalām ʻalā tilka l-bilād taḥdīdan wa taḥṭīṭan wa ʻādātuhum wa akhlāquhum wa mā taʻlaqa bi-dhālika* (Nouakchott: Muʼassasat Munīr, 1989).

Alawī, Muḥammad b. ʿAbdallāh b. Muḥammad b. al-Ṣaghīr. *Muṭrib al-sāmiʿīn al-nāẓirīn fī manāqib al-Shaykh al-Ḥājj ʿAbdallāh b. al-Sayyid Muḥammad* (Kaolack, Senegal: Maktabat al-Nahḍa, 2004).

Ali, Abdullah Yusuf. *The Meaning of the Glorious Qurʼan* (Lahore: Ashraf, 1967).

Allen, J.W.T. ʻArabic Script for Students of Swahili', *Tanganyika Notes and Records*, Supplement, November 1945, 7–78.

Allen, J.W.T. *Tendi: Six Examples of a Swahili Classical Verse Form with Translations and Notes* (London: Heinemann, 1971).

American Fact Finder. ʻSelected Population Profile in the United States: 2011–2013 American Community Survey 3-Year Estimates', American Community Survey 2013, http://factfinder.census.gov/faces/tableservices/jsf/pages/productview.xhtml?pid=ACS_13_3YR_S0201&prodType=table.

Amin, S. ʻSynthesis and Reflections', interviewed by Amady Aly Dieng, *Development and Change*, 38, 6, 2007, 1149–59.

Amin, S. *Eurocentrism: Modernity, Religion, and Democracy: A Critique of Eurocentrism and Culturalism* (New York: Monthly Review Press, 2009) 2nd edition.

Amin, S. 'Notes on the creation of CODESRIA', paper presented at the celebration of CODESRIA Day at the CODESRIA headquarters in Dakar, 1 February 2016.

Anderson, Paul. 'The Piety of the Gift: Selfhood and Sociality in the Egyptian Mosque Movement', *Anthropological Theory*, 11, 1, 2011, 3–21.

Andezian, S. *Expériences du Divin dans l'Algérie Contemporaine. Adeptes des Saints dans la Région de Tlemcen* (Paris: CNRS, 2001).

Anjum, Tanvir. 'Sufism in History and its Relationship with Power', *Islamic Studies*, 45, 2, 2006, 221–68.

Anjum, Z. *Iqbal: the Life of a Poet, Philosopher, and Politician* (India: Random House, 2015).

Appiah, Kwame Anthony. *In My Father's House: Africa in the Philosophy of Culture* (London: Methuen, 1992).

Arberry, A.J. *Sufism, an Account of the Mystics of Islam* (London: Allen & Unwin, 1950).

Arberry, A.J. *Interpretation of Koran* (New York: Macmillan, 1955).

Asad, Muhammad. *The Message of the Qur'ān: Translated and Explained* (Al-Andalus: Gibraltar, 1980).

Asad, Talal. 'The Idea of an Anthropology of Islam', *Occasional Papers Series* (Washington, DC: Center for Contemporary Arab Studies, Georgetown University, 1986).

Asad, Talal. *Genealogies of Religion: Discipline and Reasons of Power in Christianity and Islam* (Baltimore and London: Johns Hopkins University Press, 1993).

Augis, Erin. 'Aïcha's Sounith Hair Salon: Friendship, Profit, and Resistance in Dakar', *Islamic Africa*, 5, 2, 2014, 199–224.

Austen, Ralph. *TransSaharan Africa in World History* (Oxford: Oxford University Press, 2010).

Aydin, Cemil. *The Idea of the Muslim World: A Global Intellectual History* (Cambridge, MA: Harvard University Press, 2017).

B. Fodiye, 'Uthmān b. Muḥammad. *Fatḥ al-baṣā'ir litaḥqīq waḍ'i 'ulūm al-bawāṭin wa'l-ẓawāhir*, Muhammad Shareef (ed. and trans.) (Maiurno, Sudan: Sankore Institute of Islamic-African Studies International, 1996).

B. Muṣṭafā, 'abd al-Qādir (Dan Tafa). *Rawdat al-Afkaar: The Sweet Meadows of Contemplation*, Muhammad Shareef (ed. and trans.) (Maiurno, Sudan: Sankore Institute of Islamic-African Studies International, 1991).

B. Muṣṭafā, 'abd al-Qādir (Dan Tafa). *Manẓūma Iṣtilāḥāt al-Ṣūfiyya*, Muhammad Shareef (ed.) (Maiurno, Sudan: Sankore Institute of Islamic-African Studies International, 2006).

B. Muṣṭafā, 'abd al-Qādir (Dan Tafa). *al-Kashf wa'l-Bayān limā ashkala min Kitāb al-Insān*, Muhammad Shareef (ed.) (Maiurno, Sudan: Sankore Institute of Islamic-African Studies International, 2010).

B. Muṣṭafā, 'abd al-Qādir (Dan Tafa). *Kashf al-ghitā' wa'l-rayb fī dhikr anwā' mafātiḥ al-ghayb*, Muhammad Shareef (ed.) (Maiurno, Sudan: Sankore Institute of Islamic-African Studies International, 2010).

B. Muṣṭafā, 'abd al-Qādir (Dan Tafa). *Tarjuma ba'ḍ al-'ulamā' al-zamān*, Muhammad Shareef (ed. and trans.) (Maiurno, Sudan: Sankore Institute of Islamic-African Studies International, 2010).

B. Muṣṭafā, 'abd al-Qādir (Dan Tafa). *'Uhūd wa mawāthīq*, Muhammad Shareef (ed. and trans.) (Maiurno, Sudan: Sankore Institute of Islamic-African Studies International, 2016).

B. Muṣṭafā, 'abd al-Qādir (Dan Tafa). *Kashf al-Kunūz wa Ḥall al-Rumūz*, Muhammad Shareef (ed.) (Maiurno, Sudan: Sankore Institute of Islamic-African Studies International, n.d.).

Babou, Cheikh Anta. 'Educating the Murid: Theory and Practices of Education in Amadu Bamba's Thought', *Journal of Religion in Africa*, 33, 3, 2003, 310–27.

Babou, Cheikh Anta. *Fighting the Greater Jihad: Amadou Bamba and the Founding of Muridiyya of Senegal, 1853–1913* (Athens: Ohio University Press, 2007).

Babou, Cheikh Anta. 'The al-Azhar School Network: A Murid Experiment in Islamic Modernism', in Robert Launay (ed.), *Islamic Education in Africa. Writing Boards and Blackboards* (Bloomington: Indiana University Press, 2016) 173–94.

Badawī, Ṣāliḥ Muhammad 'Alī. *Al-Riyāḍ bayna maḍīhī wa ḥāḍirihi* (Lamu: Ṣāliḥ al-Badawī, 1989).

Bakari, M. 'The New 'Ulama in Kenya', in Mohamed Bakari; Saad S. Yahya (eds.), *Islam in Kenya: Proceedings of the National Seminar on Contemporary Islam in Kenya* (Nairobi: Mewa Publications, 1995).

Banafunzi, Bana; A. Vianello. 'Chimi:ini in Arabic Script: Examples from Brava Poetry', in Meikal Mumin; Kees Versteegh (eds.), *The Arabic Script in Africa* (Leiden: Brill, 2014) 293–311.

Bang, Anne K. *Sufis and Scholars of the Sea. Family Networks in East Africa, 1860–1925* (London: RoutledgeCurzon, 2003 and Routledge, 2014).

Bang, Anne K. *Islamic Sufi Networks in the Western Indian Ocean* (Leiden: Brill, 2014).

Bangstad, Sindre. 'Saba Mahmood and Anthropological Feminism After Virtue', *Theory, Culture & Society*, 28, 3, 2011, 28–54.

Bano, Masooda (ed.). *Modern Islamic Authority and Social Change, Vol 1: Evolving Debates in the Muslim-Majority Countries* (Edinburgh: Edinburgh University Press, 2018).

Barnard, Timothy P. 'The Hajj, Islam, and Power among the Bugis in Early Colonial Riau', in Eric Tagliacozzo (ed.), *South East Asia and the Middle East. Islam, Movement and the Longue Durée* (Stanford, CA: Stanford University Press, 2009) 65–82.

Barnes, Adam. 'A Comparative Spirituality of Liberation: The Anti-Poverty Struggles of the Poverty Initiative and the Tijaniyya of Kiota', PhD diss., Union Theological Seminary New York, 2014.

Barth, Heinrich. *Travels and Discoveries in North and Central Africa* (London, 1858) vol. iv.

Bates, Robert H.; V.Y. Mudimbe; Jean F. Obarr (eds.). *Africa and the Disciplines. The Contributions of Research in Africa to the Social Sciences and Humanities* (Chicago: University of Chicago Press, 1993).

Batran, Abdal-Aziz. 'An Introductory Note on the Impact of Sidi al-Mukhtar al-Kunti (1728–1811) on West African Islam in the 18th and 19th Centuries', *Journal of the Historical Society of Nigeria*, 6, 4, 1973, 347–52.

Batran, Abdal-Aziz Abdulla. 'The Qadiriyya-Mukhtariyya Brotherhood in West Africa: The Concept of Tasawwuf in the Writings of Sidi al-Mukhtar al-Kunti (1729–1811)', *Transafrican Journal of History*, 4, 1–2, 1974, 41–70.

Baudrillard, Jean. *Simulacres et Simulation* (Paris: Éditions Galilée, 1981).

Bava, S. 'Migration-Religion Studies in France: Evolving Toward a Religious Anthropology of Movement', *Annual Review of Anthropology*, 40, 1, 2011, 493–507.

Bawa, C. Yamba. *Permanent Pilgrims: The Role of Pilgrimage in the Lives of West African Muslims in Sudan* (Edinburgh: Edinburgh University Press for the International African Institute, London, 1995).

Behrman, Lucy. *Muslim Brotherhoods and Politics in Senegal* (Cambridge, MA: Harvard University Press, 1970).

Beigel, F.; R. Connell; J.B. Ouedraogo, 'Building Knowledge from Fractured Epistemologies', *METHOD(E)S: African Review of Social Science Methodology*, Special Issue on Epistemological Fractures in a Globalized World: Normalizations, Debates and Alternatives in the Social Sciences, 1–2, 2017, 62–78.

Bello, Mohammed. *Infāq al-Maysūr fī Tārīkh Bilād at-Takrūr* Bahija Chadli (ed.) (Rabat: Mohammed V University Publications of the Institute of African Studies, 1996).

Bensaid, Benaouda; Tarek Ladjal. 'The Struggle of Traditional Religious Education in West Africa: The Case of Mahdara in Mauritania', *Journal of Ethnic and Cultural Studies*, 6, 1, 2019, 152–61, 152–3.

Benton, Lauren. *Law and Colonial Cultures: Legal Regimes in World History 1400–1900* (Cambridge: Cambridge University Press, 2002).

Berkey, Jonathan Porter. *The Transmission of Knowledge in Medieval Cairo: A Social History of Islamic Education* (Princeton, NJ: Princeton University Press, 1992).

Berque, Jacques. *Ulémas, fondateurs, insurgés du Maghreb XVIIe siècle* (Paris: Sindbad, 1982).

Berriane, Johara. 'Intégration symbolique à Fès et encrages sur l'ailleurs: les Africains sub-sahariens et leur rapport à la zawiya d'Ahmad al-Tijani', *L'Année du Maghreb*, 11, 2, 2014, 139–53.

Berriane, Johara. *Ahmed al-Tijani de Fez. Un sanctuaire soufi aux connections transnationales* (Paris: L'Harmattan, 2015).

Bianchi, Robert. 'Ḥajj', *The Oxford Encyclopedia of the Islamic World*. Oxford Islamic Studies Bianchi Online, http://www.oxfordislamicstudies.com/article/opr/t236/e0289. Accessed 18 March 2019.

Birks, J.S. *Across the Savannas to Mecca. The Overland Pilgrimage Route from West Africa to Mecca* (London: Frank Cass, 1978).

Bissell, William Cunningham. *Urban Design, Chaos, and Colonial Power in Zanzibar* (Bloomington: Indiana University Press, 2010).

Bivar, A.D.H.; Mervyn Hiskett. 'The Arabic Literature of Nigeria to 1804: a provisional account', *BSOAS*, xxv, 1962, 104–48.

Blanchi, R. *Guests of God. Pilgrimage and Politics in the Islamic World* (New York: Oxford University Press, 2004).

Bledsoe, C.H.; P. Sow. 'Back to Africa: Second chances for the children of West African immigrants', *Journal of Marriage and Family*, 73, 4, 2011, 747–62.

Bobboyi, Hamid. 'Shaykh Abd Allah al-Barnawi and the world of Fes Sufism: some preliminary observations', in Fès Faculté des Lettres et des Sciences Humaines (ed.), *Fès et l'Afrique: relations économiques, culturelles et spirituelles* (Rabat: Institut des Études Africaines, 1995) 115–24.

Bobboyi, Hamid. 'Scholars and scholarship in the relations between the Maghrib and the Central Bilad al-Sudan during the pre-colonial period', in Helen Lauer; Kofi Anyidoho (eds.), *Reclaiming the Human Sciences and Humanities through African Perspectives*, Volume I (Ghana: Sub-Saharan Publishers, 2012).

Bonte, Pierre. *L'émirat de l'Adrar mauritanien: Ḫarîm, compétition et protection dans une société tribale saharienne* (Paris: Karthala, 2008).

Booth, Marilyn. 'Islamic Politics, Street Literature, and John Stuart Mill: Composing Gendered Ideals in 1990s Egypt', *Feminist Studies*, 39, 3, 2013, 596–627.

Boubakeur Hamza (trans.). *Al-Burda. Le Manteau. Poème consacré au Prophète de l'islam* (Montreuil: Imprimerie TIPE, 1980).

Boubrik, Rahal. 'Les fuqahâ' du prince et le prince des fuqahâ': discours politique des hommes de religion au pays maure (Mauritanie, XVIIe – XIXe siècle)', *Afrique et histoire*, 7, 1, 2009, 153–72.

Bousbina, Saïd. 'Les mérites de la Tijāniyya d'après 'Rimah' d'Al-Hajj Umar', *Islam et sociétés au Sud du Sahara*, 3, 1989, 253–60.

Bousbina, Sa'īd. 'Un siècle de savoir islamique En Afrique de L'Ouest, 1820–1920 analyse et commentaire de la littérature de la confrérie Tijaniyya à travers les œuvres d'al-Hajj Umar', PhD diss., in History, Université de Paris, Panthéon Sorbonne, 1996.

Bowen, John. *A New Anthropology of Islam* (New York: Cambridge University Press, 2012).

Boyce-Davies, C. 'Decolonizing the University', paper presented at the UNESCO World Humanities Conference, Liège, August 2017.

Boyce-Davies, C.; M. Gadsby; C. Peterson; H. Williams (eds.). *Decolonizing the Academy: African Diaspora Studies* (Trenton, NJ and Asmara: Africa World Press, 2003).

Boyd, J. *The Caliph's Sister: Nana Asma'u (1793–1865): Teacher, Poet, and Islamic Leader* (London: Frank Cass, 1989).

BRACED. 'Building Resilience and Adaptation to Climate Extremes and Disasters. 2015', Senegal Floods 2015, http://www.braced.org/reality-of-resilience/i/?id=3dc7ca27-bc7d-466f-a6af-4dae3bc12abd. Accessed 14 September 2016.

Brenner, Louis. 'Three Fulbe Scholars in Borno', *The Maghreb Review*, 10, 4–6, 1985, 107–13.

Brenner, Louis. *Controlling Knowledge. Religion, Power and Schooling in a West African Muslim Society* (London: Hurst & Company, 2000).

Brigaglia, Andrea. 'The Radio Kaduna tafsir (1978–1992) and the construction of public images of Muslim scholars in the Nigerian media', *Journal for Islamic Studies*, 27, 1, 2007, 173–210.

Brigaglia, Andrea. 'Learning, Gnosis and Exegesis: Public Tafsīr and Sufi Revival in the City of Kano (Northern Nigeria), 1950–1970', *Die Welt des Islams*, 49, 2009, 334–66.

Brigaglia, Andrea. 'Two Exegetical Works from Twentieth-Century West Africa: Shaykh Abu Bakr Gumi's Radd al-adhhān and Shaykh Ibrahim Niasse's Fī riyāḍ al-tafsīr', *Journal of Qur'anic Studies*, 15, 3, 2013, 253–66.

Brockelmann, Carl. *Geschichte der Arabischen Litteratur*, 2 vols. (Leiden: Brill, 1943–9).

Brown, Daniel W. *Rethinking Tradition in Modern Islamic Thought* (Cambridge: Cambridge University Press, 1999).

Brown, Jonathan. *Hadith: Muhammad's Legacy in the Medieval and Modern World* (Oxford: Oneworld Publications, 2009).

Brubaker, R. 'The "diaspora" diaspora', *Ethnic and Racial Studies*, 28, 1, 2005, 1–19.

Bulkeley, Kelly. *Dreaming in the World's Religions: A Comparative History* (New York: New York University Press, 2008).

Burgel, J.C. 'Qasida as Discourse on Power and its Islamization: Some Reflections', in S. Sperl; C. Shackle (eds.), *Qasida Poetry in Islamic Asia and Africa: Classical Traditions & Modern Meanings* (Leiden: E.J. Brill, 1996) vols. 1–2.

Burton, Richard. *Personal Narrative of a Pilgrimage to Mecca and Medina* (Leipzig: Bernhard Tauchnitz, 1874) 3 vols.

Cabral, A. *Unity and Struggle* (New York: Monthly Review Press, 1979).

Casewit, Yousef. *The Mystics of Al-Andalus. Ibn Barrajan and Islamic Thought in the Twelfth Century* (Cambridge: Cambridge University Press, 2017).

Cerulli, Enrico. 'Note sul movimento musulmano nella Somalia', in *Somalia: Scritti Vari ed Inediti, Vol. I* (Rome: Istituto Poligrafico dello Stato, 1957) 177–210.

Chakrabarty, D. *Provincializing Europe: Postcolonial Thought and Historical Difference* (Princeton, NJ and Oxford: Princeton University Press, 2000).

Chanfi, Ahmed. *AfroMecca in History. African Societies, Anti-Black Racism, and Teaching in al-Haram Mosque in Mecca* (Newcastle upon Tyne: Cambridge Scholars Publishing, 2019).

Chanfi, Ahmed. *West African ʿulamāʾ and Salafism in Mecca and Medina: Jawāb al-Ifrīqī – The Response of the African* (Leiden: Brill, 2015).

Charlier, J.-É. 'Les écoles au Sénégal: de l'enseignement officiel au daara, les modèles et leurs répliques', *Cahiers de la Recherche Sur l'Education et les Savoirs*, 3, 2004, 35–53.

Chatterjee, Partha. *Nationalist Thought and the Colonial World* (London: Zed Books, 1986).

Chaterjee, Partha. 'Colonialism, Nationalism, and Colonialized Women: The Contest in India', *American Ethnologist*, 16, 4, 1989, 622–33.

Chatterjee, P. *Our Modernity* (Rotterdam/Dakar: SEPHIS & CODESRIA, 1997).

Cheddadi, Abdesselam. *Ibn Khaldûn: l'homme et le théoricien de la civilisation* (Paris: Gallimard, 2006).

Chittick, W. *The Sufi Path of Knowledge: Ibn al-ʻArabi's Metaphysics of Imagination* (Albany: SUNY Press, 1989).

Chittick, W. *Self Disclosure of God* (Albany: SUNY Press, 1998).

Chittick, William. *Sufism: A Beginner's Guide* (Oxford: Oneworld Publications, 2000).

Chittick, William. 'Ibn Arabi', *The Stanford Encyclopedia of Philosophy,* Spring 2014, Edward N. Zalta (ed.), http://plato.stanford.edu/archives/spr2014/entries/ibn-arabi.

Choplin, Amselle. *Nouakchott: Au carrefour de la Mauritanie et du monde* (Paris: Khartala, 2009).

Cissé, Mouhamadou Alpha. 'El Hadji Omar Foutiyou Tall, une Grande Figure de la Tijāniyya en Afrique Occidentale au XIXème siècle: Pensée juridico-mystique à travers "Rimah"', PhD diss., Université Cheikh Anta Diop de Dakar, 2011.

Cisse, Mamadou. 'Langue, Etat et société au Sénégal', *Sudlangues*, 5, 2005, 99–133.

Clark, Janine. *Islam, Charity, and Activism: Middle-Class Networks and Social Welfare in Egypt, Jordan, and Yemen* (Bloomington: Indiana University Press, 2004).

Clausen, Ursel. 'Islam und nationale Religionspolitik: das Fallbeispiel Mauretanien', Hamburg, 2005, https://www.liportal.de/fileadmin/user_upload/oeffentlich/Mauretanien/ Islam_und_Religionpolitik Mauretanien.pdf. Accessed 8 February 2017.

Cleaveland, Tim. 'Ahmed Baba and His Islamic Critique of Slavery in the Maghreb', *Journal of North African Studies*, 20, 1, 2015, 42–64.

Cochrane, Laura L. 'Religious motivations for local economic development in Senegal', *Africa Today*, 58, 4, 2012, 2–19.

Cochrane, Laura. 'Land Degradation, Faith-Based Organizations, and Sustainability in Senegal', *CAFE: Culture, Agriculture, Food, and Environment*, 35, 2, 2013, 112–24.

Cochrane, Laura L. 'Addressing Global Economic Inequalities in Local Ways in Senegal's Artisanal Workshops', *Economic Anthropology*, 2, 2015, 250–63.

Cochrane, Laura L. *Everyday Faith in Sufi Senegal* (New York and London: Routledge, 2017).

Coe, C. *The Scattered Family. Parenting, African Migrants, and Global Inequality* (Chicago and London: University of Chicago Press, 2014).

Coe, C. 'Child circulation and West African migrations', in C. Ni Laoire; A. White; T. Skelton (eds.), *Movement, Mobilities, and Journeys* (Singapore: Springer Science+Business, 2017) 389–407.

Coly, Germain. *La Région de Thiès à Travers son Musée* (Thiès: Conseil Régional de Thiès, 1999).

Comaroff, J.; J. Comaroff. *Theory from the South: Or How Euro-America is Evolving Towards Africa* (New York: Routledge, 2012).

Commander, Simon. 'Structural Adjustment Policies and Agricultural Growth in Africa', *Economic and Political Weekly*, 23, 39, 1988, A98–A105.

Constitution du Sénégal de 1963. 'Articles 21–23', http://www.gouv.sn/spip.php?article794. Accessed 15 March 2012.

Copans, Jean. *Les marabouts de l'arachide* (Paris: L'Harmattan, 1988) 2nd edition.

Copans, Jean. 'Mourides des champs, mourides des villes, mourides du téléphone portable et de l'internet. Le renouvellement de l'économie politique d'une confrérie', *Afrique contemporaine*, 14, 2000, 24–33.

Cornell, Vincent. *Realm of the Saint: Power and Authority in Moroccan Sufism* (Austin: University of Texas Press, 1998).

Coulon, Christian. *Le marabout et le prince* (Paris: Pedone, 1981).

Coulon, Christian. 'The Grand Magal in Touba: A Religious Festival of the Mouride Brotherhood of Senegal', *African Affairs*, 98, 391, 1999, 195–210.

Cruise O'Brien, Donal. *The Mourides of Senegal. The Political and Economic Organization of an Islamic Brotherhood* (Oxford: Oxford University Press, 1971).

Cruise O'Brien, Donal. *Saints and Politicians: Essay on the organisation of a Senegalese Peasant Society* (Cambridge: Cambridge University Press, 1975).

Cuneen, C; S. Rowe; S. Tauri; J. Tauri. 'Fracturing the Colonial Paradigm: Indigenous Epistemologies and Methodologies', in Fernanda Beigel; Jean-Bernard Ouedraogo; Raewyn Connell (eds.), special issue on 'Epistemological Fractures in a Globalized World: Normalizations, Debates and Alternatives in the Social Sciences', *METHOD(E)S: African Review of Social Science Methodology*, 2, 1–2, 2017, 62–78.

Currie, P.M. *The Shrine and Cult of Mu'īn al-Dīn Chistī of Ajmer* (Oxford: Oxford University Press, 1989).

Dallal, Ahmad. 'The Origins and Objectives of Islamic Revivalist Thought (1750–1850), *Journal of the American Oriental Society*, 113, 3, 1993, 341–59.

Dallal, Ahmad. *Islam without Europe: Traditions of Reform in Eighteenth-century Islamic Thought. Islamic Civilization & Muslim Networks* (Chapel Hill: University of North Carolina Press, 2018).

Danner, V. *The Book of Wisdom* (New York: Paulist Press, 1978).

Dawley, Lisa. 'Social network knowledge construction: emerging virtual world pedagogy', *On the Horizon*, 17, 2, 2019, 113.

Daye, Ali. 'Grand Mosque Expansion Highlights Growth of Saudi Arabian Tourism', https://blog.realestate.cornell.edu/2018/03/21/grandmosqueexpansion/. Accessed March 2018.

De Diego González, Antonio. 'Identidad y modelos de pensamiento en África', PhD diss., Universidad de Sevilla, 2016.

De Diego González, Antonio. 'El juego geopolítico de Marruecos y Arabia Saudí en África Occidental', *Araucaria Revista Iberoamericana de Filosofía, Política, Humanidades y Relaciones Internacionales*, 21, 41, 2019, 415–38.

De Diego González, Antonio. *Populismo Islámico* (Córdoba: Almuzara, 2020).

De Diego González, Antonio. *Ley y Gnosis. Historia Intelectual de la ṭarīqa Tijāniyya* (Granada: Editorial Universidad de Granada, 2020).

De Moraes, Farias Paulo F. 'Ahmad Baba', *Encyclopaedia of Islam III* (Leiden: E.J. Brill, 2007).

Decker, Corrie. 'Investing in Ideas: Girls' Education in Colonial Zanzibar', PhD diss., University of California Berkeley, 2007.

Deeb, Lara. *An Enchanted Modern: Gender and Public Piety in Shi'i Lebanon* (Princeton, NJ: Princeton University Press, 2006).

Dell, Jeremy. 'Unbraiding the Qur'an: Wolofal and the Tafsīr Tradition of Senegambia', *Islamic Africa*, 9, 2018, 55–76.

Dia, H. 'Pratiques de scolarisation de jeunes Français au Sénégal. La construction de l'excellence par le pays des 'ancêtres', *Cahiers d'études Africaines*, 1, 221, 2016, 199–218.

Diagne, Mamousse. *Critique de la raison orale* (Paris: Karthala, 2005).

Diagne, Pathé. 'Table ronde sur 'l'éducation en Afrique', *Présence Africaine*, Nouvelle série 64, 4e trimestre 1967, 59–96.

Diagne, S.B. *The Ink of The Scholars: Reflections on Philosophy in Africa* (Dakar: CODESRIA, 2016).

Dilger, Hansjörg; Dorothea Schulz. 'Politics of Religious Schooling: Christian and Muslim Engagement with Education in Africa: Introduction', *Journal of Religion in Africa*, 43, 4, 2013, 365–78.

Diop, C.A. *The African Origin of Civilization: Myth or Reality* (New York: Lawrence Hill & Co., 1974).

Diop, Cheikh Anta. *Nations nègres et culture* (Paris: Présence Africaine, 1979).

Dodge, Bayard. *Al-Azhar. A Millennium of Muslim Learning* (Washington, DC: The Muslim Institute, 1961).

Dumont, Fernand. *L'Anti-Sultan ou Al-Hajj Umar Tal du Fouta, Combattant de la foi (1794–1864)* (Dakar and Abidjan: Nouvelles éditions africaines, 1974).

Duncan, Christopher. 'Catholicism, Poverty and the Pursuit of Happiness', *Journal of Poverty*, 12, 1, 2008, 49–76.

Duruflé, Gilles. 'Bilan de la Nouvelle Politique Agricole au Sénégal', *Review of African Political Economy*, 22, 63, 1995, 73–84.

Dussel, E. *The Invention of the Americas: Eclipse of 'the Other' and the Myth of Modernity* (New York: Continuum, 1995).

Eickelman, Dale F.; James Piscatori. *Muslim Travellers: Pilgrimage, Migration, and the Religious Imagination* (Berkeley: University of California Press, 1990).

El Adnani Jilali. 'Entre visite et pèlerinage: le cas des pèlerins oust-africains à la zâwiya Tijâniyya de Fès', *Al-Maghrib al-Ifrîqî*, 6, 2005, 7–37.

El Hamel, Chouki. *La vie intellectuelle islamique dans le Sahel ouest-africain, XVIe– XIXe siècles: une étude sociale de l'enseignement islamique en Mauritanie et au nord du Mali, XVIe–XIXe siècles* (trans. 'Fatḥ al-šakūr' by al-Bartīlī al-Walātī (mort en 1805) (Paris: L'Harmattan, 2002).

El-Kenz, Ali. *Algeria: The Challenge of Modernity* (Dakar: CODESRIA, 1991).
El-Mansour, Mohamed. *Morocco in the Reign of Mawlay Sulayman* (London: Middle East and North African Studies Press, 1990).
El-Rouayheb, Khaled. *Islamic Intellectual History in the Seventeenth Century: Scholarly Currents in the Ottoman Empire and the Maghreb* (New York: Cambridge University Press, 2015).
El-Sharif, Farah. 'The Rhetoric of Twentieth-century Damascene Anti-Salafism', *Contemporary Levant*, 5, 2, 2020, 113–25.
Elias, Jamal J. 'Sufi Poetry and the Indus Valley: Khwāja Ghulām Farīd', in John Renard (ed.), *Tales of God's Friends: Islamic Hagiography in Translation* (Berkeley: University of California Press, 2009) 249–60.
Elias, Norbert. *The Established and the Outsiders* (London: Sage Publications, 1965).
Ensel, Remco. *Saint and Servants in Southern Morocco* (Leiden: Brill, 1999).
Ernst, Carl. 'Between Orientalism and Fundamentalism: Problematizing the Teaching of Sufism', in Brannon Wheeler (ed.), *Teaching Islam* (Oxford: Oxford University Press, 2002) 108–23.
Ernst, Carl. 'Situating Sufism and Yoga', *Journal of the Royal Asiatic Society*, 15, 1, 2005, 15–43.
Escobar, A. *Encountering Development: The Making and Unmaking of the Third World* (Oxford: Princeton University Press, 1995).
Esposito, John (ed.). *Oxford Encyclopedia of Islam* (Oxford: Oxford University Press, 2009).
Esposito, John; Yvonne Yazbeck Haddad. *Islam, Gender, and Social Change* (Oxford: Oxford University Press, 1998).
Evans, Judith; Kathy Bartlett. *The Madrasa Early Childhood Programme: 25 Years of Experience* (Geneva: Aga Khan Development Network, 2008).
Fadel, Mohammed. 'The Social Logic of *Taqlīd* and the Rise of the *Mukhtaṣar*', *Islamic Law and Society*, 3, 2, 1996, 193–233.
Fair, Laura. *Pastimes and Politics: Culture, Community, and Identity in Post-Abolition Urban Zanzibar, 1890–1945* (Athens, OH and Oxford: Ohio University Press and James Currey, 2001).
Fall, P.D. 'Des francenabé aux modou-modou: géographie de la migration internationale des sénégalais', PhD diss., Université Cheikh Anta Diop Dakar, 2013.
Finnegan, Ruth. *Oral literature in Africa* (Cambridge: Open Book Publishers, 2012).
Finnegan, Ruth. *Literacy and Orality: Studies in the Technologies of Communication* (London: Callender Press, 2014).
Fodiye, B. *'Uthman b. Muḥammad, Ḥiṣn al-afhām min juyūsh al-awhām*, ed. and trans. F.R. Al-Ṣiddīqī (Kano: Quality Press, 1989).

Foley, Ellen E. *Your Pocket is What Cures You: The Politics of Health in Senegal* (New Brunswick: Rutgers University Press, 2010).

Fortier, C. 'Le corps comme mémoire: du giron maternel à la férule du maître coranique', *Journal Des Africanistes*, 68, 1–2, 1998, 197–224.

Fortier, Corinne. 'Une pédagogie coranique: Modes de transmission des savoirs islamiques (Mauritanie)', *Cahiers d'Etudes Africaines*, 169–70, 1–2, 2003, 235–60.

Foucault, Michel. 'Technologies of the self' (Les techniques de soi; Université du Vermont, octobre 1982; trans. F. Durant-Bogaert), in P.H. Hutton; H. Gutman; L.H. Martin (eds.), *Technologies of the Self. A Seminar with Michel Foucault* (Amherst: The University of Massachusetts Press, 1988).

Frauen, Wulf. *Backfire on the State? Eine Analyse zu den langfristigen Konsequenzen der Reform der Al-Azhar (1961, 1994)* (Munich: AVM, 2013).

Frede, Britta. *Die Erneuerung der Tiğānīya in Mauretanien. Popularisierung religiöser Ideen in der Kolonialzeit*, ZMO Studien, 31 (Berlin: Schwarz-Verlag, 2014).

Frede, Britta. 'Following in the Steps of ʿĀʾisha: Hassaniyya Speaking Tijānī Women as Spiritual Guides (muqaddamāt) and Teaching Islamic Scholars (limrābuṭāt) in Mauritania', *Islamic Africa*, 5, 2, 2014, 225–73.

Frede, Britta. 'Arabic Manuscripts of the Western Sahara: Trying to Frame an African Literary Tradition', *Journal of Islamic Manuscripts*, 8, 1, 2017, 57–84.

Fuglesang, Minou. 'No Longer Ghosts: Women's Notions of "Development" and "Modernity" in Lamu Town, Kenya', in G. Dahl; A. Rabo (eds.), *Kam-Ap or Take-off: Local Notions of Development* (Stockholm: Stockholm Studies in Social Anthropology, 1992) 123–56.

Gaborieau, Marc; Malika Zeghal (eds.). 'Autoritiés religieuses en Islam', *Archives des sciences sociale des religions*, 49, 125, 2004.

Gatsheni-Ndlovu, S. *Coloniality of Power in Post-Colonial Africa: Myths of Decolonization* (Dakar: CODESRIA, 2013).

Gaudefroy-Demombynes, M. *Le pèlerinage à la Mecque* (Paris: Geuthner, 1923).

Geertz, Clifford. *Local Knowledge: Further Essays in Interpretive Anthropology* (New York: Basic Books, 1983).

Gellner, Ernest. *Saints of the Atlas* (Chicago: Chicago University Press, 1969).

Gellner, Ernest. *Muslim Society* (Cambridge: Cambridge University Press, 1981).

Ghazal, Amal N. *Islamic Reform and Arab Nationalism: Expanding the Crescent from the Mediterranean to the Indian Ocean (1880s–1930s)* (London and New York: Routledge, 2010).

Gibb, H.A.R. *Modern Trends in Islam* (Chicago: University of Chicago Press, 1947).

Gilsenan, Michael. *Saint and Sufi in Modern Egypt: An Essay in the Sociology of Religion* (Oxford: Clarendon Press, 1973).

Global Partnership for Education. 'Senegal', http://www.globalpartnership.org/country/senegal. Accessed 6 October 2016.

Glover, John. *Sufism and Jihad in Modern Senegal: The Murid Order* (Rochester, NY: University of Rochester Press, 2007).

Gori, Alessandro. *Studi sulla letteratura agiografica islamica somala in lingua araba* (Florence: Dipartimento di Linguistica, Universita' di Firenze, 2003).

Grillo, R.; B. Riccio. 'Translocal development: Italy–Senegal', *Population, Space and Place*, 10, 2004, 99–111.

Grysole, A.; C. Beauchemin. 'Les allers-retours des enfants de l'immigration sub-saharienne: Les filles ou les garçons d'abord?, *Migrations Société*, 3, 4, 2013, 127–42.

Grysole, A. 'Private School Investments and Inequalities: Negotiating the Future in Transnational Dakar', *Africa*, 88, 4, 2018.

Gubara, Dahlia El-Tayeb. 'Al-Azhar in the Bibliographic Imagination', *Journal of Arabic Studies*, 2012.

Gubara, Dahlia El-Tayeb. 'Al-Azhar and the Orders of Knowledge', PhD diss., Department of History, Columbia University, 2014.

Gubara, Dahlia E.M. 'Revisiting Race and Slavery through 'Abd al-Rahman al-Jabarti's *'Aja'ib al-athar'*, *Comparative Studies of South Asia, Africa and the Middle East*, 38, 2, 2018, 230–45.

Guèye, Cheikh. *Touba: La capitale des mourides* (Paris: Karthala, 2002).

Gwarzo, H.I. 'The Theory of Chronograms as Expounded by the 18th Century Katsina Astronomer-Mathematician Muḥammad b. Muḥammad', *Research Bulletin of the Centre of Arabic Documentation*, Institute of African Studies, University of Ibadan, 3, 2, 1967, 116–23.

Haddad, Y.Y.; F. Senzai; J.I. Smith. *Educating the Muslims of America* (Oxford: Oxford University Press, 2009).

Hall, Bruce S. *A History of Race in Muslim West Africa, 1600–1960* (Cambridge: Cambridge University Press, 2011).

Hall, Bruce; Charles Stewart. 'The Historic "Core Curriculum" and the Book Market in Islamic West Africa', in Graziano Krätli; Ghislaine Lydon (eds.), *The Trans-Saharan Book Trade* (Leiden and Boston: Brill, 2011) 109–74.

Hallaq, Wael. *Authority, Continuity and Change in Islamic Law* (Cambridge: Cambridge University Press, 2004).

Hallaq, Wael B. 'What is Shari'a?', *Yearbook of Islamic and Middle Eastern Law*, 2005–2006, 12 (Leiden: Brill Academic Publishers, 2007) 151–80.

Hallaq, Wael B. *The Impossible State: Islam, Politics, and Modernity's Moral Predicament* (New York: Columbia University Press, 2014).

Hanretta, Sean. *Islam and Social Change in Africa* (New York: Cambridge University Press, 2009).

Harries, Lyndon. *Swahili Poetry* (Oxford: Clarendon Press, 1962).

Harrison, Christopher. *France and Islam in West Africa, 1860–1960* (Cambridge: Cambridge University Press, 1988).

Heer, Nicholas. 'Al-Abhari and al-Maybudi on God's Existence: A Translation of a Part of al-Maybudi's Commentary on al-Abhari's Hidayat al-Hikmah', 2009, http://faculty.washington.edu/heer/abhari-sep.pdf.

Hegel, Georg Wilhelm Friedrich. *The Philosophy of History* (New York: Willey Book Co., 1900) 99.

Hegel, Georg Wilhelm Friedrich. *Lectures on the Philosophy of World History: Volume I: Manuscripts of the Introduction and the Lectures of 1822–1823*, P. Hogdson (ed. & trans.) (Oxford: Oxford University Press, 2011).

Hill, Joseph. 'Divine Knowledge and Islamic Authority: Religious Specialization among Disciples of Baay Ñas', PhD diss. in Anthropology, Yale University, 2007.

Hill, Joseph. '"Baay is the spiritual leader of the rappers": performing Islamic reasoning in Senegalese Sufi hip-hop', *Contemporary Islam*, 10, 2, 2016, 267–87.

Hinawy, M.A. *Al-Akida and Fort Jesus* (Mombasa: Muscat Bait Alghasham for Publishing & Translating, 2015).

Hirchskind, Charles. *The Ethical Soundscape: Cassette Sermons and Islamic Counterpublics* (New York: Columbia University Press, 2006).

Hirth, Michael. *Traditionelle Bildung und Erziehung in Mauretanien. Zum entwicklungspolitischen Potential der maurischen mahadra* (Frankfurt: Peter Lang, 1991).

Hiskett, Mervyn. 'Materials related to the state of learning among the Fulani before their jihad', *Bulletin of the School of Oriental and African Studies*, 19, 3, 1957, 550–78.

Hobsbawm, Eric; Terence Ranger (eds). *The Invention of Tradition* (New York: Cambridge University Press, 1983).

Hodgson, Marshall G.S. *Rethinking World History: Essays on Europe, Islam, and World History* (New York: Cambridge University Press, 1993).

Hoechner, H. 'Mobility as a contradictory resource: peripatetic Qur'anic students in Kano, Nigeria', *Children's Geographies*, 13, 1, 2015, 59–72.

Hoechner, H. *Quranic Schools in Northern Nigeria: Everyday Experiences of Youth, Faith, and Poverty* (Cambridge: Cambridge University Press, 2018).

Hoffman, Valerie J. 'Annihilation in the Messenger of God: The Development of a Sufi Practice', *International Journal of Middle Eastern Studies*, 31, 3, 1999, 351–69.

Hountondji, P. (ed.). *Endogenous Knowledge: Research Trails* (Dakar: CODESRIA, 1997).

Human Rights Watch. 'Senegal: New Steps to Protect Talibés, Street Children', 28 July, https://www.hrw.org/news/2016/07/28/senegal-new-steps-protect-talibes-street-children. Accessed 24 August 2016.

Hunwick, John. 'Ahmad Baba and the Moroccan invasion of the Sudan (1591)', *Journal of the Historical Society of Nigeria*, 2, 1, 1962, 311–28.

Hunwick, John. 'A New Source for the study of Ahmad Baba al-Timbukti (1556–1627)', *Bulletin of the School of Oriental and African Studies*, 27, 1964, 568–93.

Hunwick, John. 'Ṣāliḥ al-Fullānī: The Career and Teachings of a West African ʿĀlim in Medina', in A.H. Green (ed.), *In Quest of an Islamic Humanism* (Cairo: AUC Press, 1984) 139–54.

Hunwick, John. 'An Introduction to the Tijani Path: being an annotated translation of the chapter headings of the *Kitab al-Rimah* of Al-Hajj Umar', *Islam et Sociétés au Sud du Sahara*, 6, 1992, 17–32.

Hunwick, John. *Timbuktu and the Songhay Empire: al-Saʿadī's Taʾrīkh al-sūdān down to 1613 and other contemporary documents* (Leiden: Brill, 2003).

Hunwick, John O. 'West Africa and the Arabic Language', *Sudanic Africa*, 15, 2004, 133–44.

Hunwick, John; R.S. O'Fahey (eds.). *Arabic Literature of Africa: Volume II, The Writings of Central Sudanic Africa* (Leiden: E.J. Brill, 1995).

Hunwick, John et al. *Arabic literature of Africa Vol. 4: Writings of Western Sudanic Africa* (Leiden: Brill Academic Publishers, 2003).

Hunwick, John; Alida Boyle. *Hidden Treasures of Timbuktu. Rediscovering Africa's Literary Cultures* (London: Thames, 2008).

Hynes, William G. *The Economics of Empire: Britain, Africa and the New Imperialism, 1870–95* (London: Longman Group Limited, 1979).

Ibn al-Shaykh ʿAbdullāh, Muḥammad. *Mādhā ʿan al-Shaykh Ibrāhīm* (Lemden, Mauritania: Muḥammad ibn al-Shaykh ʿAbdullāh, 2014).

Ibn al-Shaykh ʿAbdullāh, Muḥammad. *Rijāl wa Adwār fī Ẓill Ṣāḥib al-Fayḍah al-Tijānīyah: Al-Milaff al-Gharb Ifrīqī* (Lemden, Mauritania: Muḥammad ibn al-Shaykh ʿAbdullāh, 2014).

Ibn al-Shaykh ʿAbdullāh, Muḥammad. *Rijāl wa Adwār fī Ẓill Ṣāḥib al-Fayḍah al-Tijānīyah: Al-Milaff al-Mūrītānī* (Lemden, Mauritania: Muḥammad ibn al-Shaykh ʿAbdullāh, 2014).

Ibn al-Shaykh ʿAbdullāh, Muḥammad. *Rijāl wa adwār fī ẓill Ṣāḥib al-Fayḍah al-Tijānīyah: Al-Milaff al-Sanighālī* (Lemden, Mauritania: Muḥammad ibn al-Shaykh ʿAbdullāh, 2014).

Ibn al-Shaykh ʿAbdullāh, Muḥammad. *Āfāq al-Shiʿr fī al-Shaykh Ibrāhīm Niyās* (Lemden, Mauritania: Muḥammad ibn al-Shaykh ʿAbdullāh, 2018, vols. 1–6).

Ibn Baṭṭūṭah, M.A. *Tuḥfat al-nadhar fī Gharāʾib al-amsār wa al-asfār* (Cairo: Maṭbaʿ al-Istiqāma, 1967).

Ingram, Brannon D. *Revival from Below: The Deoband Movement and Global Islam* (Oakland: The University of California Press, 2018) 8.

Ingrams, William Harold. *Zanzibar, Its History and Its People* (London: H.F. & G. Witherby, 1931).

International Social Science Council and UNESCO. *World Social Science Report 2010: Knowledge Divides* (Paris: ISSC and UNESCO, 2010).

ISESCO. *Ahmad Baba al-Timbukti: Buḥūth al-nadwa allati 'aqadatha ISESCO bi-munāsabat murur arba'a qurun wa nisf 'ala wiladatihi*, Actes du colloque organisé par l'ISESCO quatre siècles et demi après la naissance de Ahmed Baba (Marrakesh: ISESCO, 1993).

Islamic Propagation Center. *Lengo La Maisha Ya Mwanadamu (The Goal of Human Life)*. Vol. 1. 7 vols. Darasa La Watu Wazima (Dar es Salaam: Afroplus Industries, 2003).

Islamweb, Wafāt al-'Allāma Muḥammad Sālim 'Addūd islamweb.net: tarīkh wa-ḥaḍāra, 29 April 2009, http://articles.islamweb.net/media/index.php?page=article&lang=A&id=151027. Accessed 4 July 2020.

Jackson, Sherman. *Islamic Law and the State: The Constitutional Jurisprudence of Shihāb al-Dīn al-Qarāfī* (Leiden: Brill, 1996).

Janmohamed, Shelina. *Generation M: Young Muslims Changing the World* (London: I.B. Tauris, 2016).

Jeppie, Shamil; Souleymane Bachir Diagne (eds.). *The Meanings of Timbuktu* (Cape Town: Human Sciences Research Council, 2008).

Jeppie, Shamil; Souleymane Bachir Diagne (eds.). *Tombouctou: Pour une histoire de l'érudition en Afrique de l'Ouest*, trans. Ousmane Kane (Dakar and Cape Town: CODESRIA and Human Sciences Research Council, 2012).

Ka, Thierno. *Ecole de Pir-Saniokhor et culture arabo-islamique au Sénégal du XVIIe au XXe siècle* (Dakar: GIA, n.d.).

Kane, Cissé (trans). *Jawâhirul-ma'ânî - Les joyaux des sens et l'accès aux aspirations, en l'effluve spirituel du maître, Abul 'Abbâs At-Tijânî* (Dakar: L'Harmattan, 2018).

Kane, Oumar. 'Les relations entre la communauté tijane du Sénégal et la zawiya de Fèz', *Annales de la Faculté de Lettres et des Sciences Humaines*, 24, 1994, 49–68, 65.

Kane, Ousmane. *Handlist of Manuscripts in the Libraries of Shaykh Mor Mbaye Cissé, al-Hâjj Malick Sy & Shaykh Ibrahima Niasse* (London: Al-Furqan, 1997).

Kane, Ousmane. 'Muhammad Niasse (1881–1956) et sa réplique contre le pamphlet anti-tijani de Ibn Mayaba', in Jean-Louis Triaud; David Robinson (eds.), *La Tijaniyya. Une confrérie musulmane à la conquête de l'Afrique* (Paris: Karthala, 2000) 219–236.

Kane, Ousmane. *Intellectuels non Europhones* (Dakar: CODESRIA, 2003).

Kane, Ousmane. *Muslim Modernity in Postcolonial Nigeria* (Leiden: E.J. Brill, 2003).

Kane, Ousmane. *Al-muthaqqafūn al-ifrīqiyyūn al-mutahaddithūn bi-lughāt ghayr 'urūbiyya* (Cairo: Center for Arab Studies, 2005).

Kane, Ousmane. *The Homeland is the Arena. Religion, Transnationalism and the Integration of Senegalese Muslims in America* (New York: Oxford University Press, 2011).

Kane, Ousmane. *Africa y la produccion intellectual no eurofona. Introduccion al conocimento islamico al sur del Sahara* (Madrid: Oozebap, 2011).

Kane, Ousmane. *Beyond Timbuktu. An Intellectual History of Muslim West Africa* (Cambridge, MA: Harvard University Press, 2016).

Kanté, S. 'Les Sénégalais émigrent aussi vers les États-Unis', *Population & Avenir*, 689, 4, 2008, 17–19.

Kassim, Mohamed. 'Colonial resistance and the local transmission of Islamic knowledge in the Benadir Coast in the late 19th and early 20th centuries', PhD diss., History, York University, 2006.

Kazmi, Yedullah. 'Islamic Education: Traditional Education or Education of Tradition?', *Islamic Studies*, 42, 2, 2003, 259–88.

Kea, P. 'Photography and Technologies of Care: Migrants in Britain and Their Children in the Gambia', in J. Cole; C. Groes (eds.), *Affective Circuits. African Migrations to Europe and the Pursuit of Social Regenerations* (London: University of Chicago Press, 2016) 78–100.

Keane, Webb. 'Self-Interpretation, Agency and the Objects of Anthropology: Reflections on a Genealogy', *Comparative Studies in Society and History*, 45, 2, 2003, 222–48.

Keane, Webb. *Christian Moderns: Freedom and Fetish in The Mission Encounter* (Berkeley: University of California Press, 2007).

Khayr al-dīn, al-Ziriklī. *Al-A'lām: Qāmus tarājim li-ashhur al-rijāl wa 'l-nisā min al-'arab wa 'l-musta'ribīn wa 'l-mustashriqīn* (Beirut: Dar al-'ilm lil-malayīn, 1990).

Ki-Zerbo, J. (ed.). *La natte des autres* (Dakar: CODESRIA, 1980).

Kineenewa, Mutiso. 'Archetypal Motifs in Swahili Islamic Poetry: Kasidaya Burudai', PhD diss., Department of Linguistics and African Languages, University of Nairobi, 1996.

King, R.; A. Christou. 'Of Counter-Diaspora and Reverse Transnationalism: Return Mobilities to and from the Ancestral Homeland', *Mobilities*, 6, 4, 2011, 451–66.

Kirk-Greene, A.H.H. *Barth's Travels in Nigeria* (Oxford: Oxford University Press, 1962).

Kluge, Scott A. *Sufis and Saints' Bodies: Mysticism, Corporeality, and Sacred Power in Islam* (Chapel Hill: University of North Carolina Press, 2007).

Knysh, A. *Ibn 'Arabi in the Later Islamic Traditions: The Making of a Polemical Image in Medieval Islam* (Albany: SUNY Press, 1999).

Kominko, Maja (ed.). *From Dust to Digital: Ten Years of the Endangered Archives Programme* (Cambridge: Open Book Publishers, 2015).

Kresse, K. 'Cosmopolitanism Contested: Anthropology and History in the Eastern Indian Ocean', in Roman Loimeier; Rüdiger Seesemann (eds.), *The Global Worlds of the Swahili* (Berlin: LIT Verlag, 2006).

Kresse, Kai. *Philosophising in Mombasa: Knowledge, Islam and Intellectual Practice on the Swahili Coast* (Edinburgh: Edinburgh University Press, 2007).

Kresse, K. 'Enduring Relevance: Samples of Oral Poetry on the Swahili Coast', *Wasafiri*, 2, 2011.

Lammer, Andreas. 'Eternity and Origination in the Works of Sayf al-Dīn al-Āmidī and Athīr al-Dīn al-Abharī: Two Discussions from the Seventh/Thirteenth Century', *The Muslim World*, 107, 3, 2017, 432–81.

Landau, J.M. 'Kuttab', *Encyclopaedia of Islam*, II (Leiden: E.J. Brill, 1960–2004).

Lane, William Edward. *An Account of the Manners and Customs of the Modern Egyptians: Written in Egypt During the Years 1833–1835* (Ward: Lock and Company, 1890).

Lanza, Nazarena. 'Péleriner, faire du commerce et visiter les lieux saints. Le tourisme religieux sénégalais au Maroc', *L'année du Maghreb*, 11, 2014, 157–71.

Last, Murray. *The Sokoto Caliphate* (New York: Humanities Press, 1967).

Last, M. 'Children and the Experience of Violence: Contrasting Cultures of Punishment in Northern Nigeria', *Africa: Journal of the International African Institute*, 70, 3, 2000, 359–93.

Launay, Robert (ed.). *Islamic Education in Africa. Writing Boards and Blackboards* (Bloomington: Indiana University Press, 2016).

Lawrence, Bruce. 'Sufism and Neo-Sufism', in Michael Cook (ed.), *The New Cambridge History of Islam* (Cambridge: Cambridge University Press, 2009) 355–84.

Leaman, Oliver. *An Introduction to Classical Islamic Philosophy* (Cambridge: Cambridge University Press, 2001).

Learn Religions. 'Hajj Statistics: How the Needs of 2 Million Pilgrims Are Met', Hajj Pilgrimage Statistics, 22 June 2018, https://www.learnreligions.com/hajj-by-the-numbers-2004319. Accessed February 2020.

Lecomte, Bernard. 'Senegal: The Young Farmers of Walo and the New Agricultural Policy', *Review of African Political Economy*, 55, 1992, 87–95.

Lee Kuan Yew. *From Third World to First: The Singapore Story: 1965–2000* (New York: HarperCollins Publishers, 2000).

Leichtman, Mara A. 'The Authentication of a Discursive Islam', in Mamadou Diouf; Mara Leichtman (eds.). *New Perspectives on Islam in Senegal: Conversion, Migration, Wealth, Power, and Femininity* (New York: Palgrave Macmillan, 2009) 111–38.

Lenoble, Marc. 'Les premières écoles de campement en Mauritanie', in Edmond Bernus; Pierre Boilley; Jean Clauzel; Jean-Louis Triaud (eds.), *Nomades et commandants: Administration et sociétés nomades dans l'ancienne* A.O.F (Paris: Karthala, 1993) 139–44.

Levtzion, Nehemia. 'Eighteenth Century Sufi Brotherhoods: Structural, Organizational and Ritual Changes', in Peter Riddell and Tony Street (eds.), *Islam: Essays on Scripture, thought and society: a festschrift in honor of Anthony Johns* (Leiden: Brill, 1997) 147–60.

Levtzion, Nehemia. 'Islam in the Bilad al-Sudan to 1800', in R. Pouwels; N. Levtzion (eds.), *History of Islam in Africa* (Athens, OH: Ohio University Press, 2000).

Levtzion, Nehemia; J.F.P. Hopkins. *Corpus of Early Arabic Sources for West African History* (Princeton, NJ: Markus Wiener Publishers, 2011).

Lewis, Bernard. *Islam and the West* (New York: Oxford University Press, 1993).

Lewis, Bernard. *What Went Wrong? Western Impact and Middle Eastern Response* (New York: Oxford University Press, 2002).

Limbert, Mandana E. *In the Time of Oil: Piety, Memory, and Social Life in an Omani Town* (Stanford, CT: Stanford University Press, 2010).

Lo, Mamadou. 'Un aspect de la poésie wolofal mouride: traduction et analyse de quelques titres de Sëriñ Mbay Jaxate', Master's thesis, Université Cheikh Anta Diop Dakar, 1993.

Loimeier, Roman. *Between Social Skills and Marketable Skills: The Politics of Islamic Education in 20th Century Zanzibar* (Leiden: Brill, 2009).

Ly-Tall, Madina. *Un islam militant en Afrique de l'Ouest au 19ème siècle. La Tijaniyya de Sayku Umar Futiyu contre les pouvoirs traditionnels et la puissance coloniale* (Paris: L'Harmattan, 1991).

Lydon, Ghislaine. *On Trans-Saharan Trails: Islamic Law, Trade Networks, and Cross-Cultural Exchange in Nineteenth Century Western Africa* (Cambridge: Cambridge University Press, 2009).

Mahmood, Saba. 'Rehearsed Spontaneity and the Conventionality of Ritual: Disciplines of "Salat"', *American Ethnologist*, 28, 4, 2001, 827–53.

Mahmood, Saba. *Politics of Piety: The Islamic Revival and the Feminist Subject* (Princeton, NJ: Princeton University Press, 2011).

Makdisi, George. *The Rise of Colleges: Institutions of Learning in Islam and the West* (Edinburgh: Edinburgh University Press, 1981).

Makhlūf, Muḥammad b. Muḥammad. *Shajarat al-nūr al-zakīyya fī ṭabaqāt al-Māliīīya* (Cairo: 1349/1930–1).

Mama, A.; A. Imam; F. Sow (eds.). *Engendering African Social Sciences* (Dakar: CODESRIA, 1997).

Mamdani, Mahmood. *Citizen and Subject: Contemporary Africa and the Legacy of Late Colonialism* (Princeton, NJ: Princeton University Press, 1996).

Mamdani, M. *Define and Rule: Native as Political Identity* (Cambridge, MA: Harvard University Press, 2012).

Mandaville, Peter G. *Global Political Islam* (London and New York: Routledge, 2007).

Mandaville, P. 'Islamic education in Britain: Approaches to religious knowledge in a pluralistic society', in R.W. Hefner and M.Q. Zaman (eds.), *Schooling Islam. The Culture and Politics of Modern Muslim Education* (Princeton, NJ: Princeton University Press, 2007).

Marielle, Villasante-de Beauvais (ed.). *Groupes serviles au Sahara: approche comparative à partir du cas des arabophones de Mauritanie* (Paris: Éditions du CNRS, 2000).

Martin, Bradford. *Muslim Brotherhoods in Nineteenth-Century Africa* (Cambridge: Cambridge University Press, 1976).

Masoud, Tarek. 'Using the Qur'ān to Empower Arab Women? Theory and Experimental Evidence from Egypt', *Comparative Political Studies*, 49, 12, 2016, 1555–98.

Masud, Muhammad Khalid; Brinkley Messick; David Powers (eds.). *Islamic Legal Interpretations: Muftis and their Fatwas* (Cambridge, MA: Harvard University Press, 1996).

Mbacké, Khadim. *Le pèlerinage aux lieux saints de l'islam. Participation sénégalaise, 1886–1986* (Dakar: Presses universitaires de Dakar, 2004).

Mbembe, A. 'Africa in Theory', paper for CODESRIA Point Sud conference on Africa, Dakar, CODESRIA, 2013.

Mbembe, A.; F. Sarr (eds.). *Ecrire L'Afrique-Monde* (Paris and Dakar: Philip Rey and Jimsaan, 2017).

Mbow, Penda. 'Secularism, Education, and Human Rights in Senegal', Evanston: Northwestern University, Institute for the Study of Islamic Thought in Africa Working Paper Series, 2009.

Mbuup, Samba. 'Littérature nationale et conscience historique. Essai sur la perspective nationaliste dans la littérature d'expression wolof de 1850 à nos jours', PhD diss., Université de Paris III, 1977.

McIntosh, Janet. *The Edge of Islam: Power, Personhood, and Ethnoreligious Boundaries on the Kenya Coast* (Durham, NC: Duke University Press Books, 2009).

Melvin-Koushki, M. 'Intellectual Millenarianism in Early Timurid Iran', PhD diss., Yale University, 2012.

Melvin-Koushki, M. 'The Quest for a Universal Science: The Occult Philosophy of Ṣā'in al-Dīn Turka Iṣfahānī (1369–1432)', PhD diss., Yale University, 2012.

Merolla, Daniella. 'Introduction: Orality and Technauriture of African literatures', *Tydskrif vir letterkunde*, 51, 1, 2014, 80–90.

Messick, Brinkley. *The Calligraphic State: Textual Domination and History in a Muslim Society* (Berkeley: University of California Press, 1992).

Meyer, Brigit; Peter Pels (eds.). *Magic and Modernity: Interfaces of Revelation and Concealment* (Stanford, CA: Stanford University Press, 2003).

Mignolo, W.D. *The Darker Side of The Renaissance: Literacy, Territoriality and Colonization* (Ann Arbor: University of Michigan Press, 1995).

Mignolo, W.D. *The Darker Side of Western Modernity: Global Futures, Decolonial Options* (Durham, NC and London: Duke University Press, 2011).

Mitchell, Timothy. *Colonising Egypt* (Berkeley: University of California Press, 1991).

Mittermaier, Amira. *Dreams That Matter: Egyptian Landscapes of the Imagination* (Berkeley: University of California Press, 2011).

Mkandawire, T. '"Good governance": the itinerary of an idea', *Development in Practice*, 17, 4–5, 2007, 679–81.

Montagne, Robert. *Les Berbères et le Makhzen dans le Sud marocain: essai sur la transformation politique des Berbères sédentaires (groupe chleuh)* (Paris: Alcan, 1930).

Monteil, Vincent. *L'islam Noir* (Paris: Editions Du Seuil, 1964).

Moosa, Ebrahim. *What Is a Madrasa?* (Chapel Hill: University of North Carolina Press, 2015).

Morris, James. 'Ibn 'Arabi's "Esotericism": The Problem of Spiritual Authority', *Studia Islamica*, 71, 1990, 37–64.

Mudimbe, V.Y. *The Invention of Africa: Gnosis, Philosophy, and the Order of Knowledge* (Bloomington and Indianapolis: Indiana University Press; London: James Currey, 1988).

Mudimbe, V.Y. *The Idea of Africa* (Bloomington: Indiana University Press; London: James Currey, 1994).

Muḥammad al-'Arabī b. al-Sā'īḥ. *Bughyāt al-Mustafīd li Sharḥ Munyāt al-Murīd* (Rabat: al-Ma'ārif al-Jadīda, 2017) 61.

Muḥammad al-Zajlāwī, Nawāzil, Lemtarfa Library MS, 87.

Muhammad Shareef. 'Ilaawat'l-Muttaalib Fee Shukr'l-Waahib al-Mufeeda'l-Mawaahib', https://siiasi.org/shaykh-dan-tafa/shukrl-waahib/, Sankore Institute of Islamic-African Studies International, 2013.

Müller, Christian. *Der Kadi und seine Zeugen: Studie der mamlukischen Ḥaram-Dokumente aus Jerusalem* (Wiesbaden: Harrasowitz, 2013).

Mumin, Meikal. 'The Arabic Script in Africa: Understudied Literacy', in Meikal Mumin; Kees Versteegh, *The Arabic Script in Africa. Studies in the Use of a Writing System* (Boston, MA and Leiden: Brill, 2014) 41–76.

Mumin, Meikal; Kees Versteegh. *The Arabic Script in Africa. Studies in the Use of a Writing System* (Boston, MA and Leiden: Brill, 2014).

Muyaka Abdulaziz, M.H. *19th Century Swahili Popular Poetry* (Nairobi: Kenya Literature Bureau, 1994).

Narizny, Kevin. *The Political Economy of Grand Strategy* (Ithaca, NY: Cornell University Press, 2007).

Narkissa, Aria. 'An Epistemic Shift in Islamic Law. Educational Reform at al-Azhar and Dār al-ʿUlūm', *Islamic Law and Society*, 21, 3, 2014, 209–51.

Nasr, S.H. 'Oral Transmission and the Book in Islamic Education: The Spoken and the Written Word', *Journal of Islamic Studies*, 3, 1, 1992.

Nasr, S.H. *Islamic Philosophy From its Origin to the Present, Philosophy in the Land of Prophecy* (Albany: SUNY Press, 2006).

Nelson, Kristina. *The Art of Reciting the Qur'ān* (Cairo: American University Press in Cairo, 2001).

Ngom, Fallou. 'Amadu Bamba's Pedagogy and the Development of Ajam Literature', *African Studies Review*, 52, 1, 2009, 99–123.

Ngom, Fallou. *Muslims Beyond the Arab World: The Odyssey of Ajami and the Muridiyya* (New York: Oxford University Press, 2016).

Niang, Cheikh. 'Le transnational pour argument. Socio-anthropologie historique du mouvement confrérique tidjane de Cheikh Ibrahim Niasse (Sénégal, Niger, Nigeria)', PhD diss., Anthropology, Université de Toulouse, 2014.

Niasse, Ibrahim. *Al-Ḥujjat al-bālighat fī kawn adhāat alqurān sāi'gha* (Dakar: Muḥammad al-Ma'mūn b. Ibrāhīm Niasse, 1988).

Niasse, Ibrahim. *Traduction et interprétation du Saint Coran en Wolof 1950–1960* (New York: Sall Family Publishers, 1998), 30 cassettes, with a preface by Ibrahim Mahmoud Diop.

Niasse, Ibrahim *The Removal of Confusion Concerning the Flood of the Saintly Seal Ahmad al-Tijani: A Translation of Kashif al-ilbas an fayda al-khatm abi 'abbas*, trans. Zachary Wright, Muhtar Holland and Abdullahi Okene with forewords by Sayyid Ali Cisse, Shaykh Tijani Cisse, Shaykh Hassan Cisse (Louisville, KY: Fons Vitae, 2010).

Niasse, Ibrahim. *Fī Riyāḍ al-Tafsīr li'l-Qur'ān al-Karīm* (Lemden, Mauritania: M. Ibn al-Shaykh ʿAbdullāh, 2014).

Niasse, Ibrahim. *In the Meadows of Tafsīr for the Noble Qur'an*, trans. Moctar Ba (Atlanta: FaydaBooks, 2014).

Niasse, Ibrahim. *The Spirit of Good Morals* (Atlanta, GA: Fayda Books, 2016).

NOAA. 'Climate Prediction Center's Africa Hazards Outlook September 8 – September 14', 2016, http://www.cpc.ncep.noaa.gov/products/international/africa/africa_hazard.pdf

Noor, Farish A.; Yoginder Sikand; Martin van Bruinessen (eds.). *The Madrasa in Asia: Political Activism and Transnational Linkages* (Amsterdam: Amsterdam University Press, 2008).

Noor, Farish A.; Yoginder Sikand; Martin van Bruinessen. 'Behind the Walls: Re-Appraising the Role and Importance of Madrasas in the World Today', in Farish A. Noor; Yoginder Sikand; Martin van Bruinessen (eds.). *The Madrasa in Asia: Political Activism and Transnational Linkages* (Amsterdam: Amsterdam University Press, 2008).

Norris, H.T. 'Znāga Islam during the Seventeenth and Eighteenth Centuries', *Bulletin of the School of Oriental and African Studies*, 32, 3, 1969, 509–10.

Norris, H.T. *Sufi Mystics of the Niger Desert* (Oxford: Clarendon Press, 1990).

Nouhi, Mohamed Lahbib with C.C. Stewart. 'The Maḥaẓra Educational System', in Charles C. Stewart (ed.), *Arabic Literature of Africa, Vol. 5: The Writings of Mauritania and the Western Sahara*, Vol. 1 (Leiden: Brill, 2016) 18–50.

Nurse, Derek; Thomas J. Hinnebusch. *Swahili and Sabaki: A Linguistic History* (Berkeley: University of California Press, 1993).

Nurse, Derek; Thomas Spear. *The Swahili: Reconstructing the History and Language of an African Society, 800–1500* (Philadelphia: University of Pennsylvania Press, 1985).

Nyamnjoh, F.B. *#RhodesMustFall: Nibbling at Resilient Colonialism in South Africa* (Mankon Bamenda: Langaa Research Publishing, 2016).

O'Fahey, R.S. *Enigmatic Saint: Ahmad ibn Idris and the Idrisi tradition* (Evanston, IL: Northwestern University Press, 1990).

O'Fahey, R.S.; Bernd Radtke. 'Neo-Sufism Reconsidered', *Der Islam*, 70, 1, 1993, 52–87.

Ogunnaike, O. 'From Theory to Theoria and Back Again: Decolonizing Theories of African Philosophy and Religion', paper delivered at the Meeting of the American Academy of Religion, Boston, 18–21 November 2017.

Ogunnaike, Oludamini, *Deep Knowledge: Ways of Knowing in Sufism and Ifa Two West African Intellectual Traditions* (Philadelphia: Penn State University Press, 2020).

Ong, Walter. *Orality and Literacy* (New York: Routledge, 2013).

Osswald, Rainer. *Schichtengesellschaft und islamisches Recht: die Zawāyā und Krieger der Westsahara im Spiegel von Rechtsgutachten des 16.-19. Jahrhundert* (Wiesbaden: Harrasowitz Verlag, 1993).

Osswald, Rainer. *Sklavenhandel und Sklavenleben zwischen Senegal und Atlas* (Wiesbaden: Ergon Verlag, 2016).

Ould Abdallah, Deddoud. *Dawr al-Shanāḳiṭa fī nashr al-thaḳāfa ʿarabiyya al-islāmiyya bi-gharb Ifrīḳiya ḥattā nihāyat al-ḳarn al-thāmina ʿashar li 'l-mīlād, Annales de la Fac. des Lettres et des Sciences Humaines de l'Univ. de Nouakchott*, 1989, 13–33.

Ould Ahmed Salem, Zekeria. *Prêcher dans le désert. Islam politique et changement social en Mauritanie* (Paris: Karthala, 2013).

Ould Cheikh, Abdel Wedoud. 'Théologie du désordre: Islam, ordre et désordre au Sahara', *L'année du Maghreb*, 7, 2011, 61–77.
Ould el-Bara, Yahya. 'Les théologiens mauritaniens face au colonialisme française. Etude de fatwas de jurisprudence musulmane', in David Robinson; Jean-Louis Triaud (eds.), *Le temps des marabouts. Itinéraires et stratégies islamiques en Afrique occidentale française v. 1880–1960* (Paris: Karthala, 1997) 85–117.
Ould el-Bara, Yahya. 'Les réponses et les fatâwâ des érudits Bidân face à l'occupation de la Mauritanie', in Mariella Villasante Cervello; Christophe de Beauvais (eds.), *Colonisation et héritages actuels au Sahara et au Sahel* (Paris: L'Harmattan, 2007) vol. 2, 155–92.
Park, Katharine; Lorraine Daston. 'Introduction: The Age of the New', in K. Park; L. Daston (eds.), *The Cambridge History of Science, Vol. 3: Early Modern Science* (Cambridge: Cambridge University Press, 2013) 1–18.
Patterson, Amy S. 'The Dynamic Nature of Citizenship and Participation: Lessons from Three Rural Senegalese Case Studies', *Africa Today*, 46, 1, 1999, 3–27.
Pearson, M.N. 'The Indian Ocean and the Red Sea', in Nehemia Levtzion; Randall Pouwels (eds.), *The History of Islam in Africa* (Athens, OH: Ohio University Press, 2000) 37–59.
Penrad, Jean-Claude. 'Madrassat Al-Nur. Une École Coranique de La Ville de Pierre et Son Shaykh', in Colette Le Cour Grandmaison; Ariel Crozon (eds.), *Zanzibar Aujourd'hui* (Paris: Éditions Karthala, 1998) 307–19.
Pérez-Sabater, Carmen. 'The Linguistics of Social Networking: A Study of Writing Conventions on Facebook', *Linguistik Online*, 56, 6, 2012, 81–93.
Perry, Donna L. 'Rural Weekly Markets and the Dynamics of Time, Space and Community in Senegal', *The Journal of Modern African Studies*, 38, 3, 2000, 461–86.
Peters, F.E. *The Hajj. The Muslim Pilgrimage to Mecca and the Holy Places* (Princeton, NJ: Princeton University Press, 1994).
Peters, Rudolph. *Crime and Punishment in Islamic Law: Theory and Practice from the Sixteenth to the Twenty-First Century* (Cambridge: Cambridge University Press, 2005).
Petry, C.F. *The Cambridge History of Egypt* (Cambridge: Cambridge University Press, 2008).
Philipp, Thomas; Moshe Perlmann. *ʿAbd al-Raḥmān al-Jabartī's History of Egypt: ʿAjāʾib al-thar fī 'l-Tarājim wa 'l-Akhbār* (Stuttgart: Franz Steiner Verlag, 1994).
Pollock, Sheldon. 'A new Philology: From Norm-Bound Practice to Practice-Bound Norm in Kannada Intellectual History', in Jean-Luc Chevillard (ed.), *South-Indian Horizons: Felicitation Volume for François Gros* (Pondichéry: Institut Français de Pondichéry/Ecole Française d'Extrême-Orient, 2004).

Pongiglione, Francesca. 'Mandeville on Charity Schools: Happiness, Social Order, and the Psychology of Poverty', *Journal of Philosophy and Economics*, 29, 1, 2016, 82–100.

Pouwels, R.L. *Horn and Crescent: Cultural Change and Traditional Islam on the Kenyan Coast, 800–1900* (Cambridge: Cambridge University Press, 1987).

Pratt, Nicola. 'Identity, Culture and Democratization: The Case of Egypt', *New Political Science*, 27, 1, 2005, 73–90.

Projet de réhabilitation et de viabilisation d'un site de Mbacké Kadioor, http://mbackekadior.com/mbacke-Kadior-est-situe-au-senegal-dans-la.html. Accessed 21 August 2016.

Quadri, Yasir Anjola. 'The Tijaniyyah in Nigeria. A Case Study', PhD diss., Arabic and Islamic Studies, University of Ibadan, 1981.

Quijano, Anibal. 'Coloniality and modernity/rationality', *Cultural Studies*, 21, 2–3, 2007, 168–78.

Radtke, Bernd. 'Studies on the Sources of Kitāb Rimāh Hizb al-Rahīm by Hajj Umar', *Sudanic Africa*, 6, 1995, 73–113.

Radtke, Bernd. 'Sufism in the 18th Century: an attempt at a provisional appraisal', *Die Welt des Islams*, 36, 3 1996, 326–64.

Radtke, Bernd; John O'Kane; Knut S. Vikor; R.S. O'Fahey. *The Exoteric Aḥmad Ibn Idrīs: A Sufi's Critique of the Madhāhib and the Wahhābīs: Four Arabic Texts with Translation and Commentary* (Leiden: Brill, 2000).

Rahimi, Babak; Payman Eshaghi (eds.). *Muslim Pilgrimage in the Modern World* (Chapel Hill: University of North Carolina Press, 2019).

Razy, É. 'De quelques "retours Soninké" aux différents âges de la vie. Circulations entre la France et le Mali', *Journal Des Anthropologues*, 2006, 106–7.

Razy, É. 'La famille dispersée (France/Pays Soninké, Mali). Une configuration pluriparentale oubliée?', *L'Autre*, 11, 3, 2010, 333–41.

Rebstock, Ulrich. *Maurische Literaturgeschichte* (Würzburg: Ergon, 2001) 3 vols.

Reese, Scott. 'Patricians of the Benaadir: Islamic Learning, Commerce and Somali Urban Identity in the Nineteenth Century', PhD diss., History, University of Pennsylvania, 1996.

Reese, Scott. 'The Best of Guides: Sufi Poetry and Alternate Discourse of Reform in Early Twentieth Century Somalia', *Journal of African Cultural Studies*, 14, 1, 2001, 49–68.

Reese, Scott (ed.). *The Transmission of Learning in Muslim Africa* (Leiden: Brill, 2004).

Reese, Scott. *Renewers of the Age: Holy Men and Social Discourse in Colonial Benaadir* (Leiden: Brill, 2008).

Reichmuth, Stefan. 'Autobiographical Writing and Islamic Consciousness in the Arabic Literature of Nigeria', in János Riesz; Ulla Schild, *Autobiographical Genres in Africa* (Berlin: Dietrich Reimer Verlag, 1996) 179 89.

Reichmuth, Stefan. *Islamische Bildung und soziale Integration in Illorin (Nigeria) seit ca 1800* (Münster: LIT Verlag, 1998).

Reichmuth, Stefan. 'Islamic Education in Sub-Saharan Africa', in R. Pouwels; N. Levtzion (eds.), *History of Islam in Africa* (Athens, OH: Ohio University Press, 2000) 419–40.

Reichmuth, S. *Murtaḍa al-Zabīdī (1732–1791): Life, Networks, and Writings* (Oxford: Gibb Memorial Press, 2009).

Reichmuth, Stefan. *The World of Murtaḍa al-Zabīdī* (Cambridge: Gibb Memorial Trust, 2009).

Ring, Nancy C. *Introduction to the Study of Religion* (New York: Orbis, 2007).

Robinson, Chase. *Islamic Historiography* (Cambridge: Cambridge University Press, 2003).

Robinson, David. 'The Islamic Revolution of Futa Toro', *The International Journal of African Historical Studies*, 8, 2, 1975, 185–221.

Robinson, David. *The Holy War of Umar Tal* (Oxford: Oxford University Press, 1985).

Robinson, David. *Paths of Accommodation, Muslim Societies and French Colonial Authorities in Senegal and Mauritania, 1880–1920* (Ohio and Oxford: Ohio University Press and James Currey, 2000).

Robinson, David. 'Failed Islamic States in Senegambia: Umar Tal', Pluralism and Adaptation in the Islamic Practice of Senegal and Ghana, http://aodl.org/islamicpluralism/failedislamicstates/essays/43-1A9-F/#jump. Accessed 4 January 2018.

Rogers, Carol L. 'Desertification', *Science News*, 112, 18, 1977, 282–3.

Rosenthal, Franz. *Knowledge Triumphant: The Concept of Knowledge in Medieval Islam* (Boston, MA and Leiden: Brill, 1970).

Rostow, Walt Whitman. *The Stages of Economic Growth: A Non-Communist Manifesto* (Cambridge: Cambridge University Press, 1960).

Rougier, C.B.; P. Colin; R. Grosfoguel. *Penser l'envers obscur de la modernité: une anthologie de la pensée décoloniale latino-américaine* (Limoges: Presses Universitaires de Limoges, 2014).

Rustom, M. 'Philosophical Sufism', in C. Taylor and Louis Xavier López-Farjeat (eds.), *The Routledge Companion to Islamic Philosophy* (New York: Routledge, 2016) 399–411.

Ryad, Umar (ed). *The Hajj and Europe in the Age of Empire* (Leiden: Brill, 2017).

Saad, Elias N. *A Social History of Timbuktu* (Cambridge: Cambridge University Press, 1983).

Sall, E. 'The Social Sciences in Africa: Trend, Issues, Capacities and Constraints' *Social Science Research Council Working Paper Series*, 8, 2003.

Sall, E. 'Decoloniality and Beyond', paper for the Ateliers de la Pensée 2017, Dakar, November 2017.

Sall, E.; J.B. Ouedraogo. 'Sociology in West Africa: Challenges and Obstacles to Academic Autonomy', in S. Patel (ed.), *The International Sociology Association Handbook of Diverse Sociological Traditions* (London: SAGE Publications, 2010).

Sall, Ibrahima Abou. *Mauritanie du Sud. Conquêtes et administration coloniales françaises 1890–1945* (Paris: Karthala, 2007).

Sall, M. *La mesure de l'Arabophonie au Sénégal* (Dakar: Presses universitaires de Dakar, 2018).

Sambidge, Andy. 'Hajj Pilgrims Total 3.1m, Says Saudi Arabia', *Arabian Business*, 26 June 2017, https://www.arabianbusiness.com/hajj-pilgrims-total-3-1m-says-saudi-arabia-477638.html. Accessed June 2019.

Samson, Fabienne. *Les marabouts de l'islam politique. Le Dahiratoul Moustarchidina Wal Moustachidati, un mouvement néo-confrérique sénégalais* (Paris: Karthala, 2005).

Santos, Boaventura De Sousa. *Epistemologies of the South. Justice Against Epistemicide* (Boulder, CA: Paradigm Publishers, 2014).

Sarr, F. *Afrotopia* (Paris: Philippe Rey, 2016).

Scheele, Judith. *Smugglers and Saints of the Sahara: Regional Connectivity in the Twentieth Century* (Cambridge: Cambridge University Press, 2012).

Schoeler, Gregor. *The Oral and the Written in Early Islam* (London and New York: Routledge, 2006).

Schoeler, Gregor. *The Genesis of Literature in Islam. From Aural to Read* (Cairo: The American University in Cairo Press, 2009).

Scott, J. *Against the Grain: A Deep History of the Earliest States* (New Haven, CT: Yale University Press, 2017).

Searing, James F. *'God Alone is King': Islam and Emancipation in Senegal. The Wolof Kingdoms of Kajoor and Bawol, 1859–1914* (Portsmouth, NH: Heinemann, 2002).

Seesemann, Rüdiger. 'Ziyāra: Funktionen und Bedeutungen in der Tiǧānīya (Westafrika)', *Der Islam*, 83, 1, 2006, 158–70.

Seesemann, Rüdiger. *The Divine Flood: Ibrahim Niasse and the Roots of a Twentieth-century Sufi Revival* (Oxford: Oxford University Press, 2011).

Seesemann, Rüdiger. 'Epistemology or Ideology? Toward a Relational Perspective on Islamic Knowledge in Africa', *Journal of African Religions*, 6, 2, 2018, 232–68.

Shahid, Omar. 'Why I left Britain to live in an Islamic State', 2 March 2016, https://omarshahid.co.uk/2016/03/02/why-i-left-britain-to-fight-jihad-in-an-islamic-state/. Accessed 4 July 2020.

Shareef, M. 'The Life of Shaykh Dan Tafa: The life and times of one of Africa's leading scholars and statesmen and a history of the intellectual traditions that produced him' (Maiurno, Sudan: Sankore Institute of Islamic-African Studies, n.d.).

Shareef, Muhammad. 'Ilaawat'l-Muttaalib Fee Shukr'l-Waahib al-Mufeeda'l-Mawaahib' (Maiurno, Sudan: Sankore Institute of Islamic-African Studies International, 2013).

Shihadeh, Ayman. *The Teleological Ethics of Fakhr al-Dīn al-Rāzī* (Boston, MA: Brill, 2006).

Shiohata, Mariko. 'Exploring the Literacy Environment: A Case Study from Senegal', *Comparative Education Review*, 54, 2, 2010, 243–69.

Shoshan, Boaz. *Popular Culture in Medieval Cairo* (Cambridge: Cambridge University Press, 1991).

Sieveking, Nadine. 'We Don't Want Equality; We Want to Be Given Our Rights: Muslim Women Negotiating Global Development Concepts in Senegal', *Afrika Spectrum*, 42, 2007, 29–48.

SInternational. *The Qur'ān* (Jeddah: Abul-Qasim Publishing House, 1997).

Sirriyeh, Elizabeth. *Sufi Visionary of Ottoman Damascus: 'Abd al-Ghanī al-Nābulusī, 1641–1731* (New York: Routledge, 2011).

Skali, Fawzi. *Saints et Sanctuaires de Fez* (Rabat: Marsam, 2007).

Skinner, David E. 'Conversion to Islam and the Promotion of "Modern" Islamic Schools in Ghana', *Journal of Religion in Africa*, 43, 4, 2013, 426–50.

Smith, James Howard. *Bewitching Development: Witchcraft and the Reinvention of Development in Neoliberal Kenya* (Chicago: University of Chicago Press, 2008).

Smith, Margaret. *Rābi'a the Mystic and her Fellow Saints in Islam* (Cambridge: Cambridge University Press, 1984).

Smith, Wilfred Cantwell. *Islam in Modern History* (Princeton, NJ: Princeton University Press, 1977).

Snouck-Hurgronje, C. *Mekka in the latter part of the 19th century. Daily life, customs and learning. The Moslims of the East-Indian-Archipelago* (Leiden and London: E.J. Brill Ltd and Lucaz and Co., 1931).

Soares, Benjamin. *Islam and the Prayer Economy: History and Authority in a Malian Town* (Edinburgh: Edinburgh University Press for the International African Institute, London, 2005).

Some, Aymar Narodar. *Migration au Sénégal: Profil National 2009* (Geneva: International Organisation for Migration, 2009).

Somet, Y. 'L'Egyptologie dans le programme décolonial', paper for UNESCO World Humanities Conference, Liège, August 2017.

Spencer, Ian. *A History of Beer and Brewing* (Cambridge: The Royal Society of Chemistry, 2003).

Sperl, S.; C. Shackle (eds.). *Qasida Poetry in Islamic Asia and Africa: Eulogy's Bounty, Meaning's Abundance. An Anthology* (Leiden: E.J. Brill, 1996).

Stetkevych, S.P. 'Abbasid Panegyric and the Poets of Political Allegiance: Two Poems of Al-Mutanabbi on Kafur', in S. Sperl; C. Shackle (eds.), *Qasida Poetry in Islamic Asia and Africa: Classical Traditions & Modern Meanings*, Vol. I (Leiden: E.J. Brill, 1996).

Stewart, Charles. *Islam and Social Order in Mauritania: A Case Study from the 19th Century* (Oxford: Clarendon Press, 1973).

Stewart, Charles. *Arabic literature of Africa Volume 5: the Writings of Mauritania and the Western Sahara* (Leiden: Brill, 2016) 2 vols.

Tagliacozzo, Eric (ed.). *South East Asia and the Middle East. Islam, Movement and the Longue Durée* (Stanford, CA: Stanford University Press, 2009).

Tagliacozzo, Eric; Shawkat M. Toorawa (eds.). *The Hajj. Pilgrimage in Islam* (Cambridge: Cambridge University Press, 2016).

Tāl, ʿUmar. *Kitāb Rimāh Hizb al-Rahīm ʻAlā Nuḥūr Ḥizb al-Rajīm* (Beirut: Dār al-Fikr, 1981).

Tall, S.M. 'La migration internationale sénégalaise : des recrutements de main-d'oeuvre aux pirogues', in M.-C. Diop (ed.), *Le Sénégal des migrations. Mobilités, identités et sociétés* (Paris: Karthala, 2008) 37–67.

Taylor, Edward. *Primitive Culture: Researches into the Development of Mythology, Philosophy, Religion, Art, and Custom* (New York: Harper & Row, 1958).

Ter Haar, Gerrie; Stephen Ellis. 'The Role of Religion in Development: Towards a New Relationship between the European Union and Africa', *The European Journal of Development Research*, 18, 3, 2006, 351–67.

Thurston, A. *Salafism in Nigeria. Islam, Preaching, and Politics* (Cambridge: Cambridge University Press, 2016).

Thurston, A. *Boko Haram: The History of An African Jihadist Movement* (Princeton, NJ and Oxford: Princeton University Press, 2018).

Tidjani Mohamemad al-Mansour al-Mohieddine. *Ahmad Tidjani et ses valeureux compagnons* (Paris: Albustane, 2015).

Timera, M. 'Righteous or rebellious? Social trajectory of Sahelian youth in France', in D. Bryceson; U. Vuorela (eds.), *The Transnational Family. New European Frontiers and Global Networks* (Oxford: Berg, 2002) 147–54.

Topan, F. 'Projecting Islam: Narrative in Swahili Poetry', *Journal of African Cultural Studies*, 14, 1, 2001.

Touati, Henri. *Islam and Travel in the Middle Ages*, trans. by Lydia G. Cochrane (Chicago: University of Chicago Press, 2010).

Touati, Houari. 'Les héritiers: anthropologie des Maisons de sciences maghrébines aux XIe/XVIIe et XIIe/XVIIIe siècles', in Hassan Elboudrari (ed.), *Modes de transmission de la culture religieuse en Islam* (Cairo: Publications de l'IFAO, 1993) 65–92.

Touati, Houari. *Entre Dieu et les hommes: lettrés, saints et sorciers au Maghreb 17e siècle* (Paris: Editions de l'EHESS, 1994).

Touati, Houari. 'Le prince et la bête: enquête sur une métaphore pastorale', *Studia Islamica*, 83, 1996, 101–19.

Triaud, Jean-Louis. 'Hommes de religion et confréries islamiques dans une société en crise, l'Aïr aux XIXe et XXe siècles: le cas de las Khalwatiyya', *Cahiers d'Études Africaines*, 23, 1983, 239–80.

Triaud, Jean-Louis; David Robinson (eds.). *La Tijaniyya. Une confrérie musulmane à la conquête de l'Afrique* (Paris: Karthala, 2000).

Trimingham, John Spencer. *The Influence of Islam Upon Africa* (London: Longmans, 1968).

Turki, Benyan S. 'British Policy and Education in Zanzibar, 1890–1945', PhD diss., University of Exeter, 1987.

Turner, Victor. 'The Center out There: Pilgrim's Goal', *History of Religions*, 12, 1973, 191–230.

Tyan, Emile, *Histoire de l'organisation judiciaire en pays d'Islam* (Leiden: Brill, 1960).

Tylor, Edward. *Primitive Culture: Researches into the Development of Mythology, Philosophy, Religion, Art, and Custom* (New York: Harper & Row, 1958).

'Umar Ridā Kahhāla. *Mu'jam al-mu'allifīn* (Beirut: Dār ihyā al-turāth al-'arabī, 1958).

Urs Peter, Ruf. *Ending Slavery: Hierarchy, Dependency, and Gender in Central Mauritania* (Bielefeld: Transcript Verlag, 1999).

Usmani, Taqi. *An Approach to the Qur'anic Sciences* (New Delhi: Adam Publishers, 2006).

Van Dalen, Dorrit. *Doubt, Scholarship and Society in 17th-Century Central Sudanic Africa* (Leiden: Brill, 2016).

Vertovec, S. 'Religion and Diaspora', in P. Antes; A.W. Geertz; R. Warne (eds.), *New Approaches to the Study of Religion* (Berlin and New York: Walter de Gruyer, 2004) 275–304.

Vianello, Alessandra; Mohamed M. Kassim (eds.). *Servants of the Sharia: the Civil Register of the Qadis' Court of Brava, 1893–1900* (Leiden: Brill, 2006) 2 vols.

Vianello, Alessandra. 'Dada Masiti', in Emmanuel K. Akyeampong; Henry Louis Gates (eds.), *Dictionary of African Biography* (New York: Oxford University Press, 2012) vol. 2, 150–1.

Vianello, Alessandra; Lidwien Kapteijns; Mohamed M. Kassim (eds.). *'Stringing coral beads'. The Religious Poetry of Brava (c. 1890–1975): A Source Publication of Chimiini Texts and English Translations* (Leiden: Brill, 2018).

Villalón, Leonardo A. *Islamic Society and State Power in Senegal: Disciples and Citizens in Fatick* (Cambridge: Cambridge University Press, 1995).

Voll, John. 'Neo-Sufism: Reconsidered Again', *Canadian Journal of African Studies*, 42, 2/3, 2008, 314–30.

Wade, Malick et al. 'On the Spatial Coherence of Rainfall over the Saloum Delta (Senegal) from Seasonal to Decadal Time Scales. Frontiers in Earth Science', 2015, http://dx.doi.org/10.3389/feart.2015.00030. Accessed 14 September 2016.

Walz, Terence. 'Trans-Saharan Migration and the Colonial Gaze: The Nigerians in Egypt', *Alif*, 26, 2006, 94–118.

Walz, Terence. 'Sudanese, Habasha, Takarna, and Barabira: Trans-Saharan Africans in Cairo as Shown in the 1848 Census', in Walz and Cuno (eds.), *Race and Slavery in the Middle East: Histories of Trans-Saharan Africans in 19th-Century Egypt, Sudan, and the Ottoman Mediterranean* (Cairo: American University in Cairo Press, 2011).

Walz, Terence; Kenneth Cuno (eds.). *Race and Slavery in the Middle East: Histories of Trans-Saharan Africans in 19th-Century Egypt, Sudan, and the Ottoman Mediterranean* (Cairo: American University in Cairo Press, 2011).

Wan, Abdullah Wan Hilmi. 'Muhammad Rifat and His Reciting Records', *International Journal of Islamic Thought*, 2013, 74–81.

Ware, Rudolph T., III. 'The Longue Durée of Quran Schooling, Society, and State in Senegambia', in Mamadou Diouf; Mara Leichtman (eds.), *New Perspectives on Islam in Senegal: Conversion, Migration, Wealth, Power, and Femininity* (New York: Palgrave Macmillan, 2009) 21–50.

Ware, Rudolph T., III. *The Walking Qur'an: Islamic Education, Embodied Knowledge, and History in West Africa* (Chapel Hill: University of North Carolina Press, 2014).

Ware, Rudolph; Zachary Wright; Amir Syed. *Jihad of the Pen: the Sufi Literature of West Africa* (Cairo and New York: American University in Cairo Press, 2018).

Warscheid, Ismail. 'Entre mémoire lettrée et vécu institutionnel: la compilation de nawāzil dans le grand Touat (Algérie) aux XVIIIe et XIXe siècles', *Studia Islamica*, 108, 2, 2013, 214–54.

Warscheid, Ismail. *Droit musulman et société au Sahara prémoderne: la justice islamique dans les oasis du Grand Touat (Sud algérien) XVIIe – XIXe siècles* (Leiden: Brill, 2017).

Warscheid, Ismail. 'Le Livre du désert: la vision du monde d'un lettré musulman de l'Ouest saharien au XIXe siècle', *Annales: Histoire, Sciences Sociales*, 73, 2, 2018, 359–84.

Weber, Max. *Wirtschaft und Gesellschaft: Grundriss der verstehenden Soziologie* (Frankfurt a.M: Zweitausendeins, 2005), 3rd edition.

Wikan, Unni. 'Living Conditions among Cairo's Poor: A View from Below', *Middle East Journal*, 1985, 7–26.

Wilke, Annette; Oliver Moebus. *Sound and Communication* (Berlin: Walter de Gruyter GmbH, 2011).

Willis, John Ralph. *In the Path of Allah: the Passion of al-Hajj Umar. An Essay into the Nature of Charisma in Islam* (London: Frank Cass, 1989).

Winter, Michael. *Society and Religion in Early Ottoman Egypt: Studies in the Writings of 'Abd al-Wahhāb al-Sha'rānī* (New Brunswick, NJ: Transaction Publishers, 2009).

Wiredu, J.E. 'How not to compare African traditional thought with Western thought', *Transition*, 75/76, 1997, 320–7.

Works, John A. *Pilgrims in A Strange Land. Hausa Communities in Chad* (New York: Columbia University Press, 1992).

World Bank. *Migration and Remittances Factbook 2011* (Washington, DC: World Bank, 2011).

World Bank. *Migration and Remittances Factbook 2016* (Washington, DC: World Bank, 2016) 1–232, https://doi.org/10.1017/CBO9780511550003.

Wright, Zachary Valentine. *On the Path of the Prophet. Shaykh Ahmed al-Tijani and the Tariqa Muhammadiyya* (Atlanta, GA: The African American Islamic Institute, 2005).

Wright, Zachary. 'The Kāshif al-Ilbās of Shaykh Ibrāhīm Niasse: Analysis of the Text', *Islamic Africa*, 1, 1, 2010, 109–23.

Wright, Zachary. *Living Knowledge in West African Islam: The Sufi Community of Ibrahim Niasse* (Leiden: E.J. Brill, 2015).

Wright, Zachary. *Pearls from the Flood: Select Insight of Shaykh al-Islam Ibrāhīm Niasse* (Atlanta, GA: Fayda Books, 2015).

Wright, Zachary. 'Secrets on the Muhammadan Way: Transmission of the Esoteric Sciences in 18th century scholarly networks', *Islamic Africa*, 9, 1, 2018, 77–105.

Wright, Zachary. *Realizing Islam: The Tijaniyya in North Africa and the Eighteenth-Century Muslim World* (Chapel Hill: University of North Carolina Press, 2020).

Yassin Mohamed, Abdisalam. 'Sufi Poetry in Somali: its Themes and Imagery', PhD diss., University of London, 1977.

Zaouit, Mohamed. 'Mi'raj as-su'ud et les Ajwiba: Deux consultations juridiques d'Ahmad Baba de Tombouctou relatives à l'esclavage des Noirs au Bilad al-Sudan au XVIème et début du XVIIe siècle: édition critique et analyse historique', PhD diss., History, Université de Paris 1, 1997.

Zarruq, Ahmad. 'Qawāīd at-Taṣawwuf, Principles of Sufism: an Annotated Translation with Introduction', trans. Zaineb Istrabadi, PhD diss., Indiana University, 1988.

Zeghal, Malika. 'The "Recentering" of Religious Knowledge and Discourse: The Case of al-Azhar, Radical Islam, and the State (1952–94)', in Robert Hefner; Muhammad Qasim Zaman (eds.), *Schooling Islam: The Culture and Politics of Modern Muslim Education* (Princeton, NJ: Princeton University Press, 2007) 107–30.

Zeleza, P.T. (ed.). *The Study of Africa, Volume II: Global and Transnational Engagements* (Dakar: CODESRIA, 2006).

Zimmerman, Andrew. *Alabama in Africa: Booker T. Washington, the German Empire, and the Globalization of the New South* (Princeton, NJ and Woodstock, NY: Princeton University Press, 2012).

Zine, Jasmin. 'Safe havens or religious "ghettos"? Narratives of Islamic schooling in Canada', *Race Ethnicity and Education*, 10, 1, 2007, 71–92.

Zine, J. *Canadian Islamic Schools. Unravelling the Politics of Faith, Gender, Knowledge, and Identity* (Toronto: University of Toronto Press, 2008).

Zouber, Mahmoud A. *Ahmad Baba (1556–1627). Sa vie et son œuvre* (Paris: Maisonneuve et Larose, 1977).

Zwemer, Samuel. *The Moslem World*, vol. II, 2, 1991, 218.

Index

Previously published titles in the series

Violent Conversion: Brazilian Pentecostalism and Urban Women in Mozambique, Linda Van de Kamp (2016)

Beyond Religious Tolerance: Muslim, Christian & Traditionalist Encounters in an African Town, edited by Insa Nolte, Olukoya Ogen and Rebecca Jones (2017)

Faith, Power and Family: Christianity and Social Change in French Cameroon, Charlotte Walker-Said (2018)

Contesting Catholics: Benedicto Kiwanuka and the Birth of Postcolonial Uganda, Jonathon L. Earle and J. J. Carney (2021)

Islamic Scholarship in Africa: New Directions and Global Contexts, edited by Ousmane Oumar Kane (2021)

From Rebels to Rulers: Writing Legitimacy in the Early Sokoto State, Paul Naylor (2021)

Sacred Queer Stories: Ugandan LGBTQ+ Refugee Lives and the Bible, Adriaan Van Klinken and Johanna Stiebert, with Sebyala Brian and Fredrick Hudson (2021)

Labour & Christianity in the Mission: African Workers in Tanganyika and Zanzibar, 1864–1926, Michelle Liebst (2021)

The Genocide against the Tutsi, and the Rwandan Churches: Between Grief and Denial, Philippe Denis (2022)

Competing Catholicisms: The Jesuits, the Vatican & the Making of Postcolonial French Africa, Jean Luc Enyegue, SJ (2022)

Islam in Uganda: The Muslim Minority, Nationalism & Political Power, Joseph Kasule (2022)

Forthcoming

Spiritual Contestations: The Violence of Peace in South Sudan, Naomi Ruth Pendle (2023)

Printed and bound by CPI Group (UK) Ltd, Croydon, CR0 4YY
09/06/2025
14685698-0005